T0318424

Handbook of Investors' Behavior during Financial Crises

Handbook of Investors' Behavior during Financial Crises

Edited by

Fotini Economou

Konstantinos Gavriilidis

Greg N. Gregoriou

Vasileios Kallinterakis

ACADEMIC PRESS

An imprint of Elsevier

Academic Press is an imprint of Elsevier
125 London Wall, London EC2Y 5AS, United Kingdom
525 B Street, Suite 1800, San Diego, CA 92101-4495, United States
50 Hampshire Street, 5th Floor, Cambridge, MA 02139, United States
The Boulevard, Langford Lane, Kidlington, Oxford OX5 1GB, United Kingdom

Library of Congress Cataloging-in-Publication Data
A catalog record for this book is available from the Library of Congress

British Library Cataloguing-in-Publication Data
A catalogue record for this book is available from the British Library

ISBN: 978-0-12-811252-6

For information on all Academic Press publications visit our website at
https://www.elsevier.com/books-and-journals

Working together
to grow libraries in
developing countries

www.elsevier.com • www.bookaid.org

Publisher: Candice Janco
Acquisition Editor: Scott Bentley
Editorial Project Manager: Susan Ikeda
Production Project Manager: Jason Mitchell
Cover Designer: Christian Bilbow

Typeset by Thomson Digital

Contents

Chapter 17: Herding in the Athens Stock Exchange During Different Crisis Periods 303

Fotini Economou

Chapter 18: Liquidity and Beta Herding in Emerging Equity Markets....................319

Styliani-Iris A. Krokida, Spyros I. Spyrou, Dimitris A. Tsouknidis

Chapter 19: Exchange-Traded Funds: Do They Promote or Depress Noise Trading? 335

Konstantinos Gavriilidis, Greg N. Gregoriou, Vasileios Kallinterakis

List of Contributors

Akrivi Andreou   Medbest SA, Athens, Greece

Andreas Andrikopoulos   University of the Aegean, Chios, Greece

Ruggero Bertelli   University of Siena, Siena, Italy

Natividad Blasco   University of Zaragoza, Zaragoza, Spain

Reza Bradrania   University of South Australia, Adelaide, SA, Australia

Thomas C. Chiang   Drexel University, Philadelphia, PA, United States

Alain Coën   University of Quebec at Montreal, Montreal, QC, Canada

Pilar Corredor   Public University of Navarre, Pamplona, Spain

Aurélie Desfleurs   University of Sherbrooke, Sherbrooke, QC, Canada

Mübeccel Banu Durukan   Dokuz Eylul University, Izmir, Turkey

Fotini Economou   Centre of Planning and Economic Research, Athens, Greece

Zeliha Can Ergun   Adnan Menderes University, Aydin, Turkey

Mário Pedro Ferreira   Portuguese Catholic University, Porto, Portugal

Sandra Ferreruela   University of Zaragoza, Zaragoza, Spain

William Forbes   Queen Mary University of London, London, United Kingdom

Konstantinos Gavriilidis   University of Stirling, Stirling, United Kingdom

Dimitris Georgoutsos   Athens University of Economics and Business, Athens, Greece

Evangelos Giouvris   Royal Holloway, University of London, Egham, United Kingdom

Greg N. Gregoriou   State University of New York, Plattsburgh, NY, United States

Daniel Haguet   EDHEC Business School; Institute of Business Administration, Nice Sophia Antipolis University, Nice, France

Vasileios Kallinterakis   University of Liverpool, Liverpool, United Kingdom

Dmitriy Krichevskiy   Elizabethtown College, Elizabethtown, PA, United States

Styliani-Iris A. Krokida   Athens University of Economics and Business, Athens, Greece

Huimin Li   West Chester University of Pennsylvania, West Chester, PA, United States

Xiao Li   University of South Australia, Adelaide, SA, Australia

SungKyu Lim   Royal Holloway, University of London, Egham, United Kingdom

Petros Migiakis   Bank of Greece, Athens, Greece

Christos Nastopoulos   University of the Aegean, Chios, Greece

Plamen Orecharski   University of National and World Economy, Sofia, Bulgaria

Hilal H. Özsu   Dokuz Eylul University, Izmir, Turkey

Athanasios A. Pantelous   Institute for Risk and Uncertainty, University of Liverpool, Liverpool, United Kingdom

Dhimitri Qirjo   State University of New York, Plattsburgh, NY, United States

Husaini Said   Royal Holloway, University of London, Egham, United Kingdom

Spyros I. Spyrou   Athens University of Economics and Business, Athens, Greece

Dimitris A. Tsouknidis   Cyprus University of Technology, Limassol, Cyprus

Michail D. Vamvakaris   Institute for Risk and Uncertainty, University of Liverpool, Liverpool, United Kingdom

Dimitris Voliotis   University of Piraeus, Piraeus, Greece

Camillo von Müller   CLVS-HSG University of St. Gallen, St. Gallen, Switzerland

Constantinos E. Vorlow   IMAR, International Markets and Risk, Attika, Greece

Apostolos Xanthopoulos   Mercer Investment Consulting, Chicago, IL, United States

Lei Xu   University of South Australia, Adelaide, SA, Australia

Konstantin Zuev   California Institute of Technology, Pasadena, CA, United States

Editor Bios

Dr. Fotini Economou received her PhD from the Department of Business Administration at the University of Piraeus, Greece supported by a scholarship from the Alexander S. Onassis Foundation. She is a Research Fellow at the Centre of Planning and Economic Research (KEPE), Greece as well as Adjunct Lecturer at the Hellenic Open University. Her research focuses on behavioral finance, herd behavior, investor sentiment, and international financial markets. She has published several papers in peer-reviewed financial journals (*Journal of International Financial Markets, Institutions and Money; International Review of Financial Analysis*) and has contributed to research projects for various public, private, and academic institutions.

Dr. Konstantinos Gavriilidis is Senior Lecturer of Finance at the Stirling University Management School. Before that, he held a position at the Durham University Business School, while prior to joining academia he had extensive work experience in the shipping industry. He has taught various courses related to Behavioral Finance, Corporate Finance, and Investments. His research areas include behavioral finance, shipping and tourism. He has published extensively to date in a series of peer-reviewed journals including the *Annals of Tourism Research*, the *Journal of Economic Behavior and Organization*, the *Journal of International Financial Markets, Institutions and Money*, the *International Review of Financial Analysis*, and the *Investment Management and Financial Innovations*.

Dr. Greg N. Gregoriou, a native of Montreal, obtained his joint PhD in finance at the University of Quebec at Montreal which merges the resources of Montreal's four major universities McGill, Concordia, UQAM, and HEC. Professor Gregoriou is Professor of Finance at State University of New York (Plattsburgh) and has taught a variety of finance courses, such as Alternative Investments, International Finance, Money and Capital Markets, Portfolio Management, and Corporate Finance. He has also lectured at the University of Vermont, Universidad de Navarra, and at the University of Quebec at Montreal. Professor Gregoriou has published 52 books, 75 refereed publications in peer-reviewed journals, and 27 books chapters since his arrival at SUNY Plattsburgh in August 2003. Professor Gregoriou's books have been published by McGraw-Hill, John Wiley & Sons, Elsevier-Butterworth/Heinemann, Taylor and Francis/CRC Press, Palgrave-MacMillan, and Risk Books. Four of his books have been translated into Chinese and Russian. His academic articles have appeared in well-known peer-reviewed journals, such as the *Review of Asset Pricing Studies, Journal of Portfolio Management, Journal of Futures Markets, European Journal of Operational Research, Annals of Operations Research, Computers and Operations Research*, etc. Professor Gregoriou is the derivatives editor and editorial board member for the *Journal of Asset Management* as well as editorial board member for the *Journal of Wealth Management*, the *Journal of Risk Management in Financial Institutions, Market Integrity, IEB International Journal of Finance*, and the *Brazilian Business Review*. Professor Gregoriou's interests focus on hedge funds, funds of funds, commodity trading advisors, managed futures, venture capital, and private equity. He has also been quoted several times in the New York Times, Barron's, the *Financial Times of London, Le Temps* (Geneva), *Les Echos* (Paris), and *L'Observateur de Monaco*. He has done consulting work for numerous clients and investment firms in Montreal. He was a part-time lecturer in finance at McGill University and is currently an advisory board member for the Research Center for Operations and Productivity Management at the University of Science and Technology of China's School of Management based in Hefei, China.

Dr. Vasileios (Bill) Kallinterakis is currently Senior Lecturer in Finance at the University of Liverpool Management School; he has also lectured at Durham University Business School (from where he also obtained his PhD), and Leeds University Business School. During his career, he has taught a variety of courses related to Behavioral Finance, Corporate Finance, and Econometrics. His research interests focus on behavioral finance, institutional investors, market volatility, and emerging markets. To date, he has published a series of academic articles in peer-reviewed journals including the *European Financial Management journal*, the *Journal of Economic Behavior and Organization*, the *Journal of International Financial Markets, Institutions and Money*, the *International Review of Financial Analysis*, and the *Review of Behavioral Finance*. He has contributed to the Wiley Encyclopedia of Management and has served as ad hoc referee to research projects submitted to the National Stock Exchange of India. He is currently a member of the editorial board of several peer-reviewed journals (*Economic Analysis*; *International Business Research*; *International Journal of Economics and Finance*; *Review of Behavioral Finance*).

Contributor Bios

Akrivi Andreou is currently holding the position of Finance and Operations Director at Medbest S.A. She holds a BSc in International and European Economics (major International Banking and Finance, Athens University of Economics and Business) and an MA in European Studies (University of Birmingham). She also holds a Diploma in International Financial Reporting Standards (Association of International Accountants). Her research work has been presented in international conferences.

Andreas Andrikopoulos is an Assistant Professor of finance at the Department of Business Administration of the University of the Aegean. He holds a PhD in Financial Modeling (Athens University of Economics and Business). He teaches courses on financial economics, risk management, and international finance at the University of the Aegean and the Hellenic Open University. His research work focuses on the corporate social responsibility of financial institutions, the liquidity of stock markets, and the methodology of financial economics. His work has been published in journals, such as the *Journal of Econometrics*, the *Journal of Banking and Finance*, the *Cambridge Journal of Economics*, *Transportation Research Part A*, *the International Review of Financial Analysis and Quantitative Finance*.

Ruggero Bertelli attained his degree in Economics and Banking, Postgraduate Diploma from the SSDB (Scuola di Specializzazione in Discipline Bancarie), and PhD in Banking Law and Economics, all from the University of Siena. Since 2001, he has been working as an Associate Professor in Banking and Finance at the University of Siena. He is member of the *Financial Management Association (www.fma.org)*, and has been member of the FMA Board of Directors as Program Co-Chair, 2005 European Conference in Siena and 2009 European Conference in Torino. He is lecturer in *Banking Management* (undergraduate level), and *Credit Risk Management* (postgraduate level). His major fields of research include: Asset Management, Financial Portfolio Performance Attribution and Analysis, Banking Management, Private Banking, Credit Risk management, Behavioral Finance, and Financial Advisory. Currently, he is researching into Credit Risk Models and Corporate Bond Portfolio Management, Quantitative Portfolio Strategies and Techniques, Financial Education, and Behavioral Finance.

Natividad Blasco is a Professor of Finance at the Department of Accounting and Finance (Faculty of Economics and Business Administration) at the University of Zaragoza. Her key research interests include Market Microstructure, Corporate Finance, and Behavioral Finance.

Her research has been published in peer-reviewed journals, such as *The Journal of Business Finance & Accounting*, *Journal of Accounting, Auditing and Finance*, *Journal of the Operational Research Society*, *Accounting and Finance*, *European Journal of Operational Research*, *Quantitative Finance*, *Applied Economics*, and *Journal of Behavioral Finance*. She is currently combining teaching and research with the professional collaboration with companies and private and public institutions.

Reza Bradrania holds a Master degree in Finance and Investment from Durham University in the United Kingdom and a PhD in Finance from the University of Sydney Business School. His main research interests and expertise include asset pricing, investment, and behavioral finance. He has published in premier journals and conferences and has delivered numerous lectures, seminars, and workshops for both academics and industry practitioners. He is a lecturer at the University of South Australia and has previously worked as an Associate Director, Director, and Senior Consultant in Investment Banking, Private Equity, and Management Consulting firms.

Thomas C. Chiang is a professor of finance at the LeBow College of Business, Drexel University, where he is the Marshall M. Austin Chair Professor. His research interests include financial contagion, international finance, asset pricing, behavioral finance, and financial econometrics. His articles have appeared in *the Journal of Banking and Finance*, *Journal of International Money and Finance*, *Quantitative Finance*, *Journal of Money, Credit and Banking*, *Journal of Forecasting*, *Pacific-Basin Finance Journal*, *Journal of Financial Research*, *Financial Review*, *European Financial Management*, and *Weltwirtschaftliches Archiv*, among others. Dr. Chiang received his PhD from the Pennsylvania State University, with a concentration in financial economics.

Alain Coën is Full Professor of Finance at the Graduate School of Business (ESG) of the University of Quebec in Montreal (UQAM). Before joining ESG-UQÀM, he was an Associate Professor of finance at EDHEC School of Management. He obtained his PhD in Finance from the University of Grenoble, and his PhD in Economics from the University of Paris I Panthéon-Sorbonne. He holds a Master of Arts in Economics with major in Macroeconomics from Laval University and Accreditations to supervise research (HDR in Management) from Paris-Dauphine University and (HDR in Economics) from University of Paris I Panthéon-Sorbonne. He has been visiting professor at Paris-Dauphine University, University of Paris-Ouest-Nanterre, EDHEC, Laval University, HEC-University of Liège, and University of Sherbrooke. His research interests focus on asset pricing, international finance, hedge funds, REITs, business cycles, and financial econometrics. He has published in several international journals including *Journal of Empirical Finance*, *Journal of Financial Research*, *Economics Letters*, *Finance Research Letters*, *Journal of Economics and Business*, *Finance*, *Journal of Alternative Investments*, *Real Estate Economics*... and has written a book in financial management. He is an Associate Researcher of the Ivanhoé Cambridge Real Estate Chair at ESG-UQÀM Graduate School of Business.

Pilar Corredor is Professor of Finance at the Department of Business Administration (Faculty of Economics and Business Administration) at the Public University of Navarre. Her key research interests are Derivatives, Corporate Finance, and Behavioral Finance. Her research has appeared in peer-reviewed journals, such as *Journal of the Operational Research Society, The Journal of Futures Markets, Technovation, Journal of Business Research, Accounting and Finance, Quantitative Finance, Applied Economics, European Journal of Operational Research, International Review of Financial Economics, International Business Research,* and *Journal of Behavioral Finance.*

Aurélie Desfleurs is Associate Professor in the Accounting Department at the University of Sherbrooke (Canada). She graduated from EDHEC School of Management and obtained her PhD in Finance from Laval University. She is also a Chartered Professional Accountants of Canada. She has published articles in the *Journal of Economics and Business* and the *Journal of Multinational Financial Management.* Her research focuses on financial analysts' forecasts, mergers and acquisitions, and International Financial Reporting Statements.

Mübeccel Banu Durukan received her bachelor's degree from the Faculty of Business, Dokuz Eylul University in Turkey, her MBA from Graduate School of Management, Boston University in the United States, and her doctorate degree from Graduate School of Social Sciences, Dokuz Eylul University in Turkey. She has become an Associate Professor in 2000 and a Full Professor of finance in 2006. Dr. Durukan has served as the Head of the Division of Accounting and Finance at Dokuz Eylul University Faculty of Business between 1999–2008 and 2001–2012; as an Associate Dean between 2001 and 2006; as an acting Head of the Department of International Business and Trade between 2012 and 2013. She is also a member of the Dokuz Eylul University Senate. She has taught and carried out her research activities as a guest professor at the University of Ljubljana, Faculty of Economics between 2008 and 2010, where she still teaches Corporate Finance. Her research interest includes IPOs, investments, behavioral finance, corporate governance, and capital structure. She has published articles in national and international journals, book chapters, and books. She also serves as a reviewer at national and international journals.

Zeliha Can Ergun studied International Trade and Finance at Izmir University of Economics where she received her bachelor's degree as high honors student and she also studied psychology as a double major student. She graduated from Dokuz Eylul University, Master of Accounting and Finance program with a thesis topic "The Empirical Analysis of Herd Behavior in Borsa Istanbul." She began to work as Research Assistant at the Department of Business Administration in Dokuz Eylul University and has started her PhD degree in Business Administration in 2014. Her interested research area is behavioral finance.

Mário Pedro Ferreira is a lecturer at the Oporto Catholic Business School since 1999. Bachelor in Economics from Oporto University, MBA from Cardiff Business School, and PhD from Reading University. Research active in the area of behavioral finance with several publications in international journals. Current research interests are focused on micro evidence of herding in exchange groups and the profitability of momentum trading in the Euronext.

Sandra Ferreruela is Lecturer at the Department of Accounting and Finance (Faculty of Economics and Business Administration) at the University of Zaragoza. Her research focuses on Behavioral Finance issues and Market Microstructure. She has published in peer-reviewed journals, such as *Accounting and Finance, Journal of the Operational Research Society, Quantitative Finance, and Journal of Behavioral Finance*, and her research has been presented in a variety of academic conferences internationally (e.g., EFMA, World Finance Conference, Behavioral Finance Working Group Conference, Euro Working Group on Financial Modelling).

William Forbes is a visiting Professor at Waterford Institute of Technology, Ireland, where he supervises some PhD students and the Faculty of Economics at the University of Groningen. He has taught previously at Loughborough, Glasgow, and Manchester Universities. His research areas are largely in the areas of market-based accounting, behavioral finance, and corporate governance.

Dimitris Georgoutsos is a professor of Finance at the Department of Accounting and Finance of the Athens University of Economics and Business. He has also taught at the Trinity College of the University of Cambridge, the University of Essex, and the University of Crete. He has served as Departmental Chairman and as a member of the University Council of AUEB. He has also served in the past as an economist in the Bank of Greece, in the investment committees of investment companies, and as a member in the BoD of Eurobank-Ergasias SA. He has published numerous articles in the areas of International Finance, Risk Management, and Investments, among others, the *Journal of Banking and Finance, Journal of International Money and Finance, European Economic Review, Journal of Forecasting, the European Financial Management*. He has published a research monograph on Corporate Taxation and a textbook on Bank Management. He holds a BSc in Economics from the University of Athens, an MSc in economics from the London School of Economics and Political Science, and a PhD in economics from the University of Essex.

Evangelos Giouvris (BSc, MSc, PhD, FHEA) is a Lecturer in Finance at Royal Holloway, University of London. Prior to that, he worked at Durham Business School, Grant Thornton as a consultant and SOAS, University of London. He completed his PhD in Finance from Durham Business School. His research papers have been published in various journals, such as *International Review of Financial Analysis and Journal of Business Finance and Accounting*.

Daniel Haguet is Associate Professor of Finance at EDHEC Business School since 2001 that he joined after 12 years as an executive in a large French pension fund. His teaching comprises Corporate Finance, Valuation, Asset Management, and Behavioral Finance. He also used to teach in executive education for financial planners and IFA's. His research interests are individual investor behavior and behavioral finance. Professor Haguet holds an MSc in Finance and a PhD in Finance from the French University.

Dmitriy Krichevskiy is an Assistant Professor in the Business Department at the Elizabethtown College. He has joined the college at 2011. Prior to current appointment, Dmitriy worked as a research associate for Lumina Foundation. He has completed his PhD in Economics at Florida International University in 2011. His research interests include entrepreneurship, labor, applied microeconometrics, and education.

Styliani-Iris A. Krokida holds a BSc in Business Administration from the Department of Business Administration of the University of Piraeus, Greece, and an MSc in Banking and Finance from the Department of Banking and Financial Management of the University of Piraeus, Greece. She is currently a PhD candidate on herding behavior and international financial markets at the Department of Accounting and Finance at the Athens University of Economics and Business. Her research has been published in international refereed academic journals and presented in international conferences. She has completed a 1-year internship at the Banking and Capital Market Section of the Bank of Greece.

Huimin Li is a Professor of finance at the College of Business and Public Management, West Chester University of PA. Her research interests include financial contagion, international financial markets, asset pricing, behavioral finance, and oil price dynamics. Her publications have appeared in *Journal of International Money and Finance*, *Journal of International Financial Markets, Institutions & Money*, *Quantitative Finance*, *Journal of Multinational Financial Management*, among others. She received her PhD in Business Administration from Drexel University, with concentrations in economics and finance.

Xiao Li is a postgraduate student in Banking and Finance at the University of South Australia. His research interests are Banking and impact of related regulations on banks performance.

Sungkyu Lim (BSc, MSc, PhD) is a visiting lecturer at Royal Holloway, University of London. He completed his PhD in Finance at Royal Holloway, University of London.

Petros Migiakis is a Senior Economist of the Bank of Greece at the Economic Analysis and Research Department. Within his duties as Deputy Head of the Banking Affairs and Capital Market Section, he has worked on policy proposals for public debt restructuring and ECB's projects on interest rate forecasting and risk management for monetary policy purposes. Also, his research deals with yield curve modeling for defaultable sovereign bonds, the decomposition of systemic and idiosyncratic factors, the Euro-area debt crisis, and the rationality of inflation expectations. He holds a PhD in Finance, from the Athens University of Economics and Business, while his studies also include an MSc in Mathematical Modeling from the National Technical University of Athens, an MSc in Applied Economics and Finance, from the Athens University of Economics & Business, and an MA in Business Administration from the same university. Articles published as a result of the aforementioned research can be found in the *Journal of Banking and Finance, the European Financial Management and Empirical Economics* and other journals.

Christos Nastopoulos was born in 1973, in Athens Greece. He studied physics at the University of Patras and he holds a Master's degree (MSc) in Banking (Hellenic Open University). He is currently a PhD candidate in finance, in the University of the Aegean and his research focuses mainly on the area of Critical Realist Financial Economics. He lives in Patras and works as a bank executive. His research work has been presented in international conferences.

Plamen Oresharski is Associate Professor and has been teaching finance since 1987 at the Department of Finance in the Bulgarian University of National and World Economy (UNWE). In the period 1993–97, he was appointed as Chief of the State Treasury in the Ministry of Finance with the task to create and develop the market for government debt in the country. From 1997 to 2001, Oresharski was Deputy Minister of Finance, responsible for the management of government debt and supervision of financial markets. He had an active role in the great local monetary and banking crisis in 1996–97 having done successful debt restructuring operations to rebalance the debt portfolio of the Government. He was also a Member of the Board of Directors of the Bulgarian Stock Exchange in 1997–99 and several local banks in the period 1994–2000. In 2003 until 2005, he held the post of Deputy Rector at the UNWE. In 2005, Plamen Oresharski became Minister of Finance until 2009. Under his leadership, Bulgaria realized budget surpluses and was the only country in the European Union with budget surpluses in four consecutive years. He was responsible for the most fundamental reforms in the sector, one of which is the restructuring of the tax system, whereby the flat tax of 10% was first introduced and kept until today. Nominated as a Finance Minister in Eastern Europe in 2006 by "Euromoney" and among the top 10 reformers in the World Bank ranking for 2007. In 2009, he was elected a member of the Parliament. In mid-2013, Plamen Oresharski became the Prime Minister of Bulgaria, leading an expert government at a time of intense political crisis until late 2014. He is currently continuing his academic work in the University of National and World Economy. Throughout the years, he has published several textbooks on investment and management of investment portfolios and has written numerous articles and commentaries in the press.

Hilal Özsu graduated from Suleyman Demirel University with a Bachelor's degree of Business Administration. She studied her Master's degree with accounting and finance concentration, with her thesis about financial crises. She completed her PhD in Business Management program in Dokuz Eylul University, with her thesis titled "Herd Behavior on Borsa Istanbul (BIST): An Empirical Analysis." She was appointed to Gediz University as Research Assistant and then as Lecturer. She is pursuing her academic career in Gediz University as a faculty member. Her main research interest focuses on corporate finance, behavioral finance, and investment analysis. She teaches in undergraduate and graduate programs and lectures on corporate finance, financial statement analysis, behavioral finance, investment, and portfolio analysis, capital markets.

Athanasios A. Pantelous is a Reader within the Department of Mathematical Sciences, University of Liverpool, United Kingdom. He has received two PhDs: in *Statistics* (Actuarial Science) from *Athens University of Economics and Business* (Athens, Greece) and in *Stochastic Modelling and Control Theory* (Engineering) from City University (London, UK). His research program and scholarly accomplishments involve leading research and training in several areas of applied mathematics and modelling under risk and uncertainty (e.g., actuarial science, quantitative finance, computational mathematics, applied stochastic analysis, systems and control theory) with several significant applications in finance (disappointment and loss aversion theory, decision making under risk and uncertainty, financial networks analysis, commodities), in actuarial science (optimal premium-reserve strategies in competitive insurance markets, catastrophe risk bonds, reserving, mortality modelling), and in engineering (singular systems, stochastic vibration theory) at national and international high-impact levels. Long-term perspective and sustainable impact characterize the primary research principle. He was the founder and was leading the research in Institute for Financial and Actuarial Mathematics (IFAM) at the University of Liverpool from 2011 to 2015, as well as high-quality training in actuarial and financial mathematics at large scale at local, national, and international levels through accredited UG/PGT level courses from the Institute and Faculty of Actuaries (IFoA) London UK, a big number of PhD/Post-Doc students, influential roles in professional societies, service on editorial, and advisory boards, as external advisor, expert and assessor for research councils, universities, and industry. Currently, he co-leads, as Deputy Director and co-Principal Investigator, the EPSRC and ESRC Centre for Doctoral Training (CDT) in Quantification and Management of Risk & Uncertainty in Complex Systems & Environments (2014–23). This research and training center has a total funding volume of £21 million and involves 36 industrial and academic partners from around the globe. He is the author and coauthor of more than 130 publications in journals, conference proceedings, and reports.

Dhimitri Qirjo is an Associate Professor in the Department of Economics & Finance at SUNY, Plattsburgh where he has been a faculty member since 2012. From 2010 to 2012, Dhimitri served as a postdoctoral fellow in the Vancouver School of Economics at University of British Columbia. He completed his PhD in economics at Florida International University and his undergraduate studies at Aristotle University. His research interests lie in the fields of international trade, labor economics, and environmental economics.

Husaini Said (BA, MSc) is a Doctoral Researcher in Finance. Prior to pursuing his PhD at Royal Holloway, University of London, he was an investment and treasury practitioner. He holds an MSc in Finance and Investment from Durham Business School.

Spyros I. Spyrou, Deputy Rector for Economic Affairs, is a Professor of Finance at the Department of Accounting & Finance, Athens University of Economics & Business (AUEB). He has served as a member of the University Senate, as a member of the Deanery, as the Head of the Department of Accounting & Finance, at the Managing Committee for various Postgraduate courses (MSc in Shipping, Finance, & Management, MBA International, MSc in Accounting & Finance), and as the Erasmus Program coordinator for the Department of Accounting & Finance. In previous administrative posts he has served as the Admissions Tutor for Postgraduate Courses and member of the IT Committee at the University of Durham (Department of Economics & Finance, 1999–2001), and MA Programme Leader and Postgraduate Admissions Committee at Middlesex University Business School (School of Economics) (1997–99).

He has been appointed as a Lecturer at Athens University of Economics & Business in 2001. Before that he was a Lecturer at the University of Durham (UK, 1999–2001) and Middlesex University Business School (UK, 1997–99). He holds a PhD in Finance from Brunel University (UK) in 1997. The thesis examined the functioning and efficiency of emerging equity markets. He also holds an MSc in Business Finance from Brunel University (1993) and a BSc in Economics from the National & Kapodistrian University of Athens (1990).

His research interests are in the area of asset pricing and investor behavior and has published more than 30 research articles in refereed academic journals, such as *Journal of Banking & Finance, Journal of Business Finance & Accounting, European Financial Management, Journal of Futures Markets, International Review of Financial Analysis, Applied Financial Economics, Derivatives, Use, Trading & Regulation, Applied Economics, Applied Economics Letters, Journal of Emerging Markets Finance, The Manchester School, Journal of Economic Development*, among others. Research papers have also been presented in numerous international conferences, such as the Financial Engineering & Banking Society, European Finance Association, European Financial Management Association, Multinational Finance Society, Money Macro and Finance, British Accounting Association, Hellenic Finance & Accounting Association, etc. His research has been cited more than 500 times (as of September 2015, excluding own citations) in papers that are published in journals, such as *Journal of Money, Credit & Banking, Journal of Business Finance and Accounting, European Financial Management, Review of Financial Economics, European Central Bank Working Paper Series, Applied Financial Economics, Journal of Financial Regulation & Compliance, Journal of Asset Management, International Economic Journal, Emerging Markets Review, Journal of Economic Behaviour and Organization*, among others. He is also the author of two books, *Money & Capital Markets* (LA: Greek) and *Introduction to Behavioral Finance* (LA: Greek)), and has published articles in professional journals and newspapers.

His teaching portfolio includes a large number of postgraduate modules (Money & Capital Markets, Financial Engineering, Security Investment Analysis, Portfolio Management,

Behavioral Finance, Risk Management & Derivatives) and undergraduate modules (Money & Capital Markets, Investments, Security Valuation and Portfolio Management, International Finance, Derivative Markets), taught at the University of Durham, at Middlesex University Business School, and at Athens University of Economics & Business.

Dimitris A. Tsouknidis is a faculty member (Lecturer) in the Department of Commerce, Finance, and Shipping at Cyprus University of Technology. He holds a BSc (Economics) from the University of Thessaly, Greece; an MSc (Computational Finance) from the University of Essex, UK; an MBA and a PhD (Finance) from the Athens University of Economics and Business, Greece. He has held full time academic posts at University of Bradford, UK and Regent's University London, UK and visiting research and teaching posts at Athens University of Economics and Business, Greece; University of Reading, UK; University of Valencia, Spain; and ALBA Graduate Business School, Greece.

His research interests lie in the fields of empirical asset pricing, risk management, and ship finance. His research output has been published in international peer reviewed academic journals and secured twice joint research funding from the Athens University of Economics and Business. He has contributed book chapters on financial derivatives (Oxford University Press) and serves as a referee for a number of international academic journals. He has delivered his academic work as part of professional seminar series for practitioners on shipping derivatives and provided consultancy services on credit risk modeling issues for ship-lending financial institutions.

Michail D. Vamvakaris has graduated with distinction from the School of Economics of the Aristotle University of Thessaloniki, Greece. He holds a Master's degree in Complex Systems and Networks from the Department of Mathematics from the same institute and a Research Master in Decision Making under Risk and Uncertainty from the University of Liverpool. Currently, he is a PhD candidate in the same university.

Dimitris Voliotis is Assistant Professor in Mathematical Economics and Game Theory at the Department of Banking and Financial Management at the University of Piraeus. Dimitris's research interests are in applied game theory with emphasis on monetary economics and financial markets. Prior to joining University of Piraeus in 2009, Dimitris was an Economist at the Council of Economic Advisors at the Greek Ministry of Finance.

Camillo von Müller [PhD (HSG), MA (JHU), MA(HU)] is an economist at the German Federal Ministry of Finance in Berlin. He obtained a PhD in Management/Finance at the University of St. Gallen, Switzerland, and has been a Visiting and Teaching Fellow at Harvard University's Economics Department having also taught at the Economics and Social Science Departments at the Universities of Zurich, St. Gallen, and Leuphana University. Camillo has published widely in the fields of economics, management, and finance. Prior to joining the Federal Ministry of Finance he has worked and consulted for nonprofit, public, and private sector institutions including Finance Watch in Brussels, the Ministry of Finance and Economics of Baden-Württemberg, and Deutsche Börse.

Konstantinos Vorlow is an Economist with a PhD in Finance from the University of Durham where he also worked as a Lecturer. He has also served as a Senior Economist and Quant in the Private Banking and Investment Funds sector. He specializes in Economic and Macrofinancial Early Warning Systems, Risk Management, Tactical & Strategic Asset Allocation, Trading Models & Algorithms. He is the founder and CEO of IMAR International Markets & Risk.

Apostolos Xanthopoulos has taught quantitative finance, and other business classes at a few major Universities in the Chicago area. Contemporaneously, he worked as Consultant and Senior Quant at several banking institutions, including Mercer, Alliant Credit Union, Federal Home Loan Bank, Calamos Investments, and Deerfield Capital Management. He performed numerous statistical analyses, including balance sheet sensitivity to interest rates, refined portfolio return quantification methodologies, and facilitated reporting and monitoring in risk applications. Previously, he worked with OTC financial derivatives at Bank of America, and then joined KPMG Peat Marwick's enterprise-wide risk applications. A Deutsche Asset Management, he designed and implemented programming modules of a fund performance system. Apostolos has two Master's degrees, received his doctorate from the Stuart School of Business at IIT, and has published in academic journals. He is currently involved in assessing performance of investment managers at a major investment consulting group (Mercer Investment Consulting). In addition to having seen and analyzed/rated hundreds of retail and institutional fixed income portfolios since 2013, at Mercer, he spearheaded quantitative techniques that help discern the entrenched behavior of investors, as a result of market characteristics after the financial crisis.

Lei Xu is a Senior Lecturer in Finance at the School of Commerce, University of South Australia. Prior to joining the University of South Australia in 2013, he worked as a Lecturer in Finance at the University of Adelaide, and has also worked in the banking sector in China for quite a few years. His recent research focuses on both theoretical and empirical examination of the capital and risks involved in the financial institutions, reforms in banking, and the emerging financial issues in key industries. His research in Banking and Finance has been published in premier international and national journals and conferences. He is keen on contributing to the understanding and exploring the unknown aspects and impacts of the modern finance concepts, practices, and policies, not only in business, but also for a wider community. In addition to the Justice of Peace for South Australia, Fire Warden, and First Aid Officer for the School, he has actively committed himself to various community engagements.

Konstantin Zuev is a Special Lecturer in Computing and Mathematical Sciences at the California Institute of Technology. He obtained his PhD in Mathematics (2008) from Moscow State University and PhD in Civil Engineering (2009) from the Hong Kong University of Science and Technology. Konstantin is an applied mathematician with broad research interests. Most of his research falls under the umbrella of applied probability and statistics and has a strong geometric flavor. In particular, he is interested in complex networks, Markov chain Monte Carlo algorithms, rare event estimation, and Bayesian inference. He is currently an Honorary Supervisor at the Institute of Risk and Uncertainty, University of Liverpool, UK; a Guest Editor for the ASCE-ASME Journal of Risk and Uncertainty in Engineering Systems; and a chair of the Committee on Probability and Statistics in the Physical Sciences, one of the standing committees of the Bernoulli Society for Mathematical Statistics and Probability.

Acknowledgments

We would like to thank a handful of anonymous referees in the selection of the papers for this book. In addition, we thank a few people at Elsevier: Dr. J. Scott Bentley, Susan Ikeda, and Jason Mitchell for their wonderful help, support, and guidance throughout the process. Neither the editors nor the publisher can guarantee the accuracy of each chapter of this book and it is the sole responsibility of the contributors for their own chapters.

Theoretical Perspectives of Investors' Behaviour During Financial Crises

Debt Markets, Financial Crises, and Public Finance in the Eurozone: Action, Structure, and Experience in Greece

Akrivi Andreou*, Andreas Andrikopoulos**, Christos Nastopoulos**

*Medbest SA, Athens, Greece; **University of the Aegean, Chios, Greece

Chapter Outline

1.1 Introduction and Theoretical Framework

The outburst of the Greek crisis in Europe signaled the transition to the second stage of the financial crisis which broke out in 2007 in the United States of America. The 2007 crisis spread its effects rapidly throughout the global economy, reversed positive growth rates, increased unemployment in developed economies, cut down investments and trade, and transformed the international economic system fundamentally. In that adverse environment, the Greek economy proved to be too frail and the European economy too vulnerable to come out from the turbulence unscathed. The financial system in Europe appeared pretty stable at the first stage of the global crisis, receiving strong support from European Union (EU) governments and the European Central Bank (ECB). In 2009, however, within the continuing uncertainty surrounding the global economy, destabilizing trends started to appear in the European economic system stemming mainly from two sources: the structural asymmetries between the European Monetary Union (EMU) member states and, in a wider context, the loose political and economic ties between the EU countries. To further maintain financial stability, for example, a different economic policy would need to be prescribed to the countries of the European North compared to what was needed in the periphery, while at the same time the resolution of this situation could not come of the shallow political-economic bonds of the Eurozone. At that point Greece stood out, being the first Eurozone member state to have its financial stability and sovereign debt sustainability severely questioned. Eventually, Greece was excluded from the capital markets and resorted to bilateral loans from EMU member states and the International Monetary Fund (IMF). The leading role played by Greek financial instability coupled with the expansion of the sovereign debt crisis in Portugal, Ireland, and Cyprus, as well as the serious effects on the Spanish and the Italian economy, indicating that the Greek crisis might not have been only the result of Greek economy's serious structural problems but also the effect of institutional weaknesses embedded in the Eurozone.

The economic analysis of this paper is informed by critical realism as a philosophy of science (Bhaskar, 1978) and, more particularly, as a philosophy of economics (Lawson, 1997); our methodology builds on the critical realistic approach to the study of financial markets (Andrikopoulos, 2013). In philosophy, *realism* means that the world exists independently of what we think about it, and *critical realism* means that our view of this world affects its evolution. Our critical realistic approach is based on the ascertainment that the social space, into which the events of the Greek debt crisis evolved, constitutes an open system, that is, a locus subject to constant and relentless transformation. Within this open system, we cannot observe any strict periodicity in economic phenomena, but, instead, only partial regularities. Moreover, our methodology is based on the idea that the social factor and free human will act as catalysts for economic and political developments, making their parameterization in a mathematical equation virtually impossible and ineffective. The events of the crisis emerge as a result of a rich grid of causes. While reality about causes is objective, actors' knowledge of the causes can only be partial, fallible, and subjective. The events of the crisis shape actors' experiences, revealing the meaning and perspective of their actions which, in turn and in large, reproduce the structures that caused the crisis in the first place. In certain historical moments, actors not only reproduce but also reshape and reconstruct seemingly ineradicable structures for good. Inasmuch as the structures of the economy—and the economic crisis—exist, reproduce, and evolve through actors' agential choices and experiences, the economic system is open and the events of the crisis are unique and unrepeatable in time and space. The triad Action—Experience—Structure forms the organization of this paper.[1]

To start with, we recount the main agents' actions, offering a brief chronology of the outburst of the crisis extending from autumn 2009 to spring 2014 when the Greek government returned to capital markets and issued a 5-year bond. Through analyzing this particular period we focus on the origins and initial stages of the crisis, we show the dynamics through which the crisis deepened and illustrate useful analytical paths for the exploration and understanding of more recent as well as future developments. In the third section of the paper, we present actors' experiences as those were expressed (uttered) during the course of the crisis by the actors themselves. In the fourth section of the paper, we try to identify and discuss the structures that gave birth and shaped the events of the Greek financial crisis. This way, a full analytical cycle is completed through which we come closer not only to understanding the causes of a crisis that has plagued Greek society for years, but also to a complete critical realist account of how the political-economic system, of which we are integral parts, operates. The final section concludes this paper.

1.2 The Crisis Chronology

As of the beginning of 2009, when Standard and Poor's downgraded Greece's sovereign credit rating from A to A minus, things had started looking gloomy for the Greek economy. By the fall of the same year, 12 months after the collapse of Lehman Brothers, the Greek economy was clearly showing its weaknesses: the gross domestic product (GDP) growth rate for 2009 was expected to be negative for the first time since 1993, the public debt was increasing (2007: 94.8%, 2008: 95.4%, 2009 1st semester: 111.5%, of GDP), the state budget primary surplus had already turned into a deficit and, most worryingly, the current account deficit (2007: 12.3%, 2008: 12.7% of GDP) and the general government deficit (2007: 3.5%, 2008: 3.7% of GDP) were depicting the country's increased needs for debt (Alpha Bank, 2009; Bank of Greece, 2009). Greece was already under the European Commission's surveillance of the excessive deficit procedure (EDP) since March 2009 and the adverse fiscal developments further increased capital markets' mistrust in the Greek economy's potential. The interest rate for the 10-year Greek government bond started increasing, making borrowing progressively more expensive for Greece, while at the same time the Greek government target proceeds

---

[1] Critical realism has been the philosophical framework for schools of economic thought that have sought to explain rather than forecast and have fostered discussions of open economic systems and the importance of institutions in the generation of economic phenomena. Post-Keynesian economics and the French regulation school are characteristic of this (Jessop, 2006; Jefferson and King, 2011; Rotheim, 1999). This paper is not a contribution to these schools of economic thought. We try to make a methodological contribution to applied critical-realist economics, by producing distinct accounts of the three layers of reality: the actual, the real, and the empirical.

could not be sustained due to the effects the world economic crisis had on various sectors of the domestic economy, decreasing incomes and demand and, therefore, taxables.

Amid the deteriorating economic state of affairs, the Prime Minister Konstantinos Karamanlis called early elections to get "fresh popular mandate"[2] and support for the requisite measures to confront the looming economic disaster. The, thus far, opposition party PASOK won the elections of October 4, 2010. The party's preelectoral campaign was soon epitomized in one single phrase uttered by its leader, George Papandreou, which clearly suggested that there is enough "hidden" money in the Greek economy and that one only needs to work decisively toward the correct direction to bring this money to the market fore. Having even promised marginal wage and pension increases, Papandreou managed to get a comfortable majority of 160 Parliamentary seats. It was not long after the elections, however, and instead of presenting the updated Stability and Growth Program due for the next ECOFIN[3] as provided by the EDP, that Greece revised its general government deficit to 12.5% of GDP.[4] This figure was more than double the percentage estimated by the previous government.

The revised fiscal figures flared waves of reactions from the rating agencies, the European Commission and the markets, stemming mainly from the fact that the credibility of Greek economic authorities at all levels was severely questioned. Despite the rather optimistic 2010 State Budget submitted to the Parliament on November 20, 2009, all rating agencies kept downgrading the Greek economy with the understanding that the origins of the Greek economic troubles were structural and that, therefore, they could not be addressed with something less than long-term structural measures. The European Commission published its "Report on Greek government deficit and debt statistics" on January 8, 2010 in which, using a sharp language, directly raised issues of reliability of the statistical figures provided by Greece. This publication, coming from an official European institution, irreparably shook the capital markets', the global media's and the European counterparties' trust in any economic or political account emanating from Greece. The uncertainty for the prospects of the Greek economy proliferated and the spread of the 10-year Greek government bond on January 21, 2010 reached 300 basis points. At the same time, the political pressures and criticism from abroad were escalating.[5] The global public opinion was not wondering any more whether Greece had the intention or the ability to reverse its economic track, but if it had the European guarantees to avoid its upcoming default.

---

[2] To Vima (02/09/2009), http://www.tovima.gr/politics/article/?aid=286340

[3] Economic and Financial Affairs Summit

[4] European Commission—Report on Greek Government Deficit and Debt Statistics 8/1/2010 (European Commission, 2010).

[5] The British Chancellor of the Exchequer, A. Darling stated that the Greek problem was a Eurozone and not a European Union problem while both his French counterparts, C. Lagarde and J. Almunia, a prominent member of the European Commission, refuted that a rescue plan for Greece existed. Naftemporiki (Davos 2010)—http://www.naftemporiki.gr/stream/718

On the sidelines of the European Council meeting on February 11, 2010, the European leaders[6] expressed their willingness to support Greece to its endeavor to tackle with its economic problems but at the same time they stressed out the importance of Greece's commitment to the goals set. The European Council delegated the ECOFIN to prepare a mechanism of providing economic support to Greece and ensuring the stability of the Eurozone. The ECOFIN asked the Greek government to take measures toward restructuring the institutional framework of the Greek economy and set a deficit reduction target of 8.7% of GDP for 2010 and 3% until 2012.[7]

In March, the Greek government announced the second batch of measures which would result, in total, in a net proceeds increase of 5.5 billion euro—2.5 billion of which from expenditure cuts.[8] The austerity measures were unprecedented: further public sector wage and allowance cuts, zero pension increases, controls on public sector recruitments, VAT and various other indirect tax increases, and introduction of new forms of taxation.[9] The ECB welcomed the measures announced. The ECB Governing Council noted, however, that the fiscal reforms should be combined with structural institutional reforms in order to bring economic development and tackle the increasing unemployment.[10] Within Greece the opposition parties—mainly of the Left—and trade unions reacted immediately, calling people to mobilize and organized demonstrations and strikes. The participation in the protests was great and, to a limited extent, riots broke out. That was the beginning of a long series of protests, including demonstrations and strikes, which took place in Greece between 2010 and 2012, even leading to the death of 5 people on May 5, 2010 and climaxing to the "Indignant Citizens Movement" in 2011.

Right after announcing the second batch of austerity measures, and while the bond spread had exceeded 400 basis points, George Papandreou traveled to Germany and France to secure political support, and not, as emphatically noted, to ask for economic help.[11,12] At the same time when Jose Manuel Barroso was stating that Greece had taken the measures needed to decrease its deficit and was acknowledging the role the credit default swaps (CDS) had played in the magnification of the crisis,[13] various voices from the Eurozone and the

---

[6] The President of the European Council H.V. Rompuy, the Chancellor of Germany A. Merkel, the French President N. Sarcozy, the President of the European Commission J.M. Barroso, and the President of the ECB J.C. Trichet.

[7] http://www.consilium.europa.eu/uedocs/cms_data/docs/pressdata/en/ecofin/112905.pdf

[8] The first batch of measures, which was announced a month earlier, contained a package of 800-million euro worth of measures and focused mainly on wages and allowances cut in the public sector.

[9] Eleftherotipia (enet.gr) 4/3/2010.

[10] http://www.ecb.europa.eu/press/pr/date/2010/html/pr100303.en.html

[11] To Vima (tovima.gr) 5/3/2010—http://www.tovima.gr/politics/article/?aid=318624 & http://www.youtube.com/watch?v=ocHPd7FWKrk

[12] http://www.youtube.com/watch?v=rwPyf6UhtFg

[13] http://europa.eu/rapid/press-release_SPEECH-10-80_en.htm

European Union were making clear that more measures were needed[14] and that a support mechanism could not only stem from Europe, without the participation of the International Monetary Fund.[15,16] By the end of April 2010, the bond spreads had exceeded 600 basis points, the credit rating agencies kept downgrading Greece, the European Commission had further revised the 2009 deficit to 13.9% and a Greek default seemed more than possible.[17]

On April 23, 2010, the Greek Prime Minister announced Greece's appeal to the support mechanism designed in March 2010, with the participation of the EU, the ECB, and the IMF. Greece signed a Memorandum of Understanding with the IMF and the EU agreeing on the measures that had to be taken for the support mechanism to be activated. The measures, defined in detail by the Greek Minister of Finance George Papakonstantinou on May 2, 2010, consisted of various tax increases further wage cuts in the public sector, pension cuts, real estate objective values increase, and a 1 billion euro worth of public investment cumulative cuts for 2010 and 2011. Among other institutional reforms, it was announced that the Hellenic Financial Stability Fund (HFSF) would be established.

The "Troika" consisted of representatives of the European Commission, the ECB and the IMF which would periodically evaluate the application of the terms agreed, giving opinion on each loan disbursement. The loan from the EU was 80 billion euros with a 5 year repayment period and a grace period of 3 years from each disbursement and an interest rate Euribor +3% within the grace period and +4% for the remaining period. The loan from the IMF was for 30 billion euro, with the same repayment and grace periods and an interest rate of SDR+3%.[18,19] The implementation of the funding program by the EU would be performed by the newly founded special purpose vehicle, the European Financial Stability Facility (EFSF).[20]

The continuous proclamation and, to a limited extent, introduction of austerity and restructuring measures notwithstanding, during the first months of 2011 Greece was still being downgraded

---

[14] Olli Rehn's encouraging wish addressed in Greek to Greeks during his official visit in Athens, made more than clear that more measures were coming http://www.youtube.com/watch?v=EeGe1iLhYrE

[15] The Prime Minister of Hungary, G. Bajnai, for example, openly brought up IMF's involvement Eleftherotipia (enet.gr) 16/3/2010—http://www.enet.gr/?i=news.el.article&id=141923

[16] Also see, for example, the "Statement by the heads of state and government of the euro area" published on 25/3/2010 http://www.consilium.europa.eu/uedocs/cms_data/docs/pressdata/en/ec/113563.pdf

[17] The CDS interest rates more than tripled between November 2009 and November 2010, displacing the Greek government bonds from the capital markets.

[18] http://www.hellenicparliament.gr/UserFiles/c8827c35-4399-4fbb-8ea6-aebdc768f4f7/ADANEIO.pdf. Greece: Request for Stand-By Arrangement, IMF country report 10/111—http://www.imf.org/external/pubs/ft/scr/2010/cr10111.pdf, http://www.imf.org/external/np/exr/facts/sba.htm

[19] In March 2011, the interest rate was lowered by 1% and the repayment period was extended to 7.5 years during the EU Summit.

[20] In December 2010, it was decided that a permanent organization would be established. The European Stability Mechanism (ESM) is ESFS's successor and the only active mechanism since July 1, 2013 when ESFS expired. http://www.efsf.europa.eu/about/index.htm and http://www.esm.europa.eu/about/index.htm

by the international credit agencies. In June 2011, the Greek Parliament voted for the Medium Term Fiscal Strategy 2012–15 which, apart from a wide range of further tax and spending-cut measures also contained the establishment of the Agency for Privatization (Hellenic Republic Asset Development Fund). The Fund would take ownership of public property and take all necessary actions to privatize it, reimbursing the revenue created to the Treasury for debt reduction.[21] In the meantime, understanding that Europe was in the midst of a great financial crisis, the Eurozone states along with Bulgaria, Denmark, Latvia, Lithuania, Poland, and Romania, were voting the Euro Plus Pact, a reform of the Stability and Growth Pact.

In July 2011, the EU Summit, which was called to address the Greek debt problem and to protect the euro from speculative attacks, concluded with an agreement for a new loan to Greece. The new loan was 158 billion euro, 37 of which would be contributed by the private sector through bond exchange. In the Summit Conclusions it was stated that "reliance on external credit ratings in the EU regulatory framework should be reduced." A few days after the Summit Moody's and Fitch downgraded Greece due to the private sector involvement (PSI) in the bond exchange program. Toward the end of August, it was clear that the Greek economy was off-track. The unemployment rate was over 18%,[22] the recession rate was estimated around 5%, the public revenue had decreased by 1.9 billion euro to the previous year and, at the same time, the public expenditure increased by 2.7 billion euro. The central government deficit was now estimated at 8.5% of GDP—far from the 7.6% target. The Greek government tried to persuade the Troika to loosen the deficit goal, calling upon failures at the adjustment program itself.[23] After severely disagreeing with the Minister of Finance on the ways to cover the fiscal deviation, the Troika left Greece before approving the disbursement of the sixth installment of the first support package.[24] Under the pressure of losing the installment, the government announced more fiscal and structural measures.[25] The next Euro Summit was held in October 2011 with the understanding that "further action is needed to restore confidence"[26] and to deal with the effects of the international financial crisis. After a 4-day round of consultations an agreement of increased private sector involvement was reached, providing for a voluntary exchange of a 206 billion euros worth of Greek bonds with new bonds (at face value). In nominal terms, the loss would be around 50%, and the remaining 50% of the old bonds would be covered with new, Greek government and EFSF

---

[21] http://demo.minfin.gr/sites/default/files/financial_files/MTFS.pdf

[22] ELSTAT November 2011—http://www.statistics.gr/portal/page/portal/ESYE/PAGE-consumerworks?inputA=6

[23] Skai.gr (20/8/2011)—http://www.skai.gr/news/finance/article/177826/ektos-stohou-proupologismos-esoda-dapanes-analutikoi-pinakes-/

[24] http://www.inewsgr.com/158/efyge-i-troika---diafonia-gia-nea-metra.htm

[25] Among which, the establishment of a unitary payroll system in the public sector, a decrease on the level of untaxed income, broad dismissals in state-controlled organizations, and a new tax on real estate property. https://www.youtube.com/watch?v=0QtIv44o18c

[26] http://www.consilium.europa.eu/uedocs/cms_data/docs/pressdata/en/ec/125644.pdf

bonds. Based on this agreement, a new support program of 100 billion euro and a 30 billion euro package for debt restructuring were agreed; the Greek debt would become sustainable, reaching 120% of GDP by 2020. At the same time, it was decided that the EFSF lending capacity would increase to 1 trillion euros from 440 billion euro. In Greece the agreement was taken in as controlled default, and the public reaction was severe. Under the weight of intense domestic discontent the Greek Prime Minister announced his decision to hold a referendum so that the Greek people would decide whether the new loan would be signed or not—a decision that raised waves of dissatisfaction abroad, peaking with A. Merkel and N. Sarkozy stating that Greece's stay in the Eurozone depended on the result of this referendum.

The political developments in Greece in light of the Euro Summit decisions, the forthcoming PSI and Papandreou's call for a referendum were exponential, resulting in the destabilization of the government and the formation of a national unity government. A technocrat, Lucas Papademos, Vice-President of the European Central Bank and former Governor of the Bank of Greece, was chosen as the Prime Minister. The aim of his government would be to introduce all the necessary measures already agreed with the creditors during the summer, and to successfully complete the PSI bond swap. On March 9, 2012 the bond swap was completed and on April 25, 2012 the Ministry of Finance announced a private sector voluntary participation of 96.9%. Due to the fact that the Greek government activated collective action clauses (CACs), the ISDA (International Swaps and Derivatives Association) declared a Greek credit event, triggering 3.2 billion dollars' worth of credit default swaps (Zettelmeyer et al., 2013).[27]

A few days earlier, on March 2, 2012, the EU member states were taking a big step toward further fiscal coordination by signing the treaty on stability, coordination, and governance in the economic and monetary union (known as the Fiscal Compact or the Fiscal Stability Treaty).[28] The signatories agreed to introduce a balanced budget rule in their domestic legislation. Prior to issuing new debt, the states have the obligation to inform the other member states, the Council of the EU and the European Commission and consult each other when big economic policy reforms are planned, before implementing them. The annual structural government deficit is not allowed to exceed 0.5% of the GDP and each time there is a significant deviation from the country-specific medium-term objective, a correction mechanism is going to be "triggered automatically."[29]

Some important institutional developments occurred from the side of the European Central Bank as well in 2012. The Governing Council of the ECB decided to adopt a permanent intervening procedure, activating outright monetary transactions (OMT), buying sovereign

---

[27] http://www.isda.org/dc/docs/EMEA_Determinations_Committee_Statement_09032012.pdf
[28] The Treaty was signed by the Euro Zone members and eight other EU member states, that is, Bulgaria, Denmark, Hungary, Lithuania, Latvia (later also part of the Eurozone), Poland, Romania, and Sweden.
[29] http://www.european-council.europa.eu/media/639235/st00tscg26_en12.pdf

bonds in the secondary bond. Since September 2012 this intervention is a permanent mechanism of the ECB which can be initiated only under certain conditions, that is, attached to an EFSF/ESM program. The goal was, of course, to lower the long-term sovereign bond yield and, therefore, the borrowing cost for the Eurozone states. According to De Grauwe and Ji (2013),[30] the lower 10-year bond interest rate seen during the second-half of 2012 can be explained by the successful effects of the OMT.[31]

In Greece, the relative political stability after the June 2012 elections, which resulted in a coalition government with Antonis Samaras as a Prime Minister, contributed to a, more or less, on-target implementation of the adjustment program, a normal, prompt release of debt installments and the successful recapitalization of the banking sector. The systemic banks' recapitalization[32] was completed in June 2013 and its total cost was 28.595 billion euro, 24.998 billion of which were covered by the HFSF and the remaining 3.597 billion from private shareholders. Out of the four banks, only Eurobank collected less than the 10% threshold set as the minimum private installation participation, and therefore its management was passed into the hands of the HFSF.

Yet another major structural development in the EU for 2012 was the initiation of the process to create the Banking Union. The Banking Union, which transfers supervisory and intervening jurisdictions from the national level to the EU/ECB, constitutes an important component of European economic integration and operates complementarily with the "Euro-Plus Pact" reforms and the "Europe 2020" growth strategy in ensuring a safe and robust European banking system. Since November 2014, the ECB has assumed its supervisory role. The single resolution mechanism (SRM) entered into force in January 2016 and, through a single resolution board (SRB) and single resolution fund (SRF), it will "allow bank resolution to be managed more effectively" in the "rare cases when banks fail" (ibid).

The year 2013 ended with positive signs in regards to the basic goals of the fiscal consolidation. The Minister of Finance, Yannis Stournaras, predicted a budget surplus of 812 million euro and the 2014 budget was even more optimistic, with a GDP growth of 0.6% and a deficit of 2.3% of the GDP. The fiscal improvement was accompanied with more austerity and structural measures. The deregulatory character of the bill voted in March 2014, the significant steps into fiscal consolidation, and the memories of the 2012 unstable preelection climate were the major components of the political and economic environment formed in

---

[30] Panic-driven austerity in the Eurozone and its implications—http://www.voxeu.org/article/panic-driven-austerity-eurozone-and-its-implications

[31] While ECB's policy can exert some influence on the dynamics of bond spreads, macroeconomic fundamentals remain the major determinants of yield spreads during the crisis (e.g., von Hagen et al., 2011).

[32] The Bank of Greece categorized as "systemic" four Greek banks, after a strategic evaluation study prepared in March 2012: the National Bank of Greece, Piraeus Bank, Alpha Bank, and Eurobank. http://www.bankof greece.gr/BogEkdoseis/Έκθεση_για_την_ανακεφαλαιοποίηση.pdf

Greece in March 2014. Within this framework, 4 years after the exclusion of Greece from the capital markets, the Greek government issued a 3 billion euro worth 5-year bond at an interest rate of 4.75%. Based on Bloomberg, the offers were more than 20 billion euro and the yield of the 10-year bond fell to 5.8%.[33] The international media reported extensively on Greece's return to the markets, positively commenting on the successful issuing of the bond, recognizing the progress of the Greek economy, expressing at the same time reservations as to whether the point of complete recovery had been reached or not yet and that, therefore, more time might be needed to proclaim a Greek "success story."[34] A day after the bond was issued, the German Chancellor Angela Merkel visited Athens, from where she stated that significant progress had been accomplished in the Greek public finance and the Greek economy. Similar statements were made from other voices within the European Union.[35]

The return of Greece to the capital markets was indeed a financial fact of great economic and political importance. Although it did not of course lead to a restoration from the debt crisis or liberation from the supervision of the Troika, it was an important step toward this direction. However, at the same time, the unemployment was still in unprecedented levels, the public debt remarkably high, the construction activity stock-still, direct foreign investment very limited, the banking sector still unable to provide the necessary liquidity to the economy and, last but not least, the social cohesion weak and erratic. The Greek economy was undoubtedly in a recovery course but, as proven later, that was a fragile course of low speed in fickle weather.

1.3 Experiences

Having set the framework within which the crisis developed, we can now move to the next axis of this analysis that is to reach out for the experiences of the leading actors and the ways in which these experiences reproduced and/or changed the generative structures that brought Greece and the Eurozone in an orbit of transitions.

Given the difficulty—the impossibility even—to delineate the actors' experiences and place them within strict temporal and personal limits and infallibly associate them with structures and actions related to the crisis, we approximate actors' experiences through their public statements.[36] The political communication of the crisis has played a major formative role of the crisis, affecting spreads and securities prices in the debt market (Gade et al., 2013).

---

[33] http://www.bloomberg.com/news/2014-04-10/greece-readies-bond-sale-as-athens-car-bomb-reminds-of-upheaval.html

[34] http://www.nytimes.com/2014/04/10/business/international/greece-dives-back-into-the-bond-market.html

[35] http://www.star.gr/Pages/Politiki.aspx?art=222912&artTitle=soults_endeixi_empistosynis_stin_ellada_i_epitychimeni_exodos_stis_agores&page=3

[36] Surely, the focus on specific actors as well as the selection and interpretation of specific statements of theirs, inescapably carries the weight of our own personal view and analytical vision.

1.3.1 The Greek Government

1.3.1.1 The Prime Ministers

As the president of a socialist party, George Papandreou initiated his term as a Prime Minister promising prosperity and social justice, shutting out the possibility of reaching for help to the IMF, whose practices elsewhere had shown that "trim the future of those countries."[37] A few months later he was forced to explain to his European counterparties the reasons why Greece was asking for their support to "have the gun loaded on the table to be sure that the markets will respond positively."[38] Despite the continuous denials that a debt restructuring was likely, the Greek government agreed on it in order to get the second financial package. The Prime Minister presented this agreement as a victory and recognition of the sacrifices of the Greek people.[39] However, when the next day the celebrations for the national holiday of the October 28 were marked by strong protests of unprecedented severity against the members of the government, it was clear that the Greeks did not feel the same at all about the recent developments. Only a few days later, the Prime Minister was declaring his decisiveness to hold a referendum: "at a time when the political system is disputed and attacked we have the obligation to prefix and highlight the role and the responsibility of the citizen."[40] His initiative, led to his government's overthrow and the formation of a coalition government.

Lucas Papademos originally opposed a sovereign bond haircut,[41] but when taking office, he maintained that the haircut was indispensible to Greece if it wanted to stay in the Eurozone and to its economic recovery and prosperity.[42] All during his term his public speech was highlighting the seriousness of the crisis, the importance of debt restructuring, and the necessity of fiscal and structural reforms.

Before agreeing to participate in the coalition government under Lucas Papademos, Antonis Samaras, president of the new democracy party (ND), had strongly opposed to participating in a government with PASOK and was arguing that "the Memorandum brings recession. The freezing of the economy brings recession. This recession is sucking the effectiveness of the measures taken by the government."[43] A month before forming his coalition government after the June 2012 election, he said voting for the second Memorandum was a totally different thing.[44] Samaras' government applied the commitments of the second Memorandum and planned to discuss the prolongation of the repayment period in autumn 2014. A day after Greece's readmittance to the capital markets, A. Samaras was stating: "I think that with the

---

[37] http://www.youtube.com/watch?v=728wt3ganRo (3/6/2009)
[38] http://www.youtube.com/watch?v=LbAipY5U_mI (21/3/2010)
[39] http://www.youtube.com/watch?v=67oAMfMTGlw (24/10/2011)
[40] http://www.youtube.com/watch?v=GnqFvMa3wYM (31/10/2011)
[41] http://blogs.wsj.com/economics/2011/05/09/papademos-on-what-greece-must-do-to-address-debt-crisis/
[42] https://www.youtube.com/watch?v=F7IvfI0Y87s
[43] https://www.youtube.com/watch?v=yRkhDVt7Les
[44] https://www.youtube.com/watch?v=UfWTzoy-WlQ

sacrifices of the Greek people, the solidarity of our partners and the people of Germany, today we are in a totally different fate."[45]

1.3.1.2 The Ministers of Finance

George Papakonstantinou was Minister of Finance from October 2009 until June 2011 and his term is tied up with Greece's entry to the support mechanism. The beginning of his tenure coincided with the staggering revision of the expected 2009 public deficit, which decisively shaped the dominant Greek-crisis discourse at its dawn (Lane, 2012). For Papakonstantinou, austerity measures and structural reforms was a one-way solution and any other strategic choice was associated with disaster: "we have a choice between a difficult way and the way of catastrophe."[46]

Evangelos Venizelos, who succeeded Papakonstantinou in the Ministry of Finance, had been in favor of Greece's appeal to the support mechanism right from the start. In September 2011, Venizelos was the leading actor in the breakdown of the negotiations with the Troika, which led to the delay of the sixth debt installment and later to the announcement of the referendum by Papandreou. Although initially Venizelos advocated the referendum, soon he retreated contending that "Greece's place within the Euro is a historical conquest of the country that cannot be put into question. This is a Greek people's collective attainment and it cannot depend upon the conduct of a referendum."[47] During his speech at the Parliament when the PSI plus was discussed he gave a clear account of his ideas on the role of the markets: "Unfortunately, in the asymmetric warfare with the states on the one side and the international organizations and the markets on the other, so far the markets prevail. When the Eurozone for 2012 has the obligation and will pursuit to borrow from the markets more than 1.6 trillion euro, yes, unfortunately the markets have subdued the nations."[48]

Yannis Stournaras took office as a Minister of Finance of the coalition government formed after the June 2012 election. He believed that the recessional phenomena were not results of the Memorandum, "the Memorandum is not to blame for the current difficult economic and social conjuncture in our country."[49] He insisted that Greece's stay in the Eurozone was fully interwoven with the memorandums: "the alternative solution would be the exit from the Euro. And this solution would be and is catastrophic."[50] Consistent with this political path, when Greece borrowed from the markets in April 2014, he saw it as an indication that Greece had come out of the crisis.[51]

---

[45] http://www.primeminister.gov.gr/2014/04/11/12699
[46] http://www.youtube.com/watch?v=r1vKU2TzKY8 (10/6/2011)
[47] http://www.evenizelos.gr/el/statementsgr/2790-statement
[48] https://www.youtube.com/watch?v=DinZhLic5WI
[49] https://www.youtube.com/watch?v=duEgZSaqFf4
[50] https://www.youtube.com/watch?v=MAvZAxjKejI
[51] https://www.youtube.com/watch?v=5up1EdB2lSs

Time and again since the beginning of the crisis the Greek government saw itself acrobat between achieving the European support and mitigating popular reactions to austerity measures.

1.3.2 The European Central Bank

Being one of the three constituent parts of the Troika, the ECB played a major role in the evolution of the Greek crisis, not only through the supervision of the fiscal consolidation program, but also through liquidity provision to the Greek banking system and direct purchases of Greek debt in the secondary bond market. In the early stages of the crisis, Jean-Claude Trichet, president of the ECB (2003–11), intervened mainly to fashion a more favorable climate for the markets[52] or to exhort the political actors in the EU to take action.[53,54] Mario Draghi's public statements were more dynamic than his predecessor's, climaxing to his notable statement that the ECB "…is ready to do whatever it takes to preserve the Euro. And believe me, it will be enough."[55] Draghi's promise was emblematic of a sense of political urgency (Holmes, 2014). The ECB strongly supported and promoted a closer economic integration in the EU[56] and proved to be the central policy generation mechanism in the Eurozone of the debt crisis.

1.3.3 The President of the Eurogroup

Jean-Claude Juncker, president of the Eurogroup as of January 2005, agreed with Trichet on the importance of restoring markets' confidence in the Greek economy and regarded the support mechanism as a safety net to placate the markets.[57] "For every one of us the future of Greece is clearly within the Eurozone."[58] In April 2014, as a candidate for President of the European Commission he stated: "Greece returning to the markets is a hugely positive signal. Europe's common recipe for the crisis is starting to work."[59] Jeroen Dijsselbloem, Juncker' successor, also expressed confidence in the prospects of the Greek program[60] but he has reckoned that Greece may need financial support beyond the end of the funding program, such as "further reduction of the interest rates on the Greek loan facility and co-financing of EU structural funds."[61]

---

[52] http://www.youtube.com/watch?v=xduFKIZHIwA (26/3/2010)

[53] http://www.youtube.com/watch?v=XkiUsfRLgw4 (8/4/2010)

[54] http://www.youtube.com/watch?v=kurCV18vJnc (11/10/2011)

[55] https://www.youtube.com/watch?v=Pq1V0aPEO3c (26/07/2012)

[56] http://www.youtube.com/watch?v=ii-KU99yTuc (25/1/2013)

[57] http://www.youtube.com/watch?v=QpnESXnTs5Y (11/4/2010)

[58] http://www.youtube.com/watch?v=fraZpjnlpoQ (24/1/2012)

[59] http://juncker.epp.eu/press-releases/juncker-and-daul-welcome-greece%E2%80%99s-return-bond-markets (10/4/2014)

[60] https://www.youtube.com/watch?v=gVyNTcDVy54

[61] https://www.youtube.com/watch?v=Zo6ujwgXdD8

1.3.4 The President of the European Commission

In March 2010, one and a half month before Greece appealed to the support mechanism, Jose Mauel Barroso[62] supported the program of fiscal consolidation the Greek government had presented[63]. Barroso was also criticizing the credit rating agencies' role and methods and suggested a supervising competence for the (future) European Securities and Markets Authority (ESMA).[64] When needed, the President addressed the EU governments and called upon the European ideals and the seriousness of the circumstances arguing that "in a globalized world either we act as Europe, or we are not actors at all" (…) "Euro is one of our greatest assets" and its conservation requires the biggest attempts from all sides."[65] Barroso kept a moderate stance toward Greece, focusing mainly on the stability of the Euro.

1.3.5 The European Commissioner for Economic and Monetary Affairs and the Euro

Olli Rehn was also taking distance from either inordinately friendly statements of support to the Greeks or indignant arguments for their expulsion from the Euro. His dedication to neoliberal political-economic principles and a recovery through the application of austerity measures was stable and nonnegotiable[66]. Having lost his trust in the reliability of the Greek public organizations, he supported increased European interventional and coordinative activity through on-site technical committees.[67]

1.3.6 The President of the European Council

Herman Van Rompuy,[68] often aided Juncker's endeavors for coordinative action and he was frequently taking the role of the tranquilizer: "we are not in a monetary Armageddon, further inflation will not bring back confidence, it is a political duty to keep a sense of proportion."[69] He was highlighting the fact that Greece is a unique case[70] but also that the support mechanism was not "a miracle solution."[71]

---

[62] President of the European Commission between November 2004 and October 2014, Barroso is the only President of the Commission after Jacques Delors to serve two terms in office.
[63] http://www.youtube.com/watch?v=AR9MxM3Q9zs (4/3/2010)
[64] http://www.youtube.com/watch?v=VZis-1YNtgA (6/5/2010)
[65] http://www.youtube.com/watch?v=ayejyifP17Y (20/7/2011)
[66] http://www.youtube.com/watch?v=HrUghDOw3JU (12/5/2011)
[67] http://www.youtube.com/watch?v=1nh8cgQAV7I (10/2/2012)
[68] The first President of the European Council, December 1, 2009–November 30, 2014.
[69] http://www.youtube.com/watch?v=r-jeY-mcBGA (25/5/2010)
[70] http://www.youtube.com/watch?v=yX8zutnJLow (5/5/2010)
[71] http://www.youtube.com/watch?v=lQwbdIKN_R0 (26/3/2010)

1.3.7 The German Government

At the outbreak of the Greek debt crisis, given the absence of institutionalized financial support mechanisms, the Greek government, the markets and the entirety of the political and economic world was keeping a close eye on the German political scene, trying to decode the German positions. The latter ranged from a complete disapproval and even punitive disposition toward Greece to acquiescence for financial support under conditions: The German Chancellor A. Merkel was rigorously stating that "we can't have a common currency where some get lots of holiday time and others very little" (Guillén, 2012) and that there will be no European bonds "as long as I live."[72] The German Minister of Finance, Wolfgang Schaeuble was always highlighting the importance of discipline in the application of austerity measures contending that "European solidarity isn't a one-way street."[73] In February 2010, A. Merkel was stating that "Greece is a part of the European Union and won't be left on its own, but there are rules and these rules need to be adhered to."[74] Finally, Germany agreed with the provision of help to Greece conditional to the IMF's participation in the rescue program.

The German procrastination, the divergence of views between German officials and the request of IMF's involvement can be understood if one considers the timing in which these events took place: German elections were approaching and the German public opinion was reluctant to agree on any kind of financial help toward the European South. At the same time, the liquidity of the German banks was hanging upon the viability of the Greek sovereign debt, since the German along with the French banks were holding together two thirds of it (Barth et al., 2011). In April 2010, W. Schaeuble was saying: "We cannot allow Greece to turn into a second Lehman Brothers,"[75] making clear that for the German authorities a Greek default had finally been appraised unadvisable (Mink and de Haan, 2013). A week after the "first test"[76] was passed, in April 2014, Mr. Schaeuble was insisting that "the main danger here is complacency."[77,78] Mrs. Merkel was more enthusiastic with the 5-year Greek bond issuance and appeared more supportive stating that "Greece has honored its pledges" and that it "has made it."[79] All during the crisis Germany remained faithful to a well-rooted, neoliberal social-economic model which fully rejects loose monetary and fiscal policy and prioritizes

---

[72] http://www.spiegel.de/international/germany/german-commentators-say-merkel-s-hard-line-could-cause-end-of-euro-a-841489.html

[73] http://www.worldbulletin.net/haber/90235/greek-euro-zone-exit-preventable-schaeuble

[74] http://www.euractiv.com/euro/eu-leaders-reach-deal-rescue-greece (12/2/1010)

[75] http://www.spiegel.de/international/europe/german-finance-minister-wolfgang-schaeuble-we-cannot-allow-greece-to-turn-into-a-second-lehman-brothers-a-689766.html

[76] http://www.thetoc.gr/eng/economy/article/schauble-lauds-samaras

[77] http://www.kathimerini.gr/763303/article/epikairothta/politikh/o-efhsyxasmos-einai-o-kyrios-kindynos-proeidopoiei-o-soimple

[78] http://www.thetoc.gr/eng/economy/article/schauble-lauds-samaras

[79] http://www.dailymail.co.uk/wires/ap/article-2602261/Merkel-Athens-praises-Greek-reform-progress.html

price stability—austerity was therefore the only solution to the Greek problem, the "bitter medicine" the Greek ailing economy had to take to heal.

1.3.8 The French Government

The French President, Nicolas Sarkozy advocated immediate action and a radical solution to the Greek problem. His stance, apart from his personality, was also associated with his party's Gaullist tradition, with France's leading role in the European integration process and the postwar French political tradition regarding state involvement in the financial system.[80] Sarkozy's discourse during the European debt crisis in general and the Greek issue in particular built on and around the idea of solidarity.[81,82] The differences between the German and French fiscal priorities were evident since the first violations of the Stability and Growth Pact and the disparate personal political style between N. Sarkozy and A. Merkel consisted, for many, determinant factors of the flow of events during the crisis (Bohn and De Jong, 2011; Howarth, 2004). Sarkozy was for more definite solutions without the involvement of non-European organizations, such as the IMF[83] but the German view prevailed. The new French President, Francois Hollande followed his predecessor's line, insisting on European solidarity and the unceasing Greek efforts to abide with their obligations.[84]

1.3.9 The Greek Citizen

Undeniably, the Greeks experienced in the hardest way the impact of the financial crisis and the plethora of austerity measures which reduced their income, wounded their prosperity and, above all, disoriented their perspective. During the first 4 years of the crisis, the Greek GDP decreased by 20% from 2009 to 2013, the basic salary fell from 740 to 586 euro, the unemployment rate exceeded 27% and 250,000 SMEs shut down. The aftereffect of income shrinkage was dramatically depicted on an increase of the at-risk-of-poverty rate.[85] A report on the Greek economy published by the Greek Foundation for Economic and Industrial Research in December 2013[86] shows the strong compression of the purchasing power and consumer confidence.[87] The continuing uncertainty and continuing scenarios of a Greek unregulated

---

[80] The vigorous governmental intervention in France during the 2008 credit crisis is indicative of this stance (Jabko and Massoc, 2012).

[81] https://www.youtube.com/watch?v=M0HTD0ytCdA (Bloomberg 8/3/2010)

[82] http://www.ft.com/intl/cms/s/0/db2dd602-2914-11df-972b-00144feabdc0.html#axzz3N1OQTpuC

[83] http://www.bloomberg.com/apps/news?pid=newsarchive&sid=aFoFKQDc5LJk

[84] http://www.nytimes.com/2012/08/26/world/europe/france-reassures-greece-on-euro-zone-membership.html?_r=0

[85] http://www.statistics.gr/portal/page/portal/ESYE/BUCKET/A0802/PressReleases/A0802_SFA10_DT_AN_00_2012_01_F_GR.pdf. In 2012 the rate was 23.1% or 2,535,700 citizens—in 2009 the same figure was 19.7%.

[86] http://www.iobe.gr/default_en.asp

[87] http://www.iobe.gr/docs/situation/BCS_13012014_REP_GR.pdf

default and exit from the Eurozone, led to recurring bank runs—in combination with the severe income decreases, the bank deposits decreased by 77.7 billion euro in the period 2010–12.

New political and social streams have emerged or gained power during the period 2009–14. In spring 2012, the Greeks changed the political scene irreversibly: traditionally big political parties turned into peripheral powers (PASOK got 12.28%), three new parties entered the Parliament (Independent Greeks, Golden Dawn, and Democratic Left), SYRIZA became the opposition party increasing its power to the Parliament in unprecedented levels for the Greek Left and the far-right fascist party Golden Dawn with a 6.92% won parliamentary seats for the first time in the Greek political history. The subsequent parliamentary elections of 2015 further solidified this new political landscape, with SYRIZA forming their first government.

1.3.10 The Investors

The investors were, of course, another leading actor of the Greek crisis. Their preferences and choices shaped the capital market dynamics and, through the markets, the political program of governments. The investors' transactions are, basically, opinion articulation mechanisms—the largest investors are "heard" more. The investors network is very dense and of course uncharted. As indicative of the investor experiences we used Charles Dallara statements, Managing Director of the Institute of International Finance (1993–2013) and spokesman of the private investors in Greece. His role was important particularly during the participation of the private investors in the debt restructuring, from the summer of 2011 through the spring of 2012. With his statements in July 2011 he was paving the way for the private investors' participation in the Greek debt restructuring program.[88] The characterization "Armageddon" for the Greek exit from the Eurozone depicted the investors' preference for economic and political stability in Greece and Europe.[89] The loan and the payout agreement was a political and economic case where the financial system, the political leaders, and the people were connected in a network of inextricably complex and dynamic bonds.

1.4 The Structures

In this section we are looking into the generative and reproductive structures that led to the outbreak and the evolution of the crisis until the spring of 2014 when the Greek government returned to bond markets with a 5-year bond issue. The combination of structural factors that shaped the dynamics of the crisis is summarized in Fig. 1.1.

The US financial crisis affected to a greater or lesser extent every economic entity involved in the internationalized economic system and soon it transfigured into a global systemic

---

[88] http://www.youtube.com/watch?v=-RnbWg7plWU Bloomberg 6/7/2011
[89] http://www.youtube.com/watch?v=Rdar8-0csyI Bloomberg 16/5/2012

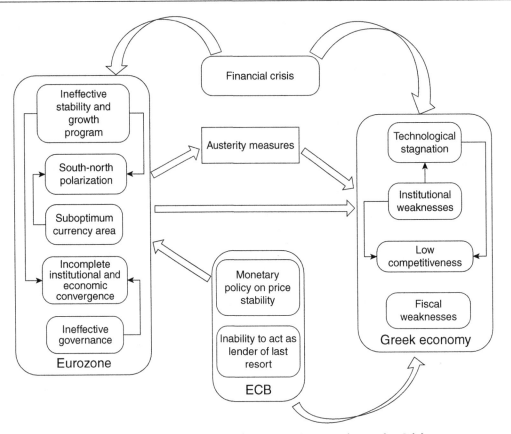

Figure 1.1: Structural Causes of the Greek Sovereign Debt Crisis.

crisis. Economies, such as the British, the Irish, and the Icelandic were shattered as they were largely based on the dynamic development of the financial sector, which enjoyed lax supervision and, for the sake of its growth, was exposed to high risk across global financial and capital markets. The central banks offered immediate liquidity to the commercial banks substituting the inert interbank market (Crouhy et al., 2008). Public budgets eased to allow larger deficits, increased public expenditure, provision of guarantees on deposits, and the recapitalization of systemic banks and, consequently, led to increased public debt, raising doubts about its viability and shifting investors' concerns in sovereign debt market. The interdependence between sovereign debt crisis and financial crisis has been studied by Reinhart and Rogoff who showed that the financial crises follow bank crises within a period of a few months and that the public debt to GDP rate is increasing after the outbreak of banking crises[90] (Reinhart and Rogoff, 2011). The banks are the main government lenders,

---

[90] Candelon and Palm (2010), employing the approach of Rogoff and Reinhart, had demonstrated the possibility of a credit event in Greek and Irish sovereign debt, based on data from 2009.

who, if need be recapitalized will burden public debt which is purchased by private creditors (Angeloni et al., 2012).

In Greece, throughout the postwar history, the banking system had been a strategic government lender and, therefore, it was heavily exposed to the risk and return of sovereign bonds (Pagoulatos, 2003). In the end of 2008 the banking system got a direct financial support of 5 billion euro (2% of GDP)—indirectly another 15 billion euro were provided in the form of guarantees and 8 billion in the form of securities.[91] The state budget was not severely charged by the support provided to the banks. However, the growth rate of the Greek economy was negative in 2008 and the recession in 2009 was −3.1%. The public debt reached 112.9% of GDP in 2008 and 129.7% in 2009. As the growth prospects of the world economy were deteriorating and the Eurozone was entering a financial crisis itself, the markets felt the Greek economy weaknesses and they started questioning the viability of the Greek debt increasing the rate of return of the Greek securities. When it was revealed that restoring confidence in the Greek economy was no longer feasible, Greece looked out for the financial support of the EU and the IMF.

1.4.1 The Structural Weaknesses of the Eurozone

But why couldn't the EU provide the necessary reassurance to the markets (both abstractly and practically) that Greece, as part of the European family, could serve its obligations and finally exit the difficult period unscathed? The reasons for this inability lie in structural weaknesses which the EU and the Eurozone carried and—somewhat diversified, but still—carry until today.

In an increasingly liberalized world, tending to deregulation and decreasing state market intervention, the creation of the Common Market was based in anticipation of its autoregulation, fair organization for the benefit of consumers, producers, and workers (Petit, 2012). In order to achieve equitable distribution of resources among numerous sides with conflicting interests, it was necessary to develop structures that would promote cohesion and solidarity among Member States. The Common Market was largely based on the German model of the Social Market Economy and ordoliberalism[92] assisted by the neo-liberal Anglo-Saxon logic. What was missing, in contrast to the German model, was a central entity to undertake the regulatory role of the state. Financial and fiscal goals are monitored and regulated (convergence criteria) at the supranational level but growth and unemployment goals (solidarity criteria) remain in the hands of the national government. The Eurozone inherited its principles from the Common Market: based on the article 104 of the Maastricht Treaty (1992), the member states did not have the obligation to rescue a member

---

[91] Law 3723/2008 (250 A).

[92] For a comprehensive account on the Social Market Economy and ordoliberalism, see Vandberg (2004).

state from insolvency. The participation in the Euro moved forward as an irreversible process, and although this strengthened the robustness and reliability of the Euro, the no-bailout clause created a political and procedural gap which would be visible only in the advent of adverse financial developments. All the Treaties that followed imposed strict conditions for the application of the Euro and compliance mechanisms. Growth would come through ensuring financial stability, low inflation, and competitiveness. However, this growth was not symmetrical for Europe. The European Regional Development Fund, the Community Support Frameworks and, in general the EU regional policy seek to smooth some of the structural differences between the member-states. In the Eurosystem, the ECB and the central banks of the Eurozone member states cooperate in the formation and application of the monetary policy. The ECB's (in)ability to buy government debt lies in the epicenter of its role in sovereign debt crisis (Lavoie, 2015). "The Eurozone has a central bank without a government, governments without central banks and banks without an effective lender of last resort" (Toporowski, 2013, p. 572).

Using the analytical tools supplied by the Optimal Currency Areas[93] theory we can evaluate the function of the Eurozone and understand its difficulty to address the dangers of asymmetric shocks in its constituency (Jager and Hafner, 2013). Influential economists, such as Eichengreen (1991) and De Grauwe (2000, 2006) had expressed concerns regarding the viability of the Eurozone and the need for reforms to enhance the stability of the EMU well before the debt crisis broke out, during which the structural weaknesses of the Eurozone became more explicit (Shambaugh, 2012). The challenges in the operation of a monetary union begin when different areas of the union are in need of dissimilar—and often incompatible—economic policy mixes while being at different points in the economic cycle. In such cases the monetary union is stable when the following conditions are met: Mobility of labor and capital, price flexibility of goods and services, commercial openness, social transfers from the surplus to the deficit regions. In the EU these conditions are often not met, at least not to the extent necessary to assure the smooth operation of the union during asymmetric shocks. This is more evident when the EU is compared to the USA, which is not an optimal currency area either (Kouparitsas (2001)). The absence of a common national identity and the existence of important language barriers render labor relatively immobile. Although the basic European capital markets have similar dynamics, the capital movements are less able to absorb economic asymmetries as this happens with the capital movements between the states in the USA (Jager and Hafner, 2013; Savva et al., 2009). Price flexibility in goods and services, as well as in the cost of labor increases competitiveness. Employee compensation fluctuations cannot be unlimited or abrupt as provided by labor law—which is also different between different Eurozone countries. Accordingly, legal and economic factors

---

[93] The bases of the Optimal Currency Area theory were set by Mundell (1961), McKinnon (1963), and Kenen (1969). Earlier, Friedman (1953) had also put forward some preliminary concerns. For a review of the related literature, see Dellas and Tavlas (2009).

restrict the competition intensity in many sectors of the economy and, consequently, goods' prices do not change easily. Trade between the Eurozone members or with third countries did not increase as a result of the adoption of the common currency (Willet et al., 2010) and therefore the Euro did not substantially improve the ability of international trade to normalize asymmetries in good times. Many of the EU policies are, basically, redistributive, but what was missing was the political will and the structural framework for direct money transfers to regions affected by severe financial problems (Holmes, 2014). This function was initiated in 2010 with the establishment of EFSF, which is not, however, a systematic coping mechanism against financial asymmetries. The fiscal union of the Eurozone members, toward which the Fiscal Compact is moving, is a component of their political union and they are both crucial for the viability of the single currency.[94]

The great heterogeneity of the European economies denotes great dissimilarities on issues, such as private consumption, credit growth, entrepreneurship, labor relations, the educational system, social welfare, fiscal policy, and public expenditure. Structural asymmetries led to repeated violations of the Stability and Growth Pact. During the crisis, the shallow examination of fiscal asymmetries and Greek structural weaknesses led to a rough diagnosis of the Greek problem and neglected the formation and application of antirecessionary policies, focusing instead on methods of fiscal sanitization and market deregulation to diminish fiscal divergence. These policies and their recessionary effects shoved Greece into a deep, long-term economic depression, often superseding the short-term benefits of financial support and of deregulatory and restructuring measures which need more time to pay.

1.4.2 Structural Weaknesses of the Greek Economy

The main axes of Greek economic development had been private consumption and construction, powered by growing liquidity and low cost of money that came with the advent of the euro. The contribution of the services sector was expanding in contrast to agriculture and industrial production which had been progressively shrinking. The accession to the Eurozone, the advantages of low and stable inflation, low cost of money, and increased liquidity did not make up the springboard for the modernization and qualitative transformation of the Greek economy or its reorientation toward more specialized and efficient productive sectors.

Public debt accumulation stems from recurring high deficits of the state budget. Despite the favorable conditions of high growth and low borrowing costs between 2000 and 2008, the Greek governments did not act counter-cyclically, missing a unique opportunity to implement a moderate fiscal policy reducing public debt to sustainable levels. Fiscal deficits partly

---

[94] The importance of a political union for the viability of a common currency has been highlighted since the first steps of the scientific dialog on economic integration (Balassa 1961).

resulted from governments' inability to achieve sufficient revenue to meet public expenditure, in large due to its inadequacy to tackle with a vast tax evasion problem. Another permanent feature of the Greek economy was the persistent and increasing current account deficit, which contributed decisively in the expansion and accumulation of public debt. In the way toward the crisis, the balance of services was positive, mainly due to inputs from land and sea transportation and tourism. At the same time, Greek exports are characterized by a high concentration of low and medium-low technology-intensive products, a characteristic which depicts the economy's limited ability to grow (Yousefi, 2013; Zeira, 1998). Oelgemoller (2013) showed that the main Greek export products are low- and medium-low-tech, such as fruit, tobacco, cotton, vegetables, fish, leather, minerals, and metals. So long as Greek exports focus on low-technology and low skills labor, the easy solution to the improvement of competitiveness will be salary reduction.

Within the Eurozone inflation differences created imbalances and reduced the Greek competitiveness, affecting product and raw material prices and production costs.[95] Higher inflation contributed to the growth of nominal unit labor costs in Greece. Furthermore, the insufficient institutional framework, the existence of oligopolies and closed professions and sectors raised consumer prices almost regardless of the intensity of demand. The competitiveness and productivity of the Greek economy are also inhibited by lagging infrastructure, poor public services, road and telecommunication networks, poor utilization of green technologies, and alternative energy sources severely affecting productivity.

Moreover, ineffective governance, corruption, lack of transparency, tax evasion, a slow justice system, are features of weak institutions which are incapable of ensuring equity and social justice and promote welfare (Pelagidis, 2009). The prevalent perception on corruption in Greece is that the Greek political system, and the political parties more particularly, are responsible for the consolidation of opacity, customer relationships in politics, and the neglect of meritocracy and equality in Greece. There is a certain temperament, forged in the historical evolution and inherited standards of the Greek society (Vryonis, 1963), which allows for the acceptance of the stereotypes that promote customer relationships and sidestep formal institutions. A paternal figure, that holds absolute power, has the ability to bypass institutions and promote customer relations to settle ordinary affairs—this father figure, a politically mutant sense of parental protection (Ramfos, 2011), permeates economic,[96] social and political institutions, and inactivates society, setting it in waiting of the central political power to solve its problems. Also, the feeling of living within a corrupt system weakens public confidence in fundamental social institutions impeding economic development. Trust

---

[95] For the period 2001–10 the average inflation rate was 1.1% in Germany, 2% in the Eurozone (12 members), and 3.1% in Greece.

[96] For example, Drakopoulou Dodd and Patra (2002) found that relatives consist 31% of the network of the Greek entrepreneurs.

between people and institutions is a key factor for a successful and creative entrepreneurship, trust favors macroeconomic stability and the relationship between trust and economic development is two-way (Knack and Zack, 2003; Sangnier, 2013; Welter, 2012). Economic development and welfare are also promoted by the stability stemming by the application of the rule of law (Boettke and Subrick, 2003), because it reveals that the State attitude toward legal issues remains stable. To achieve this, the justice system needs to be rapid and effective. Oltheten et al. (2014) reported that 23.8% of cases pending in courts in 2011 were concerning tax affairs and the average period until settlement of tax cases in Greek courts was around 7–10 years.

One of the main symptoms of institutional ineffectiveness in Greece is tax evasion. According to Transparency International, the tax collection mechanism was the second most corrupt service in Greece, after health care services. Over and above the State's inability to collect taxes, the basic structural component of tax evasion is related to the informal sector of the Greek economy (black economy or underground economy).[97] The conformation of the Greek economy around small, family enterprises, the large number of self-employed, and the missing (until recently) necessary infrastructure for the electronic interconnection of the Ministry of Finance with the taxpayers aggravate tax evasion.

Within the international literature of Development Economics there is no agreement on the institutional characteristics that fit better to the course of a country toward growth and prosperity. Effective institutions vary from country to country and from one era to the other (Chang, 2011). The unchanged application of similar principles in heterogeneous economies often poses political and economic impasses. The political crunches of the programs usually suggested by the IMF mostly stem from the attempt to apply the same treatment to substantially different patients. It goes without saying that structural reforms take several years to yield, but this can only mean that they should not have been tied to the short term Troika installments programs and that spectacular growth overthrows will be required in the near future in order to cover the ground lost during the Memorandum years.

1.5 Conclusions

The ongoing crisis is indicative of open economic systems which are driven by their dynamic structures and also by the agential choices of economic actors. Employing a critical-realist framework and implementing a novel methodology with respect to this framework, we stratify the Greek crisis in three layers: the structures which brought about economic outcomes, the experiences of economic actors, and their actions which set economic structures in motion, triggering the crisis, and still reproducing it. The evolution of the crisis

---

[97] In 2012, the informal sector accounted for 23.6% of the GDP (Schneider, 2013). In 2011, the government tax revenue was 32.4% of the GDP (the European average was 38.8%).

was shaped through the actions of its protagonists, whose actions are constitutive of their experiences, the way in which they underwent the crisis. Based on this experience, the actors chose their response, trying to avoid or deter the crisis, sometimes ending up deepening it. Some of the actors' responses produced effects of structural change: the IMF became part of the economic governance of the Eurozone, the OMT program was an institutional move of the ECB closer to a role of lender of last resort, the EFSF and the ESM challenged the no-bailout clause of the Maastricht Treaty. On the other hand, some other initiatives seemed to reproduce the structural characteristics of the Eurozone: the Fiscal Compact and the Euro Plus Pact are the institutional descendants of the Stability and Growth Pact which fostered homogeneous fiscal austerity across the European Union. Apart from emergency measures which deal with some of the crisis' painful symptoms, an effective response to the crisis should deal with its deep-rooted causes and such causes are mostly institutional. Our analysis has provided an outline of the institutional apparatus of radical economic change in times of crisis. Knowing this apparatus, we can target, design, and apply the necessary institutional changes both in Greece and the Eurozone.

References

Alpha Bank, 2009. Economic Bulletin, 110. Athens, Greece.

Andrikopoulos, A., 2013. Financial economics: objects and methods of science. Camb. J. Econ. 37 (4), 35–55.

Angeloni, C., Merler, S., Wolff, G.B., 2012. Policy lessons from the Eurozone crisis. Int. Spect. 47 (4), 17–34.

Balassa, B., 1961. The Theory of Economic Integration. Richard D. Irwin Inc, Homewood, IL.

Bank of Greece, 2009. Monetary Policy—Interim Report, Athens.

Barth, J.R., Liy, T., Prabhavivadhana, A., 2011. Greece's "unpleasant arithmetic" containing the threat to the global economy. Global Econ. J. 11 (4), 1–15.

Bhaskar, R., 1978. A Realist Theory of Science, second ed. Hemel Hempstead, Harvester Press, Sussex.

Boettke, P.J., Subrick, J.R., 2003. Rule of law, development and human capabilities. Sup. Ct. Rev. 10, 109–126.

Bohn, F., de Jong, E., 2011. The 2010 euro crisis stand-off between France and Germany: leadership styles and political culture. Int. Econ. Econ. Pol. 8 (1), 7–14.

Candelon, B., Palm, J.R., 2010. Banking and debt crises in Europe: the dangerous liaisons? De Economist 158 (1), 81–99.

Chang, H.-J., 2011. Institutions and economic development: theory, policy and history. J. Inst. Econ. 7 (4), 473–498.

Crouhy, M.G., Jarrow, R.A., Turnbull, S.M., 2008. The subprime credit crisis of 2007. J. Deriv. 16 (1), 81–110.

Dellas, H., Tavlas, G.S., 2009. An optimum-currency-area odyssey. Bank of Greece Working paper, Athens.

De Grauwe, P., 2000. Economics of the Monetary Union, fourth ed. Oxford University Press, Oxford.

De Grauwe, P., 2006. What have we learnt about monetary integration since the Maastricht Treaty? J. Common Mark. Stud. 14 (4), 711–730.

De Grauwe, P., Ji, Y., 2013. Panic-driven austerity in the Eurozone and its implications. Available from: http://www.voxeu.org/article/panic-driven-austerity-eurozone-and-its-implications

Drakopoulou Dodd, S., Patra, E., 2002. National differences in entrepreneurial networking. Entrep. Reg. Dev. 14 (2), 117–134.

Eichengreen, B., 1991. Is Europe an Optimum Currency Area? National Bureau of Economic Research, Working paper No. 3579.

European Commission, 2010. Report on Greek Government Deficit and Debt Statistics 8/1/2010. Brussels.

Friedman, M., 1953. The case for flexible exchange rates. In: Friedman, M. (Ed.), Essays in Positive Economics. University of Chicago Press, Chicago, pp. 157–203.

Gade, T., Salines, M., Glöckler, G., Strodhoff, S., 2013. Loose lips sinking markets? The impact of political communication on sovereign bond spreads. ECB working paper.

Guillén, A., 2012. Europe: the crisis within a crisis. Int. J. Polit. Econ. 41, 41–68, Fall 2012.

Holmes, C., 2014. 'Whatever it takes': polanyian perspectives on the eurozone crisis and the gold standard. Econ. Soc. 43 (4), 582–602.

Howarth, D., 2004. The ECB and the stability pact: policeman and judge? J. Eur. Public Policy 11 (5), 832–853.

Jabko, N., Massoc, E., 2012. French capitalism under stress: how Nicolas Sarkozy rescued the banks. Rev. Int. Polit. Econ. 19 (4), 562–585.

Jager, J., Hafner, K.A., 2013. The optimum currency area theory and the EMU. Intereconomics 48 (5), 315–322.

Jefferson, T., King, J.E., 2011. Michal Kalecki and critical realism. Camb. J. Econ. 35 (5), 957–972.

Jessop, B., 2006. Beyond the Regulation Approach. Edward Elgar, Cheltenham.

Kenen, P.B., 1969. The theory of optimum currency areas: an eclectic view. In: Mundell, R.A., Swoboda, A.K. (Eds.), Monetary Problems of the International Economy. University of Chicago Press, Chicago, pp. 41–60.

Knack, S.F., Zack, P.J., 2003. Building trust: public policy, interpersonal trust and economic development. Sup. Ct. Rev. 10, 91–107.

Kouparitsas, M.A., 2001. Is the United States an optimum currency area? An empirical analysis of regional business cycles. Federal Reserve Bank of Chicago Working Paper.

Lane, P.R., 2012. The European sovereign debt crisis. J. Econ. Perspect. 26 (3), 49–68.

Lavoie, M., 2015. The Eurozone: similarities and differences with Keynes's plan. Int. J. Polit. Econ. 44 (1), 3–17.

Lawson, T., 1997. Economics and Reality. Routledge, London.

McKinnon, R.I., 1963. Optimum currency areas. Am. Econ. Rev. 53 (4), 717–725.

Mink, M., de Haan, J., 2013. Contagion during the Greek sovereign debt crisis. J. Int. Money Finance 34, 102–113.

Mundell, R.A., 1961. A theory of optimum currency areas. Am. Econ. Rev. 51 (4), 657–665.

Oelgemoller, J., 2013. Revealed comparative advantages in Greece, Ireland, Postrugal and Spain. Intereconomics 48 (4), 243–253.

Oltheten, E., Sougiannis, T., Travlos, N., Zarkos, S., 2014. Greece in the Eurozone: lessons from a decade of experience. Q. Rev. Econ. Finance 53 (4), 317–335.

Pagoulatos, G., 2003. Greece's New Political Economy. Palgrave McMillan, London and New York.

Pelagidis, T., 2009. Structural and institutional divergence in the European Union. Challenge 52 (6), 101–113.

Petit, P., 2012. Building faith in a common currency: can the Eurozone get beyond the common market logic? Camb. J. Econ. 36 (1), 271–281.

Ramfos, S., 2011. The Logic of Insanity. Armos, Athens.

Reinhart, C.M., Rogoff, K.S., 2011. From financial crash to debt crisis. Am. Econ. Rev. 101 (5), 1676–1706.

Rotheim, R.J., 1999. Post Keynesian economics and realist philosophy. J. Post Keynes. Econ. 22 (1), 71–103.

Sangnier, M., 2013. Does trust favor macroeconomic stability? J. Comp. Econ. 41 (3), 653–668.

Savva, C.S., Osborn, D.R., Gill, L., 2009. Spillovers and correlations between US and major European stock markets: the role of the euro. Appl. Financ. Econ. 19 (19), 1595–1604.

Shambaugh, J.C., 2012. The Euro's three Crises. Brookings Papers on Economic Activity, Spring 2012, pp. 157–231.

Schneider, F., 2013. Size and development of the shadow economy of 31 European and 5 other OECD countries from 2003 to 2013: a further decline. Working paper.

Toporowski, J., 2013. International credit, financial integration and the Euro. Camb. J. Econ. 37 (3), 571–584.

Vandberg, V.J., 2004. The Freiburg School: Walter Eucken and ordoliberalism. Working paper.

von Hagen, J., Schuknecht, L., Wolswijk, G., 2011. Government bond risk premiums in the EU revisited: the impact of the financial crisis. Eur. J. Polit. Econ. 27 (1), 36–43.

Vryonis, S., Jr., Byzantine dēmokratia and the guild in the eleventh century, 1963, Dumbarton Oaks Papers, vol. 17, pp. 287–314.

Welter, F., 2012. All you need is trust? A critical review of the trust and entrepreneurship literature. Int. Small Bus. J. 30 (3), 193–212.

Willet, T.D., Permpoon, O., Wihlborg, C., 2010. Endogenous OCA analysis and the early Euro experience. World Econ. 33 (7), 851–872.

Yousefi, A., 2013. The impact of information and communication technology on economic growth: evidence from developed and developing countries. Econ. Innov. New Tech. 20 (6), 581–596.

Zeira, J., 1998. Workers, machines and economic growth. Q. J. Econ. 113 (4), 1091–1117.

Zettelmeyer, J., Trebesch, C., Gulati, M., 2013. The Greek debt restructuring: an autopsy Working Paper, July 2013.

Further Reading

Christopoulou, R., Monastiriotis, V., 2016. Public-private wage duality during the Greek crisis. Oxf. Econ. Pap. 68 (1), 174–196.

Ehrman, M., Soudan, M., Stracca, L., 2013. Explaining European Union citizens' trust in the European Central Bank in normal and crisis times. Scand. J. Econ. 115 (3), 781–807.

Kaplanoglou, G., Rapanos, V.T., Bardakas, I.C., 2015. Does fairness matter in the success of fiscal consolidation? Kyklos 68 (2), 197–219.

Theocharis, Y., van Deth, J.W., 2013. Causes and consequences of the Greek crisis. Working paper, Mannheim Center for European Social Research, University of Mannheim.

Wälti, S., 2012. Trust no more? The impact of the crisis on citizens' trust in central banks. J. Int. Money Finance 31 (3), 593–605.

CHAPTER 2

Investor Behavior Before and After the Financial Crisis: Accounting Standards and Risk Appetite in Fixed Income Investing

Apostolos Xanthopoulos[a]

Mercer Investment Consulting, Chicago, IL, United States

Chapter Outline

2.1 Introduction

The roots and consequences of the 2007–08 financial crisis in the United States, and the actual or the perceived effect on economies of the rest of the world have by now been extensively documented. The purpose of the present analysis is to gauge any ever-so-slight modifications in the behavior of investors before, and after the event in terms of absolute levels of wealth, as well as measure the ability of agent-portfolio managers in meeting such change, in terms of benchmark-relative performance. The investor exhibited natural predisposition to modify patters of consumption in a timeframe that is coincidental to early signs of the crisis (2004–08), and seems to return to such patterns post crisis (2012–15). But the onset of unprecedented Central Bank intervention may have been equally destabilizing,

---

[a] This article was prepared by the author in his personal capacity. The views and opinions expressed in this article are those of the author and do not necessarily reflect the views and opinions of Mercer Investment Consulting LLC or its affiliates.

as the crisis itself (2008–12). In the process, investors have learned to pursue absolute performance from large swings in financial markets. Hence, portfolio managers have attempted to generate out-performance in a benchmark-relative sense. As the principals, large institutional and retail investors exhibited tolerance toward investing in the tails and agent-portfolio managers responded by positioning portfolios suitably.

As of the time of this writing, due to the low-volatility, low-yield environment promulgated by Central Bank intervention, the investors may once again view returns out of once-critiqued "fat tails" as having become largely undemonized. The proclivity of the investor to move to the tails in search of yield can derive from a simple expansion of utility of wealth, to terms higher than portfolio-variance, in absolute terms. But the three distinct periods mentioned [crisis, quantitative easing (QE), "taper tantrum"] may reveal different levels of such investor proclivity. The pertinent question of portfolio manager response to such changes is addressed. One difficulty of standard performance metrics in industry is they do not capture current investor behavior but only reflect a paradigm of normal distributions and linear beta. The task of evaluating the performance of portfolio managers by the consulting industry should also be difficult, due to the earlier considerations. These issues are partly addressed. Estimation results illustrate the patterns in which absolute returns sought, and relative returns generated, match. The discussion is motivated by one example of the circumstances that have triggered an apparent tendency of fixed income investor to travel toward and away from market events, in the process of achieving general wealth maximization.

The main theme is that risk-taking of the investor was up before the crisis, vanished in the aftermath of crisis, and is on now back up again, to levels as high as before. In that respect, the time period of March 2004 to December 2015 was divided in three periods of 48 monthly returns each: (1) the Crisis period of March 2004 to February 2008, (2) the Quantitative Easing (QE) period of February 2008 to January 2012, and (3) Taper Tantrum period, from January 2012 to December 2015. For each period, subsamples of 36 monthly returns were rolled forward a month at a time to obtain a total of 12 rolling-sample results. The 12 rolling-sample results were averaged within each of the periods and compared to detect changes in investor behavior. Results entailed information ratio (IR) modified to account for market nonlinearities and effects attributed to a low-rate environment. Monthly data were obtained from Morningstar, for 388 retail portfolios between March 2004 and December 2015. Monthly data for eight indices were obtained for the same period, from Bloomberg: Barclays Global Aggregate, Barclays Global High Yield, Credit Suisse Leveraged Loans, Barclays US Aggregate, Barclays US High Yield, Barclays US TIPS, Bank of America Merrill Lynch Government/Corporate 1-3 Year, and JP Morgan Emerging Market Global index.

2.2 Early Signs of Trouble

Investor utility of wealth is not directly observable, especially as far as changes in resulting behavior due to the crisis are concerned. The performance of fixed income investment professionals acting as agents of the utility-maximizing investors, on the other hand, is directly measurable. It is assumed that this level of performance partly reflects behavioral changes of the investor-principal, even as standard issues with measuring manager performance partly frustrate such reflection. At the same time, during crisis times, one should expect established patterns in the relation of investor utility and manager performance to be breaking down. Yet, the basic behavioral ingredients that led to this apparent breakdown permeated the markets, all along. Before embarking on an analysis of investor behavior during the actual event, it is constructive to isolate the predisposition to such changes, which based on pivotal market elements just before, could have brought on the crisis earlier, if not in milder form. Evidence of impending imbalances was partly hidden, until it ultimately culminated with the crisis and that could be seen, in advance.

Financial crises of the 2007–08 kind, in the largest economy of the world, do not happen without any early warning signs, whatsoever. It may not be an anachronism to say that the financial crisis of 2007–08 in the United States should have occurred prior to 2005. Evidence was the massive amounts of refinancing of residential mortgages in the United States, right after what appeared to be the peak of a housing price bubble around December, 2004. The signs of this abrupt increase in refinancing were clearly visible, through the patterns of statistical data on mortgage prepayments, processed by Government Sponsored Enterprises (GSEs), the agencies created by US government to protect and support residential housing. Prepayments refer to the option of a borrower to prepay at par, at any time during the life of his or her mortgage. For a 30-year period before the financial crisis, analysis of the option to prepay was dependent only on (1) the coupon rate in relation to refinancing opportunities, (2) the age of the mortgage, (3) the season of the year, (4) the degree of mortgage burnout, and (5) the growth/recession state of the macro economy.[1] What had possibly escaped the attention of analysts and investors, was that an option to prepay (call option) and one to default (put option), should at least in theory be linked through put-call parity, with underlying values of the loan amount and the market value of property, respectively.[2] The mortgage lender substitute refinancing in place of possible default, ahead of time.

With the advent of subprime loans and the seepage of lower standards into AAA-rated mortgage pools, substitution of behavior between what should have been an interest-rate-driven call on the typical US mortgage loan (i.e., prepayment through refinancing) and what ended up as the exercise of a property-value-decline put on housing, had eluded the investor public for at least 3 years. Today it is common knowledge that prepayment may have more than quadrupled, in one single month (Bhardwaj and Sengupta, 2008). Data available in the systems of US GSEs of the FNMA, FHLMC, and the Federal Home Loan Banks would have

---

[1] Breeden, D.T., 1995. Risk, return and hedging of fixed-rate mortgages. In: Fabozzi, F.J. (Ed.), The Handbook of Mortgage-Backed Securities, fourth ed., Probus Publishing Company, United States. pp. 783–825.

[2] Pennington-Cross, A., 2002. Patterns of Default and Prepayment for Prime and Nonprime Mortgages, Working Paper 02-1, OPHEO Working Papers, Office of Federal Housing Enterprise & Oversight, Washington, D.C.

pointed to this inconsistency, almost immediately at that time.[3] As author Andrew Sorkin points in his book "Too Big to Fail" risk analysts that may have pointed to prepayment inconsistencies were often shown their way to the elevator carrying a box of personal belongings, to paraphrase.[4] The inability of the GSEs to perceive any sort of soft landing in the face of already known information was due to short-sighted self-interest of senior management, preferring the continuation of a modus operandi. A counter-argument is that the mandate of a GSE was to support the mortgage market, perhaps precluding an alternative, such as sale of mortgage portfolio at that time. Be that as it may, the investor should have been made aware of the signs of a crisis, by generally accepted accounting standards. In addressing the relevant question of how the investor could have reacted, the answer is, there was incomplete information. The substantial 2004 jump in mortgage prepayments, in pools of mortgages that backed up mortgage-backed securities, was largely disguised. The GSEs (FNMA, FHLMC, and FHLBC) had delayed until at least 2005, full adoption of relevant Financial Accounting Standard 133 (SFAS 133), whose deadline for implementation was 2000 year-end. SFAS 133 had obligated institutions in the United States to treat financial derivatives as hedging specific mortgage assets or else directly impact the variability in stated earnings. Had the GSE earnings variability been impacted, that would inadvertently emanate as a clear signal to investors that something was wrong.

Specifically, the GSEs were following an allowable "short-cut" method in linking financial derivative value to mortgage securities held in a manner that circumvented performing the cumbersome hedge ratio estimation between mortgages and traded swaps, swaptions, etc. All three GSEs were artificially showing in their balance sheets, that their hedge book of swaps, swaptions, caps, and floors, was "perfectly" offsetting mortgages at all times, including that of the precipitous decline in December 2004. What triggered the curiosity of bank examiners from the Federal Housing Finance Agency at that time was an attendant decline in the market value of equity in institutions, such as the Federal Home Loan Bank of Chicago, which could not be hidden even as this jump in prepayments had appeared as perfectly matched by derivatives, at the time period when there was no corresponding change in interest/refinance rates. Management of such financial institutions was responding negatively at that time, to the possibility that prepayments were merely postponing default in a market where rates had not moved. Misapplying a financial standard hindered alerting the investor. The often-expressed notion that there was absolutely no possible signal of trouble ahead of the crisis is too simplistic. What is more likely is that the investor was surprised when accumulated information was finally released into the markets, by 2008. A conjecture stated without formal proof, is that the surprise had been large, but the investor had already acquired a

[3] Xanthopoulos, A., 2010. Market value signal extraction and misapplication of SFAS 133 in the U.S. GSE's. J. Econ. Asymm. 7, 57–75.

[4] Sorkin, A.R., 2009. Too Big to Fail: The Inside Story of How Wall Street and Washington Fought to Save the Financial System-and Themselves, Viking Press, United States.

tendency to expect, and prudently react to, such large market swings, if detected.[5] Using data from the Federal Home Loan Bank of Chicago, I had shown that the change in balance sheet accounts around the December 2014 large prepayment was so large, that by itself it should have, at the very least, prompted investors to react early. What happened instead was that regulators did all the prompting, while management attempted to cooperate as possible in the disentanglement of accounting information in a manner that preserved this short-cut in matching.

As shown later, the fixed-income portfolio of the Federal Home Loan Bank of Chicago had market and book values of assets and liabilities, and an off-balance-sheet account that held derivative instrument positions as a risk hedge (mostly interest-rate swaps). To use an analogy discussed by management of that time, this balance sheet had resembled a child's swimming pool toy in which owner's equity was a ballast that held it upright while the durations and convexities of the asset and liability compartments were roughly matched. Liabilities were adjusted downward when asset values went down, while assets were sold when liabilities were called or allowed to mature. But such matching was not always timely, thus hedge instruments were needed to fill the difference. These practices were partly encapsulated in the spectral decomposition of the correlation matrix between the five main balance sheet accounts in Table 2.1. Principal component analysis (PCA) had revealed the internal structure of data in a way that had explained variance and reduced dimensionality by transforming them into linear combinations. The PCA eigenvectors are listed in Table 2.1. Each component of the balance sheet appeared to measure a distinct characteristic of all the balance sheet accounts. Cross-multiplication of balance sheet account values by eigenvectors produced component values. Component values were transformed to ranges between 0 and 1 to allow for a comparison to the ratio of the equity's market to book value, falling between 0 and around 1, by definition. This equity ratio was related to the five components of the balance sheet in a forecasting model. Balance sheet component values were superimposed on the level of swap rates. One can see why a typical investor would have thought that the decline in the mortgage portfolio value of a GSE was hedged with derivatives, as if formal hedge analysis had been performed. That was not the case. Since mortgage-backed-securities, an instrument once regarded as safe as US Treasury bonds, had lost value so abruptly, it is reasonable for the investor to expect, or even develop some taste for such moves.

SFAS 133 entails the recording of derivatives at fair value, and recognition of their unrealized gains and losses in the current period. When transactions are eligible for hedge accounting, the rule permits gains and losses on underlying assets or liabilities to be recognized as well, which reduces income variability. SFAS 133 treats prepayments as a call embedded in the

---

[5] The purpose of stating these facts based on experience, is to justify that the investor would have reason to try and "catch-up" on portfolio losses, both before and after the crux of the crisis in 2008. This tendency may provide support to any empirically observed trade-off between portfolio risk from variance and kurtosis-seeking risk.

Table 2.1: Correlation and eigenvectors of balance sheet accounts in 127 business days.

	AMV	LMV	HMV	ABV	LBV
			Correlation Matrix		
AMV	1.0000	0.9995	0.3397	0.9954	0.9954
LMV	0.9995	1.0000	0.3440	0.9965	0.9965
HMV	0.3397	0.3440	1.0000	0.3707	0.3674
ABV	0.9954	0.9965	0.3707	1.0000	0.9999
LBV	0.9954	0.9965	0.3674	0.9999	1.0000

	Increase in All Accounts	Market Speculation	Market Value Decline	Market Value Separation	Book Value Separation
			Eigenvectors		
AMV	0.4868	0.1282	−0.5718	0.6476	−0.0160
LMV	0.4872	0.1235	−0.4160	−0.7578	0.0072
HMV	0.2200	−0.9750	−0.0314	−0.0002	−0.0030
ABV	0.4886	0.0922	0.4915	0.0661	0.7119
LBV	0.4884	0.0961	0.5073	0.0445	−0.7020
Variance:					
explained	83.0%	16.8%	0.1%	0.0%	0.0%
cumulative	83.0%	99.8%	100.0%	100.0%	100.0%

ABV, Asset book value;
AMV, asset market value;
HMV, hedge market value;
LBV, liability book value;
LMV, liability market value.

mortgage related asset and permits the market price of the option to qualify as hedge-able risk. However, the effectiveness of such hedges is generally assessed by changes in fair value of the bifurcated option against changes in the fair value of derivatives. GSEs had elected the short cut method of SFAS 133, which basically implied an ideal matching between derivatives and hedged items, and mostly eliminated variability in earnings. In the Chicago branch of the Federal Home Loan Bank System, unimpeded use of such methods had obscured the prepayment shock.

Based on eigenvectors in Table 2.1, the first component had a weight for the market and book values of assets and liabilities of 0.49, and for the hedge account 0.22. But the weight for the hedge account in the second component was negative and large (−0.97), signifying the "hedging" of mortgage returns. In the third component, market values moved in a direction opposite to book for assets and liabilities. This third component captured pure sensitivity of the balance sheet to interest rates which largely excluded the effect of hedging as described earlier. But the third (and other) component had explained very little. Thus, the large fluctuation in mortgage-backed assets held in GSE balance sheets was effectively hidden. This fact may explain the similarities between periods (1) and (3) and the breakdown during period (2).

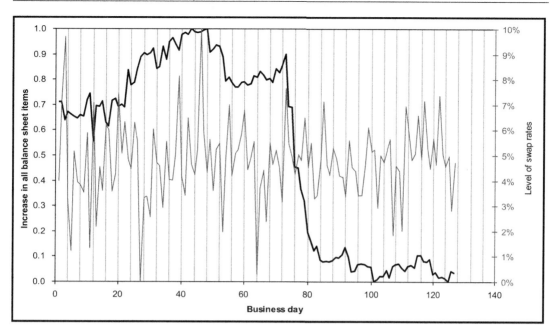

Figure 2.1: First Portfolio Balance Sheet Component and Swap Rate Level Over Time.

2.3 Investor Fat Tail-Seeking

Misapplications of SFAS 133 by GSEs most likely went undetected by the investing public, while regulators had probably recognized large prepayments as forerunners of collapse. In 2004, investors would have limited information on the patterns of refinancing activity as manifested by mortgage instruments 3 years ahead of the crisis. After the fact, any abrupt event as portrayed in Figs. 2.1–2.3 would entice the investor to anticipate, and ultimately be prompted to seek the returns from events that lie at the tail of wealth distributions.[6] If nonlinear responses of asset returns to indices introduced kurtosis in portfolio returns, quadratic utility optimizers could be viewed as kurtosis-averse, meaning that they are either platy-kurtosis-seeking or leptokurtosis-averse. But, that was not optimal. When the investor observed kurtosis, he or she moved to a "prudent" trade-off, which under assumptions led to abrupt adjustments, including crises. All that is needed to arrive at such conclusion is (1) expansion of utility of wealth to the fourth moment of kurtosis, and (2) assuming that the skew in return distributions is not affecting investor preference (focusing on only mean-preserving

---

[6] This presumed behavior pertains to optimization of wealth at a point in time, in relation to a reference index, or benchmark. This discussion does not pertain to "satisficing" behavior, such as that pertaining to liability-driven investing (LDI), target-date investing, or glide paths in investing, across time. That other discussion is undertaken in ensuing research. For this analysis the investor is assumed to maximize utility of wealth at a point in time.

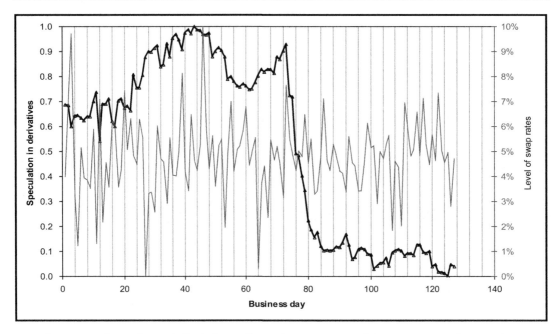

Figure 2.2: Second Portfolio Balance Sheet Component and Swap Rate Level Over Time.

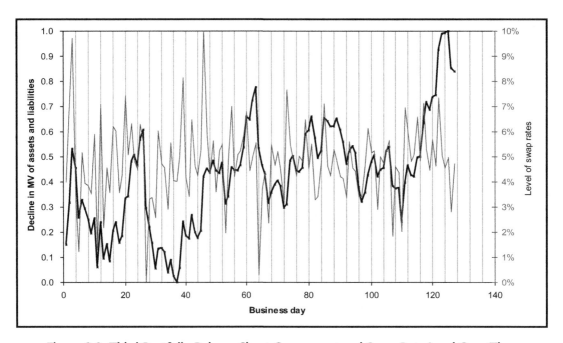

Figure 2.3: Third Portfolio Balance Sheet Component and Swap Rate Level Over Time.

moments of return distributions). The adjustment of portfolio weights then could be assumed to be taking place, in a two-stage process Eq. (2.3):

1. Investors assume normal portfolio returns, similar to what may have been the case at any time before the total 2004–15 time period ($\theta_p^4 = 3$ implies standard quadratic utility).
2. Investors observe portfolio kurtosis, as the effect of nonlinear asset returns seeped into portfolio return distributions. Portfolio weights are adjusted, according to both moments.

In the second stage, the investor views portfolio kurtosis as a parameter whose value is estimated in the first. Polynomial utility becomes quadratic in variance, in contrast to standard quadratic utility of wealth. First and second order conditions imply that the optimal point is a minimum when investors are variance averse ($\lambda > 0$) and maximum when variance seeking ($\lambda < 0$). The challenge is to assess the vertical distance between quadratic utility that decreases with portfolio variance, and polynomial that possesses a minimum beyond which volatility raises utility. If standard portfolio performance measurement metrics imply quadratic utility, and investors reveal polynomial utility instead, then the difference earlier integrated up to the "prudent point" represents a "deadweight loss" of sorts, which investors, managers, and performance evaluators must have assessed over time. It will be shown later, that benchmark-relative performance follows polynomial utility, but not the ratings.

$$\text{maximize}: E\left[U\left(r_p\right)\right] = q^T E[x \cdot b] - \frac{1}{2 \cdot \lambda} \cdot q^T \Omega q - \frac{\left(\theta_p^4 - 3\right)}{4 \cdot v} \left(q^T \Omega q\right)^2 \tag{2.1}$$

$$\text{subject to}: q^T \cdot \mathbf{1} = 1, \text{where } \mathbf{1} \text{ is a vector of 1's.}$$
$$\text{and}: \quad -1 \le q_i \le 1$$

$$E\left[U\left(r_p\right)\right] = ax^2 + bx + c; \quad a = -\frac{\theta_p^4 - 3}{4v}, \quad b = -\frac{1}{2\lambda}, \quad c = \bar{r}_p, \quad x = \sigma_p^2 \tag{2.2}$$

$$\text{FOC}: \frac{\partial E\left[U\left(r_p\right)\right]}{\partial x} = 2ax + b = 0 \Leftrightarrow \sigma_p^2\left(\theta_p^4 - 3\right) = -\frac{v}{\lambda}$$

$$\text{SOC}: \frac{\partial^2 E\left[U\left(r_p\right)\right]}{\partial x^2} = 2a \ge 0 \Leftrightarrow \left\{ \begin{array}{ll} v \le 0 & \text{when} \quad \theta_p^4 \ge 3 \\ v \ge 0 & \text{when} \quad \theta_p^4 \le 3 \end{array} \right\} \quad \text{(hedging relation)} \tag{2.3}$$

Under precrisis and postcrisis conditions, the investor seemed to behave more in line with Eq. (2.1), as long as excess kurtosis over a normal distribution, $\theta_p^4 - 3$, stayed positive. The investor operated in an environment where tails appeared at any point in time, the effect of which was not measured by adequate degrees of freedom. The increase in investor utility over quadratic, captured by the two-sided arrow in Fig. 2.4 above, portrays that the investor had "learned" before and after the financial crisis, in terms of optimizing absolute levels of

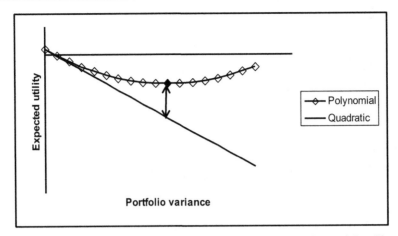

Figure 2.4: Utility of Wealth from Quadratic, Versus Polynomial Utility.

wealth, and the role of the portfolio manager would be generating relative performance that met investor expectations. In that respect, the minimum in polynomial utility was higher than quadratic utility by $\sigma_p^2 / 4\lambda$ and was a prudent point in the following sense: from zero to that point, portfolio variance reduced utility in both quadratic and polynomial. A prudent investor would not seek to raise portfolio variance beyond that point, since that adds to polynomial utility contradicting an original risk aversion statement. In plain terms, increasing variance beyond the prudent point was not a target that could be "sold" to the investor. But, raising the variance of portfolio returns up to that point would still be desirable, since it would eliminate any polynomial-to-quadratic deadweight loss in utility.

It is assumed that the investor has always had this propensity to react as portrayed in the first-order-condition (FOC) of Eq. (2.3). Perhaps due to the 2008 financial crisis, this propensity had acquired some very large amplitudes that still must be examined. At the actual time of crisis and subsequent QE, the learned investor reaction earlier appeared to have severely broken down. Manifestations of further learning from period (2) were evident in the interaction of portfolio managers and the investing principal. Implications are also manifested in the methods by which advisory/consultancy intermediaries assess the performance of portfolio managers, while the latter attempt to minimize the deadweight loss described earlier, even as they were still measured with metrics that do not reflect such minimization. Specifically, the prospect of increased utility of absolute wealth as a function of variance resulted in the controversial and largely insupportable reversal toward kurtosis seeking. There is hardly an institutional sponsor of a plan that should openly accept a preference toward fat tails, without enticing critique from beneficiaries of a retirement plan, or endowment fund. Yet, preference reversal stems directly from the second-order-condition (SOC) in Eq. (2.3), and turns the kurtosis-averse investor into kurtosis-seeking, in an apparent "hedging-like" relation that is enough to frustrate any "qualitative" method of assessment. In a friction-less market with an unlimited funding and leverage, weights approach infinity as shown in Eq. (2.5) later, pointing to the classic "fallacy of composition" that evaluators must address. These issues are controversial and hard to quantify among institutional and retail investors, portfolio/wealth managers, and intermediaries involved (researchers/consultants, etc.). The fact that commonly used metrics that measure performance rely on only two moments of returns makes resolution of these issues harder.

2.4 Investor Behavior, Pre- and Postcrisis

Investors behave in a manner that befits tail events in a noncrisis environment, and befalls as if no crisis would ever happen (based on metrics used, such as information ratio). This description appears to fit a period before and after, but not during. But that supposition, in itself, may be erroneous. It may be just that, during a crisis, the delicate relations of agents to principals, augmented by consultants as may be, underwent tremendous oscillations that were even harder to measure. For example, it may be the case that QE essentially discounted crisis-related effects into portfolio manager undertaking of risk, manifested in both variance and tails of return distributions to satisfy increased appetites by the investor. All of this discussion is coined in the framework of absolute returns of a strategy, in parallel to active returns relative to a chosen index that represents the market. The supposition that investors now expect the portfolio manager to undertake risk that exploits tails in absolute returns does not mean the investor tolerates tails in the distribution of active returns above a benchmark, it seems. Or, does it so?

Should benchmark-relative metrics, such as information ratio (IR) reflect active fat-tails? This is another difficultly the portfolio manager must navigate through. That is, produce absolute returns that "milk" the tails, but do not generate active returns over a benchmark that have tails. Implicitly, this assumes that a benchmark itself has tails that the way in which portfolios are positioned must not exceed by some large amount. Be that as it may, what creates a contradiction in the way risk is discussed versus the way it is undertaken is that under imperfect market conditions (limited liquidity and leverage) absolute wealth-maximization behavior of investors may have exacerbated the issue that this investor was also worried about, such as illiquidity and constraints on financial leverage. The weights could tend to infinity, if the portfolio manager simply followed the mandate of variance-kurtosis optimization, implicitly revealed by investors, in a classic case of the fallacy of composition: what is true for the individual (benefiting from seeking returns at the tails) appears to be true for the group. But if all investors sought tail-returns, and portfolio weights changed by infinite amounts, liquidity and leverage constraints would get exacerbated. During a crisis, investors behaved in a manner of "running to the door in an earthquake" shown in Eq. (2.5). In the case of frictionless markets with unlimited liquidity, two-asset portfolios based on utility function Eq. (2.1) earlier could generate optimal weights that approached infinity, as shown in Eq. (2.5), using Eq. (2.3) earlier. One way to resolve infinity is to assume that the investor has a long-term, constant ratio of preferences v/λ:

$$\begin{bmatrix} \dfrac{\partial E[U(r_p)]}{\partial w_1} \\[2mm] \dfrac{\partial E[U(r_p)]}{\partial w_2} \end{bmatrix} = \begin{bmatrix} E(r_1) \\ E(r_2) \end{bmatrix} - \lambda^{-1} \begin{bmatrix} \sigma_{11} & \sigma_{12} \\ \sigma_{21} & \sigma_{22} \end{bmatrix} \begin{bmatrix} w_1 \\ w_2 \end{bmatrix} - v^{-1}\left(\theta_p^4 - 3\right)\begin{bmatrix} \sigma_{11} & \sigma_{12} \\ \sigma_{21} & \sigma_{22} \end{bmatrix}\begin{bmatrix} w_1 \\ w_2 \end{bmatrix}\sigma_p^2$$

$$= \begin{bmatrix} 0 \\ 0 \end{bmatrix}$$

(2.4)

$$\begin{bmatrix} w_1 & w_2 \end{bmatrix} = \cdot\left[\lambda^{-1} + v^{-1}\left(\theta_p^4 - 3\right)\sigma_p^2\right]^{-1}\begin{bmatrix} E(r_1) & E(r_2) \end{bmatrix}\begin{bmatrix} \sigma_{11} & \sigma_{12} \\ \sigma_{21} & \sigma_{22} \end{bmatrix}^{-1}$$

$$\Rightarrow \mathbf{w}^T = \xi E[\mathbf{x}\cdot\mathbf{b}]^T \Omega^{-1}$$

$$\xi = \left[\lambda^{-1} + v^{-1}\left(\theta_p^4 - 3\right)\sigma_p^2\right]^{-1} \approx \frac{(\lambda v)_{\text{long term}}}{v + \lambda\left(\theta_p^4 - 3\right)\sigma_p^2} \to \infty$$

(2.5)

Eq. (2.4) earlier assumes that the investor has a portfolio p with two assets, whose weights and returns are w_1, w_2, and r_1, r_2, respectively. Differentiating the utility function Eq. (2.1) with respect to the weights and setting equal to zero, results in optimal weight vector $\mathbf{w}^T$, which exhibits an "amplifying" factor ξ. When optimal portfolio returns under state (1) do not exhibit fat tails ($\theta_p^4 = 3$), the investor is not "surprised" by the performance of its investment, irrespective of how it was generated or not, in a benchmark-relative mindset. In that case, this amplifying factor ξ is simply equal to λ, the tolerance that the investor has always had with respect to portfolio variance, which is not infinite. But if there is some statistically significant measure of excess kurtosis, then the amplifying factor ξ becomes infinite in (2). That means that optimal weights $\mathbf{w}^T$ are also large or infinite, given assumptions. In this framework, an intermediary between principal and agent should perhaps evaluate portfolio manager performance in a manner that "rewards" one tail-seeking investor, but not another (lest systemic collapse was induced). Of course, this discussion is coined in somewhat unrealistic, purely theoretical terms. The markets are not limitless in liquidity and leverage, while intermediaries between investors and portfolio managers play a crucial role in the efficient reallocation of investment funds across time. The concern of this chapter is whether or not there have been changes in the way investor preferences were captured and reflected.

2.5 Benchmark-Relative Performance

If the earlier analysis is representative, the task of timely portfolio performance evaluation undertaken on behalf of the principal-investor could be challenging. For one thing, metrics, such as information ratio, tracking error, alpha, and beta do not account for the type investor behavior described. For another, the investor in benchmark relative sense may only appear to not forgive deviations from fat-tails reflected in the benchmark. Another is that in a low-volatility environment, seeking returns de facto implies greater tolerance toward tails. An attempt is made to sort through these apparent contradictions, through time.

2.5.1 Nonlinearity in Asset and Portfolio Returns

The principal-agency problem implies that using a metric to measure the portfolio manager creates the incentive to "game" that measure (Goetzmann et al., 2007). But the problem in using common metrics of performance is much larger. Because the investor knows that abrupt, nonlinear or "regime-switching" events, such as the ones portrayed in Fig. 2.1 occur, the investor expects evidence of such nonlinearity through benchmark-relative optimization process of the portfolio manager. Asset returns are regime-switching and classic mean-variance exhibits fat tails based on the utility formulation earlier, which the investor would detect and respond to.[7] Nonlinear asset returns, aggregated up to a portfolio alpha and beta, reveal issues that confound standard performance measurement (with the error term ε_i not zero under expectation). Fitting a linear model on an otherwise nonlinear relationship allows market risk to seep into alpha. From there, market effects are passed as "skill" eagerly claimed by the investors' agents.

$$R_{asset(i)}(t) = \alpha_i + \beta_i \cdot R_{index}(t) + \phi_i \cdot \left(1 - \frac{2}{e^{2(\gamma_i + \delta_i \cdot R_{index}(t))} + 1}\right) + \varepsilon_i(t) \tag{2.6}$$

$$R_{portfolio}(t) = \sum_{i=1}^{n} w_i R_{asset(i)}(t) = \sum_{i=1}^{n} w_i \alpha_i + \sum_{i=1}^{n} w_i \beta_i R_{index}(t) + \sum_{i=1}^{n} w_i \phi_i - \sum_{i=1}^{n} \frac{2w_i \phi_i}{e^{2 f_i(R_{index}(t))} + 1} + \sum_{i=1}^{n} \varepsilon_i(t)$$

$$E\left[R_{portfolio}(t)\right] = \alpha_{portfolio}^{NL} + \beta_{portfolio} \cdot R_{index}(t) \tag{2.7}$$

$$\text{where } f_i(R_{index}(t)) = \gamma_i + \delta_i \cdot R_{index}(t), \alpha_{portfolio}^{NL} = \alpha_{portfolio}^{L} + \phi_{portfolio} - \sum_{i=1}^{n} E\left[\frac{2w_i \phi_i}{\left[e^{2 \cdot f_i(R_{index}(t))}\right] + 1}\right]$$

In Eq. (2.6), the returns of asset $R_{asset(i)}$ depend on market returns $R_{index(i)}$ in a model that incorporate a hyperbolic-tangent response. Standard portfolio theory assumes that either ϕ is 0, and/or γ and δ are 0. Combining asset returns $R_{asset(i)}$ into portfolio returns $R_{portfolio(i)}$ into

---

[7] Xanthopoulos, A., 2011. An interpretation of carry trade profitability. Rev. Bus. Res. 11, 65.

Eq. (2.7), points to the fact that alpha is party market-dependent [the L and NL superscripts at the bottom of Eq. (2.7) stand for "linear" and "nonlinear" respectively]. Nonlinear, but deterministic market effects escape from an error term of a basic linear model, and land into alpha. If not all $f_i(\ )$ and ϕ_i are 0, some nonlinear effect escapes into alpha from the error term, which should be enough to frustrate any "qualitative" evaluation of a portfolio manager's skill, based solely on holdings. That is because benchmark-relative performance would be generated not out of the specificity of names invested-in after careful fundamental analysis, but out of abrupt, regime-switching, and thus likely nonrepeatable changes in positions, whether underlying issuers invested-in, or capital structure slots held fell within, or without an acceptable benchmark, with concomitant implications about market timing.

2.6 Information Ratio in a Low-Volatility/Rate Environment

Roll (1992) writes that the investor-principal accepts reduced portfolio performance in absolute terms, by letting the manager track the market index. The reason is that (due to the principal-agency issue) the investor would have otherwise had to incur costs to monitor the manager.[8] In a low-yield, low volatility market environment, monitoring costs become low, as chances that a manager will produce unwanted results go down. Perhaps this low implicit cost of monitoring explains the recent popularity of strategies termed as "unconstrained" versus a market index. The complicating factors with nonlinearity in portfolio returns in Eq. (2.7), or "prudent" behavior toward variance and fat tails in Eq. (2.3) earlier, beg the question: does not-tracking a benchmark explicitly mean managers take advantage of market nuances that constitute a source of performance? Unconstrained strategies do imply a higher level of tolerance toward fat tails, captured by v, in Eq. (2.1), but the current level of low rates and low volatility frustrates reflecting the related outperformance through IR. Strategies in high-yield or bank loans may require an even greater level of v, than strategies commonly termed as unconstrained. In the results that follow, both the nonlinearity in asset returns and the tendency to alter weights substantially in a low-rate environment are addressed by a minor alteration to the information ratio as proposed, which is run on the three periods of returns.

The tendency of the investor to "overreact" notwithstanding, a low rate environment masks deviations of portfolio beta from a market index. This potential beta-masking is illustrated via restatement of the Capital Asset Pricing Model (CAPM), as shown later, while pointing to the fact that IR has been predicated on the normality of active returns and the assumption that the index used always captures pertinent market effects (R_f is the risk-free rate, R_b is benchmark returns, as earlier).

$$R_p - R_f = \alpha + \beta\left(R_b - R_f\right) + \varepsilon \Rightarrow E\left[R_p\right] = \alpha + \beta R_b + \left(1 - \beta\right)R_f, \text{ assuming } E\left[\varepsilon\right] = 0 \quad (2.9)$$

---

[8]   Roll, R., 1992. A mean/variance analysis of tracking error. J. Portf. Manage. 18(4), 13–22.

$$IR^{expost} = \frac{E\left[R_p - \beta R_b - (1-\beta)R_f\right]}{\sigma\left[R_p - \beta R_b - (1-\beta)R_f\right]} \approx \frac{E\left[R_p - R_{bp}\right]}{\sigma\left[R_p - R_{bp}\right]}, \text{ assuming } (1-\beta)R_f \approx 0 \quad (2.10)$$

The issue that may be partly circumvented by restating *IR* in Eq. (2.10) is that the low risk-free rate deviations from the stated benchmark captured by $(1-\beta)$ in Eq. (2.9) vanish as the risk-free rate R_f approaches 0, since these terms are multiplied together. To circumvent the nonlinearity of alpha shown in Eq. (2.7), as well as eliminate the potential zero-rate-boundary effects shown in Eq. (2.9), I estimate the proxy benchmark return R_{bp} for each portfolio by regressing its returns against a least-correlated set of indices, simply restricting the intercept to 0. The goal is to capture market-driven beta when subtracting index returns from the portfolio. The proxy benchmark should not contain alpha as indices do not have "skill." Such skill is thus captured by the active returns of the portfolio R_p above proxy benchmark R_{bp}. The restated IR in Eq. (2.10) is believed to offer several advantages over industry-accepted methods. For example, by restricting the intercept to 0, some of the nonlinear alpha effects described in Eq. (2.7) earlier are most likely eliminated. Most of performance is attributable to market betas. If a manager had attempted to time markets through regime switches, with the result attributable to alpha in a single-benchmark used, most of this alpha would now be extracted-out by the betas. Specifically in the case where risk-free rates are low and portfolio managers tend to deviate from index, the would-be enhancement: $R_p-(1-\beta)R_f$ when $\beta > 1$ is penalized by the restriction to 0, without deviating very much from industry practice.

2.7 Probability of Outperformance and Investor Utility of Wealth

Gauging changes in investor behavior, based on portfolio returns, is intertwined with the measurement of performance generated by manager-agents. Practitioners in performance assessment have displayed a substantial degree of "consternation" with any method that deviated from a qualitative approach postcrisis, even as parties involved used a statistical concept of *probability of outperformance* in discussions that lead to assignment of a *rating*. Perhaps ratings capture the degree to which an investor is expected to derive utility from performance, and thus may serve as further gauge of changes in investor behavior. I present this measure of quantitative performance in three simple steps. For each subperiod of (1) the crisis, (2) QE, and (3) "taper tantrum," 48 monthly returns are used to derive results.[9]

A. For each of the 388 portfolios, in each of the three periods, rolling samples of 36 months were used in estimation. For each subperiod, for each subsample, absolute returns of the 388 funds from Morningstar were regressed against the eight benchmarks, $j = 1,...,8$

---

[9] The author would like to thank Alex Huba, Technology Manager and Bloomberg Instructor at Benedictine University in Lisle, IL for assistance in assembling the data sets used in this study.

listed earlier in Eq. (2.10). Resulting alpha and beta values were averaged across all subsample s values within each subperiod, and stored for the purpose of using as explanatory variables of the expost information.

$$R_{p,s} = \alpha_{p,s} + \sum_{j=1}^{8} \beta_{p,s}\left(R_j\right) + \varepsilon_{p,s}, \Rightarrow \alpha_{p,e}, \sum_{j=1}^{8} \beta_{p,e}\left(R_j\right) \text{for } p = 1,...,388, s = 1,...,12 \quad (2.11)$$

B. For each subperiod, for each subsample, the absolute returns of 388 funds from Morningstar were regressed against the same benchmarks, with the intercept restricted to arrive at returns from the proxy benchmark R_{bp} as in Eq. (2.10). The resulting "active" returns across all subsamples s were averaged within each subperiod, and used as the main gauge for relative performance. Thus, information ratio is shown as being explained by alphas and betas of portfolio managers.

$$R_{bp,s} = 0 + \sum_{j=1}^{8} b_{p,s}\left(R_j\right) + e_{p,s} \Rightarrow IR_{p,s}^{expost}, \text{for } p = 1,...,388, s = 1,...,12 \quad (2.12)$$

$$\left\{E\left[IR_p^{expost}\right]\right\} = c_0 + c_\alpha E\left[\alpha_p\right] + \sum_{j=1}^{8} c_j E\left[\beta_{p,j}\right] + \zeta_p, \text{for } p = 1,...,388 \quad (2.13)$$

C. For each subperiod, across all 388 funds from Morningstar, information ratio IR^{expost} obtained through (B) earlier was logit-regressed against the α_p and $\beta_{p,j}$ coefficients in, (A) with the rationale that these commonly observed regression coefficients are somehow linked to outperformance, the latter measured separately with information ratio that accounts for market nonlinearities. The average IR over subsamples s for each fund p, ranks portfolios from best to worst in a peer group over time, which is one of the challenging aspects of portfolio performance evaluation: a different index may be followed, with different response levels, by peers who are still evaluated in the same relative universe (benchmark-relative). Once IR in Eq. (2.12) is estimated and linked to a manager's attributes α_p and $\beta_{p,j}$, each manager's outperformance probability is estimated in Eq. (2.15). The metric in Eq. (2.15) can rank all 388 strategies across the three periods of (1) crisis, (2) QE, and (3) taper tantrum. The information on Morningstar data are publicly available and thus it may be of interest to see where each of these 388 funds would have fallen, as the markets vacillated.

$$\hat{Logit}\left\{E\left[IR_p^{expost}\right]\right\} = \gamma_0 + \gamma_\alpha E\left[\alpha_p\right] + \sum_{j=1}^{8} \gamma_j E\left[\beta_{p,j}\right] + \zeta_p, \text{for } p = 1,...,388 \quad (2.14)$$

$$\hat{Prob}\left\{E\left[IR_p^{expost}\right]\right\} = \frac{\exp\left\{\gamma_0 + \gamma_\alpha E\left[\alpha_p\right] + \sum_{j=1}^{8} \gamma_j E\left[\beta_{p,j}\right]\right\}}{1 + \exp\left\{\gamma_0 + \gamma_\alpha E\left[\alpha_p\right] + \sum_{j=1}^{8} \gamma_j E\left[\beta_{p,j}\right]\right\}}, \text{for } p = 1,...,388 \quad (2.15)$$

Step (A) earlier is of interest for looking into the sources of manager alpha and beta to indices, which the portfolios exhibit in each of the three periods. The patterns of investor behavior clearly differ between the periods of before, during, and after the crisis. Fig. 2.5 shows the averages over all 388 funds of $\alpha_{p,e}$, $\beta_{p,e}(R_1)$, $\beta_{p,e}(R_2)$,...,$\beta_{p,e}(R_8)$ in Eq. (2.11), for periods: (1) 3/2004–2/2008, (2) 2/2008–1/2012, and (3) 1/2012–12/2015. Investors heavily relied on the Barclays US Aggregate during the period (2) with underweight exposure in high yield, inflation-protected securities, government/corporate securities of 1–3 years in maturity, and emerging markets. Betas to these last four categories recovered back to precrisis levels, in period (3). The crisis period (2) may have thus made high yield, inflation-linked, short-duration, and emerging markets "cheap," and that may partly explain the subsequent popularity of these sectors. The period (1) underweight in global high yield became an overweight in period (2) but did not fall again after the crisis. The difference between period (1) and period (3) exposures to global may have been absorbed by the rise in the value of the US dollar in the third period, in a scenario of adjustment by interest rate parity. Also, alphas shown were small, due to the number of market indices explaining performance in Eq. (2.11). Generally, the investor got scared in period (2), and ran from sector-weights to the total market aggregate. After that period, the investor went back to "business as usual" in taking exposure.

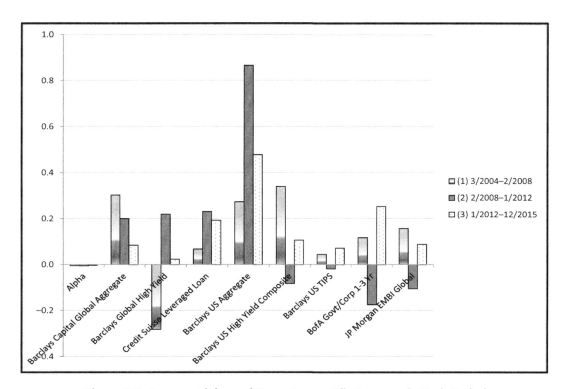

Figure 2.5: Average Alpha and Betas Across All Managers in Each Period.

Table 2.2: Impact of market betas on modified information ratio.

Information Ratio versus Betas	(1) 3/2004–2/2008	(2) 2/2008–1/2012	(3) 1/2012–12/2015
Unexplained (C_0)	−10%	−27%	−47%
Alpha (C_a) Effect	−22%	5%	−19%
Barclays Capital Global Aggregate (C_1)	11%	−15%	16%
Barclays Global High Yield (C_2)	15%	−10%	34%
Credit Suisse Leveraged Loan (C_2)	24%	8%	28%
Barclays US Aggregate (C_3)	1%	−23%	−4%
Barclays US High Yield Composite (C_4)	11%	−13%	22%
Barclays US TIPS (C_5)	17%	−34%	59%
BofA Govt/Corp 1–3 Yr (C_6)	2%	−7%	1%
JP Morgan EMBI Global (C_7)	20%	−33%	26%

Step (B) is important, since it reveals how the proxy-benchmark, and expost *IR* are estimated. This *IR* is the "outperformance" discussed earlier, which can be linked to coefficients from step (A), shown in Eq. (2.13). Table 2.2 reveals that the information ratio presented in Eq. (2.10) captures differences in performance in the three periods, the most notable of which being the importance of alpha and negative impact of market exposure during the second period. A somewhat alarming result is that of Unexplained as it verifies that nonlinearities described in Eq. (2.7) are isolated by that term, and may be increasing over time.

Step (C) moves us from the concept of "outperformance" to the concept "probability of outperformance." It reveals the impact of market betas on *IR*. The difference is that *IR* is logit-transformed while Eq. (2.15) is an approximation to this probability. During the crisis, outperformance depended on security selection.

The bars shown in Fig. 2.6 are similar to the coefficients c_0, c_α, and c_j for $j = 1,…,8$ in Eq. (2.13), except that their values are those of γ_0, γ_α, and γ_j for $j = 1,…,8$ of logistic regression that lead to probability in Eq. (2.15). Since the resulting logit-approximation to cumulative probability is a nonlinear function, the impact of each market beta is separated and linearly retransformed to add to 100%. As far as portfolio manager performance is concerned, skill as reflected in alpha, in contrast to beta-exposure, became the primary determinant of manager performance during period (2). Together with results earlier, it becomes clear that the more investment managers had increased exposure to aggregate markets in period (2), the less probability of outperformance depended on such increase. Managers could not find a solid footing in the aggregate. In contrast, during all three periods, beta to specific sectors, such as Global, Leveraged Loan, High Yield, TIPS, 1–3 Year, Emerging Market, contributed to outperformance probability almost equally. The link of alpha to outperformance was stronger in the third period, compared to the first one, pointing to the fact that selection skills were becoming partly honed-in. Still, if I refer to the seeping on nonlinear effects into alpha in

Eq. (2.7), it is hard to tell whether the crisis was what had sharpened actual selection skills, or an abrupt enticement of ϕ in the hyperbolic tangent response in Eq. (2.6) merely landed on the term that was not explained by market betas. In other words, the large intercept effect during the 2008–12 time period reflected something other than market effects. But that was not necessarily skill. At least, it can be shown that this second period had not contributed to investor utility, in the same manner as periods before and after did. In terms of utility maximization as stated in Eq. (2.1), it seems that portfolio relative performance did not capture investor utility preferences in period (2), as compared to (1) and (3). Probability of outperformance in periods before and after could be explained by an "isorisk" condition derived implied in Eq. (2.3). The conclusion is that portfolio performance resulting from a benchmark-relative process did not raise investor utility of absolute wealth, in the period of 2008–12. It is hard to attribute the period to skill, when investor wealth remained unaffected at the time. It is easy to show that investor wealth had remained unaffected in period (2). If the investor's tolerance for fat tails divided by that for variance had remained constant at a value $(\nu/\lambda)_c$, the product of portfolio variance times excess fat tails remained constant too, without affecting polynomial utility. If that ratio increased, perhaps by an investor's selecting a manager that "swings for the fences," wealth may have increased as the manager simply fulfilled the desire for the trade-off between the two, implied by investor preference. But if the product of the two goes up, then "isorisk" goes up, resulting in a higher relative performance. I simply ran a regression of the outperformance probability against the probability of isorisk for the 388 portfolio managers and found more than half of outperformance was explained by isorisk in the first and the third periods. Not in the second one, where the relation between performance against a benchmark and utility-maximizing risk had broken down. The high effect of alpha in Fig. 2.6 may just be attributable to extreme market nonlinearity, during period (2) and not to manager skill. Unlike periods (1) and (3), when more than 50% of a portfolio manager's probability of outperformance would be explained by iso-risk, almost none (0.2%) is explained in period (2) (Table 2.3).

2.8 Portfolio Ratings and Probability of Outperformance

Morningstar publishes the ratings for each of the 388 portfolios used in this study. It is of interest to find out how ratings of five, four, three, or two and below stars correspond to the measure of probability of outperformance, discussed earlier. To the degree that ratings reward different investment patterns than the ones based on probability of outperformance, investor behavior is affected differently across time. These ratings were obtained as of the last day of the complete period of data, which is December 2015. The quest was to find out if ratings reinforced different investment patterns than implied by relative performance (which follows desired investor utility) across the three periods of data. Ratings assigned depend on past information and reflect patterns of exposure to the market since the beginning of the sample, 2004. Patterns of alpha and beta exposure differ in each of three periods under examination. For this reason, α_p and $\beta_{p,j}$ coefficients estimated in Eq. (2.11) are rearranged into principal

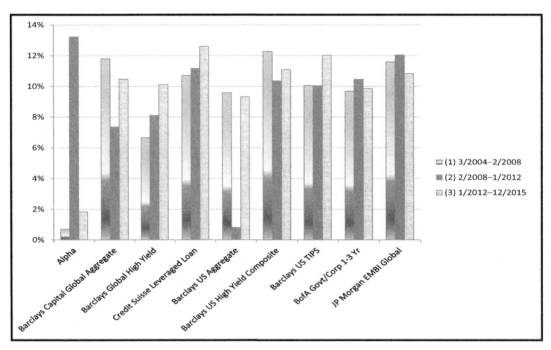

Figure 2.6: Probability of Outperformance Generated from Portfolio Alpha and Betas.

Table 2.3: Probability of outperformance explained by probability of isorisk.

Coefficient value:	(1) 3/2004–2/2008	(2) 2/2008–1/2012	(3) 1/2012–12/2015
Intercept	22.7%	46.2%	25.4%
P(isorisk)	58.8%	0.2%	53.4%
t-Statistic value:			
Intercept	5.27	28.73	7.39
P(isorisk)	6.71	4.41	7.60

components, so that patterns of investing across time are discerned, in step (D). Patterns differ across periods, as shown in Table 2.4. These numbers are the coefficients to d_0, d_α, and d_j to logistic outperformance in Eq. (2.16).

D. Nonalpha manager attributes $\beta_{p,j}$ are arranged into principal components, to detect patterns of exposure to specific indices across the three periods. The probability of outperformance that is based on information ratio, Prob$\{E[IR^{expost}]\}$ is regressed against these principal components. It is not only of interest to find out how patterns of investing differed across the three subperiods but also to see how patterns affected outperformance probability. Eq. (2.14) is restated in terms of these principal components in Eq. (2.16). The corresponding probability in Eq. (2.15) is Eq. (2.17).

Table 2.4: Contribution of principal components of alpha and betas to logit of information ratio.

(1) 3/2004–2/2008	Coefficients	*t*-Stat
Intercept	2.03	6.56
Alpha	-3.27	7.62
C1: -Barclays Global High Yield -Barclays US Aggregate	0.86	14.68
C2: +Barclays Global High Yield -Barclays US Aggregate	0.65	5.15
C3: +Barclays Capital Global Aggregate -BofA Govt/Corp 1-3 Yr	0.82	4.22
C4: -Barclays US Aggregate +Barclays US TIPS -BofA Govt/Corp 1-3 Yr	1.45	7.05
C5: -Barclays US TIPS +JP Morgan EMBI Global	1.56	3.30
C6: +Credit Suisse Leveraged Loan +Barclays US TIPS -JP Morgan EMBI Global	2.64	5.09
C7: -Barclays US High Yield Composite +Barclays US TIPS	0.17	0.29
C8: +Barclays US TIPS +JP Morgan EMBI Global	4.83	3.47
(2) 2/2008–1/2012	Coefficients	*t*-Stat
Intercept	1.78	5.37
Alpha	0.80	-1.70
C1: +Barclays US Aggregate -BofA Govt/Corp 1-3 Yr	0.20	2.77
C2: +Barclays Capital Global Aggregate -Barclays US Aggregate	0.67	5.47
C3: +Barclays Global High Yield -Barclays US High Yield Composite	1.37	6.09
C4: -Barclays Capital Global Aggregate -Credit Suisse Leveraged Loan	0.92	2.07
C5: +Credit Suisse Leveraged Loan +JP Morgan EMBI Global	0.91	2.03
C6: +Barclays Global High Yield +Credit Suisse Leveraged Loan -JP Morgan EMBI Global	4.29	7.20
C7: +Barclays US TIPS -JP Morgan EMBI Global	0.24	0.30
C8: -Barclays US TIPS -JP Morgan EMBI Global	7.56	3.69
(3) 1/2012–12/2015	Coefficients	*t*-Stat
Intercept	0.44	1.41
Alpha	-2.26	5.50
C1: -Barclays US Aggregate +BofA Govt/Corp 1-3 Yr	0.34	5.12
C2: +Barclays Capital Global Aggregate -Barclays US Aggregate	1.15	8.21
C3: +Barclays Global High Yield -Barclays US High Yield Composite	0.78	3.37
C4: -Barclays Capital Global Aggregate +Credit Suisse Leveraged Loan	2.07	5.94
C5: +Credit Suisse Leveraged Loan -Barclays US High Yield Composite	1.08	3.64
C6: +Barclays US High Yield Composite -Barclays US TIPS	1.14	1.34
C7: -Credit Suisse Leveraged Loan -Barclays US High Yield Composite +JP Morgan EMBI Global	0.64	0.68
C8: +Barclays US High Yield Composite +Barclays US TIPS	9.02	7.09

$$Logit\left\{\underset{s}{E}\left[IR_p^{expost}\right]\right\}\Bigg|_{p\in q_i} = d_{0,q_i} + d_{\alpha,q_i}\underset{s}{E}\left[\alpha_p\right] + \sum_{j=1}^{8} d_{j,q_i} PC\left\{\underset{s}{E}\left[\beta_{p,j}\right]\right\} + \eta_p, \text{for } i = 1,...,4 \quad (2.16)$$

$$\text{Prob}\left\{\underset{s}{E}\left[IR_p^{expost}\right]\right\} = \frac{\exp\left\{d_{0,q_i} + d_{\alpha,q_i}\underset{s}{E}\left[\alpha_p\right] + \sum_{j=1}^{8} d_{j,q_i} PC\left\{\underset{s}{E}\left[\beta_{p,j}\right]\right\}\right\}}{1 + \exp\left\{d_{0,q_i} + d_{\alpha,q_i}\underset{s}{E}\left[\alpha_p\right] + \sum_{j=1}^{8} d_{j,q_i} PC\left\{\underset{s}{E}\left[\beta_{p,j}\right]\right\}\right\}}, \text{for } i = 1,...,4 \quad (2.17)$$

Eqs. (2.16) and (2.17) portray the joint estimation through maximum likelihood, of the effects of alpha and beta values from Eq. (2.11) earlier, on the *IR* in each of four quadrants, and ratings,

Table 2.5: Approximate outperformance probability by quadrant and rating across three periods.

(1) 3/2004–2/2008	Quadrant	Rating	Difference
First	43.0%	31.0%	−12.0%
Second	33.0%	23.0%	−10.0%
Third	14.0%	22.0%	8.0%
Fourth	10.0%	24.0%	14.0%
	100.0%	100.0%	22.0%
(2) 2/2008–1/2012	Quadrant	Rating	Difference
First	42.0%	30.0%	−12.0%
Second	32.0%	28.0%	−4.0%
Third	20.0%	19.0%	−1.0%
Fourth	6.0%	23.0%	17.0%
	100.0%	100.0%	17.0%
(3) 1/2012–12/2015	Quadrant	Rating	Difference
First	45.0%	16.0%	−29.0%
Second	31.0%	33.0%	2.0%
Third	18.0%	28.0%	10.0%
Fourth	6.0%	23.0%	17.0%
	100.0%	100.0%	29.0%

q_i within each of the three periods under investigation. Simple quadrants of outperformance segregate the 388 funds based on four categories, after ranking funds from highest to lowest in performance. The ratings, on the other hand, segregate funds into four different categories, based on rating assigned. Then, the probabilities of outperformance for the four categories determined through quadrants, is compared to the categories in ranking. If ratings capture outperformance, then quadrant-based probability of outperformance should be equal to ranking-based probability of outperformance, across all three time periods. If, ratings-based probability is lower for a certain category, then certain constituents of that category should have been rated lower. If, on the other hand, ratings-based probability is higher for a certain category, constituents of that category should have been rated higher. Unfortunately, what seems to be the case is that these ratings do not produce outperformance that sequentially ranks the 388 funds. In other words, higher-rated funds do not have a greater probability to outperform than the ones below, with probability that declines sequentially (please refer to Table 2.5). Be that as it may, it must be stressed that the methods in this study do not specifically revolve around performance metrics that cannot be manipulated. It is a known fact that Morningstar ratings follow a quantitative methodology that accounts for the "gaming" of performance by portfolio managers, for the purpose of manipulating fees. This aspect of performance measurement (i.e., gaming) is not examined at all, in this analysis, which only relies on approximation.[10]

First, seemingly unrelated equations are estimated by segregating the 388 funds into four quadrants of equal size, by probability of outperformance for each fund, in each of

---

[10] Foster, D.P., Young, H.P., 2010. Gaming performance fees by portfolio managers. Q. J. Econ. 125(4), 1435–1458.

the four periods. Then, the system is estimated by segregating the 388 funds into four categories of ratings, as assigned by Morningstar at the end of the total sample used. The results are summarized later. Table 2.4 earlier shows the estimated coefficients d_0, d_α, and d_j for each principal component, in each of three periods, without segregating the funds on either performance, or rating. It is interesting to see what kinds of patterns of investing were most prevalent, in each of the three periods (the eigenvectors of all principal components were realigned in their sign, so that their contribution to $Logit\{E[IR]\}$ was always positive).

- Between 3/2004 and 2/2008, the two most prevalent patterns of investing across eight indices were related to Global High Yield, and Barclays US Aggregate. In the second and third periods, the indices of BofA Govt/Corp 1–3 Year entered the top component, and attributed to the onset of QE subsequent tapering. Also in these periods, Barclays Capital Global featured as a substitute to Barclays Global High Yield, as investors started looking for yield overseas in the low-rate environment for the United States. These effects are in rows C1 and C2 in each of three periods.
- Of interest is the ascension of Barclays US High Yield Composite from the seventh component C7 in the first period, to as high as the third component in the other periods. It is true that US high yield had become popular during this whole period. As of today, this sector could be overvalued.
- The last (lowest-eigenvalue) components have changed dramatically between the three periods. These investment patterns are least prevalent and more abrupt in nature, capturing the tendency of manager to "swing for the fences" in their effort to meet the isorisk tolerance of the investor. Thus, the corresponding contribution to $Logit\{E[IR]\}$ is always very large. In period (1), before the crisis, such patterns involved the sectors of US Treasury Inflation-Protected Securities (TIPS) and Emerging Market Global securities. In period (2), that pattern spilled over to both of C7 and C8 components. In period (3), the pattern disappeared. Other patterns can be detected.

The estimated coefficients in Table 2.4 pertained to the total of 388 portfolios in each of the three periods through OLS regression. For estimation pertaining to quadrants and ratings, the process was as follows:

1. Within each of the three periods, the 388 funds were segregated into four categories, but twice: once based on four quadrants of outperformance probability, and once based on the number of stars assigned by Morningstar: 5, 4, 3, and 2 or 1 stars, for a total of four such rating categories.
2. Within each of the three periods, the estimation of the four quadrants of outperformance took place in the system of unrelated equations, though maximum likelihood. Then, the estimation of four ratings took place the same way, resulting in different coefficient values for Eqs. (2.16) and (2.17).

3. The outperformance probability that corresponds to each of the components C1 through C8 was estimated, and adjusted to equal the probability of the overall quadrant or rating in Eq. (2.2), earlier, to find the difference between quadrant-probability and rating-probability for each component.[11]

Based on part 1, it is obvious that quadrants and ratings point to different outperformance probabilities. For example, in the first row of Table 2.5, in period (1) 3/2004–2/2008, the approximate probability of outperformance for the first quadrant is 43%, but the same for the first Morningstar rating (five stars) is only 31%, meaning some funds were rated too high. By contrast, the fourth quadrant and rating in the same period results in an overestimate of 14%, pointing to the fact that some funds rated low should have been rated higher. The rating process does not result in as granular a segregation of funds into four categories, as probability of outperformance does. Across all three periods, first-category ratings do not have as high a probability of outperforming as they should, and the last-category ratings do not have as low a probability of outperforming, either. In addition, this mismatch between ratings and performance appears to have improved from period (1) to period (2), but worsened from period (2) to period (3).

- By approximation, 12% of the probability of outperformance that should accrue to investors of funds in the first quadrant was not rated as high as it should have been, as it was "lost" among the other ratings, impacting disparity between quadrant and rating at another level; while 14% of the probability of outperformance that should accrue to investors in the last quadrant was not rated as low as it should, but distorted ratings above, all in period (1). If absolute values of the Difference in Table 2.5 are added (divided by 2 to avoid double counting), 22% of probability of outperformance in period (1) would be "destroyed" had the investor blindly followed ratings.
- These percentages do not change very much in period (2), in which only 17% of outperformance probability was "destroyed" across all four ratings, compared to four quadrants of performance.
- Period (3) is the worse, with 29% outperformance probability that could potentially accrue to the investor, had it been rated higher: and a total of 27% from the last two ratings that should be rated lower. In total, 29% of outperformance probability was "destroyed" by the four ratings.

The source of mismatch between quadrants and ratings, as explained by components, is illustrated in the four figures later. Fig. 2.7 illustrates the mismatch of 12.0% between the first quadrant and first rating for period (1), together with a 12.0% mismatch in same for

---

[11] The mean values of the independent variables that are the α_p and $\beta_{p,j}$ coefficients in Eq. (2.11) should vary, each time the 388 funds are segregated by quadrant or rating. The investor would not know apriori. In this approximation, the averages of α_p and $\beta_{p,j}$ coefficients over the whole of 388 funds are used in finding these probability effects.

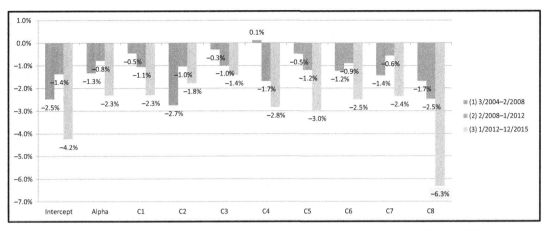

Figure 2.7: Mismatch of First Rating Based on Components of α_p and $\beta_{p,j}$ Coefficients.

period (2), and the 29.0% mismatch for period (3), broken down by principal component C1 through C8. Based on Table 2.4, the consistency of these components changes, in each of the three periods. Nevertheless, latter eigenvalue component (C8) always captures the more "regime-switching" aspects of relative performance, which generate a large portion of probability. It is not coincidence, that this component exhibits the greatest variation in the mismatch between quadrants and "qualitative" ratings. Looking at all the periods of (1) 3/2004–2/2008, (2) 2/2008–1/2012, and (3) 1/2012–12/2015, several patterns of mismatch emerge:

- In the first quadrant compared to the first rating, the mismatch becomes larger over time. The most significant source of mismatch is component C8, which is the most "tactical" and generates the largest portion of outperformance. This is the pattern that is least-observed, and hardest to evaluate. It pertains to positions that the manager may change abruptly, in an effort to capture changing market trends. To maximize utility, the investor would have liked that this component be rated in a way that is consistent with probability of outperformance (please refer to Fig. 2.7).
- That pattern is reversed in the Fig. 2.8, which depicts the second rating from the top, matched to the second quadrant for each of the three periods examined. Over time, the components C2 through C5, which are neither the most, not the least-prevalent, seemed to follow probability of outperformance better. The pattern on assessing C8 is reversed, in the third period examined.
- Some funds in the third category from the top should be rated higher. This is prevalent in the first and the third periods under investigation, but is mostly abated by events in the second period of 2/2008–1/2012. The depths of crisis and start of QE reduce the effect of funds being rated lower than what they should on relative performance (please refer to Fig. 2.9).

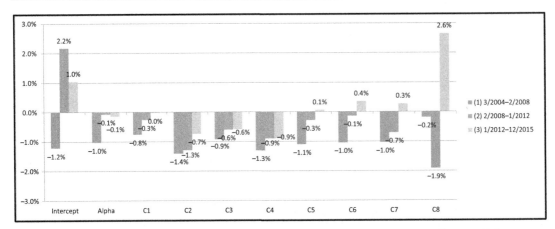

Figure 2.8: Mismatch of Second Rating Based on Components of α_p and $\beta_{p,j}$ Coefficients.

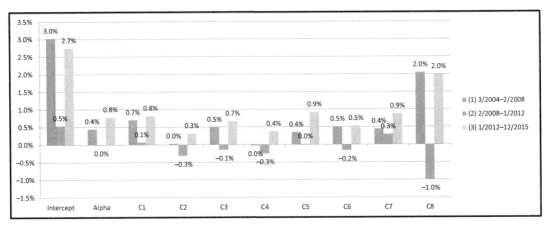

Figure 2.9: Mismatch of Third Rating Based on Components of α_p and $\beta_{p,j}$ Coefficients.

- In Fig. 2.10, the effect of funds rated lower than what they should is over all components C1 to C8. No particular component accounts for most mismatch of ratings to performance, except perhaps component C4 which, during period (2), reveals a large mismatching. Component C4 in Table 2.4 shows that the emphasis changed from underweight in US Aggregate, to underweight in Global Aggregate, while from period (1) and (2) Leveraged Loan weight changed. That particular component generated only a 0.4% probability of outperformance by the quadrants, and a 2.8% probability of outperformance by rating, for a difference of 2.4%. Probability of outperformance based on rating was higher than the actual quadrant of outperformance, for that component, in period (2). Some funds in lowest rating should have been rated higher. For all other components and in the same (last) quadrant versus rating, the phenomenon of rating-based outperformance that should be rated higher is spread equally across all components of α_p and $\beta_{p,j}$ coefficients.

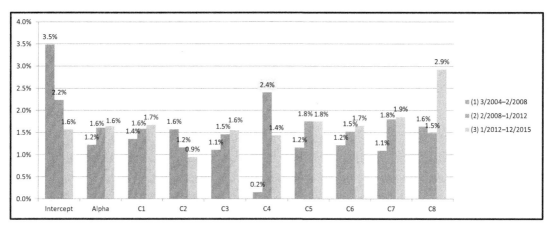

Figure 2.10: Mismatch of Fourth Rating Based on Components of α_p and $\beta_{p,j}$ Coefficients.

2.9 Conclusions

The behavior of the investor in the three periods of (1) crisis in March 2004 to February 2008, (2) QE in February 2008 to January 2012, and (3) Taper Tantrum from January 2012 to December 2015 was very different, while several similarities were found between periods (1) and (3). Most of the difference was in period (2) of 2008–12, which is attributed to a "breakdown" of the relation between investor risk preferences, and portfolio manager relative performance. Interestingly, consistent biases in rating the performance of portfolio managers may have lessened as well, during the same period, comparatively.

Early signs of the crisis in mortgage markets should have been evident as early as 2004, in which case they would have most likely affected investor behavior. However, the experience with implementation of financial accounting standards by GSEs points to the fact that such early signs were at least not in plain view. Thus the investor continued to expect performance out of a mixture of returns in the middle, as well as the tails of the return distribution in period (1) before the crisis, as well as in (3) afterward. Portfolio managers have attempted to generate outperformance in a benchmark-relative sense that matched the behavioral aspects of investors' seeking performance at the tails of return distributions, in these periods. The process of evaluating portfolio manager performance and assigning a rating may have gone from a state of being partly inaccurate toward such attempts in (1), to being equally if not more inaccurate, as markets stabilized postcrisis, in state (3). In between, that inaccuracy seemed to have abated through events related to crisis and QE. It is hard to tell, if ratings reflected the behavioral aspect of investors, best described in the trade-off between risk from variance and that derived from tails, liberally termed as "isorisk" to capture the fact that managers do travel across both. The fact that manager ratings tend to capture tail-seeking less accurately may, at the limit, be a blessing: following the fallacy of composition, if investors were pointed by ratings toward investment managers that are best in tail-seeking, then at the limit, large changes in weights would exacerbate the related underlying sources of tail events, such as illiquidity, mispricing due to market flow, etc. But ultimately, ratings should not fix the decision of the kind of risk desirable, on behalf of the investor. In retrospect, this is why environmental, social, and governance issues have become necessary in the assessment of manager performance. To mitigate ratings that could run-away with the better ability of a manager to undertake large changes in positions irrespective of the effect on markets, and other participants.

Due to asset nonlinearities, which apparently become exacerbated in a full crisis period, such as (2), the partly confusing phenomenon appears that certain managers possess better "skill" than others, when an evaluation of performance is based on standard metrics used, such as linear beta and information ratio. But, an intercept during a crisis period is not pure skill. The relation between utility of absolute levels of wealth to the investor, and benchmark-relative performance of the portfolio manager breaks down in periods of crisis. Other processes are in place during a crisis, which require methods that lie beyond the scope of this analysis. Still, there is a learning process that accrues to investors due to the actual event of the crisis, manifested in the fact that the patterns of investing captured by the portfolio betas to the indices bear similarities between periods (2) and (3). The investor is preserving the patterns of investing that were determined in period (2), for reasons alluded to low volatility, Central Bank intervention, etc. Investor behavior appears to have reverted back to the precrisis conditions. That behavior is largely captured by patterns of portfolio management. What remains to be seen, is if ratings catch up, as well.

References

Bhardwaj, G., Sengupta, R., 2008. Did Prepayments Sustain the Subprime Market? Research Division, Federal Reserve Bank of St. Louis Working Paper 2008-039A (Oct. 2008), pp. 1–44.

Goetzmann, W., Ingersoll, J., Spiegel, M., Welch, I., 2007. Portfolio performance manipulation and manipulation-proof performance measures. Rev. Financ. Studies 20, 1503–1546.

Roll, R., 1992. A mean/variance analysis of tracking error. J. Portfol. Manage. 18, 13–22.

Further Reading

Archer, W.R., David L., Gary M., 2001. Prepayment Risk and Lower Income Borrowers, Joint Center for Housing Studies, Working Paper, pp. 1–41.

Breeden, D.T., 1995. Risk, return and hedging of fixed-rate mortgages. In: Fabozzi, F.J. (Ed.), The Handbook of Mortgage-Backed Securities. fourth ed. Probus Publishing Company, Chicago, pp. 783–825.

DeLiban, N., Lancaster, B.P., 1995. Understanding and valuing mortgage security credit. In: Fabozzi, F.J. (Ed.), The Handbook of Mortgage-Backed Securities. Probus Publishing, Chicago, pp. 449–487.

Feldstein, M.S., 1969. Mean-variance analysis in the theory of liquidity preference and portfolio selection. Rev. Econ. Studies 36 (1), 5–12.

Foster, D.P., Payton Young, H., 2010. Gaming performance fees by portfolio managers. Q. J. Econ. 125 (4), 1435–1458.

Golub, B.W., Tilman, L.M., 1997. Measuring yield curve risk using principal component analysis, value at risk, and key rate durations. J. Portfol. Manage. 24, 72–84.

Grinold, R., 1989. The fundamental law of active management. J. Portfol. Manage. 15, 30–37.

Jarrow, R., Zhao, F., 2006. Downside loss aversion and portfolio management. Manage. Sci. 52 (4), 558–566.

Sorkin, A.R., 2009. Too Big to Fail: The Inside Story of How Wall Street and Washington Fought to Save the Financial System-and Themselves. Viking Press, New York.

Trippi, R.R., Turban, E., 1993. Neural Networks in Finance and Investing. Probus Publishing Company, Chicago.

Pennington-Cross, A., 2002. Patterns of Default and Prepayment for Prime and Nonprime Mortgages, Working Paper 02-1, OPHEO Working Papers, Office of Federal Housing Enterprise & Oversight, Washington, D.C.

Zellner, A., 1962. An efficient method for estimating seemingly unrelated regressions and tests for aggregation bias. J. Am. Stat. Assoc. 57, 348–368.

CHAPTER 3

Optimal Bubble Exit Strategies

Dimitris Voliotis

University of Piraeus, Piraeus, Greece

Chapter Outline

3.1 Introduction

Insofar, there are several explanations for the emergence of speculative bubbles. The mispricing of securities, that is, the departure of market prices from their fundamental value, is usually attributed to the overvaluation of investors, the herding behavior of noise traders or to the excessive risk taking of fund managers. All of them, individually or in combination, explain well how speculative bubbles emerge, nevertheless institutional investors and practitioners are not only eager to explain the phenomenon but also to find strategies that make bubbles manageable. For instance, many investors have the expertise and the experience to identify when a bull market turns to a bubble, still they can never be certain when it is going to burst. No doubt, institutional investors may possess the strategic power to trigger the burst of the bubble, nevertheless this could occur with certainty only for massive short selling and only when the price has reached an unprecedented level. Otherwise, playing against the momentum of the market may cause you to suffer severe losses. Knowing that the bubble is going to get burst, but not knowing the exact time makes imperative to form an optimal timing strategy.

This model provides an analysis of investors' behavior, when the bubble has been acknowledged but only few major investors have the strategic power to possibly prompt an abrupt correction of prices back to their fundamental values. Still, the strategic power is not always adequate. Important role also plays a bundle of unspecified determinants that attribute the complexity of the phenomenon, for which we have introduced an uncertainty factor that encompasses all these unspecified parameters of the model and determines the probability of success when some investor attempts to trigger the burst. Hence, investors should weigh both the strategic interaction with other major investors as well as the unrestrained powers of the market.

There are two specifications of the model. Both assume that there is a group of strategic investors that have the power to burst the bubble, that is, to push the price back to its fundamental value by massive short sales. The first specification assumes that strategic investors are having one shot to trigger the burst, whereas the second allows for multiple shots. Before the correction, investors have incentive to go long to the securities, maximizing speculative gains, still they will have to move out well before the burst that will evaporate all their profits.

The role of information in the analysis has a decisive role. Strategic investors have common knowledge of the characteristics of their opponents, as well as of the fundamental security prices. Although the vast literature assumes that investors perceive differently for fundamental prices, when we talk about strategic institutional investors, common knowledge of fundamental security prices seems quite reasonable. To the contrary, we assume that the uncertainty factor, that is, the probability of success will be subjectively perceived.

The model assumes two types of investors. There is a group of finite number of strategic investors, and a continuum of nonstrategic investors (or small and uninformed investors) that have no power to affect security prices, whatsoever. This is consistent with the specification of Abreu and Brunnermeier (2003) that rationalizes "bubbles" assuming the presence of a pool of "behavioral" investors that are subject to animal spirits. Strategic investors can affect prices and possess complete information of the objective function of all investors (strategic or nonstrategic). On the other hand, the pool of nonstrategic (and uninformed) investors are unaware of the strategic capabilities of the informed strategic investors. Nevertheless, we assume that all investors know a threshold price from above, that once reached, everyone understands that it is a bubble and fire sales are triggered.

The conceptual framework of the game rests upon the literature of duel games. Specifically, the game is a noisy duel with discrete number of actions. The basic framework of the game for a single shot and zero-sum payoffs is met in Dresher (1981) and is extended for multiple shots in Fox and Kimeldorf (1969). A further generalization is provided by Positselskaya (2008) for nonzero sum games, while Restrepo (1957), Teraoka (1983), and Orlowski and Radzik (2007) prove the equilibrium existence for discrete silent duels, that is, when the past behavior of the opponents is not available. Notice here that in contrast to the existing literature, the model captures the possibilities of strategic interaction not through time but in another well-ordered set, the price range of stock prices, which comes naturally in our framework.

Section 3.2 provides the basic notation, definitions, and the basic setup of the game. Section 3.3 extends the game to accommodate strategies of multiple shots by investors and discusses their strategic behavior. Section 3.4 discusses the idea of dark pools as a vehicle for some investor to "silently" trigger the burst. Finally, Section 3.5 concludes.

3.2 The Model

Consider a securities market, where investors with long positions are divided into two classes or types, a subset of investors having a small number of shares and few that have a substantial tranche of shares and can effectively influence the market price. You may think of a vast majority of small shareholders that exhibit herd behavior and follow the market developments, and a group of strategic investors, usually major institutional investors that have the market power, the technical expertise, and the relevant information to affect the market.

Suppose now a stock or a stock index that significantly moves away from its fundamental value. Price q takes values in the real interval, $[\underline{Q},\overline{Q}]$. Think of $\underline{Q}$ as the fundamental price of the stock where any value in excess of $\underline{Q}$ reflects positive expectations for excessive cash flows. The upper bound $\overline{Q}$ defines a *threshold* price that signals to all investors, both informed and uninformed, that the stock price is a "bubble" and triggers massive sales pushing the price back to its fundamental value, $\underline{Q}$.

Without loss of generality, we define a nonzero sum game between the two institutional strategic investors (strategic investors, for short) in the sense of Positselskaya (2008).[1] Both strategic investors have entered the market for price Q, that is, at its fundamental value. Their pursuit is to dominate the market and increase their *strategic power* but this does not preclude that a "bubble" situation might be profitable for both. Hence, they want to make more money and at the same time make their opponent to lose. Strategic investors $I = 1,2$ know when there is solid ground for $q > \underline{Q}$, or not. Once a "bubble" emerges they can securely make speculative profits by taking long positions, knowing that no uninformed investor can identify the bubble before $\overline{Q}$ is reached. If, however the "opponent" investor moves first by selling massively the stock at some price lower to $\overline{Q}$, the bubble might burst with positive probability and any speculative gains will be lost. If investor i has long position z_i, the speculative gains—if sells at price q—will be $u_i = z_i\left(q - \underline{Q}\right)$.

A *strategy* of informed investors is the price they opt to *get out* of the market and cash in their gains. For strategy price x of Player 1, there is positive probability for the bubble to burst, given by the cumulative distribution $P(x)$, respectively, $P(y)$ for price of Player 2. If the bubble does not burst, then the opponent investor will leave the market at $\overline{Q}$ and it's realized that speculative gain will be $\overline{Q} - \underline{Q}$. To the contrary, the nonrealized gains for the investor who left early, are $\overline{Q} - x$.

The cumulative probability $P(q)$ for $q = x,y$, attributes the probability of a bubble burst when each investor moves. Let us call this *idiosyncratic* probability P_i as the *implosion function* of investor i. We anticipate that an investor will have greater strategic power to burst the bubble

---

[1] Politselskaya calls this class of games *nonantagonistic*.

when the relative long position in the market—compared to the opponent investor—is much larger.

Assumption 2.1

The implosion function $P_i(q)$ is continuous and increasing in q.

Assumption 2.2

The implosion function $P_i(q)$ satisfies $P_i(\underline{Q})=0$ and $P_i(\bar{Q})=1$.

Assume that $P(q)$ takes the form, $P_i(q)=1-\left(\dfrac{q-\underline{Q}}{\bar{Q}-\underline{Q}}\right)^{a_i}$. The coefficient a_i for investor i will be given by the relative size of their position $a_i = z_i / (z_i + z_j)$.

The expected payoff function of investor 1 is

$$U_i(x)=\begin{cases} P_1(x)z_1\left(x-\underline{Q}\right), & x < y \\ \left[P_1(x)\left(1-P_2\left(y\right)\right)+P_2\left(y\right)\left(1-P_1(x)\right)+P_1(x)P_2\left(y\right)\right]z_1\left(x-\underline{Q}\right), & x = y \\ \left(1-P_2\left(y\right)\right)z_1\left(\bar{Q}-\underline{Q}\right), & x > y \end{cases}$$

The payoff function can be read as follows. When investor 1 moves first (i.e., $x < y$), he receives the speculative profit $z_1\left(x-\underline{Q}\right)$ with probability of success $P_1(x)$. In case of failure, he receives zero payoff with probability $1-P_1(x)$. If the opponent moves first and fails with probability $1-P_2(y)$, the investor waits until price reaches $\bar{Q}$ and makes profits amounted to $z_1\left(\bar{Q}-\underline{Q}\right)$.[2] Otherwise, when the opponent succeeds he makes no profits. When both investors move simultaneously, there are three out of four events that the "bubble" goes burst, that is, when one or both investors succeed. In this case, the realized profits of investor 1 amount to $z_1\left(x-\underline{Q}\right)$.

A *Nash equilibrium* of the game is a strategy profile (x,y) such that it holds,

$$U_1\left(x',y\right)\le U_1\left(x,y\right)\text{ and }U_2\left(x,y'\right)\le U_2\left(x,y\right),$$

For arbitrary strategies $x', y' \le \bar{Q}$.

An *approximate Nash equilibrium* of the game is a strategy profile (x,y) such that for sufficiently small $\varepsilon > 0$ it holds,

$$U_1\left(x',y\right)-\varepsilon\le U_1\left(x,y\right)\text{ and }U_2\left(x,y'\right)-\varepsilon\le U_2\left(x,y\right),$$

For arbitrary strategies $x', y' \le \bar{Q}$.

---

[2] More precisely, the investor gets out of the market for price marginally lower than $\bar{Q}$, that is, $\bar{Q}-\varepsilon$. The outcome of such strategy will be an approximate equilibrium.

Theorem 2.1

The unique Nash equilibrium of the games satisfies $P_j(x) + P_i(y) = 1$.

Proof. Suppose that the current price of the stock is $q > \underline{Q}$ Investor i has no incentive to move first once $1 - P_j(q) > P_i(q)$. That is, at price q if investor j moves first, the probability of failing to burst the bubble is higher than the probability of success of i. Indeed, the expected payoff of investor i is higher when investor j moves first,

$$\left(1 - P_2(y)\right)z_1\left(\overline{Q} - \underline{Q}\right) > P_1(x)z_1\left(x - \underline{Q}\right).$$

As q increases, both $P_i(q), P_j(q)$ increase. The maximum price that investor i is willing to wait before the move is the one that maximize his probability of success, which is when $1 - P_j(q) = P_i(q)$ or $P_j(x) + P_i(y) = 1$. □

It is important to highlight the *quasi antagonistic* character of the game since when the bubble goes burst before the terminal price $\overline{Q}$ only one investor realizes positive speculative gains whereas the other gets nil. Also, note that the two investors move simultaneously since no person will have incentive to move first, that is, investor 2 has no incentive to move as long as $1 - P_j(q) > P_i(q)$.

Example

Suppose that the price ranges in the interval [1, 50] and the long position of investor 1 is 6 mio, while for investor 2 is 2 mio. The strike price will be given for,

$$\left(\frac{q-1}{49}\right)^{1/4} + \left(\frac{q-1}{49}\right)^{3/4} = 1$$

The strike price will be q = 11,584 and the expected speculative gains will be
$EU_i = P_i(x)\left(1 - P_j(y)\right)z_1\left(x - \underline{Q}\right) = 13749314{,}544$.

3.3 The Game with Multiple Shots

Heretofore, we assume that investors opt for the price that will leave the market. Once, they leave the market and the "bubble" is still there, we assume that they don't have second chance to return back. If they do, they enter back into the market for a price well above the fundamental price and a loss may incur. However, this is not an extreme scenario. Next, we assume that investors have more than one, but a finite number, of chances to reenter the market and attempt to burst the bubble before the opponent investor do so.

Now, assume that investor 1 has m shots and investor 2 has n shots, respectively. A strategy for investor 1, thus will be a vector $x = (x_1, x_2, \ldots, x_m)$ and similarly for investor 2, $y = (y_1, y_2, \ldots, y_n)$. Each x_i (or y_i) will be a price that triggers the exit for investor and normally $\underline{Q} \leq x_1 < \cdots < x_m \leq \bar{Q}$ (or $\underline{Q} < y_1 < \cdots < y_n \leq \bar{Q}$). Also, define x_{i_j} the projection of the vector x that includes all elements greater of equal to i (similarly for investor 2 y_{i_j}). For instance, $x_{|3} = (x_3, x_4, \ldots, x_m)$.

The payoff function adjusts accordingly. The expected payoff for investor 1 is

$$
U_1(x,y) = \begin{cases}
P_1(x_i)z_1(x_i - \underline{Q}) - (1 - P_1(x_i))\left[z_1(E(q) - x_i) - EU_1(x_{|i+1}, y)\right], & x_i < y_j \\[2mm]
\begin{aligned}
&\left[P_1(x_i)(1 - P_2(y_j)) + P_2(y_j)(1 - P_1(x_i)) + P_1(x_i)P_2(y_j)\right]z_1(x_i - \underline{Q}) \\
&+ (1 - P_1(x_i))(1 - P_2(y_j))EU_1(x_{|i+1}, y)
\end{aligned} & x_i = y_j \\[2mm]
(1 - P_2(y_j))EU_1(x_{|i+1}, y_{|j+1}), & x_i > y_j
\end{cases}
$$

Some remarks are necessary here. Suppose that investor 1 moves first $(x_i < y_j)$. With probability $P_1(x_i)$ the bubble burst and the investor cash in the gains $z_1(x_i - \underline{Q})$. If "bubble" survives, investor suffers losses. Price might go up and formed to the expected level $E(q)$. Then the per unit realized losses would be $(E(q) - x_i)$. Take notice that the difference $(E(q) - x_i)$ is anticipated to be positive. Otherwise the martingale property holds and investors have no strategic power, whatsoever. Investor 1 has to pay the price difference to cover his short position and the overall loss is $z_1(E(q) - x_i)$. Once investor 1 turns again to long position, his expected payoff for the continuation game will be $EU_1(x_{|i+1}, y)$.

Suppose now, that investor 2 moves first. If the "bubble" bursts, the payoff of investor 1 is nil, since the market price adjusts automatically to its fundamental value $\underline{Q}$ Otherwise, with probability of $(1 - P_2(y))$ the payoff adjusts to the expected payoff of the continuation game.

Last, let us assume that investors move simultaneously. There are three events that make the "bubble" burst. That is, when investors together burst the "bubble," and when one investor 1 or investor 2 individually achieve to burst the "bubble." Still there is one event where the game is continued, that is, when they together fail to burst the "bubble." When the "bubble" bursts, both investors capitalize their gains, otherwise the game is continued and receive the expected payoff of the continuation game. Fox and Kimeldorf (1969) prove that at the equilibrium, a generalization of the result of Theorem 2.1 holds.

Lemma 3.1 (Fox and Kimeldorf, 1969)

At Nash equilibrium it is,

$$\prod_m \left(1 - P_1(x_i)\right) + \prod_n \left(1 - P_2(y_j)\right) = 1,$$

for $P_1(x_i), P_2(y_j) \in (0,1)$.

Their result is robust not only for zero-sum games but also for the more general nonzero-sum games, like ours. Positselskaya (2008) proves that for noisy duel games with arbitrary number of actions, we can always find an approximate Nash equilibrium and define conditions that makes the outcome Pareto optimal. *Mutadis mutandis.*

Theorem 3.1 (Positselskaya, 2008)

There are $(\tilde{x}, \tilde{y})$ strategy profiles that are approximate equilibria of the game.

The proof of the theorem follows inductively from the standard case where $m = n = 1$. Another important result that we meet in Fox and Kimeldorf (1969) and reproduced in Positselskaya (2008) is the following.

Lemma 3.2

Let the set of prices $\{q_{ij}, i, j \in N\}$ denoting price levels where investor 1 has spent his ith move and investor 2 his jth move. Then the following inequality holds,

$$\underline{Q} < q_{ij} < \min\{q_{i-1,j}, q_{i,j-1}\}.$$

The proof of the lemma can be found, *mutadis mutandis* in Positselskaya (2008). This lemma reveals us that an investor never opts to spend all of his moves before the opponent make his first move. Another interesting result is the following.

Lemma 3.3

The last attempt (x_2 or y_2) always occurs for price $\bar{Q}$.

Proof. Once the opponent investor has wasted all the opportunities to burst the "bubble," the investor has no incentive to evade profits by attempting before $\bar{Q}$. □

Lemma 3.4

The investor with the highest strategic power always moves first.

Proof. Without loss of generality suppose that investor 1 has the highest market power, $a_1 > 1 - a_1 = a_2 > 0$. Following the argument of Theorem 2.1, no investor i moves first once $1 - P_j(q) > P_i(q)$ for $q \in [\underline{Q}, \bar{Q}]$. For convenience, let $\Delta = \left(\dfrac{q - \underline{Q}}{\bar{Q} - \underline{Q}} \right)$. We claim that investor 1 moves first. Suppose not. Investor 2 moves first once it is the case,

$$P_2(q) \geq 1 - P_1(q)$$
$$1 - \Delta^{a2} \geq 1 - \left(1 - \Delta^{a1}\right) = \Delta^{a1}$$
$$1 \geq \Delta^{\alpha 1} + \Delta^{\alpha 2} = \Delta^{\alpha 1} + \Delta^{1 - \alpha 1}$$
$$\geq \Delta^{\alpha 1} + \frac{\Delta}{\Delta^{\alpha 1}}$$
$$\frac{\Delta^{\alpha 1} - \Delta}{\Delta^{\alpha 1}} \geq \Delta^{\alpha 1}$$

The numerator of the left-hand side is negative that makes the ratio negative. The right-hand side is always positive that makes the inequality impossible, unless $q = \underline{Q}$. But by assumption $P(\underline{Q}) = 0$, which excludes the move at the very beginning. Contradiction.   □

3.4 Cascading the Orders in Dark Pools

Nowadays, financial innovation allows big investors to cascade their orders from other traders. Dark pools or dark venues are trading platforms that permit opaque trading and ensure multiple benefits for their customers where can execute large trades without transmitting their valuable private information throughout the lit market. Dark pools are usually hosted by big investment banks.[3] As of April 2013, dark pools amounted to approximately 14% of all the US stock trading volume (Bloomberg Businessweek, 2013). Insofar, the regulatory framework (i.e., US SEC) allows for nonexchange trading venues that operate in parallel to official bourses. These trading venues are coined alternative trading systems (ATS) and perform all the functions of a bourse. Most commonly, trades occur via and electronic communications network (ECN), provided by brokers (mostly by Tier-1 brokers, i.e., Goldman Sachs, Deutche Bank etc.), that automatically match buy and

---

[3] Most renowned are Credit Suisse, Goldman Sachs Citi, and many others.

sell orders for execution (Banks, 2010). In this electronic marketplace, all brokerage activities are carried out by appropriately designed algorithms that will keep the anonymity of investors and minimize the price effect of their orders (Leshik and Cralle, 2011).

The rationale of cascading algorithm is to minimize the price effect cost, that is, the change in price by the quote of a big order. This is done by breaking the order is smaller parcels that are hardly identifiable and minimize the price effect. This strategic tactic is adopted by institutional traders who want to buy (or sell) hundreds and thousands of stocks, fixing each "parcel" for trade to a thousand of stocks or two (Leshik and Cralle, 2011). This appears quite relevant to our duel model of big institutional investors and reveals that speculative trading strategies are preferred to be "silent" rather "noisy" as in our standard case. The duel model is noisy in the sense that informed investors observe the moves of all others. Hence, a move is neither observable to the opponent investors nor uninformed investors can identify these moves by abrupt price changes. "Silent" moves keeps the duel private and increases the opportunities of big investors to make opponent(s) to get trapped by the bubble.

A general solution to the class of games with silent shots has been provided by Restrepo (1957). Teraoka (1983) proves that the duel game with silent shots has a mixed strategy equilibrium. Baston and Garnaev (1995) show that there are also many pure Nash equilibria, while they also provide conditions for uniqueness. The idea of equilibrium strategies has as follows. If some investor has m silent shots, he partitions the interval $\underline{Q} < q_1 < q_2 < .. < q_m < \bar{Q}$. Then he should randomly use his first shot in the interval $\left[\underline{Q}, q_1\right]$, his second shot in $\left[q_1, q_2\right]$, and so on so forth (Radzik and Raghavan, 1994).

3.5 Conclusions

Speculative bubbles appear to be inherent in economic systems and always create great opportunities for windfalls to traders. As long as bubbles evolve, prices are at disequilibrium and traders can make money out of it. However, cautious investors are fully aware that after the boom follows the burst and prices are going to fall back down at equilibrium level. This exercise addresses the problem of optimal timing for "getting off" the speculative bubble.

The model assumes that investors are long in securities and can have a single or multiple opportunities to "get off." When investors have a single opportunity to move and the "bubble" survives, they cash in their gains, nevertheless there are evaded profits since prices keep increasing when they are out. We find that the optimal timing of exit is when the probability of success equals the probability of failure of the opponent. The second and more interesting case is when investors have more than one shots. In the latter, we find some very interesting results. First, the investor with the highest strategic power has the incentive to move first. This is a normal outcome since the probability of success outweighs the probability of failure of the opponent. If opposite, the investor would have the incentive not to act but to wait the opponent to make his move. We also showed that an investor has merely to wait the "bubble" to "mature" if the opponent has spent all of his shots. Last, Lemma 3.2 illustrates that there is going to be alternating moves of some sort by investors.

In Section 3.4, we discussed the role of silent duels, and their relevance with the market practices in the evolving financial system. Dark pools are a nice place to hide while the computational trading permits the design of trading strategies that can serve the role of optimal bubble exits. Still, this is an issue that need to be further investigated and should be reserved for future research.

References

Abreu, D., Brunnermeier, M.K., 2003. Bubbles and crashes. Econometrica 71 (1), 173–204.

Banks, E., 2010. Dark Pools. The Structure and Future of Off-Exchange Trading and Liquidity. Palgrave Macmillan, London, UK.

Baston, V.J., Garnaev, A.Y., 1995. Teraoka-type two-person nonzero-sum silent duel. J. Optimiz. Theory App. 87 (3), 539–552.

Bloomberg Businessweek, 2013. Credit Suisse is making dark pools even darker.

Dresher, M., 1981. The Mathematics of Games of Strategy. Theory and Applications. The Rand Corporation, New Jersey, US.

Fox, M., Kimeldorf, G.S., 1969. Noisy duels. SIAM J. Appl. Math. 17 (2), 353–361.

Leshik, E.A., Cralle, J., 2011. An Introduction to Algorithmic Trading. Basic to Advanced Strategies. John Wiley & Sons Ltd, West Sussex, UK.

Orlowski, K., Radzik, T., 2007. Discrete silent duels with complete counteraction. Optimization 16 (3), 419–429.

Positselskaya, L.N., 2008. Equilibrium and pareto optimality in noisy discrete duels with an arbitrary number of actions. J. Math. Sci. 154 (2), 223–229.

Radzik, T., Raghavan, T.E.S., 1994. Duels. Handbook of Game Theory with Economic Applications. Elsevier, Amsterdam, The Netherlands, Chapter 20, Appendix.

Restrepo, R., 1957. Tactical problems involving several actions. In: Dresher, M., Tucker, A.W., Wolfe, P. (Eds.), Contributions to the Theory of Games 3, Annals of Mathematical Studies. Princeton University Press, New Jersey, US.

Teraoka, Y., 1983. A two-person game of timing with random termination. J. Optimiz. Theory App. 40, 379–396.

CHAPTER 4

Why History Matters to Financial Economists: The Case of Black Monday 1987

Camillo von Müller

CLVS-HSG University of St. Gallen, St. Gallen, Switzerland

Chapter Outline

4.1 Introduction

Why do investors behave the way they do? And why do they behave the way they do in times of crises? These questions are of fundamental importance to economists, regulators, savers, depositors, stock-, share-, and bondholders, and other people with claims in financial markets. As this essay is going to argue financial crises are neither necessarily resulting (exclusively) from a lack of skills of investors, nor are they necessarily due to "animal spirits" (Akerlof and Shiller, 2009). Rather, even accomplished investors can be causing their own demise by trading on the wrong rationale as result of (misguided) strategic incentives.

The subject of investor errors is a common topic in financial literature having caught attention of scholars from the days of Keynes (1936) until today (Akerlof and Shiller, 2009, 2016). But not only economists have been paying attention to this matter: Financial historians, such as Kindleberger (2005), and Dale (2016) have been contributing to the study of investor behavior today too.

Given the involvement of representatives from both the disciplines of economics and history, this essay is also going to discuss the fundamental question if and how these disciplines are complementing each other.

In a classic paper, Kenneth Arrow (1985) depicts the interplay of and differences between economic and historic inquiries by drawing an analogy "from the natural world" (p. 320). According to this analogy, geological inquiries rest both on the "underlying laws of geology," such as "the laws of physics and chemistry," as well specific concrete developments that lead to geographical formations at distinct places, for example, in form of "the history of the Appalachians and the Himalayas," or, the "movements of the Indian subcontinent" (pp. 320–321). According to this definition, the general laws of physics and chemistry manifest themselves in distinct geographical patterns at specific places on the global map. Parallel to the field of geology, Arrow (1985) categorizes events in economic history as being both the visualization and results of the general laws of economics. In the subsequent sections I will argue, however, that historic inquiries can fulfill a third function, that is, when they serve as testing grounds for economic theories. As inquiries into the history of investor and market behavior have the potential to falsify aspects of economic theory, they can add to the generalizable stock of knowledge on investor behavior, too. In the subsequent paragraphs, I will lay out this hypothesis in more detail, starting with the framework of the present argument, that is, a comparison of historical inquiries and scientific forms of analyzing investor behavior (Section 4.2), before turning to a more formal depiction of investor behavior in terms of simple game theory (Section 4.3), and its empirical discussion (Section 4.4). Section 4.5 concludes.

4.2 Analyzing Investor Behavior

The present essay examines aspects of behavioral finance under the premise of false choices. False choices, or to use a more technical term, "judgment errors" are studied by psychologists as well as by economists. Both professions agree in that they regard errors as information. If people use simplified [or one may add: inapt] procedures to judge and choose, those procedures may be seen most clearly through the errors they cause (Kamerer, 1995, p. 589). In this context, "for economists the frequency of errors is important because [reappearing] errors might affect economic efficiency, and methods for removing errors might affect economic efficiency."

4.2.1 Errors are Information

The insight that economic errors matter for reflections on economic activity is far from new. In fact, it dates back to the very beginnings of economics, that is, Adam *Smith's Wealth of Nations*. There, Smith described how "in their roles as producers" … "individuals do correctly perceive their self-interest" … "although not necessarily as consumers" (Friedman, 2011, p. 168). The notion that individuals are unable to understand their (true) self-interests and act accordingly can even be traced back to biblical interpretations as, for example, by St. Augustine who explained the Fall of Adam and Eve from paradise, by pointing at the limitations of the human intellect.

However, at least since the professionalization of economics as own branch of academic inquiry, economists have been convinced that individuals are able to act for their own good thus (unintentionally) contributing to the common weal. Richard T. Ely (1900) coined this notion "economic optimism" observing that trust in the intellect of the individual was both a specific characteristic of 18th century (providential and liberal) economists, as well as a notion that took a prominent place in the birth of American Economics in the late 19th century. The question of how to study individual behavior has been key to economic undertakings since this time.

4.2.2 Experimental Economics and Economic History

An intuitive answer to this question is the need for empirically generated data so as to enable economists to assess and examine concrete individual behaviors, and look for the root of errors through the lenses of other peoples' choices.

One way to produce this kind of data is by "the Art of Experiment" (Ledyard, 1995, p. 113). Like formal models, economic experiments are formed by virtue of abstractions and simplification, separating the world into "explicans" and "explicandum." They are a powerful tool to test and advance theoretical knowledge (e.g., in the realms of game theory), as they benefit from their proximity to the methodologies of what is commonly labeled as "hard sciences."

However, like engineers, who learn about flaws in the construction of bridges not only from physical experiments but also from bridges crashing in the real word, economists can learn about the reasons behind false economic decisions not only through experiments but also from studying individual decisions in reality.

In other words, economists who are interested in studying investor behavior can advance their theoretical knowledge by resting the latter on economic experiments and financial history. While experiments have the benefit to deliver replicable data that is transparently attributable to clearly defined causes, financial history (though quite often being messier than experiments) has the potential to offer information on aspects that the researcher had not been aware of at the beginning of her research. Moreover, experiments and historical analyses differ with regard to inferences that can be drawn from their results. While experiments allow for quantitative forecasting within their defined contexts, financial history rather gives a sense of possible outcomes and their preconditions at a specific point in time. That is, rather than delivering probabilistic results in terms of quantitative reasoning, the study of financial history can among other things help in the identification of qualitative questions essential to the evaluation of past, current, and future states of affairs.

Table 4.1: Prisoners' dilemma pay-off structure.

p_A, p_B	$b = C$	$b = D$
$a = C$	R,R	S,T
$a = D$	T,S	P,P

Source: Verhoeff, T., 1998. The Trader's Dilemma: A Continuous Version of the Prisoner's Dilemma. Faculty of Mathematics and Computing Science, Eindhoven University of Technology. Available from: http://www.win.tue. nl/~wstomv/publications/td.pdd

As I will argue in the following, inquiries into the history of investor behavior have been triggering additional dimensions of outcomes as they provided single cases that falsified then-valid theories on economic behavior thus leading in turn to new (generalizable) forms of knowledge. In this context, they have the potential to not only "fill missing places in the periodic table" of financial economics, but can even lead to changes in the vision of economists and investors thus increasing the stock of economic knowledge by more than increments comparable to William Herschel, who, "when he increased by one the time-honored number of planetary bodies, taught astronomers to see new things when they looked at the familiar heavens even with instruments more traditional than his own" (Kuhn, 1962, p. 175). This hypothesis will be discussed empirically in the subsequent sections that refer to the events of the Black Monday of October 19, 1987 and their relevance for the efficient market hypothesis as discussed by Shiller (1992).

4.3 Prisoners' Dilemma and Investor Behavior

Before examining the behavior of investors before and on October 19, 1987 in more detail, I will refer to the well-known framework of the Prisoners' Dilemmas as formal outline for discussing harmful investor behavior that leads to systematic errors.

Prisoners' dilemmas describe situations in which parties make choices so as to maximize private gains resulting in subperfect (if not harmful) total outcomes. A typical matrix-representation is stated later.

The matrix (Table 4.1) depicts a situation in which players *(A,B)* can either choose to cooperate *(C)* or to defect *(D)*. The different pay-offs are denoted as

"S is the sucker's payoff (for a forsaken cooperator),
P is the punishment (for mutual defection),
R is the reward (for mutual cooperation),
T is the temptation (for defecting a cooperator)"

(Verhoeff, 1998, p. 2).

The Prisoners'-Dilemma condition is satisfied for

"S < P < R < T"

(Verhoeff, 1998, p. 2).

That is, according to this setting, the choice to "defect" represents the stable strategy for each player so that both *(A)* and *(B)* will decide for noncooperation. As a consequence, both will be rewarded P instead of T leading thus to a suboptimal allocation of resources.

In the case of financial markets, the question persists, if it seems feasible to assume that the latter punish "cooperation," that is, if situations exist, in which cooperation of agents (be it in form of a stop, or a continuation of buying and selling activities) would be a preferable strategy; yet, incentives are such that rational investors chose to behave otherwise. This question is discussed in the subsequent two sections.

4.4 *Empirical* Observations—The Black Monday of October 1987

The "Black Monday" events refer to what has been "the first contemporary global financial crisis" (Bernhardt and Eckblad, 2013). This crisis was the result of a "chain reaction of market distress" that "sent global stock exchanges plummeting in a matter of hours. In the United States, the Dow Jones Industrial Average (DJIA) dropped 22.6% in a single trading session, a loss that remains the largest one-day stock market decline in history" (ibid). Fig. 4.1 depicts earlier-described events by representing monthly data on the S & P and NASDAQ indices.

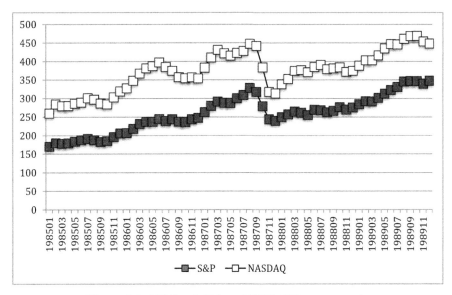

Figure 4.1: US Stock Prices (1985–89), own graph.
Source: St. Louis Fed (https://research.stlouisfed.org/publications/review/04/11/0411dwd.xls)

Bernhardt and Eckblad (2013) of Chicago FED offer a respective narrative to the data:

> Stock markets raced upward during the first half of 1987. By late August, the DJIA had gained 44% in a matter of 7 months, stoking concerns of an asset bubble. In mid-October, a storm cloud of news reports undermined investor confidence and led to the additional volatility in markets. The federal government disclosed a larger-than-expected trade deficit and the dollar fell in value. The markets began to unravel, foreshadowing the record losses that would develop a week later. Beginning on October 14, a number of markets began incurring large daily losses. On October 16, the rolling sell-offs coincided with an event known as "triple witching," which describes the circumstances when monthly expirations of options and futures contracts occurred on the same day. By the end of the trading day on October 16, which was a Friday, the DJIA had lost 4.6%. The weekend trading break offered only a brief reprieve; Treasury Secretary James Baker on Saturday, October 17, publicly threatened to devalue the US dollar in order to narrow the nation's widening trade deficit. Even before US markets opened for trading on Monday morning, stock markets in and around Asia began plunging. Additional investors moved to liquidate positions, and the number of sell orders vastly outnumbered willing buyers near previous prices, creating a cascade in stock markets. In the most severe case, New Zealand's stock market fell 60%. Traders reported racing each other to the pits to sell. In the United States, the DJIA crashed at the opening bell and eventually finished down 508 points, or 22.6%.

In a well-known paper, Shiller (1992) has attempted to explain the events of October 19, 1987 from an investor perspective. His investigation was driven by the fundamental question that something "must have been different on October 19, 1987 that caused the behavior of the market to be very different from other days. What was different on that day?" (Shiller, 1992, p. 397).

According to the efficient market hypothesis, the answer to this question is to be found in outside information processed by financial markets. This hypothesis has shaped a generation of academic financial economists, particularly through "Eugene Fama's (1970) influential survey article, "Efficient Capital Markets." "It was generally believed that securities markets were extremely efficient in reflecting information about individual stocks and about the stock market as a whole." Thus, neither technical analysis, which is the study of past stock prices in an attempt to predict future prices, nor even fundamental analysis, which is the analysis of financial information, such as company earnings and asset values to help investors select "undervalued" stocks, would enable an investor to achieve returns greater than those that could be obtained by holding a randomly selected portfolio of individual stocks, at least not with comparable risk. The efficient market hypothesis is associated with the idea of a "random walk," which is a term loosely used in the finance literature to characterize a price series where all subsequent price changes represent random departures from previous prices. The logic of the random walk idea is that if the flow of information is unimpeded and information is immediately reflected in stock prices, then tomorrow's price change will reflect only tomorrow's news and will be independent of the price changes today. But news is by definition unpredictable, and, thus, resulting price changes must be unpredictable and random. As a result, it was assumed that prices fully reflect all known information, and even uninformed investors buying a diversified portfolio at the tableau of prices given by the market will obtain a rate of return as generous as that achieved by the experts." (Malkiel, 2003, p. 59).

Thus, 1987-financial markets should have reacted efficiently by incorporating financial news that was reflected in stock price changes. Still, the analysis by Shiller (1992) of how buyers and sellers reacted to news comes to a contrary conclusion.

Table 4.2 summarizes the results reported by Shiller (1992). It shows that the "200-drop in the Dow on the morning of the October 19 is the most important" item for individual and institutional market participants (Shiller, 1992, p. 386). The latter deemed new information such as changes in the producer price index, or about the U.S. attack on an Iranian oil station relatively low (Shiller, 1992, p. 386). The low importance of the latter is deemed by Shiller (1992) to be of significance since this item "seems to be the best candidate for an important

Table 4.2: Importance of news items in 1987 stock market crash.

Relevance of news items to buyers and sellers according to their estimates: 1 = completely unimportant; 4 = moderately important; 7 = very important. For further details cf. Shiller (1992).	Individual (n = 605)					Institutional (n = 284)				
	All	Buy ers		Sell ers		All	Buy ers		Sell ers	
		Oct ober					Oct ober			
		12-19	19	12-19	19		12-19	19	12-19	19
200 point drop in Dow the morning of Oct 19	5.14	5.69	5.76	5.32	6.54	5.93	6.05	5.86	6.24	6.08
Treasury Bond Yield hit 10.5%	4.27	4.56	4.41	4.46	4.46	5.57	5.85	5.84	6.01	5.64
Drop in U.S. Stock Prices October 14–16	4.54	5.29	5.12	5.13	5.38	5.23	4.85	5.18	5.77	5.83
Baker suggested USD should slip further	4.04	4.50	4.05	4.11	5.31	4.84	4.45	4.67	5.41	5.39
Drop in Japanese or London Stock Prices	3.74	4.19	4.53	4.55	5.00	4.78	4.90	4.83	5.11	5.14
Trade d announced Oct 16, 1987	4.21	3.94	4.24	4.50	4.62	4.21	4.40	4.14	4.75	4.39
Chemical Bank raising prime rate, Oct 14	4.14	4.18	4.00	4.58	4.77	3.95	4.25	3.82	4.51	4.28
US attack on Iranian Oil Station, Oct 19	3.73	3.13	3.53	3.70	3.46	3.32	3.30	2.96	3.61	3.28
PPI index figures announced Oct 16	3.26	3.13	3.47	3.13	3.23	3.17	3.00	3.22	3.38	3.03
Prechter's short run signal of Oct 14	2.17	2.07	3.00	2.49	2.45	2.59	2.80	2.37	3.10	2.94

Source: Shiller, R.J., 1992. Investor behavior in the October 1987 stock market crash: survey evidence. In: Shiller, R.J. (Ed.), Market Volatility, MIT Press, Boston, 1992; own format.

news event that became public knowledge right on October 19 or over the weekend" before this date (p. 386).

Shiller (1992) concludes that "nothing stood out" in the reactions of buyers and sellers "beyond the price declines" (p. 387). This however, implies that investors may have been "reacting to price movements themselves" on a day "of big market drops, and not to any specific news stories" (Shiller, 1992, p. 387). In other words, "the survey did not turn up anything really important to investors that became public on October 19, 1987 or over the weekend, other than the price decline itself and the behavior of investors reacting to it and previous declines" (Shiller, 1992, p. 397). However, Shiller (1992) identified "news stories that preceded the drop by a number of days, and that were on investors' minds" (p. 398). For example, "[i]institutional investors were most concerned about the recent rise in interest rates and about Treasury Secretary James A. Baker's October 15 threat to push the dollar lower in response to increases in German interest rates" (Shiller, 1992, p. 398). Moreover, both "individual and institutional investors were confident that the marked was overpriced, worried about program trading, and were concerned about the national debt and taxes. These concerns … certainly affected individual behavior on October 19, but do not explain the events of that day" (Shiller, 1992, p. 398).

Given the absence of any "event outside the market to be immediately responsible for the market crash," Shiller (1992) assumes that the crash was "determined endogenously by investors."

In a recent Bundesbank-Working Paper, Kurz-Kim (2016) confirms the existence of "momentum trading" in the Dow Jones prior to October 19, 1987. As indicator of these strategies Kurz-Kim (2016) compares empirical probabilities of sequences of the same sign (i.e., consecutive trading days in which stock prices move in the same direction) to the theoretical probabilities of these events to happen. As a result, Kurz-Kim (2016) notes that "[b]efore Black Monday, the empirical probabilities of sequences of the same sign for both the positive and negative ... are significantly higher than those of the theoretical values" (p. 8). This leads to the conclusion that "before Black Monday, investors tended to buy when the stock return was positive and to sell when the stock return was negative (a day-to-day momentum strategy)" (p. 9). That is, investors engaged into behavior that amplified trends until the point where their behavior led to outcomes that were no longer feasible.

4.5 Conclusions

What is to conclude from the observations described earlier? First, earlier described situation in which investors where driving up prices until they felt that the level of the latter was no longer feasible bears the characteristics of a Prisoners' Dilemma as it represents a situation in which cooperation (i.e., the stop of momentum trading) would have stabilized markets whereas from the individual perspective of investors, clear disincentives for this kind of behavior existed since investors who would have been betting on falling prices would have been compensated with "a sucker pay-off for forsaken cooperation" (cf. above).

The empirical discussion of uncooperative investor behavior along with its (simple) formal representation in form of a Prisoners' Dilemma represents historic evidence that contradicts generalizable economic knowledge in form of the efficient market hypothesis. It thus serves as example for how the historic study of investor errors can depict limitations to an existing stock of economic theories and knowledge, thus in turn leading to better understanding of how investors behave in times of crises.

References

Akerlof, G.A., Shiller, R.J., 2009. Animal Spirits: How Human Psychology Drives the Economy and Why it Matters for Global Capitalism. Princeton University Press, Princeton, NJ.

Akerlof, G.A., Shiller, R.J., 2016. Phishing for Phools. The Economics of Manipulation and Deception. Princeton University Press, Princeton, NJ.

Arrow, K., 1985. Economic history: a necessary though not sufficient condition for an economist: Maine and Texas. Am. Econ. Rev. 75 (2), 320–323.

Bernhardt, D., Eckblad, M., 2013. 'Black Monday: The Stock Market Crash of 1987', Federal Reserve History. Available from: http://www.federalreservehistory.org/Events/DetailView/48

Dale, R., 2016. The First Crash. Lessons from the South Sea Bubble. Princeton University Press, Princeton, NJ.

Ely, R., 1900. A decade of economic theory. Ann. Am. Acad. Pol. Soc. Sci. 15 (2), 92–112.

Friedman, B., 2011. Economics: a moral inquiry with religious origins. Am. Econ. Rev. 101 (3), 166–170.

Kamerer, C., 1995. Individual decision making. In: Kagel, John, H., Roth, Alvin, E. (Eds.), The Handbook of Experimental Economics. Princeton University Press, Princeton, NJ.

Keynes, J.M., 1936. The General Theory of Employment, Interest, and Money. Prometheus Books, Amherst, NY.

Kindleberger, C.P., 2005. Manias, Panics, and Crashes: A History of Financial Crises. John Wiley and Sons, Hoboken NJ.

Kuhn, T.S., 1962. The historical structure of scientific discovery. The University of Chicago Press, Chicago IL, pp. 165–177.

Kurz-Kim, J.R., 2016. Black Monday, Globalization and Trading Behavior of Stock Investors. Discussion Paper Deutsche Bundesbank No 18/2016.

Ledyard, J.O., 1995. Public goods: a survey of experimental research. In: Kagel, J.H., Roth, A.E. (Eds.), The Handbook of Experimental Economics,. Princeton University Press, Princeton NJ.

Malkiel, B.G., 2003. The efficient market hypothesis and its critics. J. Econ. Perspect. 17 (1), 59–82.

Shiller, R.J., 1992. Investor behavior in the October 1987 stock market crash: survey evidence. In: Shiller, R.J. (Ed.), Market Volatility. MIT Press, Boston.

Verhoeff, T., 1998. The Trader's Dilemma: A Continuous Version of the Prisoner's Dilemma. Faculty of Mathematics and Computing Science, Eindhoven University of Technology. Available from: http://www.win. tue.nl/~wstomv/publications/td.pdd

Governing Financial Orders Which Have Been Grown and Not Made: The Origins of the Financial Crisis in Financial Gridlock

William Forbes

Queen Mary University of London, London, United Kingdom

Chapter Outline

5.1 Introduction

This paper draws upon Hayek's concept of a "Law of Liberty" which governs a financial order, which has grown and no single conscious authority has made to understand the unfolding of, and most appropriate responses to the recent financial crisis. See to argue two seemingly contradictory things in a belief their acceptance can help us understand recent crises, such as those a Enron in 2002 and Lehman in 2008.

Recognition of these two interacting currents in recurrent crises makes me favor structural reform and suspicious of ad hoc interventions even when such interventions have laudable aims of punishing the greedy, etc. In short, I advocate a government of law and not of men.[1]

New cures need to recognize the need to choose between a grown and made financial order, rather than simply assuming regulatory interventions occur in an unchanging order still largely dominated by preexisting social norms. Such intervention is rendered particularly hazardous when the underlying definition of property rights, applied to traded assets, are themselves in the process of contention and reconstruction.

5.2 Governing Financial Orders Which Have Been Grown and Not Made

> The government works best when it establishes the rules of the road, not to trying to determine the composition of the traffic.
>
> **(Epstein, 1995, p. xiii)**

This paper focuses on the role of property rights in maintaining a "law of liberty," or at least the governance structure most consistent with personal autonomy in a financial order which has been "grown" and not made by any conscious act of a unifying intelligence.

Organizations around the world have spent thousands of hours for becoming Sarbanes-Oxley compliant in order to be able to continue trading with companies in the USA. At the center of Sarbanes-Oxley was its focus on strengthening corporate governance procedures to prevent fraud and mismanagement—but the more recent chaos in the banking sector must raise a question over the success of Sarbanes-Oxley, and more significantly, over the whole idea of corporate governance as presently conceived. Madrick (2010, pp. 37) comments on the most recent financial crisis:

> people on Wall Street and mortgage brokers acted in their self interest without fear of either legal or economic reprisal.

It was the great American Judge Oliver Wendhall Holmes who stated that "the life of law has not been one of logic but of experience" (Holmes, 1963). Following this stand-point, we look at the prevailing financial order as an evolutionary state, as opposed to a purposively constructed mechanism, brought into being by any one actor's agency. In this I follow a thriving theoretical literature advancing biological metaphors to better understand the development and regulation of market processes (Dopfer, 2005).

One way of reconciling the avalanche of regulatory interventions and the escalating chaos we now see around us, comes from the insights of the later work of Friedrich Hayek, the

---

[1] In a phrase attributed to the Founding Father John Adams.

Nobel Prize-winning Economist.[2] I make tentative steps in that direction in this paper. I do so by outlining the concept of the evolution of a "law of liberty" as a way of stabilizing a financial market which is the product of a spontaneous order which has been grown and not made.

Hayek influence was at its greatest when, toward the end of World War 2, he asked in his best seller *The Road to Serfdom* (1944), whether the British were at the start of a path which eventually led to the monster that was Nazi Germany. Since then his work has been frequently invoked by those who fear "the passion for equality [will make] vain the hope for freedom."[3] In an era when free markets and social justice seem to collide (the 1% vs. the 99%) revisiting Hayek's thought seems opportune.

5.3 Common Elements in Recent Crises

The prime responsibility for any business failure must rest with its top management who took the decisions precipitating crisis. While financial crises undoubtedly have many authors, the proximate agents of corporate decline are clearly the senior management team of the failed entity. Therefore, what caused management to get things so wrong? Market pressures were driving Boards of Directors to grow their businesses and hit or exceed profit targets. Rewards for hitting these short-term targets merely reinforced executives' behavior. One clear proximate cause of crisis was the growing power of the trading floor and the inability of general managers to effectively oversee financial products they struggled to even fully understand. One of the Board's roles being to challenge and contribute toward the development of the company's strategy.

At Enron Lou Pai, who headed up Enron Capital and Trade Resources (ECT) and the general culture of the trading floor was seen to have taken over the corporation. This exposed the whole of Enron to the threat of unravelling on the emergence of any aspect of catastrophic risk as one ex-Enron Executive put it "Trading companies fall quickly—like a helicopter running out of fuel." (McLean and Elkind, 2003, p. 80). In the more recent market frenzy the credit giving rise to the alphabet soup of credit instruments, credit default obligations (CDO), CDO^2, MBO, etc).

A trading culture with loose definitions of proprietary rights, their boundaries, and constraints, characterized both the 2002 crisis and the more recent one. Manufacture of tangible goods and delivery of observable, easily valued, services became less important than the trading of complex derivatives with unclear values based upon fragmented, fungible property rights depending on future outcomes of an uncertain nature. Lev and Feng (2016)

---

[2] Although other great Economists of the same era, like Milton Friedman, had doubts about Hayek's credentials as an Economist as opposed to a social commentator or political theorist (see Ebenstein, Chapter 24).

[3] To quote Lord Acton as cited by Hayek at the head of Chapter 8 of the *The Road to Serfdom* (1944).

chronicle the way in which investment in intangible assets has greatly outstripped that in tangibles. Further they make clear the inability of our current financial reporting regime to capture value in such a "concept company" economy. Increasingly corporations both manufacturing and financial have had to be valued upon the basis of contingent cash-flows, when the contingent events were both highly uncertain and likely to be correlated across potential investments. The risks created were likely to be systemic in impact and lead to pervasive losses and resulting calls for State action. A moral hazard problem was clearly brewing. Increasingly systemically important institutions were simply "playing with other people's money" in Roberts, 2010 words.

This growing trading culture within financial institutions occurred at the very point when financial regulators, such as the Basel Committee and the FSA in Britain, were stressing their own role as simply that of overseers of self-managed risk-management protocols and metrics. An emergent "meta-regulation" allowed the State to retreat to a position of encouraging beneficial adaption of risk-management practice, driven by a process of competitive self-regulatory innovation within the banking industry (Gray and Hamilton, 2006). This created the conditions for a natural experiment of the ability of self-stabilizing financial order to grow and sustain itself. Indeed their seemed some hope initially that innovations in risk-management would facilitate such an emergent order. Even a mind as fine as Alan Greenspan's "The Maestro" (Greenspan, 2002) believed this could occur:

> *The development of our paradigms for containing risk has emphasized, and will, of necessity, continue to emphasize dispersion of risk to those willing and presumably able, to bear it. If risk is properly dispersed, shocks to the overall economic system will be better absorbed and less likely to create cascading failures that could threaten financial stability.*

This chapter traces out a few results of that experiment.

In the immediate the wake of the financial crisis an unsurprisingly unhappy electorate, faced with huge tax rises, is pressuring the government to intervene to control financial speculation before even more damage is done. This led President Obama to understandably say "we want our money back, while Senator Bernie Sanders rose on the tide of representing the 99%". The resulting state intervention has not been slow coming and the politics of jealousy has had free-rein in the context of a huge tax-payer bailout of financial institutions. In the United Kingdom, the House of Commons Treasury Committee (HC 416, 2009) and the Walker Report (2009) on the governance of UK banks are central chronicles of this response.

Both of these responses to the crisis seem to assume that since the roots of the crisis were man made, it will also be man-made plans which can deter future crises which lie ahead and depending on the evolution of the Eurozone may already be upon us. This of course echoes the Enron "show trials" where, admittedly greedy and unappealing, high-profile Executives (like Jeff Skilling and Andy Fastow) were held liable for managerial looting. Such demonization of individuals ignores a central part of the trader's function in financial markets which is "to promote an end which is no part of his intentions." (Smith, 1776, p. 421). This form of reasoning reifies an innately social process to become a story of purposive corruption, initiated by a few identifiable primary authors, who are swiftly demonized to assume their guilt. As Robert Skidelsky in his account of what Keynesian thought can add to our understanding of the recent crisis states (Skidelsky, 2009, p. 22):

> our first reaction to crisis is scapegoating; it is only by delving deeper into the sources of the mistakes that the finger can be pointed to the system of ideas which that gave rise to them.

This paper seeks to dig a bit deeper into the regulatory response to financial instability and its ability to both constrain and provoke later waves of financial distress.

5.4 Financial Reform and the Law of Liberty

The difficulty we face in reforming US and UK governance appears to lie then in precisely the fact that so much of what constitutes just law or what Hayek terms "the Law of Liberty" is beyond any one individual's will, or even cognizance, at a conscious rational level. Indeed for this just law of corporate governance to emerge it must be seen as simply stating recognized best practice or decent behavior. There is little doubt that Andrew Fastow became a convenient whipping-boy for those wishing to deny their own culpability in Enron's collapse as John Paulsen at Goldman Sachs later became one. Skilling, for example, claimed in an amazing statement for a CEO "I'm not particularly interested in the balance-sheet. It seemed to be doing well. We always had money." (McLean and Elkind, 2003, p. 164). But it is equally true that Fastow, Enron's CFO, was central to the conceit of Enron's "walk-on-water" survival of the stock market crash of early 2000.

Much good governance simply articulates some general abstract rule which is already expected practice by market participants. An example is the requirement of Sarbox Section 302 that CEO's formally attest to their assent and understanding of their employer's published accounts. The power of this legislation proceeds directly from the incredulity with which the Senate hearings received Ken Lay and Jeff Skilling's evidence that as Chairman and CEO, respectively, it was just too tedious to bother checking Andy Fastows' claims that Enron was profitable.

In approaching the reform of financial markets, it is important to recall that order in financial markets is "grown" and not "made" (Hayek, 1973). Indeed the vast, disparate and contentious information set invoked by any price equilibrium in a financial market implies this must inevitably be so. As Hayek (1973, pp. 38) states:

> Very complex orders, comprising more complex facts that any could ascertain or manipulate, can be brought about only through forces inducing the formation of spontaneous orders.

The rather frustrating thing from the perspective of an elected politician, or an aspiring regulator, is that since order arises in financial markets without the oversight of a single unifying intelligence, its improvement or reform cannot be initiated by State dictate, or centrally administered codes of conduct. In reality such actions are more than likely to induce unintended consequences due to market innovations designed to circumvent the regulatory intent. The growth of credit default swaps (CDSs), or the Eurodollar market in an earlier age, reflects this very process of market adaption to an inhibitive regulatory regime. The substantial relocation of the CDO/CDS trading to London from New York results from a very similar process of global regulatory arbitrage. Martin (2016) in commenting on the starting gun for financial reform in Britain, the "big bang," when trading commissions were deregulated[4] in 1986 quotes a senior minister in the Thatcher Cabinet as saying:

> The truth is that we did not quite know what we were doing. They did not realise what they were unleashing.
>
> **_(Martin, 2016, p. 106)._**

But this inability to effectively provide a set of rules to deter the next bubble/bust cycle should not justify the State adopting a passive, wait and see approach in financial markets. As with other self-sustaining systems, the State can intervene to create the correct conditions for a self-sustaining order to reconstitute itself in order to "fail-safe" in a crisis and to do so without taxpayers' subsidy. This view promotes a structural, framework legislation agenda as opposed to a piecemeal, regulatory authority empowering more sweeping intervention.

One proposal of this type is that for "living wills" to precommit a bank to a liquidation plan which requires no public support. Section 165(d) of the Dodd-Frank Wall Street Reform and Consumer Protection Act requires banks with assets above $50 billion in the United States to periodically submit resolution plans for inspection by the Federal Reserve. This helps keep bank Boards focused on the downside risk, especially when "gambling for resurrection" during a crisis. One essential element of such scene-setting regulatory intervention is the degree to which it devolves regulatory intervention, as opposed to regulatory intent, to individual company boards. This sort of intervention continues much of the practice of the FSA with its encouragement of Codes of Business conduct (to constrain corrosive conflicts of interest) and its comply or explain tradition. While in the wake of the crisis, this sort

---

[4] Following in the path of the NYSE's decision in 1975.

of regulatory intervention may seem tame and weak, given the scale of financial collapse recently observed, it does at least recognize the importance of building norms of good conduct, as opposed to simply proliferating rules that induce further cycles of financial innovation/regulatory arbitrage. Sunder (2005) states the argument for such code of conduct regulation as follows when discussing accounting regulation.

> The power of free and rational argument remains, I am old fashioned enough to believe, the best road to truth in human affairs. I would therefore give companies the maximum freedom to present their accounts in whatever way the thought fit, and require them to explain and justify the course they had taken.
>
> *Sunder (2005, p. 380).*

The emergence of a spontaneous order in financial markets relies of the interplay of a tangled, incoherent web of knowledge all men benefit from but no man-made institution or agency can possess. Recognition of this fact may be hindered by a focus on the computerized trading systems, like the SETS or the NASDAQ. While the settlement of trades may be highly standardized, rules based, and commoditized, the nexus of counterparties that underpins it, is certainly not. It was the unravelling of this more relationship based ecology of counterparties that began so disastrously from late 2007 within the credit default instruments market (Khandini and Lo, 2007). It seems a general maxim that the more extensive the "made" order becomes the greater will be the reliance on a "grown" order of unarticulated shared understandings Hayek states (1973, p. 49–50).

> Organisation encounters here a problem which any attempt to bring order into complex human activity meets: the organiser must wish the individuals who are to co-operate to make use of knowledge that he does not possess. In none but the most simple kind of organisation is it conceivable that all details of all activities are governed by a single mind....The more complex the order aimed at, the greater will be that part of separate actions which will have to be determined by circumstances not known to those who direct the whole, and the more dependent control will be on rules rather than specific commands.

In a similar vein Richard Epstein a Chicago Law Professor, and notable advocate of a classical liberal approach to legal disputes, points out legislative intervention can quickly degenerate into special pleading and rent-seeking by well-placed lobby groups. Epstein (1998, p. 10) states

> ...a sound legal order is one that responds to the fragility of knowledge by giving no one absolute control and power. It seeks the dispersion of power across individuals and social groups.

Recognition of the need for humility in disrupting a market order which contains its own imperfect stabilization mechanisms cautions us against too enthusiastic an advocacy of wide-ranging legislative reform of financial markets even in an age of righteous anger.

5.5 *Regulating a Grown Financial Order*

It is the impossibility of a commanded, or made, financial order which constrains the utility of supervisory regulation. A commanded order, brought into being by a regulatory authority like the FSA or SEC is likely to be inadequate, or more likely dysfunctional, in its effect. This is because for financial decision-making context is all and broad rules, to increase predictability and hence mutual reliance, are the philosopher's stone market-makers in assets seek. What is most needed is a flexible, yet functional, set of trading practices capable of adaption to changing market conditions. As the quotation at the head of the paper suggests the State should devise rules of the road rather than seek to direct the traffic.

A clear danger in the present politically charged environment is the enactment of a dramatic, but ultimately futile, legislative framework designed to appease unsurprising voter anger about the bank bailout packages. This ignores the grown, as opposed to made, nature of the financial order we observe in financial markets. As Hayek (1973, p. 65) observed:

> Law-making is necessarily a continuous process in which every step produces hitherto un-foreseen consequences for what we can or must do next.

Given this fact, it is far more important to focus on getting the regulatory structure right, abolishing or enhancing the role of the FSA rather than sweating over the drafting of any particular regulatory intervention.

Recently the Bank of England has been refining its procedures for resolving bank failure, without provoking an all-out bank run of the sort that greeted the financial distress of Northern Rock (Hall, 2008). Hall (2008) records how the dismay expressed by the House of Common's Treasury Committee at the Bank of England's inability to plan covert intervention to support a major toppling financial institution has led to a hopefully more practical bank failure resolution protocol. This evolutionary, "learning by doing," approach to supervisory legislation seems most in line with maintaining a financial order sustained by an emergent, largely self-sustaining, law of liberty.

5.6 *Fragmentation of Property Rights and Financial Order*

If what we observe before us in Anglo-Saxon financial markets is indeed a grown order, we might ask how has that growth been accomplished and entrenched? Hayek (1973, p. 163) states the central role of a clear definition of, and respect for, property rights as a precondition of the growth and maintenance of a prosperous economic order thus:

> Law, liberty and property are the inseparable trinity. There can be no law in the sense of universal rules of conduct which does not determine boundaries of the domains of freedom by laying down rules that enable each to ascertain where he is free to act.

The great value of established, enforceable property rights in growing a financial order is in reducing uncertainty about how the behavior of others will impact on my plan of action. Thus Hayek (1944, p. 88) states in his Road to Serfdom:

> ...for the Rule of Law to be effective it is more important that there should be a rule applied than what the rule is....The important thing is that the rule enables us to predict other people's behaviour correctly, and this requires that it should apply in all cases – even if in a particular instance we feel it to be unjust.

This very trinity of property, liberty and the rule of law may indeed give us a clue to the origin the parlous state corporate governance is now in. Everywhere we look at governance failures doubts over the ownership structure of shareholder rights abound. This causes us to ask whether the set of reforms currently being proposed best establishes a rule of law capable of restoring a stable financial order.

At Enron, the development of off-balance sheet Special Purpose entities, especially JEDI1 and JEDI2, fragmented and obfuscated true shareholder value. The JEDI's, while in theory entirely separately owned from Enron Corporation and unaccountable to it, were only financially viable because the underpinning bank loans (from Chase Manhattan in particular) were secured on Enron's own stock. The downside risk remained squarely on Enron's balance-sheet whether this was reported or not. This form of transaction was to be echoed and increased in scale by Ernst and Young in its Repo 105 transactions for the now bankrupt Lehman Brothers.

5.7 Illustrations of the Role of Fragmentation of Property Right in Inducing Crises

The "securitize and distribute" model of creating a structured special purpose vehicle and selling on the bundled debt in tranches, AAA, AA, etc., became the "securitize and not distribute" model as investment houses sought yield by buying each other's securitized debt issues. In a downswing, which induced fears of systemic risk, "all the correlations went to one" for defaults supposedly managed by their dispersal throughout the global financial markets. In reality a few key financial institutions, AIG, Lehman Brothers, Citibank, Royal Bank of Scotland, held huge chunks of the total portfolio of residual equity stakes in securitized debt, or simply that debt itself. When financial distress manifested itself, these institutions began to implode. Since many believed they had implicit "too big to fail" guarantees the ultimate loss was always planned to be socialized at the expense of taxpayers. The unseemly squabble over the rights of senior traders at RBS to million pounds plus bonuses is illustrative of the moral hazards created. It has truly become "heads I win, tails the taxpayer loses."

Once again the ownership rights and corresponding responsibilities of shareholders and taxpayers were confused and fungible, in this case in favor of the banks or at least their senior managers. But even before this tragicomic finale, the economic borders of the modern corporation were already been contested, transformed, and redefined.

Since at least the emergence of the junk-bond fueled leveraged buy-out of the 1980 (Bruck, 1989), US major corporations have been ripe for destabilization of their shareholder base, dissolution and subsequent reconfiguration as a new entity which may bear little resemblance its original state. The history of the United Kingdom's now romanticized retailer Woolworth's gives some idea of the rough-ride corporations "in play" can expect. The emergence of a "strong manager, weak owner" (Roe, 1994) culture, with investors' exit being the almost sole solution to poor management, contains within it a tendency for failing senior managers themselves to feel a loss of control to impersonal market forces. Ultimately control rights in the corporation are constantly contested, arbitraged and reconstituted in a financial market in which sentiment plays a significant part. This induces a fragmentation and partial dissolution of property rights that we focus upon in the latter part of this paper as a source of repeated financial crises.

5.7.1 Market Order as a Public Good

The classical liberal response to the crisis put much weight on the evolution of new rules for maintaining financial order short of coercive State intervention to impose a revised order presumably reflecting some distributional goal of penalizing "greedy bankers," etc. It certainly makes sense for banking professionals to undertake systematic reform of self-regulation given the gun now held to their head by an angry electorate who are paying for the bailout, via large tax hikes and reductions in public services. Not unreasonably the ruling political elite "want our [taxpayers'] money back." But organizing the collective action necessary to restore confidence in financial markets is by no means easy given the difficulty of excluding free-riders from the benefits of financial stability.

In judging the likelihood of success of a self-regulatory response to the crisis, it may be worth recalling an important distinction raised by Mancur Olson between inclusive and exclusive groups organized to provide a public good (in this case financial stability). In an exclusive group, a defecting member may take off a large proportion of the gains to group membership. An example here might be a rogue member of OPEC, which can just turn on the taps and sell cheap oil at below the cartel price, effectively destroying OPEC's grip on the oil market (as Russia and Nigeria have done). Such an exclusive group tends to highly participatory, but unstable. In an inclusive group, the reverse is true, no one member can substantially appropriate the public good to himself. An example here might be a bible-study or local theatre group. A member who leaves simply ceases to enjoy the public good as well as having to share in the cost of its provision.

An examples of relevance to the current discussion might be an organized market like the gilts market (a clearly exclusive group), where a few well known repeat players dominate the market and by contrast the more diffuse, ad hoc/one off deals, which characterize the over-the-counter market in unquoted stocks, or foreign-forward currency contract, markets which are characterized by less standardized contracts and hence an inclusive grouping of rapidly turned over bilateral partnerships dominates the market. Lewis (2010, pp. 124) describes how contrarian arbitrageurs with very little capital were able to get an ISDA license and start trading CDOs on the basis of a personal recommendation from contacts within Deutsche Bank.

The CDS/CDO markets were certainly far closer to this second inclusive group arrangement with calamitous effects for the provision of market integrity and liquidity provision as a public good. Beyond the confines of the over-the-counter market in which securitised debt was traded lay many pensioners and mortgage holder who relied upon the integrity of that market. For this broader social polity provision of the public good of market integrity was almost impossible without some state coercion or subsidy. Yet there was no incentive compatible mechanism to ensure its provision. The unravelling of the coalition of credit instrument traders, organized as an inclusive group, was the displaced thread that soon set financial markets into a complete unravelling.

5.8 Regulation as an Imperfect Substitute for Social Norms of Good Behavior

Few but the most zealous right-wing ideologues could believe that the State should never legislate whatever the degree of open market abuse. Even some traditionally right of center commentators have been shocked into revising their views by the sheer scale of the most recent financial crisis. So Richard Posner, a prominent figure in the Chicago Law and Economics School prefaces his book on the Crisis by stating (Posner, 2009, p. 12):

> The government's myopia passivity and blunders played a critical role in allowing the recession to balloon into a depression...But without any government regulation of the financial industry, the economy would still, in all likelihood, be in a depression.

If some market regulation is desirable, the question then arises how much? In deciding this it is easy to believe that social norms and regulation act as complements. I have never murdered anyone, this is not mainly because to do so is clearly illegal. But the fact it is illegal is most probably still a good thing.

Epstein (1998, p. 58–63) has pointed out that legal intervention can in many legal areas compromise an evolved preexisting social norm. Take the example of the terms of a Staff handbook, which many academics will know. Such a book will tell me how my rights to promotion, sickness pay, and grievance procedures can be expected to be treated by my line manager. A breach of the rule-book constitutes a disciplinary offense that I can raise with my manager's manager. Such a Staff handbook may offer superior rights to those in the general law in order to encourage internal resolution of employment disputes. Further encroachment by legislation on rights guaranteed by the Staff Handbook undermines this incentive to internal resolution of disputes. In such contexts, which really characterize any relationship based contract, like marriage, it may be better to keep laws and social norms far apart rather than to seek some reinforcement mechanism between them.

So regulation and sanctions for violation of accepted social norms, unreasonable treatment of employees, etc., must often work as substitutes not complements, then should we choose one and not the other. The most obvious solution is to regulate those abuses that carry the greatest potential for major social costs. If my employer's treatment toward me is unjustified in my eyes then the easiest and most cost effective solution is often just to find another job. But suppose my employer treats all nonwhite, or all female employees, poorly. Such widespread damage makes the case for legal intervention seem more creditable, although some like Gary Becker, make argue even discrimination by unchangeable index characteristics is self-defeating in an efficient market. Nevertheless the case of widespread systemic threats to the well-being of a defined group is a social threat which may be seen to justify a legislative intervention. In the same way, a presumption of justification for regulatory intervention can only find a sound basis if a threat of increased systemic risk is present.

5.9 Liberal Justification of Financial Regulation

The "blowing up" of an individual trader or bank is just part of the creative destruction of a competitive process. To impede such losses is to undermine the pressure for productive innovation. But once national life is threatened by a financial crisis, as it clearly now is in the PIIGS (Portugal, Italy, Ireland, Greece, and Spain), it is far more difficult to justify letting the "market work its magic."

In what follows later I seek to argue two seemingly contradictory things an understanding of which goes some way to help us grasp the whipsaw effect that generated the crisis of 2002 (WorldCom, Enron, Tyco International, and the legislative response in Sarbox) and the later financial crisis of 2008 from which we appear now to be stutteringly emerging.

- The first of these is how a fragmentation of property rights occurred, via the disintermediation of the corporation, as the "hollow"/asset lite corporation evolved and destabilized an established financial and productive order of major economies, especially the United States and United Kingdom.
- Second, the supplanting of a "grown" social order within financial markets, with their sanctions and supportive ecology by intrusive regulatory regimes has often exacerbated, not ameliorated, the underlying dissolution of clearly defined property rights. It has done so by undermining the preexisting "grown" financial order and triggering financial

innovation to avoid the desired regulatory intention without retaining the imperfect imbalance of the prior grown order. An imperfect grown order is often supplanted by a botched, dysfunctional attempt to make the prior grown financial order complete.

In commenting on a common law requirement made of US Mine Owner's to make good housing damage caused by subsidence Epstein (1998, p. 64) comments:

> The constant pressure to convert a social norm into a legal norm does not have to rectify some imperfection: rather, it gets rid of a small imperfection and replaces it with a larger one.

In what remains, we apply a similar mode of reasoning to the regulatory response to the diffusion of corporate property rights and the evolution of succeeding financial crises in the United States and United Kingdom. While legal reform was initially triggered by the dissolution of clearly defined set of property rights, the resulting legislative "cure" may indeed be worse than the illness it sought to treat. New cures need to recognize the need to choose between a grown and made financial order, rather than simply assuming regulatory interventions occur in an unchanging order still largely dominated by preexisting social norms. Such intervention is rendered particularly hazardous when the underlying definitions of property rights in traded assets are themselves in the process of contention and reconstruction.

5.10 Tragedies of the Commons, Anticommons, and Gridlock

For Hayek the great benefit of conferring ownership rights is in limiting access of others, encouraging investment and hence overall social well-being. So the challenge to those committed for maintaining a law of liberty is to establish and enforce ownership via property rights. The Tragedy of the Commons (Hardin, 1962) is that of overuse of a shared resource nobody feels belongs to them.

More recently Michael Heller has pointed out a corresponding Tragedy of the Anticommons or Gridlock economy. If the key characteristic of the Tragedy of the Commons is overuse and hence wasteful depletion then the hallmark of the Tragedy of the Anticommons is underuse or an absence of provision. Buchanan and Yoon (2000) stress the symmetrical nature of these tragedies in formal terms, the tragedy of the commons deriving from an excess of usage, the tragedy of the anticommons arising from its mirror image of an excess of exclusion rights. So if an absence of property rights induces one tragic outcome it may be an overzealous, or internally contradictory, allocation of competing property rights produces quite another. Like Goldilocks, a well-functioning financial market requires neither too few allocations of ownership rights, nor too many. The allocation of ownership rights must be balanced to be just right to facilitate an efficient financial market. The consequence of willful overuse of the Tragedy of the Commons is clear for all to see.

But the consequences of Gridlock are often some new products *not* being sold, or *not* being made available in certain markets. Heller (2008) gives an example of how the Wright Brothers struggled to commercialize their 1906 patent on an airplane. As they struggled to sell their design, other engineers claimed property rights in their product which used a myriad of complimentary or near substitute products. The Wright Brothers were caught in what an economist Carl Shapiro has called a "patent thicket" of competing and possibly contradictory claims to intellectual property rights (Shapiro, 2001).

Certainly the continual slicing, dicing, and reselling of subprime debts clouded both the responsibility for monitoring the lender's ability to repay and borrower's ability to enforce foreclosure if they failed to do so. These difficulties reflected more the gridlock induced by an excess of overlapping property rights, which were held in tension, rather than a failure of property rights to be allocated at all. So the property right challenges we now face in financial markets may not be those, Hayek originally envisaged when his call for the establishment of a law of liberty was first made.

5.11 Fragmentation of Property Rights as a Trigger for Financial Crisis and Reform

In the Hayekian vision of a grown financial order, the maintenance of properly defined property rights and the enforcement thereof takes pride of place. Certainly diffusion of property rights can be seen as central to the evolution of the two most recent financial crises. We now provide four illustrations of how a dissemblance of previously well-defined property rights induced recent financial crises, which motivated Sarbox in the United States and more recently the Turner Report in the United Kingdom. Sarbox sets the backdrop of the 2008 financial crisis, but in many ways we believe both the Enron/WorldCom crisis of 2002 and the more recent one have common origins in the fragmentation of clearly delineated property rights that underpin a spontaneously grown financial order. So breakdown of an underlying "law of liberty" within observed financial markets can be seen as an essential ingredient in the cocktail of causes of recent financial crises.

Example 1: Property rights in the housing market.

One very clear illustration of the potential of financial distress to disrupt property rights comes from considering a mortgaged homeowner. Typically like his peers without a mortgage the mortgaged homeowner has every incentive to take care of his property, which he soon hopes to own, be a good neighbor and encourage others to be the same. Now suppose a mortgaged homeowner sees default as a genuine possibility, or even probability. In this event the dampness in the bathroom is no longer a problem for the mortgagee but for the mortgage company, noisy neighbors are not worth confronting given the mortgagee may not be living here very long. A moral hazard becomes established in the mortgaged housing market. Many investments of both private and communal benefit are undermined once property rights are unclear or likely to be overthrown in the near future. Epstein (1997, p. 24) in his Ronald Coase lecture states, the dissimulation of property rights for financially distressed tenants as follows:

> Head I win, tails you lose becomes a possibility that the borrower would never own up to at the outset of the relationship, but which could become his sole possibility of salvation at the end of the day.

So financial distress can induce social breakdown of clearly defined property rights. The consequent failure of the free market system creates a presumptive case for State intervention to protect society, by making sure distressed homeowners can still refinance their debts.

An illustration of State intervention to guard against financial distress is the US Financial Institutions Reform Recovery and Enforcement Act of 1989 (FIRREA) (Epstein, 1997, p. 25).

In an attempt to curb speculative investments of the Savings and Loan Associations (S & Ls), who had recently got burned by overinvesting in "junk bonds," these institutions were required by FIRREA to mark to market the assets on their balance sheet. The idea behind this was that any increase in interest rates, an implicit warning by the Federal Reserve about an emergent housing bubble, would cause the value of the loan portfolio to decline, forcing the S&Ls to realize a loss. The problem was of course any increase in interest rates also reduced the value of liabilities, composed of outstanding borrowings, on the other side of the balance sheet. The effect of this regulatory intervention was that as interests rose in the early 1990s S&L asset's shriveled on corporate balance sheets. But since liabilities had also fallen in value S&L's had little reason to reign in their lending behavior, especially during a recession when their members needed cash. Nevertheless, many S&Ls whose published accounts showed falling assets when recorded at market values, with no offsetting reduction in liabilities calculated at historic cost, began to rack up large reductions in shareholder's equity. Liquidation and industry-wide consolidation occurred without any widespread underlying cash-flow problems being present in the S&L industry of that era.

An initial distortion in property rights allocations had induced some social costs. But the impact of a regulatory intervention was to exacerbate, rather than ameliorate, the initially perverse behavior. All the regulatory intervention did was to safeguard investors in booms, when they are fairly flush anyway, at the cost of impoverishing them in the downturn when they really needed financial help.

In what follows we point to the importance of the distortion of clearly defined property rights as causative of regulatory intervention and then trace that very same regulatory intervention's perverse impact. As such we see clearly defined and allocated property rights as a precondition of a well-functioning "grown" financial order and attempts by the State to "make things better" by regulatory interventions as ultimately making matters worse.

Establishing this proposition matters because it is above all property rights that are the hallmark of the "law of liberty" of a self-sustaining grown financial market order. In this concluding section, we show how the fragmentation of property rights and the consequent disruption of an already evolved self-sustaining "law of liberty," which had largely historically maintained order in financial markets, now served to induce systemic crisis. Challenges to some prior delineation of property rights both motivated the Sarbox reform and explain that reform's failure to offer any protection against the further spasms of 2008.

In the 2002 crisis, this unravelling of the provision of the public good of market order was played out in the equity market, while later 2007/08 it was played out in the market for securitized debt instruments. Both the 2002 and 2008 crises were united by a marked fragmentation and partial dissolution of property rights as we now proceed to try to show.

Example 2: Enron and the emergence of special purpose entities.

Andrew Fastow arrived at Enron in 1990 having built expertise in securitization of debt, and especially clever financial structures to house them at Continental Bank. When Fastow became CFO of Enron in 1998, he was determined to reap his true worth as he saw it. Fastow established the Global Finance group whose special mission was largely the creation of off-balance sheet investment vehicles capable of bridging the funding gap in Enron's operations. By the millennium, Global Finance was providing $20 billion a year in working capital to fund Enron's faltering operations. Indeed Fastow himself often described his role within Enron as to "feed the best" (McLean and Elkind, 2003, p 151).

Far from being clandestine about his basic strategy, Fastow both publicly boasted about it and was rewarded for doing so. On winning the 1999 CFO of the year award from *CFO Magazine*, he was lauded in media coverage for "thinking outside the box" and "inventing a new ground-breaking strategy" for treasury management. Skilling commented (in slight tension with his view at the Senate Investigation), "We needed someone to rethink the entire financial structure …. [Fastow] deserves every accolade tossed his way."

The "asset lite" corporation was hailed as a revolutionary new corporate strategy. The "hollowness" of a corporation and its dissimulation, to leave almost only the organizing hub for a myriad of-balance-sheet assets and partially owned joint ventures, was hailed as masterstroke of business acumen in Harvard Business School case-studies and the consulting circuit. But this withering away of clear ownership rights and reciprocal rights and duties slowly undermined traditional duties of care between the managers of corporate assets and their owners. Here the erosion and eventual dissimulation of reciprocal trust between SPE's controllers and those that funded their existence brought the massive weight of Enron's swelling Diaspora of SPEs crashing back onto Enron's balance sheet when distress hit in 2001. Since the loans provided by Fastow's favored banks were secured on Enron's stock they had never truly been separated off from Enron anyway of course.

The highly lucrative nature of investment banking services to Enron meant few financial institutions wished to rock the boat. Fastow understood this well and always played off financial institutions against each other for Enron and his own well-being. While investment banking and investment research are in theory separated by "Chinese Walls" in reality these walls can be pretty thin.

Since Enron underwrote investments made in the "independent" SPEs, this was a no downside to this investment opportunity (until the game was up and Enron folded). The fragmentation and deliberate misrepresentation of the dilution of property rights, and specifically ultimate rights of ownership and control, seem central to the genesis of both the 2002 crisis of shareholder value and our current crisis deriving from the unravelling of credit default instruments an issue we discuss next.

The ultimate impact of all of this on Enron's viability as a going concern was well understood, at least by Fastow himself. On being quizzed by a colleague what would happen to his escalating pyramid of SPE's if Enron ceased to grow and could no longer settle past prepayment bills as they matured by issuing new prepayment contracts. Fastow answered "It implodes" (McLean and Elkind, 2003, p. 151) and this it duly did in 2001. Along with it went the trust and reliance placed by many shareholders in the honoring of management's duty of care to the ultimate owners of equity stakes.

The power of Enron to trigger a widespread financial crisis was borne not out of the unique greed of the defendants but by the ubiquity of the central issue of a fragmentation and diffusion of property rights by means of financial innovation. As we shall see this fragmentation was to be mirrored, but on an amplified scale, in the later crisis of 2007/08 from which we are now slowly emerging.

Example 3: Credit default swaps as archetypes of the degeneration of ownership rights.

One way to see the emergence of the CDS market is as a sort of terminal point in the progressive dissimulation of property rights that characterized the evolution of financial markets during this century. CDS instruments were conceived of a way to "securitize and distribute" the potential losses arising on corporate bonds in the event of liquidation. This sort of instrument had a reasonably long history, which was subjected to the usual actuarial calculation of the probability of default. The extension of this sort of derivative instrument to cover potential losses on mortgage-backed securities, where only data on a very short bull market period of trading life existed, greatly amplified the risk of this derivative product.

If purchase of CDS instruments, written upon securitized, mortgage portfolios, was risky it also entrenched conflicts between potential claimants on the defaulting financial institutions assets, which were to greatly intensify the dynamics of financial collapse. This was because of the "sequentialized" nature of the sale of these instruments. CDS instruments were divided into strips, or "tranches," in the jargon, with successive levels of exposure. These were as follows:

- *Senior debt* was the least risky, many AAA rated, debt which offered the least prospect of default and hence loss,
- *Mezzanine debt* that was a bit more risky carrying a higher risk of default, but a compensating higher rate of return,
- *Junior debt,* which offered a high return but was something like "junk" with correspondingly high default rates and so losses.

Even with perfect information available to all parties, fragmented ownership induced divided loyalties among mortgage brokers trying to service the loans of distressed subprime mortgagees. A senior debt/AAA bond holder might be happy to renegotiate the mortgage to avoid a default; this suggested a patient approach to the lender's inability to pay up. Such senior debt holders realized their investment capital was only threatened by total collapse of the subprime mortgage market. But owners of subordinated junior debt might prefer to grab the home from the lender at the first sign of trouble in the hope of at least rescuing something from the mess. Hence while asymmetric information certainly intensified conflicts between CDS instrument holders, the basic structure of the instruments sale insured a tense relationship between coowners anyway. The lack of clarity in property rights initiated a gridlock in competing, and often conflicting, property rights which led ultimately to contracts being dishonoured.

To fix ideas, I discuss one illustrative deal in an Appendix to this paper. These various tranches established fertile ground for a gridlock of conflicting property rights that created a tragedy of the anticommons when it came to the provision of market liquidity. The problem was not an absence of enforceable property rights in securitized debt instruments but the proliferation of overlapping, and often conflicting, rights.

Example 4: Lehman's Repo 105 transactions.

Lehman Brothers bankruptcy as "a colossal failure of common sense" (McDonald, 2009) has now become iconic illustration of the greed and deceit that produced the most recent financial crisis. Part of that deceit it now transpires was facilitated by Ernst and Young by means of what were termed Repo 105 transactions that magically placed $50 billion of its debt off its quarterly balance sheet in a neat variation of the well-known "bed and breakfast" creative accounting tactic. We know a lot about this particular arrangement because it forms volume three of a nine volume report on Lehman's collapse by the Southern District of New York's Bankruptcy Court (Valukas, 2010), although few can doubt this was not the only plan with such a debt concealing motivation.

Sales and repurchases of assets in which Lehman raised quick cash, on the basis of collateral to be redeemed in the (typically very near) future, were a normal and very substantial part of

Lehman's business model. Usually the cash raised was recognized as an asset on the balance sheet alongside a matching liability to repay the cash in the future to restore the pawned asset. But from 2001 onward on the basis of an opinion letter issued by Lehman's London lawyers Linklaters, Lehman initiated *Repo 105 transactions which treated the temporary pawning of the asset as a sale vitiating the need to recognize the liability of cash held to redeem the asset pawned to match the quick cash raised by a standard repo transaction.* From early 2007 when Lehman, along with other investment banks, faced pressure to reduce gearing Repo 105's were catnip. Soon billions of dollars of Repo 105 transactions were set up to reduce reported net leverage by repoing assets just before the quarter's close and redeeming those assets days later.

Anton Valukas's report quotes an email from Bart McDade, then Head of Equities at Lehman, as assuring a concerned colleague to say "I am very aware it is another drug we're on" (Valukas, 2010, p. 742). While we omit here the accounting technicalities of the transaction it suffices to say Valukas's report concludes "Lehman's description of its net leverage was misleading because it omitted disclosing that the ratio was reduced by means of temporary accounting motivated transactions" (Valukas, 2010, p. 750). These words have not gone unnoticed and by mid-June of 2010, the Accounting and Auditing Disciplinary Board in the United Kingdom announced it was investigating Ernst and Young's role in instigating the Repo 105 deception.

Such off-balance sheet transactions shows how the mass-customized of practices begun within Enron proceeded in the ensuing years. Increasingly such arrangements were made available to favored clients by both law and accounting firms.

5.12 Conclusions

This article revisits the recent financial turmoil from the viewpoint of classical liberal writers, especially Friedrich Hayek. Hayek's writings were inspirational; with those attempting to create some form of self-regulation of the credit default swap markets (ISDA) and Alan Greenspan at the US Federal Reserve. But in advocating a laissez-faire line, it is now possible to see the degree to which the writings of Friedrich Hayek were distorted, or selectively sampled, as opposed to authoritatively invoked. Furthermore the danger of the violation of uniquely held property rights was not the primary trigger for the crisis. Rather the anticommons gridlock induced a thicket of overlapping and often conflicting property rights which created tensions that lead to a lack of credit monitoring and preemptive seizure of assets.

The law of liberty requires that great liberty is balanced by great responsibility. Nowhere is this requirement more pressing than in the preservation, upholding and resolution of property rights. Yet an intrinsic part of both the 2002 and 2008 crises was the fragmentation, corruption and often strategic misrepresentation of property rights. The 2002 crisis Enron shows how off-balance-sheet finance and the growth of SPE's, fueled by leverage, largely precipitated the crisis of 2002 and 2007/08. In the early noughties, financial innovation allowed property rights in securities debt to be sliced, diced, and remolded in a way that made individual bank's risk-exposure very opaque. This fragmentation and subsequent poor definition of property rights characterized both the 2002 and 2007/08 crisis.

If a Hayekian perspective helps us understand the common roots of recent crises, can a Hayekian perspective help us avoid repeating that sad history once more? This seems less likely given the prominence of classical liberals, libertarians, and Hayekians in positions of great power during the most recent crisis. All this study can do perhaps is point ahead to a more balanced and hence more credible, contribution classical liberals can make to financial market reform. Specifically regulators should not see themselves as simply providing much needed order for currently chaotic, if not completely dissolved, markets. A regulator's true role is to guide an evolved spontaneous order toward its own self-sustenance. A primary objective for doing so is ensuring the clarification, recognition, and enforcement of often overlapping and conflicted property rights.

Appendix: Ownership Fragmentation and Conflicts in the CDO/CDS Market

Ishikawa (2009, p. 68) gives an example of a CDO deal. The CDO he describes was for €3 billion and contained 300 separate loans varying in size from €10 million to €300 million in size. While on average the bonds contained in the securitization were of only AA quality, the beauty of the deal was that it allowed € 2.6 million AAA bonds to be sold to finance the deal. The rest cascading down successively into AA, A, and BBB tranches, with only a small sliver of equity being retained. Any queries about deal quality that were raised, and not many were raised, were soon quelled by the assurance that "scenario" analysis suggested that the likelihood of losses, even on BBB bonds, were very small. Of course the computer simulation underpinning this scenario analysis made projections looking forward from a period of initial creation of the CDS market, when the market was expanding and a fiscal policy that was incredibly lax by historic standards. The models worked if the future was a direct extrapolation of the past. But as we now know this was not to be.

The securitized form of these obligations meant they could now be, and largely became, traded for purely speculative purposes. Hence the "real" demand for coverage against default on a physical asset (e.g., the home of a subprime mortgagee) became hostage to a purely financial speculative trade in CDS instruments. A CDS is the separately traded insurance product purchased to cover losses on a CDO deal of the type described earlier. This division between ultimate responsibility to make good on defaulted assets and the ownership of the resulting insurance instruments, carrying with them responsibility to do so, made the likelihood of a panic response to a market downturn far greater than if ownership and financial responsibility were fused. CDS holders at the cusp of the oncoming crisis had no data to infer likely future default rates and since they were executing a highly leveraged trading strategy every incentive to assume the worst. The problem was now the gridlock of intertwined property rights chaffing against one another rather than simply the presence of clear property rights as such.

As well as a separation of loan originators and CDS holders, divisions between the interests of holders themselves now began to emerge as default rates surged. Posner (2009, pp. 61) gives the example of two counterparties involved in the liquidation of Lehman Brothers in September 2008. Suppose counterparty A had insured Lehman against as loss on its loan portfolio of $X, while another counterparty B was itself insured by Lehman against it losing $X. Logic and equity suggested when Lehman folded A would pay B $X and both would pass on their way rejoicing at a near miss. But the diffuse ownership, lack of any centralized trading platform and sudden unravelling of Lehman meant this "netting off" of financial distress could not occur. Rather both A and B had capital tied up in the Lehman melt down for months to come. This added to the financial costs of a crises deriving solely from a confusion over property rights and the ability to exercise them.

References

Bruck, C., 1989. The Predator's Ball: The Inside Story of Drexel Burham. Penguin, London.

Buchanan, J., Yoon, Y., 2000. Symmetric tragedies: commons and anticommons. J. Law Econ. 63, 1–13.

Dopfer, K., 2005. The Evolutionary Foundations of Economics. Cambridge University Press, Cambridge, England.

Epstein, R., 1995. Simple Rules for a complex World. University of Chicago Press, Chicago, Illinois, USA.

Epstein, R., 1997. Simple Rules for a Complex World. Harvard University Press, Cambridge, Massachusetts, USA.

Epstein, R., 1998. Principles of a Free Society: Reconciling Individual Liberty and the Common Good. Perseus Books, Reading, Massachusetts, USA.

Gray, J., Hamilton, J., 2006. Implementing Financial Regulation: Theory and Practice. John Wiley, Chichester, 2006.

Greenspan, A., 2002. World Finance and Risk Management [Online]. Remarks at Lancaster House on 25th of September: Federal Reserve of New York. Available from: http://www.federalreserve.gov/BoardDocs/Speeches/2002/200209253/default.htm

Hall, M., 2008. The sub-prime crisis, the credit crunch and bank "failure": an assessment of the UK authorities response. J. Financ. Regul. Compl. 16, 427–452.

Hardin, G., 1962. The tragedy of the commons. Science 162, 1243–1248.

Holmes, O.W., 1963. The Common Law, New York.

Hayek, F., 1944. The Road to Serfdom. University of Chicago Press, Chicago, USA.

Hayek, F., 1973. Law, Legislation and Liberty: Volume 1: Rules and Order. University of Chicago Press, Chicago, USA.

Heller, M., 2008. The Gridlock Economy: How Too Much Ownership Wrecks Markets, Stops Innovation and Costs Lives. Basic Books, New York.

House of Commons Treasury Committee, 2009. Banking Crisis: dealing with the failure of the UK banks, HC416.

Ishikawa, T., 2009. How I Caused the Credit Crunch: An Insiders' Story of Financial Meltdown. Icon Books, London, England.

Khandini, A., Lo, A., 2007. What happened to the Quants in August 2007? J. Invest. Manage. 5, 5–54.

Lev, B., Feng, G., 2016. The End of Accounting and The Path Forward for Investors and Managers. John Wiley & Son, Hoboken, New Jersey, USA.

Lewis, L., 2010. The Big Short. W.W. Norton & Company, New York, USA.

Martin, I., 2016. Crash Bang Wallop: The Inside Story of London's Bing Bang and a Financial Revolution that Changed the World. Sceptre, London, England.

McDonald, L., 2009. A Colossal Failure of Common Sense: The Incredible Inside Story of the Collapse of Lehman Brothers. Ebury Press, Random House, Reading, UK.

Madrick, J., 2010. At the Heart of the Crash. New York Review of Books, Vol 57, Number 10, New York, pp. 37–39.

McLean, B., Elkind, P., 2003. The Smartest Guys in the Room: The Amazing Rise and Scandalous Fall of Enron. Portfolio/Penguin Group, New York.

Posner, R., 2009. A Failure of Capitalism: The Crisis of 08 and the Descent into Depression. Harvard University Press, Cambridge, Harvard, Massachusetts, London, England.

Roberts, R., 2010. Gambling with Other People's Money: How Perverted Incentives Caused the Financial Crisis. In: Center, M., (Ed.). Mercatus Center-George Mason. Arlington, Virginia.

Roe, M., 1994. Strong Managers, Weak Owners: The Political Roots of American Corporate Governance. Princeton University Press, Princeton, NJ, USA.

Shapiro, C., 2001. Navigating the Patent Thicket: Cross-licenses, patent pools and standard setting. In: Jaffe, A. (Ed.), Innovation Policy and the Economy, MIT Press, Cambridge, Massachusetts.

Skidelsky, R., 2009. Keynes: The Return of the Master. Allen Lane, London England.

Sunder, S., 2005. Minding our manners: accounting as social norms. Br. Account. Rev. 37, 367–387.

Valukas, A., 2010. United States Bankruptcy Court Southern District of New York Report on Lehman Brothers.

Available from: http://lehmanreport.jenner.com/

Further Reading

Akerlof, G., Shiller, R., 2009. Animal Spirits: How Human Psychology Drives the Economy, and Why It Matters for Global Capitalism. Princeton University Press, Princeton.

Epstein, R., 1996. Transaction costs and property rights: Or do good fences make good neighbours, SSRN Working Paper. Available from: http://papers.ssrn.com/sol3/papers.cfm?abstract_id=36840

Evensky, J., 2005. Adam Smith's theory of moral sentiments: on morals and why they matter for a liberal society of free people and free-markets. J. Econ. Perspect. 19 (3), 109–130.

Heller, A., 2009. Ayn Rand and the World She Made. Nan A Talese/Doubleday, New York.

Hayek, F., 1960. The Constitution of Liberty. Chicago, USA.

Hayek, F, 1976. Law, Legislation and Liberty: Volume 2: The Mirage of Social Justice. University of Chicago Press, Chicago, USA.

Kuran, T., 1997. Private Truths and Public Lies: The Social Consequences of Preference Falsification. Harvard University Press, USA.

Olson, M., 1965. The Logic of Collective Action: Public Goods and the Theory of Groups. Harvard University Press, Cambridge, Massachusetts.

Tett, G., 2009. Fool's Gold: How Unrestrained Greed Corrupted a Dream, Shattered Global Markets. Little Brown, London, England.

Tulloch, G., Seldon, A., Brady, G., 2002. Government Failure: A Primer on Public Choice. Cato Institute, Washington DC.

CHAPTER 6

Overconfidence in Finance: Overview and Trends

Mário Pedro Ferreira

Portuguese Catholic University, Porto, Portugal

Chapter Outline

6.1 Market Efficiency and Investor Rationality

Investor rationality is considered as one of the basic pillars supporting mainstream neoclassical finance theories that postulate market efficiency. Among these, we can find the efficient market hypothesis (EMH) that was first presented in the seminal paper by Fama (1965). Starting from the simple finding that stock prices in the Dow Jones Industrial Average tend to follow random walks (Fama, 1965), the EMH has, since then, evolved and yielded a very substantial level of empirical research in the area of finance. Over the years, the EMH has been one of the most, if not the most discussed theory in the area of finance, with several authors either trying to confirm its validity (mostly in the 1960s and 1970s) or attempting to dispute its practical relevance (mostly after 1980s). It is a market approach that relies on solid theoretical assumptions coming from the Economics field, such as perfect markets and rational investors, the latter being defined as subjects that always take decisions based on a utility maximizing mindset. In a context of perfect symmetric information and rational investors, markets should perform flawlessly, leading to equilibrium "fair" prices (Fama, 1970) that are based on fundamentals and incorporate all available information almost instantaneously. With this level of efficiency, it is impossible to consistently "beat" the market using special portfolio diversification or timing strategies. Any attempt to obtain above-average returns can only occur if investors are willing to take above-average risks, discarding any possibility of market failures or anomalies that can be exacerbated and exploited.

The assumption of investor rationality is one of the most debated issues when it comes to supporting EMH. As expected, it is very difficult to value securities rationally consistently in the medium to long-run and overtime EMH supporters were somewhat forced to acknowledge the presence of irrationality in the mindset of investors. However, they did not take it into consideration as a fundamental market mechanism leading to long-run or structural mispricing. Instead, they saw it as a temporary source of mispricing that is rapidly corrected in order to ensure that market efficiency holds. Therefore, the presence of irrational traders is considered to be irrelevant toward final price formation, as their trades are random, uncorrelated, and tend to cancel each other out. Furthermore, if irrational traders tend to correlate their trades, leading to mispricing, they are faced with the presence of rational arbitrageurs in the market who are going to explore prices differences, via hedging against close substitutes, restoring the "fair" values. Overall, market efficiency should hold even in the presence of irrationality. This conclusion is later confirmed by Fama (1998), when he admits that market anomalies can exist, due, not to investor irrationality, but rather to chance, namely technical issues. These anomalies are essentially short-term phenomena leading to market under and overreaction, however in the long-run they level each other out and market efficiency holds.

6.2 Overconfidence

Despite the persuasive arguments of the EMH supporters, the simple fact is that market reality in the 1980s moved away from efficiency in a consistent way, opening avenues for additional explanations that needed to go beyond investor rationality. This created an opportunity for a leap forward in literature, as authors started looking into alternative explanations for the "so-called" anomalies, especially when they showed remarkable resilience. This meant the advent of the behavioral finance field with possible reasons for specific trading patterns being attributed to psychological features, leading to a sudden interest in psychology literature, namely the seminal works of Kahneman and Tversky (1972, 1973, 1979). In this new field, investors were no longer regarded as basic rational decision-makers, but they were rather seen as complex subjects responding, not only to rationality, but also to other factors, such as psychological biases and limitations in information processing.

One of the critical events marking the need for a new set of explanations more oriented toward psychological biases, namely sentiment, was the Black Monday crash that took place in October 19, 1987. An average drop in stock prices of 22.6%, a fall much larger than expected when looking at the economic context, raised questions about the possibility of investors being influenced by more than just rationality, leading to the need to search for additional explanations (Shiller, 1987; Siegel, 1992). Shiller (1987) conducted a survey about the behavior of individual and institutional investors during the Black Monday crash and found that the majority interpreted the stock price collapse as the result of other investors' psychology rather than fundamentals. Siegel (1992) could not explain the 1987 stock price crash with changes in profits and interest rates, and pointed at investor sentiment as a probable cause for this market anomaly. As expected, in this context, the concept of investor sentiment, considered as a collection of systematic biases in beliefs leading to trade based on nonfundamentals, emerged as a relevant issue to explain markets anomalies. This opened the path for a sequence of research developments that attempted to provide a more thorough view of the relationship between sentiment and asset prices (Barberis et al., 1998; Black, 1986; Daniel et al., 2001; DeLong et al., 1990).

Overtime, one of the factors behind sentiment clearly emerged as a relevant and controversial issue toward understanding investor behavior and market anomalies; overconfidence. Overconfidence is an important attribute of investors behavior leading to momentum anomalies. This idea is confirmed by the work of Daniel et al. (1998) when they consider that overconfidence and self-attribution working together can be behind overreaction and underreaction due to excessive reliance on private information. When new public information is released into the market and learning ensues, prices revert back to fundamentals. As expected, sequences of overreactions and underreactions and the subsequent corrections may be behind excess volatility, which is documented as one of the main impacts of overconfidence.

It is very difficult to define the concept of overconfidence or even to assess it, as it is nonobservable and occurs at the same time with other type of psychological phenomena in a mixture called "sentiment." There are many ways in which we can address it; we can think of it as an investor tendency to overestimate the precision of his/her knowledge about the value of an asset (Odean, 1998); as "the tendency to place an irrationally excessive degree of confidence in one's abilities and beliefs"[1] (Grinblatt and Keloharju, 2009); as "the overestimation of one's knowledge or precision of private information, or the interpretation thereof"[2] (Skata, 2008), or as "having mistaken valuations and believing in them too strongly"[3] (Daniel and Hirshleifer, 2015). All definitions focus on excess of confidence and belief, however, they differ when looking at scope and motivations. Grinblatt and Keloharju (2009) characterizes the type of excess as being clearly irrational whereas Odean (1998) and Daniel and Hirshleifer (2015) look only at asset valuation and Skata (2008) places the focus on private information. This divergence is a clear sign of lack of consensus in an area that encompasses many different perspectives and still has much to offer in terms of research.

Despite the fact that the term "overconfidence" started being widely used since the 1960s, today there is still a lot of unknowns about its sources, its implication, and its impact in finance. The intensity of the discussion regarding the concept of overconfidence is clearly a

---

[1] Page 552.
[2] Page 41.
[3] Page 61.

sign that this is not a residual topic for psychologists and finance academia. The dispute is so fierce that some simply claim that the phenomenon may not exist (Gigerenzer et al., 1991; Juslin, 1994) and may just be a glitch due to faulty methodological options applied to particular studies instead of a true cognitive bias. In fact, the flaws of the main methodology used in finance to assess this phenomenon support to a certain extent this view, as there is an enormous reliance on experiments and questionnaires, which are methods that cannot avoid biases, such as nonrepresentative sampling, small sample sizes, and artificial scenarios. Nevertheless, for others authors, these methodological flaws cannot eliminate the general validity of most tests that are based on real market data and have produced conclusive evidence that overconfidence is a relevant cognitive bias that takes different shapes (Ayton and McClelland, 1997; Glaser and Weber, 2007; Odean, 1998). In fact, DeBondt and Thaler (1995) confirms this perspective by stating that possibly one of most robust findings in the psychology of judgments is that people are overconfident.

6.3 Sources of Overconfidence

When looking at the reasons behind investor overconfidence, many issues can be considered as determinants of this behavior, but some authors (Skata, 2008; Menkhoff et al., 2013) consider that its main sources are miscalibration, better than average effect, illusion of control, and unrealistic optimism. These factors are normally assessed and explained in a separate way from a theoretical and empirical point of view, however, they tend to overlap or work together when triggering overconfidence in real market settings.

Overconfidence based on miscalibration occurs when people assign probabilities higher than they should to particular events. The confirmation bias may be one of the factors influencing this type of behavior with investors searching for and using an excessive amount of confirming evidence, while systematically neglecting contradictory evidence. Also, the "hard-easy effect" is a relevant issue (Fischhoff et al., 1977; Lichtenstein et al., 1982) with overconfidence being higher for difficult and very difficult tasks whereas easy tasks tend to be a source of underconfidence. The presence of clear and rapid feedback and the repetitive nature of a task may be important factors influencing miscalibration, however, there is still heated debate on whether overconfidence can be considered a stable feature or a dynamic process subject to external influence.

The better than average effect is based on psychological research showing that people, in general, tend to have an excessively optimistic view of themselves. Due to a very high intertwining with miscalibration, the better than average effect can be regarded as a type of miscalibration where the subject is not comparing its performance against an objective benchmark, but rather against a subjective view of other subjects' performance. In this setting, the self-serving or self-attribution bias becomes relevant (Babcock and Loewenstein, 1997; Taylor and Brown, 1988) with people assigning to themselves more responsibility for success and less for failures, not giving the appropriate credit to others. Focusing highly on self-esteem, which is a crucial feeling at this level, people associate success with internal factors (skills, knowledge) rather than external ones (luck, weather).

Illusion of control occurs when people are led to believe that they can control events (tasks) that are just determined by chance (Taylor and Brown, 1988) leading to wrong probability assessment. This bias is normally grounded on the wrong perception that subjects that apply their skills to particular tasks through choice, familiarity, and involvement can actually influence the outcome of those tasks. An example of this illusion can be the fact of a particular individual simply believing that he/she has a probability higher than 50% of getting a specific outcome when tossing coin, just because he/she actually tosses the coin. Task involvement does not justify any change in probability which keeps being purely determined by chance, but the subject erroneously believes that the simple fact of intervening in the task can increase his/her odds of being successful.

Finally, unrealistic optimism is regarded as an error in terms of the assessment of future outcomes determined simply by being "better" or "having a brighter future" effects. Subjects prone to unrealistic optimism believe that positive events are more likely to happen to them, whereas negative events are less likely to happen. This bias tend to be especially higher when there is a strong desire for a particular outcome, the probability of being successful is high and there is a clear perception of control over the actual event. Overlapping with the better than average, the biased self-attribution and the illusion of control effects, the unrealistic optimism can be persistent when there is a strong perception of control and a strong commitment or emotional attachment (Skata, 2008).

6.4 Empirical Evidence on Overconfidence

As a reflection of its importance for subjects' decision making, overconfidence has produced a relevant track of publications in the field of behavioral finance with plenty of empirical evidence supporting the significance of this cognitive bias in financial markets (DeBondt, 1998; Glaser and Weber, 2007; Odean, 1998). Nevertheless, most of the financial evidence found about this topic is a mirror of the heated debate going on theoretically and there are critical divergences emerging when looking at the impacts of overconfidence over the stock market, for example, trading volume and trading profits, or when focusing on the determinants of overconfidence, such as learning, experience, age, gender, or type of market (online vs. offline). Even though these issues will be subsequently presented in an individual way, it is important to realize that in real market conditions impacts and determinants work together and are not easily distinguishable.

In terms of the implications of overconfidence, one of the most relevant focus on the relationship with trading volume and is documented, among others, by Odean (1998), Benos (1998), Biais et al. (2005), Glaser and Weber (2007), and Grinblatt and Keloharju (2009).

These authors do not share the same view and the debate is still going on to determine whether there is any relationship between overconfidence and trading volume. On one hand, by taking a narrower approach of overconfidence and focusing mainly on miscalibration, Biais et al. (2005) and Glaser and Weber (2007) claim that there is no relationship between overconfidence and trading volume. On the other hand, by taking a broader view of overconfidence that considers different settings and contexts, the remaining authors arrived to the conclusion that overconfident investors trade more. A fact also confirmed by Glaser and Weber (2009) that in a later study, using a sample of 215 online investors, uncovered a positive relationship between better than average effect and trading frequency. Overall, overconfident investors are seen as having lower expected utilities, relying more on their private information and stock picks, and holding riskier and less diversified portfolios. This situation tends be more significant in bull markets with aggregate overconfidence having a boost and determining also higher levels of individual overconfidence. A conclusion reinforced by Chuang and Lee (2006), when showing that overconfident traders are more prone to trade on relatively riskier assets, after experiencing market gains.

When looking at the impact of overconfidence on trading profits, there is also a clear disparity in empirical evidence. Benos (1998) believes that overconfident traders are more aggressive and therefore tend to enjoy "first-mover" advantages in most trades, leading to higher profits. This is achieved only by enjoying aggressiveness benefits without incurring in high risk taking. A view shared by Hirshleifer and Luo (2001) that believe that overconfident traders exploit better mispricing. Their trading aggressiveness is justified by risk underestimation and overestimation of trading strategies, showing a superior ability to use their information in a more intensive way. On a different perspective, Gervais and Odean (2001) found that overconfident traders tend, on average, to achieve lower gains, as the additional trading volume and the additional volatility they create in markets affects negatively their trading performance. This effect is explained by excessively small asset holding time-windows, leaving no time for assets to adjust to expected values, and higher trading commissions. The same result was obtained by Cheng (2007) based on a sample of 159 students from various academic institutions in Singapore.

Moving away from impacts and looking at the determinants of overconfidence, it is relevant to observe that perspectives on the evolution of overconfidence overtime also are a source of controversy with the possibility of positive, negative, and neutral relationships between experience/learning and overconfidence. On a neutral perspective, while holding confidence levels constant, Hirshleifer and Luo (2001) consider that overconfident traders learn very little and tend to hold their confidence level even when having a bad performance. This is a relevant theoretical result that may not apply in a real market situation, as confidence levels are expected to fluctuate with feedback from past performance. Taking a different stance, Gervais and Odean (2001) propose a negative correlation between experience and overconfidence. They conducted a dynamic study in an attempt to assess changes in overconfidence levels mainly due to self-attribution bias. Unlike Hirshleifer and Luo (2001), they allowed confidence levels to change with past performance. Based on this assumption, they managed to eliminate individual overconfidence through learning, allowing traders to have frequent, rapid, and clear feedback. With an increase in experience levels, traders recognized their true skills and adjusted their overconfidence levels to zero. Nevertheless, the aggregate level of market overconfidence was not eliminated, because there was a constant entry of new overconfident traders and an exit of experienced traders. Menkhoff et al. (2013) also found results similar to Gervais and Odean (2001), in terms of individual confidence. By looking at a pool of institutional investors, investment advisors, and individual investors, these authors uncovered a negative relationship between overconfidence levels and experience, with institutional investors being, on average, the least overconfident. These results are consistent with Linnainmaa (2011) and Grinblatt and Keloharju (2009) pointing at the fact that investors at the beginning of their careers are more overconfident, trade more, and hold riskier assets. Finally, sharing a totally opposite view and focusing on a positive relationship between experience and overconfidence, there are studies pointing at the fact that more experienced subjects tend to be more overconfident (Heath and Tversky, 1991; Kirchler and Maciejovsky, 2002). Positive feedback reinforcing self-attribution of past successes and illusion of control tend to be some of the factors behind this type of relationship.

Some of the significant ambiguity found before is partly explained by the fact that age of subjects is used as a proxy for experience. However, age may not be always be an appropriate choice, because it is too general and does not directly relate to breadth and intensity of investment experience. When age is considered independently from investment experience, as shown in the study by Menkhoff et al. (2013), experience and age tend to work in opposite ways when determining overconfidence. In general, this result may point at the fact that older investors have poorer investment skills, despite their higher experience level (Korniotis and Kumar, 2011).

Gender is also a relevant topic in the research of overconfidence and one in which the level of consensus seems higher. Given the same level of knowledge, most of the empirical research in finance so far is pointing at the fact that males tend to be more overconfident than females (Barber and Odean, 2002; Benos, 1998; Odean, 1998). With men showing higher levels of self-attribution bias (Beyer, 1990; Meehan and Overton, 1986) and finance being connoted as a typical male topic, there is support to find higher overconfidence among men (Lundeberg et al., 1994) leading to higher trading activity and lower returns. In a study focused on more than 35,000 households and limited to small investors from a single large brokerage firm, Barber and Odean (2002) confirmed the male predominance in terms of overconfidence when they found higher average turnover and trading activity for accounts managed by men, leading to higher transaction costs and to lower returns. Overall, single men have 85% of portfolio turnover compared to 53% of single women.

Finally, on the issue of the impact of online trading on overconfidence, it is important to distinguish between two different perspectives. On one side, it seems that going online can be considered as a source of overconfidence due to illusion of knowledge and illusion of control. On the other side, there are reasons to believe that going online can reduce overconfidence as an isolated atmosphere can avoid distractions and lead to higher levels of concentration. Most of the evidence supporting the former view comes from the work of Barber and Odean (2002) that surveyed approximately 1600 traders that moved from telephone to Internet-based trading. With the Internet supplying a larger quantity of data and traders having higher control over trades and portfolios, there are reasons to believe that two relevant overconfidence sources may come into play: illusion of knowledge (higher quantity of information) and illusion of control (a more direct involvement in trades). The results obtained by Barber and Odean (2002) confirm this view by showing that there is a higher turnover online leading to lower average returns, however, they are disputed by some because they do not account for relevant factors, such as sensation seeking or learning effects associated the novelty of online trading. On a different note and supporting the latter view, in 2007, Chen revisited this topic and found that traders in online environments tend to have higher performance and take less risk than their offline counterparts, being therefore less overconfident (Cheng, 2007). In a context where being online is no longer a novelty, the main argument for this outcome is related with the fact that overconfidence tends to be higher in highly interactive and open offline environments where traders are exposed to very diverse and intensive stimuli, including head to head competition with peers, that can be significant distractions. In such an exposed competitive environment, overconfidence comes mainly via better than average effect with traders wanting to be seen as successful when compared to peers. On the other hand, the level of overconfidence online is smaller because there are fewer distractions, more concentration, and less competition.

6.5 What Next for Overconfidence in Finance?

By looking at the quantity and quality of publications on overconfidence in financial markets, either from a theoretical or an empirical point of view, it seems that we are now witnessing a stagnation period after an intense peak. The 1980s and especially the 1987 crisis were critical stages in the early days of the behavioral finance research boom, leading to a publishing frenzy that made its way to top journals and gave notoriety to particular authors. However, this did not mean that overconfidence became immediately a hot topic as well, as most initial approaches to behavioral finance were essentially general, lacking a clear understanding of all the specificities included in the so-called investor "sentiment." Only with time, did authors manage to get to grips and focus on the specifics of behavioral finance, and this led to a progressive surge of interest in the overconfidence topic. The peak of this interest seemed to have taken place in the period between the mid-1990s and 2007. During this time, there were several publications in reputed journals and some authors gained considerable reputation by being associated with this topic. Names like Barber, Odean, Gervais, Glaser, Weber,

Benos, Hirshleifer, among others emerged in this period, being their pioneering work still considered as main references in the area. After 2007, it seems that the quantity and quality of publications simply decreased with some of the most prominent names no longer publishing frequently in high rank journals.

The above tendency seems to be pointing at some contextual forces at play that may have led to a loss of relevance of this particular topic. From the loss of relevance of the individual investor decision making to the emergence of a new political agenda focusing mainly on promoting market efficiency, there are several factors contributing to a loss of appeal of overconfidence. All of them being reinforced by a medium-term context of market stability where anomalies have somewhat been contained due to high central bank and government intervention after the 2008 sub-prime crisis, decreasing the frequency and relevance of this type of phenomena. In such a scenario, research funds and academic interest seem to have followed the political agenda leading to a lack of interest in topics considered residual at present time.

The increasing regulation of markets, a higher level of trading/financial products complexity, higher levels of market concentration, more information disclosure, the advent of algorithm trading and high-frequency trading (HFT) seem to be overwhelming forces in today's markets leaving fewer room for individual investors and uninformed nonautomated decision making. Typically, individual investors are easier to study in behavioral finance and also tend to be the ones more prone to cognitive biases in terms of decision making, mainly overconfidence. However, their role in today's markets has been diminished because institutional traders with higher levels of experience backed by time-tested algorithms, relying on high frequency trading, and covering a higher range of information sources have increased their proportion of market participation, supporting most of the trading action. Additionally, most of the decision making these days, either in terms of institutional or experienced individual investors, is highly dependent on computers, as they are normally the ones placing final orders in an almost stand-alone automated basis, trying to reduce as much as possible the potential for any human error caused by nonrational biases. In such a scenario, it is becoming harder and harder to study and understand the psychological factors actually contributing to orders because they are not so clear.

Additionally, it seems that some of the loss of relevance of overconfidence is also due to the fact that market efficiency is now at the top of political agenda among governments and securities commissions around the globe. In fact, overtime, overconfidence has always been regarded by some as an undesired source of volatility in markets, as it normally appeared associated to crises with relevant economic impacts. Governments and securities commissions are specially affected in terms of their credibility by crises episodes and obviously do whatever they can to avoid them. In fact, most of the work done by regulators in recent years has aimed at increasing market efficiency levels by reducing the impact of many biases affecting price formation, including overconfidence. Tighter regulations, higher levels of information disclosure, trading stops, short-selling restrictions, bans on inside trading, and more intense reporting are just examples of means used to control mispricing. With the help of high-speed computing, it is now also possible for authorities to effectively have higher levels of control over trading, making life harder for investors that do not conform to established rules. This is occurring in a time where the legal and fiscal systems have also evolved to close any loopholes in terms of illicit behaviors.

At present, overconfidence is not desirable and has been somewhat subdued, however, this does not mean that overconfidence is no longer a significant force in today's real markets. There are essentially four reasons to believe that overconfidence has adjusted to present day market conditions and can still be a relevant topic in the research agenda. The first is market momentum. It is important to remember that markets have entered into a rather stable bull stage since the 2008 crisis with central banks providing safety for most investments, either based or not on fundamentals. In such a context, overconfidence may still be present at normal levels, as investors tend to be more overconfident during bull periods, however, it may not be so easy to see it, as underreaction or overreaction, which are some of the key indicators of the existence of overconfidence, are contained within controlled ranges. The second relates to the fact that algorithm trading does not eliminate overconfidence in trades even though it is aiming at that. In fact, what algorithm trading does is transferring overconfidence biases from the final decision to the choice of key indicators or corresponding weights that are going to be used in decision making. This change does not eliminate overconfidence, instead it just makes it more difficult to be identified and properly assessed. The third is higher transparency levels. Markets are now forcing listed companies to disclose more information and the internet helps more private information to become public in a faster way. This fact can contribute to better price formation and faster feedback to investors leading them to learn better, fostering lower overconfidence levels, however, it may also be responsible for higher overconfidence by reinforcing the illusion of knowledge associated with more information available. The fourth is higher market complexity. From the human investor side, it seems that higher levels of experience are now required to perform trading using more complex platforms and products. This, in principle, is expected to be a source of lower overconfidence, however, we have also seen that it can lead to higher overconfidence due to self-attribution, illusion of control, and illusion of knowledge effects associated with higher experience levels. The simple fact of addressing a higher level of complexity can lead on its own to overconfidence via the "hard-easy effect."

From a normative standpoint, and even though overconfidence has a negative connotation, it is important to realize that it should not be simply discarded as a market nuisance with no added value. To a certain extent, overconfidence can be a significant force to create opportunities and attempt new trading dynamics. It has been proven that overconfident investors research more and trade more aggressively based on private information, leading to higher incorporation of information on price formation (Hirshleifer and Luo, 2001; Odean, 1998). Therefore, when being part of a team of traders, overconfident subjects can provide the group with valuable information (Bernardo and Welch, 2001). Additionally, overconfidence motivates investors to participate in different markets or asset classes that may be unfamiliar or riskier creating new opportunities. Even though they tend to follow different paths and strategies from other investors, they provide constant challenges to the group that can help it evolve and develop new strategies. A fact recognized by active fund managers that, being aware of these benefits, tend to devise specific incentives to foster overconfidence and aggressive behavior.

6.6 Conclusions

Overall, and despite a recent downward tendency in publications, there are reasons to believe that overconfidence is still a very relevant force in today's markets and should keep fostering new avenues of research and publications in financial markets. It is now probably harder to research overconfidence in markets due to some of the inhibiting factors mentioned before, however, it may also be more rewarding. For instance, new lines of research associated with the impact of algorithm trading or increasing market complexity on overconfidence, among others, are still unexplored fields that can yield significant contributions and relevant publications. As securities' commissions and market players have a strong belief that they are now dealing with more efficient markets, I guess they would be extremely interested in knowing how efficient markets are and to what extent psychological biases are still determining actual trading decision making, because they still are.

References

Ayton, P., McClelland, A., 1997. How real is overconfidence? J. Behav. Decis. Mak. 10 (3), 279–285.

Babcock, L., Loewenstein, G., 1997. Explaining bargaining impasse: the role of self-serving biases. J. Econ. Perspect. 11 (1), 109–126.

Barber, B., Odean, T., 2002. Online investors: do the slow die first? Rev. Financ. Studies 15 (2), 455–487.

Barberis, N., Shleifer, A., Vishny, R., 1998. A model of investor sentiment. J. Financ. Econ. 49 (3), 307–343.

Benos, A., 1998. Aggressiveness and survival of overconfident traders. J. Financ. Markets 1 (3–4), 353–383.

Bernardo, A., Welch, I., 2001. On the evolution of overconfidence and entrepreneurs. J. Econ. Manage. Strat. 10 (3), 301–330.

Beyer, S., 1990. Gender differences in the accuracy of self-evaluations of performance. J. Personal. Soc. Psychol. 59 (5), 960–970.

Biais, B., Hilton, D., Mazurier, K., Pouget, S., 2005. Judgmental overconfidence, self-monitoring and trading performance in an experimental financial market. Rev. Econ. Studies 72 (251), 287–312.

Black, F., 1986. Noise. J. Finance 41 (3), 529–543.

Cheng, K., 2007. The trader interaction effect on the impact of overconfidence on trading performance: an empirical study. J. Behav. Finance 8 (2), 59–69.

Chuang, W., Lee, B., 2006. An empirical evaluation of the overconfidence hypothesis. J. Banking Finance 30 (9), 2489–2515.

Daniel, K., Hirshleifer, D., Subrahmanyam, A., 1998. Investor psychology and security market under and overreactions. J. Finance 53 (6), 1839–1885.

Daniel, K., Hirshleifer, D., 2015. Overconfident investors, predictable returns, and excessive trading. J. Econ. Perspect. 29 (4), 61–88.

Daniel, K., Hirshleifer, D., Subrahmanyam, A., 2001. Overconfidence, arbitrage and equilibrium asset pricing. J. Finance 56 (3), 921–965.

DeBondt, W., 1998. A Portrait of the Individual Investor. Eur. Econ. Rev. 42 (3–5), 831–844.

DeBondt, W., Thaler, R., 1995. Financial decision-making in markets and firms: a behavioral perspective. Jarrow, R. et al., (Ed.), Handbooks in Operations Research and Management, vol. 9, Elsevier Science, Amsterdam.

DeLong, B., Shleifer, A., Summers, L., Waldmann, R., 1990. Noise trader risk in financial markets. J. Polit. Econ. 98 (4), 703–738.

Fama, E.F., 1965. The behavior of stock-market prices. J. Bus. 38 (1), 34–105.

Fama, E.F., 1970. Efficient capital markets: a review of theory and empirical work. J. Finance 25 (2), 383–417.

Fama, E., 1998. Market efficiency, long-term returns, and behavioral finance. J. Financ. Econ 49 (3), 283–306.

Fischhoff, B., Lichstenstein, S., Slovic, P., 1977. Knowing with certainty: the appropriateness of extreme confidence. J. Exp. Psychol. 3 (4), 552–564.

Gervais, S., Odean, T., 2001. Learning to be overconfident. Rev. Financ. Studies 14 (1), 1–27.

Gigerenzer, G., Hoffrage, U., Kleinbolting, H., 1991. Probabilistic mental models: a Brunswikian theory of confidence. Psychol. Rev. 98 (4), 506–528.

Glaser, M., Weber, M., 2007. Overconfidence and trading volume. Geneva Risk Ins. Rev. 32 (1), 1–36.

Glaser, M., Weber, M., 2009. Which past returns affect trading volume? J. Financ. Markets 12 (1), 1–33.

Grinblatt, M., Keloharju, M., 2009. Sensation seeking, overconfidence and trading activity. J. Finance 64 (2), 549–578.

Heath, C., Tversky, A., 1991. Preference and belief: ambiguity and competence in choice under uncertainty. J. Risk Uncertainty 4 (1), 5–28.

Hirshleifer, D., Luo, G., 2001. On the survival of overconfident traders in a competitive securities market. J. Financ. Markets 4 (1), 73–84.

Juslin, P., 1994. The overconfidence phenomenon as a consequence of informal experimenter-guided selection of Almanac Items. Organ. Behav. Hum. Decis. Process. 57 (2), 226–246.

Kahneman, D., Tversky, A., 1972. Subjective probability: a judgment of representativeness. Cogn. Psychol. 3 (3), 430–454.

Kahneman, D., Tversky, A., 1973. On the psychology of prediction. Cogn. Psychol. Rev. 80 (4), 237–251.

Kahneman, D., Tversky, A., 1979. Prospect theory: an analysis of decision under risk. Econometrica 47 (2), 263–291.

Kirchler, E., Maciejovsky, B., 2002. Simultaneous over and underconfidence: evidence from experimental asset markets. J. Risk Uncertain. 25 (1), 65–85.

Korniotis, G., Kumar, A., 2011. Do older investors make better investment decisions? Rev. Econ. Stat. 93 (1), 244–265.

Lichtenstein, S., Fischhoff, B., Philips, L., 1982. Calibration of probabilities: the state of the art to 1980. In: Kahneman, D., Slovic, P., Tversky (Eds.), Judgment Under Uncertainty: Heuristics and Biases. Cambridge University Press, Cambridge.

Linnainmaa, J., 2011. Why do (some) households trade so much? Rev. Financ. Studies 24 (5), 1630–1666.

Lundeberg, M., Fox, P., Punccohar, J., 1994. Highly confident but wrong: gender differences and similarities in confidence judgments. J. Educ. Psychol. 86 (1), 114–121.

Meehan, A., Overton, W., 1986. Gender differences for success and performance on piagetian spatial tasks. Memill Palmer Q. 32 (4), 427–441.

Menkhoff, L., Schmeling, M., Schmidt, U., 2013. Overconfidence, experience and professionalism: an experimental study. J. Econ. Behav. Org. 86 (1), 92–101.

Odean, T., 1998. Volume, volatility, price and profit when all traders are above average. J. Finance 53 (6), 1887–1934.

Shiller, R., 1987. Investor Behaviour in the October 1987 Stock Market Crash: Survey Evidence, National Bureau of Economics Research, Working Paper No. 2446, Cambridge, Massachusetts.

Siegel, J., 1992. Equity risk premia, corporate profits forecast and investor sentiment around the stock crash of October 1987. J. Bus. 65 (4), 557–570.

Skata, D., 2008. Overconfidence in psychology and finance—an interdisciplinary literature review. Financ. Markets Inst. 4, 33–50.

Taylor, S., Brown, J., 1988. Illusion and well-being: a social psychological perspective on mental health. Psychol. Bull. 103 (2), 193–210.

CHAPTER 7

Rational Agents and Irrational Bubbles

Dmitriy Krichevskiy*, Dhimitri Qirjo**

*Elizabethtown College, Elizabethtown, PA, United States;
**State University of New York, Plattsburgh, NY, United States

Chapter Outline

7.1 Introduction

From Kipper-und Wipperzeit of 1619 or Tulip Mania of 1637, investment bubbles have captured the imaginations of people and news cycles of the day (Garber, 2016; Kindleberger, 1991). After each bubble's demise regulators, investors, and the general public demand explanations, policy changes, and often punishments. Oftentimes, demand for punishment runs ahead of the demand for explanations. Unfortunately, aside from participants themselves, there is not necessary a common cause. Bubbles differ in assets types, magnitude, growth rates, timing, and predictability.

Most recent global financial crisis exhibited numerous contributing factors, such as excessive government support for home ownership, banking deregulation, erroneous asset risk valuations, increase global market integration, and broad investment funds participation. However, we can identify a mechanism general enough to explain typical mechanics of investment bubbles. Information asymmetry, overt as well as covert governments' actions and greed, typically play a role in bubble formation, growth, and demise. Most fascinating is the scope of financial bubbles. Mass participation is the fuel that blows the bubbles so far beyond the traditional assets' fundamental price. We use the difference between the fundamental price and the market price as a definition of a bubble. It is also critical to assess who are the participating investors. Some of the investors participating in these bubbles are ill-informed or overly optimistic about their returns. At the same time, many bankers and investors are usually perceived as rational, risk-neutral market players. Bubbles' demise often spells financial ruin for many, informed or otherwise. Typically, soon after bubble bursts, there is a renewed interest in public media, regulatory agencies, policymakers, and academia alike. In addition to empirical assessment of timing, scope, and magnitude of market irregularities a mechanism for the bubble formation growth and demise is needed. We find the underlining mechanism to be the most fascinating.

A good theoretical model has to include rational and sophisticated bubble participants as well as ill-informed agents. Now that some years have passed since the demise of the latest and one of the most severe economic bubbles and crisis of 2008, a number of economic models have been put forward. The importance of the behavioral economics models into the housing market is of particular interest after the lack of understanding of the world financial crisis of 2008. Many economists believe that this huge financial crisis that initiated the well-known Great Recession has its foundation in the US residential housing market bubble that crashed in 2006 and the subprime mortgage market that crashed in 2007.

This chapter offers a theoretical model outlining this particular housing market bubble's creation, growth, and demise while utilizing both sophisticated as well as ill-informed or naïve participants. We use a theoretical application of the (Abreu and Brunnermeier, 2003) model, henceforth AB, that was originally developed to explain the dot-com financial bubble, but it is general enough and very applicable to the 2006–07 real estate bubble in the United States. The assumption of the existence of a lot of irrational investors (i.e., necessary for the development of the theoretical model) who invested in the housing market is very realistic, in particular in the United States, where a culture of homeownership was strongly encouraged by the US government. We show that the presence of a relatively low-interest rates regime that was maintained by the Federal Reserve (FED) (i.e., during the Alan Greenspan years), the high dispersion of opinions among rational investors, and the low-quality mortgages issued by the biggest and most eminent private financial institutions in the United States helped by their overvalued ratings have played a crucial role in the creation, the exponential growth and the crash of the 2006 residential housing market bubble in the United States, and the 2007 parallel subprime mortgage market bubble.

This chapter is organized as follows. In the second section, we present the model, wherein Section 7.2.1, we demonstrate the existence of an exogenous bubble for the residential housing market in the United States and for the subprime mortgage market that followed, and in Section 7.2.2, we illustrate the presence of an endogenous bubble for the same markets. The third section concludes. The references are presented in the fourth section and the graphs appear at the end of the chapter.

7.2 An Application of AB to the United States 2006–07 Housing Bubble

The inclusion of theories relaxing the assumption of rationality in an attempt to explain the existence of financial bubbles was popularized by Keynes (1936). He claimed that securities prices are often different from their fair values mainly due to households' sentiments that consist of their overoptimistic or overpessimistic behavior in contrast with rational households that are assumed to be free of such behavior toward the market. However, despite some popular models in behavioral economics, such as (AB; Avery and Zemsky, 1995; Bala and Goyal, 2000; Bikhchandani et al., 1992; Blanchard, 1979; Blume et al., 1994; Chamley and Gale, 1994; Choi, 1997; De Long et al., 1990a,b; Geanakoplos, 1992; Helling, 1982; Kahneman and Tversky, 1979; Scheikman and Xong, 2003; Shiller, 1996, 2000, 2005; Shleifer, 2000; Tversky and Kahneman, 1974), the inclusion of behavior economics in the real estate pricing models have received limited coverage until the 2006 housing bubble in the United States. This is mainly related to the general acceptance of the "Efficient Market Hypothesis" by economists. This hypothesis claims that bubbles do not exist in models that only focus on rational investors. One may argue that the above hypothesis is true in the housing market if the latter is perfectly controlled by the rational investors. These investors will eliminate any regional land bubbles because if the house prices become high, they will find it rationally to relocate in a different region and purchase the same quality of real state with a lower price (this is more common in the United States, where finding a similar job is more likely and the relocation costs and adjustment time to a newer environment are lower compared to the rest of the world).

However, in the real world, we have seen a lot of bubbles in the real estate market. This is demonstrated by plenty of empirical studies that have confirmed the existence of bubbles in the housing market. For example, in the United States, there are documented bubbles in the housing market in the late 1970s and 1980s. A lot of studies have included some sort of irrational behavior in their theoretical models in order to break the "Efficient Market Hypothesis" and leave a theoretical basis for the existence of a bubble in the housing market (for a comprehensive review of theoretical and empirical studies on housing market bubbles, see Brunnermeier, 2009; Brunnermeier and Julliard, 2008; Reinhart and Rogoff, 2009; Scherbina and Schulsche, 2012; Shefrin and Statman, 2011; Whittle et al., 2014).

We apply the AB model to the US residential real estate crises of 2006 and the parallel crises of subprime mortgage market of 2007. We focus on the role that the low interest rate, dispersion of opinions among investors combined with low quality mortgages issued by many of the biggest and more well-known private financial institutions in the United States, (which were also helped by the overvalued ratings of the national rating agencies) have played on the existence and persistence of the 2006 housing market bubble and the 2007 parallel subprime mortgage market bubble.

In most rigorous definitions, a financial bubble starts at the time where the price of an asset is higher than its fundamental price, $p_t = e^{gt}$ (fair price, hereafter, $p_t = e^{rt}$), where r is the risk-free interest rate (or the market rate). It is assumed that $g > r$. In the subprime mortgage and residential housing markets, this higher growth rate g may be viewed as a consequence of continuously positive shocks that were created in the real estate market as a result of low quality mortgages issued by the US banks. Under this setting, irrational investors (who are usually called behavior traders in the behavior economics literature) tend to believe that economy has changed as well. The existence of such behavior of investors was very common in the United States (Case, 2008; Case and Shiller, 2003), using surveys of recent homebuyers conclude that they were overoptimistic about the higher future prices of their homes and they formed bias beliefs in regards to the fair value of their home based on word of mouth and similar noisy feelings. Moreover, according to Sanders (2007), an experienced mortgage banker claimed that home buyers were very naïve. They were willing to sign everything that was put in front of them without fully understanding what they just signed. Therefore, from the early 1990 till 2006, there existed a general belief of behavior traders that the housing prices would monotonically increase. This bias belief increased the expected future home prices, which was the main force in raising the housing prices enabling the construction business to expand in the United States. In addition, according to Morgenson and Rosner (2011), a culture of homeownership was encouraged by the US government, especially during the Clinton administration. Furthermore, the profit driven corporations, such as Countrywide Financials, Merrill Lynch, UBS, AIG, and others also welcomed and encouraged the culture of homeownership by taking more risks on holding and/or issuing mortgages and mortgage securities (Shefrin and Statman, 2011). Consequently, these future expectations about the housing prices accompanied with the governmental and greedy mortgage industry corporations' encouragement to own a house contributed to behavior investors being overoptimistic about their future real estate ownings, and the intensity of demand driving the housing prices much higher than their fair value.

In the AB model, a bubble is established when a sufficient number of investors contribute to mispricing of the asset from its fair value. Thus, at time $t = 0$, $p_t = 0$. At $t > 0 \Rightarrow p_t = e^{gt}$. Nature chooses a random time $t_0 > 0$ distributed on $[0, \infty)$ with the cumulative distribution function (cdf) $\Phi\left(t_0\right) = 1 - e^{-\lambda t_0}$, where an increase of the price in a house can be explained by the increase of its real value. After t_0, $\forall~ p_t > p_{t_0}$, in addition to its fair value, p_t includes a bubble component $\beta(t - t_0)$, such that β is an increasing function of $(t - t_0)$, until it is assumed to bursts exogenously at $\overline{\beta}$ when the bubble reaches its maximum size. The bubble may also burst endogenously before it reaches $\overline{\beta}$. Mathematically, $\beta\left(t - t_0\right): [0, \overline{\tau}] \mapsto \lfloor 0, \overline{\beta} \rfloor$, where $\overline{\tau}$ represents the maximum life time of the bubble. There exists an infinite number of investors, however only the rational investors (who are the ones who become aware of the bubble) are active in this model, and we analyze their optimal strategies. The rational investors do not have the same level of satisfaction due to the dispersion of their opinions (denoted by η) about the housing and subprime mortgage markets. Thus, some of them become aware of the bubble before other rational investors. The timing of the active players in this game lie within $[t_0, t_0 + \eta]$. Thus, at time $t_0 + \eta$ all rational investors know that housing prices are above their fair values. However, since t_0 is random, investors do not know how many other investors knew about the bubble before them. The bubble will endogenously burst at $t_0 + \eta\kappa$ when there is enough selling pressure accumulated by κ rational investors. Since investors sequentially become aware of the bubble, for an investor t_i, t_0 to is in $[t_i - \eta, t_i]$ and the distribution of t_0 is

$$\Phi(t_0|t_i) = \frac{e^{\lambda\eta} - e^{\lambda(t_i-t_0)}}{e^{\lambda\eta} - 1}.$$ It is assumed that $\dfrac{\lambda}{1 - e^{-\lambda\eta\kappa}} < \dfrac{g - r}{\beta(\eta\kappa)}$ in order to guard the bubble from

unware attacks. In other words, this inequality assures that when the critical mass of investors κ know the existence of the bubble, if the probability of the burst is less than cost-benefit ratio of attacking it, the investors will hold their houses or their subprime mortgage stocks.

The strategy profile for an investor is $\sigma : [0, \infty] \times [0, \infty]°\{0, 1\}$, where each investor's active space is either 0 or 1, meaning that at 1 an investor owns only houses and/or subprime mortgage stocks, and at 0, he/she sells out all his/her real state. Thus, investors are risk-neutral. They cannot gradually sell out their real state in order to eliminate the risk. This is a simplifying assumption. The results of the model hold when allowing investor's active space to be continuum on $[0, 1]$. $\sigma(t, t_i)$ denotes the selling pressure at time t $\forall$ investor t_i. The total selling pressure for all active players with $t > t_0$ is $s(t, t_0) = \int_{t_0}^{min\{t, t_0+\eta\}} \sigma(t, t_i) dt_i$. Thus, the bubble will burst endogenously at $T^*(t_0) = \inf\{t | s(t, t_0) \geq \kappa\}$, or exogenously at $t(t_0) = t_0 + \bar{\tau}$, where $\bar{\tau} > T^*$. Hence, an investor who realizes the existence of the bubble at time t_i forms her beliefs about the bursting date from $\Pi(t|t_i) = \int_{T^*(t_0)<t} d\Phi(t_0|t_i)$. Investors' payoff is given by the difference of the subprime mortgage stock prices (or housing prices) and their transaction costs. These expected prices depend on the time of buying and selling relative to the bubble. α denotes the selling pressure in such manner that $\alpha > 0$, if the selling pressure is more than κ; otherwise, $\alpha = 0$. The expecting price is $(1 - \alpha)p_t + \alpha(1 - \beta(t - t_0)) p_t$. The payoff of a fully invested active player at a time t in the housing and/or subprime mortgage markets until he/she sells his/her entire assets on these markets is given by the following: $\int_{t_i}^{t} e^{-rs} \left(1 - \beta\left(s - T^{*-1}(s)\right)\right) p(s) d\Pi(s|t_i) + e^{-rt} p(t)\left(1 - \Pi(t|t_i)\right) - c$. It is assumed that transaction costs are constant and also an investor does not enter in these markets until the crash of their respected bubbles.

Without loss of generality, AB restricts their analysis to trigger strategies. From here the equilibrium of the game is defined as Perfect Bayesian Nash Equilibrium (for further details on the game-theoretical structure of the AB model, see Nielsen, 2009). Thus, an investor who is aware of the bubble and has stock holdings less than her maximum believes that other investors that were aware of the bubble before her also own stock holding less than their maximum. In other words, there exists a monotonicity property such that if $t_i < t_j$ then $T(t_i) < T(t_j)$. Therefore, the monotonicity property of Perfect Bayesian Nash Equilibria in this setting means that the investors who become aware of the bubble earlier, also sell out earlier in equilibrium. From here we can identify the bursting time of the bubble: $T^*(t_0) = \min\left\{T(t_0 + \eta k, t_0 + \bar{\tau})\right\}$. If an investor t_i sells at $t_0 + \eta\kappa$ enough selling pressure is being generated to burst the bubble. Of course all other investors who have become aware of the bubble before t_i have already sold out. However, the bubble may have already exploded before for exogenous reasons at $t_0 + \overline{\tau}$. In AB, it is shown that the function $T^*(\cdot)$ and its inverse $T^{*-1}(\cdot)$ are both continuous and increasing in equilibrium.

Given the strategies of all other investors, an investor t_i belief about the bursting date is given by $\Pi(t|t_i) = \Phi(T^{*-1}(t))$. Hence, the expected payoff of t_i selling out at date t can be specified as $\int_{t_i}^{t} e^{-rs}\left(1 - \beta\left(s - T^{*-1}(s)\right)\right) p(s)\pi(s|t_i) ds + e^{-rt} p(t)\left(1 - \Pi(t|t_i)\right) - c$, where $\pi(s|t_i)$ represents the conditional density at time t_i. Differentiating the expected payoff with respect to time t yields the optimal sell-out condition of investor t_i

$$\frac{\pi(t|t_i)}{1 - \Pi(t|t_i)} = \frac{g - r}{\beta\left(t - T^{*-1}(t)\right)} \tag{7.1}$$

The left-hand side of Eq. (7.1), represent the hazard rate (denoted by $h(t|t_i)$) that the bubble will burst at t. The right hand side of Eq. (7.1), represents the cost-benefit ratio of attacking the bubble (CBR). $h(t|t_i)$ represents t_i risk assignment to the bubble busting. The numerator of CBR implies the costs of being out of the market assuming that the bubble has not yet exploded at t. The denominator of CBR shows the benefits of attacking the bubble at t, measured by the bubble's size at t. Thus, if $h(t|t_i) \geq CRB$, then investor t_i leaves the market. If $h(t|t_i) < CBR$, then the investor t_i will keep her investments in the housing market.

Since investor t_i believes that the bubble started randomly at $t_0 \in [t_i - \eta, t_i]$, the latter's

distribution is $\Phi(t_0|t_i) = \dfrac{\int_{t_i-\eta}^{t_0}\left(\frac{1}{\eta}\lambda e^{-\lambda s}\right) ds}{\int_{t_i-\eta}^{t_i}\left(\frac{1}{\eta}\lambda e^{-\lambda s}\right) ds} = \dfrac{e^{\lambda\eta} - e^{\lambda(t_i-t_0)}}{e^{\lambda\eta} - 1}$. If we assume that investor

t_i believes that the bubble will burst ξ units of time after its starting date at t_0, then her

distribution about the bursting time $(\xi + t_0)$ is $\Pi(t_i + \tau|t_i) = \dfrac{e^{\lambda\eta} - e^{\lambda(\zeta-\tau)}}{e^{\lambda\eta} - 1}$ and her hazard rate is

$$h(t_i + \tau|t_i) = \frac{\lambda}{1 - e^{-\lambda(\zeta-\tau)}} \tag{7.2}$$

Using Eq. (7.1), we can easily find her optimal selling out date $(t_i + \tau)$. This is given by

$$h(t_i + \tau|t_i) = \frac{g - r}{\beta\left(t - T^{*-1}(t)\right)} = \frac{g - r}{\beta(\xi)} \tag{7.3}$$

Combining Eqs. (7.2) and (7.3) implies that if all rational investors believe that the bubble will burst at the date $(\xi + t_0)$, they will exactly sell out all their real estate properties at the time $(\tau + t_0)$, where

$$\tau = \xi - \frac{1}{\lambda}\ln\left(\frac{g - r}{g - r - \lambda\beta(\xi)}\right) \tag{7.4}$$

Therefore in Eq. (7.4), the bubble will burst exogenously if all rational investors believe that $\xi = \bar{\tau}$ and the size of the bubble will reach its maximum at $\beta(\xi) = \bar{\beta}$. Otherwise the bubble will burst endogenously at $\xi = \eta\kappa + \tau$. Hence, from here we can solve for ξ

$$\xi = min\{\bar{\tau}, \eta\kappa + \tau\} \tag{7.5}$$

Using Eqs. (7.4) and (7.5), we can find the equilibrium values for ξ and τ. Then we can figure out if the bubble will burst endogenously or exogenously and analyze each case.

7.2.1 Exogenous Bubble

Combining Eqs. (7.2), (7.3), and (7.4), it is straightforward that the bubble will burst exogenously if

$$\frac{\lambda}{1 - e^{-\lambda\eta\kappa}} \leq \frac{(g-r)}{\bar{\beta}} \tag{7.6}$$

The right-hand side of this inequality implies that the CBR of an investor does not depend on the timing of the burst. The left-hand side denotes the hazard rate. This inequality shows that if the dispersion of opinion, η is large in the real estate market, then Eq. (7.6) is more likely to hold. Under this scenario, the bubble will grow slowly and it will last until its possible maximum length of time. Substituting $\xi = \bar{\tau}$ and $\beta(\xi) = \bar{\beta}$ into Eq. (7.4) gives the equilibrium selling out condition denoted by τ^1

$$\tau^1 = \bar{\tau} - \frac{1}{\lambda}\ln\left(\frac{g-r}{g-r-\lambda\bar{\beta}}\right) < \bar{\tau} \tag{7.7}$$

AB shows that the earlier equilibrium is symmetric and unique. Therefore, all rational investors apply this optimal strategy. Intuitively, this means that rational investors that are aware of the bubble before τ^1 ride the bubble effectively by selling out before τ^1. However, rational investors that are aware of the bubble at some time after τ^1 ride the bubble but miss the optimal sell out time and can suffer large losses because after the crash the price of the stock returns to its precrash value.

It is quite possible that the residential housing market bubble in the United States can be represented by the earlier model, where inequality Eq. (7.6) is satisfied due to very high values of the excess growth rate of the housing bubble $(g - r)$, and the dispersion of opinions among rational investors η.

The portion of the mispricing in the housing market that was not justified by its fair value g, was very high during the recent housing market bubble in the United States. A lot of researchers (Brunnermeier, 2009; Coval et al., 2009; Lewis 2010; Scherbina and Schulsche, 2014; Shefrin and Statman, 2011, among others) claim that the main reason for the initial departure of the housing prices from their fair value is contributed to very popular mortgage securitization mechanism (that was newly implemented around that time) that permitted banks to sellout their own mortgages in order to diversify away the risk of volatile prices in the regional housing market. These mortgage backed securities (MBSs) were insured by credit default swaps (CDSs) and there was a biased rating by credit rating agencies.

In order get significantly inflated asset values (large g) in the housing market bubble it is not sufficient the large presence of behavioral households that believe that the positive trend on the housing market will last forever, after observing this rise in price for a short period of time. Homes bought by the majority of these households needed outside financing that was secured by various banks. In other words, a housing market bubble needs irrational investors willing to invest more in new homes, but also a parallel subprime mortgage system that fuels the outside financing of this homes possible at very low cost. This is exactly, what happened during the housing bubble in the United States that peaked in 2006. The subprime loans issued by the banks were used by the latter to manufacture AAA ranked securities. These securities became very popular mainly due to high rankings, which give investors the wrong impressions that they did not carry a lot of risks. The ranking institutions over ranked these securities in fear of losing business to other competitive rating agencies (Brunnermeier, 2009).

Some researchers claim that the low-interest rates regime that was maintained by FED especially during the Alan Greenspan years could have also contributed to the expansion of the real estate bubble of 2006 in the United States. During these years, FED was committed to lower interest rates using the intuition that lower interest rates may help the economy to increase investments in the United States, and therefore, may help the US economy recover after the dot-com bubble. In 2004, Greenspan was convinced that there was no bubble in the US housing market. However, this low interest rate policy increased the excess growth rate of the real estate market bubble $(g-r)$, and therefore, indirectly increased the inflated prices of houses in the United States. The latter caused irrational investors to invest more in this market (some households that could not afford to buy houses before used to own two houses at the peak of the housing bubble). According to Scherbina and Schulsche (2012, 2014), one of the main reasons of the initial mispricing of the housing market is contributed to the low interest rates maintained by the FED after the collapse of the dot-com bubble in 2002. For more on the persistence of low interest rates during the crises, see Fig. 7.1.

We believe that the dispersion of opinions among rational investors η was also very high and played an important role on accelerating the housing bubble in the United States. Looking back on various professional presentations, academic reports, media coverage, and articles published in newspapers and academic journals, one can easily document the high diversion of opinions among public, but also especially among rational investors in regards to the existence of the bubble in the housing market in the United States. For example, in a report published by TIAA-CREF, Richard Peach, 2005 (Vice President of FED—New York)

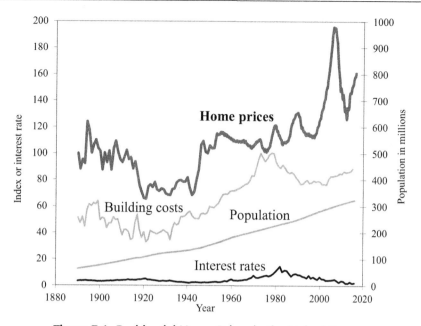

Figure 7.1: Residential Home Prices in the United States.
US Home Price and Related data, for Figure 3.1 in Shiller, R.J., 2015. Irrational Exuberance, third ed., Princeton University Press, as updated by author. See the book for description of data.

claimed that there might be some regional bubble in the United States, but the overall national housing prices represented their fair values. He argued that the national housing prices were on the rise due to lower interest rates and improvements in the quality of houses. However, in the same report, Robert Shiller (2005) (Professor of Economics at Yale University) argued that the rising trend of the home prices in the United States at that time was not normal by historical standards, and he presented arguments and potential risks in consistent with the existence of the bubble in the housing market (for a further discussion on these two opposing views, see Shefrin and Statman, 2011). Moreover, a lot of investors in Wall Street and rating agencies followed the Gaussian Cupola function developed by Li (2000) when analyzing risk of various securities related to residential housing market, and/or to subprime mortgage market, such as CDSs. On the other hand, on various economic and financial newspapers appeared a lot of information in regard to the possible existence of a bubble in the US residential housing and subprime mortgage markets (for more details, see The Economist, 2002, 2003, 2005a,b). Consequently, the disparity of opinions was high during the development of residential housing and subprime mortgage crisis in the United States.

7.2.2 Endogenous Bubble

However, it is still possible that the exogenous variables of the model (e.g., $g, r, \eta, \kappa, \overline{\beta}$) were such that U.S. economy was in the midst of an endogenous bubble in the residential real estate market that crashed in 2006 and the subprime mortgage market that crashed a bit latter in 2007. In terms of the AB model, this means that the following inequality must hold.

$$\frac{\lambda}{1-e^{-\lambda\eta\kappa}} > \frac{(g-r)}{\bar{\beta}} \tag{7.8}$$

The validity of the earlier inequality shows that when a critical amount of investors realize the existence of the bubble, the hazard rate is higher than the *CBR* of attacking the bubble at the date when the bubble reaches its maximum size. Intuitively, this implies that the bubble grows rapidly or starts quickly. In this model, using backward induction rational investors will delay the burst of the bubble for some time until the selling pressure reaches a critical point denoted by τ^*, where the bubble crashes. Therefore, it is still beneficial to rational investors that were aware of bubble to ride it until it reaches τ^*. Combining Eq. (7.4) (where we substitute $\xi = \tau^*$) with the fact that now $\lambda/1-e^{-\lambda(\xi-r)} \to \lambda/1-e^{-\lambda(\eta\kappa)}$, we find the equilibrium date for riding the bubble

$$\tau^* = \beta^{-1}\left(\frac{g-r}{\dfrac{\lambda}{1-e^{-\lambda\eta\kappa}}}\right) \tag{7.9}$$

As the crash date of the bubble is delayed by rational investors, the size of the bubble starts to diminish. The latter makes the ride of the bubble more attractive because it reduces the costs of staying invested before the burst. Using Eq. (7.9), we find the size of the bubble at the bursting date, β^*

$$\beta^* = \frac{1-e^{-\lambda\eta\kappa}}{\lambda}(g-r) \tag{7.10}$$

From Eqs. (7.9) and (7.10), it is straightforward that the hazard rate $h^* = \dfrac{\lambda}{1-e^{-\lambda\eta\kappa}}$ is constant relative to the timing of the bubble, while the CBR of attacking it, $CBR = \dfrac{g-r}{\bar{\beta}(\eta\kappa+\tau)}$ is decreasing as the bubble continues to grow. AB show that the equilibrium date of

the bubble's burst, τ^* is symmetric and unique. This implies that rational investors that realize the existence of the bubble prior to τ^* ride the bubble effectively and sell out before it crashes. However, rational investors who became aware of the bubble at some time after τ^*, ride the bubble through the crash. One may argue that this is exactly the case in the subprime mortgage crash of 2007 in the United States. For example, Goldman Sachs was among rational investors that realized early the existence of the bubble and sold out their MBSs right before the bubble crashed. Thus, they effectively rode the bubble and benefited from it in contrast with other rational investors, such as Countrywide Financials, Merrill Lynch, UBS, and AIG, who became aware of the bubble at latter stages and got the timing of the crash wrong.

Even in an endogenous crash, it can be shown that for certain values of λ, $(g - r)$, η, κ, the bursting time of an endogenous crash τ^*, is very close to the bursting time of an exogenous crash $\bar{\tau}$. This implies, that under certain condition, an endogenous bubble can also last for a long period of time.

Even if the dispersion of opinion η is not extremely high to ensure an exogenous crash described by Eq. (7.6), the existence of a high η in the housing market would increase the optimal timing of the endogenous crash τ^*, increasing the size of the bubble β^* at τ^*. Consequently, proposition 1 follows.

Proposition 1

In an endogenous crash, an increase of the dispersion of opinions among rational investors (η) increases the equilibrium bursting date of the bubble τ^*.

The proof of proposition 1 is straightforward, since $\dfrac{d\beta^*}{d\eta} = \kappa e^{-\lambda \eta \kappa}(1 + r) > 0$. Also, $\dfrac{d\tau^*}{d\beta^*} > 0$.

Hence, $\dfrac{d\tau^*}{d\eta} > 0$. One can also show directly that $\dfrac{d\tau^*}{d\eta} > 0$. Thus, differentiating Eq. (7.9) with respect to η gives us $\dfrac{d\tau^*}{d\eta} = \dfrac{(g - r)\kappa e^{-\lambda \eta \kappa} - \beta \kappa}{\beta}$. The numerator is positive due to

Eq. (7.8). We can also proof proposition 1 with the help of Fig. 7.2. The initial equilibrium is

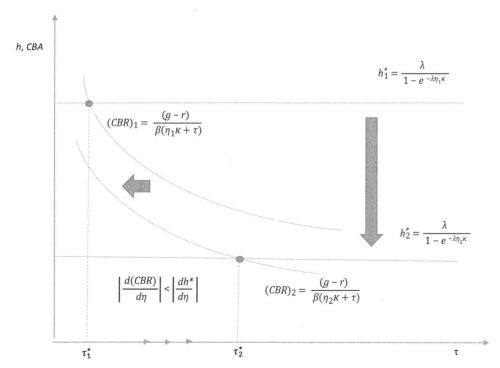

Figure 7.2: An Increase of η in an Endogenous Crash.

at τ_1^*. An increase of η will shift the hazard rate line downward $\left(\left.\dfrac{dh^*}{d\eta}\right. = -\dfrac{\kappa\lambda^2 e^{\lambda\kappa}}{\left(1-e^{-\lambda\eta\kappa}\right)^2} < 0 \quad \text{and}\right.$

simultaneously shift the CBR to the left $\left(\dfrac{dCBR}{d\eta} = -\dfrac{\kappa(g-r)}{\beta(\eta\kappa+\tau)^2}\right) < 0$. The validity of inequality

Eq. (7.8) assures that $\left|\dfrac{dCBR}{d\eta}\right| < \left|\dfrac{dh^*}{d\eta}\right|$. Hence, the new equilibrium date of the burst will be on the right of the old equilibrium.

In an analogous line of reasoning with the earlier proposition, an increase of the excess growth of the bubble $(g-r)$ would also delay the bursting date of the bubble increasing in this way its size. This may come as a result of an increase in the portion of the stock price not explained by its fair value g, and/or as a result of a decrease in the risk-free interest rate, r (see our discussion on the existence of high values of g in Section 7.2.1, and low values of r in the residential housing market and subprime mortgage market in the United States in Section 7.2.1) Consequently, proposition 2 follows.

Proposition 2

In an endogenous crash, an increase of the excess growth rate of the bubble $(g-r)$ increases the equilibrium bursting date of the bubble τ^*.

The proof of proposition 2 is analogous to proposition 1. Thus, $\dfrac{d\beta^*}{d(g-r)} = \dfrac{1-e^{-\lambda\eta\kappa}}{\lambda} > 0$. We

can also prove proposition 2 with the help of Fig. 7.2. The old equilibrium timing is at τ_1^* where the hazard rate h_1^* intercepts with the CBR_1 of attacking the bubble. An increase of the excess growth rate of the bubble $(g-r)$ due to an increase of g, and/or a reduction of r, will shift

the CBR_1 of attacking the bubble to the right (since $\dfrac{d(CBR)}{d(g+r)} = \dfrac{1}{\beta(\eta\kappa+\tau)} > 0$) as shown by

CBR_2. Since the hazard rate curve is unaffected by this change, the corresponding equilibrium bursting date of the bubble represented by τ_2^* will be on the right of the old one $\left(\tau_1^*\right)$ (Fig 7.3).

7.3 Conclusions

External factors can be responsible for initial overly optimistic asset evaluations as well as for the shocks that end the bubble. At the same time, bubbles are doomed from the very beginning even if there is no destructive shock to end it. Most importantly, bubbles formation, growth, and implosions need not rely solely on naïve or misinformed agents. Sophisticated investors willingly and knowingly participate in investment bubbles. Mass and ratio or informed to uninformed market participants change bubbles' magnitude, time to demise, compounding an impact any external factors may already have. Applying this model to the

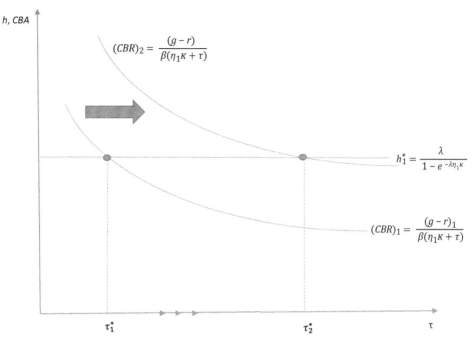

Figure 7.3: An Increase of g, and/or a Decrease of r in an Endogenous Crash.

most recent financial crisis, it is clear that increased complexity of financial instruments together with amplified global market participation have contributed significantly to external factors, such as erroneous asset evaluations and depressed interest rates.

In this chapter, we employ the AB model into the residential real estate market and the parallel subprime mortgage market bubbles in the United States. We show that if the bubble is created independently in an endogenous or exogenous way, the low interest rate regime, the homeownership culture of the irrational investors, the existence of many low quality mortgages issued by almost all financial institutions, that were able to diversify away the risk of volatile prices in the US residential real estate market (of course, helped from overvalued rating that these financial institutions received from ranking institutions), and the presence of high dispersion of opinions among rational investors played a vital part in the creation and development of the recent residential housing and subprime mortgage bubbles in the United States. We show that rational investors who became aware of the above bubbles at their early stages, such as Goldman Sachs, were able to effectively ride the bubbles. However, other rational investors, such as UBS or AIG to name a few, who got the timing of the subprime mortgage wrong due to becoming aware of the bubble at relatively latter stages, rode the bubble through the crash.

Clearly, the last bubble is not going to be the last bubble. Unfortunately, one never knows what next asset, or class of assets, will take on the reputation of a golden fleece or what asset manager is going to be the new King Midas. Since the average investor is not likely to be more informed it falls on funds managers, financial advisors, and regulators to blow a whistle before the next bubble grows too large. Unfortunately, the applications of the AB model in the residential housing market bubble in the United States that crashed in 2006, and the parallel subprime mortgage bubble that crashed in 2007 show that investors have a real interest to participate in the bubble and "ride the wave" even if they are well informed.

References

Abreu, D., Brunnermeier, M.K., 2003. Bubbles and crashes. Econometrica 71 (1), 173–204.

Avery, C., Zemsky, P., 1995. Multi-dimensional uncertainty and herd behavior in financial markets. Am. Econ. Rev. 88 (4), 724–748.

Bala, V., Goyal, S., 2000. A noncooperative model of network formation. Econometrica 68 (5), 1181–1231.

Bikhchandani, S., Hirshleifer, D., Welch, I., 1992. A theory of fads, fashion, custom and cultural change as informational cascades. J. Polit. Econ. 100 (5), 992–1026.

Blanchard, O., 1979. Speculative bubbles, crashes, and rational expectations. Econ. Lett. 3 (4), 387–389.

Blume, L., Easley, D., O'Hara, M., 1994. Market statistics and technical analysis: the role of volume. J. Finance 49 (1), 159–181.

Brunnermeier, M.K., 2009. Deciphering the liquidity and credit crunch of 2007–2008. J. Econ. Perspect. 23 (1), 77–100.

Brunnermeier, M.K., Julliard, C., 2008. Money illusion and housing frenzies. Rev. Finan. Studies 21 (1), 135–180.

Case, K.E., 2008. The central role of home prices in the current financial crises: how will the market clear? Brookings Pap. Econ. Act. 39 (2), 161–193.

Case, K.E., Shiller, Jr., R., 2003. Is there a bubble in the housing market? Brookings Pap. Econ. Act. 34 (2), 299–342.

Chamley, C., Gale, D., 1994. Information revelation and strategic delay in a model of investment. Econometrica 62 (5), 1065–1085.

Choi, J.P., 1997. Herd behavior, the 'penguin effect', and the suppression of informational diffusion: an analysis of informational externalities and payoff interdependency. Rand J. Econ. 28 (3), 407–425.

Coval, J., Jurek, J., Stafford, E., 2009. The economics of structured finance. J. Econ. Perspect. 23 (1), 3–25.

De Long, Jr., B., Scheilfer, A., Summers, L.H., Waldmann, Jr., R., 1990a. Noise trader risk in financial markets. J. Polit. Econ. 98 (4), 703–738.

De Long, Jr., B., Scheilfer, A., Summers, L.H., Waldmann, Jr., R., 1990b. Positive feedback investment strategies and destabilizing rational speculation. J. Finance 45 (2), 375–395.

Garber, P., 2016. Tulipmania. In: Jones, G. (Ed.), Banking Crises: Perspectives From the New Palgrave Dictionary. Palgrave Macmillan, New York, NY.

Geanakoplos, J., 1992. Common knowledge. J. Econ. Perspect. 6 (4), 53–82.

Helling, M., 1982. Rational expectations equilibrium with conditioning on past prices: a mean-variance example. J. Econ. Theory 26 (2), 279–312.

Kahneman, D., Tversky, A., 1979. Prospect theory: an analysis of decision under risk. Econometrica 47 (2), 263–292.

Keynes, J.M., 1936. The General Theory of Employment, Interest, and Money. McMillan, London.

Kindleberger, C.P., 1991. The economic crises of 1619–1623. J. Econ. Hist. 51 (1), 149–175.

Lewis, M., 2010. The Big Short, first ed. W. W. Norton, New York, NY.

Li, D.X., 2000. On default correlation: a Copula function approach. J. Fixed Income 9 (4), 43–54.

Morgenson, G., Rosner, Jr., 2011. Reckless Endangerment: How Outsized Ambition, Greed, and Corruption Led to Economic Armageddon. Times Books, Henry Holt, New York.

Nielsen, S., 2009. A game-theoretical analysis of price bubbles in financial markets. Student thesis, Aarhus University.

Peach, R., 2005. Is there a housing bubble? In: TIAA-CREF Report, Exchange: Ideas and Viewpoints. Which Direction Will Home Prices Take? TIAA-CREF, Summer 2005.

Reinhart, C.M., Rogoff, K., 2009. This Time is Different: Eight Centuries of Financial Folly, first ed. Princeton University Press, Princeton, NJ.

Sanders, S., 2007. Mortgage Guide. Available from: www.fhaloanpros.com/2007/10fha-mortgage-reformthanks-but-no-thanks-says-mba

Scheikman, J., Xong, W., 2003. Overconfidence and speculative bubbles. J. Polit. Econ. 111 (6), 1183–1219.

Scherbina, A., Schulsche, B., 2012. Asset bubbles: an application of residential real estate. Eur. Finan. Manag. 18 (3), 464–491.

Scherbina, A., Schulsche, B., 2014. Asset price bubbles: a survey. Quant. Finance 14 (4), 589–604.

Shefrin, H., Statman, M., 2011. Behavioral Finance in the Financial Crisis: Market Efficiency, Minsky, and Keynes. Santa Clara University, Mimeo.

Shiller, Jr., R., 1996. Speculative booms and crashes. In: Capie, F., Wood, G.E. (Eds.), Monetary Economics in the 1990s. McMillan, London, pp. 58–74.

Shiller, Jr., R., 2000. Irrational Exuberance, first ed. Princeton University Press, Princeton, NJ.

Shiller, R., Jr., 2005. Homes are a risky long-term investment. In: TIAA-CREF Report, Exchange: Ideas and Viewpoints. Which Direction Will Home Prices Take? TIAA-CREF, Summer 2005.

Shleifer, A., 2000. Inefficient Markets—An Introduction to Behavior Finance. Oxford University Press, Oxford.

The Economist, 2002. House prices going through the roof: the economist's new global house-price index confirms that spring is in the air. But will the housing boom in America, Britain and elsewhere end in a bust? The Economist print edition. Available from: www.economist.com/node/1057057/print

The Economist, 2003. House of cards: in many countries, the stock market bubble has been replaced by a property-price, bubble, sooner or later it will burst, says Pam Woodall, our economist, editor. The Economist print edition. Available from: www.economist.com/node/1794873/print

The Economist, 2005a. The global housing boom: in come the waves: The worldwide rise in housing prices is the biggest bubble in the history. Prepare for the economic pain when it pops. The Economist print edition. Available from: www.economist.com/node/4079027/print

The Economist, 2005. House prices after the fall: soaring housing prices have given a huge boost to the word economy. What happens when they drop? The Economist print edition. Available from: www.economist.com/node/4079458/print

Tversky, A., Kahneman, D., 1974. Judgement under uncertainty. Heuristics and biases. Science 185 (4157), 1124–1131.

Whittle, R., Davies, T., Gobey, M., Simister, Jr., 2014. Behavioral economics and house prices: a literature review. Bus. Manag. Horizons 2 (2), 15–28.

CHAPTER 8

The Similarities Between the Bulgarian Local Financial Crisis in 1997 and the Global Financial Crisis in 2008

Plamen Orecharski

University of National and World Economy, Sofia, Bulgaria

Chapter Outline

8.1 Introduction

Ten years before the collapse of financial markets, as a result of Lehman Brothers bankruptcy and the unfolding global financial crisis, quite identical financial disaster took place at a small and emerging market, such as Bulgarian. Due to the small size and peripheral location to global financial centers, this crisis was not spotted. A careful observation at its characteristics, undoubtedly reveals the similarities to the global crisis of 2007–08. The analysis of the prerequisites, main stages of development, the behavior of major market players, as well as the reactions of the wider investor audience shows a striking similarity.

Moreover, the conclusions taken out of the Bulgarian crisis last century largely cover the main conclusions widely discussed in the period after global crisis 2008.

In purely functional plan, modern financial instruments, such as Mortgage Backed Securities (MBS), Collateralized Debt Obligations (CDO), or the different credit derivatives, such as Credit Default swaps (CDS) were unknown to the Bulgarian financial market. They were barely introduced to the global markets during the 1990s of the last century. Essentially similar effects to those of the global financial crisis at the beginning of 21st century were achieved at Bulgarian local crisis only by the use of traditional financial instruments, without using innovative instruments of financial engineering. Impressive is the fact that some of the instruments used by the Bulgarian monetary and fiscal authorities were applied by the large and developed economies in an attempt to counteract the global financial crisis after 2008. Some solutions to mitigate or overcome the negative effects of the crisis in 1997 in Bulgaria proved to be quite successful. They can be identified as empirical tested tools and to serve as appropriate benchmarks in the search for better solutions to overcome the effects of future shocks and distortions in financial markets.

8.2 The Face of the Bulgarian Crisis

During the last months of 1996 and early 1997, in Bulgaria a large-scale monetary and financial crisis took place. It was the logical conclusion of inconsistently implied reforms in Bulgaria, started during the early 1990s of the last century and irrational behavior of the investors during this period, mainly influenced by the lack of sufficient knowledge and experience in terms of free-functioning financial markets. The main characteristics of the crisis were:

- Shocking devaluation of the Bulgarian national currency (BGN) and impairment over 10 times during short period of several months.
- Depletion of foreign currency reserves of the Bulgarian Central Bank (BNB) and inability to maintain stable exchange rate of the local currency.
- Falling into a liquidity failure of the banking system and subsequent bankruptcy of one-third of functioning commercial banks.
- Complete collapse in monetary and interbank markets and operations.
- Expanding the budget deficit to double digits figures, although greatly reduced public spending.
- Actual impossibility to "roll-over" domestic government debt, due to sharp decrease in the demand for treasury bills and bonds. Acquisition of treasury instrument from the

Bulgarian National Bank, in order to compensate for the lack of investor's interest and monetarization of the debt.

- Enormous difficulties in servicing external government debt and partial suspension of payments on it.
- Loss of confidence by the local investors in local currency, and in the banking and financial system as whole, consequently led to the outflow of deposits from the banking system and intensive transition to "dollar economy."
- Negative impact by the financial turbulence over the real economy and the economic downsize of about 10% annually.
- Political and governmental crisis which led to early parliamentary elections.

A general overview of the characteristics mentioned earlier, allows to highlight comparative lines to any typical financial crisis, with exceptions of some specifics arising from the condition of the Bulgarian financial sector during that period. It is completely understandable not so much by similarities of the fundamental factors in the particular situation of the financial markets in Bulgaria and other countries that have undergone severe distress, but mainly due to the similarities in perceptions and reactions of the investors. Despite persistent attempts by various analysts to impose local regional specificity, the reactions of investors in its core areas remain identical. In most parts, the highlights of the crisis are rather similar, than opposites.

Even general overview of the characteristics of the local Bulgarian crisis, are quite convincing to show us the similarities to the global financial crisis 2007–08. As mentioned earlier, these conclusions are not based on equal fundamental factors, but mainly due to investor' behavior of the local and developed global markets.

8.3 On the Edge of the Crisis

In the early 1990s of the last century, like other Eastern European countries part of the former Soviet Union, Bulgaria launched ambitious economic reforms toward the establishment of normal functioning of market economy and liberalization of financial markets. The processes were hampered by the collapse of former Yugoslavia on the one hand and a debt moratorium announced immediately after the collapse of the centralized type of economy on the other. These circumstances predetermined shortage of capital due to the inherited debt problems generated during reformation period and small interest demonstrated by potential foreign investor, due to the high levels of regional risk. The loss of traditional Eastern markets and underfunding resulted in large state manufacturing companies to prebankruptcy state, and in many cases to technical bankruptcy.

The development of the financial sector was also facing a series of challenges. Most emerging financial institutions, primarily banks did the subprime lending and speculative operations on the currency market. Therefore, their employees were rewarded with formal and informal bonuses without taking into account the risk profile of the concerned bank customer. It was a complete analogy with the statements of several executives of large investment banks during the hearing in front of the United States Congress committee after 2008, where they shared opinion about suspected low quality and high risk investment products (2008 Financial Crisis and the Federal Reserve, Day 1, Part 1) (2008 Financial Crisis, 2016). Main incentive were the existing system of operation and the solid bonuses offered. Securities markets were unregulated and developed spontaneously. They dominated operators with a tendency to develop speculative schemes known as "Ponzi." They offered the audience imitations of various types of equity or debt securities, which were considered very attractive by the small investors. Some commercial banks, although monitored by the banking supervision authorities, also applied controversial practices.

The supervisory authorities in the most developed markets were also unable to identify a high-risk profile and provide innovative investment instruments for the entire period from the beginning of the century until the 2007–08 year. Rating agencies awarded their highest ratings for the same type of securities. This environment created favorable conditions for expansions of the prerequisites of the global crisis.

On this background, the Bulgarian investment community should adopt a rather cautious behavior. Instead, we observed completely irrational tendency to financial optimism.

The initial effects of economic liberalization and the first successes in the financial operations generated strong and significantly overvalued confidence in the future upstream developments on financial markets. High, double-digit nominal interest rates and negative real ones confused depositors, as they were completely in charge of "money illusion." As the professional financial community and small investors perceived higher asset values to their appropriate market prices and at the same time underestimated the risks posed by unstable macroeconomic situation and the poor financial situation of companies in the real sector of the economy. The behavior of the global investment community in the precrisis year 2007–08 was not any different.

8.4 Investor Overconfidence

Often investor's overconfidence is the characteristic sign preceding each financial crisis. The situation before 1996–97 year in Bulgarian financial system and precrisis 2007–08 on global financial markets were very similar. Bulgarian investor community demonstrates overoptimism unrealistic and inflated expectations of their own investment decisions. Similarly, global investors perceived trends in financial markets. Bulgarian investors' confidence that the upward trend will continue indefinitely maintain the new local Bulgarian market for financial instruments at the end of the last century, as global investors admired mortgage-based instruments and credit derivatives on global markets at the beginning of this century.

As Bulgarian banking system before the local crisis and banks in developed markets before the global crisis generated plenty of lending, which further inflate asset prices. Rising asset prices created a "wealth effect" (Altissimo, 2005). It, in own terms, stimulate aggressive behavior of both investors and the general public and create conditions for increasing debt. Well-known fact before 2008, but similar was the Bulgarian economic reality in the mid-1990s of last century.

On the eve of the big local monetary and financial crisis Bulgarian investors believed in the limitless possibilities of the emerging private sector and magical qualities of financial instruments to generate money from money itself. Similarly, the global investment community in the wake of the collapse of the United States and other major financial markets, were convinced that this time is not within the scope of a large stock bubble. They believed that this time is different because of the new technologies, the development of financial engineering, and limitless possibilities of the insurance industry. It is essential to remember how glamorous looked investment world from just before the dot com crisis to the collapse of the US mortgage market in 2007. World driven by greed impatient and arrogant defense of the right of quick profits, that any comments for higher risk exposures are presented for outdated approach to understanding investment realities (Rapp, 2009).

Even evolved several relatively large scale of the Bulgarian market financial pyramids closely corresponding to the similar nature of Madoff's investment scheme, collapsed immediately after the peak of the global financial crisis in 2008 (Henriques, 2011).

It is true that in the initial period of economic reforms and modernization of the financial systems, majority of the Bulgarian audience had low financial knowledge even for traditional financial instruments. They were relatively new to the Bulgarian financial environment. This was one of the leading causes of good investor demand for high-risk and low-quality financial products.

The situation with the newly introduced collateralized debt obligations and new derivative instruments was very much alike on the global financial market (Allen, 2013). They were also new to the global investment community and helped to inflate the bubble of the US mortgage market, which quickly jumped over the American borders and covered virtually the rest of the World (Navarro, 2012).

The author of these comments back in 1995 already delivered a report to the Bulgarian banking community that contained warnings of the high risks in bank portfolios and some weaknesses in banking supervision. His conclusions and findings were underestimated. Similarly, the signals by the few analysts to some disturbing trends in global financial markets in the period before the 2007–08 year found no proper response among financial audiences (Rajan, 2005). In such conditions, financial crashes followed and led to the significant scars both for the Bulgarian market at the end of the last century and the global financial markets at the beginning of this century.

8.5 The Development of the Bulgarian Financial Crisis

On the eve of the local crisis Bulgarian commercial banks were heavily contaminated with loan portfolios, but it was not a barrier to continue to give out risky loans. On this basis, reporting high current profits at the expense of destroying the capital base of its institutions and paying disproportionately for Bulgarian standard large salaries and bonuses to employees and chairmen. Nonbank financial institutions continued to market the speculative and fraudulent nature tools in the absence of effective regulation of emerging capital markets. These tools were well received by the investment public.

The key reasons leading to the mismanagement of the global investment banking sector were indeed very similar to the one caused the Bulgarian financial crisis:- the bonus system for employees and management of the financial institutions and in particular the investment banking sector- Investment initiatives to acquire high level of Collateral debt obligations (CDO) and Credit default swaps (CDS), also correctly named afterwards "Toxic Assets" (Ferrell, O.C., Fraedrich, J. & Ferrell, L., 2010).

In this environment of high but unsustainable gains and total liquidity crisis in the financial system was needed a spark to kindle the fire of crisis. Such was relatively unexpected bankruptcy of two of the largest commercial banks in mid-1996, by analogy, the signal sent to the global investor community collapse of Bear Stearns in the first half of 2008 (Greenberg and Singer, 2010). However, local investor audience was only shaken, but not determined to withdraw from the market of financial products. As well as global investors continued to believe that the crisis will remain local, within the US financial system and limited in scale. Additional pressure brought depletion of foreign exchange reserves of the Bulgarian National Bank as a result of payments on the foreign debt, and due to constant refinacing of troubled commercial banks. So the autumn of 1996 left the exchange rate trend, by which it moved in recent months and took over direction of accelerating depreciation. The signal was even more pronounced and financial audiences started to taste the looming financial disaster. The reactions were immediate—both large and small investors changed their expositions from local currency to more secured positions in USD and German Deutschmark (DEM) (by that time both currency were considered with high degree of consumer trust). The distrust in the local currency was quickly combined with the distrust in local financial institutions, including commercial banks. The trend of outflows of deposits and capital outside of Bulgaria was instantly formed (current currency regime was not particularly strict) or so called "treasury" of savings of the smallest investors occurred. The banking system fell another shock—mass withdrawals of deposits.

The Central Bank has taken disciplinary measures and strongly restrict the refinacing of commercial banks in an attempt to stabilize accelerating devaluation of the local currency. Followed the failure of a whole group of commercial banks, including such systemic importance to the financial system. Nothing could prevent the total collapse of local financial markets.

In the same way, the bankruptcy of Lehman Brothers was the last negative signal that accelerated the global financial crash in September 2008 (Dillian, 2012).

8.5.1 Dramatic Devaluation of the Local Currency

As noted, one of the visible signs of the biggest financial crisis in Bulgaria by the end of the last century was the dramatic devaluation of the local currency—probably the only manifestation that has no analogs in the global financial crisis of 2007–08 years. The reasons are obvious to any attempt to seek an analogy between local and global crises—the second is not characterized by large currency fluctuations. The growing distrust in local currency escalated for several reasons. More early stages of acceleration of depreciation was greeted by investors with a gradual dollarization and currency conversion in foreign currency positions.

The trend was reinforced due to the ongoing parallel destruction of confidence in the banking system and shaped the process of withdrawal of deposits out of commercial banks. Due to the limited size of capital markets, savings turned to the foreign exchange market. For multiple deadlines, whole economy was dollarized. At the end of 1996 and beginning of 1997, the pace of devaluation gained acceleration so that within some days the depreciation of the local currency was measured by tens of percentage. For a short period, this process came closer to the familiar hyperinflation of the early 1920s in Weimar Germany[1] (Anon, 2012).

Calm down of the dynamics of the exchange rate occur was fairly unexpected. At the height of the financial crisis, when it became political, with the resignation of the government and announcements for developed and adopted stabilization measures, including the adoption of a fixed exchange rate known as the introduction of currency board, the local currency was even recovered, and returned to the levels that financial audiences perceived as a long overcome. In this case, there were no fundamental factors affecting the reverse dynamic behavior of the exchange rate. Foreign exchange reserves of the country continued to be at the lowest level in recent years, and banks continued to hold high level of nonperforming loan, but the audience could see good prospects. The normalization of the exchange rate behavior in local currency happened only because the fundamental change in expectations of general investors in terms of future equilibrium level of the exchange rate in the local currency.

8.5.2 The Behavior of Commercial Banks

Local financial crisis in Bulgaria by the end of the last century manifest a certain extent and banking crisis. Within a few months one-third of functioning commercial banks went into bankruptcy and credit markets. Even with the adoption of a more restrictive

---

[1] Hyperinflation of the early 1920s of the last century is presented in a remarkable way by Erich Maria Remarque in "Black Obelisk" and it remains one of the most convincing descriptions of a similar process, although only in a literary form.

policy on refinancing by the Central Bank, commercial banks have sharply reduced their lending activity. This practical was frozen immediately after the announcement of a dozen commercial banks insolvent. Hindering their access to the resources of the Central Bank in relation to the ongoing contraction of its deposit base and the apparent onset of the economic recession do not allow any other type of behavior.

Interbank markets virtually ceased to function. Commercial banks corresponded with the Central Bank in managing their liquidity. Trust between them was completely destroyed.

Rumors, which bank will be closed, next spread not only among small investors, but in the professional banker circles, as far as most banks were heavily contaminated with portfolios of nonperforming and/or under watched loans. Central Bank and representatives of government were forced to make statements that do not outline new bank failures to restore the shaken confidence in the banking system. Quite identical reactions were of European banks in the period after the bankruptcy of Lehman Brothers. They sharply restricted their lending activity. Management of their liquidity shifted from interbank markets to the European Central Bank (ECB), at least for the large commercial banks.

ECB governor and Government leaders of the Eurozone countries made similar statements that they will not allow the bankruptcy of another systemic bank like the case of Lehman Brothers.

Finance ministers of the member states at the October ECOFIN meeting in 2008 (Council, 2008) discussed and approved the decision to increase the threshold of guaranteed deposits initially to EUR 50,000, and next year this minimum guarantee deposit was increased to EUR 100,000. The aim was to bring peace among bank depositors and to prevent further outflow of resources from commercial banks, as well as to avoid arbitration of deposits between commercial banks from different countries due to different levels of deposit protection. Of course, the conclusions of this parallel between the reactions of the audience and the investment banking institutions in a purely local crisis in a small Bulgarian economy and the global financial crisis of 2007–08 year are not surprising. They only show that despite various fundamental factors in both cases, the behavioral responses of both institutional and personal investors of small and large markets are too identical.

8.5.3 Experiment with Index-Linked Bonds

In an attempt to offer an alternative investment for small investors, Bulgarian Treasury (at the time the author led this department in the Ministry of Finance) issued a 1-year government bond index clause. The debate on the index were focused on the US dollar as acceptable and most often applied in such cases benchmark. The objective was to return the outflowing from banks local currency and bring it back in circulation by offering the most secure tool— government securities with dollar clause protecting investors from the ongoing depreciation of the local currency.

However, the choice departs toward the dynamics of consumer prices, instead of the US dollar in the role of an index. The arguments focused on the reluctance to signal small investors that the US dollar is the anchor of last resort, which perceive the official Bulgarian financial institutions. Investor audience took a highly positive this instrument. The index bonds were the only financial instrument in local currency that was demanded on the market.Perhaps, if one year term bond with the dollar index clause was selected, the same audience directly would prefer to directly go to the currency market and invest in USD. That would have additionally lead to higher demand for USD and consequently undermine the measure itself.

8.5.4 Rollover of Domestic Debt

One of the biggest challenges during the development of the Bulgarian financial crisis in 1996–97 was to roll over the domestic debt denominated in local currency. The development of the economic and financial situation in Bulgaria in the months before the sharpest stages of the financial crisis of 1996–97 bode recent suspension of service on domestic government debt. The same has gained speed in the previous few years as a result of large budget deficits, nationalization of deficits in corporate sector, and financing of foreign debt payments at the expense of issues of domestic financial markets. Although its size has not exceeded that of foreign debt, the limited liquidity of domestic financial markets hampered its normal servicing even before the crisis. Additional problems came along several lines. Accelerating devaluation of the local currency and increased inflationary pressures shorten the investment horizons to a few weeks. The general macroeconomic uncertainty and unpredictability of the trend movement in key macroeconomic indicators, also were factors forcing the investors to look only for short term investment instruments. Increased basic interest rate of the Central Bank to 300% on simple annual basis in order to stabilize the national currency sharply raised interest payments, as far as the vast majority of domestic bonds were issued with floating interest coupons. In these conditions, the interest of financial institutions at the primary auctions of government securities faded completely. Outlined a new risk—a moratorium on domestic government debt and practical disintegration of the financial system. In these conditions, Bulgarian Treasury amend in its issuance policy. In the first stage were harmonized maturities of government securities in accordance with the weekly calendar of primary auctions—3-month Treasury bills agreed maturity of 91 days, 6 month—182 days, and annual—364 days. This new type of calendar and specific maturity of the treasury bonds, ensured that on the maturity date of any old government instrument, a new one was issued, allowing smooth transition. Facility for commercial banks— the main holders of domestic government debt at that time apparently attracted high demand for new treasury instruments at the primary market.

However, when investment horizons shrank to a month, as mentioned already, the demand for government securities again shrank dramatically. Then 7 and 28 days treasury bills were introduced and issuing of bonds with longer maturities was stopped. The issue calendar of Treasury became daily, and the Central Bank closed the open market, that is, stop short

REPOs (Repurchase Agreement). So, Treasury took over the functions of the regulator liquidity of financial institutions in the money markets, while keeping all free liquidity. Commercial banks received daily liquidity from maturing Treasury securities at the same time and were able to use free liquidity and direct it toward new daily issues by Treasury. The new system introduced by the Ministry of Finance gave an extra dose liquidity of treasury instruments and partially regained investor confidence.

In the most critical moments, in terms of rollover of the domestic government debt, the Central Bank was buying unrealized volumes of Treasury securities in the primary market. The earlier mentioned market innovations treasury instruments have helped to rollover debt without the same can be monetized substantially. Support from the Central Bank in emissions of Treasury securities gave additional dose of tranquility as primary dealers, and all holders of government debt and stabilize the demand for instruments treasure. As a result, Bulgarian monetary and financial crisis was one of the few of this type in which servicing of domestic debt was stopped. The reputation of central institutions was protected and investor confidence in the ability of monetary and fiscal authorities to manage the financial system in crisis situations was restored.

Going back to the debt crisis in the Eurozone a few years ago will find that it emerged and evolved under similar circumstances. The most significant of them was incurred distrust among the investment community in the ability of several European countries on the southern periphery to serve their public debt. The hesitation of the ECB policy at first, which did not give clear signals that will support these countries in their efforts to deal with debt problems also helped.

Countries whose treasury bonds were bought by the ECB eventually able to scroll their debts and avoid disruptions in economic development. Investors continued to buy their bonds not because they were convinced of their fiscal capacity to implement seamless payments on debt instruments, but because they believed that the ECB will intervene and will not allow insolvency of those countries (Sinn, 2014).

Ultimately, the adoption of a more interventionist policy by the ECB preserve financial stability in the Eurozone and prevent euro crashes itself as a collective currency. Conversely, if the ECB had continued with its initial conservative line in terms of market interventions of government debt, threats to the Eurozone came not by fundamental factors, but form lack of sufficient confidence of investors in the determination of the ECB to protect by unambiguous manner the euro itself.

8.5.5 Why was it Important to Serve the Domestic Debt?

Looking at the assets of the commercial banks during the crisis showed that possible moratorium on the domestic debt repayments will impact most negatively on the banks with the largest share of the attracted personal savings. (*At that point, the guarantee of deposit was not yet implemented even for the smallest amounts and the whole impact would have rebounded on the State treasury.*) For instance, one of the commercial banks that had attracted more than 50% of all personal savings, had invested three-fourth of its assets in Government bonds. Each suspension of the repayments lead by the State Treasury meant bankruptcy for the earlier mentioned bank or blocking of the deposits of small investors. Allowing such a scenario would have destroyed the residual amount of trust in the central institutions and the recovery period would have been extended indefinitely. Considering the earlier scenario, the efforts to collateralize the roll-out of the internal government debt were worth it—this roll-out kept the trust of the small investors in the institutions and made possible fast economical and financial recovery.

Similar was the sought effect of the insistence of the ECB in front of the State Member leaders not to allow the bankruptcy of any of the banks in the Eurozone after the bankruptcy of Lehman Brothers (Varoufakis et al., 2011). The concerns of the ECB were reasonable. In case of bankruptcy of any bank in the Eurozone, the quake would have been vast and the consequences for the whole financial system would have been unpredictable.

8.6 The Recovery of the Trust in the Financial System

The Bulgarian crisis from the end of the last century is characterized with one more relatively rare achievement—recovery within several months. At the beginning of 1997, the crisis was at its peak while in the middle of the same year the situation looked completely different in terms of fast stabilization of the overall macroeconomic and financial situation. The main prerequisites can be grouped as follows:

- Successful overcome of the political crisis, a rapid change in the government and the scheduling of new parliamentary elections.
- Adopted decision of introduction of Currency board and fixing of the exchange rate pegged to the German mark.
- Reasonable and in some aspects, innovative monetary and fiscal politics in the period until the stabilization of the Currency board.

Key role in all of the three factors outlined earlier, played by the behavioral reaction of the institutional and personal investors as well as the recovered trust in the capability of the central monetary and fiscal authorities to proceed with the reforms of the financial system and to maintain under control the risks related to postcrisis recovery. Moreover in mid-1997, the fundamental factors were in worse condition compared to the economic situation a year earlier. The public perceptions though were changed. Expectations of fast recovery and development were formed after the crisis based on decisiveness in the society for cardinal economic reforms. This had an impact and the stability of the financial system was achieved in unexpectedly short period.

Among the most important factors for the rapid restoration of the public trust and the establishment of macroeconomic balance was the expectation of the fixing of the exchange rate. Without being officially announced, in the minds of the investment community was layered expectation of a certain level around which the exchange rate was established on the market until actual introduction of the Currency board. This played the role of informational quantitative anchor (Shleifer, 2000; Kuhnlenz, 2014) which gave confidence to the investors and blocked the speculative attacks on the current exchange rate of the local currency.

8.6.1 Overcoming of the Political Crisis

As a consequence of the shocking devaluation of the national currency, high inflationary pressures, real decrease of the income, and loss of the savings in the bankrupt banks, broad public dissatisfaction to the actions of the Government and the Central Bank was formed. The public unrest in front of the Parliament was the expression of the earlier situation. The negative public attitude made the Government to resign, the Parliament to dissolve, and the scheduling of new parliamentary elections. Temporary Government was formed, headed by the mayor of the capital, popular at this time. This Government invalidated the negative public attitude. There were no negative regard arising from the past toward it and due to temporary character, it did not concentrate any aspirations for the future except for the hopes of current stabilization. In 3 months, a regular Government was chosen from the central-right wing party that won the parliamentary majority from the elections.

By itself, the change of the Government in the midst of the crisis responded to the changed public attitudes and expectations which was an important prerequisite for the recovery of the investors' trust.

Although there cannot be complete comparison, parts of the political situation in Bulgaria during the crisis resembled the change in the President administration in the United State of America immediately after the spread of the crisis in year 2007–08. The dissatisfaction of the broad US audience was concentrated in its major part toward the financial institutions on Wall Street, not toward the political structure (Carother, 2015). Despite that, the similarity in the periods of incorporating stabilization procedures and the election of new president was favorable in terms of the perceptions and attitude of the broad audience as well as the investors community.

8.6.2 New Monetary Regime and Regulations

In the years prior to the Bulgarian monetary and financial crisis in years 1996–97, perceptions toward the negative role of the Central Bank politics regarding refinancing of the commercial banks and governmental budgets were displayed publicly. Indeed, in the portfolio of the Central Bank, the receivables from the commercial banks increased at an accelerated pace. The bank was also buying Treasury bonds mainly from the financial markets, but also occasionally directly from the primary auctions of the treasury instruments. Analytical comments explained to the investing public that the relatively high inflation and the volatility of key macroeconomic variables is due to this exact unreasonable politic of the Central Bank. The critical assessments deepened in the midst of the crisis.

In this environment, not only the investors' community but also the broad public welcomed the announced decisions for restructuring of the overall operations of the Central Bank, the bank to begin to function on the basis of Currency board and to improve the administrative and functional capacity of the banking supervision.

The introduction of the Currency board cannot be assessed unambiguously. From one side, the rejection of a proactive monetary politics denies the central authorities an effective tool to manage the economic cycle. The fixed exchange rate of the local currency adversely affects the competitiveness of the Bulgarian export and implies increase of the current account deficit of the balance of payments. On the other hand, the automation of the money supply ensured by the Currency board is a barrier against the continuation of the adopted bad practice to refinance commercial banks under speculative corporate pressure and deficits of the governmental budgets in order to serve political considerations. The fixing of the exchange rate of the local currency serves as the anchor for all remaining macroeconomical variables and stabilizes the overall financial system and macroeconomical framework. The level of predictability of the economy increases and the investment horizons extend.

In a situation of negative sentiment layered into the public against the bad policy of the Central Bank until the period of the crisis, the perception of the investors' community on the positives of the forthcoming introduction of the Currency board and the oblivion of the negatives, were quite understandable. This contributed to the rapid restoration of the confidence in the financial system and the national currency. The decisions to strengthen the Banking supervision based on review and improvement of the legislative and regulatory framework received additional approval as well.

New laws regulating the activities of both the Central Bank and commercial banks were introduced. The independence of the Central Bank was strengthened. The responsibility of the managers was increased and the bad practice to hand out unsecured loans was criminalized. The regulations on the stock markets and their supervision improved.

In late 2008, after the shock of the bankruptcy of Lehman Brothers on the financial market, most frequently mentioned measures to overcome the global economic and financial crisis were new architecture of financial markets and institutions and more robust regulations of the financial markets. They went into the programs and discussions and into the meetings of the G20. Both in the United States and European Union, the legislative and regulatory framework were improved, new institutions with supervisory functions were created, and the existing ones were strengthened (G20, 2008).

8.6.3 Monetization of the Sovereign Debt—The Role of Psychological Perceptions

In the course of the preparation for the introduction of the Currency board lasting several months specially designed and quite unusual recovery plan for the financial markets and the investor confidence in them, was applied.

The basis of the plan was the refinancing of the Ministry of Finance by the Central Bank up to the amount of maturing government securities in the domestic public debt and the acquiring of government bonds from the secondary market by the Central Bank. This measure is twofold.

On one hand, the financial system is loaded with liquidity in local currency, which was necessary after the shocking devaluation in the midst of the already mastered financial crisis. The commercial banks received additional liquidity through the purchases of longer-term government securities from their portfolios by the Central Bank.

On the other hand, the abundant refinancing of maturing government securities by the Central Bank and the purchases of such securities from the secondary market allowed for the vast majority of domestic government debt to concentrate in the portfolio of the Central Bank. In practice, the internal government debt was transformed from receivables of the commercial banks from the Government to receivables of the Central Bank by the Government. The further idea was that this same government debt to be cancelled in the transformation of the Central Bank into a Currency board.

In this way, in mid-1997 the closing balance sheet of the Central Bank was prepared and the next day a new institution, in its essence, was launched. It comes back to a Central Bank, but functioning on the principles of Currency Board. In the peculiar transformation of the Central Bank, an exchange of assets and liabilities between it and the Ministry of Finance, was realized. All receivables of the Central Bank from the government in the form of government securities and direct credit lines were cancelled in exchange for the transfer of the Ministry of Finance of all liabilities of the Bank to the International Monetary Fund and additional equalizing exchange of assets. As a result, the domestic government debt was reduced to minimum levels at the start of the new monetary regime—a prerequisite for a more streamlined issuance policy of the Government of the domestic financial and capital markets in the subsequent period of sustained recovery of the macroeconomic and financial stability. It was only a first step toward the subsequent extremely prudent fiscal and, in particular, debt policy, leading to a reduction of government debt of over 120% of GDP in the commented 1997 to 14% of GDP in 2008.

And so, from the early to mid-1997, the Bulgarian Central Bank was purposefully purchasing Government bonds and refinancing the Ministry of Finance on the payment of maturing ones. An absolutely unacceptable practice in a normal economic environment. However, in the situation of a postcrisis recovery, this measure definitely had a positive role.

At the same time, the actions of the central monetary and fiscal authorities did not receive wide publicity. The investment community remained with the perceptions from the originally announced plan for economic stabilization. One of the leading measures was suspending the practice of the Central Bank to refinance government spending on any occasion. Even professional observers commented publicly that the basis of the rapid macroeconomic and financial stabilization is the refusal of the Central Bank to finance the Ministry of Finance. Notable analyzes and conclusions with one flow though—they were based on inaccurate facts.

In fact, the relatively rapid stabilization of the economic and financial environment actually had in its basis the belief of both the investors and the general public that the Central Bank no longer is going to refinance the Government. This happened only after mid-1997 with the introduction of the Currency board. If the developed and implemented recovery plan with measures based on which the Central Bank continued to refinance Ministry of Finance for several more months, was made public than most likely the investors would deepen their distrust of the actions of the central institutions and the recovery would be postponed for an indefinite period time, with all the negatives of that transparency.

The direct or indirect financing from the Central Bank to ease the efforts of the Government in repayment of its debt is not considered conventional tool of the monetary policy. The resulting monetization of the government debt or the noise of "printing presses" was never favored by the economic analysts. The author of these comments included the measure in the recovery plan in 1997 being fully aware of it, but also of the goals pursued in that period. Even he didn't think though that a little more than 10 years later, in the midst of the debt crisis in the Eurozone, the purchase of government bonds by the ECB would be the most effective rescue measure to tackle the crisis and the only tool to regain the confidence of the investment community in the creditworthiness of the issuers of sovereign debt of southern European periphery (Richardson and Richardson, 2015).

8.6.4 Market Interest Rates—The Role of the Arbitration

In the beginning of 1997, one of the numerous challenges for the economic and financial recovery was the excessively high interest rates. The basic monthly interest rate of the Central Bank was 18%—a result of its interest policy during the crisis. A transition to a market determination of interest rates in the economy was expected, as the upcoming Currency board did not have any functions regarding the determination of the interest rates.

Discussions on the necessary market interest base ended in favor of the 3 months Treasury bill's yield. This segment of the financial market was the most profound and its interest rates were comparatively the most representative ones, as the money markets did not function and operations were sporadic.

With the initially set double digit monthly interest rates, the market mechanisms did not predict the rapid decrease of the short-term treasury bills' yield. The primary dealers with governmental securities continued to require a high yield despite the achieved consistency of the exchange rate and the announcement that it will be fixed close to the current levels. The Baltic and the Argentinean experience showed that these economies reached single digit interest rates between the first and the second year after the introduction of the Currency board in their countries.

The interest rates in the Bulgarian financial system were focused around the three-month treasury bonds yields. The bonds were focused on the similar, in terms of maturity, German treasury bonds with relatively low spread above them. This spread was considerably lower compared to the perceptions for the Bulgarian country risk.

Financial operators saw excellent arbitration opportunities. Combining the purchase of long-term treasury instruments together with currency forward contracts, they managed to fix a huge, very low risk yield. The Public treasury's response was identical to the one of the arbitration operations, but in the other direction. Making use of the official external funding and delaying part of the public expenses, the Public treasury abruptly reduced the number of offered issues of treasury instruments of the primary auctions. In the same time, the orders of the primary dealers that had aggressively low prices with huge average deviations, were rejected. As a result, the reference interest rate was considerably reduced in just couple of weeks. This trend continued up until the middle of the year when the Currency board was introduced with single digit annual interest rates. In this way one of the main risk factors—the high basic interest rates—was successfully overcome. In the beginning of the new monetary regime, the yield of the Bulgarian Treasury bonds was oriented around the yield of the German Treasury bonds with higher spread corresponding with the higher country risk.

Immediately after the onset of the crisis in 2007–08 year, the central banks of the developed financial centers drastically reduced the reference interest rates. Of course, they did it in a conventional way without the need for more complex management schemes, but the sought final effect was identical—counteracting cooled economic environment and quicker overcoming of the economic recession (The Economist, 2013).

8.6.5 To Prudent Fiscal Policies After a Crisis

Bulgarian financial crisis was not the result of irresponsible fiscal policy, or at least fiscal policy was not the leading factor in the collapse of the financial sector. Although in previous years, government budgets had deficit, the accumulated public debt was mainly due to budgetary interventions to support the banking sector.

The monetary and financial crisis sent a strong signal in the direction of keeping a prudent fiscal policy, not only to the management elite, but also to society. Both local and foreign investors welcomed the lowest budget deficits after the crisis of 1996–97. This policy continued in the beginning of this century. Moreover, during the credit boom prior to the global crisis of 2007–08 fiscal year, Bulgarian policy was used as a counter-cyclical tool. Thus, for the period 2005–08 year, the Bulgarian government budget had surpluses ranging from 3% to 3.6% for each of the 4 years. Perhaps this is a kind of world record for a country that is not dependent on oil or other deposits. The memory of the devastating crisis had made so that the political and managerial elite strictly followed the rules for keeping prudent public finances and the general public relatively uncritically accepted this type of fiscal policy.

After the devastating global crisis of 2007–08 year, we have seen calls for fiscal consolidation not just within the Eurozone, but the entire European Union. Repeatedly changed fiscal pact aimed to discipline public finances across the European Union. Although any similar regulation has its shortcomings and risks, efforts to consolidate public finances were welcomed by the global investor community and helped to restore confidence in credibility of European issuers of sovereign debt (Ubillos, 2013).

8.6.6 Impulses for Structural Actions

Any financial crisis discloses functional and/or institutional asymmetries in the economy and requires structural action to achieve a sustainable recovery and economic growth. This was the case with the Bulgarian financial crisis of 1996–97, as well as with the global financial crisis in 2007–08 year.

One of the most important conclusions from the Bulgarian financial crisis was not only the need for fiscal consolidation, but clearly outlined the need for deeper structural reforms—economic restructuring, accelerating the unfinished privatization of state assets, streamlining of the government spending, modernizing the field of public works and services. In the period after the crisis, governments focused their efforts in these areas. Initially, we witnessed a more targeted activity. Largely this was dictated by the behavior of local and foreign investors, who made similar recommendations to the government of the country.

With the passing of the crisis and the entry of economic development in a more normal mainstream, structural actions weakened. The period of accelerated economic growth as a result of the global credit boom of the early years of the century to 2008 quite blunt the impulses to reform the economic and social sphere. Therefore, the Bulgarian economy was not strong enough to meet the challenges of the global crisis. The consequences of that were mitigated only by the strong precrisis fiscal position of the country.

Not a small part of the European economies, especially those from the southern periphery, found themselves in a similar situation after the global crisis of 2007–08 year. In the ensuing, great recession investors have clearly stated the need for structural adjustments in these countries by refusing to accept their sovereign debt.

In terms of the constricted economic activity and decreasing budget revenues, most European economies did not show enough flexibility in terms of public spending and worryingly increased their fiscal deficits. Markets, however, showed no previous inclination to fund them and thus shape the debt crisis in the Euro Zone. In order not to fall into insolvency, these countries enjoyed official financing (by the EC and the IMF, or only by the EC), which was packed with programs for economic reforms. A typical example of this was Greece. Caught in the debt trap and loitering of any structural measures in the beginning, Greece has not yet recovered its economy, despite the partially accepted structural measures. Other countries had more progress, but generally none reorganized their economy and public sphere to the extent that would make them more competitive.

8.7 Conclusions

Reviewing the Bulgarian monetary and financial crisis of 1996–97 showed a lot of fragments all seen in more recent global crisis that began in the 2007–08 year. This was not so much in the specific mechanisms and even less in financial instruments. Rather, the similarities are emerging in the behavior of both investors and the general public, and to a certain extent of the key players from the financial sector.

Despite the perfectly various financial instruments that operators used during both crises, the final effects are strikingly identical—on the eve of crises portfolios of both Bulgarian banks and the large cross-border financial conglomerates are filled with bad, toxic assets. In the previous period, the main culprits for the deterioration of portfolio exposures are generously rewarded with bonuses for temporary profits. In both observed crises investors were overly optimistic, willingly take risks that in normal conditions could be identified without great effort and are not willing to accept any warning signals.

In the period preceding the local Bulgarian crisis and the global crisis pyramid scheme type "Ponzi" were developed—a sure sign that the greed of the investment public is dulled their risk tolerance and one of the indirect signs that the assets are overvalued. Investors have similar preferences in Bulgarian public debt and sovereign debt of European countries to support the same from the Bulgarian National Bank, respectively the ECB. Restoring investor confidence in debt markets in both crises occurs when the relevant central banks submit clear signals that support the efforts of issuers play through their debts. The preferences of investors in Bulgarian public debt and sovereign debt of European countries are very similar and aim at supporting the same from the Bulgarian National Bank, respectively the ECB. Restoring investor confidence in debt markets in both crises occurred when the relevant central banks submitted clear signals that support the efforts of issuers to rollover their debts.

Strengthening of the regulations was the natural reaction of the authorities and after the local crisis in Bulgaria, as well as the global crisis in developed economies. Such were the expectations of investors and the general public. Another illustration was the change in the sociopolitical attitudes in Bulgaria and in the countries that were hit the hardest by the global financial crisis. The two crises—local Bulgarian crisis since the end of last century and the global crisis since the beginning of this century sent strong signals to the authorities on the need for fiscal consolidation and structural actions. The first signal for disciplining public finances played a role and the fiscal position of Bulgaria and the other affected countries by the global crisis was tightened. The main contribution to this process, however, belongs to the investors whose impact was more effective—demand for sovereign bonds issued by the governments of these countries. The second signal, however, was not supported by effective pressure from the investment community—it just does not have the tools to put such pressure. Therefore, this signal continues to be underestimated, probably until the next crisis.

During the local Bulgarian crisis, local analysts commented on it as a result of immaturity of development and the absence of necessary experience in managers in the private sector and in senior government administrators to conduct prudent policies. One of the explanations was the delay in deregulation and in the process of establishing neoliberal norms of behavior. There was criticism for some of the measures of the central fiscal and monetary authorities from positions of pure market mechanisms and naive behavior of investors.

Ten years later, the global crisis of 2007–08 year convinced us that "overdevelopment" of financial markets and excessive experience of managers from the private sector could also lead to failures. Apparently it became that deregulation and neoliberalism are the basis of financial disaster. Faithful libertarians of the 1990's watched with astonishment how in the most liberal economies—the United States and old Europe—private companies with centuries of history have been nationalized and how under the slogan of "quantitative easing" colossal amount of money was printed. It turned out that global investors were no less naive than those in less developed and undeveloped markets such as the Bulgarian at the end of last century.

References

2008 Financial Crisis, 2016. 2008 Financial Crisis and the Federal Reserve, Day 1, Part 1, C-SPAN, Available from: https://www.c-span.org/video/?292886-1/2008-financial-crisis-federal-reserve-day-1-part-1

Allen, L., 2013. The global economic crisis: a chronology. Reaktion Books, London.

Altissimo, F., 2005. Wealth and asset price effects on economic activity, Frankfurt am Main: European Central Bank.

Anon, 2012. Hyperinflation in the Weimar Republic, Betascript Publishing.

Carother, T., 2015. The Complexities of Global Protests. Available from: http://carnegieendowment.org/2015/10/08/complexities-of-global-protests-pub-61537

Council, 2008. Council Conclusions on a coordinated EU response to the economic slowdown. Available from: http://www.consilium.europa.eu/ueDocs/cms_Data/docs/pressData/en/ecofin/103203.pdf

Dillian, J., 2012. Street Freak: A Memoir of Money and Madness. Simon & Schuster, New York.

Ferrell, O.C., Fraedrich, J., Ferrell, L., 2010. Business Ethics: Ethical Decision Making and Cases: 2009 Update. South-Western Cengage Learning, Mason, OH.

G20, 2008. Declaration of the Summit on Financial Markets and the World Economy November 15, 2008, Washington DC. Available from: http://www.un.org/ga/president/63/commission/declarationg20.pdf

Greenberg, A.C., Singer, M., 2010. The Rise and Fall of Bear Stearns. Simon & Schuster, New York.

Henriques, D.B., 2011. The Wizard of Lies: Bernie Madoff and the Death of Trust. Times BOOKS/Henry Holt, New York.

Navarro, A., 2012. Global Capitalist Crisis and the Second Great Depression: Egalitarian Systemic Models for Change. Lexington, Lanham.

Rajan, R., 2005. Has financial development made the world riskier? Working Paper 11728. Available from: http://www.nber.org/papers/w11728

Rapp, D., 2009. Bubbles, Booms, and Busts: The Rise and Fall of Financial Assets. Copernicus Books, New York, NY.

Richardson, J.J., Richardson, J., 2015. Constructing a policy-making state? Policy dynamics in the EU. Oxford University Press, Oxford.

Shleifer, A., 2000. Inefficient Markets. An Introduction to Behavioral Finance. Oxford University Press, Oxford.

Sinn, H.-W., 2014. The Euro Trap: On Bursting Bubbles, Budgets, and Beliefs. Oxford University Press, Oxford.

Kuhnlenz, S., 2014. Economic Bubbles: A Story of New Eras, Emotional Contagion and Structural Support, Anchor Academic Publishing.

The Economist, 2013. Six years of low interest rates in search of some growth. Available from: http://www.economist.com/news/briefing/21575773-central-banks-have-cushioned-developed-worlds-economy-difficult-period-they-have-yet

Ubillos, J.B., 2013. The Economic Crisis and Governance in the European Union: A Critical Assessment. Routledge, Abingdon, Oxon.

Varoufakis, Y., Halevi, J., Theocarakis, N., 2011. Modern Political Economics: Making Sense of the Post-2008 World. Routledge, Abingdon, Oxon.

Empirical Evidence on Investors' Behaviour During Financial Crises

CHAPTER 9

Herding, Volatility, and Market Stress in the Spanish Stock Market

Natividad Blasco*, Pilar Corredor**, Sandra Ferreruela*

*University of Zaragoza, Zaragoza, Spain; **Public University of Navarre, Pamplona, Spain

Chapter Outline

9.1 Introduction

The existence of collective phenomena, such as herding (Shefrin, 2000; Thaler, 1991) can be studied in the framework of investor behavior in financial markets. This area of finance suggests that stock prices are not the only relevant information in the market. Broader shades of meaning can therefore be applied to the usual definition of market efficiency within a bounded rationality paradigm.

Herding occurs in a market when investors opt to imitate the observed decisions of other agents in the market, who they supposed to be better informed, instead of following their own information and beliefs. Avgouleas (2010) says that herding also means that disclosed information is ignored in favor of the safer "follow the herd" strategy. Thus, herding places a very powerful limitation on what are usually considered to be rational reactions to all kinds of disclosed information. The main causes for herding suggested in the literature to date are imperfect information (Chari and Kehoe, 2003; Puckett and Yan, 2008), reputation (Trueman, 1994), and compensation schemes (Brennan, 1993; Maug and Naik, 2011; Rajan, 1994; Roll, 1992; Scharfstein and Stein, 1990). The paper by Hirshleifer and Teoh

(2003) provides a thorough review of the various explanations that have been offered for this phenomenon in the literature.

Herding can be regarded as a rational strategy for less sophisticated investors who try to imitate the activities of successful investors since obtaining and processing their own information would lead to greater costs (Khan et al., 2011). The presence of extreme market movements could exacerbate this behavior. The cost and time of processing the amount of information generated during such periods is higher than usual, increasing the incentives to herd. Extreme down market movements and periods of stress have been linked to herding both directly and indirectly through market volatility (Karunanayake et al., 2010; Patev and Kanaryan, 2003; Schwert, 1990; show that crises significantly increase market volatility). Kodres and Pritsker (2002) claim that bad news and financial crises increase informational asymmetries and generate contagion and imitation. Policymakers also suggest that the herding behavior of market participants exacerbates market volatility, destabilizes markets, and increases the fragility of the financial system. It is in fact one of the potential explanations for simultaneous market drops. Brock (1999) indicates that some explanations for financial crises focus on the idea that market participants who invest by imitation are especially concerned about the short term, and this can occasionally lead to panic situations in the market. Avgouleas (2010) argues that institutional herding has been recognized as one of the main builders and amplifiers of crises and especially as one of the causes of the global financial crisis of 2008.

In this vein, some herding measures suggested in the literature (Chang et al. 2000; Christie and Huang, 1995, among others) presuppose that, if the phenomenon appears, it would be stronger under extreme market conditions, that is, when sharp rises and falls are taking place. This idea is confirmed by several papers focused on the effects of the Asian crisis (Choe et al. 1999; Ghysels and Seon, 2005, among others). However, Hwang and Salmon (2004) conclude precisely the opposite for the market index. They find that herding behavior is more intense during periods of market calm.

The link between volatility and investor behavior is not new in the literature. Friedman (1953) was the first to suggest that irrational investors destabilize markets by buying when prices are high and selling when they are low, whereas rational investors move prices closer to their fundamental value by buying when they are low and selling when they are high. More recently, several authors have pointed out the influence on volatility of investors who imitate other investors (Alper and Yilmaz, 2004; Choe et al., 1999; Froot et al., 1992). This relationship has been documented by Avramov et al. (2006) who claim that the activity of some investors (those showing herding behavior and those showing contrarian behavior) has a noticeable effect on daily volatility. However, Bohl et al. (2009) conclude that herding and positive feedback trading behavior are not necessarily evidence in favor of a destabilizing effect on stock prices. Authors, such as Blasco et al. (2012), Ouarda et al. (2013),

Di Guilmi et al. (2014), Karanasos et al. (2016), or Huang et al. (2015), among others, suggest that there is a link between herding and volatility.

We aim to test whether the existing relationship between volatility and herding is affected by extreme conditions in the market (abnormally large average price movements), and whether the effects hold for both bullish and bearish extreme market periods. Given the different psychological implications of extreme bullish markets (e.g., the disposition effect) and extreme bearish markets (e.g., panic), we expect to find asymmetrical effects of herding on volatility. We chose the Spanish stock market because it is one of the biggest markets by capitalization in Europe. According to the classification of the World Federation of Exchanges for 2014, the BME Spanish Exchange is the fourth group by capitalization, preceded by the London SE Group, NYSE Euronext (Europe), and Deutsche Börse. Also, the existence of herding and the influence of this behavior on volatility have already been tested and confirmed (Blasco and Ferreruela, 2007, 2008; Blasco et al., 2011). Both characteristics make it the perfect framework for our purposes.

This paper focuses on two main questions. The first is to test whether investor herding intensity increases significantly during crisis periods. The second is to measure the impact of herding behavior on volatility during both bullish and bearish extreme market periods. During stress periods, the stability of the financial system and the effectiveness of portfolio management are questioned. Assessing what happens in the markets during these periods can thus be useful for both portfolio managers (who diversify to minimize risks) and policymakers (who need to calibrate the functioning of market systems). Additionally, we consider that studies of the influence of human behavior on financial markets is of great interest in that they help to understand market reactions that cannot be explained by fundamentals.

This paper contributes to the financial literature in various ways. First, it directly analyzes investor behavior during several extreme market situations with different intensities and implications. Following Christie and Huang (1995), we use two criteria to define extreme market movements: the 1% and the 5%. The 1% (5%) criterion restricts extreme days as 1 (5)% of the lower tail and 1 (5)% of the upper tail of the market return distribution. The results are enriched by assessing how herding intensity reacts to both bearish and bullish market situations. Second, the implications of herding (which can be regarded as a form of uninformed trading) on market volatility during extreme market periods are studied. Both realized volatility and conditional volatility models are used, improving the robustness of the results. Moreover, we use conditional volatility models because they offer a wider perspective of the concept of volatility. To the best of our knowledge, these models have not previously been applied to the problem posed here. In the third place, a measure of herding which does not presuppose a higher level of herding during stress moments is applied. This avoids bias in our results, providing them with greater reliability and robustness. Some papers studying the relationship between market stress and herding suffer a major drawback when trying to test the relationship since the models used implicitly add extreme market movements to the herding measure.

The remainder of the paper is structured as follows. Section 9.2 describes the database used, while Section 9.3 shows the construction of the different variables considered and the methodology as well as the main results. Section 9.4 summarizes the main conclusions derived from the study.

9.2 Data

Our data set contains data for the Ibex-35 index and also for the stocks belonging to it during the sample period. The period under analysis goes from January 1, 1997 to December 31, 2003, a total of 1750 trading days. This period is chosen basically for two reasons. The first is due to the availability of data and its processing, and the second is because some of the most significant crises that affected some markets locally occurred in this period. We have avoided the recent global crisis because its widespread impact in all markets makes it difficult to attribute the results to a specific variable, such as herding.

The Ibex-35 index is a capitalization-weighted index comprising the 35 most liquid Spanish stocks traded in the continuous market. The liquidity of the assets belonging to the Ibex-35 index allows us to calculate the herding measure, given that a substantial amount of data is necessary. The Ibex-35 index is not a closed set of stocks. It is revised every 6 months by adding the most liquid stocks of the semester and removing those which are not so liquid. In order to select the most liquid, both the volume traded and the quality are taken into account.

The data have been provided by the Spanish Sociedad de Bolsas SA. Two databases have been used: one related to individual stocks and the other to the market index. The former has intraday frequency and is used in the construction of the herding intensity measure. It contains, for each and every transaction in the period under study, the date, the time in which it took place measured in hours, minutes, seconds, the stock code, the price, and the volume traded (measured in number of stocks). We need to highlight that the number of data fluctuates between 25,000 and 150,000 transactions a day, so the computational effort needed for processing the intraday frequency dataset is intense. The data used refer to transactions in the stocks belonging to the Ibex-35 during the official trading hours of the Spanish market. We exclude from the analysis all trades executed outside regular trading hours (10:00 a.m. to 5:00 p.m. for the whole of 1997, later extended by stages from 9:00 a.m. to 5.30 p.m. by 2003). Hence, the data used in this analysis cover all trades executed on Ibex-35 stocks at any time during regular stock exchange trading hours.

For the purpose of our analysis, we used daily data of the composition of the Ibex-35, the volume traded in both Euros and number of stocks, together with the daily closing price series for the period. Further, we used Ibex-35 15 min price data.

Table 9.1: Annual descriptive of Ibex-35 return series, volume traded in thousands (Vol), number of trades (NT), realized volatility (VR), and herding intensity measures (H_a and H_b).

Year	Variation Rent (%)	Vol	NT	VR	H_a	H_b
1997	40.75	572,858	14,089	0.0095	−6.023	−6.204
1998	35.58	935,926	25,351	0.0137	−8.468	−8.490
1999	18.35	853,401	25,804	0.0105	−7.620	−7.309
2000	−21.75	1,522,887	40,456	0.0123	−8.798	−8.479
2001	−7.82	1,411,571	34,802	0.0136	−9.347	−9.282
2002	−28.11	1,279,675	38,074	0.0148	−10.941	−10.800
2003	28.17	1,283,267	34,292	0.0097	−10.526	−10.535
Average	9.31	1,122,383	30,397	0.01202	−8.815	−8.726

Table 9.1 shows some descriptive statistics for the Ibex-35 index. More precisely, it shows the percentage variation in returns year by year, the volume traded and the number of trades, as well as the volatility measures used. The evolution in the level of herding intensity as described in the following section is also shown.

9.3 Methodology and Results

9.3.1 Herding Intensity Measure

Detecting the existence of herding and its effects is not an easy task. There have been multiple attempts to measure it. Lakonishok et al. (1992) suggested a measure which has been used particularly in the study of herding among institutional investors, while other measures have been proposed by Christie and Huang (1995), Chang et al. (2000), and Patterson and Sharma (2006) (henceforth PS). It is in practice difficult to empirically distinguish between intentional herding (deliberately following other investors) and spurious herding (individuals behaving in the same way when facing the same information set). There is a plethora of factors which can potentially affect an investment decision. Despite the difficulties involved, analyzing the effects of herding is worthwhile and may produce useful results.

To measure herding intensity in the market, this study uses the measure proposed by PS, which is based on the information cascade models of Bikhchandani et al. (1992), where herding intensity is measured in both buyer- and seller-initiated trading sequences. This measure has a major advantage over others in that it is constructed from intraday data, since this has been considered to be the ideal frequency of data to test for the presence of this kind of investor behavior (Henker et al., 2006). It has the additional advantages for our purposes that it does not assume herding to be revealed only under extreme market conditions, as occurs in other methodological proposals, and that it considers the market as a whole rather than being limited to a few institutional investors as has been the case in many empirical studies.

Following the model of Bikhchandani et al. (1992), market participants receive an imperfect signal G (good news which can make stock prices rise) or B (bad news which can make stock prices fall) about the future value of an asset. Investors know their own signal but not those of other investors, although they can infer these by observing their investment decisions. In this model, investment decisions are made sequentially, hence the observation of preceding acts can become crucial when taking an investment decision. Information cascades occur when investors base their decisions on the actions they observe in others, which they allow to override their own information.

Following the scheme presented in Bikhchandani and Sharma (2001), the simplest operative sequence could be summarized as follows. The first agent to make a decision (I#1) only has his own signal to go by; having no other investor to observe, he acts upon his own private information. The second investor (I#2) has, in addition to his own signal, the information revealed by I#1's decision. If I#1 invested and I#2's signal is G, he will buy. If the two signals are contradictory, Bayes' theory tells us that there is 0.5 probability of a positive return. In this case, the second investor will decide completely at random whether or not to buy. When it is I#3's turn to decide, if the first two investors have invested, he will know that I#1's signal was G, and that I#2's was also most probably positive; he will therefore invest even if his signal is B. After I#3, no new information regarding investment decisions will be passed on to later investors, since all the existing information is based on the decisions of the first investors. This is the point at which the investment cascade begins, since people will invest whatever signal they receive. An investment cascade will therefore commence if, and only if, the number of previous investors that decide to invest is two or more than the number of those who do not invest. The probability of a cascade is very high even when only a few of the earliest investors have made their decision. If an investment cascade starts, then we would expect to observe long sequences of buy or sell trades. In particular, we would expect to see fewer buy or sell runs than we would in the case where each investor followed his or her own signal.

PS propose a statistic to establish the measure of herding intensity in the market by comparing the number of sequences. For the purposes of the analysis, we need to infer the direction of trade using intraday trading data. Following PS, we use the tick-test with respect to traded prices to infer if a trade is buyer or seller initiated.[1] A trade is classified as buyer-initiated if the current trade price is higher than the previous trade price (up-tick). Similarly, a trade is classified as seller-initiated if the current trade price is lower than the previous trade price (down-tick). In a traditional tick-test, if there is no change in the current trade price with respect to the previous trade price (zero-tick), then the trade is classified using the last trade price which differs from the current trade price. However, as the sequence of zero-ticks gets longer, it may be difficult to justify the use of the earlier mentioned method to classify zero-tick trades. Therefore, we separate the zero-ticks from up-ticks and down-ticks.

---

[1] There are different means to identify a transaction as a buy or a sell. Finucane (2000) demonstrates how this method yields similar results to others. This, together with the unavailability of a database that included the bid-ask spread, led us to opt for the tick-test to categorize trades.

We formally define $\{Tr_{jt}\}$ as the entire number of trades in stock j throughout all the t_k moments of the t-th trading session.

$$\{Tr_{jt}\} = \{Tr_{jt_k}, \ldots Tr_{jt_m}\} \quad \text{with} \quad k \leq \cdots \leq m \tag{9.1}$$

Let PTr_{jtk} be the trade price. We define sequences $S_{jt} = \{Tr_{jt_k}, Tr_{jt_{k+1}} \ldots Tr_{jt_{k+l-1}}\}$ as a subgroup of consecutive trades in stock j on day t. We identify buyer initiated, seller initiated, and zero-tick sequences (S_{ijt}, i = buyer initiated, seller initiated, zero-tick) if, respectively,

$$
\begin{aligned}
PTr_{jt_k} &< PTr_{jt_{k+1}} < \cdots < PTr_{jt_{k+l-1}} \\
PTr_{jt_k} &> PTr_{jt_{k+1}} > \cdots > PTr_{jt_{k+l-1}} \\
PTr_{jt_k} &= PTr_{jt_{k+1}} = \cdots = PTr_{jt_{k+l-1}}
\end{aligned}
\tag{9.2}
$$

In order to determine the significance of the sequence test, we follow a procedure commonly used in this kind of analysis. We call $x(i, j, t)$ the estimated difference in the number of sequences of a certain type i. This difference is calculated by comparing the real number of sequences in the market (r_i) to those which should be found in theory.

$$r_i = \sum I_i(S_{jt}) \tag{9.3}$$

where $I_i(S_{jt})$ is an indicator which takes value 1 if the sequence S_{jt} is of type i, and 0 otherwise.

$$x(i, j, t) = \frac{(r_i + 1/2) - np_i(1 - p_i)}{\sqrt{n}} \tag{9.4}$$

where r_i is the real number of sequences of type i (upward, downward, or zero-tick), n is the total number of trades executed in security j during the trading day t, $\frac{1}{2}$ is a discontinuity adjustment parameter, and p_i is the probability of finding a sequence of type i (a priori $p_i = 1/3$).[2] The variable $x(i, j, t)$ is asymptotically normally distributed with zero mean and variance:

$$\sigma^2(i, j, t) = p_i(1 - p_i) - 3p_i^2(1 - p_i)^2 \tag{9.5}$$

Let $H(i,j,t)$ be a measure of buyer-initiated or seller-initiated herding for stock j on date t. This measure could be computed as:

$$H(i, j, t) = \frac{x(i, j, t)}{\sqrt{\sigma_i^2(i, j, t)}} \xrightarrow{a.d} N(0,1) \tag{9.6}$$

---

[2] Under the null hypothesis that stock prices follow a random walk, the probability assignable to each type of price sequence should be the same. However, Blasco et al. (2012) show that stock markets may reflect other tendencies or phenomena than herd behavior that may influence such probability, although the significance and the conclusions do not change significantly. We therefore use the case of $p_i = 1/3$.

where i can take one of three different values according to whether the trade is buyer-initiated, seller-initiated, or zero-tick, which gives three series of H statistics. H_a represents the buyer-initiated (upward) herding measure series, H_b represents the seller-initiated (downward) herding measure series, and H_c represents the zero-tick herding series. We calculate H_c as a different measure in order not to make H_a and H_b artificially higher which could lead us to say that there is herding where actually there is not, but for the purposes of the analysis we only show the results for H_a and H_b. If investors herd, then the actual number of buyer initiated/seller initiated runs would be lower than expected. This would result in a statistically significant negative $H(i,j,t)$. Therefore, the more negative the $H(i,j,t)$, the greater the probability of herding. For large samples, $H(i,j,t)$ is normally distributed with mean 0 and variance 1 under the twin assumptions that the variable under study is *iid* and continuously distributed.

We then obtain H_a and H_b statistics for each day of the study period on all the stocks listed in the Ibex-35 and finally obtain average H_a and H_b series for the Ibex-35.

The appropriate way to detect herding is to compare the fraction of the sample having statistically significant herding intensity to what is expected by pure random chance. The results of the herding intensity measures for both the whole sample period and each of the years under study are shown in Table 9.1. On average, the herding measure is negative and significant for buyer initiated and seller initiated sequences. It should be noted that the average level of herding intensity is significant for all the years in the sample, increasing considerably during the last 2 years.

9.3.2 Market Stress and Herding Intensity

Herding behavior and other collective phenomena can be exacerbated when the market suffers extreme conditions. Hence these conditions can contribute to an increase in the effects of a crisis because that is when the contagion effect is most likely to be at its peak. Kodres and Pritsker (2002) argue that in such moments more intense herding behavior is likely to appear due to the confluence of information asymmetries and bad news. Additionally, information costs and their effect on herding behavior may become more relevant during crises. Herding can also be affected by the existence of extreme bullish periods, when great amounts of information are generated in the market and less sophisticated investors do not have the time or the tools to process it.

In this section, we set out to assess whether this phenomenon takes place in the Spanish market. Further, we analyze whether it holds for up- and down-market situations considering the market as a whole. The level of herding is modeled including variables representing the stress periods or otherwise.

The period under study contains several dates that have been considered extreme up-market days and extreme down-market days. Following Christie and Huang (1995), we

Table 9.2: Number of extreme market days by year.

Year	Extreme up days (5%)	Extreme down days (5%)	Extreme up days (1%)	Extreme down days (1%)
1997	7	6	1	2
1998	17	15	4	7
1999	4	4	2	1
2000	12	15	1	1
2001	16	19	2	3
2002	25	22	7	3
2003	6	6	0	0

The first two columns show the extreme days identified taking the 5% upper and lower tails of the distribution of the returns as extreme days. The last two columns show the number of extreme days by year when taking the 1% upper and lower tails of the distribution as extreme.

consider two different criteria to determine what an extreme market day is. The 5% criterion restricts extreme days to 5% of the lower tail and 5% of the upper tail of the market return distribution. The 1% criterion is more restrictive as it only considers 1% of the lower tail and 1% of the upper tail to be extreme days. Globally speaking, the 5% criterion characterizes 174 days as extreme days (87 up and 87 down), 27% of them during 2002. The more restrictive 1% criterion detects 34 extreme days during the period under study, of which 32% belong to the year 1998 and 29% belong to the year 2002 (Table 9.2). The months of September and October of 1998 deserve a special mention, given that the falls were greater than 7%.

Taking into account these periods, four fictitious variables are created: two related to extreme falls and the other two related to extreme rises. The variables related to significant falls take a value of 1 for those days when extreme negative returns were recorded and 0 otherwise (for the 5% lower tail the variable is D_{D5} and when we apply the 1% criterion the variable is D_{D1}). The variables related to extreme rises take a value of 1 when extreme positive returns were recorded and 0 otherwise (D_{U5} takes a value of 1 for the 5% upper tail of the distribution of returns and 0 otherwise, and D_{U1} is the dummy variable for the 1% criterion).

We set out to determine whether extreme falls or extreme bullish days affect the herding level of the market, and whether they do so in a similar way and with the same intensity. We pose a system of equations taking into account the two kinds of herding described earlier (H_a and H_b) which we solve following the seemingly unrelated regression (SUR) methodology:

$$H_{at} = \alpha_{a0} + \delta_{aj} \sum_{j=1}^{k} H_{at-j} + \alpha_{a1} D_{ijt} + u_{at}$$

$$H_{bt} = \alpha_{b0} + \delta_{bj} \sum_{j=1}^{k} H_{bt-j} + \alpha_{b1} D_{ijt} + u_{bt}$$

(9.7)

Table 9.3: Results of the SUR (seemingly unrelated regression) estimation of the herding intensity levels regarding extreme market periods.

	H_a	H_b
D_{US}	-0.3213	-1.8082
t-statistic	$(-1.99)^b$	$(-11.27)^c$
D_{DS}	-1.6297	-0.3208
t-statistic	$(-10.98)^c$	$(-2.02)^b$
D_{U1}	-0.6056	-2.0044
t-statistic	$(-1.66)^a$	$(-5.38)^c$
D_{D1}	-2.1775	-0.7849
t-statistic	$(-6.76)^c$	$(-2.32)^b$

H_a and H_b are respectively the herding intensity measures for upward and downward sequences. D_{ij} takes four different values depending on the hypothesis under study: D_{US}, D_{DS}, D_{U1}, and D_{D1}. Model:

$$H_{at} = \alpha_{a0} + \delta_{aj} \sum_{j=1}^{k} H_{at-j} + \alpha_{a1}D_{ij} + u_{at}$$

$$H_{bt} = \alpha_{b0} + \delta_{bj} \sum_{j=1}^{k} H_{bt-j} + \alpha_{b1}D_{ij} + u_{bt}$$

[a]Significant at 10%.
[b]Significant at 5%.
[c]Significant at 1%.

where H_{at} and H_{bt} mean upward and downward herding intensity, respectively. D_{ijt} is the dummy variable (D_{US}, D_{DS}, D_{U1}, or D_{D1}). In addition, some lags of the dependent variable are included to correct the autocorrelation of the series.

The results of the estimation are shown in Table 9.3. This only gives the coefficients of the dummy variables under study. The results indicate that the level of herding behavior increases during stress periods, but the influence of extreme up markets and extreme down markets is not the same. Extreme bullish days affect herding in seller initiated sequences (H_b) more intensely than herding in buyer initiated sequences (H_a), whereas during extreme bearish days herding in buyer initiated sequences grows more than in seller initiated sequences. It seems that investors follow the unexpected more than the expected, that is, when the prices are falling and the returns are negative, herding is more intense on the buy side, and when prices rise and the returns are positive then herding takes place on the sell side. Such trades are seen as something extraordinary, given the market situation on those days, and therefore they are intensely followed. It seems that the relevant actions on a bad day are buyer initiated trades while on a good day seller initiated trades are the most mimicked. This phenomenon is more intense when we look at the dummy variables calculated with the 1% CH criterion. That makes sense given that those dummy variables refer to the most extreme days of the period.

9.3.3 Volatility Measure

The volatility measure used in this paper is realized volatility. It is obtained by summing the squares of intraday returns calculated from high frequency data. Andersen et al. (2001) prove that under general conditions, the variance of these discrete returns over a day is conditional on the sample path $\{\sigma_{t-\tau}^2\}_0^1$ is $\overline{\sigma_t^2} = \int_0^1 \sigma_{t-\tau}^2 \, d\tau$. In the literature, $\overline{\sigma_t^2}$ is known as integrated variance and is a natural measure of the true daily volatility. The estimator of this variance is known as realized volatility and is obtained as follows:

$$\overline{\sigma_t^2}(m) = \sum_{k=1,2,\ldots m} r_{t+k/m}^2 \tag{9.8}$$

where m is the number of intervals within a day. Andersen et al. (2001) show that under weak regularity conditions, $\overline{\sigma_t^2}(m)$ converges in probability to the integrated variance, as $m \to \infty$. Hence, it seems that the higher the data frequency, the closer to true volatility the estimator will be. Most papers consider 5 min intervals to be a good frequency. The availability of data for the Ibex-35 only allows us to calculate realized volatility through 15 min data. In any case, since Andersen et al. (2000) find that volatilities start to stabilize at 30 min intervals, the results obtained can be considered free of significant error, thanks to the data frequency used. Table 9.1 gives the annual average of the volatility measure.

9.3.4 Volatility, Herding Intensity, and Market Stress

Following the theory of Noisy Rational Expectations, Hellwig (1980) and Wang (1993) assert that volatility is driven by uninformed or liquidity trading, given that price adjustments arising from uninformed trading tend to revert. The latter author observes that information asymmetry may drive volatility and that uninformed investors largely tend to follow the market trend, buying when prices rise and selling when they fall. Uninformed trading is not equivalent to herding, but we could say that herding is a type of uninformed trading, given that investors ignore their own information and beliefs and act following the actions of other investors. Hellwig (1980), Wang (1993), and Avramov et al. (2006) find a more or less direct relationship between volatility and herding (or uninformed trading), thus indicating that collective behavior is a volatility enhancing factor. Blasco et al. (2012), using several volatility measures, confirm that herding has a direct linear impact on volatility for all of the volatility measures considered (the higher the observed level of herding intensity, the greater the volatility expected), although the corresponding intensity is not always the same. They also find that herding variables seem to be useful in volatility forecasting. Ouarda et al. (2013) find evidence of herding behavior that contributes to a bearish situation characterized by strong volatility and a trading volume. Di Guilmi et al. (2014), introduce a theoretical model to show that trend chasing, switching, and herding all contribute to market volatility. Huang et al. (2015) find that financial crisis enhances herding, especially in portfolios with larger idiosyncratic volatility, and Karanasos et al. (2016) indicate a continuous herding behavior during crisis periods of increased market volatility.

French and Roll (1986) argue that trading entails volatility. This means that we always need to include a measure of the traded volume in any study of market volatility. There is a vast amount of literature regarding the relationship between traded volume and volatility. Jones et al. (1994) separate daily volume into the number of trades and the average trade size and observe that the former affects volatility to a higher degree. Chan and Fong (2000) consider that the important factor in volatility is order imbalance. Given that it is not clear which is the best volume measure for these purposes, following Chan and Fong (2006) we consider both the volume traded and the number of trades in order to obtain robust results.

The next step is to determine whether herding affects volatility in a different way during extreme market periods. Previously we have detected an influence of extreme days on the herding level. Hence, intuitively we think that this effect could be reflected in volatility. In order to carry out this analysis we estimate the following models for the realized volatility measures:

$$RV_t = \alpha_0 + \alpha_1 M_t + \sum_{j=1}^{12} \rho_j RV_{t-j} + \alpha_2 V_t + \alpha_3 H_{i,t} + \alpha_4 D_{ijt} H_{it} + \mu_t \qquad (9.9)$$

$$RV_t = \alpha_0 + \alpha_1 M_t + \sum_{j=1}^{12} \rho_j RV_{t-j} + \alpha_2 NT_t + \alpha_3 H_{i,t} + \alpha_4 D_{ijt} H_{it} + \mu_t \qquad (9.10)$$

where RV_t is realized volatility as described previously, M_t is the Monday dummy variable, which takes a value of 1 on Mondays and 0 otherwise. V_t is the volume traded on day t, NT_t is the number of trades on day t, and H_{it} are two variables related to the herding level in the market (H_a and H_b). D_{ijt} is the variable representing the extreme market period under study and it takes the four different values already explained. Hence, each of these equations is estimated 8 times, considering a different kind of herding intensity every time and also the different extreme market variables that we have described earlier.

Table 9.4 gives the results of these regressions. The coefficients of the herding variables in the stress moments considered are shown. If we observe the effect of extreme bullish days, the results show that herding increases volatility less than on the rest of the days, regardless of the volume measure considered, the type of herding, and the criterion used to determine what is extreme. On the other hand, during extreme down-market days herding makes volatility rise more than usual. This result holds for both herding measures and for both the 1% and the 5% criterion.

Table 9.4: Results of the estimation of the influence of herding on volatility during market stress.

	Eq. (9.9)			
	D_{US}	D_{DS}	D_{U1}	D_{D1}
$\alpha_3 H_a$	−0.0005	−0.0003	−0.0005	−0.0004
t-statistic	(−5.83)[c]	(−4.02)[c]	(−5.87)[c]	(−4.96)[c]
$\alpha_4 H_a$	0.0001	−0.0004	0.0004	−0.0010
t-statistic	(2.34)[b]	(−8.37)[c]	(3.14)[c]	(−10.14)[c]
$\alpha_3 H_b$	−0.0002	−0.0002	−0.0002	−0.0002
t-statistic	(−2.78)[c]	(−2.21)[b]	(−2.64)[c]	(−2.50)[b]
$\alpha_4 H_b$	0.0001	−0.0006	0.0004	−0.0013
t-statistic	(2.42)[b]	(−9.50)[c]	(3.12)[c]	(−11.35)[c]
	Eq. (9.10)			
	D_{US}	D_{DS}	D_{U1}	D_{D1}
$\alpha_3 H_a$	−0.0002	−0.0001	−0.0003	−0.0002
t-statistic	(−2.92)[c]	(−1.32)	(−2.96)[c]	(−1.85)[a]
$\alpha_4 H_a$	0.0001	−0.0004	0.0004	−0.0010
t-statistic	(2.38)[b]	(−8.54)[c]	(2.99)[c]	(−10.49)[c]
$\alpha_3 H_b$	0.0000	0.0000	0.0000	0.0000
t-statistic	(−0.18)	(0.18)	(−0.04)	(0.23)
$\alpha_4 H_b$	0.0001	−0.0005	0.0003	−0.0013
t-statistic	(2.04)[b]	(−9.08)[c]	(2.84)[c]	(−11.47)[c]

$$RV_t = \alpha_0 + \alpha_1 M_t + \sum_{j=1}^{12} \rho_j RV_{t-j} + \alpha_2 V_t + \alpha_3 H_{it} + \alpha_4 D_{ijt} H_{it} + \mu_t \tag{9.9}$$

$$RV_t = \alpha_0 + \alpha_1 M_t + \sum_{j=1}^{12} \rho_j RV_{t-j} + \alpha_2 NT_t + \alpha_3 H_{it} + \alpha_4 D_{ijt} H_{it} + \mu_t \tag{9.10}$$

[a]Significant at 10%.
[b]Significant at 5%.
[c]Significant at 1%.

These results are consistent with the idea of volatility as destabilization or turbulence, which are probably greater in bearish periods when investors may panic, than during bullish days when investors are more relaxed. Schwert (1990) studied the October 1987 crash and showed that stock volatility jumped dramatically during and after the crash. Patev and Kanaryan (2003) studied four Central European markets and found strong evidence of a huge influence over market volatility caused by the Asian and Russian crises. Karunanayake et al. (2010) show that both the Asian crisis and the more recent global financial crisis significantly increased the stock return volatilities across all of the four markets in their study.

We find that it is during extreme down market days and not during bullish days when the behavior of investors, imitative or otherwise, affects volatility to a higher degree.

9.3.5 Conditional Volatility Models and Herding

This section sets out to analyze whether the effect of herding on conditional volatility can be significant during crisis periods. In order to carry out this analysis, we propose the conditional volatility model Garch$(1,1)^3$ in which we include the variables related to herding and its effect during extreme market days. This inclusion is in line with Lamoreux and Lastrapes (1990a) and with the incorporation of traded volume in the conditional volatility model.

$$R_t = \beta_0 + \beta_1 * R_{t-1} + \beta_2 * D_{ijt} + u_t \text{ where } u_t \text{ follows a } N(0,\ \sigma_t^2) \qquad (9.11)$$

$$\sigma_t^2 = \alpha_0 + \alpha_1 u_{t-1}^2 + \alpha_2 \sigma_{t-1}^2 + \alpha_3 H_{i,t} + \alpha_4 H_{i,t} D_{ijt} \qquad (9.12)$$

In addition, model GJR$(1,1)^4$ is estimated. The average specification is similar and the variance is as follows:

$$\sigma_t^2 = \alpha_0 + \alpha_1 u_{t-1}^2 + \alpha_2 \sigma_{t-1}^2 + \alpha_3 H_{i,t} + \alpha_4 H_{i,t} D_{ijt} + \alpha_5 S_{t-1}^- u_{t-1}^2 \qquad (9.13)$$

where S_t^- equals 1 when u_t is smaller than zero and equals 0 when u_t is larger than or equal to 0.

Table 9.5 shows the results of the estimations. The coefficients related to the impact of herding on the conditional volatility during extreme days as well as the herding variable itself are shown. For the bearish days, the conclusions are similar to those of the realized volatility previously analyzed, whereas in the case of extreme positive returns days, the coefficient of the effect of herding on volatility is no longer significant. The coefficient of herding during extreme bearish days appears significant and negative regardless of the criterion used to determine the extreme days and the type of herding under analysis. The results for the bearish days are consistent with those obtained for the other volatility measure. This confirms that conditional volatility is also affected by herding levels during extremely bearish moments in the market.

9.4 Conclusions

This paper has analyzed in depth the highly relevant question of the effect that herding behavior has on the market and how this is affected by extreme positive or negative returns days, in other words, days of market stress. First, we analyzed the influence of extreme market days on the mimicking behavior of investors. We concluded that during such days, investors follow each other more intensely than when the market is calm or merely bullish/ bearish, but that the effect is not homogenous. During extreme bullish days, investors mimic

---

[3] Following Lamoreux and Lastrapes (1990b) this model is a parsimonious representation of the conditional variance which adequately adjusts to financial series.

[4] This model takes into account the possibility of non symmetrical impacts of information on volatility Glosten et al. (1993).

Table 9.5: Results of the estimation of the influence of herding and financial crises on conditional volatility.

	GARCH			
	D_{US}	D_{DS}	D_{U1}	D_{D1}
$\alpha_3 H_a \, (\times 10^{-5})$	−0.727	0.004	−0.031	−0.031
z-statistic	(−13.51)[c]	(0.29)	(−1.20)	(−1.31)
$\alpha_4 H_a \, (\times 10^{-5})$	1.010	−0.547	0.309	−1.440
z-statistic	(17.93)[c]	(−3.49)[c]	(0.59)	(−2.13)[b]
$\alpha_3 H_b \, (\times 10^{-5})$	−0.021	0.009	0.002	−0.005
z-statistic	(−0.77)	(0.78)	(0.13)	(−0.30)
$\alpha_4 H_b \, (\times 10^{-5})$	0.129	−0.624	0.172	−1.630
z-statistic	(1.14)	(−3.45)[c]	(0.34)	(−2.13)[b]
	GJR			
	D_{US}	D_{DS}	D_{U1}	D_{D1}
$\alpha_3 H_a \, (\times 10^{-5})$	−0.056	0.012	−0.020	−0.005
z-statistic	(−1.47)	(1.17)	(−0.73)	(−0.17
$\alpha_4 H_a \, (\times 10^{-5})$	0.233	−0.486	0.415	−1.420
z-statistic	(1.69)[a]	(−3.57)[c]	(0.78)	(−2.40)[b]
$\alpha_3 H_b \, (\times 10^{-5})$	−0.034	0.012	−0.007	0.001
z-statistic	(−1.00)	(1.24)	(−0.28)	(0.08)
$\alpha_4 H_b \, (\times 10^{-5})$	0.185	−0.557	0.235	−1.670
z-statistic	(1.53)	(−3.50)[c]	(0.43)	(−2.42)[b]

Models follow:

$$R_t = \beta_0 + \beta_1 * R_{t-1} + \beta_2 * D_{ct} + u_t \text{ where } u_t \text{ follows a } N(0, \sigma_t^2) \quad (9.11)$$

$$\text{GARCH}(1,1) \text{ model } \sigma_t^2 = \alpha_0 + \alpha_1 u_{t-1}^2 + \alpha_2 \sigma_{t-1}^2 + \alpha_3 H_{i,t} + \alpha_4 H_{i,t} D_{ct} \quad (9.12)$$

$$\text{GJR}(1,1) \text{ model } \sigma_t^2 = \alpha_0 + \alpha_1 u_{t-1}^2 + \alpha_2 \sigma_{t-1}^2 + \alpha_5 S_{t-1}^- u_{t-1}^2 + \alpha_3 H_{i,t} + \alpha_4 H_{i,t} D_{ct} \quad (9.13)$$

where S_t^- equals 1 when u_t is smaller than 0 and 0 otherwise.
[a]Significant at 10%.
[b]Significant at 5%.
[c]Significant at 1%.

more intensely on the sell side, while during extreme bearish days they are more prone to follow the buys. We have also assessed whether herding significantly affects market volatility during stress periods. The results indicate the great importance of herding behavior, especially at such moments. We observe an asymmetrical effect of herding on volatility. When the market is undergoing extreme falls in prices, herding affects volatility more than on nonextreme days. However, investor herding behavior has a lesser influence on volatility during extreme market rises.

Colander et al. (2008) blame economists for contributing to crises by not including abnormal situations in their models. They recommend the introduction of contagion and herding behavior in macroeconomic models as well as extending the scope of the models beyond calm market environments. The present work lends support to this recommendation. This paper also sheds light on a question of considerable relevance today. During extreme bearish days, psychological biases may arise affecting the whole financial system leading to a greater need for assessing investment risks. Adding elements which include behavioral factors to such assessments may prove to be highly valuable in the risk management field.

Acknowledgments

The authors wish to acknowledge financial support from the Spanish Ministry of Economy and Competitiveness (ECO2012-35946-C02-01), (ECO2013-45568-R), ECO2016-77631-R (AEI/FEDER, UE) and the Government of Aragón/European Social Fund (S14/2).

References

Alper, C.E., Yilmaz, K., 2004. Volatility and contagion: evidence from the Istanbul stock exchange. Econ. Syst. 28, 353–367.

Andersen, T.G., Bollerslev, T., Diebold, F.X., Ebens, H., 2000. Great realizations. Risk 13, 105–108.

Andersen, T.G., Bollerslev, T., Diebold, F.X., Ebens, H., 2001. The distribution of realized stock return volatility. J. Financ. Econ. 61, 43–76.

Avgouleas, E., 2010. What future for disclosure as a regulatory technique? Lessons from the global financial crisis and beyond. In: MacNeil, I., O'Brien, J. (Eds.), The Future of Financial Regulation. Hart Publishing, pp. 211–231.

Avramov, D., Chordia, T., Goyal, A., 2006. Liquidity and autocorrelations in individual stock returns. J. Financ. 61 (5), 1242–1277.

Bikhchandani, S., Sharma, S., 2001. Herd behaviour in financial markets. IMF Staff Papers, Int. Monetary Fund, 47(3), 279–310.

Bikhchandani, S., Hirshleifer, D., Welch, I., 1992. A theory of fads, fashion, custom, and cultural change as informational cascades. J. Polit. Econ. 100, 992–1026.

Blasco, N., Ferreruela, S., 2007. Comportamiento Imitador en el Mercado Bursátil Español: Evidencia Intradiaria. Revista de Economía Financiera 13, 56–75.

Blasco, N., Ferreruela, S., 2008. Testing intentional herding in familiar stocks: an experiment in an international context. J. Behav. Financ. 9 (2), 72–84.

Blasco, N., Corredor, P., Ferreruela, S., 2011. Detecting intentional herding: what lies beneath intraday data in the Spanish Stock Market. J. Oper. Res. Soc. 62 (6), 1056–1066.

Blasco, N., Corredor, P., Ferreruela, S., 2012. Does herding affect volatility? Implications for the Spanish stock market. Quant. Financ. 12 (2), 311–327.

Bohl, M.T., Brzeszczynski, J., Wilfling, B., 2009. Institutional investors and stock returns volatility: empirical evidence from a natural experiment. J. Financ. Stability 5, 170–182.

Brennan, M., 1993. Agency and asset prices. Finance Working Paper No. 6-93, UCLA.

Brock, H.W., 1999. Explaining global market turmoil: a fresh perspective on its origins and nature Proceedings of a conference capital flows and the international financial system, Economic Group Reserve Bank of Australia.

Chan, K., Fong, W.M., 2000. Trade size, order imbalance, and the volatility-volume relation. J. Financ. Econ. 57, 247–273.

Chan, K., Fong, W.M., 2006. Realized volatility and transactions. J. Bank. Financ. 30 (7), 2063–2085.

Chang, E.C., Cheng, J.W., Khorana, A., 2000. An examination of herd behavior in equity markets: an international perspective. J. Bank. Financ. 24, 1651–1679.

Chari, V.V., Kehoe, P., 2003. Financial crises as herds. Federal Reserve Bank of Minneapolis, Research Department Staff Report 316.

Choe, H., Kho, B.-C., Stulz, R.M., 1999. Do foreign investors destabilize stock markets? The Korean experience in 1997. J. Financ. Econ. 54, 227–264.

Christie, W.G., Huang, R.D., 1995. Following the pied piper: do individual returns herd around the market? Financ. Anal. J. 51(4), 31–37.

Colander, D., Follmer, H., Goldberg, M., Haas, A., Juselius, K., Kirman, A. Lux, T., Sloth, B., 2008. The financial crisis and the systemic failure of academic economics. Working group on Modelling of Financial Markets, 98th Dahlem Workshop.

Di Guilmi, C., He, X.-Z., Li, K., 2014. Herding, trend chasing and market volatility. J. Econ. Dyn. Control 48, 349–373.

Finucane, T.J., 2000. A direct test of methods for inferring trade direction from intra-day data. J. Financ. Quant. Anal. 35, 553–576.

French, K.R., Roll, R., 1986. Stock return variances: the arrival of information and the reaction of traders. J. Financ. Econ. 17 (1), 5–26.

Friedman, M., 1953. The case for flexible exchange rates. In: Friedman, M. (Ed.), Essays in Positive Economics. University of Chicago Press, Chicago, IL.

Froot, K.A., Scharfstein, D.S., Stein, J.C., 1992. Herd on the street: informational inefficiencies in a market with short-term speculation. J. Financ. 47, 1461–1484.

Ghysels, E., Seon, J., 2005. The Asian financial crisis: the role of derivative securities trading and foreign investors in Korea. J. Int. Money Financ. 24, 607–630.

Glosten, L.R., Jagannathan, R., Runkle, D.E., 1993. On the relation between the expected value and the volatility of the nominal excess return on stocks. J. Financ. 48 (5), 1779–1801.

Hellwig, M.F., 1980. On the aggregation of information in competitive markets. J. Econ. Theory 22, 477–498.

Henker, J., Henker, T., Mitsios, A., 2006. Do investors herd intraday in Australian equities? Int. J. Manager. Financ. 2 (3), 196–219.

Hirshleifer, D., Teoh, S.H., 2003. Herd behaviour and cascading in capital markets: a review and synthesis. Eur. Financ. Manag. 9 (1), 25–66.

Huang, T.-C., Lin, B.-H., Yang, T.-H., 2015. Herd behavior and idiosyncratic volatility. J. Bus. Res. 68 (4), 763–770.

Hwang, S., Salmon, M., 2004. Market stress and herding. J. Emp. Financ. 11, 585–616.

Jones, C.M., Kaul, G., Lipson, M.L., 1994. Transactions, volume, and volatility. Rev. Financ. Studies 7, 631–651.

Karanasos, M., Yfanti, S., Karoglou, M., 2016. Multivariate FIAPARCH modelling of financial markets with dynamic correlations in times of crisis. Int. Rev. Financ. Anal. 45, 332–349.

Karunanayake, I., Valadkhani, A., O'Brien, M., 2010. Financial crises and international stock market volatility transmission. Aust. Econ. Papers 493, 209–221.

Khan, H., Hassairi, S., Viviani, J.L., 2011. Herd behavior and market stress: the case of four European countries. Int. Bus. Res. 43, 53–67.

Kodres, L., Pritsker, M., 2002. A rational expectations model of financial contagion. J. Financ. 57 (2), 769–799.

Lakonishok, J., Shleifer, A., Vishny, R.W., 1992. The impact of institutional trading on stock prices. J. Financ. Econ. 32, 23–43.

Lamoreux, C.G., Lastrapes, W.D., 1990a. Heteroskedasticity in stock return data: volume versus GARCH effects. J. Financ. 45 (1), 221–229.

Lamoreux, C.G., Lastrapes, W.D., 1990b. Persistence in variance, structural change and the GARCH model. J. Bus. Econ. Statistics 8 (2), 225–234.

Maug, E., Naik, N., 2011. Herding and delegated portfolio management: the impact of relative performance evaluation on asset allocation. Q. J. Financ. 01 (02), 265–292.

Ouarda, M., El Bouri, A., Bernard, O., 2013. Herding behaviour under markets condition: empirical evidence on the European financial markets. Int. Econ. Financ. Issues 3 (1), 214–228.

Patev, P., Kanaryan, N., 2003. Stock market volatility changes in central europe caused by asian and russian financial crises. Tsenov Academy of Economics Department of Finance and Credit Working Paper, No. 03-01.

Patterson, D.M., Sharma, V., 2006. Do traders follow each other at the NYSE? Working Paper, University of Michigan-Dearborn.

Puckett, A., Yan, X., 2008. Short-term institutional herding and its impact on stock prices, Working Paper.

Rajan, R.G., 1994. Why credit policies fluctuate: a theory and some evidence. Quart. J. Econ. 436, 399–442.

Roll, R., 1992. A mean/variance analysis of tracking error. J. Portfolio Manage. 18, 13–22.

Scharfstein, D.S., Stein, J.C., 1990. Herd behavior and investment. Am. Econ. Rev. 80, 465–479.

Schwert, W., 1990. Stock volatility and the crash of '87. Rev. Financ. Studies 31, 77–102.

Shefrin, H., 2000. Beyond Greed and Fear; Understanding Behavioral Finance and the Psychology of Investing. HBS Press, Cambridge.

Thaler, R., 1991. Quasi-rational economics. Russel Sage Foundation, New York.

Trueman, B., 1994. Analyst Forecasts and herding behaviour. Rev. Financ. Studies 7, 97–124.

Wang, J., 1993. A model of intertemporal asset prices under asymmetric information. Rev. Econ. Studies 60, 249–282.

CHAPTER 10

Did Security Analysts Overreact During the Global Financial Crisis? Canadian Evidence

Alain Coën*, Aurélie Desfleurs**

*University of Quebec at Montreal, Montreal, QC, Canada; **University of Sherbrooke, Sherbrooke, QC, Canada

Chapter Outline

10.1 Introduction

The seminal work of De Bondt and Thaler (1990) has introduced an important literature devoted to the analysis of financial analysts' (hereafter FA) behavior. Their study is motivated by the previous work of Shiller (1987), describing the overreaction of investors: *"they react to each other during crashes, rather than to hard economic news."*[1] This behavioral attitude has been later qualified as "animal spirits" by Akerlof and Shiller (2010). It is also an echo of the fundamental work of Kahneman and Tversky (1973). *"They found that people's intuitive forecasts have a tendency to overweight salient information, such as recent news,*

---

[1] De Bondt, W.F.M., Thaler, R., 1990. Do security analysts overreact? Am. Econ. Rev. 80 (2), pp. 52.

169

and underweight less salient data, such as long-term averages."[2] The crucial role of financial analysts' forecasts (FAF) in investment decisions on developed and emerging financial markets has been highlighted in numerous studies. Their forecast "overoptimism" has been often severely criticized (Alford and Berger, 1999; Barlett, 1997; Brown, 1997; Brown et al., 1987; Chopra, 1998... among many others).

In this article, we suggest analyzing the evolution of their forecasts from 2005 to 2014 on the Canadian stock markets, using the global financial crisis (hereafter GFC) of 2008 as a potential breakdown. Our main objectives are to analyze whether financial analysts exhibit specific behaviors during the GFC. Therefore we divide our sample in three periods: before the GFC (2005–07); during the crisis (2008–10); and after the crisis (2011–14). We use two acknowledged metrics in the behavioral finance literature. We focus indeed on financial analysts' forecast accuracy and forecast bias to estimate the relative evolution of their performance and level of optimism. We conjecture that the period after the GFC may reasonably have led to an improvement of FAF accuracy and a drop of the level of overoptimism (or a decline of FAF bias). Moreover, it seems to be relevant to show whether financial analysts are pessimistic when they forecast earnings profits and less overoptimistic for losses forecasts. Therefore we use these two specific metrics and compare their evolution in a contrasted environment. Our sample based on the Canadian market includes 11 industrial sectors as defined by the I/B/E/S database: Basic industries, Capital goods, Consumer durables, Consumer nondurables, Consumer services, Energy, Finance, Health care, Public utilities, Technology, and Transportation. This choice is justified by our aim to illustrate a potential diversity of reactions among the financial analysts' community. It is well acknowledged by the literature, that they tend to be specialized by industrial sectors.

This article is organized as follows. The conceptual framework is briefly presented and motivated in Section 10.2. The data and the definitions of FAF accuracy and FAF bias are described in Section 10.3. The results are reported and analyzed in Section 10.4. Finally in Section 10.5, we summarize the main findings and draw our conclusions.

10.2 Conceptual Framework

As far as our main objective is to shed light on the behavior of financial analysts during the GFC, we use two important topics of FAF (FAF accuracy and FAF bias), following the same methodology already used in previous studies by Coën and Desfleurs (2004) for emerging Pacific Rim markets, (2014) for the analysis of FAF for REITs on Asian markets, and (2016) for Eastern frontier markets.

---

[2] De Bondt, W.F.M., Thaler, R., 1990. Ibid. pp. 52.

10.2.1 Financial Analysts' Forecast Accuracy

The financial literature acknowledges that FAF accuracy (and FAF bias) is influenced by special factors. We may mention that the skill of individual analysts (e.g., Clement, 1999; Mikhail et al., 1997…), the firm size and analyst coverage (Alford and Berger, 1999; Chang et al., 2006; Hong et al., 2000; Lang et al., 2004; Yu, 2008), the level of diversification (Thomas, 2002…), the level of disclosure (O'Brien, 1990…), the financing decisions (Bradshaw et al., 2006…), the type of earnings (Ciccone, 2005…), or country and industry effects (Black and Carnes, 2006; Byard et al., 2011; Capstaff et al., 1998; Chee et al., 2010; Coën et al., 2009; Katz et al., 2000; Patel et al., 2002; Tan et al., 2011, among others…) are among the main topics studied and analyzed to explain FAF. Here to shed light on the behavior of FA during a crisis, we have chosen to analyze the trend of FAF accuracy during a period marked by the global financial crisis. This specific event is also associated with a significant increase of information disclosure and a high level of competition. Following the results of Basu et al. (1998), Alford and Berger (1999), or Coën and Desfleurs (2004), we consider that the performance of financial analysts on the Canadian financial market during the 2005–14 period should have improved. We suggest the study of FAF in the 11 industrial sectors describing the global economy in Canada. We can reasonably expect that FAF accuracy may seriously differ among industrial sectors.

10.2.2 Financial Analysts' Forecast Bias

Earnings forecasts may be biased exhibiting a certain kind of overoptimism (when the financial analysts' forecast error is positive) or pessimism (when the forecast error is negative). This bias casts doubt on the role of FA and on their real independence and autonomy, especially during periods of high uncertainty (Das et al., 1998; Ke and Yu, 2006; Sadique et al., 2010). The literature documents that FAF bias is related to a sentiment of overoptimism on average. Focusing on the Canadian market and grouping firms by industrial sectors, during the GFC, we may expect contrasted results with significant differences between subperiods. Intuitively, the bias should increase during the crisis period and then decrease. The amplitude of the crisis in 2008 and the adoption of reforms after the GFC should support this intuition.

10.3 Data and Methodology

Extending the previous work of De Bondt and Thaler (1990) and following Coën and Desfleurs (2004), we have chosen to use three metrics to analyze three dimensions of FAF for our sample of Canadian industrial sectors. First, we analyze FAF accuracy conceptually defined as the absolute difference between the reported and forecasted earnings. Second, we compare FAF errors (hereafter FAFE) with forecast errors generated by a naïve statistical model. Our main objective with this approach is to simply shed light on the specific role of financial analysts, questioning their relative accuracy with respect to a simple benchmark.

Third, we model and focus on the concept of overoptimism, the so-called FAF bias, as often described in the financial literature. Therefore we analyze the first metric (with the sign: positive or negative). A positive value may be interpreted as a kind of overoptimism while a negative value is a sign of pessimism.

10.3.1 Data

To define earnings FAF we use the standard consensus annual forecast data as provided by the International Brokers Estimate System (I/B/E/S) summary database (available on Thomson One 5.0.) for a sample of 11 industrial sectors (as defined by the standard I/B/E/S nomenclature) for Canada from fiscal year 2005 to fiscal year 2014. We consider three subperiods: before the GFC (2005–07); during the GFC (2008–10); and after the GFC (2011–14). We also report the results for the full period. Contrary to De Bondt and Thaler (1990), we have chosen to shed light on the potential behavioral differences among analysts, focusing on the industrial sectors in a specific country (namely Canada). We observe indeed an important heterogeneity among industries (and firms). We may add that analyst coverage differs significantly. Thus, we use 11 industrial sectors as defined by I/B/E/S: Basic industries, Capital goods, Consumer durables, Consumer non-durables, Consumer services, Energy, Finance, Health care, Public utilities, Technology, and Transportation. We also reduce the influence of extreme outliers: forecasts errors are winsorized at the 5% and 95% levels. We may mention that we use simple Ordinary least squares (OLS) procedure (with a standard correction for heteroscedasticity). After these adjustments, our sample includes 7930 observations from 2005 to 2014 (also reported in Table 10.1).

10.3.2 Financial Analysts' Forecast (FAF) Accuracy: A Definition

Following the financial literature, we report the definition of the FAF as the absolute difference between the consensus annual earnings forecast and the reported earnings per share for fiscal year t divided by reported earnings (the absolute FAF errors or |FAFE|). The FAF error is often deflated by stock price but this deflator may induce acknowledged problems directly related to the evolution of market conditions. To avoid these potential problems, we decide to use reported earnings as deflator. We follow the motivations of our previous studies (Coën and Desfleurs, 2004; Coën et al., 2009; Coën and Desfleurs, 2014), among others using the same approach). The FAF accuracy is analytically defined by the following equation:

$$\left| FAFE \right| = \left| \frac{e_{j,t(h)}}{RE_{j,t}} \right| = \left| \frac{F_{j,t(h)} - RE_{j,t}}{RE_{j,t}} \right| \tag{10.1}$$

Where $FAFE_t$ = the financial analyst forecast error for firm j divided by earnings per share (EPS) for fiscal year t, $e_{j,t}$ = the forecast error of earnings per share for firm j for fiscal year

Table 10.1: Descriptive statistics of absolute analysts forecast errors and naive errors for each country and each subperiod.

Variables	Number of Observations		Mean		T-Test: Mean = 0		Median		Performance of Analysts		Adjusted T-Test[c,d]; Difference Between the Subperiods		
	|FAFE|	|NFAFE|	|FAFE|	|NFAFE|	|FAFE|	|NFAFE|	|FAFE|	|NFAFE|	Sup. |FAFE|/ |NFAFE|	T-test sup.	Before/ after crisis	Before/ during crisis	During/ after crisis
All sectors													
2005–07	2315	1732	0.316[a]	0.497[a]	44.363	57.390	0.160	0.412	2.202[a]	31.136	−2.90[a]	−1.64	−1.15
2008–10	2344	2033	0.332[a]	0.573[a]	46.838	68.336	0.183	0.544	2.391[a]	35.169			
2011–14	3271	2916	0.343[a]	0.537[a]	55.871	77.029	0.200	0.495	1.845[a]	32.519			
2005–14	7930	6681	0.332[a]	0.538[a]	85.295	117.524	0.182	0.484	2.105[a]	56.552			
Basic industries													
2005–07	472	339	0.404[a]	0.581[a]	24.138	31.074	0.286	0.585	1.982[a]	12.710	0.19	−0.35	0.62
2008–10	582	477	0.412[a]	0.620[a]	28.428	37.567	0.333	0.657	2.100[a]	14.600			
2011–14	968	813	0.400[a]	0.611[a]	35.545	47.724	0.295	0.615	1.763[a]	17.458			
2005–14	2022	1629	0.404[a]	0.607[a]	51.507	68.189	0.300	0.617	1.910[a]	26.007			
Capital goods													
2005–07	127	95	0.318[a]	0.515[a]	10.106	13.715	0.144	0.438	2.267[a]	7.916	2.78[a]	2.18[b]	0.42
2008–10	117	104	0.225[a]	0.509[a]	7.812	13.415	0.085	0.407	2.621[a]	7.485			
2011–14	156	146	0.210[a]	0.432[a]	9.093	14.645	0.083	0.291	2.179[a]	9.172			
2005–14	400	345	0.249[a]	0.478[a]	15.532	24.030	0.104	0.356	2.336[a]	14.130			
Consumer durables													
2005–07	45	39	0.248[a]	0.434[a]	5.181	6.787	0.095	0.214	1.920[a]	4.594	1.18	0.38	0.79
2008–10	49	46	0.223[a]	0.491[a]	5.082	8.729	0.063	0.543	2.826[a]	7.506			
2011–14	53	53	0.178[a]	0.341[a]	4.946	7.683	0.078	0.199	1.876[a]	4.869			
2005–14	147	138	0.214[a]	0.417[a]	8.795	13.300	0.074	0.210	2.195[a]	9.584			

(Continued)

Table 10.1: Descriptive statistics of absolute analysts forecast errors and naive errors for each country and each subperiod. (*cont.*)

Variables	Number of Observations		Mean		T-Test: Mean = 0		Median		Performance of Analysts		Adjusted T-Test[c,d]; Difference Between the Subperiods		
	|FAFE|	|NFAFE|	|FAFE|	|NFAFE|	|FAFE|	|NFAFE|	|FAFE|	|NFAFE|	Sup. |FAFE|/ |NFAFE|	T-test sup.	Before/ after crisis	Before/ during crisis	During/ after crisis
Consumer nondurables													
2005-07	50	40	0.245[a]	0.372[a]	6.108	7.297	0.158	0.286	1.268[b]	2.448	0.50	−0.60	1.07
2008-10	47	44	0.283[a]	0.477[a]	5.642	8.482	0.116	0.360	2.194[a]	4.126			
2011-14	67	61	0.219[a]	0.412[a]	6.583	8.666	0.069	0.283	2.445[a]	5.592			
2005-14	164	145	0.245[a]	0.421[a]	10.569	14.115	0.119	0.297	2.024[a]	7.118			
Consumer services													
2005-07	219	184	0.192[a]	0.369[a]	10.536	15.639	0.073	0.265	2.438[a]	11.566	−1.79	−0.48	−1.20
2008-10	192	181	0.205[a]	0.352[a]	9.660	13.426	0.068	0.200	2.099[a]	10.153			
2011-14	255	243	0.241[a]	0.391[a]	11.817	16.737	0.085	0.228	1.965[a]	10.883			
2005-14	666	608	0.215[a]	0.372[a]	18.490	26.430	0.074	0.229	2.147[a]	18.770			
Energy													
2005-07	521	362	0.400[a]	0.575[a]	24.729	30.989	0.250	0.569	2.008[a]	13.169	−2.67[a]	0.97	−3.88[a]
2008-10	555	452	0.379[a]	0.709[a]	25.785	43.884	0.262	0.929	2.759[a]	19.981			
2011-14	762	675	0.456[a]	0.631[a]	33.693	45.470	0.352	0.676	1.380[a]	11.112			
2005-14	1838	1489	0.417[a]	0.641[a]	48.873	69.306	0.286	0.700	1.949[a]	24.095			
Finance													
2005-07	311	243	0.209[a]	0.361[a]	12.678	16.524	0.087	0.210	2.644[a]	13.730	−1.80	−2.44[b]	0.95
2008-10	339	309	0.268[a]	0.496[a]	14.811	23.106	0.108	0.376	2.528[a]	15.356			
2011-14	508	461	0.247[a]	0.427[a]	18.378	25.006	0.116	0.276	2.032[a]	14.252			
2005-14	1158	1013	0.243[a]	0.432[a]	26.710	37.491	0.102	0.270	2.330[a]	24.668			

Health care												
2005–07	183	133	0.293[a]	0.477[a]	13.292	15.681	0.190	0.372	1.997[a]	8.092	−0.33	0.57
2008–10	116	103	0.327[a]	0.557[a]	11.154	15.321	0.224	0.513	1.865[a]	5.788	−0.93	
2011–14	133	119	0.305[a]	0.602[a]	11.289	18.547	0.196	0.645	2.613[a]	7.953		
2005–14	432	355	0.306[a]	0.542[a]	20.724	28.356	0.200	0.467	2.164[a]	12.634		
Public utilities												
2005–07	99	87	0.256[a]	0.432[a]	7.794	10.540	0.107	0.254	1.929[a]	5.531	−0.21	0.79
2008–10	101	96	0.304[a]	0.491[a]	8.593	12.157	0.124	0.354	2.287[a]	6.905	−0.99	
2011–14	111	110	0.266[a]	0.465[a]	8.071	12.175	0.103	0.287	1.746[a]	6.065		
2005–14	311	293	0.275[a]	0.464[a]	14.142	20.199	0.108	0.307	1.978[a]	10.681		
Technology												
2005–07	242	169	0.288[a]	0.586[a]	13.807	21.485	0.148	0.545	2.754[a]	12.821	0.39	0.65
2008–10	200	177	0.297[a]	0.581[a]	12.809	20.594	0.167	0.556	2.663[a]	10.525	−0.29	
2011–14	200	180	0.276[a]	0.524[a]	11.582	18.865	0.120	0.400	2.356[a]	10.101		
2005–14	642	526	0.287[a]	0.563[a]	22.103	35.070	0.154	0.500	2.589[a]	19.118		
Transportation												
2005–07	46	41	0.269[a]	0.471[a]	5.889	8.036	0.146	0.351	2.187[a]	3.829	−0.65	1.64
2008–10	46	44	0.429[a]	0.638[a]	8.077	11.735	0.350	0.718	1.736[a]	5.209	−2.28[b]	
2011–14	58	55	0.312[a]	0.543[a]	6.556	10.329	0.113	0.525	2.154[a]	5.591		
2005–14	150	140	0.335[a]	0.552[a]	11.703	17.197	0.176	0.505	2.026[a]	8.241		

[a]Indicate statistical significance at 1% level, respectively.
[b]Indicate statistical significance at 5% level, respectively.
[c]FAFE is the mean forecast error at the end of the fiscal year divided by the annual reported earnings and defined by Eq. (10.1).
[d]*T*-test on mean differences is adjusted using de Satterthwaite's procedure if necessary

t, $F_{j,t}$ = the consensus earnings per share forecast for firm j and fiscal year t, and $RE_{j,t}$ = the reported earnings per share form firm j and fiscal year t.

Following Coën and Desfleurs (2004, 2016), we also introduce a metric for a naïve statistical model based on time series. The naïve FAF error (NFAFE) for firm j and fiscal year t is given by the following equation:

$$|NFAFE| = \left| \frac{RE_{j,t-1} - RE_{j,t}}{RE_{j,t}} \right| \tag{10.2}$$

The naïve model is based on the simple assumption that the earnings forecast for fiscal year t is the previous reported earnings (for fiscal year $t-1$). To analyze the relative performance of FAF, we also use a second metric initially developed by Brown et al. (1987):

$$SUP_{j,t} = \ln\left(\left| \frac{RE_{j,t-1} - RE_{j,t}}{F_{j,t-1} - RE_{j,t}} \right|^2 \right) \tag{10.3}$$

The interpretation is straightforward. A ratio statistically positive highlights the precision of FA with respect to a naïve statistical model: FA are more performant.

10.3.3 FAF Bias: A Definition

Following the financial literature, we define the FAF bias as the relative FAF error (forecast error with its sign) as follows (the parameters have already been defined in the previous section):

$$FAFE = \frac{e_{j,t(h)}}{|RE_{j,t}|} = \frac{F_{j,t(h)} - RE_{j,t}}{|RE_{j,t}|} \tag{10.4}$$

FAF error is considered to be not biased if FAFE is not statistically different from zero. FAF error is considered to be not biased. FA are qualified as overoptimistic if FAF is higher than reported earnings: the FAFE is indeed statistically positive. On the contrary, if the difference is statistically negative they are considered as pessimistic (or underpessimistic).When FAFE is statistically positive (FAF is higher than reported earnings), FA can be reasonably qualified as overoptimistic. On the contrary, they are considered as pessimistic or underpessimistic when the difference is statistically negative.

As our main objective is to analyze the evolution of FAF bias during the GFC, we use the well-known methodology introduced by De Bondt and Thaler (1990). We may also report that this approach is now a standard in the financial literature and has been extensively used: for example, we refer to Paudyal et al. (1997) and Coën and Desfleurs (2004) (among others). Therefore, we regress the variation of earnings forecast on the difference between the final FAF for year t and the reported earnings for $t-1$:

$$\frac{RE_{j,t} - RE_{j,t-1}}{\left|RE_{j,t-1}\right|} = \alpha + \beta \frac{F_{j,t} - RE_{j,t-1}}{\left|RE_{j,t-1}\right|} + \varepsilon_{j,t} \text{ with } \varepsilon_{j,t} \sim N\left(0, \sigma^2\right) \qquad (10.5)$$

Where:

$\dfrac{RE_{j,t} - RE_{j,t-1}}{\left|RE_{j,t-1}\right|}$: the variation of reported earnings between fiscal years t and $t-1$.

$\dfrac{F_{j,t} - RE_{j,t-1}}{\left|RE_{j,t-1}\right|}$: the difference between FAF of the fiscal year t and the reported earnings of $t-1$.

According to the seminal work of De Bondt and Thaler, if $\alpha = 0$ and $\beta = 1$ (at standard statistical level of confidence) jointly, no bias is statistically reported. Inversely, we can reject the absence of bias if $\alpha \neq 0$ and/or $\beta \neq 1$. As reported by Coën and Desfleurs (2004) (among others), a negative coefficient estimate for α may be related to overestimation (a so-called optimistic bias). On the contrary, a positive coefficient estimate highlights the presence of underestimation (pessimistic bias). Moreover, as reported by De Bondt and Thaler (1990), a coefficient estimate $\beta < 1$ is interpreted as an overreaction among FA while a coefficient estimate $\beta > 1$ reveals an underreaction. As well acknowledged, FA tend to exhibit overoptimism in their earnings forecasts (Alford and Berger, 1999; Allen et al., 1997; Ang and Ma, 2001; Basu et al., 1998; Brown et al., 1987; Chopra, 1998; Coën and Desfleurs, 2004; Coën et al., 2009; De Bondt and Thaler, 1990; Hope, 2003; Loh and Mian, 2002; Tan et al., 2011). This phenomenon should be observed for our sample with potential differences in amplitudes before, during and after the GFC.

10.3.4 FAF by Subperiods and Types of Earnings

To analyze the evolution of FAF before, during, and after the GFC, we divide our sample in three subperiods using the GFC as a potential breakdown: before the crisis, 2005–07; during the crisis, 2008–10, and after the crisis, 2011–14. Moreover, we also focus on the types of earnings, adding another behavioral dimension to our analysis of FAF accuracy and FAF bias. We follow Coën and Desfleurs (2004, 2014) and separate earnings profits from earnings losses, on one hand, and earnings increases from earnings decreases, on the other hand. As suggested by Ciccone (2005) and Coën and Desfleurs (2004, 2014) for Asian financial markets, the GFC may indeed change the behavior of FA and modify FAF accuracy and FAF bias (as suggested by Ciccone, 2005; Coën and Desfleurs, 2004, 2014 for Asian financial markets, among others).

10.4 Analysis of FAF on Canadian Industrial Sectors

In this section, first, we analyze the evolution of FA forecasts for a large sample of 11 industrial sectors in Canada from 2005 to 2014. Second, we suggest shedding light on the impact and consequences of the GFC on FA's behavior, specifically on FAF accuracy and FAF bias.

10.4.1 Analysis of FAF Accuracy: Canadian Industrial Sectors Evidence

To analyze FAF accuracy, we compare the mean of absolute FAF errors (|FAFE|) with the mean generated by a statistical naïve model, as defined by Eq. (10.2) (|NFAFE|). Descriptive statistics for each industrial sector and each subperiod are reported in Table 10.1. We note that the mean of absolute FAF errors (|FAFE|) is statistically different from zero for the full sample period, and for each subperiod, with a value of 0.332 (or 33.2%) and lower than the errors induced by a naïve model (|NFAFE|, 0.538). For all subperiods and all industrial sectors, FA perform better than a naïve model. We also observe a significant increase of |FAFE| before (0.316) and after the GFC (0.343) as reported by the adjusted T-test of −2.90 (significant at 1%). This result should be nuanced when we focus on the different industrial sectors. FA exhibit the better accuracy for Consumer durables (0.214), Consumer services (0.215), and Finance (0.243). |FAFE| are the highest for Energy (0.417), Basic Industries (0.404), and Transportation (0.335). For |NFAFE|, we report the same trend: Energy (0.641), Basic Industries (0.607), Technology (0.563), and Transportation (0.552). To shed light on the analysis of FAF accuracy, we focus now on each subperiod and each industrial sector.

10.4.1.1 Before the GFC: 2005–07

We report that the FAF accuracy is the best for Consumer services with an absolute |FAFE| of 19.2% (0.192) and Finance (0.209), followed by Consumer nondurables (0.245) and durables (0.248).The highest |FAFE| are reported for Basic industries (0.404), followed by Energy (0.400), and Capital goods (0.318). Interestingly, we note that FAF accuracy is statistically better for each industrial sector than this induced by a naïve statistic model. As an illustration, the |NFAFE| is 36.9% for Consumer services (0.369 compared to |FAFE| = 0.192) or 57.5% (0.575 compared to 0.400) for Energy. We may also report an interesting result related to the evolution of accuracy. If for all sectors, we report a decrease as mentioned earlier (adjusted T-test of −2.90), for individual industrial sector the result is contrasted. The differences of FAF accuracy before and after the GFC are not statistically significant except for Capital goods with an increase (T-test of 2.78) and inversely for Energy with a significant decrease (T-test of −2.67). At this level, we cannot draw any conclusion as far as the results are mitigated. We observe a decline of FAF accuracy, even nonsignificant, in six sectors (Consumer services, Energy, Finance, Health care, Public utilities, and Transportation) and an increase in five sectors (Capital goods, significant and nonsignificant for Consumer durables,

Consumer nondurables, Technology, and Basic industries). With these results, we cannot conclude that the negative effects of the financial crisis have been solved. Globally, there is a significant decline of the performance of FA on the Canadian market after the GFC.

10.4.1.2 During the GFC: 2008–10

For the full subsample (all sectors), we report a decrease of FAF accuracy introduced by the breakdown of the GFC. The |FAFE| reaches 31.6% before the GFC and 33.2% during the crisis. Nevertheless, this decrease is not statistically highly significant for eight industries, we observe a decline. For Finance (|FAFE| = 0.268) and Transportation (0.429), the decline of FAF accuracy is statistically significant. Inversely, for three industries an increase could be mentioned (Capital goods, Consumer durables, and Energy). This improvement of FAF accuracy is only significant for Capital goods (0.225).

10.4.1.3 After the GFC: 2011–14

After the crisis, standing as a potential breakdown, we are able to report a decrease of FAF accuracy for the group including all 11 sectors, as mentioned earlier: |FAFE| reaches 0.343 after the crisis from 0.332 during and 0.316 before the crisis. The most important decline can be reported for Energy (from 0.400 to 0.456). For the other industrial sectors, we observe a relative improvement, but not statistically significant just after the 2008–10 period.

10.4.2 Analysis of FAF Bias: Canadian Industry Sectors Effects

Our main objective in this section is to analyze the evolution of the mean of forecast errors, the so-called forecast bias. Following an important literature, we can reasonably anticipate a change in the behavior of FA. According to previous studies (including Chopra, 1998; Ciccone, 2005; Coën and Desfleurs, 2004, among others), an increase of FAF accuracy and a relative decline of overoptimism should be expected. Tables 10.2 and 10.3 report our detailed results for each industrial sectors and subperiods.

As expected, the data clearly report that FAF are highly statistically positive, highlighting the presence of a significant optimism among FA for "all sectors" FAFE range from 15.0% before the crisis to 11.7% during the crisis. For the 11 industrial sectors, FAFE range from 19.7% for Energy, followed by 15.4% for Basic industries (13.3% for Transportation) to 7% for Consumer durables, followed by Finance (8.2%), and Public utilities (8.2%). While we observe a relative decline of this overoptimism for six sectors (Basic industries: from 20.5% before the crisis to 12.9% after the crisis; Capital goods: from 18.1% to 8.7%; Consumer durables: from 12.3% to 1.5%; Consumer nondurables: from 13.7% to 8.8%; Health care: from 15.8% to 11.8%; and Technology: from 12.7% to 8.1%), we note an inverse trend for five industrial sectors exhibiting an increase of optimistic forecasts (Consumer services: from 10.9% to 13.1%; Energy: from 20.2% to 23%; Finance: from 5.8% to 9.0%; Public utilities:

Table 10.2: Descriptive statistics of forecast errors (FAFE) at the end of the fiscal year.

FAFE[a] (Bias)	Periods	Number of Observations	Mean	T-Student	Standard Deviation	Median	% Optimism
All sectors	2005–07	2315	0.150[b]	16.410	0.441	0.039	57.47
	2008–10	2344	0.117[b]	12.211	0.463	0.029	53.82
	2011–14	3271	0.137[b]	16.677	0.471	0.045	56.28
	2005–14	7930	0.120[b]	22.660	0.475	0.035	55.90
Basic industries	2005–07	472	0.205[b]	8.837	0.504	0.113	63.58
	2008–10	582	0.152[b]	7.063	0.519	0.097	59.03
	2011–14	968	0.129[b]	7.803	0.516	0.116	59.55
	2005–14	2022	0.154[b]	13.413	0.515	0.111	60.33
Capital goods	2005–07	127	0.181[b]	4.618	0.441	0.033	51.97
	2008–10	117	0.063	1.800	0.380	0.000	48.31
	2011–14	156	0.087[b]	3.124	0.346	0.000	47.44
	2005–14	400	0.110[b]	5.618	0.390	0.000	49.13
Consumer durables	2005–07	45	0.123[c]	2.134	0.387	0.006	51.11
	2008–10	49	0.082	1.546	0.371	0.000	46.00
	2011–14	53	0.015	0.333	0.317	0.000	48.15
	2005–14	147	0.070[c]	2.378	0.358	0.000	48.32
Consumer nondurables	2005–07	50	0.137[b]	2.775	0.349	0.022	54.00
	2008–10	47	0.176[b]	2.930	0.411	0.063	54.17
	2011–14	67	0.088[c]	2.133	0.338	0.009	54.93
	2005–14	164	0.128[b]	4.516	0.363	0.011	54.44
Consumer services	2005–07	219	0.109[b]	5.141	0.313	0.007	51.36
	2008–10	192	0.050[c]	1.936	0.356	0.000	46.63
	2011–14	255	0.131[b]	5.458	0.383	0.010	52.16
	2005–14	666	0.100[b]	7.294	0.355	0.005	50.30
Energy	2005–07	521	0.202[b]	9.141	0.505	0.097	61.44
	2008–10	555	0.149[b]	7.124	0.491	0.077	57.19
	2011–14	762	0.230[b]	11.660	0.544	0.178	62.18
	2005–14	1838	0.197[b]	16.329	0.518	0.118	60.47
Finance	2005–07	311	0.058[b]	2.896	0.353	0.004	52.24
	2008–10	339	0.091[b]	4.016	0.418	0.011	52.63
	2011–14	508	0.090[b]	5.338	0.380	0.007	51.07
	2005–14	1158	0.082[b]	7.232	0.385	0.007	51.84
Health care	2005–07	183	0.158[b]	5.505	0.388	0.103	64.86
	2008–10	116	0.035	0.825	0.455	0.021	52.59
	2011–14	133	0.118[b]	3.253	0.420	0.091	60.00
	2005–14	432	0.113[b]	5.594	0.418	0.091	60.09
Public utilities	2005–07	99	0.052	1.256	0.413	0.000	49.49
	2008–10	101	0.107[c]	2.350	0.456	0.000	48.04
	2011–14	111	0.086[c]	2.113	0.430	0.005	51.33
	2005–14	311	0.082[b]	3.344	0.432	0.003	49.68
Technology	2005–07	242	0.127[b]	4.763	0.415	0.019	51.82
	2008–10	200	0.102[b]	3.336	0.431	0.000	47.29
	2011–14	200	0.081[b]	2.694	0.428	0.000	47.34
	2005–14	642	0.105[b]	6.275	0.424	0.002	49.01
Transportation	2005–07	46	0.085	1.422	0.404	0.022	56.52
	2008–10	46	0.169[c]	2.133	0.537	0.016	51.06
	2011–14	58	0.144[c]	2.396	0.458	0.005	51.72
	2005–14	150	0.133[b]	3.503	0.467	0.011	52.98

[a]FAFE is the mean forecast error at the end of the fiscal year divided by the annual reported earnings and defined by Eq. (10.4).
[b]Indicate statistical significance at 1% level, respectively.
[c]Indicate statistical significance at 5% level, respectively.

Table 10.3: Test on the difference of forecast biases (FAFE).

Sectors	Bias[a]	Before Crisis	During Crisis	After Crisis	Tests on Mean Differences	Adjusted T-Test
All sectors	FAFE	0.150[b]	0.117[b]	0.137[b]	Before/after crisis	1.05
					Before/during crisis	2.53[c]
					During/after crisis	−1.63
Basic industries	FAFE	0.205[b]	0.152[b]	0.129[b]	Before/after crisis	2.62[b]
					Before/during crisis	1.67
					During/after crisis	0.82
Capital goods	FAFE	0.181[b]	0.063	0.087[b]	Before/after crisis	1.97
					Before/during crisis	2.22[c]
					During/after crisis	−0.53
Consumer durables	FAFE	0.123[c]	0.082	0.015	Before/after crisis	1.53
					Before/during crisis	0.53
					During/after crisis	0.99
Consumer nondurables	FAFE	0.137[b]	0.176[b]	0.088[c]	Before/after crisis	0.76
					Before/during crisis	−0.50
					During/after crisis	1.24
Consumer services	FAFE	0.109[b]	0.050[c]	0.131[b]	Before/after crisis	−0.70
					Before/during crisis	1.77
					During/after crisis	−2.29[c]
Energy	FAFE	0.202[b]	0.149[b]	0.230[b]	Before/after crisis	−0.91
					Before/during crisis	1.77
					During/after crisis	−2.82
Finance	FAFE	0.058[b]	0.091[b]	0.090[b]	Before/after crisis	−1.23
					Before/during crisis	−1.10
					During/after crisis	0.04
Health care	FAFE	0.158[b]	0.035	0.118[b]	Before/after crisis	0.85
					Before/during crisis	2.50[c]
					During/after crisis	−1.50
Public utilities	FAFE	0.052	0.107[c]	0.086[c]	Before/after crisis	−0.59
					Before/during crisis	−0.89
					During/after crisis	0.34
Technology	FAFE	0.127[b]	0.102[b]	0.081[b]	Before/after crisis	1.13
					Before/during crisis	0.63
					During/after crisis	0.47
Transportation	FAFE	0.085	0.169[c]	0.144[c]	Before/after crisis	−0.69
					Before/during crisis	−0.85
					During/after crisis	0.26

[a]FAFE is the mean forecast error at the end of the fiscal year divided by the annual reported earnings and defined by Eq. (10.4).
[b]Indicate statistical significance at 1% level, respectively.
[c]Indicate statistical significance at 5% level, respectively.

from 5.2% to 8.6%; and Transportation: from 8.5% to 14.4%). Interestingly we report that the GFC is not the period of the lowest level of optimism for seven industrial sectors. For four sectors, it coincides with the highest level of overoptimism (Consumer nondurables: 17.6%; Finance: 9.1%; Public utilities: 10.7%; and Transportation: 16.9%).

In Table 10.3, we report the statistical significance of these contrasted trends. First, we focus on the decline of overoptimism. It is statistically significant for "all Canadian sectors" before and during the GFC (Capital goods: from 18.1% to 6.3%; and Health care: from 15.8% to 3.5%). For Basic industries, the decline is statistically significant before and after the crisis (from 20.5% to 12.9%). For Consumer services, a significant increase of overoptimism may be reported. FAFE rise from 10.9% before crisis to 13.1% after crisis (Table 10.4).

Following the seminal work of De Bondt and Thaler (and afterward Capstaff et al., 1998; Coën and Desfleurs, 2004, 2016), we compare FAF variations to reported earnings variations defined by Eq. (10.5) (Table 10.5).

We note that for all industrial sectors and all subperiods, the coefficient estimate β is below 1 and very often statistically different from 1 except for Consumer durables. As mentioned previously, a coefficient estimate $\beta < 1$ indicates that FA tend to overreact with an increase of information flow. We also report that the coefficient estimate α is negative (and highly significant for all sectors) and all subperiods: from -2.6% before the crisis to -3.9% after the crisis. This result highlights an increase of overoptimism. A negative coefficient is indeed synonym of overoptimism. This negative coefficient is observed for all sectors (even nonsignificant) except for Consumer durables where the coefficient is positive but not significant (and Consumer services during the crisis). For this industrial sector, we cannot report the presence of an overoptimism phenomenon and neither an overreaction. For Health care, Public utilities, Technology, Transportation, and Consumer nondurables, α estimates are always negative but never statistically different from zero. While overoptimism is not detected, overreaction signals are present as reported by F test.

We improve our behavioral analysis adding two dimensions. First, we focus on profits and losses forecasts. Second, we consider earnings increases and earnings decreases forecasts. It is well acknowledged in the financial literature that FA face difficulties to forecast losses and earnings decreases.

10.4.3 Analysis of the Evolution of FAFE by Types of Earnings

10.4.3.1 Earnings profits versus earnings losses: Canadian evidence

As expected from the devoted literature, the amplitude of FAFE is more important for earnings losses than for earnings profits. This result is reported for FAF accuracy and FAF bias.

Table 10.4: Regression of reported earnings variation on forecasted earnings variation.

Sectors	Periods	Number of Observations	α	T-test: $\alpha = 0$	β	T-test: $\beta = 0$	F-test: $\beta = 1$	Adjusted R^2 (%)
Canada	2005–07	1199	-0.026^a	-3.267	0.804^a	42.801	109.54^a	60.45
	2008–10	1372	-0.030^a	-3.719	0.797^a	46.202	138.42^a	60.88
	2011–14	2007	-0.039^a	-5.704	0.758^a	48.814	243.45^a	54.28
	2005–14	4578	-0.033^a	-7.535	0.782^a	79.324	491.82^a	57.89
Basic industries	2005–07	200	-0.061^b	-2.372	0.677^a	12.776	37.30^a	44.91
	2008–10	305	-0.062^a	-2.710	0.740^a	17.435	37.43^a	49.92
	2011–14	564	-0.055^a	-3.716	0.753^a	24.466	64.31^a	51.49
	2005–14	1069	-0.058^a	-5.176	0.735^a	32.717	139.51^a	50.03
Capital goods	2005–07	62	-0.018	-0.389	0.762^a	7.131	4.95^b	44.97
	2008–10	76	-0.010	-0.543	0.976^a	21.607	0.28	86.13
	2011–14	120	-0.047^b	-2.438	0.866^a	17.503	7.30^a	71.96
	2005–14	258	-0.032^b	-2.085	0.869^a	23.243	12.27^a	67.72
Consumer durables	2005–07	28	0.010	0.273	0.929^a	6.940	0.28	63.59
	2008–10	30	0.023	0.554	$1.053^{a,b}$	7.396	0.14	64.93
	2011–14	42	0.008	0.327	0.951^a	10.794	0.31	73.80
	2005–14	100	0.011	0.602	0.977^a	14.867	0.12	68.97
Consumer nondurables	2005–07	29	-0.008	-0.200	0.986^a	8.074	0.01	69.63
	2008–10	33	-0.015	-0.386	0.813^a	10.057	5.33^b	75.78
	2011–14	50	-0.036	-1.062	0.824^a	9.599	4.20^b	65.03
	2005–14	112	-0.025	-1.207	0.845^a	16.149	8.80^a	70.06
Consumer services	2005–07	156	-0.027	-1.531	0.935^a	18.282	1.63	68.25
	2008–10	156	0.036^b	2.165	0.723^a	13.276	25.81^a	53.07
	2011–14	192	-0.008	-0.411	0.676^a	10.814	26.98^a	37.78
	2005–14	504	0.001	0.130	0.770^a	23.001	47.36^a	51.21
Energy	2005–07	219	-0.031	-1.596	0.812^a	19.505	20.27^a	63.51
	2008–10	251	-0.051^b	-2.511	0.828^a	23.380	23.66^a	68.58
	2011–14	355	-0.069^a	-3.557	0.666^a	18.089	82.18^a	47.96
	2005–14	825	-0.056^a	-4.816	0.752^a	34.218	127.04^a	58.67
Finance	2005–07	207	-0.007^a	-4.816	0.836^a	21.904	18.50^a	69.92
	2008–10	219	-0.020	-1.270	0.868^a	20.655	9.94^a	66.13%
	2011–14	351	-0.013	-0.971	0.840^a	23.572	20.03^a	61.31%
	2005–14	777	-0.013	-1.665	0.849^a	38.047	46.08^a	65.09%
Health care	2005–07	103	-0.037	-1.432	0.832^a	13.118	7.06^a	62.65%
	2008–10	80	0.003	0.081	0.773^a	10.977	10.36^a	60.20%
	2011–14	83	0.008	0.224	0.800^a	11.925	8.91^a	63.26%
	2005–14	266	-0.013	-0.765	0.809^a	21.329	25.33^a	63.14%
Public utilities	2005–07	65	-0.027	-0.850	0.787^a	10.216	7.66^a	61.76%
	2008–10	71	-0.044	-1.377	0.771^a	9.024	7.17^a	53.47%
	2011–14	84	-0.013	-0.398	0.804^a	8.539	4.33^b	46.42%
	2005–14	220	-0.027	-1.456	0.790^a	16.098	18.38^a	54.10%
Technology	2005–07	103	-0.022	-0.920	0.906^a	17.567	3.35	75.10%
	2008–10	121	-0.030	-1.019	0.833^a	13.391	7.20^a	59.77%
	2011–14	130	-0.029	-1.267	0.884^a	17.054	5.01^b	69.20%
	2005–14	354	-0.027	-1.791	0.871^a	26.982	15.83^a	67.32%

Table 10.4: Regression of reported earnings variation on forecasted earnings variation. (*cont.*)

Sectors	Periods	Number of Observations	α	T-test: $\alpha = 0$	β	T-test: $\beta = 0$	F-test: $\beta = 1$	Adjusted R^2 (%)
Transportation	2005–07	27	0.034	1.070	0.789[a]	9.416	6.34[b]	77.13%
	2008–10	30	−0.011	−0.162	0.751[a]	4.750	2.49	42.65%
	2011–14	36	−0.051	−2.009	1.009[a]	13.130	0.01	83.04%
	2005–14	93	−0.015	−0.588	0.851[a]	12.656	4.95[b]	63.37%

[a]Indicate statistical significance at 1% level, respectively.
[b]Indicate statistical significance at 5% level, respectively. Regression is given by Eq. (10.5).

For all Canadian sectors and for the full period, |FAFE| is 23.3% for earnings profits compared to 47.6% for earnings losses. The accuracy tends to be stable during the period even if we must report an expected decrease during the crisis: from 21.7% before the crisis to 24.5% after (for profits); and from 48.7% to 48.1% with a value of 45.9% during the GFC. For the 11 industrial sectors, we observe globally the same trend with some nuances. For five industries, we may report a small decrease of FAF accuracy for earnings profits (Basic industries: from 25.6% to 31.7%; Energy: from 27.3% to 34.8%; Finance: from 17.5% to 20.7%; Health care: from 27.6% to 35.8%; and Transportation: from 16.6% to 20.5%), while we note the inverse trend for six industries (Capital goods: from 20.1% to 16.6%; Consumer durables: from 16.4% to 12.4%; Consumer non-durables: from 19.1% to 18.6%; Consumer services: from 15.1% to 14.7%; Public utilities: from 21.7% to 15.9%; and Technology: from 20.7% to 18.1%).

We may also mention that FAF accuracy is at the highest level for four industries during the GFC (Capital goods: 15.5%; Consumer durables: 11.7%; Consumer nondurables: and 12.2%; Consumer services: 13.2%).

When we focus on earnings losses, we report the same contrasted results. For six industries an increase of accuracy could be highlighted (Basic industries: from 55.0% to 45.2%; Capital goods: from 59.3% to 36.7%; Consumer durables: from 45.2% to 44.1%; Consumer non-durables: from 43.4% to 30.8%; Energy: from 62.5% to 57.1%; and Health care: from 29.8% to 28.3%) while a decrease is observed for five industries (Consumer services: from 33.1% to 56.6%; Finance: from 45.6% to 49.9%; Public utilities: from 41.9% to 65.4%; Technology: from 41.0% to 43.3%; and Transportation: from 53.2% to 72.2%).

For FAF bias, values are positive or not statistically different from zero and much higher for losses than for profits. For all Canadian sectors, the FAFE for the full period are 3.5% for profits compared to 28.0% for losses. A decline of the bias could be reported for losses during the period (from 34.9% to 25.3%) while an increase is noted for profits (from 3.6% to 5.6%).

Table 10.5: Descriptive statistics of forecast errors in absolute mean (|FAFE| measure of financial analyst accuracy) and in mean (FAFE. measure of forecast bias) distinguishing reported earnings profits from reported earnings losses.

Sectors	Periods	Reported Earnings Profits			Reported Earnings Loss		
		Number of Observations	Accuracy: |FAFE|	Bias: FAFE	Number of Observations	Accuracy: |FAFE|	Bias: FAFE
All sectors	2005–07	1471	0.217[a]	0.036[a]	844	0.487[a]	0.349[a]
	2008–10	1309	0.232[a]	0.004	1035	0.459[a]	0.260[a]
	2011–14	1912	0.245[a]	0.056[a]	1359	0.481[a]	0.253[a]
	2005–14	4692	0.233[a]	0.035[a]	3238	0.476[a]	0.280[a]
Basic industries	2005–07	234	0.256[a]	0.030	238	0.550[a]	0.377[a]
	2008–10	254	0.303[a]	0.018	328	0.496[a]	0.255[a]
	2011–14	371	0.317[a]	0.087[a]	597	0.452[a]	0.156[a]
	2005–14	859	0.296[a]	0.051[a]	1163	0.485[a]	0.229[a]
Capital goods	2005–07	89	0.201[a]	0.038	38	0.593[a]	0.516[a]
	2008–10	78	0.155[a]	−0.026	39	0.366[a]	0.242[a]
	2011–14	122	0.166[a]	0.041	34	0.367[a]	0.249[a]
	2005–14	289	0.174[a]	0.022	111	0.444[a]	0.338[a]
Consumer durables	2005–07	32	0.164[a]	0.106[b]	13	0.452[a]	0.164
	2008–10	35	0.117[a]	0.005	14	0.488[a]	0.274
	2011–14	44	0.124[a]	−0.022	9	0.441[a]	0.193
	2005–14	111	0.133[a]	0.024	36	0.463[a]	0.214[b]
Consumer nondurables	2005–07	39	0.191[a]	0.060	11	0.434[a]	0.412[a]
	2008–10	31	0.122[a]	0.026	16	0.596[a]	0.466[a]
	2011–14	49	0.186[a]	0.055	18	0.308[a]	0.180[b]
	2005–14	119	0.171[a]	0.049	45	0.441[a]	0.338[a]
Consumer services	2005–07	169	0.151[a]	0.055[b]	50	0.331[a]	0.290[a]
	2008–10	149	0.132[a]	−0.027	43	0.459[a]	0.315[a]
	2011–14	198	0.147[a]	0.067[a]	57	0.566[a]	0.352[a]
	2005–14	516	0.144[a]	0.036[a]	150	0.457[a]	0.321[a]
Energy	2005–07	333	0.273[a]	0.055[b]	188	0.625[a]	0.463[a]
	2008–10	244	0.284[a]	−0.011	311	0.453[a]	0.274[a]
	2011–14	393	0.348[a]	0.077[a]	369	0.571[a]	0.392[a]
	2005–14	970	0.306[a]	0.047[a]	868	0.541[a]	0.365[a]
Finance	2005–07	274	0.175[a]	0.012	37	0.456[a]	0.398[a]
	2008–10	277	0.217[a]	0.042	62	0.500[a]	0.312[a]
	2011–14	438	0.207[a]	0.045[b]	70	0.499[a]	0.370[a]
	2005–14	989	0.201[a]	0.035[a]	169	0.490[a]	0.355[a]
Health care	2005–07	42	0.276[a]	0.064	141	0.298[a]	0.186[a]
	2008–10	22	0.354[a]	−0.167	94	0.321[a]	0.082
	2011–14	39	0.358[a]	−0.054	94	0.283[a]	0.190[a]
	2005–14	103	0.323[a]	−0.030	329	0.300[a]	0.157[a]
Public utilities	2005–07	80	0.217[a]	0.024	19	0.419[a]	0.171
	2008–10	73	0.196[a]	0.001	28	0.586[a]	0.382[a]
	2011–14	87	0.159[a]	0.017	24	0.654[a]	0.335[b]
	2005–14	240	0.190[a]	0.015	71	0.564[a]	0.310[a]

(Continued)

Table 10.5: Descriptive statistics of forecast errors in absolute mean (|FAFE| measure of financial analyst accuracy) and in mean (FAFE. measure of forecast bias) distinguishing reported earnings profits from reported earnings losses. (*cont.*)

Sectors	Periods	Reported Earnings Profits			Reported Earnings Loss		
		Number of Observations	Accuracy: |FAFE|	Bias: FAFE	Number of Observations	Accuracy: |FAFE|	Bias: FAFE
Technology	2005–07	146	0.207[a]	0.007	96	0.410[a]	0.309[a]
	2008–10	114	0.221[a]	−0.013	86	0.398[a]	0.254[a]
	2011–14	125	0.181[a]	0.024	75	0.433[a]	0.177[a]
	2005–14	385	0.203[a]	0.007	257	0.413[a]	0.252[a]
Transportation	2005–07	33	0.166[a]	0.022	13	0.532[a]	0.244
	2008–10	32	0.326[a]	0.042	14	0.665[a]	0.460[a]
	2011–14	46	0.205[a]	0.029	12	0.722[a]	0.585[a]
	2005–14	111	0.228[a]	0.031	39	0.638[a]	0.426[a]

[a]Indicate statistical significance at 1% level, respectively.
[b]Indicate statistical significance at 5% level, respectively.

10.4.3.2 Earnings increases versus earnings decreases: Canadian evidence

First, we analyze FAF accuracy. As reported by Table 10.6 for the full period, FAF accuracy is higher (30.7%) for earnings increases than for decreases (37.4%) for all Canadian sectors. This result is always reported for each industrial sector. We can reasonably conclude that FA face serious difficulties to forecast earnings decreases on the Canadian market.

As mentioned in the previous section, results are mitigated. Focusing on reported earnings increases, an increase of accuracy can be reported for six industries (Capital goods: from 24.6% to 19.9%; Consumer durables: from 18.7% to 8.2%; Consumer non-durables: from 21.6% to 18.1%; Public utilities: from 17.3% to 16.7%; Technology: 25.1% to 21.4%; and Transportation: 21.5% to 19.1%) while five sectors exhibit a decrease (Basic industries: from 38.8% to 40.9%; Consumer services: from 16.0% to 21.0%; Energy: from 39.0% to 44.6%; Finance: from 17.4% to 21.6%; and Health care: from 30.9% to 31.9%). The highest |FAFE| are reported during the crisis for only four sectors (Consumer non-durables: 25.9%; Finance: 22.5%; Public utilities: 27.5%; and Transportation: 50.4%). We also can observe that the metric for the accuracy is always lower than the metric for the bias. When we analyze earnings decreases, we note that an increase of accuracy is reported for five industries (Basic industries: from 43.1% to 39.3%; Capital goods: from 48.7% to 23.1%; Consumer durables: from 38.3% to 32.4%; Consumer non-durables: from 29.6% to 26.6%; and Technology: from 38.3% to 36.9%) while six industries show a decrease (Consumer services: from 25.9% to 30.9%; Energy: from 42.3% to 47.2%; Finance: from 30.1% to 30.5%; Health care: from 27% to 28.2%; Public utilities: from 39.1% to 39.7%; and Transportation: from 38.5% to 44.2%).

Table 10.6: Descriptive statistics of forecast errors in absolute mean (|FAFE| measure of financial analyst accuracy) and in mean (FAFE measure of forecast bias) distinguishing reported earnings increases from reported earnings decreases.

Sectors	Periods	Reported Earnings Increase			Reported Earnings Decrease		
		Number of Observations	Accuracy: |FAFE|	Bias: FAFE	Number of Observations	Accuracy: |FAFE|	Bias: FAFE
All sectors	2005–07	1549	0.286[a]	0.096	725	0.375[a]	0.262[a]
	2008–10	1408	0.307[a]	0.041	901	0.370[a]	0.238[a]
	2011–14	1989	0.322[a]	0.052	1206	0.377[a]	0.278[a]
	2005–14	4946	0.307[a]	0.063	2832	0.374[a]	0.261[a]
Basic industries	2005–07	301	0.388[a]	0.151[a]	157	0.431[a]	0.303[a]
	2008–10	372	0.385[a]	0.052	201	0.456[a]	0.335[a]
	2011–14	568	0.409[a]	0.016	369	0.393[a]	0.304[a]
	2005–14	1241	0.396[a]	0.060[a]	727	0.419[a]	0.312[a]
Capital goods	2005–07	89	0.246[a]	0.091[b]	34	0.487[a]	0.387[a]
	2008–10	66	0.171[a]	0.028	49	0.306[a]	0.111
	2011–14	96	0.199[a]	0.033	59	0.231[a]	0.175[a]
	2005–14	251	0.208[a]	0.052	142	0.318[a]	0.204[a]
Consumer durables	2005–07	31	0.187[a]	0.008[b]	14	0.383[a]	0.377[a]
	2008–10	25	0.170[a]	−0.041	23	0.277[a]	0.232[a]
	2011–14	32	0.082[a]	−0.024	21	0.324[a]	0.073
	2005–14	88	0.144[a]	−0.017	58	0.319[a]	0.210[a]
Consumer nondurables	2005–07	32	0.216[a]	0.081	18	0.296[a]	0.237[a]
	2008–10	26	0.259[a]	0.107	21	0.313[a]	0.261[a]
	2011–14	37	0.181[a]	0.014	28	0.266[a]	0.175[a]
	2005–14	95	0.214[a]	0.062	67	0.289[a]	0.219[a]
Consumer services	2005–07	151	0.160[a]	0.058[b]	65	0.259[a]	0.222[a]
	2008–10	119	0.171[a]	−0.015	70	0.264[a]	0.153[a]
	2011–14	167	0.210[a]	0.065[b]	85	0.309[a]	0.264[a]
	2005–14	437	0.182[a]	0.041[b]	220	0.280[a]	0.216[a]
Energy	2005–07	344	0.390[a]	0.166[a]	172	0.423[a]	0.277[a]
	2008–10	337	0.375[a]	0.100[a]	209	0.387[a]	0.232[a]
	2011–14	457	0.446[a]	0.146[a]	282	0.472[a]	0.358[a]
	2005–14	1138	0.408[a]	0.139[a]	663	0.433[a]	0.297[a]
Finance	2005–07	226	0.174[a]	0.027	82	0.301[a]	0.153[a]
	2008–10	192	0.225[a]	0.002	147	0.325[a]	0.208[a]
	2011–14	323	0.216[a]	0.032	177	0.305[a]	0.205[a]
	2005–14	741	0.206[a]	0.023	406	0.311[a]	0.196[a]
Health care	2005–07	112	0.309[a]	0.119[a]	66	0.270[a]	0.228[a]
	2008–10	80	0.291[a]	−0.041	33	0.412[a]	0.205[b]
	2011–14	89	0.316[a]	0.084	44	0.282[a]	0.188[a]
	2005–14	281	0.306[a]	0.062[b]	143	0.306[a]	0.210[a]
Public utilities	2005–07	64	0.173[a]	−0.034	34	0.391[a]	0.186[b]
	2008–10	50	0.275[a]	−0.049	50	0.338[a]	0.264[a]
	2011–14	64	0.167[a]	−0.050	45	0.397[a]	0.306[a]
	2005–14	178	0.199[a]	−0.044	129	0.373[a]	0.258[a]

(Continued)

Table 10.6: Descriptive statistics of forecast errors in absolute mean ($|FAFE|$ measure of financial analyst accuracy) and in mean (FAFE measure of forecast bias) distinguishing reported earnings increases from reported earnings decreases. (*cont.*)

Sectors	Periods	Reported Earnings Increase			Reported Earnings Decrease		
		Number of Observations	Accuracy: $|FAFE|$	Bias: FAFE	Number of Observations	Accuracy: $|FAFE|$	Bias: FAFE
Technology	2005–07	170	0.251[a]	0.064[b]	67	0.383[a]	0.276[a]
	2008–10	119	0.245[a]	0.047	74	0.370[a]	0.204[a]
	2011–14	126	0.214[a]	0.000	68	0.369[a]	0.224[a]
	2005–14	415	0.238[a]	0.040[b]	209	0.374[a]	0.234[a]
Transportation	2005–07	29	0.215[a]	−0.042	16	0.385[a]	0.319[a]
	2008–10	22	0.504[a]	0.099	24	0.361[a]	0.233[b]
	2011–14	30	0.191[a]	−0.035	28	0.442[a]	0.336[a]
	2005–14	81	0.285[a]	−0.001	68	0.400[a]	0.296[a]

[a]Indicate statistical significance at 1% level, respectively.
[b]Indicate statistical significance at 5% level, respectively.

Second, we shed light on FAF bias with a striking result: the FAF bias for reported earnings increases is globally not statistically significant except for Energy (where the bias is positive and always highly significant). For earnings decreases the bias is highly significant. For the full period, for all Canadian sectors, FAFE are 26.1% for decreases compared to 6.3% for increases. The bias is quite stable: from 9.6% to 5.2% (for increases); and from 26.2% to 27.8% (for decreases). We observe that the bias is the lowest during the crisis: 4.1% for increases and 23.8% for decreases. FA are less optimistic during the GFC.

Our results are in line with the previous conclusions drawn by the literature: FA make more errors when they forecast decreases and losses and they are very optimistic (all measures are positive and highly significant for earnings decreases). As highlighted by the contrasted results, we are not able to report a significant improvement after the GFC. They are overoptimistic and continue to overreact.

10.5 Conclusions

In this study, we have revisited the seminal work of De Bondt and Thaler (1990) and shed a new light on the main characteristics of FA's forecasts on the Canadian stock markets, focusing on the industrial sectors from 2005 to 2014. Our main objective was to analyze the consequences of the GFC of 2008, considered as a potential breakdown, on FA's behavior. To analyze the overreaction and the overoptimism of FA's forecasts, we have used two metrics related to FAFs accuracy (|FAFE|: the absolute financial analysts' forecast error) and bias (FAFE: the financial analysts forecast error with the sign) respectively. We have analyzed their evolution and variation among industrial sectors. Therefore we have divided our sample in three subperiods: before the GFC from 2005 to 2008; the crisis, from 2008 to 2010; and after the crisis, from 2011 to 2014.

Our results report contrasted results for the different industrial sectors on the Canadian stock markets, and thus shed a new light on the evolution of FAFs. They also lead to the conclusion that FAFs tend to systematically exhibit a certain kind of overoptimism and an overreaction before, during, and after the GFC, confirming the position defended by De Bondt and Thaler (1990).

References

Akerlof, G.A., Shiller, R.J., 2010. Animal Spirits: How Human Psychology Drives the Economy, and Why It Matters for Global Capitalism. Princeton University Press, Princeton.

Alford, A.W., Berger, P.G., 1999. A simultaneous equations analysis of forecasts accuracy, analysts following, and trading volume. J. Acount. Audit. Finance 14, 219–246.

Allen, A., Cho, J.Y., Jung, K., 1997. Earnings forecasts errors: comparative evidence from the Pacific-Basin capital markets. Pacific-Basin Finance J. 5, 115–129.

Ang, J.S., Ma, Y., 2001. The behavior of financial analysts during the Asian financial crisis in Indonesia, Korea, Malaysia, and Thailand. Pacific-Basin Finance J. 9, 233–263.

Barlett, B., 1997. Financial analysts often biased. Opinion Editorial. National Center for Policy Analysis, 17 December.

Basu, S., Hwang, L.S., Jan, C.L., 1998. International variation in accounting measurement rules and analysts' earnings forecast errors. J. Bus. Finance Account. 25, 1207–1247.

Black, E.L., Carnes, T.A., 2006. Analysts' forecasts in Asian-Pacific markets: the relationship among macroeconomic factors, accounting systems, bias and accuracy. J. Int. Financ. Manag. Account. 17, 208–227.

Bradshaw, M., Richardson, S., Sloan, R., 2006. The relation between corporate financing activities, analysts' forecasts and stock returns. J. Account. Econ. 42, 53–85.

Brown, L.D., 1997. Analysts forecasts errors: additional evidence. Financ. Anal. J. 53, 81–88.

Brown, L.D., Richardson, G., Schwager, S., 1987. An information interpretation of financial analyst superiority in forecasting earnings. J. Account. Res. 25, 49–67.

Byard, D., Li, Y., Yu, Y., 2011. The effect of mandatory IFRS adoption on financial analysts' information environment. J. Account. Res. 49, 69–96.

Capstaff, J., Paudyal, K., Ree, W., 1998. Analysts' forecast of German firms' earnings: a comparative analysis. J. Int. Financ. Manag. Account. 9 (2), 83–116.

Chang, X., Dasgupta, S., Hilary, G., 2006. Analyst coverage and financing decisions. J. Finance 61, 3009–3048.

Chee, S.C., Sujin, K., Zurbruegg, R., 2010. The impact of IFRS on financial analysts' forecast accuracy in the Asia-Pacific region: the case of Australia, Hong Kong and New Zealand. Pacific Account. Rev. 22 (2), 124–146.

Chopra, V.K., 1998. Why so much error in analysts' earnings forecasts? Financ. Anal. J. 54, 35–42.

Ciccone, S., 2005. Trends in analyst earnings forecast properties. Int. Rev. Financ. Anal. 14, 1–22.

Clement, M.B., 1999. Analyst forecast accuracy: do ability, resources, and portfolio complexity matter? J. Account. Econ. 27, 285–303.

Coën, A., Desfleurs, A., 2004. The evolution of financial analysts' forecasts on Asian emerging markets. J. Multinat. Financ. Manag. 14 (4–5), 335–352.

Coën, A., Desfleurs, A., 2014. The evolution of financial analysts' forecasts for Asian REITs and real estate companies. In: Gregoriou, G.N., Lee, D., (Eds.). Handbook of Asian Finance. Elsevier, Academic Press, Cambridge, MA.

Coën, A., Desfleurs, A., 2016. Another look at financial analysts' forecast accuracy: recent evidence from eastern European frontier markets. In: Andrikopoulos, P., Gregoriou, G.N., Kallinterakis, V., (Eds.). Handbook of Frontier Markets. Elsevier, Academic Press, Cambridge, MA.

Coën, A., Desfleurs, A., Lher, J.F., 2009. The relative importance of determinants of the quality of financial analysts' forecasts: international evidence. J. Econ. Bus. 61, 453–471.

Das, S., Levine, C., Sivarmakrishnan, K., 1998. Earnings predictability and bias in analysts' earnings forecasts. Account. Rev. 73, 277–294.

De Bondt, W.F.M., Thaler, R., 1990. Do security analysts overreact? Am. Econ. Rev. 80 (2), 52–57.

Hong, H., Lim, T., Stein, J.C., 2000. Bad news travels slowly: size, analyst coverage, and the profitability of momentum strategies. J. Finance 55, 265–295.

Hope, O.-K., 2003. Disclosure practices, enforcement of accounting standards and analysts' forecast accuracy: An international study. J. Account. Res. 41 (3), 235–272.

Kahneman, D., Tversky, A., 1973. On the psychology of prediction. Psychol. Rev. 80, 237–251.

Katz, J.P., Zarzeski, M.T., Hall, H.J., 2000. The impact of strategy, industry and culture on forecasting the performance of global competitors: a strategic perspective. J. Bus. Strat. 17 (2), 119–143.

Ke, B., Yu, Y., 2006. The effect of issuing biased earnings forecasts on analysts' access to management and survival. J. Account. Res. 44, 965–1000.

Lang, M., Lins, K., Miller, D., 2004. Concentrated control, analyst following and valuation: do analysts matter most when investors are protected least? J. Account. Res. 42 (3), 589–623.

Loh, R.K., Mian, M., 2002. The quality of analysts' earnings forecasts during the Asian crisis: evidence from Singapore. J. Bus. Finance Account. 30 (5–6), 715–747.

Mikhail, M.B., Walther, B.R., Willis, R.H., 1997. Do security analysts improve their performance with experience. J. Account. Res. 35, 131–166.

O'Brien, P.C., 1990. Forecast accuracy of individual analysts in nine industries. J. Account. Res. 28, 286–304.

Patel, S.A., Balic, A., Bwakira, L., 2002. Measuring transparency and disclosure at firm-level in emerging markets. Emerg. Markets Rev. 3, 325–337.

Paudyal, K., Saadouni, B., Briston, R., 1997. Earnings forecasts in Malaysia: an empirical analysis. Adv. Pacific Basin Financ. Markets 4, 311–334.

Sadique, S., In, F.H., Veeraraghavan, M., 2010. Analyst bias, firm characteristics, and stock returns in the Australian stock market. Working Paper. Available from: http://ssrn.com/abstract=158273

Shiller, R.J., 1987. Investor behavior in the October 1987 stock market crash: Survey evidence. Working Paper, Cowles Foundation, Yale University, November 1987, and NBER WP 2446.

Tan, H., Wang, S., Welker, M., 2011. Analyst following and forecast accuracy after mandated IFRS adoptions. J. Account. Res. 49, 1307–1357.

Thomas, S., 2002. Firm diversification and asymmetric information: evidence form analysts' forecasts and earnings announcements. J. Financ. Econ. 64, 373–396.

Yu, F., 2008. Analyst coverage and earnings management. J. Financ. Econ. 88 (2), 245–271.

CHAPTER 11

Bank Failures and Management Inefficiency During the Global Financial Crisis

Reza Bradrania, Xiao Li, Lei Xu

University of South Australia, Adelaide, SA, Australia

Chapter Outline

11.1 Introduction

The economic turbulence has often resulted in bank failures which in turn lead to wide-spread fear among the public and more bank failures due to bank run. The systematically destructive bank failures could also lead to wide-spread corporate failures and put the economy into deeper recession.

During the economic downturn between 1987 and early 1990, around six banks per year per state collapsed in the United States (FDIC, 2016). This rate of failure is close to the collapse of four banks per year during the economic expansion of 2000–07 reported by Federal Deposit Insurance Corporation (FDIC) and may not be indicative.

However, FDIC reported 325 bank failures between 2008 and 2010, which is about 108 bank failures per year during the recent global financial crisis (GFC) (FDIC, 2016). This could be a systemic shock to the banking system in the United States similar to the Great Depression in the 1930s. Due to explicit deposit insurance schemes in place and unprecedented large scale of government bailouts, the recent GFC did not experience many bank runs or wide-spread

Handbook of Investors' Behavior during Financial Crises
http://dx.doi.org/10.1016/B978-0-12-811252-6.00011-6

systemic collapse. The largely confined damage of bank failures during the GFC may also be attributed to financial safety nets, mandatory regulations, and the market discipline. For example, banks are required by Basel Accords to keep certain capital buffers to mitigate the likelihood of failures during the economic downturns. Market discipline could further help banks monitor their risky situations through efficient market mechanism.

However, the high magnitude of failure rate during the recent GFC compared to previous ones raised an important question about the factors that contribute to US bank failures during this downturn. In this paper, we examine management inefficiency as a possible explanation for the bank failure in the United States during GFC. Given the scale of bank failures and government bailouts during the recent GFC, there could be more theoretical and empirical discussions over government interventions, bank performance, and the financial safety nets.

The financial system in the United States is market-based, and therefore markets could reduce the inherent inefficiencies associated with banks and enhance economic growth (Boot and Thakor, 2000; Levine, 2002). However, the efficient market mechanism might be questioned during the recent GFC since there was a lack of systematic alarm for many bank failures. In recent decades, there have been an extensive mandatory regulations and supervisory efforts to avoid banking failures (Barth et al., 2004), but the anecdotal evidence from the GFC suggests examining the recent bank failures using conventional measurements of management efficiency. While current literature examines the banks failure factors during previous recessions, to the best of our knowledge, ours is the first study to apply efficiency analysis techniques for bank failures during the recent GFC.

In this study, we examine management performance of the 325 failed banks in the United States between 2008 and 2010. We employ three management efficiency proxies; cost efficiency, input efficiency, and output efficiency. We find that management inefficiency has been one of the main causes of bank failures in the United States during the GFC. Our study provides guidance for the efficiency indicators that can be used to anticipate bank failures. The practical implication of our study is to improve management efficiency as a main factor to avoid bank failures.

The rest of the paper is organized as follows. Section 11.2 provides a brief background. Sections 11.3, 11.4 explains the data and research methodology, respectively. Section 11.5 provides the results, and Section 11.6 concludes.

11.2 Background

Several studies have focused on management performance of the banking sector and show that better management performance could help banks avoid bankruptcies. Amel and Rhoades (1989) examine the determinants of bank failures between 1980 and 1985 in the United States, and find that banks with higher earnings are less likely to fail. Ferrier and

Lovell (1990) use two efficiency measurements over bank performance in the United States and show that banks with lower performance are more likely to fail. Berger and Humphrey (1991) and Kaparakis et al. (1994) provide further evidence that shows the importance of management performance and efficiency in bank failures in the United States. Market discipline could also minimize the likelihood of bank failures because the underperforming banks are more likely to become targets of mergers and acquisitions by their well-performed counterparts (Hannan and Rhoades, 1987).

Besides the performance management and market discipline, other determinant factors in bank failures are banks' assets, liquidity ratios, and capital buffers. Hadlock et al. (1999) suggest that banks with relatively less liquid or lower quality assets and less capital buffers are more likely to fail. However, Hannan and Rhoades (1987) and Hadlock et al. (1999) argue that there is a lack of relationship between bank earnings and the likelihood of bank failures.

11.3 Data

Our sample covers all banks with total assets above US$50 million between 2007 and 2010. Quarterly balance sheets, income statements, and stockholder equity statement of all banks including 325 failed banks are collected from FDIC. Data collected from FDIC for the failed banks and the rest are comparable. We also collect performance and quality ratios of the banking sector from FDIC.

Following Wheelock and Paul (1995), we adopt the following proxies for costs, inputs, and outputs in our management efficiency measurement.

Costs:
- Average interest cost per dollar of interest-bearing deposits greater than US$100,000 (we exclude certificates of deposits (CDs);
- Average interest cost per dollar of purchased funds and other borrowed money;
- Average annual wage per employee;
- Average cost of premises and fixed assets.

Outputs:
- Loans to individuals for household, family, and other personal expenses;
- Real estate loans;
- Commercial and industrial loans;
- Federal funds sold and securities purchased under agreement to resell, plus total securities held in trading accounts.

Inputs:
- Interest-bearing deposits (excluding CDs) greater than US$100,000;
- Purchased funds (CDs greater than US$100,000, federal funds purchased, and securities sold plus demand notes) and other borrowed money;

- Number of employees;
- Premises and fixed assets.

11.4 Methodology

11.4.1 Cost Efficiency Measures

Cost efficiency is the extent to which a bank's cost is used to achieve the best performance at a given level of input or output under certain business conditions. A competitive and efficient bank minimizes its operating and interest costs to achieve a given output.

Efficient frontiers are theoretically constrained by technical and allocative efficiencies. These efficiency conditions are necessary to define cost efficiency. Cost efficiency is the difference between a bank's costs and efficient cost frontier, given a certain level of technology. The smaller the difference, the more efficient the bank is. As technologically feasible cost functions could not be directly observed, efficient frontier can only be estimated from observed data in reality.

Aigner et al. (1977) and Berger (1993) introduce the stochastic frontier approach (SFA) and the distribution-free approach (DFA), respectively, to measure individual bank efficiency. SFA and DFA are parametric and similar in that they both assume a functional form for the cost frontier that allows for random errors. However, they separate inefficiency from random errors in different ways. As inefficiencies could not be negative, SFA assumes that inefficiencies and random errors follow either an asymmetric distribution, such as a truncated or half-normal distribution, or a symmetric distribution, such as standard normal distribution. They are also orthogonal to the input prices, outputs, and country-level variables in the estimation equation. However, DFA allows the distribution of inefficiencies to follow any form, and treat the inefficiency as a constant regardless of the pace of the organization or technology changes. Furthermore, DFA assumes that random errors can be averaged over time.

In this study, we follow the intuition of Coelli et al. (1997) and employ an SFA approach. They propose the following general cost frontier model

$$Ln\,C_j = f(w_j, y_j, z_j) + lnv_{jc} + lnu_{jc} \tag{11.1}$$

Where C represents cost for bank j, f is the functional form, wj is an input price vector, yj is the variable output vector, zj is the fixed net puts vector, vjc is a random variable which denotes inefficiency that increases cost, and ujc is the traditional random error. $lnvjc + lnujc$ is treated as an error component.

$$CE_j = \frac{C_{min}}{C_j} = \frac{\exp\big[f(w_j, y_j, z_j)\big] \times \exp\big[lnu_{jc}\big]}{\exp\big[f(w_j, y_j, z_j)\big] \times \exp\big[lnv_{jc} + u_{jc}\big]} \tag{11.2}$$

The CE, cost efficiency measure, for bank j is defined as the ratio between the minimum cost (C_{min}), given by a bank in the frontier (assuming $C_{min} = 0$), and the actual cost for bank j (C_j), given the same exogenous variables (i.e., w, y, and z).

It can be shown that Eq. (11.2) will be transform to

$$CE_j = \frac{1}{v_{jc}}$$
(11.3)

The range for the *CE* is [0, 1] and the value of the *CE* has the negative relationship with the level of efficiency, that is, the higher the value of the *CE*, the lower the efficiency of the bank. $CE = 1$ suggests that the bank is 100% inefficient, while $CE = 0$ means it has been 100% efficient.

11.4.2 Input and Output Efficiency Measurements

Farrell (1957) considers imperfect operations of a bank instead of efficient input-output allocations. He explains that cost inefficiency depends on the difference between costs of a bank and efficient cost frontier, given a certain level of technology. The efficient frontier is determined by two components, the technical efficiency, which is the minimum use of inputs, and the allocative efficiency, which is the optimal mix of inputs and outputs.

For the efficiency estimation purpose, both parametric and nonparametric approaches can be considered. The parametric approach uses statistical measurements, while nonparametric approach applies linear programming measurements. In addition, the parametric (and not nonparametric) approach takes functional form, and distributional assumptions for the efficiency frontier. However, both approaches allow for random errors in input–output observations.

The distance function is closely related to production frontiers of a bank. Without specifying management objectives of a bank, such as maximization of its profits, the distance function allows to measure multiinput and multioutput technology of a bank.

Following Coelli and Perelman (1998), we adopt an output-distance function in our measurement of bank outputs.

Given a technology set of a bank, let's assume x represents its input vector, y represents its output vector, and $P(x)$ represents the set of all production vectors.

$y = R^M$, where R is the commodity space and M is the number of commodities. $P(x)$ can be produced using the input vector, x as R^M+ …

That is,

$$P(x) = \{y = R^M + \ldots : x \text{ can produce } y\}$$
(11.4)

We assume that the technology satisfies the axioms listed in Fare and Primont (1995). The output-distance function D_o can further be defined on $P(x)$ and a parameter vector θ as

$$D_o(x,y) = \min\{\theta : (y/\theta) = P(x)\} \tag{11.5}$$

The value of $D_o(x, y)$ is no more than 1. Since the output vector y is an element of the feasible production set $P(x)$, $D_o(x, y) < 1$ if $y = P(x)$. The value of $D_o(x, y)$ is isoquant (equals) to 1 if y is located on the outer boundary of the production possibility set. So

$$D_o(x,y) = 1 \text{ if } y = Isoq\, P(x) \tag{11.6}$$

$$D_o(x,y) = \{y : y = P(x), wy \neq P(x), w > 1\} \tag{11.7}$$

where w is the vector of exogenously given input prices. Lovell et al. (1994) suggest that $D_o(x, y)$ is nondecreasing, y is positively and linearly homogeneous and convex, and x is decreasing. In other words, the higher the value of $D_o(x, y)$, which is between 0 and 1, the higher the output efficiency of the bank.

We also take an input-distance function in measuring of inputs efficiency. The input-distance function could be defined in a similar way (Coelli and Perelman, 1998). However, different from the output-distance function, the output vector is the fixed variable when looking at how the input vector might be proportionally expanded. The input-distance function D_i can be defined on the input set, $L(y)$, as

$$D_i(x,y) = \max\{\beta : (x/\beta) = L(y)\} \tag{11.8}$$

where, the input set $L(y)$ represents a set of all input vectors, $x = R^K+$, which can produce the output vector, $y = R^K+\ldots$. In other words, $L(y) = \{x = R^K+: x \text{ can produce } y\}$. Lovell et al. (1994) suggest that $D_i(x, y)$ is nondecreasing, x is positively linearly homogeneous and convex, and y is decreasing. The distance function, the value of $D_i(x, y)$ is no less than 1 if the input vector, x is an element of a feasible production set, $L(y)$. That is, $D_i(x, y) > 1$ if $x = L(y)$. Moreover, the distance function equals to 1, if x is located on the inner boundary of the input set. Therefore, the higher the estimated value of $D_i(x, y)$, which is always greater than 1, the less the input efficiency of a bank. The value of 1 means that the bank is the most input efficient.

11.5 Results and Discussions

11.5.1 Cost Efficiency

Our cost efficiency measurement values fall into the range between 0 and 1. As discussed in Section 11.4, a smaller number close to 0 suggests that the bank has greater cost efficiency. Alternatively, a greater value close to 1 suggests that the bank is less cost efficient.

Table 11.1: Cost efficiency.

Year	Quarter	Number of All Banks	Number of Failed Banks	Mean of Cost Efficiency	
				All Banks	Failed Banks
2007	1	8650	0	0.5756	NA
	2	8614	0	0.5652	NA
	3	8559	0	0.5837	NA
	4	8533	2	0.5937	0.8355
2008	1	8494	1	0.5673	NA
	2	8451	2	0.5913	0.8423
	3	8384	5	0.5798	0.7982
	4	8305	11	0.5904	0.8641
2009	1	8246	20	0.5379	0.6754
	2	8195	21	0.5707	0.8012
	3	8099	42	0.5463	0.6752
	4	8012	36	0.5553	0.7122
2010	1	7934	34	0.5439	0.6877
	2	7830	41	0.5647	0.6315
	3	7761	33	0.5714	0.7749
	4	7657	27	0.5722	0.7256
Mean		8146	21	0.5681	0.7520

This table presents number of all banks, failed banks, and the annualized mean of cost efficiency for all and failed banks in the United States from 2007 to 2010.

Table 11.1 reports the cost efficiency values for both failed and other banks during GFC. During the GFC, most of the banks surprisingly improved their levels of cost efficiency despite a little change in the sector's operating costs. The fixed asset of banks decreases in value due to the market shocks. Interestingly, the average costs of banks remain stable or even decreases during the crisis which improves cost efficiency. The cost efficiency value on average improves from more than 0.59 in Q4 of 2007 to less than 0.54 in Q4 of 2009. However, the improvement in cost efficiency did not last long among the banks; by Q4 of 2010, the average cost efficiency value moves back to that of early 2007.

However, failed banks could not stabilize their cost efficiency level during the GFC. The reports by these banks demonstrate significant lower cost efficiency compared to other banks. Consistent with sharp deteriorating values of cost efficiency, these banks declares bankruptcies. The average value of cost efficiency among the failed banks is close to 0.75, which is much higher than that of the other banks with higher management performance. In Q4 of 2008, the average value of cost efficiency among the failed banks (other banks) is over 0.86 (0.59). In short, banks were able to maintain the outputs at an efficient level, if they could effectively improve the cost efficiency, which is highly related to the management quality of banks. In other words, high management performance could decrease the average cost inefficiency level and help bank operate more efficiently.

11.5.2 Outputs Efficiency

Output distance function Eq. (11.5) estimates the maximum feasible proportionate expansion of outputs, holding inputs fixed. The output variables are listed in Section 11.3. The value of D_o (x, y) in Eq. (11.5) is equal to or less than 1, indicating that the bank is efficient; the less the values for D_o (x, y), the lower the efficiency of banks. Table 11.2 presents the outputs measurement values for failed and other banks. The results show that the average outputs inefficiency of all banks is about 0.5. However, the mean of the measure of outputs inefficiency for failed banks is less and ranges from 0.0735 to 0.2264. These results suggest a high level of inefficiency for the failed banks, which is affected by the low quality of management during the GFC.

11.5.3 Inputs Efficiency

The input distance function Eq. (11.8) estimates the maximum feasible proportionate reduction in inputs, holding outputs fixed, and subject to the existing technology. The inputs variables are listed in Section 11.3. The value of D_i in Eq. (11.8) is equal to or greater than 1, indicating efficiency of the bank; the larger the D_i, the greater the inefficiency of the bank (Shephard, 1970). Table 11.3 provides the results.

The average inputs inefficiency of all banks is about 2.4. However, this value for the failed banks is significantly higher and changes between 25.31 and 195.14. This suggests the high level of inefficiency for the failed banks, which is due to poor management during the GFC.

Table 11.2: Outputs efficiency.

Year	Quarter	Number of All Banks	Number of Failed Banks	Mean of Output Efficiency	
				All Banks	Failed Banks
2007	1	8650	0	0.48	NA
	2	8614	0	0.4962	NA
	3	8559	0	0.5095	NA
	4	8533	2	0.542	0.0735
2008	1	8494	1	0.5368	NA
	2	8451	2	0.5301	0.0877
	3	8384	5	0.5345	0.0975
	4	8305	11	0.5349	0.1695
2009	1	8246	20	0.4741	0.1316
	2	8195	21	0.4438	0.0934
	3	8099	42	0.434	0.1594
	4	8012	36	0.4241	0.1711
2010	1	7934	34	0.5454	0.2955
	2	7830	41	0.5378	0.2328
	3	7761	33	0.5031	0.2202
	4	7657	27	0.494	0.2264
Mean		8146	21	0.5013	0.1632

This table presents number of all banks, failed banks, and the annualized mean of outputs efficiency for all and failed banks in the United States from 2007 to 2010.

Table 11.3: Inputs efficiency.

Year	Quarter	Number of All Banks	Number of Failed Banks	Mean of Input Efficiency All Banks	Mean of Input Efficiency Failed Banks
2007	1	8650	0	2.58	NA
	2	8614	0	2.61	NA
	3	8559	0	2.56	NA
	4	8533	2	2.47	138.38
2008	1	8494	1	2.29	NA
	2	8451	2	2.4	46.31
	3	8384	5	2.25	195.14
	4	8305	11	2.04	41.62
2009	1	8246	20	2.25	149.47
	2	8195	21	2.45	158.96
	3	8099	42	2.37	71.43
	4	8012	36	2.5	74.29
2010	1	7934	34	2.47	72.27
	2	7830	41	2.48	87.91
	3	7761	33	2.46	103.6
	4	7657	27	2.57	56.45
Mean		8146	21	2.3971	99.6525

This table presents number of all banks, failed banks, and the annualized mean of inputs efficiency for all and failed banks in the United States from 2007 to 2010.

We further categorize the banks into nine groups based on their size of assets and compute the average of the input efficiency measure for each group. Since noninterest-bearing deposits can be regarded as an exogenous to inputs of banks, we consider these deposits as a quasifixed input where banks are takers of such deposits without any explicit price. Therefore, the quantity of these deposits rather than their price is included in the cost function (Kaparakis et al., 1994). Table 11.4 provides the estimates.

Table 11.4: Inputs efficiency per asset group.

Group	Asset size	Number of All Banks	Number of Failed Banks	Mean of Input Efficiency All Banks	Mean of Input Efficiency Failed Banks
1	0–50	1900	20	0.0737	0.1136
2	50–100	1698	36	0.0633	0.0971
3	100–200	1350	56	0.0613	0.0732
4	200–500	1780	82	0.0697	0.073
5	500–1000	1260	41	0.0756	0.0858
6	1000–2000	206	18	0.0844	0.0417
7	2000–5000	203	15	0.0797	0.0903
8	5000–10,000	127	4	0.1089	0.1213
9	10,000+	119	3	0.1174	0.1153

This table presents number of all banks, failed banks, and the annualized mean of inputs efficiency per asset group for all and failed banks in the United States from 2007 to 2010.

The results show that the average inefficiency rises with size of banks' assets, except for the group with asset size between $20 billion to $50 billion, suggesting that larger banks are less efficient. The results also show that for banks with assets over $10 billion, the average value of the inefficiency measure is 11.7% which is higher than that of all banks. Note that failed banks during GFC with the same asset level have higher inefficiency level than other banks. As the input inefficiency is a measure of management performance of banks, higher inefficiency level indicates that failed banks have more management problems than other banks.

11.6 Conclusions

In this paper, we investigate management quality as a potential factor that contributes to the US banks failures during the recent GFC. We mainly focus on three measures of inefficiency as proxies for management quality; cost, input, and output inefficiencies. We show that management performance is in fact a key determinant of the US bank failures during the financial crisis. Our research results are consistent with the findings as that by Ferrier and Lovell (1990). With new evidence from the recent GFC, we argue that traditional measurements over bank efficiency, such as costs, outputs, and inputs are still reliable indicators for bankruptcy studies over the financial sector. The implication of this study is to provide guidelines for banks to focus on their management performance by considering underlying factors for the three efficiency measures. Investigation of other contributed factors, other than those related to management quality, such as market discipline (Hannan and Rhoades, 1987) is suggested for the future research.

References

Aigner, D., Lovell, C.A.K., Schmidt, P., 1977. Formulation and estimation of stochastic frontier production function models. J. Econom. 6 (1), 21–37.

Amel, D.F., Rhoades, A.S., 1989. Empirical evidence on the motives for bank mergers. East. Econ. J. 15 (1), 17–27.

Barth, J.R., Caprio, G., Levine, R., 2004. Bank regulation and supervision: what works best? J. Financ. Intermed. 13, 205–248.

Berger, A.N., Humphrey, D.B., 1991. The dominance of inefficiencies over scale and product mix economies in banking. J. Monetary Econ. 28 (1), 117–148.

Berger, A.N., 1993. Distribution-free estimates of efficiency in the US banking industry and tests of the standard distributional assumptions. J. Product. Anal. 4 (3), 261–292.

Boot, A.W., Thakor, A.V., 2000. Can relationship banking survive competition? J. Finance 55, 679–713.

Coelli, T., Perelman, S., 1998. A comparison of parametric and non-parametric distance function. Eur. J. Oper. Res. 117, 326–339.

Coelli, T.D.S., Prasada, R., Battese, G.E., 1997. An Introduction to Efficiency and Productivity Analysis. Springer, Boston.

Farrell, M.J., 1957. The measurement of productive efficiency. J. R. Stat. Soc. 120 (3), 253–290.

Fare, R., Primont, D., 1995. Multi-Output Production and Duality: Theory and Applications. Kluwer Academic Publishers, Boston, MA.

Federal Deposit Insurance Corporation (FDIC), 2016. Failed Bank List. Available from: https://www.fdic.gov/bank/individual/failed/banklist.html

Ferrier, G.D., Lovell, C.A.K., 1990. Measuring cost efficiency in banking: econometric and linear programming evidence. J. Econom. 46 (1–2), 229–245.

Hannan, T.H., Rhoades, A.S., 1987. Acquisition targets and motives: the case of the banking industry. Rev. Econ. Stat. 69 (1), 67–74.

Kaparakis, E.I., Miller, S.M., Noulas, A., 1994. Short-run cost inefficiency of commercial banks: a flexible stochastic frontier approach. J Money Credit Bank. 26 (4), 875–893.

Levine, R., 2002. Bank-based or market-based financial systems: which is better? J. Financ. Intermed. 11, 398–428.

Lovell, C.A.K., Richardson, S., Travers, P., Wood, L.L., 1994. Resources and Functionings: A New View of Inequality in Australia, Models and Measurement of Welfare and Inequality. Springer, Berlin, pp. 787–807.

Shephard, R.W., 1970. Theory of Cost and Production Functions. Princeton University Press, Princeton.

Wheelock, D.C., Paul, W.W., 1995. Explaining bank failures: deposit insurance, regulation, and efficiency. Rev. Econ. Stat. 77 (4), 689–700.

Further Reading

Battese, G.E., Corra, G.S., 1977. Estimation of a production frontier model: with application to the Pastoral Zone of Eastern Australia. Aust. J. Agric. Resour. Econ. 21 (3), 169–179.

Berger, A.N., Humphrey, D.B., 1997. Efficiency of financial institutions: international survey and directions for future research. Eur. J. Oper. Res. 98 (2), 175–212.

Hadlock, C., Houston, J., Ryngaert, M., 1999. The role of managerial incentives in bank acquisitions. J. Bank. Finance 23 (2–4), 221–249.

Kumbhakar, S.C., Lovell, C.A.K., 2000. Stochastic Frontier Analysis. Cambridge University Press, Cambridge.

Jondrow, J., Lovell, K., Materov, I., Schmidt, P., 1982. On the estimation of technical inefficiency in the stochastic frontier production function model. J. Econ. 19, 233–238.

Meeusen, W., van Den Broeck, J., 1977. Efficiency estimation from Cobb-Douglas production functions with composed error. Int. Econ. Rev. 18 (2), 435–444.

Schmidt, P., Sickles, R.C., 1984. Production frontiers and panel data. J. Bus. Econ. Stat. 2 (4), 367–374.

Wheelock, D.C., 2011. Have acquisition of failed banks increased the concentration of the U.S banking markets? Fed. Reserve Bank ST. 93 (3), 155–168.

CHAPTER 12

Financial Crisis and Herd Behavior: Evidence from the Borsa Istanbul

Mübeccel Banu Durukan*, Hilal H. Özsu*, Zeliha Can Ergun**

*Dokuz Eylul University, Izmir, Turkey; **Adnan Menderes University, Aydin, Turkey

12.1 Introduction

The literature on herd behavior in developed and emerging markets using different approaches to herd behavior measurement has expanded over the recent years. Herd behavior plays an important role in the stability and liquidity of the financial markets (Ionescu, 2012; Poon et al., 2013). Understanding the behaviors of different groups of investors, such as institutional or foreign investors is especially crucial in a globalized financial environment. The behavior of foreign and institutional investors may influence especially the emerging markets more deeply since they have substantial shares in the trades in these markets, making them more vulnerable to shocks. Hence more researchers are investigating the herd behavior of different groups of investors.

Trading behavior of investors may also differ under different market conditions, such as up and down markets, or during periods of crisis. The investigation of herd behavior before, during, and after crisis periods yields valuable information.

Within this context, the current study aims to investigate the herd behavior of foreign investors in an emerging market, namely Borsa Istanbul (BIST), during the global financial

203

crisis. In this study, foreign investors were examined particularly because of their crucial role in the Turkish stock market. Foreign portfolio investments in Turkey are liberalized since 1989 and the share of foreign investors in BIST has ranged between 51% and 78%. Hence there are many studies analyzing and providing evidence on the impact of foreign investor trading activities and the returns on BIST (Baklaci, 2007; Bolaman Avci, 2015; Kesik et al., 2016; Yılmaz and Yılmaz, 1999). Other researchers focused on the analysis of the factors affecting their investment decisions and choice of stocks (Aksoy, 2013; Demireli and Hepkorucu, 2014; Kandır, 2008; Sevil et al., 2012). Gökdemir (2010) has investigated herd behavior by foreign investors in BIST. However, to the best of our knowledge there is no study examining the herd behavior of foreign investors in BIST during crisis periods.

In light of the earlier explanations, the study aims to contribute to the literature in three areas: first by extending the investigation of herd behavior to an emerging market where there is inconclusive evidence of herd behavior; second by focusing on the behavior of foreign investors during times of crisis, namely the global financial crisis which is not studied before; third, to the best of our knowledge, by being the first study to utilize the CMAX methodology developed by Patel and Sarkar (1998) to determine the before, during, and after crisis periods.

The rest of the study is structured as follows: the literature review on herd behavior is provided in the next section. The methodology covering the CMAX method and the herd behavior measures used in the study are discussed next. The empirical findings are followed by conclusion.

12.2 Literature Review

There are three main approaches proposed and tested by the current literature to detect herd behavior in various markets and to investigate the behavior of different types of investors. Lakonishok, Shleifer, and Vishny (LSV) measure, which is the pioneer of the empirical measurement of herd behavior, assesses the buying and selling tendencies of investors for a particular stock (Lakonishok et al., 1991). It enables the researchers to test the trading behavior of different types of investors since it uses market transactions of investors in the analysis.

Lakonishok et al. (1991) employed this measurement in order to examine herd behavior in 769 all-equity pension funds and found no evidence of herd behavior among the US pension funds. However, based on their analysis they concluded that herd behavior could generally be detected in smaller stocks due to limited information availability regarding these stocks. LSV measure was utilized by many researchers to investigate herd behavior of different types of investors. Wylie (2005) using this method found significant evidence of herd behavior of English investment funds. Also, Hsieh (2013) investigated herd behavior in Taiwan stock market for individual and institutional investors independently, providing evidence for higher tendency of herd behavior for institutional investors. In Turkey, LSV measure was employed by Gökdemir (2010) in BIST during the period 1997–2006 and herd behavior by foreign investors under certain conditions was found.

Cross-Sectional Dispersion of Stock Returns developed by Christie and Huang (1995) and Chang et al. (2000) is the most commonly used herd behavior measure in the literature. They mainly argue that when there is herd behavior in the market; dispersions from the mean return are expected to be lower. Christie and Huang (1995) argued that investors under nonnormal conditions, such as extreme movements, behave in a similar way imitating each other and this results in lower deviation of returns from the average. Hence a reduction in cross-sectional standard deviation (CSSD) can be accepted as an indicator of herd behavior.

Christie and Huang (1995) employed CSSD as a measurement of dispersion and measured herd behavior in extreme market movements (lower and upper tails) in a linear model. Since CSSD could easily be affected from the outliers, Christie and Huang (1995) and Chang et al. (2000) later used cross-sectional absolute deviation (CSAD) as a more accurate measurement of dispersion. Christie and Huang (1995) measured herd behavior for both daily and monthly US stock returns, and they could not find any evidence of herd behavior.

On the other hand, as indicated by Chang et al. (2000) when herd behavior is present in the market, the level of equity return dispersion decreases or increases at a decreasing rate when the market return increases. Therefore their argument is based on the idea that there may be a nonlinear relationship between CSAD and the average market return. They also argued that, the effect of herd behavior could be asymmetric in the up and down markets, so they also developed a model that analyzes this possibility. They measured herd behavior in the United States, Hong Kong, Japanese, South Korean, and Taiwanese stock markets, and they found evidence of herd behavior in all sampled markets except the United States and Hong Kong markets. Demirer et al. (2010) examined herd behavior in Taiwan stock exchange and found no significant evidence of herd behavior by using the linear model, but when they used the nonlinear model they observed herd behavior.

Furthermore in Turkey, this method was used in many studies to investigate herd behavior in BIST. Altay (2008) examined the presence of herd behavior in BIST in the period of 1997–2008 based on daily data and found supporting evidence. Dogukanlı and Ergun (2011) on the other hand used monthly closing prices of stocks for the period 2000 and 2010 and could not find any evidence of herding. Ozdogan (2009), Ulusan et al. (2013), and Cakan and Balagyozgan (2014) examined herd behavior for the banking sector stocks. Except the study of Cakan and Balagyozgan (2014), their findings did not provide evidence of herd behavior. Hence the herd behavior literature provides inconclusive results for BIST.

State space model developed by Hwang and Salmon (2004) is based on the linear factor model that shows the relation between sentiment and herd behavior. They argued that when there is herd behavior in the market portfolio, both the beta and the expected asset return will be affected. They used this method in order to analyze herd behavior in the United States and South Korean stock markets, and they found significant herding in both. Recently, the state space model has been utilized by many studies. Wang (2008) analyzed herd behavior in particularly developed and emerging financial markets, and they found higher level of herding in emerging markets when compared to developed markets.

In Turkey, Solakoglu and Demir (2014) employed the state space model to analyze herd behavior in BIST 30 stocks and Second National Market (SNM) stocks in the period 2000–13, and found no evidence of herd behavior in BIST 30, but found significant herd behavior in SNM. Demir et al. (2014) examined herd behavior in BIST 100 stocks by using monthly data in the 2000–11 period and found significant evidence of herding. In this current study, state space model will be employed to test herd behavior for the whole market for the before, during, and after crisis periods.

Besides the testing of herd behavior using different methodologies by using daily, weekly, monthly data in different markets, recently more studies focus on the trading behavior of investors during special events or periods. Galariotis et al. (2014) analyzed herd behavior in the United States and United Kingdom during the periods of critical macroeconomic announcements, such as the changes in the US federal funds rate and changes in the Bank of England base rate. Consequently, they found significant evidence of herd behavior during these periods.

Gavriilidis et al., 2016 analyzed herd behavior in Ramadan. Their starting point was that during Ramadan, investors have positive mood so there can be higher tendency for herd behavior during these days. Their analyses were based on the seven majority Muslim countries and they found significant evidence of herd behavior during Ramadan in most of the sample markets.

Moreover, few studies focused on detecting herd behavior during the financial crisis periods, majority analyzing the Asian crisis. Hwang and Salmon (2004) argued that herd behavior goes down when investors are faced with extreme events, such as the crisis. However, Kallinterakis et al. (2007) examined herd behavior in the Argentina financial crisis, and found significant evidence of herding in both before and after the crisis periods. Caporale et al. (2008) examined herd behavior in the Athens stock exchange (ASE) on daily, weekly, and monthly basis and found that during and after the stock market crisis, there is a statistically significant herd behavior in the market.

Ourda et al. (2013) and Angela-Maria et al. (2015) investigated herd behavior during the global financial crisis in European financial markets and Central Eastern European stock markets, respectively. Both studies found supporting evidence for herd behavior during the financial crisis. Contrary to the stock markets, the empirical findings of Galariotis et al. (2016) study provided no evidence of herding in the bond market during the European financial crisis.

Lai and Lau (2004) investigated the Malaysian investors' behavior during the Asian crisis and conclude that the investors herd during the Asian crisis, which is a down market whereas they found no evidence of herding during up markets. Ourda et al. (2013) have also provided evidence of herd behavior during the Asian crisis. Khan and Park (2009), further, provide strong evidence of herding contagion between Thailand, Malaysia, Indonesia, Korea, and the Philippines during the Asian crisis.

Even though many studies focus on crisis periods, there is limited number of studies specifically focusing on the behavior of different types of investors during crisis. As different categorizes of investors have access to different cascades of information, their behaviors may differ. Kim and Wei (2002) and Bowe and Domuta (2004) investigate the herd behavior of foreign and domestic investors before, during, and after the Asian crisis and conclude that all investors exhibit a tendency to herd whereas foreign investors herd more in general and even more during the crisis period. Kim and Wei (2002) further present evidence that nonresident foreign investors herd more than resident foreign investors and attribute this to informational asymmetry. Choe et al. (1999), on the other hand, report that herding falls during the crisis period.

12.3 Data and Methodology

The main purpose of this study is to investigate the existence of herd behavior of foreign investors during the financial crisis at BIST between 2006 and 2015. In this context, first the financial crisis periods for BIST are determined based on CMAX methodology developed by Patel and Sarkar (1998). Then, to test the existence of herd behavior during these financial crisis periods, the state space model developed by Hwang and Salmon (2004) is used. Lakonishok et al. (1992) methodology is then employed to test whether herding activity of foreign investors affect stock market in BIST during the crisis period.

12.3.1 Determining the Crisis Periods Using CMAX Methodology

To test herd behavior during crisis, at first, financial crisis periods are determined by using the CMAX methodology designed by Patel and Sarkar (1998) for the period between 2006 and 2015. CMAX is calculated by using the ratio of the current value of the BIST 100 Index to its maximum value over the previous 2 years:

$$CMAX_{i,t} = \frac{P_{m,t}}{max(P_{m,t-24........}, P_{m,t})}$$

where $P_{m,t}$ is the closing price of the market at time t.

$$C_{m,t} = 1 \quad \text{if } CMAX_{m,t} < CMAX_m - 2\sigma_m$$
$$C_{m,t} = 0, \qquad\qquad \text{otherwise.}$$

A crisis is observed when CMAX falls below a threshold set at the mean of CMAX minus 2 standard deviations. In other words, a crisis is detected if CMAX equals 1 indicating price increases over the period. If prices decrease more, CMAX is closer to 0 or more. To determine precrisis and postcrisis periods, the following steps are defined based on the CMAX methodology: the start of the crisis is the point where the price reaches its historical maximum level over a 2-year period. The date of recovery is the first month after the crisis when the index reaches the precrisis maximum.

Fig. 12.1 indicates crisis periods in BIST. As seen, while precrisis period is between October 2007 and September 2008, financial crisis is observed between the periods from October 2008 to April 2009. The Index has reached its precrisis maximum value in April 2010. Hence, postcrisis period is defined for the period of May 2009–April 2010. Based on the CMAX methodology no other crisis is determined for BIST over the 2006–15 period. This crisis period corresponded with the global financial crisis.

12.3.2 Model of Cross-Sectional Volatility of Beta Coefficients

To investigate whether there is herd behavior or not during financial crisis periods (October 2007–April 2010), the state space model based on cross-sectional volatility of beta coefficients was employed (Hwang and Salmon, 2004). To analyze, daily closing prices of stocks and BIST 100 index were obtained for the periods from January 1, 2006 to December 31, 2015.

Daily closing prices were converted to daily logarithmic returns to calculate the dispersions. The following formula was used to calculate returns:

$$R_{i,t} = ln(P_{i,t} / P_{i,t-1})$$

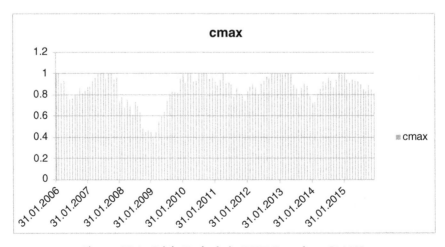

Figure 12.1: Crisis Periods in BIST Based on CMAX.

where $R_{i,t}$ is the return of stock i at time t, $P_{i,t}$ is the closing price of stock i at time t, and $P_{i,t-1}$ is the closing price of stock i on the day before.

Following Hwang and Salmon (2004), to be used in the analysis of cross-sectional standard deviation, beta coefficients were calculated by the following formula:

$$E_t(r_{it}) = \beta_{imt} E_t(r_{mt})$$

where r_{it} is the excess return on stock i at time t, r_{mt} is the excess return on the market at time t, β_{imt} is the systematic risk measure, and E_t is conditional expectation at time t.

Daily returns and risk-free rate (r_f) were used to calculate the excess returns on asset i and the market at time t $(r_t - r_f)$. As the risk-free rate, yearly compounded interest rates of treasury discounted auctions were obtained from the official website of Undersecretariat of Treasury (www.treasury.gov.tr) and converted to daily rates.[1]

To obtain the CSSD of the beta coefficients on the market portfolio, the following equation was used as in Hwang and Salmon (2004):

$$Std_c\left(\beta_{imt}^b\right) = \sqrt{\frac{\sum_{i=1}^{N_t}\left(\beta_{imt}^b - \overline{\beta_{imt}^b}\right)^2}{N_t}}$$

where $\overline{\beta_{imt}^b} = \frac{1}{N_t}\sum_{i=1}^{N_t}\beta_{imt}^b$ and N_t is the number of stocks in month t.

To examine herding level over time, first, logarithms of the equation were taken as $log\,Std_c\left(\beta_{imt}^b\right)$ and then the following regression equation is analyzed:

$$log\left[Std_c\left(\beta_{imt}^b\right)\right] = \mu_m + H_{mt} + v_{mt}$$
$$H_{mt} = \phi_m H_{mt-1} + \eta_{mt}$$

where $\eta_{mt} \sim iid\left(0, \sigma_{m\eta}^2\right)$.

The equation of $log\left[Std_c\left(\beta_{imt}^b\right)\right]$ is the measurement equation and the equation of H_{mt} is the transition equation of the standard state space model. To extract H_{mt}, the standard state space model was applied by using Kalman Filter, as in Hwang and Salmon (2004). A significant H_{mt} is expected in the existence of herding. The magnitude of H_{mt} indicates the degree of herding. For instance, if $H_{mt} = 1$, there is perfect herding.

---

[1] Daily interest rates are calculated by dividing yearly interest rates to number of months in 1 year, number of weeks in 1 month, and then number of days in 1 week, as in Altay (2008).

12.3.3 LSV Measure

Herd behavior is defined as following others' decisions in the literature. Christie and Huang (1995), Chang et al. (2000) and many other researchers used stock returns to test existence of herd behavior. However, investors tend to make stock prices unstable, if they act based on positive feedback investment strategy which relies on the past performances of the stocks (Lakonishok et al., 1992, p. 35). This methodology measures the herding activity by computing the proportion of stock holdings (Bellando, 2010, pp. 2–3). From this point, excess demand of investors buying (selling) a stock is used and measured by the dollar ratio (*Dratio*) in this study following Lakonishok et al. (1992). *Dratio* in a given period, *i* is computed as:

$$Dratio(i) = [\$buys(i) - \$sells(i)] / [\$buys(i) + \$sells(i)]$$

where *$buys(i)* is the total dollar increases by foreign investors in the month *i*, and *$sells(i)* is the total dollar decreases in holdings. To sum up, *Dratio* is defined as the difference between net trading value scaled by total activity.

It is expected that more than 50% of foreign investors increase their holdings while the others decrease (Lakonishok et al., 1992, p. 29) and trading activities of foreign investors lead to changes in stock prices on BIST in the presence of herd behavior.

12.4 Empirical Findings

The study first tests for herding in BIST by employing the state space model and the LSV measure during the whole period and the crisis period comparatively. Table 12.1 provides the regression results for the following equation of the state space model:

$$log\left[Std_c \left(\beta_{imt}^b \right) \right] = \mu_m + H_{mt} + v_{mt}$$

To test the effect of crisis on herd behavior among investors, analysis period is divided into two subperiods. Significant coefficient of σ_{mn}, supports the existence of herd behavior at a rate of 51% toward the market portfolio by taking into account the whole period.

Table 12.1: Regression results for cross-sectional volatility of beta coefficients.

Whole Period (January 2006–December 2015)			Financial Crisis Periods (October 2008–April 2009)		
σ_{mn}	F	Proportion of signal	σ_{mn}	F	Proportion of signal
0.5111 (101.3)*	10261.15*	0.5046	0.8651 (198.0)*	7976.04*	0.4369*

t-statistic in parentheses.
*Significance at 1%.

Table 12.2: Herding statistics of LSV measure.

Whole Period (January 2006–December 2015)		Financial Crisis Periods (October 2008–April 2009)
Mean	0.036 (0.04)	0.013 (0.006)
Median	0.008	0.013

Standard errors in parentheses.

According to the signal-proportion value,[2] herding also explains around 50% of the total variability in cross-sectional volatility of beta coefficients. *F* value verifies the validity of the model at the 1% significance. By contrast with the results of the whole period, the table indicates the existence of herd behavior at a higher degree of 87% during the crisis periods.

Table 12.2 presents descriptive of foreign investor herding measure following the LSV approach. The mean herding measure, 0.036, is the most important indicator exhibiting the average increases of changes. If the expected proportion of purchases in the given period is 0.50, then it can be said that 53.6% of the foreign investors changes their holdings in the same direction in the given period. The smaller mean value for the crisis period, 0.013, indicates foreign investor herd less during the financial crisis period. Lakonishok et al. (1992, p. 31) argue that low coefficients are expected because herding can be examined within subgroups of investors.

12.4.1 Herd Behavior Conditioned on Size

Although less herding is observed during financial crisis periods based on the LSV measure, more foreign investor herding effect can be examined on stocks of a particular size or performance. First, size is included and monthly market capitalization values were used as size measure between the periods from January 2006 to December 2015, including subperiods. The sample is divided into five quintiles, approximately, 45 stocks and herding coefficients are computed for each quintile. Table 12.3 reports summary statistics of herd behavior conditioned on market capitalization. While more herding is observed among investors, foreign investors tend to herd less during crisis periods, as mentioned earlier. Also, Table 12.3 exhibits that there is no clear relationship between foreign investor herding and size during precrisis, crisis, and postcrisis periods, as well.

However, the coefficients may be low due to the fact that total trading activities of investors decrease during the crisis periods, as seen in Fig. 12.2.

To analyze whether the reason of less herding effect in Table 12.3 is low trading values of foreign investors during crisis periods or not, *Dratios* are divided into five quintiles for each

---

[2] Proportion of Signal value is calculated by dividing σ_{mn} by the time series standard deviation of the logarithmic cross-sectional standard deviation of the betas, which according to Hwang and Salmon (2004) indicates what proportion of the cross-sectional volatility of the betas is explained by herding (Gavriilidis et al., 2013, p. 19).

Table 12.3: Herding conditioned on size.

Q1(Small)	Q2	Q3	Q4	Q5(Large)
Precrisis (October 2007–September 2008)				
–0.044 (0.032)	–0.044 (0.031)	–0.030 (0.025)	–0.028 (0.022)	–0.029 (0.024)
Crisis (October 2008–April 2009)				
0.030 (0.033)	0.024 (0.049)	0.018 (0.053)	0.014 (0.061)	–0.001 (0.072)
Postcrisis (May 2009–April 2010)				
0.017 (0.034)	0.016 (0.045)	0.010 (0.045)	0.010 (0.044)	0.004 (0.051)
Whole period (January 2006–December 2015)				
0.013 (0.035)	0.010 (0.031)	0.008 (0.025)	0.007 (0.022)	0.007 (0.020)

Standard errors in parentheses.

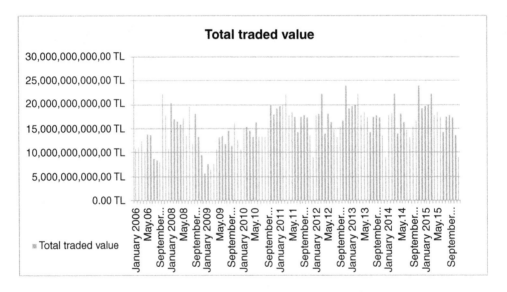

Figure 12.2: Traded Value by Foreign Investors.

firm size quintile, separately. Table 12.4 reports that the coefficient reaches from 0.062 to 0.181 based on investors' trading volumes for the first-smallest size category during precrisis period. Nevertheless, while herding measure is 0.001 for larger firms, it reaches 0.030 for smaller firms during the crisis period, indicating less impact of foreign investors on larger ones, consistent with Lakonishok et al. (1992) and Bowe and Domuta (2004). This may be due to the larger fraction of repurchasing or issuing activity in small firms rather than herding effect (Lakonishok et al., 1992, p. 32). Bowe and Domuta (2004) state that group trading patterns may be explained by less liquidity in small firms.

Similar results are found for other size categories, approximately, supporting the assumption that foreign investors may not affect stock market much during crisis because they trade less during these volatile periods. The higher the total value traded, the higher the herding effect.

Table 12.4: Stock performance conditioned on size quintiles.

	Q1(small)	Q2	Q3	Q4	Q5(large)
Dratios	Precrisis (October 2007–September 2008)				
1(low)	0.062 (0.035)	0.050 (0.012)	0.040 (0.012)	0.034 (0.003)	0.038 (0.018)
2	0.077 (0.035)	0.038 (0.043)	0.090 (0.050)	0.078 (0.062)	0.021 (0.063)
3	0.169 (0.024)	0.068 (0.023)	0.069 (0.025)	0.078 (0.035)	0.073 (0.034)
4	0.181 (0.028)	0.151 (0.266)	0.120 (0.016)	0.086 (0.025)	0.069 (0.018)
5(high)	0.307 (0.030)	0.263 (0.027)	0.211 (0.016)	0.150 (0.020)	0.111 (0.025)
	Crisis (October 2008–April 2009)				
1(low)	0.063 (0.094)	0.043 (0.054)	0.038 (0.028)	0.023 (0.056)	0.012 (0.065)
2	0.064 (0.031)	0.062 (0.072)	0.052 (0.080)	0.055 (0.099)	0.039 (0.125)
3	0.141 (0.023)	0.088 (0.059)	0.080 (0.015)	0.011 (0.007)	0.056 (0.017)
4	0.150 (0.027)	0.097 (0.028)	0.076 (0.038)	0.053 (0.036)	0.017 (0.007)
5(high)	0.152 (0.020)	0.108 (0.012)	0.096 (0.012)	0.060 (0.022)	0.001 (0.010)
	Postcrisis (May 2009–April 2010)				
1(low)	0.036 (0.012)	0.026 (0.007)	0.019 (0.011)	0.016 (0.011)	0.016 (0.012)
2	0.045 (0.014)	0.033 (0.017)	0.017 (0.011)	0.015 (0.020)	0.008 (0.027)
3	0.243 (0.055)	0.186 (0.059)	0.160 (0.070)	0.139 (0.050)	0.098 (0.065)
4	0.316 (0.040)	0.289 (0.044)	0.299 (0.040)	0.176 (0.045)	0.124 (0.025)
5(high)	0.536 (0.032)	0.546 (0.035)	0.464 (0.026)	0.397 (0.016)	0.305 (0.009)
	Whole period (January 2006–December 2015)				
1(low)	0.084 (0.080)	0.095 (0.067)	0.064 (0.055)	0.046 (0.048)	0.044 (0.044)
2	0.204 (0.195)	0.110 (0.182)	0.099 (0.146)	0.083 (0.136)	0.072 (0.123)
3	0.285 (0.310)	0.118 (0.272)	0.108 (0.235)	0.025 (0.224)	0.016 (0.190)
4	0.349 (0.342)	0.460 (0.295)	0.377 (0.246)	0.308 (0.226)	0.345 (0.179)
5(high)	0.928 (0.371)	0.721 (0.338)	0.471 (0.240)	0.365 (0.195)	0.262 (0.185)

Standard errors in parentheses.

There is also evidence that the results exhibit lowest relationship between foreign investor herding and firm size for crisis period in comparison with pre- and postcrisis periods. Higher and more significant relationship between foreign investor herding and size may also support higher trading values of foreign investors for the whole period. Thus, it can be concluded that trading activities of foreign investors do not extremely affect market movements in BIST during crisis periods.

12.4.2 Herd Behavior Conditioned on Stock Return

To test the relation between foreign investor herding and stock return, first, monthly market capitalization values are divided into five quintiles, and herding coefficients are computed for each size quintile as before. Then, monthly returns of the stocks for each size quintile are added to the model. Regression results are reported for three crisis periods in Table 12.5.

Although the coefficients are low again, the tendency of herd behavior is clearly observed for smaller stocks rather than larger stocks during crisis periods analyzed. Thus, it can be

Table 12.5: Herding conditioned on stock return quintiles.

Q1(Small)	Q2	Q3	Q4	Q5(Large)
Precrisis (October 2007–September 2008)				
0.014 (0.021)	0.013 (0.022)	0.011 (0.022)	0.008 (0.021)	0.001 (0.023)
Crisis (October 2008–April 2009)				
0.030 (0.034)	0.024 (0.049)	0.018 (0.053)	0.014 (0.061)	0.001 (0.07)
Postcrisis (May 2009–April 2010)				
0.082 (0.048)	0.089 (0.053)	0.084 (0.057)	0.072 (0.060)	0.048 (0.087)
Whole Period (January 2006–December 2015)				
0.013 (0.008)***	0.009 (0.006)***	0.007 (0.006)	0.006 (0.006)	0.006 (0.007)

Standard errors in parentheses.
***Significance at 10%.

said that price changes of small stocks are affected by foreign investor trading activities more. This might be an indicator of spurious herding (Lakonishok et al., 1992). Investors might make similar decisions for small stocks because of accessing the same limited information and interpreting this information similarly. Conversely, they might have much complicated information for larger stocks and herd intentionally, prefer to follow the consensus after observing the others. Investors buy well-performing small stocks or sell poorly performing stocks to window dress their portfolios, consistent with unintentional herding.

Table 12.6 indicates herding measurements conditioned on stock returns by dividing *Dratios* into five quintiles for each firm size quintile, again. It can be argued that stock prices are affected less (more) when foreign investors trade less (more). At the highest level of trading volumes measured by *Dratios*, especially for precrisis and crisis periods, the herding coefficients and thus, stock performances are higher and more significant.

12.5 Conclusions

The trading behavior of investors is an important issue to understand for both policy makers and financial analysts. Especially the behavior of foreign investors who hold international portfolios may have substantial effects on the emerging markets through their trading activities. Herd behavior is a phenomenon experienced in all markets under certain conditions. The majority of the studies on the topic focus on the detection of herd behavior employing different approaches and measures. However, the literature provides limited evidence on foreign investor herd behavior during crisis.

This study aimed to investigate herd behavior of foreign investors in an emerging market, namely, BIST during the global financial crisis including the period 2006–15. The before, during, and after crisis periods are determined by using the CMAX methodology. Following

Table 12.6: Stock performance conditioned on return quintiles.

	Q1(Small)	Q2	Q3	Q4	Q5(Large)
Dratios	Precrisis (October 2007–September 2008)				
1(low)	0.044 (0.017)	0.030 (0.023)	0.024 (0.024)	0.020 (0.024)	0.015 (0.023)
2	0.124 (0.026)	0.078 (0.025)	0.061 (0.024)	0.045 (0.023)	0.014 (0.027)
3	0.114 (0.012)	0.097 (0.013)	0.096 (0.012)	0.086 (0.013)	0.092 (0.013)
4	0.135 (0.020)	0.077 (0.025)	0.047 (0.028)	0.028 (0.024)	0.009 (0.027)
5(high)	0.199 (0.022)	0.192 (0.035)	0.191 (0.069)	0.183 (0.025)	0.171 (0.017)
	Crisis (October 2008–April 2009)				
1(low)	0.081 (0.098)	0.016 (0.047)	0.013 (0.042)	0.006 (0.035)	0.009 (0.027)
2	0.257 (0.070)	0.010 (0.023)	0.102 (0.009)	0.106 (0.002)	0.112 (0.007)
3	0.253 (0.095)	0.072 (0.061)	0.065 (0.053)	0.062 (0.052)	0.056 (0.052)
4	0.242 (0.083)	0.235 (0.102)	0.227 (0.124)	0.195 (0.121)	0.214 (0.105)
5(high)	0.459 (0.044)	0.423 (0.041)	0.432 (0.213)	0.462 (0.009)	0.468 (0.023)
	Postcrisis (May 2009–April 2010)				
1(low)	0.017 (0.017)	0.017 (0.017)	0.019 (0.012)	0.017 (0.013)	0.009 (0.028)
2	0.064 (0.031)	0.067 (0.028)	0.059 (0.032)	0.053 (0.033)	0.015 (0.046)
3	0.076 (0.034)	0.046 (0.019)	0.025 (0.021)	0.017 (0.017)	0.018 (0.014)
4	0.138 (0.466)	0.056 (0.023)	0.040 (0.019)	0.046 (0.016)	0.057 (0.014)
5(high)	0.212 (0.034)	0.191 (0.030)	0.160 (0.028)	0.163 (0.026)	0.030 (0.036)
	Whole period (January 2006–December 2015)				
1(low)	0.019 (0.174)	0.026 (0.059)	0.011 (0.120)	0.010 (0.054)	0.001 (0.006)
2	0.039 (0.034)	0.028 (0.035)	0.022 (0.046)	0.022 (0.039)	0.021 (0.028)
3	0.069 (0.065)	0.042 (0.060)	0.028 (0.058)	0.010 (0.060)	0.018 (0.067)
4	0.101 (0.169)	0.074 (0.158)	0.064 (0.162)	0.055 (0.217)	0.006 (0.193)
5(high)	0.129 (0.117)	0.100 (0.116)	0.082 (0.099)	0.075 (0.094)	0.076 (0.100)

Standard errors in parentheses.

the determination of the crisis periods, first the herd behavior in BIST is tested by employing the state space model which detected increased herding during the crisis period by all investors in the market. Then the herd behavior of foreign investors for the whole period and crisis period are tested using the LSV measure. In this case, the findings provided less herding by foreign investors during the crisis period.

Hence these findings provide evidence against the argument that because of information asymmetry between local and foreign investors, foreign investors herd more during crisis. The decreased herding behavior during the crisis may be due to the effect of lower trading by foreign investors during the crisis.

Foreign investor herd behavior is also tested conditioned on size and stock returns using the LSV measure. The findings support the argument that herd behavior by foreign investors effect small stocks more in general but less during financial crisis periods due to lower trading. Hence the effect is higher in the pre- and postcrisis periods.

References

Aksoy, M., 2013. Istanbul Menkul Kıymetler Borsası'nda Finansal Kriz Döneminde Yabancı Yatırımcıların Hisse Senedi Tercihlerinin Analizi' İ.Ü. Siyasal Bilgiler Fakültesi Dergisi, 48, pp. 135–150.

Altay, E., 2008. Sermaye Piyasasında Sürü Davranışı: IMKB'de Piyasa Yönünde Sürü Davranışının Analizi. BDDK Bankacılık ve Finansal Piyasalar 2 (1), 27–57.

Angela-Maria, F., Maria, P.A., Miruna, P.M., 2015. An empirical investigation of herding behavior in CEE stock markets under the global financial crisis. Procedia Econ. Finance 25, 354–361.

Baklaci, H.F., 2007. Do Foreign Investors Chase or Impact Returns in Turkey?, International Conference on Globalization and its Discontents, Co-Organized by Izmir Economy University and State University of New York, June 8–9, pp. 22–39.

Bellando, R., 2010. Measuring Herd Intensity: A Hard Task, Working Papers. Available from: http://ssrn.com/abstract=1622700

Bolaman Avci, O., 2015. Effect of foreign investor transactions on stock market returns. Hacettepe University J. Econ. Admin. Sci. 33 (4), 29–38.

Bowe, M., Domuta, D., 2004. Investor herding during financial crisis: a clinical study of the Jakarta stock exchange. Pacific-Basin Finance J. 12, 387–418.

Cakan, E., Balagyozgan, A., 2014. Herd behaviour in the Turkish banking sector. Appl. Econ. Lett. 21 (2), 75–79.

Caporale, G.M., Economou, F., Philippas, N., 2008. Herding behavior in extreme market conditions: the case of Athens stock exchange. Econ. Bull. 7 (17), 1–13.

Chang, E.C., Cheng, J.W., Khorana, A., 2000. An examination of herd behavior in equity markets: an international perspective. J. Banking Finance 24 (10), 1651–1679.

Choe, H., Kho, B., Stulz, R.M., 1999. Do foreign investors destabilize stock markets? The Korean experience in 1997. J. Financ. Econ. 54, 227–264.

Christie, W.G., Huang, R.D., 1995. Following the pied piper: do individual returns herd around the market? Financ. Anal. J. 51 (4), 31–37.

Demir, N., Mahmud, S.F., Solakoglu, M.N., 2014. Sentiment and beta herding in the Borsa Istanbul (BIST). In: Batten, J.A., Wagner, N.F. (Eds.). Risk Management Post Financial Crisis: A Period of Monetary Easing (Contemporary Studies in Economic and Financial Analysis) vol. 96. Emerald Group Publishing Limited, United Kingdom, pp. 389–400.

Demireli, E., Hepkorucu, A., 2014. Yabancı Yatırımcıların Sermaye Piyasası Algısı: Borsa Istanbul Uzerine Bir Uygulama. J. Acad. Res. Studies 6 (10), 2–22.

Demirer, R., Kutan, A.M., Chen, C.D., 2010. Do investors herd in emerging stock markets? Evidence from the Taiwanese market. J. Econ. Behav. Org. 76 (2010), 283–295.

Dogukanlı, H., Ergun, B., 2011. İMKB'de Sürü Davranışı: Yatay Kesit Değişkenlik Temelinde Bir Araştırma. Çukurova Ünivsersitesi İşletme Fakültesi Dergisi 12 (2), 227–242.

Galariotis, E.C., Rong, W., Spyrou, S.I., 2014. Herding on fundamental information: a comparative study. J. Banking Finance 50 (2015), 589–598.

Galariotis, E.C., Krokida, S., Spyrou, S.I., 2016. Bond market investor herding: evidence from the European financial crisis. Int. Rev. Financ. Anal. 48, 367–375. Available from: http://dx.doi.org/10.1016/j.irfa.2015.01.001

Gavriilidis, K., Kallinterakis, V., Leite-Ferreira, M.P., 2013. Institutional industry herding: intentional or spurious? J. Int. Financ. Markets Inst. Money 26 (1), 192–214.

Gavriilidis, K., Kallinterakis, V., Tsalavoutas, I., 2016. Investor mood, herding and the Ramadan Effect. J. Econ. Behav. Organ. 132, 23–38.

Gökdemir, G., 2010. Yabancı Yatırımcıların İMKB'dekiIMKB'deki Fiyat ve Sürü Güdüsü Etkileri. Unpublished Doctoral Dissertation. Istanbul: Kadir Has University Graduate School of Social Sciences.

Hsieh, S.F., 2013. Individual and institutional herding and the impact on stock returns: evidence from Taiwan stock market. Int. Rev. Financ. Anal. 29 (2013), 175–188.

Hwang, S., Salmon, M., 2004. Market stress and herding. J. Empirical Finance 11 (2004), 585–616.

Ionescu, C., 2012. The herd behavior and the financial instability. Ann. Univ. Petroşani Econ. 12 (1), 129–140.

Kallinterakis, V., Gavriilidis, K. and Micciullo, P., 2007. The Argentine Crisis: A Case for Herd Behaviour? Available from: https://ssrn.com/abstract=980685

Kandır, S.Y., 2008. Yabancı Yatırımcıların Türkiye'deki Yatırım Tercihlerinin Araştırılması. Muhasebe ve Finansman Dergisi 38, 199–209.

Kesik, A., Canakci, M., Tunali, H., 2016. Analyzing impact of non-rezidents' holdings of equities on BIST (Istanbul Stock Exchange) 100 Index. J. Econ. Finance Account. 3 (2), 166–179.

Khan, S., Park, K.W., 2009. Contagion in the stock markets: the Asian financial crisis revisited. J. Asian Econ. 20 (5), 561–569.

Kim, W., Wei, S.J., 2002. Foreign portfolio investors before and during a crisis. J. Int. Econ. 56 (2002), 77–96.

Lai, M., Lau, S., 2004. Herd behavior and market stress: the case of Malaysia. Acad. Account. Financ. Studies J. 8 (3), 85–101.

Lakonishok, J., Shleifer, A., Vishny, R.W., 1991. Do institutional investors destabilize stock prices? Evidence on herding and feedback trading, NBER Working Paper No. 3846.

Lakonishok, J., Shleifer, A., Vishny, R.W., 1992. The impact of institutional trading on stock prices. J. Financ. Econ. 32 (1), 13–43.

Ourda, M., El Bouri, A., Bernard, O., 2013. Herding behavior under markets condition: empirical evidence on the European financial markets. Int. J. Econ. Financ. Issues 3 (1), 214–228.

Ozdogan, S., 2009. Investor Behavior in a Stock Market: The Case of Bank Stocks in the Istanbul Stock Exchange. Unpublished Master Dissertation. Istanbul: Istanbul Bilgi University Faculty of Economics and Administrative Sciences.

Patel, S.A., Sarkar, A., 1998. Crisis in developed and emerging stock markets. Financ. Anal. J. 54 (6), 50–61.

Poon, S.-H., Rockinger, M., Stathopoulos, K., 2013. Market liquidity and institutional trading during the 2007-8 financial crisis. Int. Rev. Financ. Anal. 30 (2013), 86–97.

Sevil, G., Özer, M., Kulali, G., 2012. Foreign investors and noise trade in Istanbul stock exchange. Int. J. Bus. Soc. Sci. 3 (4), 93–101.

Solakoglu, M.N., Demir, N., 2014. Sentimental herding in Borsa Istanbul: informed versus uninformed. Appl. Econ. Lett. 21 (14), 965–968.

Ulusan, M., Hancı, G. Paksoy, M., 2013. Borsa Istanbul'daIç ya da Dış Denetim Odaklı Bireyler Açısından Bankacılık Hisseleri Bazında Sürü Davranışın Incelenmesi. Available from: http://efinans.co/wp-content/uploads/2013/11/80-92.pdf

Wang, D., 2008. Herd behavior towards the market index: evidence from 21 financial markets. IESE Business School Working Paper No. 776. Available from: https://ssrn.com/abstract=1316783

Wylie, S., 2005. Fund manager herding: a test of the accuracy of empirical results using U.K. data. J. Bus. 78 (1), 381–403.

Yılmaz, M.K., Yılmaz, A., 1999. Yabancı Yatırımcıların Istanbul Menkul Kıymetler Borsası Hisse Senetleri Piyasası Üzerindeki Rolü', Iktisat Dergisi, February–March, 9–19.

CHAPTER 13

Doctor Jekyll and Mr. Hyde: Stress Testing of Investor Behavior

Ruggero Bertelli

University of Siena, Siena, Italy

Chapter Outline

13.1 Loss Aversion During Economic Crises: The Results of a Questionnaire

13.1.1 Financial Markets and Choices Under Conditions of Uncertainty

Today's investors are called upon to make choices under conditions of great uncertainty and in a difficult environment. Throughout our lives, we must make decisions under conditions of uncertainty—that is, before future outcomes are known. In order to make such decisions, a high degree of confidence in the available data is necessary. Nevertheless, each decision contains some degree of uncertainty that affects its outcome. Deciding to get married or to have a child; deciding which school or university to attend; booking a summer vacation or a ski trip: there are countless examples of "choices under conditions of uncertainty."

A specific and worrying type of uncertainty affects financial choices. We perceive investment choices as more uncertain than other decisions, since these choices have to do with "the market." By their very nature, markets set prices that vary day by day (or even hour by hour)!

The fact that prices change every day contributes to our perception of finance as something quite particular; real estate does not give us the same impression. A company we have shares in is just as concrete as real estate, but real estate prices do not change by the day. This is the only difference. But this is of great impact for our mind.

We are emotionally invested in "money," but this does not make us greedy or mean. The fact is that our money contains our values, our sacrifices or those of our families. It represents a worry-free old age, the joy that our children give us, the achievement of important goals. We have an emotional connection to "money."

Our savings are very important. We save money because we have ambitious goals. Financial markets offer many opportunities, but also plenty of risks. Some behaviors come natural. We can defend ourselves from being excessively emotional and making mistakes by setting clear goals and not fretting over them. We often feel secure when we buy real estate, and we do not worry if prices drop this year. We have long-term goals and we tell ourselves that prices will bounce back. Real estate has long-term value, and this is reassuring.

But when we are dealing with stocks and mutual funds, it is very difficult for us to think in terms of value rather than price. We are under the impression that decisions need to be made quickly, urgently. When a sudden thunderstorm breaks out we must urgently seek shelter, otherwise we will get soaked. And what about when prices drop precipitously? We can calmly say that they will rise just as they have fallen. And our clothes stay perfectly dry. This is what experience teaches us.

Instead of looking at financial markets through our timeframe, we adapt to market timeframes. And the timeframes of financial markets are not "natural." The market is faster than we are, it is more global than we can possibly imagine. Certain market storms come from very far away and at surprising speed—and they pass just as quickly. And we feel a little awkward when we rush to buy a raincoat, pay for it, and the sun is shining by the time we are back outside.

The timeframe necessary to assess the outcome of our decisions is usually much longer than financial market responses. When we move into a new house, buy a new car, or decide to study a foreign language; when our child decides which college to attend or gets married: these are all difficult choices, whose outcomes can only be evaluated in the long run.

Imagine that there are daily odds on your child finding a job after graduation. What would change in terms of which major to choose? If in the last year engineering gains 20% and medicine loses 35%, does this mean that by the end of her college career (in 5–6 years), your child will have an easier time finding a job if she chooses engineering? I think all of us would tell our children: "your success does not depend on the major you choose, but on your commitment; and your commitment depends on you choosing something you like and that motivates you." We do not apply the same wisdom to financial choices.

In other words, a long-term outlook—*our* outlook, the one we use for the choices we make— does not seem to apply to financial markets. Is it a problem with finance, or is it *our* problem?

Behavioral finance shows us that it is mostly our problem. Simply put, we don't know how to invest. Investors systematically make mistakes—in terms of reasoning and preferences—that are difficult to reconcile with rational choices. These mistakes are reflected in "behavioral anomalies" resulting in low participation in the stock market, perception errors regarding risk/revenue ratios, poor diversification, and excessive portfolio changes (Linciano, 2010).

In summary, we can say that it has been proven that we do not know how to invest successfully. We make mistakes in what we buy (stocks, bonds, funds), in when we buy and sell, in taking on risk (which can be unnecessary or indispensable), and in succumbing to performance anxiety (Barberis and Thaler, 2003). While this generally holds true, during times of market, stress conditions can arise that lead to a change in our value system. Mister Hyde wins when we are under stress, and causes us to make mistakes that we acknowledge once we are back to being Doctor Jekyll (Ariely, 2010).

13.1.2 The Results of a Questionnaire

On behalf of *Il Sole—24 Ore*, an Italian financial newspaper, I put together a simple questionnaire to assess attitudes toward financial investments. It was published during a time of market stress (20 February, 2016).[1] It comprises five simple questions, and about 3,000 readers took part. The results are interesting, in part because *Il Sole*'s readers are far more competent than average in financial matters, and keep constantly abreast of the evolution of the market. The questionnaire, which was published in the newspaper on a Saturday, was available online for a full week.

Unfortunately, it was not possible to collect information on the participants, other than they are readers of a financial newspaper and took part in the questionnaire on a voluntary basis. Additionally, the questionnaire was published during a time of strong market volatility. Here are *Il Sole—24Ore*'s headlines:

- Wednesday 10/2/2016: The crisis shakes up markets and interest rates. Milan stock exchange—3.2%.
- Friday 12/2/2016: Stock markets and oil prices crash. Rising spread.[2]
- Saturday 13/2/2016: Markets in the eye of the storm.
- Tuesday 15/2/2016: Stock markets and bonds rise, led by banking and automotive sectors.
- Thursday 18/2/2016: Stock markets and oil prices rally. Milan stock exchange up 2.5%.

The questionnaire's contents and answers are summarized in Table 13.1. Here we comment the answers of the majority.

---

[1] *Il Sole—24 Ore*, February 20, 2016, "*Valuta quanto puoi resistere allo stress*".

[2] The difference between the interest rate on 10-year Italian treasury bonds and 10-year German bonds. This is a measure of market stress closely watched by private investors in Italy, who together with Italian banks are among the main holders of Italian treasury bonds.

Table 13.1: Questionnaire: are you sure you know how to invest (and not lose your money?).

	Number	%
1. Which of the following statements do you most agree with?		
a. I do not have a precise timeframe for investment. I prefer to be free to decide on the basis of market trends.	464	15.45
b. The destination of my savings (goals, investment timeframe) is very clear to me, but I prefer to make my investment choices (stocks and funds) on the basis of market trends.	511	17.01
c. The destination of my savings (goals, investment timeframe) is very clear to me, but my investment choices do not depend on short-term market trends.	1336	44.48
d. I prefer short-term investments that minimize risk and aim to achieve earnings (avoiding losses).	692	23.04
2. At the beginning of 2015, you invested 100,000 euros in a stock market fund. Since early 2016, it has loss 20%. Which of the following statements do you most agree with?		
a. I am not worried. Volatility of 20% is normal in the stock market. Perhaps it is an opportunity to buy.	1809	60.24
b. I am worried. I wish I had not invested in that fund. I let my broker convince me, and now (I knew it) I am losing money. I won't sell, but from now on no more stocks.	501	16.68
c. I am emotionally affected by the volatility of stock markets. I figured I would have earned something. It is not the right solution for me. As soon as the market rallies a bit, I will sell. I do not want to be trapped by stocks like in 2007, when I bought bank stock and lost 70%.	426	14.18
d. I am thrilled; market crashes like this one are always great opportunities to buy. I have seen "sale" prices for certain stocks: I will sell my fund and rush to buy stocks.	270	8.99
3. Coin toss. Which of the following alternatives do you prefer?		
a. One thousand consecutive tosses. Heads I win 15 euros, tails I lose 10.	670	22.31
b. One hundred consecutive tosses. Heads I win 10 euros, tails I lose 5.	258	8.59
c. Ten consecutive tosses. Heads I win 6 euros, tails I lose 1.	619	20.61
d. One toss only. Heads I win 5 euros, tails I lose nothing.	1467	48.85
4. An expert, I trust, told me it is a good time to buy high-yield bonds. She told me it is a risky investment. Why of the following alternatives do I most agree with?		
a. I look for a good bond to invest in, while seeking all necessary information.	706	23.51
b. I do not trust high-yield bonds since I don't know what they are	690	22.97
c. I ask the expert if buying high-yield bonds is in keeping with my investment goals and timeframe.	1168	38.89
d. I ask the expert what the return is on a high-yield bond, so I can decide based on the numbers.	454	15.12
5. I invested 100,000 euros in a balanced fund at the beginning of the year, once the treasury bonds in my portfolio expired (I did not renew them). At the end of the year, I have about 115,000 euros. At the end of the first trimester of the following year, after some market turmoil, my fund is now worth 105,000 euros. Which of the following statements do I most agree with?		
a. I am losing 10,000 euros, I am not satisfied.	336	11.19
b. I am earning 5,000 euros, I am not satisfied.	425	14.15
c. I am earning 5,000 euros, I am satisfied.	853	28.41
d. Too little time has passed to evaluate the investment.	1411	46.99

Forty-four percent of the sample stated: "the destination of my savings (goals, timeframe of investment) is very clear to me and my investment choices do not depend on short-term market trends." In the face of losses of 20% from the beginning of 2016, 60% of readers claim they would not worry. Indeed "volatility of 20% is normal for the stock market. Perhaps it is an opportunity to buy." Thirty-eight percent of the sample of readers replied that, when gauging the opportunities provided by high-yield bonds, they would ask their stock broker "whether the purchase of high-yield bonds is coherent with their investment goals and timeframe." Forty-six percent of readers say that in the face of significant losses registered by a balanced fund during the first trimester of the year, "too little time has passed to evaluate the investment."

These were the most frequent responses. They are those of a perfect investor and financial planner, who is aware of risks and invests in accordance with set goals and timeframes. This is too good to be true. Perhaps readers of *Il Sole—24 Ore* are not a representative sample of Italian investors. Leaving majorities aside, as they might be distorted by the nature of the sample, we can say that 56% of respondents do not have such clear ideas; 40% worry about short-term market trends; 62% do not consult their stock broker to assess risky investments; and 54% assess the results of a balanced fund too frequently. Nevertheless, the impression is that the average respondent is an investor who carefully evaluate his or her response, and in most cases, behaves ideally.

I did put a trick question in the questionnaire, however, one of the classics of behavioral finance, namely loss aversion. Let's see how the knowledgeable readers of *Il Sole* responded to the stress of making choices under uncertain conditions, a (mysterious and worrying) coin toss. Here is the question:

> *Coin toss. Which alternative do you prefer?*
> * *1000 consecutive tosses. Heads I win 15 euros, tails I lose 10*
> * *100 consecutive tosses. Heads I win 10 euros, tails I lose 5*
> * *10 consecutive tosses. Heads I win 6 euros, tails I lose 1*
> * *1 toss only. Heads I win 5 euros, tails I lose nothing*

Most of the 3,000 readers (to be exact, 48.85% of a sample of 3,014) answered: "1 toss only." It is all too clear why: it was the only alternative that ensured no losses. These 1,462 people literally threw away the 2,500 euros—more or less—they would have gained with the first option. Of course, this has an emotional cost, as winnings are not certain. Loss aversion translates into a feverish search for certainty, at any price.

By doing this, investors miss out on important opportunities. Why? Basically, because there is a lack of trust, and this fuels fear under conditions of stress, even when fear is entirely groundless, as in this case, when the distribution of loss probabilities is largely intuitive. The law of small numbers prevails in the minds of many people, even when it is obvious that it is the law of large numbers that governs the phenomenon at hand. The likelihood of sustaining losses after 1,000 coin tosses is 1 out of an 11-digit number (7 out of 100 billion to be exact). Within a 99% confidence interval we will earn 1,581 euros. Is this really too much uncertainty for our weak hearts? Or is our mind playing tricks on us? The "second choice" was—predictably enough—10 coin tosses (20.46% of readers). Why was it predictable (Ariely, 2010)? Because in behavioral finance losses count twice as much as earnings (Pompian, 2006). And earning 6 euros while risking losing one seems reasonable. "It's worth it."

In summary, 70% of the readers of a financial newspaper fell into the loss aversion trap in a context in which this cognitive attitude is entirely groundless. In addition, most of these people have clearly proven that they have a rational approach to the other issues in the questionnaire. Doctor Jekyll and Mister Hyde is indeed an appropriate metaphor. When faced with the same question, my mother, who is a youthful 86 years old, answered: better to win 6 and lose 1. Then over the phone she told me: "I know, I was wrong, I should have picked 1,000 coin tosses." "Mom—I replied—it's only a matter of timeframe." I know I can kid around with my mother.

13.2 Investor Behavior and Market Oscillations

13.2.1 Some Simple Thoughts on the Practical Implications of Prospect Theory

Is it better to accept a sure 5% or to toss a coin: heads 10%, tails 0%?

The answer is obvious. The rational choice is the sure 5%. The average expected result is 5%, but to obtain it we must run a risk. And most investors will choose certainty. We are risk-averse, and rightly so (Kahneman and Tversky, 1979). First and foremost, being risk averse is perfectly normal and rational. A gambler (someone with a high propensity for risk) would choose to toss the coin even if the option were 8% against 0%. This is wrong, because the expected return is less than 5%. But a gambler would reply that 8% is higher than 5%. He will take his risks even with numbers.

Let's imagine we are proposing a structured bond to an investor (Thorsten and Rieger, 2009). After 12 months, upon maturity, the return is linked to the outcome of a coin toss. Heads returns 108, tails returns the invested capital. This is the same situation as earlier. But pay attention to the "optical illusion": if the coin comes up tails, does the investor lose? Or does he perceive a loss? The answer is no, because a full return of the invested capital is not perceived as a loss (of capital).

The first problem is that investors are not always able to make financially sound comparisons. In the case of the structured bond earlier, the important thing is the comparison with the certain return (in our case, 5%). Thus, the structured bond has a lower return than the risk-free investment and should be rejected. But if it is described as an "opportunity to earn 8% without risking capital," investors could easily be fooled (Weber et al., 2005). They could latch on to 8%, compared it with 5% and immediately conclude that 8 is more than 5. In other words, the problem lies in an "emotional" definition of risk (I will not lose my capital) rather than a "rational" definition (comparison with average expected return, volatility of negative and positive outcomes). "Whereas technologically sophisticated analysts employ risk assessment to evaluate hazards, the majority of citizens rely on intuitive risk judgments, typically called: risk perceptions. For these people, experience with hazards tends to come from the news media, which rather thoroughly document mishaps and threats occurring throughout the world" (Slovic, 1987). Therefore, while we are all risk averse, sometimes we find ourselves gambling with our money, even though we do not really want to (Gentile et al., 2015; Veld and Veld-Merkoulova, 2008; Wang et al., 2011 note the low correlation between perceived risk and historical risk measures).

Let's imagine that we have overcome this misunderstanding, and that the difference between the expected return on a risky investment and a certain return is clear. Being risk-averse means that in order to take a risk, we must expect a reward. Indeed, if we replace 10% with 20% when heads comes up, we might want to take that risk. There is no cognitive problem here. The theory of risk aversion holds true. We take a risk because the expected return is higher than the certain return (Ricciardi, 2008). While it might not sound nice, "we all have a price" after all.

Second cognitive problem: in light of market uncertainty, under which circumstances would we expect a reward and thus take a risk? In other words, when would we tell ourselves that it is time to buy stocks? This is the cognitive problem: when will we feel that the market "rewards risk"? The answer is as simple as it is "terrible": when historic performances are so good that we will be convinced the trend will go on forever. This is called confirmation bias. In order to decide, we need confirmation—and what better confirmation than a market that has earned 40% over the last 12 months?

How many of us have read about a stock (or fund) that is performing well? The first time around, we tell ourselves: it's risky, it's not for me. If after a few days, we read that the stock is still performing well, our interest is piqued, and from that moment on our bias that it is a "good" stock will find plenty of confirmation, after which we will decide to buy. And of course, the stock price will begin to fall immediately thereafter. In other words, buying when the price is high is normal. One would at least have to hope that the price is only "relatively" high. Is it better to accept a sure loss of 5% or to toss a coin: heads we lose 10%, tails we lose nothing?

While a sure loss closes the door on any hope, the coin toss gives us a chance not to lose any money. And so we will choose to toss the coin. Warning: while it seems rational, it is actually the exact opposite of the previous scenario (choosing a certain 5%). This change of perspective only took place because of the switch from the "earning" mode to the "loss" mode, and for this reason only.

And so we wise and prudent investors, who need a reward in order to take a risk, have suddenly become risk takers. We have violated the basic principle according to which risks should be taken only if there is a reward. And all we can do is hope. Of course: "hope is the last to die!" (Lopes, 1987).

But if we are a little unlucky, the first coin toss will come up heads, and we will lose another 10%. At this point, do we give up or toss another coin? Obviously, we toss another coin. And if we are a little unlucky. In other words, our propensity to take risks generates what are known as drawdowns, a series of accumulating losses, which can eventually seem to become irreversible. An investor despairing over the repeated losses will say that the coin toss is rigged. She might blame "the world of finance," "the banks," or dishonest brokers. And she might stop playing after heavy losses. Of course: "hope is the last to die... but it is not immortal!"

For investors oscillating between risk aversion and risk taking, there is an interesting paradox. The most risk-averse (or prudent) investors are not unwilling to take risks, but they need higher rewards to do so. They will do so if they feel the reward is worth it. But what do they do when they perceive a reward as undeniable? In light of the earlier, when the performances of risky markets are outstanding, such investors will also decide to move away from risk-free returns. This is a situation in which the market has reached the peak of an upward trajectory. What will a prudent investor do? They will enter a bull market, when the risk of a significant drawdown is highest. But prudent investors are also the most risk averse. And thus they nearly instantly turn into "predictably irrational" risk takers, with the concrete likelihood of sustaining significant losses.

Let us ask another question. When to feel we are "earning" and when to feel we are "losing"? It might seem like a trivial question, but in behavioral finance it is fundamental (Thaler, 1999). The answer is simple: if we buy a house for 100,000 euros and sell it for 200,000, we have earned money. If instead we sell it for 80,000 then we lost money. True, because our house does not have a market value, one that appears every day in the stock market listings in the newspaper. But if the stock index goes from 20,000 to 40,000 then back down to 25,000—and we have stocks in our portfolio—are we earning or losing money? How do we feel? In all likelihood, we will feel as if we have lost a lot. Indeed, the media will keep reminding us that the stock market is still far from last year's high and that the road to recovery is still long and uncertain. Controversial point, how much does the purchase price matter? (Kahneman and Rieple, 1998).

This sensation will influence our investment choices. And we might forget that when the market was at its peak we did not invest any money—and thus, in practical terms, those market peaks mean little if anything for our money.

13.2.2 Financial Markets Over the Last 20 Years: An Ideal Context for Investor Errors

As for the coin toss discussed earlier, investors struggled to believe in the long-term returns historically offered by a liquid and diversified stock market. They thus concentrated on short-term stock index fluctuations, and constantly oscillated between risk aversion and risk taking. By the same token, investors failed to perceive the wide fluctuations of the market, which provided plenty of earning opportunities even with the simple application of a long-term moving average. Emotionally, short-term price fluctuations are a type of information that has an immediate impact (Kahneman and Tversky, 1974) and prevails over mid-term trends or fundamental predictions.

By experiencing market stress on a daily basis, investors lose sight of the notion of growth. Additionally, by constantly adjusting their mental points of reference, they believe they have invested when the market was at its peak even if this is not true. When observing the market, they confuse actual losses—the difference between the price of purchase and the price of sale—with capital losses, or the difference between top and current market values. As we have said, according to prospect theory this results in a shift from risk aversion to risk taking and subsequent reactions to an often groundless fear of losing everything.

In summary, investors transfigure Fig. 13.1 into Fig. 13.2, the drawdown graph, which never rises and always shows losses. From an emotional point of view, the drawdown graph

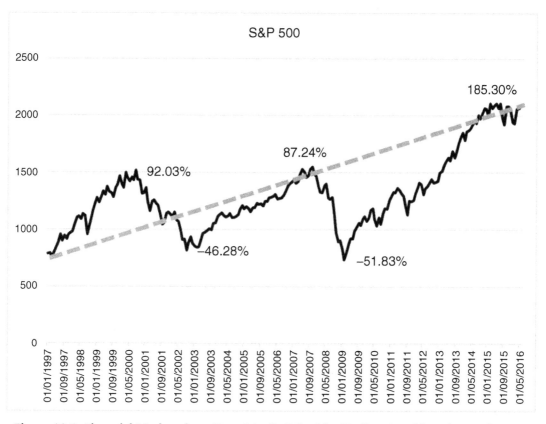

Figure 13.1: Financial Markets have Been Ideally Suited for Fueling Cognitive Bias on the Part of Investors Over the Last 20 Years.

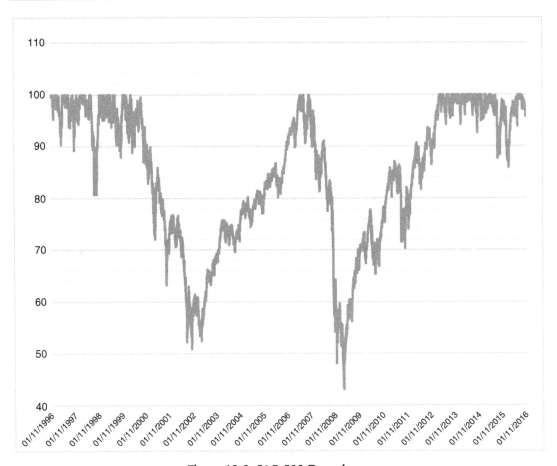

Figure 13.2: S&P 500 Drawdown.

identifies a situation in which investors always bought at the highest prices. It is a depiction of the constant shifting of the emotional reference point along the well-known, asymmetric utility curve between earnings and losses.

Fig. 13.1 depicts the large-cap stock market in the United States of America from January 1997 to the end of June 2016. It is the most liquid and diversified stock market in the world. The best market in which to risk obtaining long-term earnings. This is what history teaches us. Today, it is undoubtedly preferable to diversify as much as possible by globalizing our investments. But historical examples can usefully be based on the American market.

The dollar value at the beginning of the period was 786.16; it increased to 2098.86 by the end of the period. Long-term investors, those who "buy and hold," achieved earnings of 167% in 20 years, a compound annual rate of 5%. One hundred thousand dollars turned into 267,000 (price index, without reinvesting dividends). This is a rational reading of the numbers. Is it a difficult market? The answer is yes. It is a difficult market because it "unleashes emotions": +92% from 1997 to 2000; −46% from 2000 to 2002; then +87% until 2007 followed by −51% by the end of 2008. The market then began to climb again, and continues to do so (+185%). How much did we invest in 2000, and how much in early 2003? How much at the end of 2007 and how much in March 2009?

If we are honest with ourselves, the conclusion is sadly inescapable: we can pretty much say "I bought high and sold low." Mind you, we might not have been so obviously "stupid." Nevertheless, a close look will show that during a bull market our investments in stocks peaked (with very few liquid assets), while during a bear market we held lots of cash or short-term bonds while minimizing our stock. If we look at our new savings, in all likelihood, they were invested in stocks during a bull market and in liquid assets during a bear market. It is only normal, but in hindsight (which is always 20/20), it is a missed opportunity.

13.2.3 The Behavior of Italian Investors: Stock Market Purchases and Sales During Times of Stress

Every month, the Bank of Italy publishes the net purchases of Italian and foreign stocks (purchases minus sales) on the part of investment funds[3]; that is, on the part of Italians who decided to entrust their savings to fund managers. Within a certain margin of error, we can claim to know the purchasing behavior of the "most sophisticated" Italians: those who invest in stocks using a wise diversification tool.

Fig. 13.3 depicts all net monthly stock market purchases, or whether Italians added or removed stocks from their investment portfolios. Of course, it does not only cover US stocks. But since the US market is the reference market for the rest of the world, we can safely say that US market trends drive the confidence of investors, who may then decide to purchase stocks from other countries. As we can see, there is a very vigorous response to the +92% growth. Purchases of stocks peak along with the market. No surprise there. But what happens later "punishes" this sort of behavior. Italians get scared and begin to reduce the percentage of stocks in their portfolios. It is interesting to know that in the "boom" times of 2003–07, the percentage of stocks still fell, causing investors to lose the opportunities provided by the market. As stock prices rally back to their previous levels (when they were bought), they are sold: the "end of a nightmare" that caused a great deal of anxiety, but also a lost opportunity to actually gain back what was lost.

Fig. 13.3 shows that stocks accounted for the smallest share in the portfolio of Italians just as their prices fell to their lowest levels in 2009—the percentage of stocks fell back to 1997

---

[3] Banca d'Italia, *Supplementi al bollettino statistico, Indicatori monetari e finanziari, Mercato finanziario,* table TDEE0250, September 15, 2016.

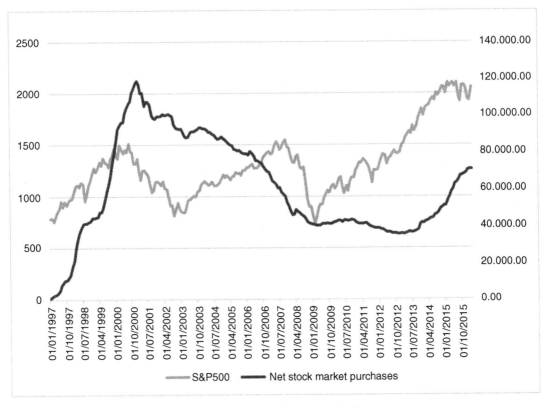

Figure 13.3: Net Stock Market Inflows.

levels. According to Bank of Italy data, it wasn't until the end of 2013 that confidence in stocks began to rise anew.

How much does such emotional behavior cost?

Consider this experiment: let us take the value of purchases (and sales, if negative) and multiply them by the stock market performance of the following month. If at the beginning of the month, Italian investors believe the market will rise, they will buy. If they think it will fall, they will sell. Of course, the market will not necessarily behave the way Italian investors expect based on their purchasing patterns. At the end of each month, then, Italian investors will have earned money if they bought stock before price increases, and lost it if they bought them before prices fell; conversely, they will have earned money if the sold stock before falling prices, and lost it if they sold before price increases. Using Bank of Italy data, we can examine trends to quantify successes and failures. This is what Fig. 13.4 shows. The S&P500 line shows market trends (taking the S&P500 as the reference). The scale on the left begins with a value of 786.16 on January 01, 1997. The *cumulative net earnings* (CNE) line shows cumulative net earnings of Italian investors (the values are on

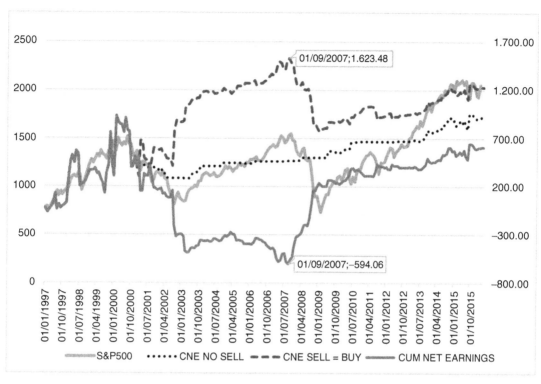

Figure 13.4: S&P 500 (left) and Cumulative Net Earnings (right).

the right, and start with zero). Until 2000, Italian investors earned money (up to 1 billion euros), then began sustaining heavy losses, to the point of losing all profits and going almost 600 million euros in the hole. They sustained losses from September 2002 to August 2008, a real nightmare. At the end, though, cumulative net earnings amounted to +650 million euros.

If we analyze the data carefully, we will see that during the first stock market crisis (tech bubble), there were extensive purchases following market trends (in keeping with risk aversion). When the stock market fell in 2001–02, heavy losses were sustained that were not recouped until the bull market of 2007. These results are coherent with the theory of risk aversion that shifts toward risk taking (prospect theory).

According to our experiment, as markets rally, purchasing 1 month late (trend following) implies lost opportunities but not actual losses if the trend continues for another month. As markets fall, on the other hand, selling takes longer due to the reluctance to sell in the face of losses (loss aversion) (Odean, 1998). This "contrarian" delay exists even if there are evident signs of trend inversion due to loss aversion (which fuels hopes of recovery). On the other hand, fear (or losing the hope of recovery) causes investors to sell just before trend inversion

(Shefrin and Statman, 1985). The marked recovery that took place starting in September 2007, when the stock market reached a new high, should be explained.

According to prospect theory, investor behavior is not driven by actual market trends, but by the way their minds interpret them. In the entire period between the market peak in 2000 and the new highs of 2007, investors were in "loss" mode compared to the reference point (2000 market peak). This is why purchases did not follow the rising trends of 2003–07. The result is a radical difference in behavior compared to the euphoria that led to the 2000 market peak and the subsequent behavioral reaction. Up until 2000, investors were in the "earning" mode. We all remember Alan Greenspan's famous speech from December 1996 on the irrational exuberance of markets. Indeed, this is when the analysis presented in Fig. 13.1 begins. It is useful to point out that the same graph as in Fig. 13.1 appears in the previous 20 years (1976–96, Fig. 13.5). The two graphs are on a linear scale: we cannot expect the average investor to behave on the basis of logarithmic scales.

Investors are thus in loss mode for the entire period after the market bottomed out in late 2002. They cannot see any rewards for taking risks on the stock market, and they sell every time the price recovers to the previous reference point. This is quite clearly noticeable as the market rallies to the new highs of 2007, when sales accelerated right before the market peak. It is very interesting to note that cumulative net purchases at the end of 2009 were back at 1998 levels. A behavioral cycle thus came to an end that was characterized by a peak in 2000

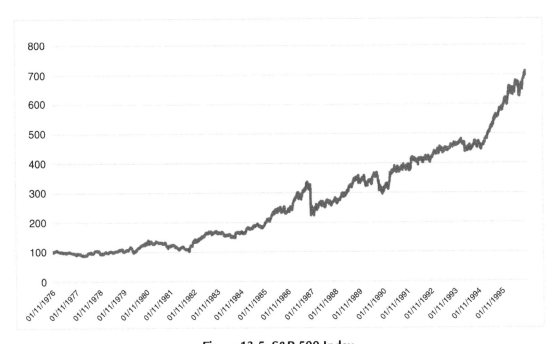

Figure 13.5: S&P 500 Index.

when investors shifted from risk aversion to risk taking. During the risk-taking phase, sales took place gradually as values returned to previous levels.

The 2008–09 crisis caught investors during the risk-taking phase, and selling accelerated as the fear took hold that the new crisis would have jeopardized capital recovery. Selling stopped at the previous lows. This explains the gains of 2007–09. Sales went hand-in-hand with a constant drop in the market, and according to the rules of our experiment, this implies earnings (sales before a price fall). As the previous highs are surpassed, we have now entered a new phase: investors are once again risk averse and thus open to a shift toward becoming risk takers, should the market enter a downturn.

We can use the same data to quantify the behavioral costs of prospect theory. Let us imagine that a broker interprets sales as "fear," and advises investors not to sell, as fear should never be a motivator. This advice should not be misinterpreted. The broker is not suggesting making long-term investments—indeed the timeframe is only of about a month. He is only advising his clients not to give in to fear and not sell in that particular month.

We should define fear-driven selling. In our experiment, this means that the investor, after delaying selling due to loss aversion (irrational expectation of recovering losses), loses hope and accepts the losses. In light of this definition, refraining from selling once it is too late to do so should have advantages. The result is the CNE NO SELL line Fig. 13.4. Through his advice, the broker has prevented certain errors that would have led to losses. Ultimately net earnings amounted to about a billion, and most importantly there were no losses. The fear of losing causes one to lose money!

Now comes a final piece of provocative advice. Every time a client asks to sell (motivated by fear, as the broker sees it), the broker advises to do the exact opposite and buy. The result is the CNE SELL = BUY line. Net earnings improve once again to 1.3 billion euros. It is true that during 2009, investors would have seen their earnings fall. In 2008–09, the CNE SELL = BUY line was the mirror image of the CUM NET EARNINGS one. If selling leads to earnings, buying leads to losses.

13.3 Investor Assessments and Coherence with Actual Behaviors

13.3.1 Perhaps Investors Know What is to be Done

Every month, Professor Robert Shiller (and the Yale School of Management) publishes the "Stock Market Confidence Index," on the basis of a questionnaire submitted to individual and institutional investors.

Fig. 13.6 (the red line's scale is on the right, the blue line represents S&P500) depicts the Valuation Confidence Index. The question it asks is essentially the following: do you think the stock market is overvalued? The index represents the percentage of subjects who believe

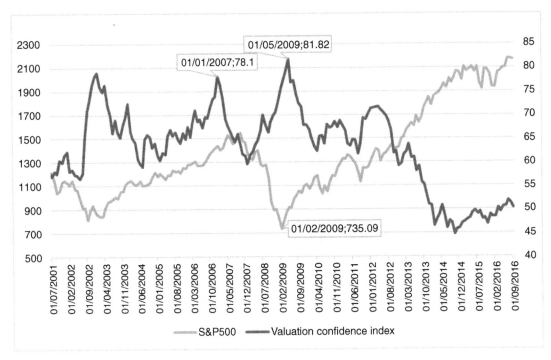

Figure 13.6: Value Confidence Index versus the S&P 500.

the market is *not* overvalued. Therefore, the higher the index, the higher the confidence in the market (the S&P 500). If the market is not overvalued, it will likely grow, or at the very least not crash.

This is an interesting question because it forces investors to think about the comparison between price and value in stock markets, as pointed out in *The Intelligent Investor* by Benjamin Graham: *The investor cannot enter the arena of the stock market with any real hope of success unless he is armed with mental weapons that distinguish him in kind—not in a fancied superior degree—from the trading public. One possible weapon is the indifference to market fluctuations (...). He must deal in values, not in price movements.*

In Fig. 13.6, the red line depicts the opinion of individuals: for example, in May, 2009 (in the midst of the economic crisis), over 80% of respondents felt the market was not overvalued (and thus that buying was a good option). The blue line shows the level of the S&P500, which was just above 900 then. In early 2007, almost 80% of respondents felt the market was not overvalued. The S&P500 index was around 1,500. As of September, 2016 (the most recent available data), respondents were evenly split: 50% think it is better to buy or at least not sell; the other 50% thinks it is best to sell. The S&P500 index is around 2,100.

Is it wise for an investor to follow the opinions expressed by this index, and to buy or sell on the basis of the mood of survey respondents?

We built three portfolios on the basis of the data in the valuation index:

- A "balanced" portfolio: 50% stocks and 50% money market investments;
- a "balanced" portfolio in which when the Valuation Confidence index rises—when the opinion of Americans on the stock market improves—the percentage of investment in stocks *increases*; and
- a "balanced" portfolio in which when the Valuation Confidence index rises—when the opinion of Americans on the stock market improves—the percentage of investment in stocks *decreases*.

The question is: which portfolio will have the best performance?

The answer is in Fig. 13.7, where PTF_BIL is the balanced portfolio; PTF_VCI is the portfolio that reflects the mood of the respondents; and PTF VCICO is the "contrarian" portfolio, which does the opposite of what most respondents would. In other words, the figures compare an investor who follows her own mood, as represented by the valuation index, with one that does the exact opposite, and increases her stock holdings when she feels stocks are overvalued, while reducing it when she feels stocks are undervalued.

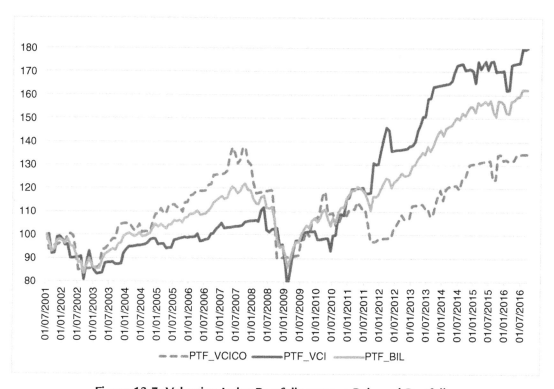

Figure 13.7: Valuation Index Portfolios versus Balanced Portfolio.

As can be seen in Fig. 13.7, when investors are asked about fundamentals (is the market overvalued?), they know that during times of crisis they *should* invest. Indeed, if we are wise and focus on value instead of price, we should come out ahead over time. As can be seen, this is not easy, and it does not always hold true. But we will not be condemned to make mistakes if, as Graham suggests, we manage to think in terms of value and not price.

13.3.2 ...But They are Not Able to Do It

Prof. Shiller also asks Americans to express their opinions about "price," and not value. To keep things short, I am only discussing the index that I feel is the most "emotional," but simulations have been carried out using the other indexes as well, with analogous results.[4]

Fig. 13.8 depicts the trend of the "Buy on Dips" index. It represents the percentage of respondents who expect the market to bounce back after falling by 3% in 1 day.[5] This index assesses investor confidence in the market in the face of exceptional volatility.

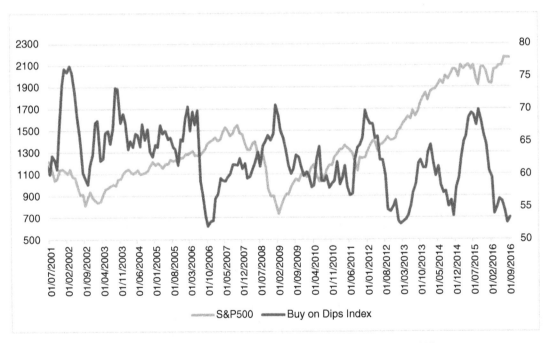

Figure 13.8: Buy on Dips Confidence Index versus S&P 500.

---

[4] The other indexes are the "Crash Index," which measures the percentage of Americans who deem a market crash in the next 6 months to be unlikely; and the "One Year Confidence Index," which measures the percentage of respondents who expect the stock market to rise in the next year.

[5] Keep in mind that between January 1950 and the present (16,797 days) a 1-day drop of over 3% has only happened 100 times (0.60% of cases). As such, it should be considered a rare event.

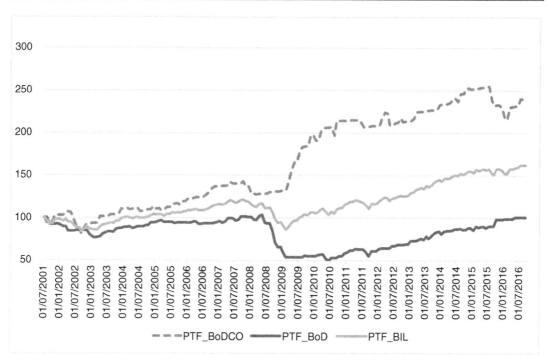

Figure 13.9: Buy on Dips Index Portfolios versus Balanced Portfolio.

As shown in Fig. 13.9, most investors feel it is opportune to buy after a market drop of 3%. But there are times when that percentage reaches 70%. On the basis of this index, we once again put together the portfolios discussed earlier: a balanced one (PTF_BIL); one that reflects the mood of respondents (PTF_BoD); and a contrarian one that does the exact opposite (PTF_BoDCO). The results are presented in Fig. 13.9. This time behavioral costs are very high. Our minds are not very good at dealing with price volatility.

By following their emotional responses to short-term price fluctuations, investors only recover the capital they invested after 15 years (PTF_BoD). By investing in a balanced portfolio—without changing it over time, and thus without giving in to emotional impulses—100 dollars will turn into 162 dollars (PTF_BIL) (Alemanni and Franzosi, 2006; Barber and Odean, 2000). Let us now modify the portfolio by doing the exact opposite as the previous one. We will increase our share of stocks when the Buy on Dips Index falls, and reduce it when the Buy on Dips Index rises. The new contrarian portfolio is depicted in the PTF_BoDCO line in Fig. 13.9: 100 dollars become nearly 240 dollars.

13.4 Conclusions

An experiment conducted on 3,000 participants, all readers of a financial newspaper, once again shows the clear presence of the best-known cognitive bias affecting financial choices during times of uncertainty: loss aversion. This cognitive and emotional response is truly blinding. Even in the face of very clear long-term gains, the fear of losing prevents us from taking advantage of them. This simple questionnaire also highlighted a second factor: since long-term gains are not certain, the albeit very limited uncertainty around them undermines trust. Since we are not fully convinced, we fall into the trap at the first sign of trouble.

Prospect theory teaches us that investors oscillate between risk aversion and risk taking around a well-defined reference point. Risk taking is based on the hope of recouping losses. Once this hope is lost, irrational fear takes over, and the assets are sold far too late, undermining any chance to recover one's losses. On the financial market, where prices appear to be the only thing that is tangible, the market value of the portfolio becomes a natural, instinctive reference point. Investors thus shift from risk aversion to risk taking when the market peaks.

By observing investor behavior using aggregate data from Italy, we were able to conclude that the two market peaks of 2000 and 2007 had opposite effects on investors: while the former certainly led to a shift from risk aversion to risk taking, with significant behavioral costs, investor attitude during the second peak seemed to be different. We believe that during 2007, peak investors were still in "loss" mode (risk taking) because the reference point of 2000 was not surpassed. Investor priorities throughout the 2003–07 stock market rally were to sell in order to recoup capital: the hope that drives the behavior of investors who are averse to losses.

Now that previous market highs have been surpassed (at least in the US stock market) new behavioral scenarios are emerging. Investors are setting higher "reference points" and are thus evaluating the extent to which the market rewards risks. They are once again ready for the shift from risk aversion to risk taking during adverse times. The analysis of Shiller's confidence indexes helped stress a point I feel is quite important: the behavior of investors under normal conditions (Dr. Jekyll) is not irrational. Investors are able to correctly perceive the difference between price and value, give or take a margin of error. But when price movements prevail and become available information, the behavior of investors' changes, and Mr. Hyde drives their choices. In this case, behavioral costs are systematic and inevitable, and independent from long-term market trends. Investors are no longer able to perceive the difference between price and value, and are driven exclusively by short-term price movements.

References

Alemanni, B., Franzosi, A., 2006. Investors psychology of high frequency online traders. Second Report on the Italian Stock market. BItNotes 16, 1–48.

Ariely, D., 2010. Predictably Irrational. Harper, New York, NY.

Barber, B.M., Odean, T., 2000. Trading is hazardous to your wealth: the common stock investment performance of individual investors. J. Finance 55 (2), 773–806.

Barberis, N., Thaler, R.H., 2003. A survey of behavioral finance. In: Constantinides, G., Harris, M., Stultz, R. (Eds.), Handbook of the Economics of Finance. Elsevier Science, Amsterdam.

Gentile, M., Linciano, N., Lucarelli, C., Soccorso, P., 2015. Financial disclosure, risk perception and investment choice. Evidence From a Consumer Testing Exercise. CONSOB Quaderni di Finanza 82, Milan.

Kahneman, D., Rieple, M.W., 1998. Aspects of investor psychology. J. Portfol. Manag. 24 (4), 52–65.

Kahneman, D., Tversky, A., 1974. Judgment under uncertainty: heuristics and biases. Sci. New Series 185 (4157), 1124–1131.

Kahneman, D., Tversky, A., 1979. Prospect theory: an analysis of decision under risk. Econometrica 47 (2), 263–291.

Linciano, N., 2010. Errori conglitivi ed instabilità delle preferenze nelle scelte di investimento dei risparmiatori retail. Le indicazioni di policy della Finanza Comportamentale. CONSOB Quaderni di Finanza 66, Milan.

Lopes, L., 1987. Between hope and fear: the psychology of risk. Adv. Exp. Soc. Psychol. 20 (2), 255–295.

Odean, T., 1998. Are investors reluctant to realize their losses? J. Finance 53 (5), 1775–1798.

Pompian, M.M., 2006. Behavioral Finance and Wealth Management. John Wiley & Sons, Hoboken, NJ.

Ricciardi, V., 2008. Risk: traditional finance versus behavioral finance. In: Fabozzi, Frank J. (Ed.), Handbook of Finance Volume 3 Valuation, Financial Modeling, And Quantitative Tools. John Wiley & Sons, Hoboken, NJ.

Shefrin, H.M., Statman, M., 1985. The disposition to sell winners too early and ride losers too long: theory and evidence. J. Finance 40 (3), 777–790.

Slovic, P., 1987. Perception of risk. Science 236 (4799), 280–285.

Thaler, R.H., 1999. Mental accounting matters. J. Behav. Decision Making 12 (3), 183–206.

Thorsten, H., Rieger, M.O., 2009. Why do Investors Buy Structured Products? (February 10, 2009). EFA 2009 Bergen Meetings Paper. Available from: https://ssrn.com/abstract=1342360

Veld, C., Veld-Merkoulova, Y.V., 2008. The risk perception of individual investors. J. Econ. Psychol. 29 (2), 226–252.

Wang, M., Keller, C., Siegrist, M., 2011. The less you know, the more you are afraid of—a survey on risk perception of investment products. J. Behav. Finance 12, 9–19.

Weber, E.U., Siebenmorgen, N., Weber, M., 2005. Communicating asset risk: how name recognition and the format of historic volatility information affect risk perception and investment decisions. Risk Anal. 25 (3), 597–609.

Further Reading

Barberis, N., Huang, M., 2001. Mental accounting, loss aversion and individual stock returns. J. Finance 56 (4), 1247–1292.

Jonson-Laird, P.N., Legrenzi, P., Girotto, V., Sonino Legrenzi, M., Caverni, J.P., 1999. Naive probability: a mental model theory of extensional reasoning. Psychol. Rev. 106 (1), 62–88.

CHAPTER 14

Market Sentiment and Contagion in Euro-Area Bond Markets

Dimitris Georgoutsos*, Petros Migiakis**

*Athens University of Economics and Business, Athens, Greece; **Bank of Greece, Athens, Greece

Chapter Outline

14.1 Introduction

The creation of the euro-area had already attracted the attention of academic researchers as early as the first years of the existence of the European Monetary Union (EMU). They had been trying to investigate empirically the degree of integration of the Eurozone sovereign bond markets, since one of the main reasons for the creation of a single currency area was to lay down the foundations for the existence of a single market for financial assets in the Eurozone. Although the studies that were conducted varied methodologically, the main conclusion they reached was that the euro-area bond markets shared, up to the outbreak of the global financial crisis, a high degree of integration (Abad et al., 2010). This literature shows that the convergence of the euro-area sovereign bond markets, both in terms of the interest rate levels and their conditional and unconditional volatility, should be attributed to the elimination of the exchange rate uncertainty and the adoption of a common monetary policy (Ehrman et al., 2011). Still, the persistence of small spreads could be related to idiosyncratic risks, that is solvency and liquidity risks (Favero and Missale, 2012).

The outbreak of the subprime loans crisis led to a dramatic increase in the sovereign bond spreads, on the Bunds, of the euro-area periphery countries. The initial response of the people in the media and a number of academics was to blame the poor fiscal performance of the noncore Eurozone countries for these developments. This interpretation of the events led to the adoption of fiscal consolidation measures, which were then followed by a severe economic recession that fed back the worsening fiscal stance measures of the initially hit countries. However from the very beginning of the global crisis many economists and market participants felt uneasy with this interpretation since it could not be compromised with the evidence that in the early EMU years, very small spreads, among many Euro-area countries, coexisted with considerably varying government deficit and debt ratios. The apparent mispricing of the sovereign debt of the Eurozone countries appears to have continued after 2008, since serious disparities in the reaction of their spreads were not always accompanied by similarly dramatic changes of the underlying fundamentals. Therefore, a burgeoning literature has been developed which is trying to explain the apparent nonrationality of the "markets" in pricing sovereign debt issues. The verdict on this discussion has far-reaching consequences since the policy recommendations are quite different. On the one hand, if loosening on the fiscal front is to blame for the disintegration of the euro-area bond markets, the policy prescription should be focusing on fiscal consolidation measures. On the other, there is plenty of scope for the common monetary policy if contagion, generated from liquidity shortages or the herding behavior from the investors, is causing the instability in the markets.

Up to now the results obtained from this research endeavor converge on a number of alternative explanations. The first one is that the dynamic generation process for the spreads changed after 2008–09 (Afonso et al., 2015; Bernoth and Erdogan, 2012). Market participants started pricing fiscal imbalances and growth prospects more aggressively than before (Beirne and Fratzscher, 2013). This behavior is rationalized by the increased risk aversion of investors as an outcome of the uncertainties the subprime loans crisis generated and is manifested through the reallocation of portfolios in favor of sovereign bonds issued by countries sharing the "safe haven" status. The second explanation is proposing that investors were misinformed before the subprime crisis about the fiscal imbalances, the growth prospects of many Eurozone countries as well as the implicit bail-out clauses that fiscally weak euro-area member countries presumably enjoyed. Under these circumstances, there must have been an event that triggered the shift in investors' behavior. By now, it is widely accepted that this event is identified with the developments in Greece in late 2009 which made clear to the world financial community that the Greek government was unable to refinance the country's debt through the markets (Arghyrou and Kontonikas, 2012).

In the present paper, we try to shed more light on the issue of the sovereign spreads determinants. We diverge from the rest of the literature on two fronts. First, we compare the impact of spread determinants over two periods, from 2009 to mid-2012 when the Eurozone crisis erupted and intensified, and the period from mid-2012 till the beginning of 2016 when a series of institutional interventions were implemented which intended to immunize the Eurozone economies from the still unresolved country-specific problems. Although the first period has been intensively investigated there is, comparatively, much scarcer evidence on the determinants of sovereign spreads for the latter period.

The second area of our departure from the existing literature is in the use of a panel vector autoregression methodology (PVAR), which allows the estimation of a dynamically interrelated system of variables in an unrestricted way and in samples spanning a very limited period of time. We apply the PVAR methodology on two panels, one consisting of four peripheral Eurozone countries, that is, Italy, Spain, Ireland, and Portugal, and the other of five core Eurozone countries, that is, France, Austria, the Netherlands, Belgium, and Finland. Each unit in the panel is represented by six variables, that is, the country's spread over the German Bund, its growth rate, the budget balance, an economic sentiment indicator (ESI), and the stock market volatility. The second and third variables account for the effect of the growth prospects and the fiscal imbalances on spreads, while the ESI variable captures not only the expectations for the future development of the two previous variables but also all the other variables that shape the economic sentiment in an economy. For instance, the ESI captures the effect of the global and regional systemic risk factors on the economic sentiment in each country or it reflects beliefs which have been shaped from a herding reaction to certain events. Finally, the stock market volatility variable represents the degree of uncertainty in each market since the frequent reshuffling of portfolios increases stock returns volatility. A sixth common variable, the Greek spreads, is added in each unit with the intension to capture contagious effects triggered by the weakest, financially, country in the Eurozone. Developments in Greece were considered by incompletely informed analysts and investors as portents of expected events to come for other Eurozone countries experiencing fiscal and financial imbalances.

The rest of the paper is organized as follows. In Section 14.2, we offer a brief and selective review of the main papers dealing with the determinants of sovereign bond spreads in the recent Eurozone crisis. In Section 14.3, we present the PVAR model and the testing procedure we follow while in Section 14.4, we present the results and we comment on them. In the last section, we present our main conclusions and we draw some policy recommendations.

14.2 Literature Review

The origins of the sovereign debt crisis in Eurozone can be traced back to the outbreak of the global financial crisis in 2007 and the measures undertaken by almost all EMU governments which were meant to insulate their banking sector from the direct or indirect consequences of that crisis. All the measures that were adopted, varying from capital injections and guarantees for bank liabilities to asset support programs and the extension of deposit insurance schemes, had as a side-effect the development of severe fiscal imbalances. Motivated by these events, part of the research in this area set out to study the "sovereign-bank" loop that was generated and it was reflected in the increased correlation between sovereign and bank default risk. Initially, causality was detected which was running from banks' to sovereigns' CDS spreads but the deterioration of the fiscal position of most EMU countries and their perceived inability to support their banking sectors soon reversed the direction of this causality (Acharya et al., 2014; Ejsing and Lemke, 2011). The intertwined default risk of sovereigns and banks is also reported when excess correlations, that are conditional on the presence of common factors, are being studied. De Bruyckere et al. (2013) find that excess correlations increased substantially over the 2009–10 period and then they move on to establish the presence of a number of channels (guarantees, asset cross-holdings, collaterals) that account for these findings.

As soon as the banking crisis was contained, the discussion shifted on the structural problems of some peripheral euro-area economies, as being the causes of their fiscal imbalances, and cast doubts on their ability to sustain their existing levels of private and public debt. Independently of the factors that caused this fiscal expansion, the major part of the relevant literature dealt with the examination of the significance of fiscal performance measures for the formation of the spreads. The accumulated evidence up to now has unequivocally reached the conclusion that although fiscal performance matters for the sovereign bond spreads, its significance is, at best, moderated by the presence of other factors. These may vary from the impact of global systemic risk factors to the presence of liquidity crashes and an array of other factors which are crucial for determining the economic sentiment prevailing in each euro-area country.

Favero and Missale (2012) claim that a country's fiscal fundamentals do not matter per se but because they determine the sensitivity of its sovereign debt spreads to the perceived global financial risk. Therefore, during low global risk periods, as captured by global spreads, poor fiscal fundamentals are not priced in domestic yield spreads. However, in periods when global risk is high, countries will be affected from their fiscal fundamentals the closer they are to fiscally troubled countries. Similarly, fiscally sound countries even in turbulent periods will not experience any substantial increase of their yield spreads. In a similar vein, Beirne and Fratzscher (2013) report results showing that the price of sovereign risk has become more sensitive to fundamentals during the euro-area debt crisis. Jaramillo and Weber (2013), using panel threshold estimation techniques, show that it does matter what state a country faces in terms of the global environment. During tranquil periods, market participants are mainly worried about macroeconomics shocks and their effect on inflation and economic growth rates. However, when global risk aversion is high, there is enhanced awareness to country specific fiscal fundamentals.

The view that sovereign spreads should be attributed mainly to global systemic financial risk factors and secondary only to domestic fundamentals has also been supported in studies by Longstaff et al. (2011) and Ang and Longstaff (2013). Furthermore, Camba-Méndez and Serwa (2016) manage to identify separately the probability of default (PD) and the loss given default (LGD) in the CDS prices of a number of euro-area countries. Then, they show that their estimates of both the PDs and the LGDs were positively correlated with global risk indicators, like the iTraxx, and weakly only related to economic fundamentals and institutional factors. Gómez-Puig et al. (2014), by making use of an exhaustive compilation of data, show that local macroeconomic variables can partially only explain the rise in sovereign risk in core and peripheral euro-area countries. Instead, regional macroeconomic fundamentals as well as local, regional and global sentiment factors had a more crucial explanatory power which got stronger after the outbreak of the sovereign debt crisis. In another paper, Gómez-Puig and Sosvilla-Rivero (2016) evaluate the extent of contagion in the euro-area, where they associate it with the existence of increased Granger-causality between pairs of sovereign bond yield spreads. Their results indicate that both the deterioration of the debt sustainability in the euro-area as well as market sentiment factors lie behind the observed increase in the sovereign risk premium. If anything, macroeconomic fundamentals seem to play a more important role for the core Eurozone countries while peripheral countries seem to be more vulnerable to episodes triggered in other countries in the periphery of the euro-area (see also, Arghyrou and Kontonikas, 2012; De Santis, 2014).

In a series of papers, De Grauwe and Ji (2013, 2014) explain how participation in a monetary union may lead member countries with high debt-to-GDP ratios to self-fulfilling liquidity crises, which then degenerate to solvency problems, in the absence of a lender of last resort function for the Central Bank. These self-fulfilling dynamics do not exist for nonunion countries which issue government debt in a currency they control. Also, the fragility of a monetary union, justified by the nonrealization of the hoped-for sovereign bailouts, the substantial cross-holdings of government bonds and the importance of the interbank market for banks' funding, can lead to the prevalence of panic conditions and the realization of bad equilibria. Ghosh et al. (2012) have reached to similar results through the concept of fiscal space. They explain that bond rates for peripheral countries were below the level they should have, according to their fiscal space, since they enjoyed a bonus from currency union membership. Finally, Saka et al. (2015) have provided empirical support to the Eurozone fragility hypothesis.

14.3 Data and the Setup of the Empirical Analysis
14.3.1 Data

Our data set consists of quarterly observations that span the period 2009:1–2016:1. We run our estimations on two subperiods; 2009:1–2012:2 and 2012:3–2016:1. The first one marks the period of time when the EMU sovereign debt crisis burst although there is some controversy about its starting and ending points. The EMU sovereign debt crisis is believed to have started in November 2009 with the announcement of the revised Greek public finance statistics. However, on January 9, 2009, Standard and Poor's published a negative watch announcement and shortly after, on January 15, 2009, it downgraded Greece from A to the A⁻ status. Other researchers, using statistical techniques, find that financial markets had started pricing sovereign debt risk as early as the end of 2008 (Bernoth and Erdogan, 2012; Georgoutsos and Migiakis, 2013b). Gómez-Puig and Sosvilla-Rivero (2016) show that two-thirds of all structural breaks occurred after November 2009 while Afonso et al. (2015) offer evidence that the significance of EMU sovereign debt determinants increased for some countries after 2009.

We could highlight several stylized facts that make a sample separation to the period before and after the end of the second quarter of 2012 warranted. At the end of the second quarter of 2012, we could trace the starting point for the stabilization/deescalation of the sovereign bond spreads of the peripheral countries. The second quarter of 2012 is crucial because a series of events, on the institutional front, have marked it as the turning point for the EMU sovereign debt crisis. Most prominent among those events are the Greek debt restructuring in February 2012 and the euro area Summit, in June 29, when the foundations for the forthcoming banking union were set. On the other hand, the third quarter marks the credible commitment of the ECB for the irreversibility of the Eurozone, with the *"Whatever it takes"* speech by M. Draghi in July 2012 and the subsequent introduction of the Outright Monetary Transactions (OMT) program in August 2012. In Fig. 14.1, we present the spreads series and the relevance of splitting the sample in mid-2012 becomes evident. Up to that period the spreads of the sovereign bonds, of both the core and the peripheral euro-area countries, were rising but thereafter they started falling.

Coming to the data we use, the price of sovereign risk is captured by the 10-year yield spread against the German bund. This variable has been extensively used in related studies and it incorporates in addition to the risk premium for the cost of insolvency, a premium for the liquidity risk as well. The series of the spreads of the core and peripheral euro-area countries, as well as the Bund, have been retrieved by Datastream.

The growth rate variable is expressed by the percentage change of GDP in a given quarter, as this is measured in the quarterly releases of national accounts, relative to the same quarter a year ago. In this way, a rate of growth of the economic activity is constructed that is of higher frequency than the annual GDP growth rate. Source of the GDP data is Ameco, the European Commission's economic database.

From the same database, we have collected data on quarterly public revenues and expenses, for the countries of our sample. After adjusting them for seasonality, with the use of the Census X12 filter, we construct the fiscal balance (i.e., surplus if balance > 0 or deficit if balance < 0), as the difference of revenues to expenses proportional to the level of government revenues at the end of each quarter. This variable compares to the fiscal balance-to-GDP ratio that is often employed in similar studies.

However, we believe that this measure of fiscal balance expresses better and more timely the fiscal position of each country as it captures the current status of fiscal imbalances rather than the potential one when the GDP appears in the denominator. In particular, as our study aims to reflect the stand point of investors, we find it highly unlikely that investors will wait until the quarterly data for GDP are released with one to three quarters lag, until they form their expectations on the fiscal figures of a euro-area country; instead investors are more likely to monitor the monthly

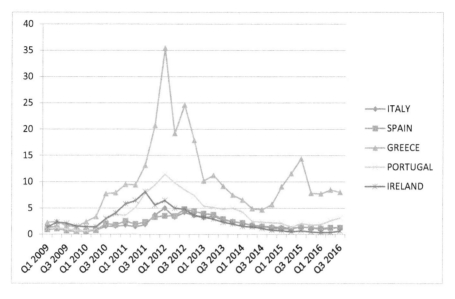

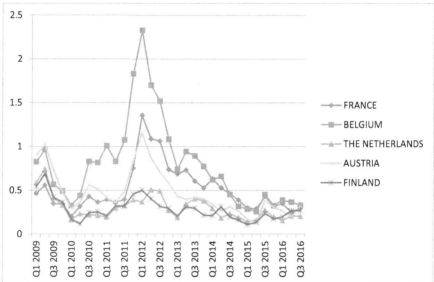

Figure 14.1: Spreads of 10-Year Eurozone Government Bond Yields Over the German Ones.

fiscal performance bulletins published by the Ministries of Finance each month.[1] Note that the latter contain figures only for the expenses and revenues; as a result we deem more likely that investors will have already formed their stance based on the monthly available information for revenues and expenses than wait until the quarterly data of GDP are released.

---

[1]   In this case, the GDP indicates the potential tax base of each country rather than the actual tax revenues raised by it. Depending on a number of factors, like changes in tax rates, the definition of the tax base or the efficiency of the tax authorities, a change in GDP does not imply that tax revenues change equiproportionately.

Finally, the economic and market sentiment in each country is being expressed by two variables, each of them collected by Datastream. The first one is the ESI issued by Eurostat for the member countries of European Union. The economic sentiment, or else "economic confidence," indicator is comprised by consumer, business, industrial, and retail confidence subcomponents, that measure the degree of optimism/pessimism of the corresponding economic agents as with regards to both the current and the upcoming prospects of their economic activities; the threshold of 100 denotes the level above (below) which economic agents are optimistic (pessimistic) on the economic outlook. As a result, it may be taken as a reflection of the growth outlook of the economy, as gauged by consumers, producers, and salesmen. We take the quarterly changes of the economic sentiment indicator (or the consumer confidence, in the case of Ireland), which are then interpreted as reflecting an improvement (in case of positive changes) or deterioration (in case changes are negative) in the expectations of domestic economic agents for the economic activity in any of the euro-area countries we examine.

The second variable that we use in order to reflect investor sentiment is the historical stock market volatility calculated as the standard deviation of daily returns of the domestic general stock market price index for each particular quarter (Gómez-Puig and Sosvilla-Rivero, 2016; Gómez-Puig et al., 2014).[2] We note that stock market volatility, either implied or historical, is often used as a "fear-gauge" or else as a measure of investors' risk aversion; it is a stylized fact, ever since the global financial crisis, that stock market volatility is one of the "early warning signals" for market turbulence and, thus, is used in order to reflect the tendency of investors to avoid exposure to risks (the so-called "market risk sentiment").

14.3.2 Setup of the Empirical Analysis

We employ a PVAR methodology. In a PVAR, all variables in the system are treated as endogenous, as in a traditional VAR model, and also, in resemblance to a panel-data approach, the presence of unobserved individual heterogeneity is being allowed for. Consider that Y_t is a stacked version of a Gx1 vector of endogenous variables y_t, each one of which corresponds to N units, that is, $Y_t = (y'_{1t}, y'_{2t}, ... y'_{Nt})$. Then a p-order PVAR is given by:

$$y_{it} = A_0 + A_1 y_{i,t-1} + ... + A_p y_{i,t-p} + f_i + u_t, \quad i = 1, ..., N, \quad t = 1, ... T \tag{14.1}$$

where $u_t \sim$ iid $(0, \Sigma)$ and f_i is a (N×1) vector of time invariant fixed effects. In the PVAR shown in Eq. (14.1), we do not allow for dynamic interdependencies in the sense that the lags of the same unit endogenous variables only appear. Also, we do not allow either for cross-sectional heterogeneities, since the coefficient matrices are the same across all units, or for static interdependencies since we assume that $cov(u_{it}, u_{jt}) = 0$, for $i \neq j$ (Love and Zicchino, 2006).

---

[2] We opted for this variable since implied volatility indices were not available for all countries.

In our case, we employ $G = 6$ variables and 2 alternative panels consisting of $N = 5$ or 4 units, which represent either core Eurozone countries (Austria, Belgium, Germany, France, and The Netherlands) or Eurozone Periphery countries (Spain, Portugal, Italy, and Ireland). The spreads series on Greece has been reserved to act as a "wake-up" factor and therefore it does not appear as an additional unit in the panel of the peripheral countries but only as an additional common endogenous variable in both panels.

For the estimation of the PVAR, we used the Stata program of Love and Zicchino (2006). The estimation method is the generalized method of moments (GMM) where the individual country fixed effects are removed through the Helmert transformation, by applying forward mean-differencing. This is a necessary procedure since the usually applied mean-differencing technique does not address the problem of lack of orthogonality between lagged regressors that are used as instruments and fixed effects. Arellano and Bover (1995) have suggested that we remove the mean of all future observations available for each unit and period and then estimate model Eq. (14.1) by GMM.[3]

Our testing procedure is the following. We first test each one of our series for being characterized as an $I(1)$ or $I(0)$ process. We apply the Im et al. (2003) panel unit root test statistic. This test allows for heterogeneity across units in the coefficient of the autoregressive component as well as for different serial correlation properties, across different units, of the error term. The testing procedure relies on separate ADF test statistics for each unit which are then combined to a final test statistic that follows the normalized standard distribution. The results show that in all cases we were unable to accept the null hypothesis for the existence of a unit root (Table 14.1).

Table 14.1: Panel unit root test (Im et al., 2003), sample period 2009:Q1–2016:Q1.

	Peripheral Countries		Core Countries	
Variable	*t*-ratio	*p*-value	*t*-ratio	*p*-value
Spread	−4.847	0.000	−4.779	0.000
Volatility	−6.749	0.000	−6.313	0.000
ESI	−4.171	0.000	−3.984	0.000
Growth	−4.763	0.000	−4.674	0.000
Balance	−9.703	0.000	−6.960	0.000

Note: Similar results are obtained for the subperiods (2009:Q1–2012:Q2; 2012:Q3–2016:Q1). The Im et al. (2003) test has the unit root as the null hypothesis. The critical values are: −2.44 (1%), −2.16 (5%), and −2.02 (10%).

---

[3] Binder et al. (2005) show that the quality of GMM estimators in PVAR models depend on the ratio of the variance of the individual effects relative to the variance of the errors in Eq. (14.1). The higher from one the value of this ratio is, the worse the performance, both asymptotically and in finite samples, of the GMM estimator gets. Also, the GMM estimator is not appropriate for datasets with a large number of time periods and few cross-section units, which is not the case in our model.

Since the series do not exhibit nonstationary properties, we have estimated the PVAR on the first differences of the data.[4] We consider one lag for the dynamic structure of the system, on the basis of the satisfactory misspecification test results it gives and the quarterly frequency of our data. Next, we apply a Cholesky decomposition of the variance-covariance matrix in order to identify the shocks with specific variables. In our case, we treat the shock of the growth rate variable as being unrelated, instantaneously, with the other variables while on the other end we consider the shock on spreads to be instantaneously related with the shocks of all the other variables.[5] Under these assumptions we obtain the dynamic response of the PVAR dependent variables to shocks related to each one of the other variables as well as to its own shocks. Impulse responses are obtained within a band representing a 95% confidence interval estimated by Monte Carlo simulations (1000 iterations). Then, variance decompositions are calculated in order to provide a measure of the proportion of the movements in the dependent variables that are due to their own shocks or shocks to the other variables in the PVAR model. Our main goal is to show the relative importance of fundamental variables, that is, the growth rate and budget deficit, as compared to variables expressing the market sentiment and/or triggers for the revision of investors' information set as possible determinants of the government bond spread changes for both peripheral and core Eurozone countries.

14.4 Empirical Evidence

In Table 14.2, we present the results from the Forecast Error Variance Decomposition Analysis (FEVD) for the two periods 2009:Q1–2012:Q2 and 2012:Q3–2016:Q1 and for both Eurozone Periphery and Core countries. Starting from the peripheral countries in Table 14.2A, we notice that the spread changes were mainly determined by shocks of the Greek spread (27.2%) and secondary by the ESI variable (15.5%). The fundamental variables, the growth rate and the budget balance, as well as the stock market volatility had a much smaller contribution. We can also notice that the ESI variable is mainly driven by the growth

---

[4] It is well recognized that unit root tests are not accurate in disentangling unit root from near unit root processes. Under these circumstances and in order to make sure that our model is not misspecified, we have also tested for the presence of panel cointegration. We applied the testing procedure suggested by Westerlund (2007) under which one set of the proposed tests is designed for the existence of cointegration for the panel as a whole, while the other set for the case when at least one unit is cointegrated. For both panels, all tests indicated failure to reject the null hypothesis of no cointegration (the results are available upon request).

[5] The ordering of the variables might be crucial for the results we get but Lütkepohl (1991) argues that it makes little difference when the residuals' correlation is small. In our case, reordering the variables in the Cholesky decomposition does not affect quantitatively, to a great extent, but definitely qualitatively the results we report. Also, the residuals correlation for all the pairs is, in the great majority of case, below ($\pm$)0.5 (these evidence is available upon request).

Table 14.2: Forecast error variance decompositions.

A: Peripheral Countries (2009:Q1–2012:Q2)

Response	Impulse					
	Growth	Balance	ESI	Volatility	Gr_Spread	Spread
Growth	0.870	0.056	0.042	0.022	0.007	0.000
Balance	0.077	0.860	0.004	0.049	0.005	0.002
ESI	0.259	0.083	0.636	0.016	0.000	0.002
Volatility	0.022	0.030	0.096	0.792	0.039	0.018
Gr_Spread	0.012	0.007	0.035	0.076	0.859	0.008
Spread	0.056	0.033	0.155	0.039	0.272	0.443

B: Peripheral Countries (2012:Q3–2016:Q1)

Response	Impulse					
	Growth	Balance	ESI	Volatility	Gr_Spread	Spread
Growth	0.909	0.003	0.010	0.071	0.001	0.004
Balance	0.022	0.945	0.022	0.005	0.000	0.002
ESI	0.054	0.008	0.907	0.008	0.018	0.002
Volatility	0.021	0.040	0.056	0.853	0.000	0.027
Gr_Spread	0.010	0.050	0.025	0.324	0.588	0.000
Spread	0.003	0.035	0.081	0.0886	0.175	0.617

C: Core Countries (2009:Q1–2012:Q2)

Response	Impulse					
	Growth	Balance	ESI	Volatility	Gr_Spread	Spread
Growth	0.641	0.106	0.205	0.022	0.005	0.018
Balance	0.027	0.923	0.008	0.000	0.019	0.019
ESI	0.090	0.253	0.575	0.034	0.013	0.031
Volatility	0.019	0.156	0.262	0.394	0.037	0.129
Gr_Spread	0.039	0.118	0.148	0.080	0.566	0.047
Spread	0.019	0.148	0.240	0.048	0.101	0.441

D: Core Countries (2012:Q3–2016:Q1)

Response	Impulse					
	Growth	Balance	ESI	Volatility	Gr_Spread	Spread
Growth	0.880	0.000	0.085	0.020	0.003	0.008
Balance	0.000	0.975	0.003	0.010	0.004	0.005
ESI	0.038	0.005	0.827	0.027	0.004	0.096
Volatility	0.003	0.022	0.053	0.905	0.001	0.012
Gr_Spread	0.010	0.006	0.102	0.486	0.385	0.008
Spread	0.003	0.035	0.060	0.230	0.084	0.586

Note: 20 steps ahead.

(25.9%) and the budget balance (8.3%) variables.[6] All in all these results give credit to the theory that developments in Greece have triggered a revision of the beliefs concerning the solvency risks of government bonds issued by countries in the periphery of Eurozone. However, the results also endorse the argument that fundamentals matter, indirectly, through their influence on the economic confidence which amount to 25.9% for the growth rate and 8.3% for the budget balance. The ESI variable however might be influenced by many other factors like the systemic global financial risk or a herding behavior which are not featured in our model but have been identified in a great number of other studies (Beirne and Fratzscher, 2013; Georgoutsos and Migiakis, 2013a; Gómez-Puig et al., 2014).

The qualitative features of the picture that emerged during the crisis period are carried forward to the next period but the impact of the Greek wake-up factor and of the ESI variable are substantially subdued. The Greek spread accounts for 17.5% and the ESI for 8.1% of the Forecast Error Variance (FEV) of the bond spreads of the other peripheral countries when in the previous period, the same variables amounted to 27.2% and 15.5%, respectively. It is also worth noticing that now the FEV of the ESI variable is not affected by the growth and budget balance variables but it is almost entirely explained, up to 90.7%, by factors which are not represented in the parsimonious model we examine. Another remark worth making is that the FEV of the Greek spread is partially attributed, up to 32.4%, to shocks identified with the volatility in the stock markets of the other peripheral countries. An interpretation for this finding is that whenever uncertainty hits the periphery of Eurozone, this has severe repercussions for Greece which is considered to be the weakest financially member of this group.

In Tables 14.2C and 14.2D, we present the results for the core Eurozone countries. During the first period, the Greek "wake-up" factor still seems to explain 10.1% of the FEV of the spreads of the core countries although the most important contributing factor, amounting to 24%, is the economic sentiment that prevailed in these countries. Also, the budget balance contributes 14.8% to the FEV of the spreads which implies that for the core countries, during the crisis period, markets priced fiscal fundamentals independently from the general economic environment.[7] Over the next period, spreads in core countries are affected basically by the stock market volatility index which reflects the investors' uncertainty. Also, the ESI gets more idiosyncratic since up to 90.5% of its FEV is explained by its own shocks. This result has a striking similarity with the evidence from the peripheral countries over the same

---

[6] This evidence is in agreement with the conclusions derived by Favero and Missale (2012) that fiscal fundamentals do not matter per se but only indirectly through the global risk factors (captured by global spreads). In this setting fiscal fundamentals only determine the reference group each country belongs to and therefore this country's sensitivity to global risk factors. In our case the effect of the global risk factor is captured by the ESI of each country.

[7] Similar results for the core countries have been reported by Gómez-Puig et al. (2014). In their case local macroeconomic variables and local, regional and global market sentiment factors are the determinants of sovereign bond spreads.

period of time and indicates that global systemic risk factors are more heavily represented in the ESI than domestic factors.[8]

In Fig. 14.2, we present the impulse response functions (IRF) of the spread changes to a one standard deviation shocks on each one of the other variables appearing in the estimated PVAR models. Some common features are prominent from a simple inspection of these figures. The first one is that the 95% bands of the calculated IRF include the zero bound except for a small number of cases, where the calculated impulse responses at the first step (quarter) are statistically different from 0. For instance, this is the case with the reaction of the core countries' spreads to a shock in Greek spreads or shocks in the ESI variable. The second worth mentioning feature is that the direction of the reaction of the spreads, to the various shocks, has been correct and in accordance to the theory. There is only one case where this is not happening and this refers to the reaction of spreads to budget balance shocks. The graphs show a positive reaction, that is, an improvement of the budget balance is causing an increase of the spreads. Although this appears to be counter-intuitive, it can be rationalized if the improvement of the fiscal performance measures has been generated not by the increased economic activity but by the application of higher tax rates and the enforcement of stricter fiscal compliance measures which in turn imply a worsening economic environment.

14.5 Conclusions

The accumulated evidence in the literature dealing with the determinants, in the Eurozone, of the sovereign bond yields vis-à-vis the German ones has a number of undisputable conclusions. First, fiscal fundamentals seem to matter marginally during turbulent periods and for financially weak countries only, second, the global financial risk aversion levels are important determinants for the pricing of sovereign bonds and, third, variables expressing the prevalent market sentiment appear to explain a large part of the movement of spreads. The market sentiment index might be dependent on an array of different factors, like for instance the evolution of the expectations for macroeconomic fundamentals or on some trigger variables that help investors to revise their information sets in a world fraught with uncertainties.

In the present paper, we have reexamined the question on the determinants of sovereign bond spreads and we contribute to the existing literature on two fronts. First, this is one of the rather few studies which are making use of a sample that covers a period up to the present time, that is it includes the after mid-2012 period. Second, we rely on a parsimonious PVAR model which allows the calculation in a variance decomposition analysis of the percentage contribution of each one of the variables appearing in the model and at the same time it

---

[8] This is not surprising. The measures that were taken at the ECB and the European Community level, in order to confine the sovereign debt problem, have shifted part of the burden of the peripheral countries onto the rest of the EMU countries. This in its turn has increased the systemic risk carried by those countries.

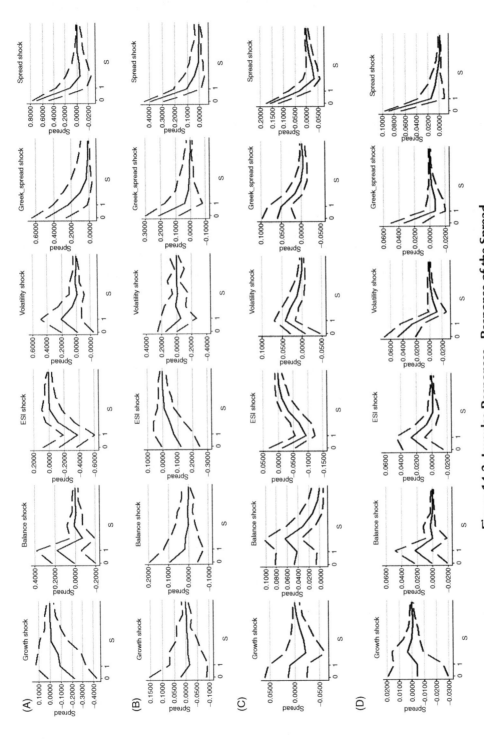

Figure 14.2: Impulse Responses—Response of the Spread.

(A) Periphery, 2009:Q1–2012:Q2; (B) Periphery, 2012:Q3–2016:Q1; (C) Core, 2009:Q1–2012:Q2 (D) Core, 2012:Q3–2016:Q1. Notes: The figures show the reaction of the spreads, in first differences, to shocks of the variables appearing on the top of each graph. The 95% bands have been generated by Monte-Carlo simulations (1000 iterations).

accommodates for the presence of dynamic interrelationships. The results we obtain are in accordance to the majority of those encountered in other studies, in the sense that they highlight the importance of the market sentiment index and the effect of the Greek crisis on leading investors to have second thoughts about the future of the Eurozone.

The policy prescriptions that emerge from the empirical research as well as from the incidence of the change in ECB's monetary policy after mid-2012 indicate that the adoption by the ECB of the "lender of last resort" function has been crucial for the containment of the negative market sentiments shared by many market participants. It remains to be seen whether this suffices for the resolution of the sovereign debt crisis.

References

Abad, P., Chulià, H., Gomèz-Puig, M., 2010. EMU and European government bond market integration. J. Bank. Finance 34 (12), 2851–2860.

Acharya, V., Drechsler, I., Schnabl, P., 2014. A pyrthic victory? Bank bailouts and sovereign credit risk. J. Finance 69 (6), 2689–2739.

Afonso, A., Arghyrou, M., Bagdatoglu, G., Kontonikas, A., 2015. On the time-varying relationship between EMU sovereign spreads and their determinants. Econ. Model. 44 (2), 363–371.

Ang, A., Longstaff, F.A., 2013. Systemic sovereign credit risk: lessons from the U.S. and Europe. J. Monetary Econ. 60 (5), 493–510.

Arellano, M., Bover, O., 1995. Another look at the instrumental variable estimation of error component models. J. Econom. 68 (1), 29–51.

Arghyrou, G., Kontonikas, A., 2012. The EMU sovereign debt crisis: fundamentals, expectations and contagion. J. Int. Financ. Markets Inst. Money 22, 658–677.

Beirne, J., Fratzscher, F., 2013. The pricing of sovereign risk and contagion during the European sovereign debt crisis. J. Int. Money Finance 36 (12), 3444–3468.

Bernoth, K., Erdogan, B., 2012. Sovereign bond yield spreads: a time-varying coefficient approach. J. Int. Money Finance 31 (3), 639–656.

Binder, M., Hsiao, C., Pesaran, M.H., 2005. Estimation and inference in short panel vector autoregressions with unit roots and cointegration. Econom. Theory 21 (4), 795–837.

Camba-Méndez, G., Serwa, D., 2016. Market perception of sovereign credit risk in the euro area during the financial crisis. N. Am. J. Econ. Finan. 37, 168–189.

De Bruyckere, V., Gerhardt, M., Schepens, G., Vander Vennet, R., 2013. Bank/Sovereign risk spillovers in the European debt crisis. J. Bank. Finance 37 (12), 4793–4809.

De Grauwe, P., Ji, Y., 2013. Self-fulfilling crises in the Eurozone: an empirical test. J. Int. Money Finance 34, 15–36.

De Grauwe, P., Ji, Y., 2014. How much fiscal discipline in a monetary union? J. Macroecon. 39 (part B), 248–260.

De Santis, R.A., 2014. The euro area sovereign debt crisis: identifying flight-to-liquidity and the spillover mechanisms. J. Empir. Finance 26, 150–170.

Ehrman, M., Fratzscher, M., Gürkaynak, R., Swanson, E., 2011. Convergence and anchoring of yield curves in the euro area. Rev. Econ. Stat. 93, 350–364.

Ejsing, J., Lemke, W., 2011. The Janus-headed salvation: sovereign and bank credit risk premia during 2008-09. Econ. Lett. 110 (1), 28–31.

Favero, C., Missale, A., 2012. Sovereign spreads in the Euro area: which prospects for a Eurobond? Econ. Policy 27, 117–198.

Georgoutsos, D., Migiakis, P., 2013a. Heterogeneity of the determinants of euro-area sovereign bond spreads: what does it tell us about financial stability? J. Bank. Finance 37, 4650–4664.

Georgoutsos, D., Migiakis, P., 2013b. European sovereign bond spreads: financial integration and market conditions. Appl. Financ. Econ. 23, 1609–1623.

Ghosh, A., Ostry, J., Qureshi, M., 2012. Fiscal Space and sovereign risk pricing in a currency union. J. Int. Money Finance 34, 131–163.

Gómez-Puig, M., Sosvilla-Rivero, S., 2016. Causes and hazards of the euro area sovereign debt crisis: pure and fundamentals-based contagion. Econ. Model. 56, 133–147.

Gómez-Puig, M., Sosvilla-Rivero, S., Ramos-Herrera, María del Carmen, 2014. An update on EMU sovereign yield spread drivers in times of crisis: a panel data analysis. North Am. J. Econ. Finance 30 (C), 133–153.

Im, K.S., Pesaran, M.H., Shin, Y., 2003. Testing for unit roots in heterogeneous panels. J. Econom. 115, 53–74.

Jaramillo, L., Weber, A., 2013. Bond yields in emerging economies: it matters what state you are in. Emerg. Markets Rev. 17, 169–185.

Longstaff, F.A., Pan, J., Pedersen, L.H., Singleton, K.J., 2011. How sovereign is sovereign credit risk? Am. Econ. J. 3 (2), 75–103.

Love, I., Zicchino, L., 2006. Financial development and dynamic investment behavior: evidence from panel VAR. Quart. Rev. Econ. Finance 46, 190–210.

Lütkepohl, H., 1991. Introduction to Multiple Time Series Analysis. Springer, Berlin.

Saka, O., Fuertes, A.-M., Kalotychou, E., 2015. ECB policy and Eurozone fragility: was De Grauwe right? J. Int. Money Finance 54, 168–185.

Westerlund, J., 2007. Testing for error correction in panel data. Oxford Bull. Econ. Stat. 69, 709–748.

CHAPTER 15

Regime Switching on the Relationship Between Stock Returns and Currency Values: Evidence From the 1997 Asian Crisis

Huimin Li*, Thomas C. Chiang**

*West Chester University of Pennsylvania, West Chester, PA, United States;
**Drexel University, Philadelphia, PA, United States

Chapter Outline

15.1 Introduction

The transmission of financial shocks across countries and across assets has been observed during the 1997 Asian crisis. The devaluation of the currencies in the crisis countries affected the rest of the economy, including the stock market. There are two channels through which the devaluation of a currency could affect these Asian economies. The first channel is through the effect on real economy (Jones, 1977). In order for the devaluation of a currency to provide a boost to the real sector, other currencies in competing countries need to hold their values steady; otherwise the competition in devaluation will offset the price advantage. Moreover, the advantage from devaluation of a currency might not be substantial if the import content of major items of exports constitutes a large part in the crisis countries' economies.[1]

---

[1] Bartov and Bodnar (1994) argue that the impact of the exchange rate change on a firm depends on whether the firm has long or short economic position in the foreign currency. US firms with a net long economic position (including exporters and firms with future cash inflows in foreign currency) will benefit (suffer) from a depreciation (appreciation) of the dollar, while US firms with a net short economic position (including importers and firms with future cash outflows in foreign currency) will suffer (benefit) from a depreciation (appreciation) of the dollar.

Table 15.1: Current account balance and foreign liabilities in the crisis countries.

	1995	1996	1997	1998	1999	2000	2001
A. Current account balance (percentage of GDP):							
Thailand	−8.1	−8.1	−2.0	12.7	10.1	7.6	5.4
Indonesia	−3.2	−3.4	−2.3	4.3	4.1	5.2	n.a.
Malaysia	−9.7	−4.4	−5.9	13.2	15.9	9.3	n.a.
Philippines	−2.7	−4.8	−5.3	2.4	10.4	11.3	6.3
Korea	−1.7	−4.4	−1.7	12.7	6.0	2.7	2.0
Hong Kong	n.a.	n.a.	n.a.	2.4	7.3	5.5	7.4
Taiwan	1.8	4.0	2.3	3.1	2.8	3.0	6.6
Singapore	17.9	14.1	19.0	24.7	26.3	23.5	n.a.
Japan	0.0	0.0	0.0	0.0	0.0	0.0	0.0
B. Foreign liabilities in deposit money banks (billions of national currency):							
Thailand	1164	1,249	1,904	1,066	718	566	462
Indonesia	26,952	29,744	70,434	97,842	100,375	92,674	68406
Malaysia	16	28	48	35	28	26	23
Philippines	168	378	616	498	483	515	449
Korea	24,361	36,454	47,418	35,464	31,348	31,366	27964
Hong Kong	4,797	4,486	4,627	3,465	2,890	2,488	2061
Taiwan	n.a.	483	489	479	462	458	540
Singapore	66	77	105	84	89	102	115
Thailand	1,164	1,249	1,904	1,066	718	566	462

n.a., Not available. Data for Taiwan are from central bank of Taiwan.
Source: International Financial Statistics from IMF.

Finally, a rational economic agent would expect a tighter monetary policy with a rise in domestic price as a result of devaluation and, therefore, a dampening in economic activity (Rakshit, 2002). The data of current account balance as a percentage of GDP in Panel A of Table 15.1 support this viewpoint. Current accounts in these economies were generally in deficit except Singapore and Taiwan in 1996. In 1997 and 1998, the current account balances were much higher in all of them except Taiwan and Japan.[2]

The second channel is through financial sector, which can have an impact on emerging economies that adopt a pegged or a fixed exchange rate system. It is well known that banks and companies in the crisis countries had borrowed heavily, in forms of short-term loans in foreign currency, from international money markets before the Asian crisis to work through the interest rate differential. Since most of the countries pegged their currencies to the US dollar before the crisis, these borrowers did not anticipate the possibility of currency risks and therefore did not hedge the risks. When devaluation of a currency occurred during the currency crisis, banks and companies suffered from a great loss due to currency and maturity

---

[2]   The low frequency data available for macroeconomic indicators here might not illustrate the short-run dynamics in the currency market and stock market, but rather provide a picture of the long run impact.

mismatches in their balance sheets. Their inability to roll over their short-term debts in the international capital markets caused financial losses in the stock markets.[3] Evidence of the seriousness of the exchange rate risk during a period of a currency crisis is provided in Panel B of Table 15.1, which shows that foreign liabilities in terms of national currency in 1997 increased dramatically after the devaluation or depreciation of the national currency.

However, both channels can also work simultaneously. In this study, the objective is not to specifically identify the transmission channel, but rather focus on the dominant effect of the channel at different times. While the financial contagion across countries has been studied by many researchers (Chiang et al., 2007b; Forbes and Rigobon, 2002), the financial contagion across different assets has not. This is especially the case when the currency markets experienced two different exchange rate regimes. Most of the countries, with the exceptions of Hong Kong and Malaysia, changed from a pegged system to a managed floating system during the Asian crisis. Hong Kong still kept its currency board system and Malaysia adopted a fixed exchange rate system after September 1998. This change of exchange rate regime could lead to different perceptions about the exchange rate risks, resulting in nonlinear relationship between stock returns and exchange rate changes.

The two channels' ability to transmit currency market shocks to stock markets indicates that the relationship between stock returns and exchange rate fluctuations might be nonlinear. The dominating channel will determine the direction and magnitude of the relationship. This study examines the contagion from currency markets to stock markets and the nonlinear relationships between stock returns and exchange rate changes using a Markov regime-switching process (Chen and Chiang, 2016; Gray, 1996; Hamilton, 1989; Hamilton and Susmel, 1994). It endogenously determines the regimes at any time and provides different estimates of exchange rate exposure of the stock markets at different times. Our study supports the hypothesis that the financial channel is more dominant during the crisis period (or "high volatility" regime), while the real channel is more dominant during the tranquil period (or "low volatility" regime). None of the existing literature has distinguished these two possible channels of contagion across assets but rather only considers the impact of the real channel.

The remainder of this paper is organized into four sections: Section 15.2 introduces the literature on exchange rate risk and regime-switching models. Section 15.3 presents the data

---

[3] Chang and Velasco (1998) set up a model that explains international illiquidity as a necessary and sufficient condition for financial crashes and/or balance-of-payments crises. As they define, international illiquidity is a maturity mismatch of a financial system's international assets and liabilities. The model assumes a bank that can accept demand deposits from domestic residents and borrow in the world market and can invest either in the world asset (liquid asset) or the long run asset to maximize its profits (zero profit in competitive markets). However, when domestic depositors and foreign creditors lose confidence in the banks as they did in 1997, they will try to withdraw their money or refrain from rolling over their loans in the short run. Banks will then have to liquidate some of their long-term assets, which is costly.

and methodology used in this study. Section 15.4 shows the empirical results and Section 15.5 summarizes the findings.

15.2 Literature Review

Most of the studies in the literature have focused on multifactor asset pricing model framework and examined whether the exposure to exchange rate risk is priced into stock returns. Starting with Jorion (1991), many papers have measured the exchange rate exposure of US firms and portfolio returns (Bartov and Bodnar, 1994). Further on, empirical analyses were extended to international studies, such as Germany, Japan, United Kingdom, and Mexico, using national stock index or firm/industry level data (e.g., Bailey and Chung, 1995; Dumas and Solnik, 1995; He and Ng, 1998). However, the results are mixed. Jorion (1991) finds that only a few US industries are significantly exposed to exchange rate risk. Bartov and Bodnar (1994), on the other hand, find that lagged changes in the dollar are a significant variable in explaining current abnormal returns of their selected sample firms. Japanese industry or firm level data, however, indicate the exchange rate risk is priced into the Japan's stock market (Choi et al., 1998) and firms that have a higher level of export are more impacted by the change in exchange rates.

The earlier mentioned studies primarily investigate the developed economies with a floating exchange rate system and do not involve a change in exchange rate system. This paper examines different exchange rate exposures that the Asian economies faced when the exchange rate system changed dramatically during the Asian crisis. To capture the dramatic change of the exchange rate system, we use a regime-switching model.

The finance literature has long realized the heteroskedasticity of high-frequency financial series and used GARCH type of models to show the properties of the time-varying volatility (see Bollerslev et al., 1992 for a detailed survey). On the other hand, research has also acknowledged the importance of large sudden shifts in volatility and its implication for estimating volatility persistence, and has used different techniques to deal with it in the GARCH models (Lastrapes, 1989). While some sudden shifts are exogenously determined, other structural changes are endogenous, which leads to popular use of regime-switching models (Hamilton, 1989; Hamilton and Susmel, 1994). In these models, both the mean equation and variance equation are assumed to follow a Markov-process, which finds that most of the persistence in stock price volatility is attributed to the persistence of low-, moderate-, and high-volatility regimes, which typically last for several years. Later on, the approach was extended and the well-known path dependency problem was solved (Dewachter, 2001; Dueker, 1997; Gray, 1996; Klaassen, 2002). At each time step, the conditional variance is obtained by aggregating the conditional variances from the two states in the previous period weighted by the regime probabilities. This aggregate conditional variance is then used to compute the conditional variance for the next period. This model setup assumes that the conditional variance at certain time steps is only dependent on the current regime, but not the entire past sequence of the regimes. This assumption makes the GARCH/regime-switching model tractable.

The finance literature contains many applications of regime-switching models, especially those related to: stock returns by Hamilton and Susmel (1994), Schaller and Norden (1997), Dueker (1997); Hess (2003); Chen and Chiang (2016); exchange rates by Fong (1998); Dewachter (2001); Klaassen (2002); the interest rate by Gray (1996); and oil prices by Fong and See (2002), to name a few.

Although, all the earlier studies find regime-switching models to be a good fit for the targeted financial assets, none of them has been applied to examine the relationship between exchange rate changes and stock returns using regime-switching models. In fact, the closest proximity to this type of investigation can be seen in the Holmes and Maghrebi (2002) study that examined the relationship between stock returns and exchange rate changes by assuming a constant variance within each regime. But even their examination failed to address the issue of time-varying variance process. The different channels of exchange rate exposure during the crisis give us an opportunity to study the financial contagion effect across assets.

This paper contributes to the literature by looking at the exchange rate exposures through different channels in different regimes. With this examination, we can answer the question why the exchange rate exposure differs across regimes. Empirical regularity suggests that a regime-switching model is appropriate to distinguish the two regimes endogenously. In this study, the regime-switching GARCH model developed by Gray (1996) is used for both the mean and variance equations of the stock returns as dependent on two regimes.

15.3 Data and Methodology

Daily stock indices and exchange rates of nine Asian countries are obtained from Datastream during the period of January 1, 1990 to March 21, 2003, the period that covers the events involving the Asian currency crisis. Stock returns and exchange rate changes are obtained by taking first differences of natural logs of the two variables. In Fig. 15.1, the bilateral exchange rate is defined as units of local currency per the US dollar. A similar pattern among Indonesia, Korea, Malaysia, the Philippines, and Thailand is striking. All the exchange rates were pegged to the US dollar and fluctuated within a small band before the crisis. However, after a sharp devaluation that occurred during the Asian crisis, the exchange rates were in a managed floating pattern except those in Malaysia, which adopted the fixed system. Fig. 15.2 shows the exchange rate changes of these economies. Not surprisingly, the turmoil during the crisis brought extremely high volatility of the exchange rates. Descriptive statistics in Table 15.2 are consistent with those seen in Figs. 15.1 and 15.2. The exchange rate changes, which are highly skewed and leptokurtic, indicate the existence of extreme values and volatility clustering.

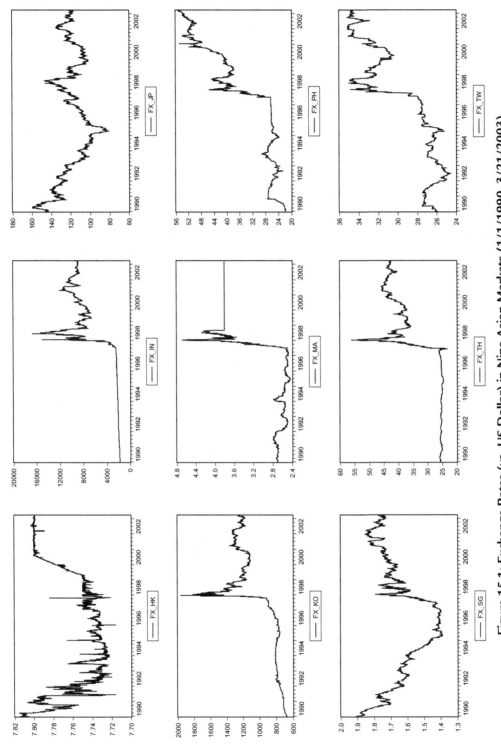

Figure 15.1: Exchange Rates (vs. US Dollar) in Nine Asian Markets (1/1/1990–3/21/2003).

FX_HK, FX_IN, FX_JP, FX_KO, FX_MA, FX_PH, FX_SG, FX_TH, and FX_TW represent the bilateral exchange rates defined as units of local currency per US dollar in Hong Kong, Indonesia, Japan, Korea, Malaysia, the Philippines, Singapore, Thailand, and Taiwan.

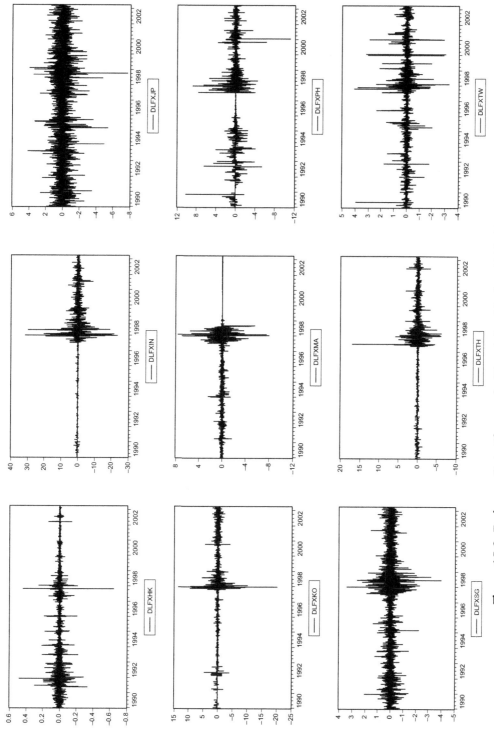

Figure 15.2: Exchange Rate Changes in Nine Asian Market (1/1/1990–3/21/2003).

DLFXHK, DLFXIN, DLFXJP, DLFXKO, DLFXMA, DLFXPH, DLFXSG, DLFXTH, and DLFXTW denote the bilateral exchange rate changes (first differences in natural logs) in Hong Kong, Indonesia, Japan, Korea, Malaysia, the Philippines, Singapore, Thailand, and Taiwan.

Table 15.2: Descriptive statistics of stock returns and exchange rate changes.

	Mean	Standard Deviation	Skewness	Kurtosis	Jarque Bera
Stock return:					
Thailand	−0.026	1.831	0.268[a]	4.622[a]	3,111.013[a]
Indonesia	−0.001	1.539	0.353[a]	11.246[a]	18,247.266[a]
Malaysia	0.001	1.614	0.531[a]	25.954[a]	96,963.928[a]
Philippines	−0.002	1.612	0.556[a]	8.882[a]	11,515.081[a]
Korea	−0.013	1.994	0.0002	3.719[a]	1,987.565[a]
Hong Kong	0.034	1.669	−0.021	9.648[a]	13,376.878[a]
Taiwan	−0.021	2.011	−0.030	3.130[a]	1,408.332[a]
Singapore	0.004	1.339	0.234[a]	10.640[a]	16,299.706[a]
Japan	−0.046	1.502	0.261[a]	3.471[a]	1,770.943[a]
Exchange rate changes:					
Thailand	0.015	0.685	4.097[a]	130.285[a]	2,448,991.539[a]
Indonesia	0.047	1.941	2.693[a]	83.078[a]	996,041.159[a]
Malaysia	0.010	0.556	0.082[b]	63.748[a]	583,998.268[a]
Philippines	0.027	0.708	1.504[a]	58.809[a]	498,311.227[a]
Korea	0.018	0.894	−1.408[a]	129.789[a]	2,421,928.284[a]
Hong Kong	-2.27×10^{-5}	0.035	−0.701[a]	651.555[a]	544,802.851[a]
Taiwan	0.008	0.319	1.813[a]	49.074[a]	347,977.469[a]
Singapore	−0.002	0.367	−0.617[a]	16.795[a]	40,755.535[a]
Japan	−0.005	0.726	−0.824[a]	8.001[a]	9,590.757[a]

Notes: The sample period is from January 1, 1990 through March 21, 2003. Stock returns are 100 times first differences of natural log of stock indices while exchange rate changes are 100 times first differences of natural log of exchange rates. Jarque-Bera statistics test for Normality.
[a]Indicates significance levels of 1%, respectively.
[b]Indicates significance levels of 10%, respectively.

To start with, the impact of the exchange rate exposure on national stock returns is specified as a single regime linear model, which is described in Eq. (15.1):

$$R_t = \mu + \phi R_{t-1} + \omega R_{t-1}^{US} + \theta X_{t-1} + \varepsilon_t, \varepsilon_t \sim N(0, h) \tag{15.1}$$

where R_t, R_t^{US}, and X_t are the stock return in country i, stock return in the United States and exchange rate change in country i. The one-day lagged US stock return, R_{t-1}^{US}, is used to account for global shocks. The 1-day lagged exchange rate change, X_{t-1}, is used to avoid endogeneity problem.[4] The exchange rate exposure is measured by the coefficient θ. In the real income channel, θ is expected to be positive, indicating a depreciation of the local currency will benefit the economy in terms of an improvement in trade balances

---

[4] Bartov and Bodnar (1994) find that lagged changes in the dollar are significant in explaining abnormal returns while contemporary changes in the dollar are not.

and, therefore, boost the stock market.[5] It could also be insignificant because of high import content or rational expectation. However, as discussed before, the possible financial channel through borrowers' balance sheets creates the possibility that θ might be negative (Jorion, 1991).

Second, to distinguish different channels of currency market shocks, the stock return is modeled with the mean equation dependent on two regimes:

$$R_t = \mu_{S_t} + \phi_{S_t} R_{t-1} + \omega_{S_t} R_{t-1}^{US} + \theta_{S_t} X_{t-1} + \varepsilon_{S_t}, \varepsilon_{S_t} \sim N(0, h) \tag{15.2}$$

The intercept and coefficients are all assumed to be dependent on the unobserved state S_t. The variance of the residual is assumed to be constant throughout the sample period. Switching probabilities S_t is assumed to have a first order Markov structure:

$$Pr[S_t = 1 | S_{t-1} = 1] = P11$$
$$Pr[S_t = 2 | S_{t-1} = 1] = 1 - P11$$
$$Pr[S_t = 1 | S_{t-1} = 2] = 1 - P22$$
$$Pr[S_t = 2 | S_{t-1} = 2] = P22$$

In order to estimate the parameters and the probabilities, the following conditional likelihood function needs to be maximized:[6]

$$L = \sum_{t=1}^{T} \log \left[p_{1t} \frac{1}{\sqrt{2\pi h}} \exp Z_1 + (1 - p_{1t}) \frac{1}{\sqrt{2\pi h}} \exp Z_2 \right], \text{ where}$$

$$Z_1 = \frac{-(R_t - \mu_1 - \phi_1 R_{t-1} - \omega_1 R_{t-1}^{US} - \theta_1 X_{t-1})^2}{2h}, \quad Z_2 = \frac{-(R_t - \mu_2 - \phi_2 R_{t-1} - \omega_2 R_{t-1}^{US} - \theta_2 X_{t-1})^2}{2h},$$

$$p_{1t} = Pr(S_t = 1 | \Phi_{t-1})$$

$$= (1 - P22) \left[\frac{g_{2t-1}(1 - p_{1t-1})}{g_{1t-1} p_{1t-1} + g_{2t-1}(1 - p_{1t-1})} \right] + P11 \left[\frac{g_{1t-1} p_{1t-1}}{g_{1t-1} p_{1t-1} + g_{2t-1}(1 - p_{1t-1})} \right].$$

To derive p_{1t}, we need to calculate the conditional density functions as follows:

$$g_{1t-1} = f(R_{t-1} | S_{t-1} = 1), \quad g_{2t-1} = f(R_{t-1} | S_{t-1} = 2)$$

where $f(R_{t-1} | S_{t-1} = i) = f(R_{t-1} | S_{t-1} = i, \Phi_{t-2})$

---

[5] It is also required to satisfy the Marshall-Lerner condition that suggests the absolute sum of the long-term export and import demand elasticities are greater than unity (Jones, 1977).
[6] For details of estimation procedure, see Gray (1996).

$$= \frac{1}{\sqrt{2\pi h}} \exp\left\{ \frac{-(R_{t-1} - \mu_i - \phi_i R_{t-2} - \omega_i R_{t-2}^{US} - \theta X_{t-2})^2}{2h} \right\}.$$

In Eq. (15.2), θ could have different signs in different regimes. If the economic force running from currency market to stock market is mainly through the real channel, then it could be positive, negative, or insignificant; however, if the economic effect is through the financial channel, then it could have a negative sign.

Indeed, the constant variance assumption in Eq. (15.2) is not realistic. It is recognized that the high frequency financial series exhibits a volatility-clustering phenomenon, which justifies volatilities in two different regimes. Therefore, the following equation assumes constant volatility within each regime but different volatility across regimes. Thus, it is legitimate to account for regime switching in volatility as:

$$R_t = \mu_{S_t} + \phi_{S_t} R_{t-1} + \omega_{S_t} R_{t-1}^{US} + \theta_{S_t} X_{t-1} + \varepsilon_{S_t}, \varepsilon_{S_t} \sim N(0, h_{S_t}) \tag{15.3}$$

To test the regime switches in the exchange rate exposure, another restricted version of Eq. (15.3) is also estimated and then likelihood ratio tests are conducted.

$$R_t = \mu_{S_t} + \phi_{S_t} R_{t-1} + \omega_{S_t} R_{t-1}^{US} + \theta X_{t-1} + \varepsilon_{S_t}, \varepsilon_{S_t} \sim N(0, h_{S_t}) \tag{15.4}$$

Eq. (15.4) assumes constant exchange rate exposure (with θ remaining constant over different regimes) during the entire sample period, while still keeping other parameters in the equation dependent on two different regimes.

The likelihood ratio test is calculated as:

$$LR = -2(l_r - l_u) \sim \chi^2(n)$$

where l_u and l_r are the maximized values of the (Gaussian) log likelihood function of the unrestricted and restricted models, respectively. Under the null that the additional parameters are not jointly significant, the LR statistic has an asymptotic distribution with degrees of freedom equal to the number of restrictions. Relative to Eq. (15.3), which is the unrestricted model here, both Eqs. (15.2) and (15.4) are restricted models. Eq. (15.2) imposes the restriction that the variance is constant across regimes, while Eq. (15.3) imposes the restriction that the exchange rate exposure is constant. The number of restrictions is one.

Since the literature has shown tremendous evidence of GARCH effects in high frequency financial data, the discrete division of the regimes into two may not be sufficient. However, the traditional GARCH model will encounter the path-dependency problem because conditional variance at time t depends on the conditional variance at time $t-1$, which depends on the regime at time $t-1$ and on the conditional variance at time $t-2$, and so on.

Consequently, the conditional variance at time t depends on the entire sequence of regimes up to time t. Gray (1996) suggests aggregation of conditional variance across regimes to eliminate path dependence. The conditional density of the residuals from the mean equation is assumed to be a mixture of distributions with time varying mixing parameters and the variance equation is modeled as:

$$h_{S_t,t} = \lambda_{S_t} + \alpha_{S_t}\varepsilon_{t-1}^2 + \beta_{S_t}h_{t-1} \tag{15.5}$$

$$h_{t-1} = p_{1t-1}[\tau_{1t-1}^2 + h_{1t-1}] + (1 - p_{1t-1})[\tau_{2t-1}^2 + h_{2t-1}] - [p_{1t-1}\tau_{1t-1} + (1 - p_{1t-1})\tau_{2t-1}]^2 \tag{15.6}$$

$$\varepsilon_{t-1} = R_{t-1} - [p_{1t-1}\tau_{1t-1} + (1 - p_{1t-1})\tau_{2t-1}] \tag{15.7}$$

where p_{1t} is the conditional probability of staying in regime 1 at time t, $\tau_{1t-1} = \mu_1 + \phi_1 R_{t-2} + \omega_1 R_{t-2}^{US} + \theta_1 X_{t-2} + \varepsilon_{1t-1}$, and $\tau_{2t-1} = \mu_2 + \phi_2 R_{t-2} + \omega_2 R_{t-2}^{US} + \theta_2 X_{t-2} + \varepsilon_{2t-1}$.

The coefficients for the variance equations are expected to be significant, and $(\alpha + \beta) < 1$ so that the variance is stationary. The value of $\dfrac{\lambda}{1 - \alpha - \beta}$ is the unconditional variance. One important assumption in this model is that the residual is assumed to be normal distribution, so that at each time step of the conditional variance can be aggregated at each step and be used to compute the conditional variances at the next time step.

15.4 Empirical Results on Mean Equations with Regime Switching

As stated earlier, various specifications of the Markov regime-switching models are estimated by maximizing the log likelihood function. For comparison purposes, the single regime model in Eq. (15.1) is estimated first (Table 15.3). Mean reversion in stock returns (negative ϕ) does not appear to exist in any cases except in Japan. The US stock return seems to have consistently high impact on the Asian economies, corroborating its leading economic position in the global market (Chiang et al., 2007a; Rapach et al., 2013). The foreign exchange exposure is shown to be only significantly positive in the cases of Thailand and Hong Kong, insignificant in Indonesia's case, but significantly negative in all other six cases. This dominance in negative foreign exchange exposure contradicts the traditional viewpoint of transmission of currency shocks through the real channel and indicates the possibility that the financial channel may be the conduit.

It follows that Eq. (15.2) is estimated with regime switches in all the parameters in the stock return equation, assuming the same variance is present in different regimes. Regime 1 is defined as a "high return" regime; Regime 2 is defined as a "low return" regime. As can be seen from the estimation results in Table 15.4, the drift terms are generally in opposite signs. Mean reversion occurs in the "high return" regime in Thailand, Indonesia, Hong Kong, Taiwan, Singapore, and Japan. Interestingly, the exchange rate exposure has negative

Table 15.3: Single regime model.

	μ	ϕ	ω	θ	LB^2(15)
Thailand	−0.034	0.120[a]	0.350[a]	0.090[b]	1079.46[a]
Indonesia	−0.007	0.194[a]	0.258[a]	0.003	725.87[a]
Malaysia	−0.005	0.066[a]	0.342[a]	−0.293[a]	1357.34[a]
Philippines	−0.006	0.171[a]	0.332[a]	−0.172[a]	228.66[a]
Korea	−0.023	0.014	0.457[a]	−0.132[a]	984.92[a]
Hong Kong	0.019	−0.015	0.593[a]	1.305[c]	1325.92[a]
Taiwan	−0.028	0.029[c]	0.362[a]	−0.236[b]	2718.17[a]
Singapore	−0.009	0.102[a]	0.428[a]	−0.241[a]	650.20[a]
Japan	−0.059[b]	−0.058[a]	0.415[a]	−0.011	483.36[a]

Note: Estimation results for Eq. (15.1): $R_t = \mu + \phi R_{t-1} + \omega R_{t-1}^{US} + \theta X_{t-1} + \varepsilon_t, \varepsilon_t \sim N(0, h)$. LB^2(15) is the Ljung-Box statistics for the squared residuals from the regression for up to 15 days.
[a]Indicates significance levels of 1%, respectively.
[b]Indicates significance levels of 5%, respectively.
[c]Indicates significance levels of 10%, respectively.

Table 15.4: Two-regime model in the mean equation with constant variance.

	μ	ϕ	ω	θ	h	P11	P22	LB^2(15)	Log Likelihood
Thailand	−0.081[a]	−0.066[a]	0.216[a]	0.170[b]	1.589[a]	0.832[a]	0.199[a]	302.62[a]	−6730.06
	0.264[c]	0.935[a]	0.784[a]	−0.180[b]		[6]	[1]		
Indonesia	0.018	−0.073[b]	0.135[a]	−0.030	1.282[a]	0.726[a]	0.249[a]	193.40[a]	−6021.51
	−0.103[b]	1.043[a]	0.491[a]	0.116[b]		[4]	[1]		
Malaysia	−0.008	0.239[a]	0.255[a]	−0.036	1.369[a]	0.955[a]	0.305[a]	1491.77[a]	−6131.95
	0.042	−0.599[a]	0.900[a]	−5.417[a]		[22]	[1]		
Philippines	0.007	0.037[b]	0.261[a]	−0.019	1.378[a]	0.863[a]	0.143[a]	46.63[a]	−6231.00
	−0.066	1.148[a]	0.537[a]	−1.218[a]		[7]	[1]		
Korea	−0.119[a]	0.018	0.396[a]	0.0004	1.772[a]	0.980[b]	0.381[a]	275.49[a]	−7074.60
	3.845[a]	−0.475[a]	2.101[a]	−1.323[a]		[50]	[2]		
Hong Kong	0.092[a]	−0.036[b]	0.540[a]	1.183	1.407[a]	0.991[a]	0.450[b]	289.60[a]	−6240.29
	−5.565	−0.575	1.628	−7.275		[111]	[2]		
Taiwan	0.042	−0.217[a]	0.264[a]	−0.206[c]	1.812[a]	0.771[b]	0.405[a]	989.59[a]	−7149.61
	−0.189[c]	0.595[a]	0.571[a]	−0.303		[4]	[2]		
Singapore	0.042	−0.101	0.305[a]	−0.139	1.108[a]	0.783[c]	0.272[a]	202.81[a]	−5490.29
	−0.181[b]	0.735[a]	0.823[a]	−0.109		[5]	[1]		
Japan	−0.046[b]	−0.048[a]	0.378[a]	−0.009	1.379[a]	0.992[a]	0.338[a]	432.93[a]	−6094.09
	−2.169[a]	−0.506[a]	4.192[a]	−0.664[a]		[125]	[2]		

Notes: Estimation results for Eq. (15.2): $R_t = \mu_{S_t} + \phi_{S_t} R_{t-1} + \omega_{S_t} R_{t-1}^{US} + \theta_{S_t} X_{t-1} + \varepsilon_{S_t}, \varepsilon_{S_t} \sim N(0, h)$. P11 and P22 are the transition probabilities. h is the constant variance. LB^2(15) is the Ljung-Box statistics for the squared standardized residuals for up to 15 days. Log likelihood is the function value achieved by the estimation. Average number of days in each regime is calculated and shown in brackets.
[a]Indicates significance levels of 1%, respectively.
[b]Indicates significance levels of 5%, respectively.
[c]Indicates significance levels of 10%, respectively.

signs in the "low return" regime in all cases except Indonesia, indicating the existence of a financial channel. In the other regime, it is either significantly positive (in Thailand case), or significantly negative (in Taiwan case), or insignificant (in all other cases). The "high return" regime, which lasts between 4 and 111 days, seems to be more persistent, while the "low return" regime, which lasts only about 1 or 2 days, is less persistent.[7] Diagnostic statistic $LB^2(15)$ is calculated to determine the presence of time-varying volatility. The large significant Ljung-Box statistic for the squared standardized residuals strongly suggests the possibility of different volatility in the regimes.

Eq. (15.3) is estimated with different variances in two regimes and results are shown in Table 15.5. After accounting for different variances, the drift terms mostly become insignificant and therefore difficult to identify as "high-return" and "low-return" regimes. Also, the mean reversion phenomena disappear except in Japan's case. However, two regimes according to

Table 15.5: Two-regime model in the mean equation with different variances.

	μ	ϕ	ω	θ	H	P11	P22	$LB^2(15)$	Log Likelihood
Thailand	−0.019	0.110[a]	0.169[a]	0.051	1.096[a]	0.967[a]	0.925[a]	669.02[a]	−6410.34
	−0.069	0.117[a]	0.635[a]	0.107	2.732[a]	[30]	[13]		
Indonesia	0.004	0.258[a]	0.135[a]	−0.013	0.662[a]	0.947[a]	0.876[a]	554.55[a]	−5273.44
	−0.021	0.178[a]	0.393[a]	0.005	2.500[a]	[19]	[8]		
Malaysia	0.009	0.200[a]	0.172[a]	0.106[b]	0.789[a]	0.966[a]	0.894[a]	1194.22[a]	−5464.55
	−0.053	0.014	0.675[a]	−0.390[a]	2.765[a]	[29]	[9]		
Philippines	−0.027	0.188[a]	0.181[a]	−0.067[c]	0.891[a]	0.965[a]	0.933[a]	146.33[a]	−5872.22
	0.031	0.152[a]	0.573[a]	−0.239[a]	2.295[a]	[29]	[15]		
Korea	−0.034	0.018	0.169[a]	0.009	1.143[a]	0.981[a]	0.972[a]	594.35[a]	−6693.13
	−0.001	0.006	0.654[a]	−0.151[a]	2.688[a]	[53]	[36]		
Hong Kong	0.073[a]	0.029	0.435[a]	0.922	0.983[a]	0.982[a]	0.956[b]	845.85[a]	−5893.94
	−0.123	−0.051	0.826[a]	2.001	2.409[a]	[56]	[23]		
Taiwan	−0.002	0.006	0.272[a]	−0.127	1.309[a]	0.980[a]	0.939[a]	1346.80[a]	−6781.77
	−0.094	0.036	0.547[a]	−0.497[c]	3.232[a]	[50]	[16]		
Singapore	−0.004	0.139[a]	0.322[a]	0.052	0.776[a]	0.973[a]	0.909[a]	445.84[a]	−5064.25
	−0.009	0.065[a]	0.574[a]	−0.516[a]	2.150[a]	[37]	[11]		
Japan	−0.044[c]	−0.066[a]	0.379[a]	0.069[c]	1.014[a]	0.982[a]	0.961[a]	221.64[a]	−5866.52
	−0.092	−0.060[c]	0.452[a]	−0.125	2.076[a]	[56]	[26]		

Notes: Estimation results for Eq. (15.3): $R_t = \mu_{S_t} + \phi_{S_t} R_{t-1} + \omega_{S_t} R_{t-1}^{US} + \theta_{S_t} X_{t-1} + \varepsilon_{S_t}, \varepsilon_{S_t} \sim N(0, h_{S_t})$. P11 and P22 are the transition probabilities. $LB^2(15)$ is the Ljung-Box statistics for the squared standardized residuals for up to 15 days. Log likelihood is the function value achieved by the estimation. Average number of days in each regime is calculated and shown in brackets.
[a]Indicates significance levels of 1%, respectively.
[b]Indicates significance levels of 5%, respectively.
[c]Indicates significance levels of 10%, respectively.

---

[7] The persistence of each regime is calculated as $\dfrac{1}{1-P11}$ and $\dfrac{1}{1-P22}$ for regime 1 and 2, respectively.

volatility can be identified—"high volatility" and "low volatility" regimes. The first row in each country's case is the "high volatility" regime and the second row is the "low volatility" regime. Compared with the "low volatility" regime, the volatility ranges from at least 1 time higher to almost 3 times higher in the "high volatility" regime. In the "high volatility" regime, five out of nine cases (Malaysia, the Philippines, Korea, Taiwan, and Singapore) turn out to have significant and negative foreign exchange exposure and two cases (Indonesia and Japan) have insignificant and negative exposure. It is somewhat surprising that both the coefficients for exchange rate exposure turn out to be positive for Thailand, although not significant. However, in Thailand's case, this result may stem from the early devaluation of the Thai baht, which gave Thailand companies a competitive advantage in the export sector, therefore alleviating the balance sheet effect.[8] In the "low volatility" regime, only Malaysia and Japan have significant and positive foreign exchange exposure and only the Philippines show statistically significant and negative exposure. All of the other six cases have insignificant exposure to exchange risk. This result is consistent with the hypothesis that during the "high volatility" regime, the exchange rate exposure is channeled through the balance sheet effect, while during the "low volatility" regime, the exchange rate exposure is channeled through the real sector effect.[9]

There is persistence in both regimes with P11 and P22, each exceeds or closes to 0.9. The average number of days for each regime is calculated and entered in the brackets below each transition probability. For example, for Thailand, the "low volatility" regime on average lasts about 30 days, while the "high volatility" regime on average lasts 13 days, indicating the "low volatility" regime is more persistent than the "high volatility" regime. Some diagnostic statistics are reported. There is still significant autocorrelation in the squared standardized residuals, shown in $LB^2(15)$, but the statistics are much lower than those in Table 15.4. The log likelihood function value enables us to conduct likelihood ratio test to see which equation is a better fit. In Eq. (15.2), the variances are assumed to be constant, so it is considered the restricted model and Eq. (15.3) is considered the unrestricted model. The test statistics are reported in the second column of Table 15.6, which shows a better fit of the unrestricted model—Eq. (15.3) with regime switching in the variance.

To further test whether regime switching in the foreign exchange exposure is warranted, Eq. (15.4) is estimated and the likelihood ratio test is conducted. The estimation results are reported in Table 15.7 and the likelihood ratio test statistics are shown in the third column of Table 15.6. As can be seen from Table 15.7, the estimation results are quite similar to Table 15.5. The regimes are divided between "high volatility" and "low volatility" and the persistence of each regime is almost the same as in Table 15.5. $LB^2(15)$ statistics are slightly lower in all cases in Table 15.5 except the Philippines case. The likelihood ratio test shows

---

[8] From Table 15.1 it can also be seen that Thailand improved its current account condition in 1997 compared with 1996 and 1995 while the others had a much smaller improvement.

[9] A word of caution, though, is that the "high volatility" regime is not limited to the crisis period and might include other periods of local political turmoil, regional chaos, or other disturbances.

Table 15.6: Likelihood ratio tests.

Restricted Model	Eq. (15.2)	Eq. (15.4)	Eq. (15.3)
Unrestricted Model	Eq. (15.3)	Eq. (15.3)	Eq. (15.5)–(15.7)
Thailand	639.44[a]	3.62[c]	1596.94[a]
Indonesia	1496.14[a]	0.24	2034.34[a]
Malaysia	1334.80[a]	14.72[a]	1847.26[a]
Philippines	717.56[a]	4.04[b]	1700.98[a]
Korea	762.94[a]	7.10[a]	1514.96[a]
Hong Kong	692.70[a]	0.26	1432.66[a]
Taiwan	735.68[a]	1.06	1614.36[a]
Singapore	852.08[a]	12.22[a]	1476.18[a]
Japan	455.14[a]	3.72[c]	1245.58[a]

Notes: Likelihood ratio test statistic is $LR = -2 * (L_r - L_u)$, where L_u and L_r are the maximized values of the (Gaussian) log likelihood function of the unrestricted and restricted regressions, respectively. Under the null that the additional parameters are not jointly significant, the LR statistic has an asymptotic distribution with degrees of freedom equal to the number of restrictions. For the second and the third columns, the critical values for $\chi^2(1)$ are 6.64, 3.84, and 2.71 at 1%, 5%, and 10% level, respectively. For the fourth column, the critical values for $\chi^2(4)$ are 13.277, 9.488, and 7.779 at 1%, 5%, and 10% level, respectively.
[a]Indicates significance levels of 1%, respectively.
[b]Indicates significance levels of 5%, respectively.
[c]Indicates significance levels of 10%, respectively.

Table 15.7: Two-regime model in the mean equation with different variances, but constant exchange exposure.

	μ	ϕ	ω	θ	h	P11	P22	LB²(15)	Log Likelihood
Thailand	−0.020	0.111[a]	0.169[a]	0.078	1.093[a]	0.966[a]	0.923[a]	680.61[a]	−6412.15
	−0.067	0.115[a]	0.632[a]		2.727[a]	[29]	[13]		
Indonesia	0.003	0.258[a]	0.136[a]	−0.004	0.660[a]	0.946[a]	0.877[a]	560.57[a]	−5273.56
	−0.020	0.177[a]	0.392[a]		2.497[a]	[19]	[8]		
Malaysia	0.006	0.195[a]	0.172[a]	−0.079	0.793[a]	0.967[a]	0.896[a]	1196.86[a]	−5471.91
	−0.054	0.043	0.694[a]		2.786[a]	[30]	[10]		
Philippines	−0.025	0.188[a]	0.181[a]	−0.112[a]	0.892[a]	0.965[a]	0.933[a]	128.27[a]	−5874.24
	0.026	0.159[a]	0.573[a]		2.301[a]	[29]	[15]		
Korea	−0.033	0.016	0.168[a]	−0.098[a]	1.141[a]	0.981[a]	0.972[a]	622.58[a]	−6696.68
	−0.003	0.012	0.652[a]		2.683[a]	[53]	[36]		
Hong Kong	0.072[a]	0.029	0.434[a]	1.059[c]	0.984[a]	0.983[a]	0.958[b]	875.98[a]	−5894.07
	−0.122	−0.052	0.827[a]		2.409[a]	[59]	[24]		
Taiwan	−0.003	0.004	0.273[a]	−0.162[c]	1.307[a]	0.980[a]	0.940[a]	1379.42[a]	−6782.30
	−0.097	0.040	0.540[a]		3.220[a]	[50]	[17]		
Singapore	−0.005	0.138[a]	0.324[a]	−0.046	0.782[a]	0.974[a]	0.907[a]	460.98[a]	−5070.36
	−0.014	0.079[a]	0.579[a]		2.191[a]	[38]	[11]		
Japan	−0.043[c]	−0.067[a]	0.382[a]	0.026	1.008[a]	0.982[a]	0.962[a]	227.75[a]	−5868.38
	−0.090	−0.055[c]	0.451[a]		2.064[a]	[56]	[26]		

Notes: Estimation results for Eq. (15.4): $R_t = \mu_{S_t} + \phi_{S_t} R_{t-1} + \omega_{S_t} R_{t-1}^{US} + \theta X_{t-1} + \varepsilon_{S_t}, \varepsilon_{S_t} \sim N(0, h_{S_t})$. P11 and P22 are the transition probabilities. h is the constant variance. LB²(15) is the Ljung-Box statistics for the squared standardized residuals for up to 15 days. Log likelihood is the function value achieved by the estimation. Average number of days in each regime is calculated and shown in brackets.
[a]Indicates significance levels of 1%, respectively.
[b]Indicates significance levels of 5%, respectively.
[c]Indicates significance levels of 10%, respectively.

that Eq. (15.3) is a better fit for Thailand, Malaysia, the Philippines, Korea, Singapore, and Japan, while for the other three economies, Eq. (15.4) seems to be a better fit and more parsimonious. For Hong Kong, this result is not surprising, because it kept its currency board system during the crisis, reducing the exchange rate risks for companies in the region. Generally speaking, the two-regime models in the mean equation with different variances are a better fit for describing the exchange rate risk at different regimes.

After fitting the data with the two-regime model in the mean equation with different variances, both the stock return and the conditional probability in the "high volatility" regime for each country are shown in Fig. 15.3. The stock return volatility seems to correspond with the low versus high regimes defined in the previous text. A common observation of the graphs for each stock market is that during the Asian crisis, the conditional probability of being in the "high volatility" regime was more frequent and stock markets moved more sharply across regimes. Although these graphs do not give us a clear answer of when the exchange rate regimes changed during the crisis, they do show that the stock markets are frequently changing between two regimes as underlying economic fundamentals changed.

As can be seen, Tables 15.5 and 15.7 still show significant autocorrelation in the squared standardized residuals, which justifies the use of regime-switching GARCH models to account for not only large shifts in volatility across regimes, but also the impact of small shocks on the conditional variance. Eqs. (15.5) through (15.7) as well as the mean Eq. (15.3) are estimated simultaneously and the results are reported in the Table 15.8. The results seem to be very different from those in Table 15.4. Most of the significant exchange rate exposure effects disappear except for those in Malaysia and Taiwan. Thailand, on the other hand, turns out to have the wrong direction of signs for the exchange rate exposure, although significant. According to the unconditional variance calculated from $\dfrac{\lambda}{1-\alpha-\beta}$, the regimes again are divided into "low volatility" and "high volatility" regimes, with the former on the first row and the latter on the second row for each country. However, it is counter-intuitive that the "high volatility" regime is more persistent than the "low volatility" regime in all cases except for Indonesia and Malaysia. It is not surprising that the persistence of the shocks $(\alpha + \beta)$ is much lower than 1 after accounting for regime shifts in variance equations. This result is consistent with the literature, which generally finds conditional variance in traditional GARCH models very close to 1 due to an inability to incorporate large shifts (Lastrapes, 1989).

Diagnostic statistics show that after incorporating GARCH effects, the autocorrelation of the squared standardized effects becomes much smaller, although still significantly. Likelihood ratio tests of the regime-switching GARCH model versus two-regime model in the mean equation with different variances are shown in the fourth column of Table 15.7. The regime-switching GARCH model, in terms of diagnostic statistics, is a better fit than the two-regime model in the mean equation with different variances. However, in terms of an intuitive

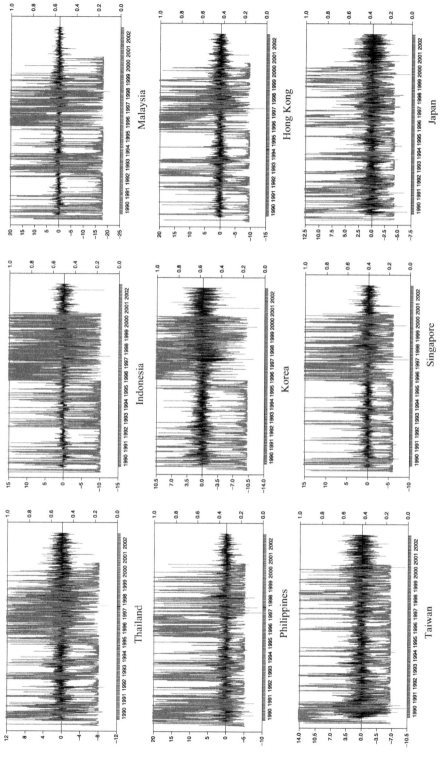

Figure 15.3: Stock Returns and Conditional Probabilities of Being in "High Volatility" Regime.

Table 15.8: Two-regime GARCH (1,1) model.

	μ	ϕ	ω	θ	λ	α	β	$\frac{\lambda}{1-\alpha-\beta}$	P11	P22	LB^2(15)	Log Likelihood
Thailand	-0.128^b	1.043^a	0.041	-0.093^c	0.141^a	0.349^a	0.000^a	0.217	0.140^a [1]	0.763^a [4]	163.50^a	-5616.87
	0.003	0.183^a	0.128^a	0.045^b	0.560^a	0.134^a	0.022^a	0.664				
Indonesia	0.002	0.982^a	0.001	-0.020	-0.0001	0.516^a	0.085^a	0.000	0.464^a [2]	0.158^a [1]	305.27^a	-4256.27
	-0.005	0.239^a	0.103^a	-0.013	0.343^a	0.183^a	0.015^c	0.428				
Malaysia	-0.016^b	0.314^a	0.107^a	-0.004	0.269^a	0.249^a	0.062^a	0.390	0.982^b [56]	0.904^a [10]	775.95^a	-4540.92
	-0.100	0.549^a	0.292^a	-0.224^c	0.986	0.132^a	0.019^a	1.161				
Philippines	-0.0004	0.964^a	0.026	0.002	0.107^a	0.397^a	0.012	0.181	0.297^a [1]	0.893^a [9]	194.40^a	-5021.73
	-0.017	0.225^a	0.149^a	-0.058^c	0.425^a	0.180^a	0.030^a	0.538				
Korea	0.038	0.992^a	0.038	-0.011	0.163^a	0.331^a	0.006	0.246	0.146^a [1]	0.758^a [4]	246.70^a	-5935.65
	-0.035	0.123^a	0.144^a	0.021	0.616^a	0.122^a	0.012^a	0.711				
Hong Kong	-0.162^a	0.792^a	0.131^b	0.383	0.183^a	0.353^a	0.064^a	0.314	0.341^a [1]	0.733^a [4]	224.04^a	-5177.61
	0.082^b	0.037^b	0.286^a	0.602	0.502^a	0.138^c	0.006^c	0.586				
Taiwan	-0.010	0.959^a	0.156^a	0.072	0.226^a	0.299^a	0.020^a	0.332	0.117^a [2]	0.655^a [4]	219.19^a	-5974.59
	-0.022	0.068^a	0.134^a	-0.128^b	0.619^a	0.112	0.014^a	0.708				
Singapore	-0.048	0.841^a	0.203^a	0.071	0.129^b	0.409^a	0.045	0.236	0.277^b [1]	0.747^b [4]	202.98^a	-4326.16
	-0.004	0.141^a	0.184^a	-0.068	0.391^a	0.178^a	0.018	0.486				
Japan	0.171^a	0.639^a	-0.071	0.062	0.140^a	0.354^a	0.098^a	0.255	0.208^a [1]	0.714^a [3]	144.70^a	-5243.73
	-0.126^a	0.031	0.379^a	-0.009	0.553^a	0.132^a	0.006^b	0.642				

Notes: Estimation results for Eq. (15.3): $R_t = \mu_{S_t} + \phi_{S_t} R_{t-1} + \omega_{S_t} R_{t-1}^{US} + \theta_{S_t} X_{t-1} + \varepsilon_{S_t}$, and Eqs. (15.5)–(15.7): $h_{S_t,t} = \lambda_{S_t} + \alpha_{S_t} \varepsilon_{t-1}^2 + \beta_{S_t} h_{t-1}$,
$h_{t-1} = p_{1t-1}[\tau_{1t-1}^2 + h_{1t-1}] + (1-p_{1t-1})[\tau_{2t-1}^2 + h_{2t-1}] - [p_{1t-1}\tau_{1t-1} + (1-p_{1t-1})\tau_{2t-1}]^2$, $\varepsilon_{t-1} = R_{t-1} - [p_{1t-1}\tau_{1t-1} + (1-p_{1t-1})\tau_{2t-1}]$. τ_{1t} and τ_{2t} are the conditional means of the stock return in the two regimes, respectively. p_{1t} is the conditional probability of staying in regime 1 at time t. The other notes are same as Table 15.4.
[a]Indicates significance levels of 1%, respectively.
[b]Indicates significance levels of 5%, respectively.
[c]Indicates significance levels of 10%, respectively.

explanation, the latter does a better job. One reason might be that the assumption for the regime-switching GARCH model may not be realistic because the stock returns are well known to be nonnormal and can be seen from the descriptive statistics in Table 15.2.

15.5 Conclusions

This paper examines the exchange rate exposure of the national stock returns for the nine Asian economies during the period from 1990 through 2003. Two possible transmission channels of currency shocks to stock markets are proposed. The first is through the real sector, which can potentially have a sequence of effects on exchange rate changes for exports, imports, and stock prices. The second is through the financial sector whose impacts can be determined by evaluating changes in the liabilities and assets of companies' balance sheets. The hypothesis is that the financial channel is more dominant during the crisis period (or "high volatility" regime), while the real channel is more dominant during the tranquil period (or "low volatility" regime). To date none of the literature has distinguished the two possible channels of spillovers across assets, but rather only considered one channel.

This study applies regime-switching models to investigate this question and finds strong support for the hypothesis. Although the regime-switching GARCH model is a better fit, it does not provide an intuitive explanation of the coefficients. On the other hand, the two-regime model in the mean equation with different variances turns out to have a good fit and shows consistent results across economies. The "low volatility" and "high volatility" regimes are identified and the former is more persistent. The evidence consistently shows that the exchange rate exposure is channeled mainly through the balance sheet effects during the "high volatility" regime, but through the real sector effect during the "low volatility" regime. However, in Thailand's case, the real sector effect seems to be strong in both regimes, which makes sense because of the early devaluation of its currency during the crisis.

Improvements can be made to this study. First, firm or industry level data, if available for the crisis economies, would have served as a better sample for investigating different exchange rate exposures at different times. Aggregate national stock indices may incorporate both export and import firms that can cancel out some of the real sector effects. Second, the methodology could be improved by modeling both stock returns and exchange rate changes as endogenous and dependent on the two regimes. Exchange rate changes are endogenous variables, although in this case they are more controlled before the crisis.

References

Bailey, W., Chung, Y.P., 1995. Exchange rate fluctuations, political risk, and stock returns: some evidence from an emerging market. J. Financ. Quant. Anal. 30 (4), 541–561.

Bartov, E., Bodnar, G.M., 1994. Firm valuation, earnings expectations, and the exchange-rate exposure effect. J. Finance 49 (5), 1755–1785.

Bollerslev, T., Chou, R.Y., Kroner, K.F., 1992. ARCH modeling in finance: a review of the theory and empirical evidence. J. Econom. 52 (1–2), 5–59.

Chang, R., Velasco, A., 1998. Financial Fragility and the Exchange Rate Regime. NBER Working Paper No. 6469.

Chen, C.Y., Chiang, T.C., 2016. Empirical analysis of the intertemporal relation between downside risk and expected returns: evidence from time-varying transition probability models. Eur. Financ. Manag. 22 (5), 749–796.

Chiang, T.C., Chen, C.W.S., So, M.K., 2007a. Asymmetries in return & volatility and composite news from stock markets. Multinat. Fin. J. 11 (3–4), 179–210.

Chiang, T.C., Jeon, B.N., Li, H., 2007b. Dynamic correlation analysis of financial contagion: evidence from Asian markets. J. Int. Money Finance 26 (7), 1206–1228.

Choi, J.J., Hiraki, T., Takezawa, N., 1998. Is foreign exchange risk priced in the Japanese stock market. J. Financ. Quant. Anal. 33 (3), 361–382.

Dewachter, H., 2001. Can Markov switching models replicate chartist profits in the foreign exchange market. J. Int. Money Finance 20 (1), 25–41.

Dueker, M.J., 1997. Markov switching in GARCH processes and mean-reverting stock-market volatility. J. Bus. Econ. Stat. 15 (1), 26–34.

Dumas, B., Solnik, B., 1995. The world price of foreign exchange risk. J. Finance 50 (2), 445–479.

Fong, W.M., 1998. The dynamics of DM/£ exchange rate volatility: a SWARCH analysis. Int. J. Finance Econ. 3 (1), 59–71.

Fong, W.M., See, K.H., 2002. A Markov switching model of the conditional volatility of crude oil futures prices. Energy Econ. 24 (1), 71–95.

Forbes, K., Rigobon, R., 2002. No contagion, only interdependence: measuring stock market co-movements. J. Finance 57 (5), 2223–2262.

Gray, S.F., 1996. Modeling the conditional distribution of interest rates as a regime-switching process. J. Financ. Econ. 42 (1), 27–62.

Hamilton, J.D., 1989. A new approach to the economic analysis of nonstationary time series and the business cycle. Econometrica 57 (2), 357–384.

Hamilton, J.D., Susmel, R., 1994. Autoregressive conditional heteroskedasticity and changes in regime. J. Econom. 64 (1–2), 307–333.

He, J., Ng, L.K., 1998. The foreign exchange exposure of Japanese multinational corporations. J. Finance 53 (2), 733–753.

Hess, M.K., 2003. What drives Markov regime-switching behavior of stock markets? The Swiss case. Int. Rev. Financ. Anal. 12 (5), 527–543.

Holmes, M.J., Maghrebi, N., 2002. Non-linearities, regime-switching and the relationship between Asian equity and foreign exchange markets. Int. Econ. J. 16 (4), 121–139.

Jones, R.W., 1977. Two-ness in trade theory: costs and benefits. Special Papers in International EconomicsPrinceton University Press, Princeton, NJ, pp. 1–47.

Jorion, P., 1991. The pricing of exchange rate risk in the stock market. J. Financ. Quant. Anal. 26 (3), 363–376.

Klaassen, F., 2002. Improving GARCH volatility forecasts with regime-switching GARCH. Empir. Econ. 27, 363–394.

Lastrapes, W.D., 1989. Exchange rate volatility and U.S. monetary policy: an ARCH application. J. Money Credit Banking 21 (1), 66–77.

Rakshit, M., 2002. The East Asian Currency Crisis. Oxford University Press, New Delhi.

Rapach, D.E., Strauss, J.K., Zhou, G., 2013. International stock return predictability: what is the role of the United States? J. Finance 68 (4), 1633–1662.

Schaller, H., Norden, S.V., 1997. Regime switching in stock market returns. Appl. Finan. Econ. 7 (2), 177–191.

CHAPTER 16

Illiquidity, Monetary Conditions, and the Financial Crisis in the United Kingdom

Husaini Said, Evangelos Giouvris

Royal Holloway, University of London, Egham, United Kingdom

Chapter Outline

16.1 Introduction

Ever since Amihud and Mendelson (1986) highlighted that stock returns is an increasing function of illiquidity, illiquidity (or liquidity) has become a common part of finance literature. Nevertheless, the study of illiquidity has become more prominent due to the developments in the financial sector that have resulted in greater funding access (Rajan, 2006) and more importantly the recent financial crisis (Brunnermeier, 2009; Crotty, 2009).

Furthermore, Kacperczyk and Schnabl (2010) mentioned that due to the crisis, safe products, such as commercial paper,[1] which is considered to be a safe asset due to its short maturity and

---

[1] Commercial paper is an unsecured short-term debt instrument issued by companies.

high credit rating before the crisis, has nearly dried up and ceased being perceived as a safe haven. Obviously, the flight-to-safety from other kinds of debt as well as stocks, could cause damage to an economy by making it more expensive for businesses to finance their daily operations (Bajaj, 2008). Thus, the effect of the liquidity crisis is not only confined to financial companies.[2] Obviously, the seriousness of the crisis can also be seen at country level.[3]

Goyenko and Ukhov (2009) show that there is a relationship between liquidity and monetary conditions, specifically an expansionary monetary policy coincides with increasing market liquidity. (Chordia et al., 2001; Söderberg, 2008).

Due to the importance of liquidity and monetary policy in combating the financial crisis, we felt that it is time that we update current *United States (US)* focused research by studying the *United Kingdom (UK)* market. Our research hopes to investigate any possible relationship between monetary conditions and illiquidity by using Jensen and Moorman (2010) framework. Jensen and Moorman (2010) focus on the US market, while we on the contrary, focus on the UK market and also discuss the financial crisis.

We feel that the UK market has strong research potential as its stock market is considered as one of the largest stock markets by capitalization and turnover ratio indicating that the market is quite liquid and therefore the results will be as immune as possible from biases, such as infrequent trading (Galariotis and Giouvris, 2007). In relation to the two monetary condition measures chosen here, namely the *Bank of England (BOE) base rate* and the *London Interbank Offered Rate (LIBOR),* the former is essentially similar to the Federal Reserve System in the US,[4] while LIBOR is widely used by institutions globally and its links to financial instruments are quite significant, whereby about USD 300 trillion financial contracts are pegged to it (Zibel, 2008).

We start our research by investigating if there are any unconditional return differences for illiquid and liquid stocks as Amihud and Mendelson (1986) indicated in their study. This

---

[2] For example, during the crisis, Keogh (2008) highlighted that the credit ratings of *United Parcel Service Inc* and *Toyota* were downgraded while *General Electric Co.*, which has held the *Standard & Poor (S&P)*'s top rating since 1956, longer than any other company, was in danger of being downgraded which would have cost $233 million more in annual payments on the $23.3 billion GE Capital Corp. raised in the US bond market in the first half of 2008, according to data compiled by Bloomberg. Eventually, General Electric Co. did lose its perfect credit rating when Standard & Poor's downgraded the company to "AA+" from "AAA". S&P expects the worsening economy to cause GE's holdings to deteriorate in value (Goldman, 2009). After 5 years, General Electric Co. have not recovered their perfect ratings but at least their 'AA+' long-term corporate credit rating outlook remains stable (StreetInsider.com, 2014).

[3] As expected, there is a domino effect following the liquidity crisis, which is due to the nation's political process and budget issues. Detrixhe (2011) reported it even resulted in S&P downgrading US' AAA credit rating for the first time, causing stock markets to fall including the *Dow Jones Industrial Average (DJIA)*, which endured its sharpest one-day decline since the financial crisis in 2008 (Browning, 2011). Three years after the downgrade, S&P maintains US' credit ratings as AA+ but the outlook on ratings is stable (Detrixhe and Katz, 2014).

[4] Decisions of BOE Monetary Policy Committee (MPC) are also being tracked by global markets.

is followed by a conditional monetary policy investigation, which is further separated into two related exercises starting with the relationship between market liquidity and monetary conditions. The next step is to look into zero-cost portfolio[5] returns and monetary conditions. It should be noted that similar to Jensen and Moorman (2010), our study focuses mainly on changes of all monetary conditions over the sample periods but we will also discuss the financial crisis when we conduct our monthly event study.

Overall, our research of the UK market shows that illiquid stocks generate higher returns compared to liquid stocks and when considering monetary conditions, expansive monetary conditions result in an increase in market liquidity, and higher zero-cost portfolio returns. However, prior to expansive shifts, investors' liquidity concerns heighten resulting in funding constraints and higher risks, making investors to reduce their holdings of illiquid stocks and moving to the less risky liquid stocks, signifying a flight-to-liquidity. Moreover, the crisis had an effect on market liquidity and illiquidity premium but it was more noticcable for the former.

The remainder of this paper is organized as follows. Section 16.2 presents the literature review while Section 16.3 describes the data and variables. In Section 16.4, the methodology and empirical results are discussed followed by our conclusion in Section 16.5.

16.2 Literature Review

16.2.1 Unconditional Returns for Illiquid and Liquid Stocks

Amihud and Mendelson (1986) who studied the relationship between expected returns and bid-ask spreads in the *New York Stock Exchange (NYSE)* discovered that average returns are an increasing function of the bid-ask spread. Similarly, using three different liquidity measures, Jensen and Moorman (2010) found evidence that the zero-cost portfolio earns returns that are both economically and statistically significant, suggesting that returns increase with increase in illiquidity. Amihud and Mendelson (1989); M. J. Brennan and Subrahmanyam (1996); Kiyotaki and Moore (2012) provide similar results. Moreover, Acharya and Pedersen (2005), using liquidity adjusted *capital asset pricing model (CAPM)*, provide evidence signifying the importance of liquidity on asset prices.

However, there are some contradictory results, which show that illiquid stocks do not necessarily provide consistently higher returns. Ben-Rephael et al. (2008) study of NYSE find evidence that the profitability of trading strategies based on liquidity premium[6] has declined over the past 4 decades, rendering such strategies virtually unprofitable especially

---

[5] Zero-cost portfolio = long the Illiquid portfolio and short the Liquid portfolio. Therefore, it is similar to the illiquidity premium as described by other researchers such as Eleswarapu and Reinganum (1993).

[6] Illiquidity premium or liquidity premium is the premium that investors received for holding a more illiquid asset/portfolio. Usually it is calculated as follows = illiquid asset/portfolio minus liquid asset/portfolio.

when using volume as a liquidity measure.[7] Furthermore, Eleswarapu and Reinganum (1993) found evidence that the premium is reliably positive only during the month of January suggesting a strong seasonal component while Brennan et al. (2013) who used the Amihud (2002) measure of illiquidity and its role in asset pricing, stated that in general, only the down-days element commands a return premium. Nevertheless, Datar et al., 1998, who investigated the liquidity-return relationship for all nonfinancial firms on the NYSE, highlighted that the liquidity effect is prevalent throughout the year and is not restricted to the month of January alone.

We believe that due to conflicting evidence, conducting research on liquid and illiquid stocks still has its merits.

16.2.2 Market Liquidity (Aggregate Illiquidity Innovation, ε_t) and Monetary Conditions

There is more research on the effect of monetary conditions on market liquidity than the relationship between illiquidity premium and monetary conditions. Specifically, Söderberg (2008) studied the ability of 14 macroeconomic variables, such as interest rate to forecast changes in monthly market liquidity on three Scandinavian order-driven stock exchanges.[8] Acharya and Pedersen (2005) highlighted that an investor should also be concerned with market liquidity, as the combined effect of both market and individual asset liquidity can affect asset prices. Thus, suggesting that by understanding how monetary conditions affect market liquidity will allow us to explore how monetary conditions affect prices as well as the illiquidity premium.

Chordia et al. (2001) study the effects of several explanatory variables (inclusive of short-term interest rates[9]) confirm that short-term interest rates significantly affect market liquidity as well as trading activity (Fernández-Amador et al., 2013; Fujimoto, 2004; Goyenko and Ukhov, 2009; Jensen and Moorman, 2010). Nevertheless, Chordia et al. (2005) obtained results indicating monetary expansions are associated with increased equity market liquidity but only during crisis periods. Even Söderberg (2008) highlighted that although some of the macroeconomic variables are able to predict the market liquidity of the specific stock markets, not a single variable is able to predict the market liquidity of all three Scandinavian stock markets. Therefore, implying that not a single macroeconomic variable has the same effect on all three stock markets.

---

[7] Although liquidity measures not related to volume did show some evidence of liquidity premiums, they are considered weak (Ben-Rephael et al., 2008).

[8] Copenhagen (Denmark), Oslo (Norway), and Stockholm (Sweden).

[9] Nevertheless, their study focuses on more macroeconomic variables, such as Gross Domestic Product (GDP), the unemployment rate, and the Consumer Price Index (CPI).

16.2.3 Illiquidity Premium Across Monetary Conditions

Even though there is limited research on the relationship between illiquidity premium and monetary conditions, there is some research on the relationship between stock prices and business conditions. In particular, Fama and French (1989) highlighted that further research on monetary policy should be done. Hence, by extending Fama and French (1989) research, Jensen et al. (1996) found evidence to suggest that the monetary environment actually influences investors' required returns. Amihud (2002) even highlighted that expected market illiquidity affects exante stock excess return positively over time, signifying that if there is an expansionary shift (market liquidity increase), stock returns are expected to decrease.

However, in contrast to Fama and French (1989) and Amihud (2002), Thorbecke (1997) who also studied the US market found evidence to indicate that expansionary policy increases expost stock returns. Thus, if *market liquidity (expansionary) increases*, stock returns are expected to also increase.

16.2.4 Flight to Liquidity

Amihud (2002) also highlighted that the effects of both expected and unexpected market illiquidity are stronger on the returns of small firm's stock portfolios. Since small firms are usually known to be more illiquid compared to larger firms, their study also indicated that market liquidity affects illiquid stocks more compared to liquid stocks meaning that small stocks are subject to greater illiquidity risk. Such a relationship can also be linked to the *"flight-to-liquidity"* or *"flight-to-quality"* phenomenon as in times of dire liquidity large stocks seem relatively more attractive compared to small stocks due to the illiquidity risk.

Brunnermeier and Pedersen (2009) provided a model to indicate that there are associations between an asset's market liquidity[10] and investors' funding liquidity.[11] Their model actually establishes various findings, such as market liquidity has commonality across shares and is subject to flight-to-quality (Acharya and Pedersen, 2005; Goyenko and Ukhov, 2009; Jensen and Moorman, 2010).

Nevertheless, Rajan (2006) mentioned that in times of ample liquidity supplied by the central banks (low interest rates), investors have a tendency to engage in riskier investments to earn higher returns. Therefore, during expansive monetary policy periods where market liquidity is expected to increase, it is likely that investors will increase their holdings of riskier illiquid stocks causing the price of illiquid stocks to increase.

---

[10] *Market liquidity* means how easily an asset is traded.
[11] *Funding liquidity* relates to degree of difficulty/easiness investors can obtain funding.

16.2.5 Sensitivity of Illiquid Quintile and Liquid Quintile

Another point that Amihud and Mendelson (1986) discovered is that there is a clientele effect, whereby stocks with higher spreads are held by investors with longer holding periods resulting in the returns of higher-spread stocks (illiquid stocks) to be less spread-sensitive. Therefore, such illiquid stock investors would react slowly to changes in liquidity of the stocks as they tend to hold the stocks for longer.

However, using turnover as a measure of liquidity and a sample of 48 stock exchanges,[12] Dey (2005) supports a negative relationship between turnover and returns but they find that turnover is significant for the emerging market portfolios only. They highlighted that due to the high liquidity of developed markets, liquidity is not a concern for investors. Therefore, since the UK market is a developed market, investors may not be as concerned with liquidity, resulting in asset prices to be less sensitive to changes in liquidity.

Furthermore, Bekaert et al. (2013) mentioned that lax monetary policy (increased market liquidity) decreases both risk aversion and uncertainty of expected market volatility by studying the VIX.[13] Therefore, it is expected that investors will prefer illiquid stocks making it to be more sensitive compared to liquid stocks during expansive monetary conditions.

16.3 Data and Variables
16.3.1 Data

We use stocks listed under the *FTSE All-Share index* to capture the UK stock market. Our sample starts in January 1987 and ends in December 2013. All data are obtained from Datastream. Outliers are eliminated and the final data set contains around 621 stocks.

16.3.2 Liquidity Measures

Choosing the right liquidity measure may be complicated. As Amihud et al. (2005) highlighted, there is hardly a single liquidity measure that can capture all aspects of estimating the effect of liquidity on asset prices. Therefore, similar to Jensen and Moorman (2010) and in order to address the issues highlighted by Amihud et al. (2005), we decided to use three liquidity measures namely: (1) *Amihud illiquidity measure* (Amihud, 2002), (2) *High-low spread (adjusted[14])* (Corwin and Schultz, 2012), and (3) *Roll estimator* (Roll, 1984). Please refer to Table 16.1 for more information.

---

[12] 48 stock exchanges consisted of 22 exchanges from Europe, 7 exchanges from North America, 13 exchanges from Asia/Pacific, 5 exchanges from South America, and 1 exchange from Africa.

[13] VIX = Chicago Board Options Exchange (CBOE) Volatility Index, which is the stock market option-based implied volatility of the US S&P500 index.

[14] Corwin and Schultz (2012) makes a few assumptions for calculating the High-low spread, where one measure is adjusted for overnight price changes whereas the second is not. We decided to use the one that is adjusted for overnight price changes. Nonetheless, the difference in spreads for the two techniques are quite minimum.

Table 16.1: Descriptive statistics of liquidity measures: January 1987 to December 2013.

	Correlation			Mean	Standard Deviation
	AMH	HLA	RE		
AMH	1.00000 —			2.42280	1.36766
HLA	0.67312 (0.0001)	1.00000 —		0.00477	0.00226
RE	0.64433 (0.0003)	0.56259 (0.0023)	1.00000 —	0.00522	0.00123

This table shows descriptive statistics including the correlation of the three liquidity measures used throughout the paper. The measures are derived from daily data but are averaged to produce monthly measures. However, for the correlations, the monthly measures are further averaged to yield annual measures. The sample uses companies listed on FTSE All Share Index between January 1987 and December 2013 (324 months).

1. The Amihud illiquidity measure (ILLIQ) or AMH is calculated for each company, c, every month as follows:

$$AMH_{cm} = \frac{1}{t}\sum_{t} \frac{1,000,000 \times |return_t|}{price_t \times volume_t}$$

   Where t is a trading day within the year the measure is calculated.
2. The High-low spread (Adjusted) or HLA is calculated for each company, c, every month as follows:

$$HLA_{cm} = \frac{2(e^{\alpha} - 1)}{1 + e^{\alpha}}$$

   Where negative values are converted to zero (0) and the following equations are used to calculate α which is inserted in the above HLA equation

$$\alpha = \frac{\sqrt{2\beta} - \sqrt{\beta}}{3 - 2\sqrt{2}} - \sqrt{\frac{\gamma}{3 - 2\sqrt{2}}}$$

$$\beta = \sum_{j=0}^{1} \left[ln\left(\frac{H_{t+j}^{0}}{L_{t+j}^{0}} \right) \right]^2$$

$$\gamma = \left[ln\left(\frac{H_{t,t+1}^{0}}{L_{t,t+1}^{0}} \right) \right]^2$$

   Where t is a trading day within the year the measure is calculated.
3. The roll estimator or RE is calculated for each company, c, every month as follows:

$$RE_{cm} = 2\sqrt{-Cov\left(\Delta P_t, \Delta P_{t-1} \right)}$$

   Where t is a trading day within the year the measure is calculated.
Source: All data were obtained from Datastream.

Since all three measures are mainly used to measure illiquidity, it is expected that there will be strong correlations between the measures but as Goyenko et al. (2009) mentioned, different measures capture different aspects of liquidity. Table 16.1 provides results that are consistent with expectations as the three liquidity measures are positively correlated to each other and the results are statistically significant at least at 1% level. Nevertheless, since the correlations are not perfect ($\rho < 1$), it shows the uniqueness of each of the three liquidity measures.

16.3.3 *Monetary Policy Measures*

In order to identify shifts in Federal Reserve's monetary policy, Jensen and Moorman (2010) uses two alternative measures namely the *Federal funds rate* and *Fed*[15] *discount rate*. *Federal funds rate* is used to represent monetary policy *stringency* and to identify adjustments in federal *stringency* while the second measure, *Fed discount rate* is used to represent monetary policy *stance* in order to identify fundamental shifts in the overall Fed monetary policy.

Stance can be defined as the contribution made by monetary policy to the economic, financial, and monetary developments (ECB, 2010). Fed uses it to identify fundamental shifts in the overall Fed monetary policy (Jensen and Moorman, 2010). The *BOE base rate* is the best alternative measure for stance in the UK as it is the key interest rate used by BOE to manage monetary policy, which would be a good indicator of economic and financial development in the UK. The BOE base rate is also the rate that the BOE charges banks for secured overnight lending. Changes to the UK *BOE base rate* (if any), is decided and made by the *Monetary Policy Committee* of the BOE on a monthly basis (Bank-of-England, 2014a). This is similar to the Fed discount rate, which is decided by the *Federal Open Market Committee (FOMC)* but they meet only around 8 times per year (Board-of-Governors-of-the-Federal-Reserve-System, 2014).

Jensen and Moorman (2010) mentioned that *stringency* can be defined as the degree of monetary strictness while Maddaloni and Peydró (2013) defined it as how stringent the capital requirements of the banking sector are within a country. Hence, the *UK 3 months LIBOR* might be the best alternative measure for stringency in UK as it is the 3 months average interest rates estimated by leading banks in London and it has been known to serve as the benchmark reference for debt instruments, such as government bonds and even retail financing. Moreover, LIBOR is the interbank rate in the UK, which is similar to *Federal fund rate*, the rate used to represent stringency in the US. However, the FOMC also decides the Federal funds rate (Board-of-Governors-of-the-Federal-Reserve-System, 2014), unlike the LIBOR which is decided by leading banks in UK. Thus, the two alternative monetary policy measures that we will be using are UK *BOE base rate* and UK 3 months *LIBOR* rate as an indicator of *stance* and *stringency*, respectively.

Similar to Jensen and Moorman (2010), the variables are measured as binary variables since we are identifying shifts in monetary conditions. The variables are considered as *expansive* for a given month (*t*) whenever the rate (either *BOE base rate* or *LIBOR*) decreases from month (*t*−1) to month (*t*) while *restrictive* for a given month (*t*) is whenever the rate (either *BOE base* rate or *LIBOR*) increases from month (*t*−1) to month (*t*). If there are no changes from month *(t−1)* to month *(t)*, the previous month *(t−1)* classification will be maintained for month *(t)*. In order to avoid look-ahead bias, stock returns are measured subsequent to the identified shifts in monetary policy.

---

[15] *Fed* is the short and informal name of the *Federal Reserve System*.

Although the two measures are used to represent different aspects of monetary conditions, Panel A in Table 16.2 indicates that the two monetary policy measures are highly positively correlated to each other. Furthermore, Table 16.2 shows that the mean is higher for *LIBOR* but *BOE base rate* has a slightly higher standard deviation indicating higher volatility and risks.

Panel B and C of Table 16.2 reports changes (expansive or restrictive) of the two monetary conditions proxies over the 324 months period. Panel B considers the two measures independently showing that there are more months with expansive monetary conditions than restrictive monetary conditions for either stance or stringency, which is in contrast with Jensen and Moorman (2010) who have more restrictive than expansive months. This could be due to the current financial crisis which has resulted in prolonged expansive periods, which is part of the data sample.

Table 16.2: Descriptive statistics for measures of monetary conditions: January 1987 to December 2013.

Panel A: Correlation of Measures of Monetary Conditions				
	Correlation			
	BOE	**LIBOR**	**Mean**	**Standard Deviation**
BOE	1.00000 -----		5.80216	3.78182
LIBOR	0.99734 (0.0000)	1.00000 -----	6.01542	3.76820

Panel B: Months Across Monetary Conditions: Measures Separated			
	Number of Months in Alternative Monetary Conditions		
Monetary State Measure	**Expansive**	**Restrictive**	**All**
UK BOE Base Rate (Stance)	199	125	324
UK 3M LIBOR (Stringency)	181	143	324

Panel C: Months Across Monetary Conditions: Measures Intersected			
	Number of Months in Alternative Monetary Conditions		
	UK Stance (BOE)		
UK Stringency (3M LIBOR)	**Expansive**	**Restrictive**	
Expansive	128	53	
Restrictive	71	72	
			All = 324

This table shows descriptive statistics for measures of monetary conditions used throughout the paper. *Stance* is derived from the monthly *United Kingdom (UK) Bank of England (BOE)* Base Rate, which is the key interest rates used by BOE to manage monetary policy. *Stringency* is determined based on UK 3 months *London Interbank Offered Rate (LIBOR)*, which is the average interest rates estimated by leading banks in London that the banks would offer to other banks if they borrowed from them. An increase in the rate from the prior month is labelled *"Restrictive"* and a decrease is labelled *"Expansive."* For each rate, whenever there is no change from 1 month to the next, the prior label is maintained. Statistics are derived from the period between January 1987 and December 2013.
Source: All data are obtained from Datastream.

Panel C identifies the intersection of the two measures. Again contrasting to Jensen and Moorman (2010), Panel C shows that there are also more months when both stance and stringency are expansive (128 months) compared to when both are restrictive (72 months). Panel C also shows the uniqueness of the two monetary policy measures, as out of the 324 months, the two monetary policy measures did not intersect for 124 months indicating that the leading banks in London, which determine the *LIBOR*, does not necessarily follow the BOE whenever the BOE change their *base rate*.

16.4 Methodology, Empirical Results, and Analysis

16.4.1 Unconditional Returns Difference Between Illiquid and Liquid Stocks

Our research starts with an investigation of portfolio returns across illiquidity quintiles without regard to monetary conditions that is the unconditional returns of the quintiles. This would allow us to assess the pricing of illiquidity before any external variables are considered.

Table 16.3 shows the equally weighted average monthly returns of the quintiles over the sample period. The prior year ($t-1$) average of the illiquidity measure is used to construct the quintiles for the returns calculation for a given year (t). Therefore, the illiquidity measure for the year 1987 is used to construct the quintiles and then calculate the quintile returns for the year 1988. Using one of the illiquidity measures at a time, the stocks are ranked and the two portfolios that are ranked top 20% and bottom 20% are classified as either liquid or illiquid quintiles. The quintiles are rebalanced annually.

Table 16.3: Monthly returns on liquidity ranked portfolios (unconditional portfolio returns): January 1988 to December 2013.

Liquidity Measure	Mean Monthly Portfolio Return (%)					Illiquid–Liquid
	Liquidity Portfolio					
	Liquid	2	3	4	Illiquid	
Amihud	0.79068%	0.84669%	0.99227%	1.00362%	1.37744%	**0.58675%** **(0.0348)**
High low spread (adjusted)	0.87038%	0.90009%	1.06716%	1.04422%	1.31145%	**0.44106%** **(0.0498)**
Roll estimator	1.10231%	0.81193%	0.66244%	1.48521%	1.71233%	0.61003% (0.1271)

This table shows equally-weighted, average monthly returns (in percentage format) for quintile portfolios formed based on the three liquidity measures described in Table 16.1. Quintile portfolio ranks are determined by the value of the liquidity measure in the year prior to the year in which returns are measured and are rebalanced annually. Thus, the returns sample period is from January 1988 to December 2013. The *"Illiquid–Liquid"* portfolio is a portfolio that takes a long position in the quintile of stocks with the lowest level of liquidity and a short position in the quintile of stocks with the highest liquidity. Newey-West *p*-values for long-short portfolios are reported in brackets and underneath the monthly average returns, whereby bold figures denote statistically significance coefficient at least at 10% level. The bandwidth parameter for the Newey-West *p*-value is calculated using the Newey-West automatic lag selection.
Source: All data are obtained from Datastream.

The final column in Table 16.3 shows the zero-cost portfolio returns, which takes a long position on the illiquid portfolio and a short position on the liquid portfolio [*illiquid minus liquid stocks portfolio (IML)*]. Table 16.3 shows, similar to past research, such as Amihud and Mendelson (1986), that the zero-cost portfolio of the first two liquidity measures earns returns that are both positive and statistically significant. However, although the zero-cost portfolio returns for the *roll estimator* showed the highest positive returns, results are not statistically significant. Therefore, there is a positive significant zero-cost portfolio returns observed in our data sample based on *Amihud* and *HLA* indicating that illiquid portfolios earn higher returns compared to liquid portfolios.

Jensen and Moorman (2010) also discovered that returns are increasing monotonically with stock illiquidity for all three liquidity measures, which means they observed a decrease in returns when moving away from the low liquidity quintile (Illiquid) to the high liquidity quintile (Liquid). However as shown in Table 16.3, our research indicated that out of the three liquidity measures, only *Amihud* showed returns that increase monotonically with decrease in liquidity.

16.4.2 Aggregate Illiquidity Innovations, ε_t

We will now proceed with our main research objective of investigating how different monetary conditions affect illiquidity premium but as highlighted before, other than Jensen and Moorman (2010), there is not much research available that investigates such a relationship.

Nevertheless, there is some research on the relationship between market liquidity and monetary conditions, such as Chordia et al. (2005) who discovered that during the crisis periods, monetary expansions are associated with increased equity market liquidity (or decrease in aggregate illiquidity). Thus, it would be beneficial if we studied aggregate illiquidity (market liquidity) in order to understand the effects of monetary conditions on illiquidity premium. As Acharya and Pedersen (2005) stated, each stock's required return depends not only on its own expected liquidity but also on the market liquidity (aggregate illiquidity).

In this section, we investigate the relationship between aggregate illiquidity and monetary conditions exploring whether aggregate illiquidity changes with different monetary conditions.

Similar to the regression technique adopted by Pastor and Stambaugh (2003) and described by Jensen and Moorman (2010), we used the *aggregate Illiquidity Innovation, ε_t* as an aggregate measure of illiquidity which is obtained using a market-wide version of *Amihud (ILLIQ)*. Please refer to Table 16.4 for more details.

The residuals, ε_t from the regression, are considered to be the *aggregate illiquidity innovations, ε_t*, which provide a dynamic measure of market liquidity conditions (Jensen and Moorman, 2010). Using the *aggregate illiquidity innovations, ε_t* three analyses are conducted in order to investigate the relationship between aggregate illiquidity and monetary conditions. The first analysis

Table 16.4: Aggregate illiquidity innovations and monetary conditions.

Monetary Policy	Aggregate Illiquidity Innovation Stance (UK BOE)		
Stringency (LIBOR)	Expansive	Restrictive	All
Expansive	**−0.71828**	0.14693	**−0.46694**
	(0.0502)	(0.6284)	**(0.0757)**
Restrictive	0.70925	0.46145	0.58449
	(0.3273)	(0.2504)	(0.1576)
All	−0.20639	0.32956	0.00000
	(0.3185)	(0.2938)	(1.0000)

This table shows average monthly innovations in aggregate illiquidity across monetary conditions and the method used, was described by Jensen and Moorman (2010) and Pastor and Stambaugh (2003).

The measure is derived from the monthly market wide version of *ILLIQ* that is reported in Table 16.1. The aggregate value of illiquidity (*AILLIQ*) is calculated as follows:

$$AILLIQ_t = \frac{1}{N_t}\sum_{i=1}^{N} ILLIQ_{i,t}$$

Where N_t includes all firms with an observation for *ILLIQ* in month t except for the highest and the lowest 1% of $ILLIQ_{i,t}$. Monthly changes in aggregate illiquidity are calculated for each month t as follows:

$$\Delta AILLIQ_t = \frac{m_{t-1}}{m_1}\left(AILLIQ_t - AILLIQ_{t-1}\right)$$

Where m_{t-1} is the total market value at the beginning of month $t-1$ for all firms with an observation for $ILLIQ_{i,t}$ in month t. m_1 is the total market value at the beginning of January 1987 for all firms with an observation for $ILLIQ_{i,t}$ in January 1987. We regress the monthly change in aggregate illiquidity on its lag and the scaled lagged value of aggregate illiquidity as follows:

$$\Delta AILLIQ_t = \alpha + \beta\Delta AILLIQ_{t-1} + \lambda\left(\frac{m_{t-1}}{m_1}\right)AILLIQ_{t-1} + \varepsilon_t$$

Aggregate illiquidity innovations are the fitted values of the regression residual, ε_t.

Monetary conditions, as labelled in month $t-1$, were assigned to a value of ε_t in month t. Measures of monetary conditions are detailed in Table 16.2. Newey-West p-values are reported in brackets and underneath the monthly average, whereby bold figures denote a statistically significant coefficient at least at 10% level. The bandwidth parameter for the Newey-West p-value is calculated using the Newey-West automatic lag selection. Values are calculated over the period from January 1987 through December 2013.

Source: All data are obtained from Datastream.

investigates the relationship between *aggregate illiquidity innovation, ε_t and monetary conditions* followed by the monthly event study, which is achieved by examining *cumulative aggregate illiquidity innovation, ε_t* around a directional change in the BOE base rate. The last analysis involves *aggregate illiquidity innovations, ε_t* within the most illiquid and most liquid quintile.

16.4.2.1 Aggregate Illiquidity Innovation, ε_t and Monetary Conditions

Table 16.4 is constructed by assigning monetary conditions in month $(t-1)$ to an *aggregate illiquidity innovation ε_t* in month (t). Since we are using *aggregate illiquidity innovation ε_t*, a negative *aggregate illiquidity innovation ε_t* value is considered as a decrease in aggregate illiquidity (or increase in market liquidity) whereas a positive *aggregate illiquidity innovation ε_t* value is considered as an increase in aggregate illiquidity (or decrease in market liquidity).

Although the *values* (positive or negative) are similar to past research as Table 16.4 shows the values are negative following expansive monetary conditions and vice-versa, the *p*-value indicates that the results are generally not significant especially for restrictive periods. Table 16.4 also highlights that market liquidity is highest and significant when both stance and stringency are expansive, which is also observed by Jensen and Moorman (2010). Interestingly, the result seems to show that stringency (LIBOR) matters more than stance (BOE base rate), as it produces significant results for expansive periods.

16.4.2.2 Monthly event study: cumulative aggregate illiquidity innovation, ε_t around a directional change in the Bank of England base Rate (Shifts in monetary policy)

Fig. 16.1, shows the timing of adjustments in *aggregate illiquidity innovation* ε_t, which involves examining the changes in *aggregate illiquidity innovation* ε_t around shifts in monetary policy by conducting a "*Monthly Event Study.*" It is assumed that an "*event*" is an incident when there is a shift in monetary policy through a statement or decision issued by the

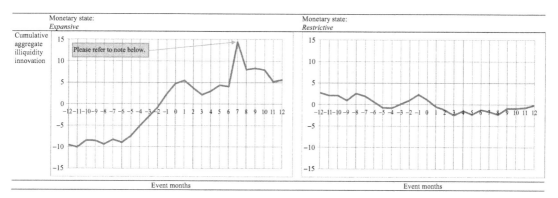

Figure 16.1: Monthly Event Study: Aggregate Illiquidity Innovations, ε_t.
This figure shows the event time average of cumulative aggregate illiquidity innovations, ε_t, around a directional change in the UK BOE Base Rate (shift in *Stance*). The monthly version of aggregate illiquidity innovations detailed in Table 16.4 is used. A monetary condition is labelled as "*Expansive*" if the prior interest rate change was a decrease or "*Restrictive*" if the prior change was an increase. Numbers on the horizontal axis are event months. The sample period is from January 1988 through December 2013.
Note: Based on our analysis, the unexpected significant increase of the event-time average of cumulative aggregate illiquidity innovations, ε_t are caused by three major happenings of which two are from the recent financial crisis, which occurred 7 months after the *directional change in the UK BOE Base Rate (event),* as follows:
1. September 11 attacks in the US (7 months after event—September 2001).
2. The fall of one of US leading mortgage lenders IndyMac Bank (7 months after event—July 2008).
3. Due to investors' concerns after the fall of Fannie Mae and Freddie Mac shares, resulting in the US government plan of saving them (7 months after event—July 2008).
All data are obtained from Datastream.

BOE. A change in interest rate (expansive to restrictive or vice-versa) is considered as a shift in monetary policy. Moreover, we also assumed that *"broad shift"* means *"long-term shift."* Hence, we are investigating long-term shifts in monetary policy.

Data of shifts in monetary policy was obtained from the BOE website (Bank-of-England, 2014b), which publishes changes in interest rates since 1694. Between January 1987 and December 2013, there are 94 changes in interest rates but only 18 are actual changes from expansive to restrictive or vice-versa (shifts in monetary policy). The remaining 76 changes are further (continued) increase or decrease in interest rates in the direction of the prior shifts.

The *"monthly event study"* investigates the behavior of the markets, 1 year (12 months) before and after an event (directional change in BOE base rate or stance) has occurred whereby month "0" is considered as when the event occurred. If there is a shift within the 12 months period before and after an event, this is considered only as a *temporary shift* and is not included in our research, as our main intention is to investigate only *a long-term shift* in monetary policy. Nevertheless, we have also included the financial crisis period even though there was a minor temporary shift. Thus, including the financial crisis period, which obviously resulted in monetary policy shifts, there are only eight monetary policy shifts between January 1987 and December 2013, namely four expansion and four restrictive shifts.

The left side of Fig. 16.1 shows that 6 months before the expansive events, *cumulative aggregate illiquidity innovation* started increasing prior to an expansive shift, indicating that aggregate illiquidity increases (or market liquidity decreases). However, cumulative aggregate illiquidity innovation started decreasing after the expansive event, signifying that market liquidity has improved but there are some interruptions 7 months after the event. These are due to (1) the September 11, 2001 attacks on the US (McAndrews and Potter, 2002), (2) the fall of one of US leading mortgage lenders, IndyMac Bank (Clifford and Chris, 2008), and (3) Fannie Mae and Freddie Mac shares plummeting due to investors' concerns (Luhby, 2008). Therefore, with the exception of the interruptions, our findings are somehow consistent to our previous findings as market liquidity improves following an expansive monetary condition.

The right side of Fig. 16.1 shows that the reaction after restrictive monetary shifts are less noticeable compared to expansive monetary conditions indicating that during restrictive monetary policy periods, changes in aggregate illiquidity would have limited implications for pricing of liquidity as investors are less concerned with liquidity, which is similar to the findings of Jensen and Moorman (2010).

16.4.2.3 Aggregate illiquidity innovations: most illiquid quintile and most liquid quintile

Panel A and B in Table 16.5 shows the average monthly innovations in *aggregate illiquidity innovation* ε_t across monetary conditions for the most liquid and illiquid quintiles respectively.

Table 16.5: Aggregate illiquidity innovations, εt, and monetary conditions: most illiquid quintile and most liquid quintile.

Panel:	A: Most Liquid Quintile			B: Most Illiquid Quintile			C: Illiquid Minus Liquid		
	Mean Monthly Illiquidity Innovation			Mean Monthly Illiquidity Innovation			Mean Monthly Illiquidity Innovation		
Monetary Policy	*Stance (BOE)*			*Stance (BOE)*			*Stance (BOE)*		
Stringency (LIBOR)	Expansive	Restrictive	All	Expansive	Restrictive	All	Expansive	Restrictive	All
Expansive	−0.00655	−0.00438	−0.00592	−2.15471	−0.95894	−1.84612	−1.94456	−0.73326	−1.59268
	(0.0978)	(0.5425)	**(0.0866)**	(0.1425)	(0.1553)	**(0.0848)**	(0.1456)	(0.1854)	**(0.0858)**
Restrictive	0.00783	0.00700	0.00741	2.83524	1.52680	2.20115	2.66768	1.32894	1.99363
	(0.3419)	(0.1014)	(0.1203)	(0.3195)	(0.3034)	(0.1927)	(0.3218)	(0.3006)	(0.1965)
All	−0.00140	0.00223	0.00000	−0.31775	0.56146	0.00000	−0.29068	0.46415	0.00000
	(0.5870)	(0.6306)	(1.0000)	(0.8112)	(0.6318)	(1.0000)	(0.8106)	(0.6385)	(1.0000)

This table shows average monthly innovations in aggregate illiquidity across monetary conditions separately for the quintile of the most illiquid stocks and the quintile of the most liquid stocks. The aggregate illiquidity innovation measure is detailed in Table 16.4. Panel C shows the difference in aggregate illiquidity innovations for the most illiquid and the most liquid quintile. Newey-West p-values are reported in brackets and underneath the monthly average, whereby bold figures denote statistically significant coefficient at least at 10% level. The bandwidth parameter for the Newey-West p-value is calculated using the Newey-West automatic lag selection. Values are calculated over the period from January 1987 through December 2013.
Source: All data are obtained from Datastream.

Similar to Table 16.4, although the values (either positive or negative) are consistent with past research, the results in Table 16.5 are generally not significant. The only significant results are when stringency is expansive as well as when both stance and stringency are expansive for the most liquid quintile.

By looking only at significant results under *stringency*, Panel A and B of Table 16.5 shows that the most illiquid quintile experiences greater change in *aggregate illiquidity innovation* ε_t values compared to the most liquid quintile, which exhibits minimum changes. Panel C in Table 16.5 presents the difference in *aggregate illiquidity innovation* ε_t between the most illiquid and most liquid quintiles. It shows that the values are not affected by the most liquid quintile confirming that the most liquid quintile experiences only a minimum change in *aggregate illiquidity innovation* ε_t due to monetary conditions.

As before, Table 16.5 seems to indicate again that stringency seems to be more important for the UK market as it generates significant results.

16.4.3 Monetary Conditions and Returns to Illiquid, Relative to Liquid Stocks

Up to this point, our UK findings do not fully support Jensen and Moorman (2010) but there are some significant results indicating that expansive monetary conditions are associated with eased funding constraints (increase in market liquidity). To investigate the relationship between illiquidity premium and monetary conditions, we undertake four different exercises focusing on the *zero-cost portfolio* or *illiquid minus liquid portfolio (IML)*.

The first exercise investigates the *average return of the IML portfolio across monetary conditions*, which is achieved by examining the IML portfolio equally-weighted average monthly returns across different monetary conditions based on the three different liquidity measures. The second exercise examines the *terminal wealth in different monetary conditions*, which is done by assessing the terminal growth of £100 invested in the IML portfolio within different monetary conditions over 26 years. The third exercise is a monthly event study involving the *cumulative IML portfolio returns* around a directional change in the BOE base rate (shifts in stance monetary policy). The last exercise looks into illiquidity and monetary conditions *beta*, β to determine whether stocks with the highest or lowest illiquidity levels drive the relationship between returns and monetary conditions.

16.4.3.1 Average return to the zero-cost portfolio across monetary conditions

Table 16.6 shows the IML portfolio equally-weighted average monthly returns across different monetary conditions based on the three liquidity measures. As before, returns are measured in a given month (t) based on monetary conditions determined in the previous month ($t-1$).

Table 16.6: Illiquid minus liquid portfolio returns across monetary conditions: January 1988 to December 2013.

Panel:	A: Amihud			B: High Low Spread (Adjusted)			C: Roll Estimator		
	Mean Monthly Return (%)			Mean Monthly Return (%)			Mean Monthly Return (%)		
	Stance (BOE)			Stance (BOE)			Stance (BOE)		
Monetary policy Stringency (LIBOR)	Expansive	Restrictive	All	Expansive	Restrictive	All	Expansive	Restrictive	All
Expansive	1.5292%	−0.5968%	0.9075%	0.9002%	0.0881%	0.6628%	1.0928%	1.0353%	1.0760%
	(0.0000)	(0.0889)	(0.0053)	(0.0345)	(0.7361)	(0.0397)	(0.1693)	(0.1189)	(0.0660)
Restrictive	0.3376%	0.1229%	0.2287%	0.2184%	0.1796%	0.1987%	0.3662%	−0.3248%	0.0158%
	(0.4529)	(0.8332)	(0.5952)	(0.5189)	(0.6531)	(0.4611)	(0.1878)	(0.7624)	(0.9751)
All	1.0964%	−0.1745%	0.5868%	0.6526%	0.1418%	0.4411%	0.8289%	0.2373%	0.6100%
	(0.0001)	(0.6227)	(0.0348)	(0.0337)	(0.5538)	(0.0498)	(0.1139)	(0.7287)	(0.1271)
Unconditional	0.5868%			0.4411%			0.6100%		
	(0.0348)			(0.0498)			(0.1271)		

This table shows illiquid minus liquid (zero-cost) portfolio, equally-weighted average monthly returns (in percentage format) across different monetary conditions. Each return is for a portfolio long in the quintile of stocks with the lowest liquidity and short in the quintile of stocks with the highest liquidity. Returns are measured in month (t) based on monetary conditions determined in month ($t-1$) and the portfolios are rebalanced on an annual basis based on the three respective liquidity measures. Liquidity and monetary conditions measures are detailed in Tables 16.1 and 16.2, respectively. Newey-West p-values are reported in brackets and underneath the monthly average returns, whereby bold figures denote a statistically significant coefficient at least at 10% level. The bandwidth parameter for the Newey-West p-value is calculated using the Newey-West automatic lag selection.
Source: All data are obtained from Datastream.

Table 16.6 demonstrate that a relationship exists between IML portfolio returns and monetary conditions for all three liquidity measures but it is considerably less noticeable for the *Roll estimator*. Table 16.6 also shows that the IML portfolio return is different across the two monetary conditions. It shows that expansive monetary conditions consistently result in higher IML portfolio returns compared to restrictive monetary conditions [see *Amihud* (Panel A)]. Following periods of expansive shifts for *stance (stringency)*, the IML portfolio returns is 1.0964% (0.9075%) whereas after restrictive periods, the IML portfolio returns is −0.1745% (0.2287%). Our results also show that the average IML portfolio returns are generally statistically insignificant when either of the monetary conditions are restrictive. Moreover, the IML portfolio returns are the highest when both monetary conditions are expansive and the results are significant for both *Amihud* and *HLA* measures. In fact, the returns (conditional returns) for the two liquidity measures are more than twice the return of their respective unconditional returns which was discussed before, in Table 16.3. Also unlike aggregate illiquidity in Table 16.4, Table 16.6 shows that stance (BOE base rate) has a stronger effect on IML than stringency (LIBOR).

Overall, there is some relationship between the zero-cost portfolio returns and monetary conditions even though the three liquidity measures do not capture the same aspects of illiquidity. Nevertheless, Table 16.6 shows that there is a relationship between monetary conditions and the price of liquidity.

16.4.3.2 Terminal wealth in different monetary conditions

Fig. 16.2 shows the growth of £100 after 26 years period (January 1988 to December 2013) by investing in the IML (zero-cost portfolio) under different monetary conditions. It is assumed that £100 is invested in the beginning (January 1988) growing cumulatively across the respective monetary conditions.

Although for a short period of time, portfolio growth during restrictive conditions can actually be higher than during expansive conditions (noticeably for the Roll estimator), the figure shows that in the long run, the IML portfolio for all three liquidity measures consistently resulted in higher growth during expansive monetary conditions relative to restrictive monetary conditions. This is also important as Table 16.2 indicated that there are more expansive periods compared to restrictive periods.

16.4.3.3 Monthly event study: cumulative illiquid minus liquid (IML) portfolio returns around a directional change in the Bank of England base rate (shifts in monetary policy)

So far Table 16.6 and Fig. 16.2 established the existence of a relationship between zero-cost portfolio returns and monetary conditions to a certain extent. However, the behavior of the temporal relationship between zero-cost portfolio returns and monetary policy shifts remains uncertain. Therefore, to investigate the temporal relationship around a directional change in

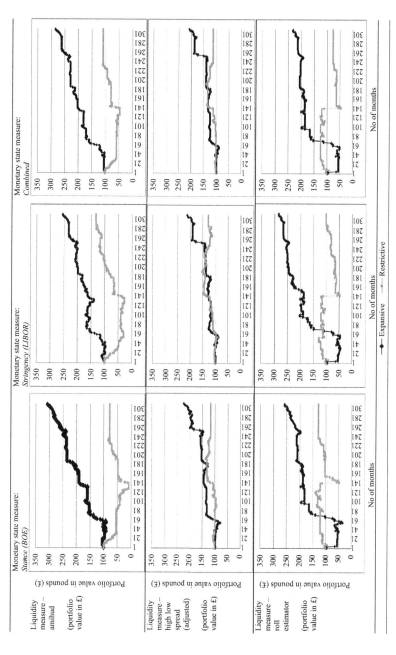

Figure 16.2: Illiquid Minus Liquid Portfolio Growth of £100 Across Different Monetary Conditions (Stringency): January 1988 to December 2013.

This figure shows the growth of £100 invested in the following strategy: long illiquid stocks and short liquid stocks in different monetary conditions over the 26 years study period. The *black line* shows the dollar growth for investing in the long-short strategy for either stance or stringency during expansive conditions and not investing during restrictive periods. The *grey line* shows the dollar growth for investing in the long-short strategy for either stance or stringency during restrictive conditions and not investing during expansive policy periods. If monetary conditions are expansive for both *Stringency* and *Stance*, then "*Combined*" is labelled expansive and it involves investing when both monetary conditions are expansive and not investing during other periods. If monetary conditions are restrictive for both *Stringency* and *Stance*, then "*Combined*" is labelled restrictive and it involves investing when both monetary conditions are restrictive and not investing during other periods. All data are obtained from Datastream.

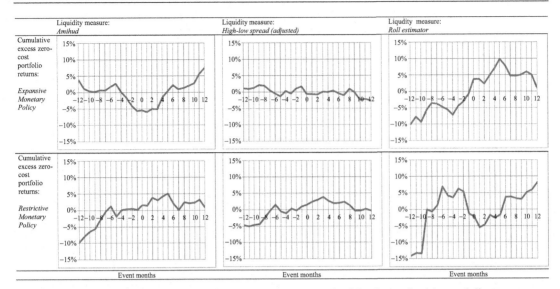

Figure 16.3: Monthly Event Study: Cumulative Excess Illiquid Minus Liquid Portfolio Returns.
This figure shows cumulative excess illiquid minus liquid portfolio returns around a directional
change in the UK BOE Base Rate (shift in *Stance*). *The illiquid minus liquid portfolio is a strategy that is long
the quintile portfolio of illiquid stocks and short the quintile portfolio of liquid stocks.* The line shows the event
time average of cumulative monthly returns in excess of the sample period mean for the long-short
strategy. A monetary condition is labelled as *"Expansive"* if the prior interest rate change is a decrease
or *"Restrictive"* if the prior change is an increase. Numbers on the vertical axis are percentages.
Numbers on the horizontal axis are event months. *All data are obtained from Datastream.*

the BOE base rate (shifts in stance monetary policy), we conduct a *monthly event study* for
the three liquidity measures similar to before.

The top row of Fig. 16.3 shows the event-time average of *"cumulative excess zero-cost
portfolio returns"* around an expansive directional change in BOE base rate (shifts in stance)
while the bottom row shows the event-time average of *"cumulative excess zero-costs portfolio
returns"* around a restrictive directional change in BOE base rate (shifts in stance).

Unlike Jensen and Moorman (2010), the return patterns of the zero-cost portfolio for the three
liquidity measures are different proving that the three liquidity measures are able to capture
different aspects of illiquidity. Nevertheless, among the three liquidity measures, *Amihud*
seems to provide results that are more consistent to our previous findings as the IML portfolio
returns increased following an expansive monetary condition.

Based on *Amihud*, our findings are consistent with Jensen and Moorman (2010) when there
is an expansive shift. Fig. 16.3 shows that 5 months prior to the event, cumulative IML
portfolio returns started decreasing reaching their lowest point. This signifies that prior to
an expansive shift, investors' liquidity concerns heightened resulting in funding constraints

and higher risks. Due to this, investors reduce their holdings of illiquid stocks moving to the less risky liquid stocks (flight-to-liquidity), resulting in the reduction of price and returns of illiquid stocks in comparison to liquid stocks. Nevertheless, after the event, cumulative IML portfolio returns started to stabilize and increase. The pattern after the event indicates that liquidity concerns have improved, resulting in better funding and less risk. Thus, as explained by Rajan (2006), due to the market liquidity increase, investors are less concerned with illiquidity risks and started moving from liquid to the riskier illiquid stocks causing the price of illiquid stocks to increase. Similar to Fig. 16.1, there is slight interruption 7 months after the event due to September 11 attacks and the financial crisis involving IndyMac Bank but it is less noticeable.

Using *Amihud,* when there is a restrictive shift, Fig. 16.3 shows results that are in the opposite direction of expansive shifts. Five months before the event, IML portfolio returns started increasing, reaching peak 5 months after the event before decreasing. However, similar to Fig. 16.1, the reaction is less noticeable compared to expansive monetary conditions signifying that during restrictive monetary policy periods, investors are less concerned with liquidity.

As highlighted earlier, *HLA* and the *Roll estimator* do not seem to demonstrate results similar to Jensen and Moorman (2010). For *HLA*, Fig. 16.3 shows that the price of liquidity adjusts relatively little around a monetary policy shift whereas the *Roll estimator*, after a restrictive shift seems to demonstrate a contradictory pattern that would normally be seen following an expansive shift.

Overall, the pattern observed does show that the price of liquidity adjusts considerably in the months around an expansive monetary policy shift.

16.4.3.4 Illiquidity and monetary conditions beta, β

In this section, we investigate whether the relationship between portfolio returns and monetary conditions is driven by strong returns for stocks with either the highest or lowest illiquidity levels. The regressions framework (as explained in Table 16.7) are used for the three liquidity measures, in order to obtain the beta, β, which is used to explore the hypothesis that sensitivities to monetary conditions vary with the level of stock illiquidity.

Similar to Jensen and Moorman (2010), our findings in Table 16.7 reveal that illiquid portfolios have higher betas than the liquid portfolios indicating that monetary conditions have the largest effect on the returns of illiquid stocks. This is consistent with Table 16.5, which also shows that monetary conditions have the largest effect on the aggregate illiquidity of illiquid stocks. Overall, the results provide further support on the relationship between illiquidity premium and monetary conditions.

Table 16.7: Liquidity and sensitivity to monetary conditions: January 1988 to December 2013.

Panel A: Amihud	Monetary Conditions Beta, β					
	Liquidity Portfolio					
Monetary Conditions Measure	Liquid	2	3	4	Illiquid	Illiquid–Liquid
BOE	−0.00498	−0.00026	0.00346	0.00415	0.00773	**0.01271** **(0.0068)**
LIBOR	0.00735	0.01131	0.01419	0.01268	0.01414	0.00679 (0.1037)
Combined	0.00293	0.00935	0.01320	0.01338	0.01811	**0.01518** **(0.0007)**
Panel B: High Low Spread	Liquidity Portfolio					
Monetary Conditions Measure	Liquid	2	3	4	Illiquid	Illiquid–Liquid
BOE	0.00043	0.00153	0.00291	0.00224	0.00553	0.00511 (0.1912)
LIBOR	0.01164	0.01270	0.01254	0.01322	0.01628	0.00464 (0.2137)
Combined	0.01022	0.01177	0.01182	0.01276	0.01753	**0.007306** **(0.0977)**
Panel C: Roll Estimator	Liquidity Portfolio					
Monetary Conditions Measure	Liquid	2	3	4	Illiquid	Illiquid–Liquid
BOE	0.00049	0.00112	0.00033	0.00159	0.00641	0.00592 (0.4749)
LIBOR	0.00966	0.00847	0.00869	0.00790	0.02026	0.01060 (0.1508)
Combined	0.01279	0.00664	0.00593	0.00979	0.02088	0.00809 (0.3370)

This table reports the coefficient, β from the following regression:

$$ret_t = \gamma + \beta \times Monetary\,Conditions_{t-1} + \varepsilon_t$$

Where ret_t is the equally-weighted return in month t either from a liquidity ranked quintile portfolio or from a portfolio long in the quintile of stocks with the lowest liquidity and short in the quintile of stocks with the highest liquidity (Illiquid–Liquid). For the monetary condition measures *Stance* and *Stringency*, *Monetary Conditions$_{t-1}$* is a dummy variable that is one in month $t-1$ when the monetary condition measure is *"Expansive"* and is zero when the measure is *"Restrictive."* For the monetary condition measure *Combined*, *Monetary Conditions$_{t-1}$* is a dummy variable that is one in month $t-1$ if the monetary condition is *"Expansive"* for both *Stance* and *Stringency* and is zero in other months. Newey-West p-values are reported in brackets for the low liquidity minus high liquidity portfolio, whereby bold figures denote statistically significant coefficient at least at 10% level. The bandwidth parameter for the Newey-West p-value is calculated using the Newey-West automatic lag selection. *Source: All data are obtained from Datastream.*

16.5 Conclusions

This study looks into monetary conditions and how they affect market liquidity and the illiquidity premium for different liquidity portfolios in the UK including the financial crisis period. We started our research by considering *unconditional returns*, where we find evidence similar to past research, such as Amihud and Mendelson (1986) to suggest that in general illiquid portfolios generate higher returns relative to liquid portfolios for all three liquidity measures. However, our research indicates that out of the three liquidity measures, only *Amihud* provided a monotonically increase in portfolio returns with decrease in liquidity, which is similar to Jensen and Moorman (2010).

Since our research is on the financial crisis, we felt that it is important to conduct a research on how monetary conditions affect *aggregate illiquidity (market liquidity)*. Generally speaking, our findings indicate that aggregate illiquidity decreases (market liquidity increases) when monetary conditions are expansive. Nevertheless, the results are generally not always significant[16] particularly for restrictive conditions.[17] This could be a result of the high liquidity of the UK market, as Dey (2005) stated that investors of developed markets may be less concerned with liquidity.

We also consider how monetary conditions affect the illiquidity premium and on most occasions, our findings revealed that illiquid portfolio returns are higher relative to liquid portfolio when monetary conditions are expansive compared to restrictive and the highest returns occurred when both stance and stringency are expansive. Our research also explored the uniformity of the changes in liquidity across liquidity quintiles and it generally shows that monetary condition changes have more effect on illiquid stocks relative to liquid stocks.

Our monthly event study found evidence to indicate that market liquidity increases after expansive shifts, but with some interruptions due to major events, such as the September 11 attacks in the US and the financial crisis. However, it is less noticeable during restrictive periods, signifying investors are less concerned with liquidity. The monthly event study on IML portfolio returns indicate that out of the three liquidity measures, only *Amihud* presents patterns that are consistent to past studies. The IML portfolio returns increase following expansive monetary shifts, signifying that illiquid stocks become more popular during expansive monetary conditions. As Rajan (2006) highlighted investors are willing to take

---

[16] We also did a stock migration investigation using Amihud as measure of liquidity but using quartiles instead of quintiles between January 1991 and December 2014. Basically, our investigation looks into stock migration from each quartile in year (t) (sorting year) to other quartiles in year ($t+1$) (performance year). The quartiles are only rebalanced annually meaning that stocks are held for at least 1 year. Our overall results show (not presented here to keep the number of tables as low as possible) that over the period, on average 78.45% of stocks remain in the same quartiles. This could be one of the reasons why our results are not always significant.

[17] Table 16.2 showed that there are more expansive periods compared to restrictive periods, which may be another reason for results that are not significant during restrictive periods.

more risks during high market liquidity, causing illiquid stock prices to increase. However, prior to the expansive monetary policy shifts, illiquid stocks became less popular signifying "flight-to-liquidity."

Using three different liquidity measures, we also obtained evidence to suggest that the three measures capture different aspects of liquidity since there can be some divergence on the results obtained. Our research shows that out of the three measures, *Amihud* seems to produce the most consistent results. Interestingly, we also discovered that the aggregate illiquidity and IML portfolio have different reaction toward BOE base rate and LIBOR. It shows that investors who are concerned with IML portfolio and aggregate illiquidity should focus on BOE decisions and LIBOR respectively. Nevertheless, it can be deducted that when there is an intersection between the two monetary conditions, the reaction is stronger.

In conclusion, our evidence generally shows that illiquid portfolios are found to supersede liquid stocks returns. Market liquidity, stock prices, and illiquidity premium are affected by changes in monetary conditions but interestingly enough, it seems that stringency (LIBOR) is more effective than stance (BOE base rate). However, in the long run, the monthly event study did show the usefulness of stance. This justifies the intervention of central banks or monetary authority when required during the financial crisis.

Nevertheless, in comparison to Jensen and Moorman (2010), we obtained weaker evidence probably due to the shorter data sample as well as the different characteristics of the UK market compared to the US market. According to Bartram et al. (2012), the UK market is less volatile compared to the US market considering companies with similar characteristics. A higher level of volatility will definitely affect prices and consequently market liquidity (Hameed et al., 2010; Stoll, 1978; Vayanos, 2004).[18]

References

Acharya, V.V., Pedersen, L.H., 2005. Asset pricing with liquidity risk. J. Financ. Econ. 77 (2), 375–410.

Amihud, Y., 2002. Illiquidity and stock returns: cross-section and time-series effects. J. Financ. Markets 5 (1), 31–56.

Amihud, Y., Mendelson, H., 1986. Asset pricing and the bid-ask spread. J. Financ. Econ. 17 (2), 223–249.

Amihud, Y., Mendelson, H., 1989. The effects of beta, bid-ask spread, residual risk, and size on stock returns. J. Finance 44 (2), 479–486.

---

[18] Stoll (1978) showed that bid-ask spreads (illiquidity) are positively affected by return volatility. Vayanos (2004) discovered that during volatile times, investors reduce their willingness to hold illiquid assets, illiquidity premia increase followed by market betas of illiquid assets. Hameed et al. (2010) mentioned that negative market returns decrease stock liquidity, with the effect being strongest for high volatility firms and during times of market funding tightness. Hameed et al. (2010) also document that market volatility affect liquidity commonality positively. Overall, it shows that there is a relationship between volatility and illiquidity and due to the difference in market volatility between the UK and the US, it would result in different findings for us compared to Jensen and Moorman (2010).

Amihud, Y., Mendelson, H., Pedersen, L.H., 2005. Liquidity and asset prices. Foundations Trends Finance 1 (4), 269–364.

Bajaj, V., 2008. Financial crisis enters new phase. Available from: http://www.nytimes.com/2008/09/18/business/18markets.html?pagewanted=all&_r=0

Bank-of-England, 2014a. Monetary Policy Committee (MPC). Available from: http://www.bankofengland.co.uk/monetarypolicy/Pages/overview.aspx

Bank-of-England, 2014b. Monetary Policy Committee Decisions. Available from: http://www.bankofengland.co.uk/monetarypolicy/Pages/decisions.aspx

Bartram, S.M., Brown, G., Stulz, R.M., 2012. Why are US stocks more volatile? J. Finance 67 (4), 1329–1370.

Bekaert, G., Hoerova, M., Lo Duca, M., 2013. Risk, uncertainty and monetary policy. J. Monetary Econ. 60 (7), 771–788.

Ben-Rephael, A., Kadan, O., Wohl, A., 2008. The diminishing liquidity premium. CFS Working Paper, http://nbn-resolving.de/urn:nbn:de:hebis:30-62317.

Board-of-Governors-of-the-Federal-Reserve-System, 2014. Federal Open Market Committee. Available from: http://www.federalreserve.gov/monetarypolicy/fomc.htm

Brennan, M., Huh, S.W., Subrahmanyam, A., 2013. An analysis of the Amihud illiquidity premium. Rev. Asset Pricing Studies 3 (1), 133–176.

Brennan, M.J., Subrahmanyam, A., 1996. Market microstructure and asset pricing: on the compensation for illiquidity in stock returns. J. Financ. Econ. 41 (3), 441–464.

Browning, E.S., 2011. Downgrade Ignites a Global Selloff. Available from: http://online.wsj.com/articles/SB10001424053111904007304576496631521538522

Brunnermeier, M.K., 2009. Deciphering the liquidity and credit crunch 2007-2008. J. Econ. Perspect. 23 (1), 77–100.

Brunnermeier, M.K., Pedersen, L.H., 2009. Market liquidity and funding liquidity. Rev. Financ. Studies 22 (6), 2201–2238.

Chordia, T., Roll, R., Subrahmanyam, A., 2001. Market liquidity and trading activity. J. Finance 56 (2), 501–530.

Chordia, T., Sarkar, A., Subrahmanyam, A., 2005. An empirical analysis of stock and bond market liquidity. Rev. Financ. Studies 18 (1), 85–129.

Clifford, C., Chris, I., 2008. The Fall of IndyMac. Available from: http://money.cnn.com/2008/07/12/news/companies/indymac_fdic/

Corwin, S.A., Schultz, P., 2012. A simple way to estimate bid-ask spreads from daily high and low prices. J. Finance 67 (2), 719–760.

Crotty, J., 2009. Structural causes of the global financial crisis: a critical assessment of the 'new financial architecture'. Cambridge J. Econ. 33 (4), 563–580.

Datar, V.T., Naik, N.Y., Radcliffe, R., 1998. Liquidity and stock returns: an alternative test. J. Financ. Markets 1 (2), 203–219.

Detrixhe, J., 2011. US Loses AAA Credit Rating as S&P Slams Debt Levels, Political Process. Available from: http://www.bloomberg.com/news/2011-08-06/u-s-credit-rating-cut-by-s-p-for-first-time-on-deficit-reduction-accord.html

Detrixhe, J., Katz, I., 2014. US Credit Rating Affirmed by S&P with Stable Outlook. Available from: http://www.bloomberg.com/news/2014-06-06/u-s-sovereign-credit-rating-affirmed-by-s-p-with-stable-outlook.html

Dey, M.K., 2005. Turnover and return in global stock markets. Emerg. Markets Rev. 6 (1), 45–67.

ECB, 2010. The ECB'S Monetary Policy Stance During the Financial Crisis. Available from: https://www.ecb.europa.eu/pub/pdf/other/art1_mb201001en_pp63-71en.pdf

Eleswarapu, V.R., Reinganum, M.R., 1993. The seasonal behavior of the liquidity premium in asset pricing. J. Financ. Econ. 34 (3), 373–386.

Fama, E.F., French, K.R., 1989. Business conditions and expected returns on stocks and bonds. J. Financ. Econ. 25 (1), 23–49.

Fernández-Amador, O., Gächter, M., Larch, M., Peter, G., 2013. Does monetary policy determine stock market liquidity? New evidence from the Euro zone. J. Empir. Finance 21, 54–68.

Fujimoto, A., 2004. Macroeconomic Sources of Systematic Liquidity. Unpublished Working Paper, University of Alberta.

Galariotis, E.C., Giouvris, E., 2007. Liquidity commonality in the London stock exchange. J. Bus. Finance Account. 34 (1–2), 374–388.

Goldman, D., 2009. GE Loses Top Rating in Downgrade. Available from: http://money.cnn.com/2009/03/12/news/companies/ge_credit_downgrade/index.htm?iid=EL

Goyenko, R.Y., Holden, C.W., Trzcinka, C.A., 2009. Do liquidity measures measure liquidity? J. Financ. Econ. 92 (2), 153–181.

Goyenko, R.Y., Ukhov, A.D., 2009. Stock and bond market liquidity: a long-run empirical analysis. J. Financ. Quant. Anal. 44 (01), 189–212.

Hameed, A., Kang, W., Viswanathan, S., 2010. Stock market declines and liquidity. J. Finance 65 (1), 257–293.

Jensen, G.R., Mercer, J.M., Johnson, R.R., 1996. Business conditions, monetary policy, and expected security returns. J. Financ. Econ. 40 (2), 213–237.

Jensen, G.R., Moorman, T., 2010. Inter-temporal variation in the illiquidity premium. J. Financ. Econ. 98 (2), 338–358.

Kacperczyk, M., Schnabl, P., 2010. When safe proved risky: commercial paper during the financial crisis of 2007-2009. J. Econ. Perspect. 24 (1), 29–50.

Keogh, B., 2008. Immelt Fights to Keep GE's AAA as Cost of Cut Surges (Update4). Available from: http://www.bloomberg.com/apps/news?pid=newsarchive&sid=a59gngOiy2c8&refer=us

Kiyotaki, N., Moore, J., 2012. Liquidity, Business Cycles, and Monetary Policy. National Bureau of Economic Research. Working Paper.

Luhby, T., 2008. US Plan to Save Fannie and Freddie. Available from: http://money.cnn.com/2008/07/13/news/economy/fannie_freddie_sunday/index.htm?postversion=2008071405

Maddaloni, A., Peydró, J.L., 2013. Monetary policy, macroprudential policy, and banking stability: evidence from the euro area. Int. J. Central Banking 9 (1), 121–169.

McAndrews, J., Potter, S., 2002. Liquidity effects of the events of September 11, 2001. Econ. Policy Rev. 8 (2.).

Pastor, L., Stambaugh, R.F., 2003. Liquidity risk and expected stock returns. J. Polit. Econ. 111 (3), 642–685.

Rajan, R.G., 2006. Has finance made the world riskier? Eur. Financ. Manag. 12 (4), 499–533.

Roll, R., 1984. A simple implicit measure of the effective bid-ask spread in an efficient market. J. Finance 39 (4), 1127–1139.

Söderberg, J., 2008. Do Macroeconomic Variables Forecast Changes in Liquidity? An Out-of-Sample Study on the Order-Driven Stock Markets in Scandinavia. Paper Presented at the CESifo Conference Centre, Munich.

Stoll, H.R., 1978. The supply of dealer services in securities markets. J. Finance 33 (4), 1133–1151.

StreetInsider.com, 2014. S&P Affirms GE (GE) at 'AA+/A-1+'; Comments on Alstom Bid. Available from: http://www.streetinsider.com/Credit+Ratings/S%26P+Affirms+GE+(GE)+at+AA%2BA-1%2B%3B+Comments+on+Alstom+Bid/9425802.html

Thorbecke, W., 1997. On stock market returns and monetary policy. J. Finance 52 (2), 635–654.

Vayanos, D., 2004. Flight to Quality, Flight to Liquidity, and the Pricing of Risk. National Bureau of Economic Research, Working Paper.

Zibel, A., 2008. Q&A: What is Libor, and How Does it Affect You? Available from: http://www.seattletimes.com/business/qa-what-is-libor-and-how-does-it-affect-you/

CHAPTER 17

Herding in the Athens Stock Exchange During Different Crisis Periods

Fotini Economou

Centre of Planning and Economic Research, Athens, Greece

Chapter Outline

17.1 Introduction

Crisis periods are expected to facilitate or even generate market anomalies and significant deviations from stock market efficiency with important implications for optimum asset allocation, portfolio diversification, and financial stability in general (Economou et al., 2016). Herd behavior in financial markets, that is, imitation in the investment decision making process resulting in correlated trading behavior (Bikhchandani et al., 1992; Hirshleifer and Teoh, 2003), is expected to emerge particularly during crisis periods when individual investors prefer to follow the market consensus despite of their own personal information and beliefs (Chang et al., 2000; Christie and Huang, 1995).

Herding has been extensively examined in different contexts internationally (stock market, bond market, derivatives market, commodities market, exchange rates, mutual funds, hedge funds etc.), referring to institutional investors, analysts, individual investors, and financial markets both in developed and emerging/frontier markets (Chen, 2013; Chiang and Zheng, 2010; Chiang et al., 2010; Economou, 2016b; Economou et al., 2011, 2015; Mobarek et al., 2014; Tan et al., 2008). This behavior may be either rational when it refers to limited knowledge or reputation and compensation based motives (Devenow and Welch, 1996;

303

Economou et al., 2015) or irrational when it is driven by sentiment (Christie and Huang, 1995; Hwang and Salmon, 2004). Spurious herding may even exist in case of correlated trading patterns resulting from either common available information or common investment strategies (Bikhchandani and Sharma, 2000; Gavriilidis et al., 2013).[1]

In this paper, we examine herding in the Athens Stock Exchange (ASE) for a large time period, from January 1998 to May 2016, covering different crises. Fig. 17.1 presents the evolution of the ATHEX Composite index for the period under examination, which reached its maximum value on September 17, 1999 and its minimum value on February 11, 2016. The ASE is a small stock market in terms of market value with low trading volume and high market volatility. The market was characterized as a developed one since 2001. It was under review for downgrade by MSCI since June 2012, and in November 2013 it was downgraded to the emerging market status. Total ASE capitalization closed up at €39.87 billion in May 2016 from €110.11 billion in May 2001, while the participation of foreign investors has significantly increased reaching 60.31% of the total ASE capitalization from 21.62% in May 2001, according to the ASE Monthly Statistics Bulletins. The ASE provides an interesting analysis setting having experienced several crisis periods including the 1999 bubble and the subsequent crash, the global financial crisis as well as the ongoing Greek debt crisis and the imposed capital controls since June 2015.

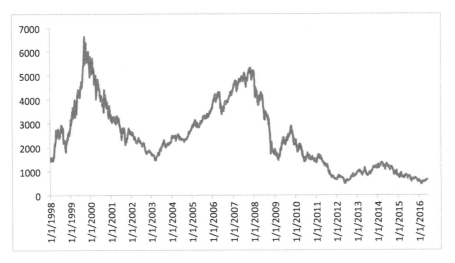

Figure 17.1: The Evolution of the ATHEX Composite Index (January 1998–May 2016).
Thomson Reuters Eikon Database

---

[1] See Spyrou (2013) for a comprehensive review of theoretical and empirical findings on herding.

Caporale et al. (2008) examined herding in the ASE for the period 1998–2007 providing empirical evidence of herding, especially during up market days. The authors were the first to document herding during the 1999 bubble also indicating the short-term nature of the phenomenon being better captured by daily data instead of weekly or monthly. In the same spirit, Tessaromatis and Thomas (2009) confirmed the existence of herding in the ASE from 1998 to 2004. Economou et al. (2011) further examined the ASE along with other three South European stock markets, that is, Italy, Spain, and Portugal, from 1998 to 2008. The authors tested for herding asymmetries under different market states and potential cross market herding effects. The empirical results indicated increased herding on days with positive market returns and no evidence of asymmetry regarding market volatility and trading volume for the period under examination. Mobarek et al. (2014) also tested for herding in European stock markets for the period 2001–12 identifying herding in the ASE during the Eurozone crisis (May 2010–February 2012). Messis and Zapranis (2014) confirmed herding in the ASE from 1998 to 2003, as well as from early 2008 to April 2010 (the last month of their sample) employing the state space model of Hwang and Salmon (2004). Recently, Economou et al. (2016) examined herding in the ASE from January 2007 to May 2015 documenting the impact of size effect on herding estimations. When testing for asymmetries, they identified stronger herding in down market, high market volatility, high trading volume, and low 10-year sovereign bond spread days. Finally, Economou (2016a) tested for herding in the ASE for the period 2004–15 taking into consideration the impact of trading volume on herding estimations. The author identified herding asymmetry regarding investor sentiment providing evidence of herding on days with increased uncertainty, as it is captured by the KEPE GRIV implied volatility index.

In this paper, we extend previous literature regarding herding in the ASE providing empirical results that cover a long period (January 1998–May 2016), as well as endogenously defined subperiods applying the cross-sectional dispersion approach of Chang et al. (2000). We test for herding under different market states with reference to market performance, market volatility, trading volume, liquidity, and the 10-year sovereign bond spread. Moreover, we augment the traditional Chang et al. (2000) model with a liquidity factor. We compare the empirical findings during different crisis periods and come up with interesting conclusions regarding investor behavior in the ASE. Finally, we test for the impact of the imposed capital controls since June 2015. The results have practical implications for asset allocation, international diversification and potential spill-over effects, especially in the light of recent empirical findings documenting that herding behavior contributed to different bubbles and crises in the US stock market, even in the global financial crisis (Litimi et al., 2016).

The rest of the paper is structured as follows: Section 17.2 describes the employed methodology and data, Section 17.3 reports the empirical results, while Section 17.4 concludes.

17.2 Methodology and Data

The cross-sectional dispersion approach proposed by the seminal papers of Christie and Huang (1995) and Chang et al. (2000) has been widely used in order to examine herding behavior in the financial markets.

The first step is to calculate a quite simple but intuitive measure of dispersion of the individual equity returns with reference to the market return, which was initially proposed by Christie and Huang (1995) and it is calculated as follows:

$$CSAD_t = \frac{\sum_{k=1}^{N} \left| R_{i,t} - R_{m,t} \right|}{N} \tag{17.1}$$

where $R_{i,t}$ is the return of equity i on day t, $R_{m,t}$ is the market return, that is, the equally weighted average return of all the individual equities on day t and N is the number of all listed equities in the market on day t. Highly correlated trades are expected result in lower CSAD levels. However, this is not enough to identify herding behavior.

Chang et al. (2000) tried to capture herding behavior using a nonlinear model that estimates the relationship between the CSAD and the market return as follows:

$$CSAD_t = \gamma_0 + \gamma_1 \left| R_{m,t} \right| + \gamma_2 R_{m,t}^2 + u_t \tag{17.2}$$

where $CSAD_t$ is the cross-sectional absolute deviation of the individual equity returns on day t and $R_{m,t}$ is the market return on day t. According to the rational asset pricing models, the estimated relationship is expected to be linear and increasing, that is, coefficient γ_1 is expected to be positive and statistically significant, since individual equities display different betas (sensitivity) with reference to the market return. A nonlinear negative relationship, that is, a negative and statistically significant coefficient γ_2, implies the existence of herding behavior under extreme market conditions. In this case, the CSAD measure increases but at a decreasing rate. This empirical finding is enough to document herding in the stock market under examination.

Eq. (17.2) is then reestimated for several subperiods that cover different crises in the ASE, since herding behavior may significantly differ testing for different crisis periods (Galariotis et al., 2015). In fact, we have endogenously identified four statistically significant structural breaks, that is, 25/9/2000, 24/6/2004, 12/9/2008, and 26/9/2011 employing the multiple breakpoint Bai-Perron tests (Bai and Perron, 1998, 2003). In this way, we avoid defining our subperiods in an arbitrary or subjective manner.

---

[2] On 15/9/2008, Lehman Brothers went bankrupt.

In fact, the identified structural breaks coincide with significant changes in the ASE. The first subperiod (2/1/1998–25/9/2000) covers the 1999 bubble in the ASE, that is, a period of explosive returns, as well as the subsequent burst of the stock market bubble. During this period, the ASE attracted many retail investors that experienced significant losses. The collapse began in September 1999, and continued over the following few years. The second subperiod (26/9/2000–24/6/2004) covers the significant down turn that followed the 1999 bubble. The ATHEX Composite index reached 1,467.3 units on 31/3/2003 from its record high of 6,633.92 on 17/9/1999 (Fig. 17.1). On the other hand, the third subperiod (25/6/2004–12/9/2008) covers the upward trend of the ASE up to the outbreak of the global financial crisis.[2] The ATHEX Composite index reached its highest value for the period on 31/10/2007 (5,334.5 units). The fourth subperiod (13/9/2008–26/9/2011) covers the significant stock market losses of the global financial crisis up to 2009, as well as the beginning of the European sovereign debt crisis and the Greek sovereign debt crisis. On 8/8/2011, the ATHEX Composite index fell below 1,000 units. The last subperiod (27/9/2011–31/5/2016) covers the escalation of the ongoing Greek debt crisis, as well as the imposed capital controls since June 2015. The main characteristics of this period are the increased uncertainty and lack of trust in the financial system in general.

Moreover, we test for asymmetric herding behavior under different market states employing a single model equation in line with previous literature (Chiang and Zheng, 2010; Economou et al., 2011). To begin with, we employ a dummy variable to differentiate between days of positive and negative market returns as follows:

$$CSAD_t = \gamma_0 + \gamma_1 D^{up} \left| R_{m,t} \right| + \gamma_2 (1 - D^{up}) \left| R_{m,t} \right| + \gamma_3 D^{up} R_{m,t}^2 + \gamma_4 (1 - D^{up}) R_{m,t}^2 + u_t \qquad (17.3)$$

where D^{up} is a dummy variable that takes the value 1 on days with positive market returns and 0 otherwise.

In the same spirit, we test for asymmetric herding behavior with reference to market volatility, trading volume, average equity liquidity, and the Greek 10-year sovereign bond spread as follows in Eqs. (17.4), (17.5), (17.6), and (17.7), respectively:

$$CSAD_t = \gamma_0 + \gamma_1 D^{up\,vlt} \left| R_{m,t} \right| + \gamma_2 (1 - D^{up\,vlt}) \left| R_{m,t} \right| + \gamma_3 D^{up\,vlt} R_{m,t}^2 + \gamma_4 (1 - D^{up\,vlt}) R_{m,t}^2 + u_t \qquad (17.4)$$

where $D^{up\,vlt}$ is a dummy variable that takes the value 1 on days with high market volatility and 0 otherwise.

$$CSAD_t = \gamma_0 + \gamma_1 D^{up\,vol} \left| R_{m,t} \right| + \gamma_2 (1 - D^{up\,vol}) \left| R_{m,t} \right| + \gamma_3 D^{up\,vol} R_{m,t}^2 + \gamma_4 (1 - D^{up\,vol}) R_{m,t}^2 + u_t \qquad (17.5)$$

where $D^{up\,vol}$ is a dummy variable that takes the value 1 on days with high market trading volume and 0 otherwise.

$$CSAD_t = \gamma_0 + \gamma_1 D^{up\,liq} \left| R_{m,t} \right| + \gamma_2 (1 - D^{up\,liq}) \left| R_{m,t} \right| + \gamma_3 D^{up\,liq} R_{m,t}^2 + \gamma_4 (1 - D^{up\,liq}) R_{m,t}^2 + u_t \qquad (17.6)$$

where D^{upliq} is a dummy variable that takes the value 1 on days with high average equity liquidity and 0 otherwise.

$$CSAD_t = \gamma_0 + \gamma_1 D^{up\,spr} |R_{m,t}| + \gamma_2 (1 - D^{up\,spr}) |R_{m,t}| + \gamma_3 D^{up\,spr} R^2_{m,t} + \gamma_4 (1 - D^{up\,spr})$$
$$R^2_{m,t} + u_t \tag{17.7}$$

where D^{upspr} is a dummy variable that takes the value 1 on days with high 10-year Greek bonds spread and 0 otherwise.

As far as equity liquidity is concerned, we use the Amihud (2002) illiquidity measure modified according to Karolyi et al. (2012) in order to measure liquidity instead of illiquidity, in line with Galariotis et al. (2016). In fact, the liquidity measure is calculated as follows:

$$Liq_{i,t} = -\log\left(1 + |R_{i,t}| / \left(P_{i,t} VO_{i,t}\right)\right) \tag{17.8}$$

where $P_{i,t}$ is the closing price of equity i on day t and $VO_{i,t}$ is the trading volume of equity i on day t. We then obtain the average equity liquidity in the market as follows:

$$Liq_{m,t} = \frac{\sum_{k=1}^{N} Liq_{i,t}}{N} \tag{17.9}$$

In order to define high market volatility, volume, average equity liquidity, and spread days we compare the variable's value on day t with the previous 30-day moving average. When it is higher, the relative dummy variable takes the value 1 and 0 otherwise. If herding asymmetries are present, we expect coefficients γ_3 and γ_4 to have a statistically significant difference in Eqs. (17.3)–(17.7). These equations have also been reestimated for the five subperiods previously identified. We also employ the Wald test in order to test for the hypothesis H_0: $\gamma_3 = \gamma_4$. Even though the results in the empirical literature are not unanimous, relevant studies have identified herding being more pronounced on days with either up (Economou et al., 2011) or down market returns (Chiang and Zheng, 2010; Economou et al., 2016; Mobarek et al., 2014) depending on the market and time period under examination, high market volatility and trading volume (Economou et al., 2011, 2016; Tan et al., 2008), high average equity liquidity in the market (Galariotis et al., 2016), and low spread (Economou et al., 2016).

Moreover, we augment the traditional Chang et al. (2000) model with the average equity liquidity factor as follows:

$$CSAD_t = \gamma_0 + \gamma_1 |R_{m,t}| + \gamma_2 R^2_{m,t} + \gamma_3 Liq_{m,t} + u_t \tag{17.10}$$

Eq. (17.10) is calculated both for the whole period under examination, as well as for the five subperiods defined earlier.

Finally, we test for the impact of the imposed capital controls in the Greek banking system since June 26, 2015. To this end we employ a dummy variable $D^{cap.control}$ that takes the value 1 since 3/8/2015, when the ASE opened after the imposition of capital controls in June 2015 and the subsequent stock market trading suspension. The relevant equation is structured as follows:

$$CSAD_t = \gamma_0 + \gamma_1(1 - D^{cap.control})\left|R_{m,t}\right| + \gamma_2 D^{cap.control}\left|R_{m,t}\right| + \gamma_3(1 - D^{cap.control})$$
$$R_{m,t}^2 + \gamma_4 D^{cap.control} R_{m,t}^2 + u_t \tag{17.11}$$

17.2.1 Data

In order to examine herding during different crisis periods, we construct a survivor bias free dataset that includes both active and dead stocks at any time from January 1998 to May 2016. Daily returns for all listed equities are calculated as follows:

$$R_{i,t} = 100 \times (\ln(P_{i,t}) / \ln(P_{i,t-1})) \tag{17.12}$$

where $P_{i,t}$ is the daily closing price of every stock i on day t. We derive data on closing prices and trading volume from the Thomson Reuters Eikon database. We also calculate the equally weighted market portfolio return $R_{m,t}$, which is needed to calculate the CSAD measure in Eq. (17.1). It has to be mentioned that we only employ stocks that displayed trading activity on day t in order to reduce the impact of thin trading that may result in biased herding estimations. As a result, the sample size of active stocks ranges between 73 and 340 stocks during the period under examination.

Table 17.1 reports the descriptive statistics for the whole sample period as well as for the five endogenously derived subperiods. The whole sample period (2/1/1998–31/5/2016) consists of 4,564 daily observations. The first subperiod that includes the 1999 bubble (2/1/1998–25/9/2000) displays the highest average daily return (+0.3063%). This was a period of significant market fluctuations also displaying the highest standard deviation of returns (2.734%). On the other hand, the lowest average daily return is reported for the fourth subperiod 13/9/2008–26/9/2011 (−0.1671%), while the lowest daily standard deviation is reported for the third subperiod 25/6/2004–12/9/2008 (1.2264%).

17.3 Empirical Results

Table 17.2 reports the results of the standard Chang et al. (2000) model for the whole period under examination and the five endogenously defined subperiods. All estimations were derived using Newey and West (1987) heteroscedasticity and autocorrelation consistent standard errors. Coefficient γ_1 is positive and statistically significant in all cases consistent with rational asset pricing models. There is evidence of herding, that is, negative and statistically significant coefficient γ_2, for the subperiods 2/1/1998–25/9/2000 and 26/9/2000–24/6/2004. Herding is more pronounced during the first subperiod that includes the 1999 bubble.

Table 17.1: Descriptive statistics.

	2/1/1998–31/5/2016		2/1/1998–25/9/2000		26/9/2000–24/6/2004		25/6/2004–12/9/2008		13/9/2008–26/9/2011		27/9/2011–31/5/2016	
	CSAD	Market return	CSAD	Market return	CSAD	Market return	CSAD	Market return	CSAD	Market return	CSAD	Market return
Mean	2.6253	0.0094	2.6635	0.3063	1.9280	−0.1486	1.9761	−0.0017	2.7477	−0.1671	3.6984	0.0883
Median	2.4598	0.0680	2.6298	0.4648	1.8300	−0.1575	1.9150	0.0757	2.6753	−0.0829	3.5786	0.1684
Maximum	10.0215	10.0683	5.3126	8.4553	3.9026	7.2592	3.7207	5.4071	6.2249	10.0683	10.0215	6.0790
Minimum	0.8029	−16.8049	0.8029	−9.8808	1.1174	−10.1654	1.2515	−7.6840	1.7501	−12.3454	2.1262	−16.8049
Standard Deviation	0.9201	1.8885	0.6576	2.7340	0.4845	1.9911	0.3574	1.2264	0.4970	1.7742	0.8471	1.7303
Observations	4,564	4,564	685	685	930	930	1,057	1,057	759	759	1,133	1,133

Table 17.2: Estimation of the Chang et al. (2000) model.

	2/1/1998–31/5/2016		2/1/1998–25/9/2000		26/9/2000–24/6/2004		25/6/2004–12/9/2008		13/9/2008–26/9/2011		27/9/2011–31/5/2016	
	Coefficient	p-value	Coefficient	p-value	Coefficient	p-value	Coefficient	p-value	Coefficient	p-value	Coefficient	p-value
γ_0	2.309[a]	0.00	2.469[a]	0.00	1.547[a]	0.00	1.742[a]	0.00	2.407[a]	0.00	3.169[a]	0.00
γ_1	0.260[a]	0.00	0.233[a]	0.00	0.287[a]	0.00	0.269[a]	0.00	0.262[a]	0.00	0.432[a]	0.00
γ_2	−0.008	0.50	−0.038[a]	0.00	−0.010[b]	0.06	0.000	0.99	0.003	0.36	−0.001	0.67
Adj-R^2	9.93%		5.56%		43.02%		42.26%		50.78%		37.70%	

Notes: Estimation of the model: $CSAD_t = \gamma_0 + \gamma_1|R_{m,t}| + \gamma_2 R^2_{m,t} + u_t$, where $CSAD_t$ is the cross-sectional absolute deviation of the individual stock returns on day t and $R_{m,t}$ is the market return on day t. All estimations are given using Newey and West (1987) heteroscedasticity and autocorrelation consistent standard errors.
[a]Indicates significance levels of 1%, respectively.
[b]Indicates significance levels of 10%, respectively.

The empirical results regarding asymmetric herding effects shed light into investor behavior under different market states. To begin with, there is evidence of herding during positive market return days for the whole sample as well as for the subperiods 2/1/1998–25/9/2000 and 26/9/2000–24/6/2004 (Table 17.3). For the first sub–period, there is also evidence of herding during down market days with herding being more pronounced on up market days as confirmed by means of Wald test. Moreover, there is evidence of herding

Table 17.3: Estimation of the Chang et al. (2000) model during periods of up and down market returns.

	2/1/1998–31/5/2016		2/1/1998–25/9/2000		26/9/2000–24/6/2004		25/6/2004–12/9/2008		13/9/2008–26/9/2011		27/9/2011–31/5/2016	
	Coefficient	p-value	Coefficient	p-value	Coefficient	p-value	Coefficient	p-value	Coefficient	p-value	Coefficient	p-value
γ_0	2.267[a]	0.00	2.448[a]	0.00	1.545[a]	0.00	1.746[a]	0.00	2.412[a]	0.00	3.194[a]	0.00
γ_1	0.425[a]	0.00	0.340[a]	0.00	0.322[a]	0.00	0.276[a]	0.00	0.250[a]	0.00	0.324[a]	0.00
γ_2	0.231[a]	0.00	0.147[b]	0.01	0.266[a]	0.00	0.223[a]	0.00	0.258[a]	0.00	0.471[a]	0.00
γ_3	−0.047[a]	0.00	−0.061[a]	0.00	−0.016[c]	0.05	0.014[c]	0.08	0.010[b]	0.01	0.022	0.13
γ_4	0.000	0.99	−0.020[b]	0.02	−0.007	0.24	0.005	0.26	0.001	0.70	−0.004[b]	0.05
Adj-R^2	11.12%		8.11%		43.25%		43.68%		51.16%		38.22%	
Wald test: H_0: $\gamma_3 = \gamma_4$												
$\gamma_3 - \gamma_4$	−0.047[a]		−0.041[a]		−0.008		0.009		0.009[c]		0.026[c]	
Standard error	0.015		0.010		0.009		0.007		0.005		0.014	

Notes: Estimation of the model: $CSAD_t = \gamma_0 + \gamma_1 D^{up}|R_{m,t}| + \gamma_2(1-D^{up})|R_{m,t}| + \gamma_3 D^{up}R^2_{m,t} + \gamma_4(1-D^{up})R^2_{m,t} + u_t$, where $CSAD_t$ is the cross-sectional absolute deviation of the individual stock returns on day t, $R_{m,t}$ is the market return on day t and D^{up} is a dummy variable that takes the value 1 on days with positive market returns and 0 otherwise. See also Notes to Table 17.2.
[a]Indicates significance levels of 1%, respectively.
[b]Indicates significance levels of 5%, respectively.
[c]Indicates significance levels of 10%, respectively.

during down market return days for the recent Greek debt crisis period 27/9/2011–31/5/2016.

Further testing for asymmetries, we identify herding during down volatility days for the whole sample period and herding during high volatility days for the highly volatile period of 2/1/1998–25/9/2000 (Table 17.4). Moreover, there is evidence of herding during high market volume days for the whole sample period and the first three subperiods (2/1/1998–25/9/2000, 26/9/2000–24/6/2004, and 25/6/2004–12/9/2008) (Table 17.5). For the first subperiod, there is also evidence of herding during down market trading volume days with herding being more pronounced on high volume days as confirmed by means of Wald test. As far as average equity liquidity is concerned, there is evidence of herding on high liquidity days for the whole period and the first two subperiods (2/1/1998–25/9/2000, 26/9/2000–24/6/2004), as well as on down liquidity days during 27/9/2011–31/5/2016 (Table 17.6). For the first subperiod, there is also evidence of herding during down liquidity days but the coefficients' difference is not statistically significant. Consequently, there was herding during both up and down average equity liquidity during 2/1/1998–25/9/2000. Finally, there is evidence of herding during down spread days for the whole period and for the 2/1/1998–25/9/2000 period (Table 17.7). Empirical results also indicate herding during high spread days for the 26/9/2000–24/6/2004 period.

Table 17.4: Estimation of the Chang et al. (2000) model during periods of up and down market volatility.

	2/1/1998–31/5/2016		2/1/1998–25/9/2000		26/9/2000–24/6/2004		25/6/2004–12/9/2008		13/9/2008–26/9/2011		27/9/2011–31/5/2016	
	Coefficient	p-value	Coefficient	p-value	Coefficient	p-value	Coefficient	p-value	Coefficient	p-value	Coefficient	p-value
γ_0	2.247[a]	0.00	2.571[a]	0.00	1.514[a]	0.00	1.760[a]	0.00	2.347[a]	0.00	3.130[a]	0.00
γ_1	0.268[a]	0.00	0.221[a]	0.00	0.289[a]	0.00	0.262[a]	0.00	0.263[a]	0.00	0.412[a]	0.00
γ_2	0.435[a]	0.00	0.095	0.38	0.368[a]	0.00	0.195[a]	0.01	0.399[a]	0.00	0.437[a]	0.00
γ_3	−0.007	0.54	−0.039[a]	0.00	−0.009	0.12	0.000	0.92	0.004	0.29	0.001	0.49
γ_4	−0.057[b]	0.10	−0.004	0.91	−0.033	0.14	0.039	0.29	−0.009	0.79	0.085	0.24
Adj-R^2	10.15%		5.69%		43.12%		42.25%		52.10%		38.99%	
	Wald test: H_0: $\gamma_3 = \gamma_4$											
$\gamma_3 - \gamma_4$	0.050[b]		−0.035		0.024		−0.039		0.013		−0.084	
Standard error	0.027		0.028		0.022		0.035		0.033		0.072	

Notes: Estimation of the model: $CSAD_t = \gamma_0 + \gamma_1 D^{up\,vlt}|R_{m,t}| + \gamma_2(1 - D^{up\,vlt})|R_{m,t}| + \gamma_3 D^{up\,vlt} R^2_{m,t} + \gamma_4(1 - D^{up\,vlt})R^2_{m,t} + u_t$, where $CSAD_t$ is the cross-sectional absolute deviation of the individual stock returns on day t, $R_{m,t}$ is the market return on day t, and $D^{up\,vlt}$ is a dummy variable that takes the value 1 on days with high market volatility and 0 otherwise. See also Notes to Table 17.2.
[a]Indicates significance levels of 1%, respectively.
[b]Indicates significance levels of 10%, respectively.

Table 17.5: Estimation of the Chang et al. (2000) model during periods of up and down market trading volume.

	2/1/1998–31/5/2016		2/1/1998–25/9/2000		26/9/2000–24/6/2004		25/6/2004–12/9/2008		13/9/2008–26/9/2011		27/9/2011–31/5/2016	
	Coefficient	p-value	Coefficient	p-value	Coefficient	p-value	Coefficient	p-value	Coefficient	p-value	Coefficient	p-value
γ_0	2.327[a]	0.00	2.517[a]	0.00	1.589[a]	0.00	1.761[a]	0.00	2.423[a]	0.00	3.182[a]	0.00
γ_1	0.358[a]	0.00	0.355[a]	0.00	0.341[a]	0.00	0.317[a]	0.00	0.269[a]	0.00	0.472[a]	0.00
γ_2	0.156[b]	0.02	0.098[b]	0.05	0.140[a]	0.00	0.151[a]	0.00	0.208[a]	0.00	0.378[a]	0.00
γ_3	−0.021[b]	0.01	−0.057[a]	0.00	−0.019[a]	0.00	−0.009[b]	0.04	0.002	0.56	−0.007	0.24
γ_4	0.002	0.91	−0.021[a]	0.01	0.018[b]	0.04	0.035[a]	0.00	0.016	0.13	0.002	0.24
Adj-R^2	11.42%		10.74%		46.55%		44.19%		50.89%		37.97%	
	Wald test: H_0: $\gamma_3 = \gamma_4$											
$\gamma_3 - \gamma_4$ Standard error	−0.023 0.015		−0.036[a] 0.011		−0.037[a] 0.009		−0.044[a] 0.009		−0.014 0.011		-0.009 0.006	

Notes: Estimation of the model: $CSAD_t = \gamma_0 + \gamma_1 D^{up\,vol}|R_{m,t}| + \gamma_2(1 - D^{up\,vol})|R_{m,t}| + \gamma_3 D^{up\,vol}R_{m,t}^2 + \gamma_4(1 - D^{up\,vol})R_{m,t}^2 + u_t$, where $CSAD_t$ is the cross-sectional absolute deviation of the individual stock returns on day t, $R_{m,t}$ is the market return on day t, and $D^{up\,vol}$ is a dummy variable that takes the value 1 on days with high market trading volume and 0 otherwise. See also Notes to Table 17.2.
[a]Indicates significance levels of 1%, respectively.
[b]Indicates significance levels of 5%, respectively.

Table 17.6: Estimation of the Chang et al. (2000) model during periods of up and down market liquidity.

	2/1/1998–31/5/2016		2/1/1998–25/9/2000		26/9/2000–24/6/2004		25/6/2004–12/9/2008		13/9/2008–26/9/2011		27/9/2011–31/5/2016	
	Coefficient	p-value	Coefficient	p-value	Coefficient	p-value	Coefficient	p-value	Coefficient	p-value	Coefficient	p-value
γ_0	2.290[a]	0.00	2.484[a]	0.00	1.518[a]	0.00	1.753[a]	0.00	2.417[a]	0.00	3.279[a]	0.00
γ_1	0.337[a]	0.00	0.293[a]	0.00	0.389[a]	0.00	0.215[a]	0.00	0.214[a]	0.00	0.001	0.99
γ_2	0.261[a]	0.00	0.170[a]	0.00	0.253[a]	0.00	0.250[a]	0.00	0.245[a]	0.00	0.469[a]	0.00
γ_3	−0.030[a]	0.00	−0.048[a]	0.00	−0.016[a]	0.00	0.040[a]	0.00	0.035[c]	0.06	0.104[a]	0.00
γ_4	−0.007	0.57	−0.029[a]	0.00	−0.006	0.40	0.000	0.90	0.005	0.21	−0.005[b]	0.03
Adj-R^2	10.04%		6.37%		46.20%		43.30%		51.03%		41.89%	
	Wald test: H_0: $\gamma_3 = \gamma_4$											
$\gamma_3 - \gamma_4$ Standard error	−0.023[b] 0.011		−0.016 0.012		−0.010 0.008		0.039[a] 0.011		0.030[c] 0.018		0.110[a] 0.019	

Notes: Estimation of the model: $CSAD_t = \gamma_0 + \gamma_1 D^{up\,liq}|R_{m,t}| + \gamma_2(1 - D^{up\,liq})|R_{m,t}| + \gamma_3 D^{up\,liq}R_{m,t}^2 + \gamma_4(1 - D^{up\,liq})R_{m,t}^2 + u_t$, where $CSAD_t$ is the cross-sectional absolute deviation of the individual stock returns on day t, $R_{m,t}$ is the market return on day t and $D^{up\,liq}$ is a dummy variable that takes the value 1 on days with high market liquidity and 0 otherwise. See also Notes to Table 17.2.
[a]Indicates significance levels of 1%, respectively.
[b]Indicates significance levels of 5%, respectively.
[c]Indicates significance levels of 10%, respectively.

Table 17.7: Estimation of the Chang et al. (2000) model during periods of up and down 10-year Greek bonds spread.

	2/1/1998– 31/5/2016		2/1/1998– 25/9/2000		26/9/2000– 24/6/2004		25/6/2004– 12/9/2008		13/9/2008– 26/9/2011		27/9/2011– 31/5/2016	
	Coefficient	p-value	Coefficient	p-value	Coefficient	p-value	Coefficient	p-value	Coefficient	p-value	Coefficient	p-value
γ_0	2.259[a]	0.00	2.517[a]	0.00	1.555[a]	0.00	1.742[a]	0.00	2.401[a]	0.00	3.197[a]	0.00
γ_1	0.307[a]	0.00	0.137	0.13	0.276[a]	0.00	0.257[a]	0.00	0.270[a]	0.00	0.452[a]	0.00
γ_2	0.376[a]	0.00	0.243[a]	0.00	0.272[a]	0.00	0.282[a]	0.00	0.289[a]	0.00	0.325[a]	0.00
γ_3	0.001	0.93	−0.021	0.28	−0.012[b]	0.02	0.004	0.49	0.003	0.48	−0.003	0.22
γ_4	−0.046[a]	0.00	−0.041[a]	0.00	−0.004	0.41	−0.004	0.48	−0.011	0.47	0.023[c]	0.07
Adj-R^2	13.00%		5.83%		43.28%		42.22%		50.76%		38.03%	
	Wald test: H_0: $\gamma_3 = \gamma_4$											
$\gamma_3 - \gamma_4$	0.047[a]		0.020		−0.007		0.008		0.013		−0.026[b]	
Standard error	0.010		0.021		0.007		0.007		0.015		0.013	

Notes: Estimation of the model: $CSAD_t = \gamma_0 + \gamma_1 D^{up\,spr}|R_{m,t}| + \gamma_2(1 - D^{up\,spr})|R_{m,t}| + \gamma_3 D^{up\,spr}R^2_{m,t} + \gamma_4(1 - D^{up\,spr})R^2_{m,t} + u_t$, where $CSAD_t$ is the cross-sectional absolute deviation of the individual stock returns on day t, $R_{m,t}$ is the market return on day t, and $D^{up\,spr}$ is a dummy variable that takes the value 1 on days with high 10-year Greek bonds spread and 0 otherwise. See also Notes to Table 17.2.
[a] Indicates significance levels of 1%, respectively.
[b] Indicates significance levels of 5%, respectively.
[c] Indicates significance levels of 10%, respectively.

Another interesting finding is reported in Table 17.8 regarding the impact of the liquidity factor on herding estimations. In fact, average equity liquidity seems to have a negative impact, further decreasing CSAD for the whole period under examination as well as for the periods 25/6/2004–12/9/2008, 13/9/2008–26/9/2011, and 27/9/2011–31/5/2016. This finding suggests that correlated trading is easier to emerge in more liquid markets with high trading

Table 17.8: Estimation of the Chang et al. (2000) model augmented with the liquidity factor.

	2/1/1998– 31/5/2016		2/1/1998– 25/9/2000		26/9/2000– 24/6/2004		25/6/2004– 12/9/2008		13/9/2008– 26/9/2011		27/9/2011– 31/5/2016	
	Coefficient	p-value	Coefficient	p-value	Coefficient	p-value	Coefficient	p-value	Coefficient	p-value	Coefficient	p-value
γ_0	1.458[a]	0.00	2.563[a]	0.00	1.485[a]	0.00	1.602[a]	0.00	1.975[a]	0.00	1.294[a]	0.00
γ_1	0.266[a]	0.00	0.226[a]	0.00	0.277[a]	0.00	0.260[a]	0.00	0.230[a]	0.00	0.299[a]	0.00
γ_2	−0.009	0.20	−0.038[a]	0.00	−0.010[b]	0.08	−0.001	0.80	0.004	0.19	−0.001	0.55
γ_3	−5.331[a]	0.00	2.124	0.14	−1.303	0.20	−1.634[a]	0.00	−1.999[a]	0.00	−6.255[a]	0.00
Adj-R^2	62.27%		6.50%		43.47%		44.51%		55.43%		60.80%	

Notes: Estimation of the model: $CSAD_t = \gamma_0 + \gamma_1|R_{m,t}| + \gamma_2 R^2_{m,t} + \gamma_3 Liq_{m,t} + u_t$, where $CSAD_t$ is the cross-sectional absolute deviation of the individual stock returns on day t, $R_{m,t}$ is the market return on day t, and $Liq_{m,t}$ is the liquidity factor calculated in Eqs. (17.8) and (17.9). See also Notes to Table 17.2.
[a] Indicates significance levels of 1%, respectively.
[b] Indicates significance levels of 10%, respectively.

activity and it is in line with Galariotis et al. (2016) who found significant evidence of herding for high liquidity stocks for most of the G5 countries.

Finally, we test for the impact of the imposed capital controls in the Greek banking system. The results of the estimation are reported in Eq. (17.13), as follows:

$$CSAD_t = 2.255 + 0.308(1 - D^{cap.control})\left|R_{m,t}\right| + 1.049\,D^{cap.control}\left|R_{m,t}\right|$$
$$-0.021(1 - D^{cap.control})R_{m,t}^2 - 0.037\,D^{cap.control}R_{m,t}^2 + u_t \quad (17.13)$$
$$\text{Adj.}R\text{-squared} = 17.01\%$$

where all coefficients are statistically significant at the 1% level. According to the results, there is evidence of herding both before and after the imposed capital controls with herding being more pronounced after the imposition of capital controls. This finding is confirmed by means of Wald test for the respective coefficients ($\gamma_3 - \gamma_4 = 0.016$, Std. err. = 0.009) and it is consistent with the results reported by Economou (2016a).

17.4 Conclusions

In this paper, we examine herding behavior under different market states for a long time-period that includes several crises. To this end, we employ the cross-sectional dispersion of returns approach using a survivor bias free dataset from 2/1/1998 to 31/5/2016.

According to the empirical results there is evidence of herding in several cases. Summarizing the empirical findings, herding is present during positive market return, high trading volume, and average equity liquidity days, as well as during low volatility and spread days for the whole period under examination. However, the results differ for the subperiods under examination. For the first subperiod (2/1/1998–25/9/2000), there is strong evidence of herding being more pronounced during positive market return, high volatility and trading volume, and low spread days. Herding is present both in high and low average equity liquidity days. For the second subperiod (26/9/2000–24/6/2004), the empirical results indicate herding being more pronounced during positive market return, high trading volume, average equity liquidity, and spread days. For the third subperiod (25/6/2004–12/9/2008), there is evidence of herding only on high trading volume days. For the forth subperiod (13/9/2008–26/9/2011), there is no evidence of herding. For the fifth subperiod (27/9/2011–31/5/2016), herding is present on negative market return and low average equity liquidity days. Finally, we document the negative impact of the liquidity factor on herd behavior as well as the impact of the imposed capital controls promoting stronger herding behavior in the ASE.

The empirical results have important implications for asset allocation and portfolio diversification, especially during crisis periods. It is evident that herding exists in the ASE under extreme up or down market conditions, such as the 1999 bubble and the ongoing Greek debt crisis, in specific market states. All in all, it seems that in both cases uncertainty is the common factor that may fuel imitation and correlated trading patterns in the ASE.

References

Amihud, Y., 2002. Illiquidity and stock returns: time series and cross-section effects. J. Financ. Markets 5 (1), 31–56.

Bai, J., Perron, P., 1998. Estimating and testing linear models with multiple structural changes. Econometrica 66 (1), 47–78.

Bai, J., Perron, P., 2003. Critical values for multiple structural change tests. Econom. J. 6 (1), 72–78.

Bikhchandani, S., Hirshleifer, D., Welch, I., 1992. A theory of fads, fashion, custom, and cultural change as informational cascades. J. Polit. Econ. 100 (5), 992–1026.

Bikhchandani, S., Sharma, S., 2000. Herd behavior in financial markets. IMF Econ. Rev. 47 (3), 279–310.

Caporale, G.M., Economou, F., Philippas, N., 2008. Herd behaviour in extreme market conditions: evidence from the athens stock exchange. Econ. Bull. 7 (17), 1–13.

Chang, E.C., Cheng, J.W., Khorana, A., 2000. An examination of herd behavior in equity markets: an international perspective. J. Bank. Finance 24 (10), 1651–1679.

Chen, T., 2013. Do investors herd in global stock markets? J. Behav. Finance 14 (3), 230–239.

Chiang, T.C., Zheng, D., 2010. An empirical analysis of herd behavior in global stock markets. J. Bank. Finance 34 (8), 1911–1921.

Chiang, T.C., Li, J., Tan, L., 2010. Empirical investigation of herding behavior in Chinese stock markets: evidence from quantile regression analysis. Global Finance J. 21 (1), 111–124.

Christie, W.G., Huang, R.D., 1995. Following the pied piper: do individual returns herd around the market? Financ. Anal. J. 51 (4), 31–37.

Devenow, A., Welch, I., 1996. Rational herding in financial economics. Eur. Econ. Rev. 40 (3), 603–615.

Economou, F., 2016a. The impact and the evolution of investment psychology in the Greek Stock Market. Greek Econ. Outlook 29, 79–86.

Economou, F., 2016b. Herd behavior in frontier markets: evidence from Nigeria and Morocco. Andrikopoulos, P., Gregoriou, G., Kallinterakis, V. (Eds.), Handbook of Frontier Markets, The African, European and Asian Evidence, vol. 1, Academic Press, Elsevier, Amsterdam, pp. 55–69.

Economou, F., Gavriilidis, K., Goyal, A., Kallinterakis, V., 2015. Herding dynamics in exchange groups: evidence from Euronext. J. Int. Financ. Markets Inst. Money 34, 228–244.

Economou, F., Katsikas, E., Vickers, G., 2016. Testing for herding in the Athens Stock Exchange during the crisis period. Finance Res. Lett. 18, 334–341.

Economou, F., Kostakis, A., Philippas, N., 2011. Cross-country effects in herding behavior: evidence from four South European markets. J. Int. Financ. Markets Inst. Money 21 (3), 443–460.

Galariotis, E.C., Krokida, S., Spyrou, S.I., 2016. Herd behavior and equity market liquidity: evidence from major markets. Int. Rev. Financ. Anal. 48, 140–149.

Galariotis, E.C., Rong, W., Spyrou, S.I., 2015. Herding on fundamental information: a comparative study. J. Bank. Finance 50, 589–598.

Gavriilidis, K., Kallinterakis, V., Leite Ferreira, M.P., 2013. Institutional industry herding: intentional or spurious? J. Int. Financ. Markets Inst. Money 26, 192–214.

Hirshleifer, D., Teoh, S.H., 2003. Herd behaviour and cascading in capital markets: a review and synthesis. Eur. Financ. Manag. 9 (1), 25–66.

Hwang, S., Salmon, M., 2004. Market stress and herding. J. Empir. Finance 11 (4), 585–616.

Karolyi, A., Lee, K.H., Van Dijk, M., 2012. Understanding commonality in liquidity around the world. J. Financ. Econ. 105 (1), 82–112.

Litimi, H., BenSaïda, A., Bouraoui, O., 2016. Herding and excessive risk in the American stock market: a sectoral analysis. Res. Int. Bus. Finance 38, 6–21.

Messis, P., Zapranis, A., 2014. Herding behaviour and volatility in the Athens Stock Exchange. J. Risk Finance 15 (5), 572–590.

Mobarek, A., Mollah, S., Keasey, K., 2014. A Cross-country analysis of herd behavior in Europe. J. Int. Financ. Markets Inst. Money 32, 107–127.

Newey, W., West, K., 1987. A simple, positive semi-definite, heteroskedasticity and autocorrelation consistent covariance matrix. Econometrica 55 (3), 703–708.

Spyrou, S., 2013. Herding in financial markets: a review of the literature. Rev. Behav. Finance 5 (2), 175–194.

Tan, L., Chiang, T.C., Mason, J.R., Nelling, E., 2008. Herding behavior in Chinese stock markets: an examination of A and B shares. Pacific-Basin Finance J. 16 (1), 61–77.

Tessaromatis, N., Thomas, V., 2009. Herding behavior in the Athens Stock Exchange. Invest. Manag. Financ. Innov. 6 (3), 156–164.

CHAPTER 18

Liquidity and Beta Herding in Emerging Equity Markets

Styliani-Iris A. Krokida*, Spyros I. Spyrou*, Dimitris A. Tsouknidis**

*Athens University of Economics and Business, Athens, Greece; **Cyprus University of Technology, Limassol, Cyprus

Chapter Outline

18.1 Introduction

Herd behavior may be defined as the process where market participants are imitating each other and/or base their decisions upon the actions of the previous decision maker (Hwang and Salmon, 2004; Welch, 2000; among others). Although this behavior has been extensively investigated for both mature and emerging markets, there are still many issues related to this behavior that need further research. For instance, as Galariotis et al. (2016) point out, an issue that has been neglected in the empirical literature on market-based herding is the relationship between liquidity and herding; they examine mature markets and report evidence of herd behavior only for stocks that exhibit high liquidity.

Motivated by this, we examine the relationship between equity market liquidity and herd behavior for a sample of important emerging equity markets. To the best of our knowledge, this is the first study to examine this issue for emerging markets. Note that the empirical literature on herding may be divided into two main strands, one that examines institutional investor herding (Lakonishok et al., 1992; among others), and one that examines herding toward the average behavior (consensus) using market data (Chang et al., 2000; among others). Our study falls within the second strand and examines the seven largest, in terms of market capitalization, emerging equity markets (Argentina, Brazil, Chile, China, India, South Korea, and Turkey), for a long sample period (1992–2015).

More specifically, for every emerging market in the sample, we first estimate the four-factor asset pricing model of Carhart (1997); that is, in addition to the excess market return factor, we estimate the value, size, and momentum factors (Fama and French, 1993). We subsequently employ these factors in order to adjust betas and compute the standardized beta herding measure of Hwang and Salmon (2009). This herding measure represents a direct measure of equity market herding over time as opposed to measures, such as the cross-sectional standard deviation (CSAD). In order to proxy for stock liquidity, we employ the Amihud (2002) illiquidity ratio for every sample stock, and based on these ratios we compute market wide measures of liquidity. Next, we employ vector autoregressive (VAR) modeling, variance decomposition tests, and Granger causality tests, in order to examine the relationship between market liquidity and herd behavior in each of the sample markets.

To anticipate the results, contrary to recent evidence on mature markets, we find that overall the relationship between liquidity and herding is very weak for the major emerging markets. Liquidity seems to explain moderate percentages of the variance of the standardized beta herding measure for Brazil, China, and South Korea only during the financial crisis period (2007–2009). For example, during the financial crisis significant herding variance percentages, such as 10.01% for South Korea, 9.08% for China, and 7.74% for Brazil, seem to be explained by illiquidity. To compare with recent evidence on developed markets consider that, for the United States, approximately 29.43% of the liquidity variance is due to return clustering (Galariotis et al., 2016). A possible explanation for our results is that in this study, we adjust the betas we employ to estimate the herding measure with the four-factor asset pricing model of Carhart (1997). In other words, the pronounced relationship reported in mature markets may not hold for emerging markets once risk has been accounted for. In addition, the Hwang and Salmon (2009) beta herding measure that we employ differs from the more traditional CSAD measure in that it takes into account the intentional aspect of herding as well as market wide sentiment.

The rest of this chapter is organized as follows: Section 18.2 briefly reviews the related literature; Section 18.3 describes the data and outlines the methodology; Section 18.4 presents the empirical results; Section 18.5 discusses the main findings and concludes the chapter.

18.2 Literature Review

The empirical literature on herd behavior may be broadly divided into two dominant strands (for an extended review see Spyrou, 2013). One strand concentrates on institutional investor herding (Dasgupta et al., 2011; Lakonishok et al., 1992; Sias, 2004; among others), while the other strand focuses on herding toward the consensus, using models based on the cross-sectional variability of returns (Chang et al., 2000; Christie and Huang, 1995; Hwang and Salmon, 2009, 2004; among others). Evidence on global emerging markets to date suggests higher investor herding, compared to developed markets. This has been attributed to the unique characteristics of emerging markets, that is, the structural environment and institutional presence (Chang, 2010).

Note that studies on herd behavior for emerging markets can be found in both strands. For example, Choe et al. (1999) study South Korea and find that herding and positive feedback trading by foreign investors are present before the Korean economic crisis (a finding which is reversed during the crisis); Jeon and Moffett (2010) examine the impact of foreign institutional herding on stock returns in the Korean market and find significant evidence of herding and intrayear positive feedback trading by foreign investors. Borensztein and Gelos (2003) investigate the behavior of emerging market mutual funds and find that although herding exists is lower than might be expected. In the same vein, Chang (2010) using order flow data finds that the trading of qualified foreign institutions (QFIIs), dealers, margin traders, and mutual funds is interrelated and that the level of disclosure of QFIIs trading activity plays an important role in herding behavior. In other studies, Voronkova and Bohl (2005) show that pension fund managers in Poland are more prone toward herd behavior than managers in mature markets, while Bowe and Domuta (2004) study investment patterns in Indonesia and also report evidence of herding during the 1997 crisis.

Other emerging market studies use aggregate market data to study herding toward the consensus, with mixed results. For example, Demirer and Kutan (2006) examine the Chinese equity markets (Shanghai and Shenzhen markets) and find no evidence of herding behavior; Tan et al. (2008), however, find that herding activity is present in both the Shanghai and Shenzhen A-share and B-share markets. Demirer et al. (2010) examine the Taiwanese market with three different herding measures and find evidence consistent with herding during down markets. Chiang and Zheng (2010) study herding on a global scale using data for 18 emerging markets and their results indicate the presence of herding in Asian markets and advanced markets (except the United States). Chen (2013) uses data for 69 countries categorized into three subgroups including developed, emerging, and frontier markets and three different herding measures. The results indicate that herd behavior is present in the majority of the markets, with herding being more pronounced in developed markets. There is also evidence to suggest that, in emerging markets, herding may be related to thin trading. For example, Kallinterakis (2007) examines the Vietnamese market and finds that herd behavior weakens once thin trading is taken into account.

The relationship between herd behavior and stock market liquidity has been investigated in both strands of the literature discussed earlier. According to Tan et al. (2008) differences in the market conditions may strengthen or weaken herding activity, while Devenow and Welch

(1996) argue that deeper (more liquid) markets offer a favorable environment for investors' clustering and this is attributed to liquidity being viewed as a positive externality. In a related study, Wermers (1999) suggests that institutional investors may share an aversion for smaller stocks which are considered less liquid due to their greater need of funds for liquidity. In another study, Poon et al. (2013) finds that higher bid-ask spreads as well as greater liquidity risk are associated with institutional sell side herding. According to Taylor (2002), there is a higher possibility for illiquid stocks to accommodate herd behavior since information asymmetry is more likely to prevail in these stocks. However, Galariotis et al. (2016) provide evidence of higher herd behavior in high liquidity stocks using data on the G5 international equity markets.

Several herding measures have been proposed in the behavioral finance literature. One of the most prominent measures is proposed by Chang et al. (2000) and is based on the dispersion of returns. In particular, using the CAPM as a benchmark model, the authors suggest that the relation between the dispersion of returns and the time-varying market expected returns is linearly increasing. Thus, the addition of a nonlinear factor to the model (squared market return) enables the detection of possible deviations from rationality. The intuition behind this measure is that during turbulent periods, market participants will tend to follow the market consensus. A reflection of this behavior will be found in the disproportionately reduced dispersion of returns contrary to what is expected by rational asset pricing. This model allows for the detection of herding activity during discrete periods. Furthermore, it does not facilitate the discrimination between what Bikhchandani and Sharma (2000) mention as "spurious" herding and herding due to intent unless, the dispersion measure is decomposed to fundamental and nonfundamental driven as in Galariotis et al. (2015).

However, Hwang and Salmon (2004) argue that herding is an evolutionary process and propose a new measure which takes into account the dynamic aspect of herding behavior. Specifically, their measure focuses only on intentional rather than spurious herding. The former implies that investors neglect fundamentals as well as their own information and imitate each other, leading to inefficient outcomes, while the latter is consistent with market efficiency and defined as a common reaction to fundamental news. In particular, Hwang and Salmon (2004) beta herding measure is based on the cross-sectional variability of CAPM betas. The assumption underlying their methodology is that when market participants alter their beliefs in favor of the consensus, individual returns move toward the direction of the market. Hence, individual betas collectively deviate from their equilibrium values. In the same vein, Hwang and Salmon (2004, 2009) propose the so-called standardized beta herding, a measure which takes into account the dynamic and intentional aspect of herding as well as market wide sentiment. The use of the standardized beta herding measure of Hwang and Salmon (2009) in this study allows the explicit examination of herding in comparison with stock market liquidity. This is an important feature of this study, since previous papers on the issue typically use the cross-sectional absolute deviation (CSAD) between each stock's returns and the market return as an indication of herding but not as an explicit measure of herding in an equity market.

18.3 Data and Methodology

For the empirical analysis, we employ the universe of listed stocks for the largest stock exchanges, in terms of total market capitalization, for the following countries (name of stock exchange): Argentina (Buenos Aires), Brazil (Sao Paulo), Chile (Santiago), China (Shenzhen), India (National India), South Korea (Korea), Turkey (Borsa Instabul). All major securities and primary quotes in the respective stock exchanges are included in the sample; we only include main market stocks (primary assets) and exclude financials and foreign companies. For each equity issue, monthly time series of the following variables are obtained through Thomson Reuters Datastream (datatype): equity price (P), total return (RI), market value (MV), number of shares (NOSH), trading volume (VO), and common equity (CEQ). The sample spans the period between July 1992 and December 2015. The sample examined starts in 1992 since prior to this date data availability in Thomson Reuters Datastream is substantially limited for emerging equity markets. All data are expressed in US dollars, while companies with negative or missing common equity values are excluded.

18.3.1 Measuring Herding

The beta herding measure introduced by Hwang and Salmon (2004) is one way to capture the extent to which investors are driven by herd-related behavioral biases. These biases may distort investors' perception of the risk-return relationship. Specifically, if investors herd toward the consensus, then the estimated betas of individual stock returns are expected to drift away from what standard asset pricing models would suggest. Thus, the deviation of betas from their equilibrium values can provide a market-based measure for herd behavior. Hwang and Salmon (2004) assume the following relationship between the equilibrium beta (β_{imt}) and the behaviorally biased beta (β_{imt}^b):

$$\frac{E_t^b(r_{it})}{E_t(r_{mt})} = \beta_{imt}^b = \beta_{imt} - h_{mt}(\beta_{imt} - 1) \tag{18.1}$$

In Eq. (18.1), r_{it} and r_{mt} are the excess returns on asset i and the market at time t, respectively. $E_t(.)$ is the expectation conditional on the information available at time t, superscript b reflects the bias due to cross-sectional mispricing, h_{mt}, represents the level of herding in betas driven by cross-sectional mispricing, that is, cross-sectional herding. When $0 < h_{mt} < 1$, there is heading toward the consensus. When $h_{mt} = 1$, there is perfect herding toward the market consensus, that is, all individual assets move in accordance to the market portfolio. When $h_{mt} = 0$, there is no evidence of herding and the asset pricing model (e.g., the CAPM) holds in equilibrium and reflects the level of herding in betas. Negative values of h_{mt} (<0) suggest adverse herding.

Hwang and Salmon (2009) define beta herding as:

$$H_{mt} = \frac{1}{N} \sum_{i=1}^{N_t} \left(\beta_{imt}^s - 1 \right)^2 \tag{18.2}$$

In Eq. (18.2), β_{imt}^s expresses the beta in the presence of the behavioral bias of cross-sectional herding and sentiment and N_t is the number of stocks at time t (for details on beta herding measure derivation see, Hwang and Salmon, 2004, 2009).

Then, they extend this idea to a standardized beta herding measure as follows:

$$H_m^* = \frac{1}{N} \sum_{i=1}^{N} \left(\frac{\hat{\beta}_{im}^s - 1}{\hat{\sigma}_{\hat{\beta}_i}} \right)^2 \tag{18.3}$$

In Eq. (18.3), $\hat{\sigma}_{\hat{\beta}_i}$ is the standard error of $\hat{\beta}_{im}^s$. The standardized beta herding measure (H_m^*) can be estimated as the cross-sectional variance of the t-statistics of the estimated coefficients on the market portfolio. The intuition is that the original beta herding measure in Eq. (18.2) may be biased due to the presence of cross-sectional average estimation errors (CAEE).

In order to implement the beta herding measure as in Eq. (18.3), in this paper, we employ the four-factor asset pricing model of Carhart (1997); that is, in addition to the excess market return factor that is commonly employed in this type of studies, we also adjust betas for the size, value, and momentum factors (Fama and French, 1993). To construct the four factors, we follow the methodology of Gregory et al. (2013), who calculate these factors for the UK equity market.

Once the four factors are estimated, we apply the Hwang and Salmon (2009) methodology to calculate the standardized beta herding measure. Specifically, we use the initial 60 monthly observations to obtain OLS estimates of betas and t-statistics using Newey-West heteroskedasticity robust standard errors for each stock and then calculate H_m^* as in Eq. (18.3). Excess returns are computed by subtracting the 1-month US Treasury-bill rate. Next, we add one observation at the end of the sample and drop the first and continue with the next 60 observations to reestimate the beta herding measure. This is equivalent to use a rolling sample of 60 monthly observations with a constant step of 1 monthly observation. Finally, we employ a statistical trimming on the resulting beta herding measure where the bottom and top 1% of standardized beta estimates are omitted.[1]

---

[1] We also employ a winsorizing statistical process in the standardized beta herding measure obtained. The winsorizing process involves setting the observations below the 1st and over the 99th percentiles equal to these values. However, winsorizing does not affect the results of this study qualitatively.

As empirical estimates of betas exhibit some well-known limitations and following Hwang and Salmon (2009), we further impose the following criteria when estimating the beta herding measure. Specifically, liquidity declines severely during crises periods and this may induce a bias in the expectations of investors for stock prices. In order to mitigate this effect along with the effects of microstructure issues and thin trading, we apply several filters. Stocks included have at least 60 past monthly observations available and their stock price needs to be over 1$ (nonpenny stocks). Since the 1$ is too restrictive and excludes a large percentage of the available sample for some emerging markets, due to the currency exchange between the USD and the national currency, we impose a 1% price cut-off point. That is, all stocks whose price belongs to the lower 1% across all prices on a given month are excluded from the sample.

Furthermore, a small number of stocks may be extremely illiquid and/or volatile. In order to avoid extremely illiquid stocks bias, we exclude stocks whose turnover (trading volume over number of shares outstanding) belongs to the bottom 1%. Imposing criteria to exclude thin trading stocks is also supported by evidence in Andronikidi and Kallinterakis (2010) who show that beta herding estimates are severely affected in the presence of thin trading. Finally, we exclude stocks whose volatility of returns during the past 60 months belongs to the top and bottom 1% of the sample for the same period. Alternative cut-off points have been used for the criteria described earlier but none affects the results of this study qualitatively.

18.3.2 Measuring Liquidity

Liquidity measures can be classified into four main categories, with each category capturing a different aspect of liquidity. For example, measures based on the bid-ask spread capture the transaction cost aspect of liquidity; volume based measures capture the breadth and depth dimensions of liquidity; price based measures capture market resiliency, (e.g., quick order flow and fast adjustment to fundamentals); market impact measures discriminate between price movements attributed to liquidity and price movements due to other factors (Sarr and Lybek, 2002). This paper employs a commonly used liquidity measure, the Amihud (2002) illiquidity ratio, that provides a standard measure of stock liquidity and has been shown to form a reliable proxy for price impact (Goyenko et al., 2009), although it should be interpreted with caution in the presence of thin trading (Chelley-Steeley et al., 2015).

The Amihud ratio is defined as:

$$Liq_{i,t} = \frac{|R_{i,t}|}{P_{i,t}VO_{i,t}} \tag{18.4}$$

In Eq. (18.4), $R_{i,t}$, $P_{i,t}$, and $VO_{i,t}$ is the return, price, and trading volume of stock i at time t.

We obtain these ratios for all sample stocks and for all sample markets and then obtain the cross-sectional average monthly illiquidity ratio at the market level as follows:

$$Liq_{m,t} = \frac{1}{N}\sum_{i=1}^{N} Liq_{i,t} \tag{18.5}$$

In order to investigate the relationship between liquidity and herding in the emerging markets of the sample, we estimate bivariate country-specific VAR models of the stock market illiquidity measure ($Liq_{m,t}$) and the standardized beta herding measure (H_m^*), and estimate a series of variance decomposition tests and Granger causality tests.

18.4 Empirical Results

Table 18.1 presents descriptive statistics for the standardized beta herding measure (Panel A) and the Amihud illiquidity measure (Panel B), for all sample markets. As can be seen in Table 18.1 (Panel A), Chile exhibits the largest average values for the standardized beta herding measure (3.370) indicating low evidence of herding, whereas Turkey exhibits the lowest average value (1.714) suggesting high levels of herding. Standard deviations of the standardized beta herding measure exhibit notable differences among equity emerging markets with Argentina (1.580) and Chile (1.104) exhibiting the largest values of standard deviations, whereas China (0.221) and Turkey (0.316) exhibit the lowest. Median values are close to average values reported in all cases, thus suggesting the absence of extreme values. Argentina exhibits the highest range of values with a maximum value of 9.193 and a minimum value of 0.362, indicating (along with the large value of the standard deviation for Argentina) largely volatile levels of herding in this market when compared to the rest of the emerging markets examined. Excess skewness and kurtosis are observed in the standardized beta herding measure for the majority of the emerging markets examined. Jarque and Bera (1980) test strongly reject the null hypothesis of normality at the 5% significance level for all the countries examined apart from Chile and China. The values of the Augmented Dickey and Fuller (ADF) (Dickey and Fuller, 1981) unit root test suggest that the standardized beta herding measure is $I(0)$, for all markets.

In Panel B (Table 18.1), the descriptive statistics for the Amihud illiquidity ratio are presented. Mean values of the illiquidity ratio indicate that India (228.425) and Argentina (41.341) are the most illiquid markets on average when compared to the rest of the markets examined in this study. In contrast, China (0.388) and Turkey (11.562) appear to be the most liquid markets in the sample examined. Median values are close to mean values apart from India, thus suggesting the absence of extreme values for the Amihud illiquidity ratio. Range values and standard deviations are decreasing in line with the decreasing order of the mean values presented earlier. The values of skewness and kurtosis are closer to the normal distribution values of 0 and 3, respectively, when compared to the same values for the

Table 18.1: Descriptive statistics beta herding measure/illiquidity measure.

Statistics	Argentina	Brazil	Chile	China	India	South Korea	Turkey
Panel A: Beta herding measure							
Mean	2.708	2.448	3.370	1.529	2.073	2.300	1.714
Median	2.345	2.266	3.206	1.507	2.006	2.294	1.675
Minimum	0.362	0.605	1.066	0.979	1.400	1.392	1.120
Maximum	9.193	6.516	6.305	2.086	3.165	3.543	2.601
Standard Deviation	1.580	0.825	1.104	0.221	0.383	0.604	0.316
Skewness	0.966	2.152	0.316	0.173	0.558	0.115	0.535
Kurtosis	3.712	9.209	2.554	2.476	2.734	1.609	2.797
Observations	222	222	222	222	222	222	222
Jarque-Bera statistics	39.250	528.151	5.552	3.647	12.186	18.376	11.005
[p-value]	[0.0000]	[0.0000]	[0.0622]	[0.1614]	[0.0022]	[0.0001]	[0.0040]
ADF	−3.384	−4.159	−3.431	−3.330	−4.141	−3.376	−2.987
[p-value]	[0.0115]	[0.0008]	[0.0104]	[0.0136]	[0.0005]	[0.0121]	[0.0401]
Panel B: Amihud illiquidity measure							
Mean $(\times 10^{-6})$	41.341	16.252	17.856	0.388	228.425	4.667	11.562
Median $(\times 10^{-6})$	38.411	12.241	13.852	0.437	121.525	3.718	10.642
Minimum $(\times 10^{-6})$	7.405	3.535	6.962	0.109	47.742	2.262	2.305
Maximum $(\times 10^{-6})$	74.451	50.852	40.752	0.707	444.525	8.645	26.855
Standard Deviation $(\times 10^{-6})$	18.852	13.151	10.267	0.188	151	1.90	7.841
Skewness	−0.128	1.197	0.974	−0.188	0.264	0.716	0.239
Kurtosis	1.912	3.296	2.646	1.683	1.232	2.069	1.543
Observations	222	222	222	222	222	222	222
Jarque-Bera statistics	11.541	53.841	36.301	17.340	31.481	26.987	21.754
[p-value]	[0.0031]	[0.0000]	[0.0000]	[0.0001]	[0.0000]	[0.0000]	[0.0000]
ADF	−3.762	−3.421	−3.374	−2.981	−3.399	−3.566	−2.980
[p-value]	[0.0087]	[0.0114]	[0.0120]	[0.0415]	[0.0113]	[0.0101]	[0.0416]

Note: This table presents descriptive statistics for the standardized beta herding measure and the Amihud illiquidity measure. Mean, median minimum, and maximum are the arithmetic average, the 50th percentile, the minimum and the maximum monthly observations of the sample data, respectively. Skewness and kurtosis are the estimated centralized third and fourth moments of the data. J-B is the Jarque and Bera (1980) test for normality; the statistic is $\chi^2(2)$ distributed. ADF stands for the Augmented Dickey and Fuller (1981) test. The ADF regressions include an intercept term. The lag length of the ADF test is determined by minimizing SBIC (Schwarz, 1978). Numbers in square brackets [.] indicate *p*-values. Sample period 1997–2015.

standardized beta herding measure reported in Panel A of Table 18.1. However, the Jarque and Bera (1980) test statistic strongly rejects the null hypothesis of normality at the 5% significance level for all the emerging markets examined. The ADF unit root tests suggest that the Amihud illiquidity ratio is $I(0)$ for all markets examined.

Fig. 18.1 plots the standardized beta herding measure over time for each emerging market examined. Higher values of the measure suggest lower herding activity and vice versa. China and Turkey exhibit the highest level of investors herding behavior among all emerging equity

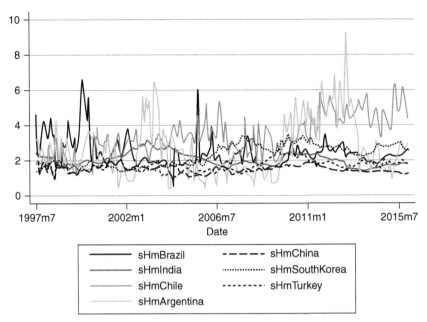

Figure 18.1: Beta Herding Measure for Emerging Equity Markets (1997–2015).
Notes: The graph presents the standardized beta herding measure of Hwang and Salmon (2009) for emerging equity markets over time. Higher values of the measure indicate lower investors' herding behavior and vice versa. *sHm* denotes the standardized beta herding measure.

markets examined in this study. South Korea and Brazil exhibit moderate levels of herding, whereas Argentina and Brazil exhibit the lowest levels of investors herding historically.

Tables 18.2–18.4 report the variance decomposition results (Monte Carlo standard errors, 100 repetitions) of bivariate unrestricted VAR models between the standardized beta herding measure and the cross-sectional Amihud illiquidity measure for each emerging equity

Table 18.2: Variance decomposition before the crisis (1997–2007).

	Variance Decomposition of Illiquidity				Variance Decomposition of Beta Herding			
	Period 1		Period 2		Period 1		Period 2	
	Beta herding	Illiquidity	Beta herding	Illiquidity	Beta herding	Illiquidity	Beta herding	Illiquidity
Argentina	0.000	100	2.311	97.695	99.831	0.162	99.841	0.162
Brazil	0.000	100	0.514	99.483	99.907	0.105	99.765	0.242
Chile	0.000	100	0.015	99.992	99.412	0.582	99.441	0.566
China	0.000	100	3.332	96.673	99.934	0.065	98.319	1.692
India	0.000	100	0.095	99.914	99.067	0.931	97.689	2.326
South Korea	0.000	100	1.302	98.705	99.966	0.037	99.817	0.196
Turkey	0.000	100	1.151	98.856	100.062	0.002	99.797	0.212

Notes: This table presents results for decomposing the variance of the variables during the precrisis period (1997–2007), based on an unrestricted VAR model with two lags as indicated by the Schwarz (1978) Bayesian information criterion (SBIC).

Table 18.3: Variance decomposition during the crisis (2007–09).

	Variance Decomposition of Illiquidity				Variance Decomposition of Beta Herding			
	Period 1		Period 2		Period 1		Period 2	
	Beta herding	Illiquidity	Beta herding	Illiquidity	Beta herding	Illiquidity	Beta herding	Illiquidity
Argentina	0.000	100	1.417	98.583	98.973	1.027	96.796	3.212
Brazil	0.000	100	8.609	91.363	92.253	7.748	88.442	11.567
Chile	0.000	100	1.822	98.186	98.676	1.329	97.086	2.921
China	0.000	100	0.259	99.742	90.916	9.087	90.242	9.755
India	0.000	100	0.754	99.242	99.128	0.875	97.492	2.507
South Korea	0.000	100	0.875	99.126	89.989	10.016	88.187	11.823
Turkey	0.000	100	0.150	99.857	95.242	4.755	95.303	4.702

Notes: This table presents results for decomposing the variance of the variables during the crisis period (2007–09). See also Notes in Table 18.2.

Table 18.4: Variance decomposition postcrisis (2009–15).

	Variance Decomposition of Illiquidity				Variance Decomposition of Beta Herding			
	Period 1		Period 2		Period 1		Period 2	
	Beta herding	Illiquidity	Beta herding	Illiquidity	Beta herding	Illiquidity	Beta herding	Illiquidity
Argentina	0.000	100	3.043	96.965	99.756	0.243	94.573	5.427
Brazil	0.000	100	0.048	99.952	99.634	0.367	99.326	0.674
Chile	0.000	100	3.004	96.997	99.352	0.645	99.333	0.667
China	0.000	100	0.158	99.842	99.982	0.018	99.952	0.050
India	0.000	100	6.013	93.989	99.795	0.210	99.076	0.928
South Korea	0.000	100	8.129	91.871	99.726	0.276	99.452	0.548
Turkey	0.000	100	0.033	99.975	99.692	0.313	98.945	1.056

Notes: This table presents results for decomposing the variance of the variables during the crisis period (2007–09). See also notes in Table 18.2.

market examined, for three subperiods, that is, a precrisis (1997–2007), a crisis period (2007–09), and a postcrisis period (2009–16), respectively. The aim here is to examine what percentage of the variance of each variable is explained by the other variable. The lag structure tests indicate a lag length of 2 in all cases based on the Schwarz (1978) Bayesian information criterion (SBIC). As can be seen in Table 18.2, during the precrisis period, the variance decomposition for illiquidity suggests that, for one period, 100% of the variance is idiosyncratic for all emerging equity markets examined. For two periods, however, the beta herding measure is able to explain 3.33% of illiquidity variance for China and 2.31% for Argentina. In turn, the variance decomposition of the standardized beta herding measure indicates that, for one period, negligible variance percentage (0.93% being the maximum for India) can be explained due to the illiquidity measure. However, for two periods, 2.32% of the variance can be explained by the illiquidity measure for India, followed by 1.68% for China.

During the financial crisis (Table 18.3), the variance decomposition of illiquidity for one period is again 100% idiosyncratic—as in the precrisis period—for all emerging equity markets examined. However, for two periods, the standardized beta herding measure is able to explain a significant 8.60% for Brazil—followed by 1.82% for Chile—of the illiquidity variance. Larger interactions between beta herding and illiquidity are observed for the variance decomposition of the standardized beta herding measure. Specifically, for one period, significant herding variance percentages (10.01% for South Korea, 9.08% for China, and 7.74% for Brazil) can be explained by illiquidity. Similar and moderately increased values are observed for two periods. For example, in the case of Brazil the variance of beta herding measure explained by the illiquidity ratio is increased to 11.56% from 7.74% in one period.

During the postcrisis period (Table 18.4), the variance decomposition of illiquidity for one period is again 100% idiosyncratic for all emerging equity markets examined. However, for two periods, the standardized beta herding measure is able to explain a significant 8.12% for South Korea and 6.01% for Chile of the variance of illiquidity. Notably, a negligible 0.04% of explained variance is observed for the case of Brazil, whereas during the crisis the respective percentage was 8.60%. In turn, for one period, only negligible variance percentages can be explained by the illiquidity ratio for the beta herding measure. However, for two periods, a notable 5.42% of the variance of beta herding measure can be explained by the illiquidity ratio for the equity market of Argentina, while the rest of the explained percentages are negligible.

Overall, the largest percentages between the beta herding measure and the illiquidity ratio are observed during the crisis period. More specifically, in South Korea, China, and Brazil, a larger percentage of the variance of the beta herding measure is accounted for by the illiquidity ratio, for both one and two periods. Moreover, Brazil exhibits a large variance percentage of the illiquidity ratio that can be explained by the beta herding measure, for two periods. It has to be noted, however, that although percentages are increased during the crisis, they are still short of the values compared to the similar values obtained in Galariotis et al. (2016) for the G5 equity markets. This suggests the lower interaction between herding and liquidity in the case of emerging equity markets when compared to the G5 equity markets.

Table 18.5 presents *p*-values from pairwise Granger causality tests with two lags. The lag structure chosen is based on the SBIC. The null hypothesis is that each variable "does not Granger cause" the other. The test examines the variance percentage of current and lagged values of standardized beta herding (Illiquidity) explained by current and lagged values of Illiquidity (standardized beta herding). Therefore, the Granger test does not indicate if the one variable is the effect of the other; rather it indicates that one variable contains information about the other. More specifically, the results suggest one-way causality from beta herding to illiquidity for China during the precrisis period and the opposite one-way relationship for Chile during the crisis period (significant at 1% level). Furthermore, during the postcrisis period, a strong two-way Granger causality is detected for South Korea (significant at

Table 18.5: Granger causality tests.

	Argentina	Brazil	Chile	China	India	South Korea	Turkey
Precrisis period (1997–2007)							
Illiquidity does not Granger cause Herding	0.794	0.842	0.997	0.241	0.157	0.901	0.853
Herding does not Granger cause Illiquidity	0.183	0.115	0.989	0.002	0.911	0.377	0.153
Crisis period (2007–09)							
Illiquidity does not Granger cause Herding	0.753	0.233	0.003	0.964	0.565	0.630	0.885
Herding does not Granger cause Illiquidity	0.876	0.311	0.566	0.698	0.565	0.156	0.981
Postcrisis period (2009–15)							
Illiquidity does not Granger cause Herding	0.052	0.866	0.947	0.169	0.069	0.038	0.715
Herding does not Granger cause Illiquidity	0.067	0.919	0.150	0.211	0.057	0.011	0.305

Notes: The table reports *p*-values for pairwise Granger causality tests with two lags. The null hypothesis is that each variable "does not Granger cause" the other. The test examines the variance percentage of current and lagged values of standardized beta herding (Amihud) explained by current and lagged values of Amihud (standardized beta herding). Therefore, the Granger test does not indicate if the one variable is the effect of the other; rather it indicates that one variable contains information about the other. See also Notes in Table 18.2.

5% level), whereas weaker two-way relationships are suggested for Argentina and India (significant at 10% level).

18.5 Conclusions

This chapter explores the relationship between herd behavior toward the consensus and stock market liquidity in selected emerging equity markets. Herding activity is measured by the standardized beta herding measure of Hwang and Salmon (2009), while equity liquidity is captured by the well-known Amihud (2002) illiquidity measure. In order to explore the effect of global financial crisis on our results we split the sample in three subperiods: the precrisis period (1997–2007), the crisis period (2007–09), and the postcrisis period (2009–15). Variance decompositions resulting from the estimation of bivariate country-specific VAR models reveal that during the crisis period, liquidity explains around 10% of the variation observed in investors' herding for South Korea, China, and Brazil emerging equity markets. However, Granger causality tests suggest one-way causality from standardized beta herding to liquidity for China during the precrisis period and the opposite one-way relationship for Chile during the crisis period. Furthermore, during the postcrisis period, a strong two-way Granger causality is detected for South Korea, whereas weaker two-way relationships are suggested for Argentina and India. In other words, contrary to recent evidence on mature markets, we find that, overall, the relationship between liquidity and herding is very weak for the major emerging markets. A possible explanation is that in this study we adjust the betas we employ to estimate the herding measure with the four-factor asset pricing model of Carhart (1997); that is, the pronounced relationship reported in mature markets may not hold for emerging markets once risk has been accounted for.

References

Amihud, Y., 2002. Illiquidity and stock returns: cross-section and time-series effects. J. Financ. Markets 5 (1), 31–56.

Andronikidi, A., Kallinterakis, V., 2010. Thin trading and its impact upon herding: the case of Israel. Appl. Econ. Lett. 17 (5), 1805–1810.

Bikhchandani, S., Sharma, S., 2000. Herding Behavior in Financial Markets: A Review. IMF Working Papers.

Borensztein, E., Gelos, R.G., 2003. A panic-prone pack? The behavior of emerging market mutual funds. IMF Staff Papers 50 (3), 43–63.

Bowe, M., Domuta, D., 2004. Investor herding during financial crisis: a clinical study of the Jakarta Stock Exchange. Pacific-Basin Finance J. 12 (4), 387–418.

Carhart, M.M., 1997. On persistence in mutual fund performance. J. Finance 52 (1), 57–82.

Chang, C., 2010. Herding and the role of foreign institutions in emerging equity markets. Pacific-Basin Finance J. 18 (2), 175–185.

Chang, E.C., Cheng, J.W., Khorana, A., 2000. An examination of herd behavior in equity markets: an international perspective. J. Bank. Finance 24 (2), 1651–1679.

Chelley-Steeley, P.L., Lambertides, N., Steeley, J.M., 2015. The effects of non-trading on the illiquidity ratio. J. Empir. Finance 34 (2), 204–228.

Chen, T., 2013. Do investors herd in global stock markets? J. Behav. Finance 14 (2), 230–239.

Chiang, T.C., Zheng, D., 2010. An empirical analysis of herd behavior in global stock markets. J. Bank. Finance 34 (2), 1911–1921.

Choe, H., Kho, B.C., Stulz, R.M., 1999. Do foreign investors destabilize stock markets? The Korean experience in 1997. J. Financ. Econ. 54 (3), 227–264.

Christie, W.G., Huang, R.D., 1995. Following the pied piper: do individual returns herd around the market? Financ. Anal. J. 51 (2), 31–37.

Dasgupta, A., Prat, A., Verardo, M., 2011. The price impact of institutional herding. Rev. Financ. Studies 24 (2), 892–925.

Demirer, R., Kutan, A.M., 2006. Does herding behavior exist in Chinese Stock Markets? J. Int. Financ. Markets Inst. Money 16 (2), 123–142.

Demirer, R., Kutan, A.M., Chen, C.D., 2010. Do investors herd in emerging stock markets? Evidence from the Taiwanese market. J. Econ. Behav. Org. 76 (2), 283–295.

Devenow, A., Welch, I., 1996. Rational herding in financial economics. Eur. Econ. Rev. 40 (2), 603–615.

Dickey, D.A., Fuller, W.A., 1981. Likelihood ratio statistics for autoregressive time series with a unit root. Econometrica 49 (2), 1057–1072.

Fama, E.F., French, K.R., 1993. Common risk factors in the returns on stocks and bonds. J. Financ. Econ. 33 (2), 3–56.

Galariotis, E.C., Krokida, S.A., Spyrou, S.I., 2016. Herd behavior and equity market liquidity: evidence from major markets. Int. Rev. Financ. Anal. 48, 140–149.

Galariotis, E.C., Rong, W., Spyrou, S.I., 2015. Herding on fundamental information: a comparative study. J. Bank. Finance 50 (2), 589–598.

Goyenko, R.Y., Holden, C.W., Trzcinka, C.A., 2009. Do liquidity measures measure liquidity? J. Financ. Econ. 92 (2), 153–181.

Gregory, A., Tharyan, R., Christidis, A., 2013. Constructing and testing alternative versions of the Fama–French and Carhart models in the UK. J. Bus. Financ. Account 40, 172–214.

Hwang, S., Salmon, M., 2009. Sentiment and Beta Herding (SSRN Scholarly Paper No. ID 299919). Social Science Research Network, Rochester, NY.

Hwang, S., Salmon, M., 2004. Market stress and herding. J. Empir. Finance 11 (2), 585–616.

Jarque, C.M., Bera, A.K., 1980. Efficient tests for normality, homoscedasticity and serial independence of regression residuals. Econ. Lett. 6 (2), 255–259.

Jeon, J.Q., Moffett, C.M., 2010. Herding by foreign investors and emerging market equity returns: evidence from Korea. Int. Rev. Econ. Finance 19 (4), 698–710.

Kallinterakis, V., 2007. Herding and the Thin Trading Bias in a Start-up Market: Evidence from Vietnam. Available from: SSRN 1105976.

Lakonishok, J., Shleifer, A., Vishny, R.W., 1992. The impact of institutional trading on stock prices. J. Financ. Econ. 32 (3), 23–43.

Poon, S.H., Rockinger, M., Stathopoulos, K., 2013. Market liquidity and institutional trading during the 2007-8 financial crisis. Int. Rev. Financ. Anal. 30 (2), 86–97.

Sarr, A., Lybek, T., 2002. Measuring Liquidity in Financial Markets (SSRN Scholarly Paper No. ID 880932). Social Science Research Network, Rochester, NY.

Schwarz, G., 1978. Estimating the dimension of a model. Ann. Stat. 6 (2), 461–464.

Sias, R.W., 2004. Institutional herding. Rev. Financ. Studies 17 (2), 165–206.

Spyrou, S., 2013. Herding in financial markets: a review of the literature. Rev. Behav. Finance 5 (3), 175–194.

Tan, L., Chiang, T.C., Mason, J.R., Nelling, E., 2008. Herding behavior in Chinese stock markets: an examination of A and B shares. Pacific-Basin Finance J. 16 (2), 61–77.

Taylor, N., 2002. Competition on the London Stock Exchange. Eur. Financ. Manag. 8 (2), 399–419.

Voronkova, S., Bohl, M.T., 2005. Institutional traders' behavior in an emerging stock market: empirical evidence on Polish pension fund investors. J. Bus. Finance Account. 32 (7), 1537–1560.

Welch, I., 2000. Herding among security analysts. J. Financ. Econ. 58 (3), 369–396.

Wermers, R., 1999. Mutual fund herding and the impact on stock prices. J. Finance 54 (3), 581–622.

CHAPTER 19

Exchange-Traded Funds: Do They Promote or Depress Noise Trading?

Konstantinos Gavriilidis*, Greg N. Gregoriou**, Vasileios Kallinterakis†

*University of Stirling, Stirling, United Kingdom; **State University of New York, Plattsburgh, NY, United States; †University of Liverpool, Liverpool, United Kingdom

Chapter Outline

19.1 Introduction

The introduction of exchange-traded funds (ETFs, hereafter) constitutes one of the most notable innovations of the finance industry during the past couple of decades, largely due to ETFs' ability of synthesizing properties of both closed-ended (they are publicly listed) and open-ended (they are benchmarked against an index) funds. ETFs invest in specific assets with the purpose of replicating the composition and performance of the benchmark (e.g., a market or sector index) to which they are linked, thus allowing their investors to trade that benchmark through the ETF's single stock. This renders trading equity-baskets easier, promotes risk-diversification, and has attracted considerable investors' participation.[1] Although traditionally viewed (see the excellent review by Deville, 2008) as an investment option for rational investors (e.g., as a tool for hedging risk), ETFs bear characteristics rendering them appealing to individual investors, while a series of studies (e.g., Curcio et al., 2004) has recently suggested that retail investors' position in ETF-trading is far from negligible. However, retail investors constitute the key candidates for

---

[1] According to the US Investment Company Institute, the total value of the assets under the management of US-domiciled ETFs was in excess of a trillion US dollars ($1,045 billion) in November 2011 (source: http://www.ici.org/etf_resources/research/etfs_11_11).

noise traders (Barber et al., 2009) and as research (Antoniou et al., 2005) has indicated, the prevalence of noise trading in markets can generate implications in terms of a market's efficiency and volatility. An issue, therefore, arises regarding the impact of the introduction of ETFs over market dynamics; this issue has received almost no attention in research and our study aims at addressing it to contribute to its understanding.

We address this issue on the premises of the established approach proposed by Sentana and Wadhwani (1992) which allows for the empirical identification of several facets of market dynamics (noise trading; return-autocorrelation; volatility) in the context of a model-framework assuming the existence of two trader-types (rational; feedback). Based on a sample of eight European markets, our results indicate that the introduction of ETFs has led to a reduction in the significance both of market inefficiencies as well as of feedback trading. More specifically, most European markets prior to the ETF-introduction exhibit significant first-order autocorrelation, while a few of them are also characterized by significant positive feedback trading. The significance of the above dissipates following the ETFs' introduction; this is further confirmed even after controlling for the impact of the ongoing global credit crisis as well as for longer memory in feedback trading. Furthermore, the reduction in the significance of feedback trading post-ETF in those few cases where its significance was witnessed pre-ETF did not lead to a migration of noise traders toward the ETF-market following the latter's launch, since feedback trading is found to be insignificant for all ETFs. The impact of the ETF-introduction over volatility seems to be less significant, since volatility in all markets appears strongly persistent and significantly asymmetric, both before and after the launch of ETFs.

Our results are particularly encouraging for regulatory authorities and policymakers, as they suggest the beneficial effect of ETFs in terms of both enhancing efficiency and reducing noise trading in capital markets. Since our study involves developed market settings, the findings reported here bear implications for emerging markets, where ETFs have either not been launched yet or are at their initial stages of development. As far as the investment community is concerned, the evidence presented here implies that ETFs are by and large in the hands of rational investors, thus rendering them less prone to mispricing—and hence, more attractive as products. The rest of our paper is organized as follows: Section 19.2 introduces ETFs as financial tools and presents the rationale for the noise trader hypothesis in their context. Section 19.3 describes the data and methodology employed and presents some descriptive statistics. Section 19.4 outlines and discusses the empirical results while Section 19.5 concludes.

19.2 Exchange-Traded Funds and the Noise Trader Hypothesis

An ETF is a fund investing in a set of assets with the purpose of replicating the performance of a predefined benchmark, which can be an equity index, a basket of stocks related to a specific investing style, a fixed-income index, a currency, or a commodity among others (Deville, 2008). The first ETF known as TIPs (Toronto Index Participation units) was launched in Canada in 1989 and was benchmarked against the Toronto 35 Index. However, the proliferation of ETFs as investment tools was realized initially in the context of the American Stock Exchange (AMEX) following the launch of the SPDRs (Standard & Poor's 500 Depositary Receipts; popularly known as "Spiders") in 1993 which was benchmarked against the S&P 500 index and which led to the massive launch of ETFs in the US markets in the late 1990s. The rest of the world's markets followed suit in establishing their own ETF-industries (Deville, 2008), with ETFs nowadays numbering several thousand[2] internationally.

A key characteristic of ETFs is that that they combine the public listing feature of closed-ended funds with the index-benchmarking feature of open-ended ones. In other words, they allow their holders to trade[3] an index through the ETF's stock alone and (contingent upon each market's regulations) allow investors to engage through it in short-selling, stop-loss orders, limit orders, and margin trading. This characteristic makes ETFs more attractive to investors, as it is obviously easier to hold an ETF investing in an index' constituents than to invest in each and every one of those constituents. Some other features of ETFs that have contributed to their popularity include: tax-efficiency; low management fees; dividend-treatment; transparency; and risk-diversification. Regarding their *tax-efficiency*, taxes are levied upon the ETF-shareholder only upon liquidation of his position in the ETF. Unlike with open-ended funds, redemption by one investor does not trigger the sale of underlying shares by the fund's manager, thus reducing the transactions involved—and the possibility that the remaining shareholders will be subject to taxation in case of capital gains being realized through those transactions (Kostovetsky, 2003). Another feature of the ETFs is their *low management fees*, which are the result of their benchmark-tracking nature. Given the latter, there is little need for active management on behalf of their managers, thus leading to management fees being substantially lower[4] compared to open-ended mutual funds, where investors need to incur annual management

---

[2] According to the World Federation of Exchanges (WFE), there were 6,892 ETFs listed internationally as of November 2011. The leader in numbers of ETFs listed was the NYSE Euronext Group with 2,055 (1,361 of which were listed in NYSE and 694 in Euronext's four European markets, namely Belgium, France, the Netherlands, and Portugal), followed by the London Stock Exchange Group (1,519) and the Deutsche Börse (898).

[3] Aside from their trading in the secondary market, the option exists for authorized participants (primarily institutional investors or market makers) to acquire ETF-shares through in-kind unit-creation by borrowing batches of shares from trusts (usually pension funds) and then depositing them with the ETF's custodian company alongside an additional amount of cash in return for ETF-shares. In the case of redeeming ETF-shares, investors return their (in-kind created) ETF-units in return for the batches of stocks and an amount of cash. The cash-amount in both cases (creation-redemption) represents the difference between the ETF's net asset value and the value of the basket of stocks necessary to form an ETF-unit. The number of shares in each creation-unit varies; Cherry (2004) notes that it may range between 25,000 and 600,000.

[4] Management expenses in ETFs are considered the lowest among comparable investment vehicles, such as open-ended (i.e., mutual) funds. Anderson (2008) mentions that US ETFs maintain expense ratios equal to around 0.1%. Of course, one should keep in mind that an ETF's expense ratio is an inverse function of the ETF's liquidity which in turn is an increasing function of the liquidity of the underlying benchmark. ETFs investing in illiquid (mainly emerging) markets or narrow sectors obviously face greater delays in their trades which result in higher transaction costs.

fees, exit fees, deferred sales charges, and the cost of the board of directors.[5] With respect to *dividend-treatment*, ETFs credit any dividends received to the accounts of their investors who nevertheless have the option of having the dividends reinvested in their ETF-position (contrary to open-ended funds that reinvest dividends automatically). *Transparency* is a key advantage of ETFs over open-ended funds; whereas the latter usually disclose their holdings quarterly, the composition of ETFs' stock baskets is available intradaily from exchange resources and information providers (Ho, 2006), thus rendering it easier for ETF-shareholders to monitor their investments. Finally, ETFs allow for greater *risk-diversification* since the purchase of a single ETF-share allows for quick diversity and exposure to a group of stocks.

In view of the above features, it would be reasonable to expect ETFs to be most appealing to sophisticated clienteles, such as institutional investors, due to their ability to serve a series of purposes in terms of portfolio- and risk-management (Hill and Teller, 2010). Survey evidence[6] indicates that US institutional investors are increasingly opting for ETF-trading, with institutional participation estimated at about half the total funds invested in ETFs in the United States (Greenwich Associates, 2010). According to Ünal (2009), ETFs are popular among specific types of institutional investors[7] as tools in, among others, tactical portfolio allocation (to gain instant asset-class exposure or shift between asset-classes), fund-setup[8] and core-satellite strategies.[9] Regulation permitting, ETFs can be used to execute the same trade-types as common stocks, such as short-selling, margin trading, and stop-loss orders and these are practices traditionally identified (Luskin, 1988; Osler, 2002) with nonretail investors, such as funds, brokerages, and other financial institutions. The impact of rational investors over ETFs can also be tacitly inferred through evidence indicating that ETFs' introduction is associated with reduced mispricing in the underlying spot and futures' markets (Kurov and Dennis Lasser, 2002; Park and Switzer, 1995; Switzer et al., 2000), and insignificant deviations of ETF-prices from their net asset values (Ackert and Tian, 2000; Elton et al., 2002).

Despite institutional investors commanding a key position in ETF-trading, retail investors have embraced ETFs with evidence (particularly from practitioners' publications) indicating rising participation rates in ETF-shareholdings on their behalf. Curcio et al. (2004), for example, reported that retail traders accounted for over three-quarters of the NASDAQ-100 Index Tracking Stock's (one of the world's most actively traded ETFs launched in the late

---

[5] ETF investors only incur brokerage commissions and bid-ask spreads; see Kostovetsky (2003).

[6] This reference is made here with respect to the 2010 Greenwich Associates Report titled "ETFs Gain Foothold in Institutional Market."

[7] He defines these as: hedge funds, traditional mutual funds, single-/multi-family offices, private wealth management entities, funds-of-funds, and foundations/trusts.

[8] Namely, using ETFs as the basis of a fund's portfolio until the fund's size grows.

[9] A core-satellite strategy is one where a series of passive investment instruments (the "core", comprised, e.g., by ETFs, index futures etc.) is combined with a portfolio of individual assets (the "satellite", including, for example, selected stocks, bonds etc) whose composition is chosen such that it contributes to the desired risk-return profile of the entire (core-satellite) portfolio.

1990s) capitalization in 2001. Several sector-studies (Deloitte Research, 2009; Ellis, 2009) predict that ETFs will increase their share in the funds' industry, leading the share of traditional open-ended funds to exhibit a decline in the United States as a result. With retail investors constituting the key participants of open-ended funds, these studies suggest that ETFs will further increase their popularity with that investors' class in the future. ETF-trading in Australia[10] and Japan[11] is reportedly dominated by retail investors, while a recent Financial Times article[12] confirmed the increased retail investors' presence in the UK ETF market (ASX investors' update newsletter, 2011; Financial Times, 2011).

However, an issue arises given the susceptibility of retail investors to behavioral biases (Barber et al., 2009), since one would expect this to generate changes to the trading dynamics of both ETFs and their underlying spot market. In this context, our study approaches ETFs from the perspective of the noise trader hypothesis by presenting its theoretical background and investigating it empirically. To that end, we now turn to describe how ETFs can attract retail traders by appealing to specific behavioral traits of their decision to invest; these traits are presented below:

1. *Recognition heuristic*: The recognition heuristic (Boyd, 2001) claims that when an investor is presented with two assets, he will evaluate more positively the one that is easier for him to recognize. To illustrate its relevance to ETFs, consider the S&P500, which consists of the 500 largest US listed stocks. Assuming that the average US retail investor is asked to state whether each of these 500 stocks' names is more, less, or equally recognizable to the S&P500's, it is fair to expect that there would be a considerable number of stocks appearing less recognizable than the S&P500. If that investor were later presented with all possible portfolio-combinations of (two, three, four, and so on) S&P500-stocks and asked to state whether each of these portfolios appears more, less, or equally recognizable to the S&P500, we would still expect many of these portfolios to be less recognizable than the S&P500, since they would contain at least one stock the investor would not recognize. Compared, therefore, to a fund investing in any particular combination of stocks, an ETF linked to the S&P500 would, on average,[13] be more appealing to the US retail traders as its underlying index would be recognized by all.

---

[10] See Skelly (2011) report from Russel Investments and the article "Where the ETF market is heading" published in the June 2011 Investors' Update newsletter issued by the ASX (Australian Stock Exchange). Available online at: http://www.asx.com.au/resources/investor-update-newsletter/201106-where-the-etf-market-is-heading.htm.

[11] Cited in Y. Konuma's article "TSE nears ETF target, but looks for institutional growth" published on 16/2/2011 in The Trade. Available online at: http://www.thetradenews.com/newsarticle.aspx?id=5544 (The Trade, 2011).

[12] "ETF launches reveal investors want broader portfolios," October 14, 2011. Available online at: http://www.ft.com/cms/s/0/3b1aeb5a-f401-11e0-b221-00144feab49a.html#axzz1j46uPCi1.

[13] The expression "on average" is used here because the recognition of a stock increases in its size (capitalization). A stock (or a portfolio of stocks) from the top capitalization decile of the S&P500 would be more likely to be as easy to recognize as the S&P500 itself compared to a stock (or a portfolio of stocks) from the bottom capitalization decile. Since, at the very best, a stock/portfolio of stocks will be as recognizable as the S&P500—and with this recognition dwindling as one moves to lower layers of capitalization—the average retail investor would indeed "on average" be expected to recognize the S&P500 by name more easily.

2. *Familiarity bias*: If an asset is easier to recognize, it also generates a greater sense of familiarity. If the average US retail investor cannot recognize all 500 S&P500-constituents, it is doubtful he feels familiar with all of them either. In fact, even with regards to those he recognizes by name, he may know little more about them. What is more, it is highly unlikely that each and every one of these 500 stocks will receive equal daily coverage on the news; conversely, the S&P500-values would be reported on the news on a daily basis. Consequently, an S&P500-linked ETF would emit an enhanced sense of familiarity (Huberman, 2001) to retail investors, since it would invest not just in any basket (whose selection-criteria may be based on a strategy the investor may not fully comprehend) but in the specific basket of the market's main index.

3. *Ambiguity aversion*: The concept of portfolio-diversification entails greater ambiguity for retail investors who are less sophisticated, possess less investment experience, and have fewer resources at their disposal than their institutional counterparts and this is reflected in the underdiversification often characterizing their portfolios (Barberis and Huang, 2001). An ETF can help remove this ambiguity by allowing them instant exposure to the portfolio of a sector or the market as a whole. What is more, an ETF removes the ambiguity in terms of performance, since it is bound, by design, to track the performance of its underlying index. Consequently, an investor who does not feel particular confidence in his portfolio-building skills and wishes to invest in a particular market or sector would view investing in an ETF linked to that market/sector more favorably.

4. *Limited Attention*: Complex environments create more uncertainty as they increase in detail and this uncertainty is bound to be felt the most among those investors with the least sophisticated processing capacity—the retail traders. Limited attention (Hirshleifer and Teoh, 2003; Hirshleifer et al., 2011) per se refers to the situation where individuals' attention is unable for some reason to capture all elements of a multifaceted issue. The relationship between ETFs and limited attention can best be reflected through the problem of stock-selection; whereas the sell-decision involves selecting among the stocks one already holds, the buy-decision involves choosing stocks from the market's universe. An investor holding a portfolio trying to replicate the performance of a market's index will have to regularly monitor the performance of his stocks, compare it to some predetermined point in the past, and rebalance his portfolio according to each stock's performance and the performance of the index itself. Conversely, holding an ETF linked to that index reduces the above procedure to the comparison versus a single benchmark—the index. An ETF can, therefore, help tackle the limited attention inevitably involved in stock-selection, since, by allowing investors to hold the portfolios of entire sectors—not to mention the entire market—through a single stock, it essentially bypasses the issue of stock-picking and the costs relevant to it.

5. *Overconfidence*: If ETFs enhance familiarity and simplification in the trading process for retail investors as discussed earlier, this raises the possibility that these investors are

more likely to underestimate the extant risks involved.[14] Under these circumstances, one would expect investors to invest in ETFs due to their overconfidence, as they would underestimate the probability of realizing losses. Overconfidence further promotes aggressiveness in trading among retail investors (Barber and Odean, 2000, 2008; Barber et al., 2009) and the fact that less trading costs will be incurred when trading the ETF alone rather than individual stocks in the context of a portfolio can only contribute to this trading aggressiveness in ETF-trading.

Consequently, the above discussion indicates that ETFs are appealing to several behavioral forces relevant to retail investors, thus bearing the potential of triggering noise trading in both ETFs and their underlying spot markets. This renders the noise trader hypothesis in the ETF-context an issue, more so since its empirical testing has been largely ignored in research; exception here is the study by Kallinterakis and Kaur (2010)[15] who explored this issue on the premises of a narrow sample (France; Germany, UK) using the Sentana and Wadhwani (1992) rational-feedback-trader framework. Their evidence suggested the absence of noise trading in these three markets be it prior to or after the introduction of ETFs, with the latter leading to improvements in market efficiency, without, however, bearing much impact over market volatility. Our study investigates this issue using a wider sample of eight European markets and the same empirical design extended to account, among other things, for the impact of the ongoing global crisis and the possibility of noise trading having a longer memory. A detailed presentation of the data and empirical framework employed in this study is outlined in the next section.

19.3 Data and Methodology

19.3.1 Data-Descriptive Statistics

Our sample includes eight European markets, namely Belgium, Finland, France, Germany, the Netherlands, Sweden, Switzerland, and the United Kingdom (UK). The choice of these markets was based on the fact that we wished to have a post-ETF launch period the majority of which would not be consumed by the ongoing global credit crisis. Assuming the start of the latter to coincide with September 2007, when most Western markets began to exhibit their

---

[14] Realistically, an investor can lose money from trading on an ETF similar to trading on a portfolio of stocks of his choice. First of all, an ETF is naturally exposed to its underlying benchmark's risk; a FTSE100-linked ETF will be exposed to the UK's market risk. Second, ETFs are always subject to the tracking error, which could be price-tracking or NAV-tracking. Price-tracking errors occur when there exist deviations between the returns of the ETF and the returns of its underlying index. NAV-tracking errors occur when there exist differences between the returns of the ETF's net asset value and the returns of its underlying index. Currency risk should not be underestimated here when trading ETFs in overseas markets, while issues of political risk might be relevant, particularly in the case of emerging markets.

[15] It is important to note here that Kallinterakis and Kaur (2010) did not expand on the noise trader hypothesis in relation to ETFs from a theoretical perspective.

first descending trends, our objective was for our markets to have a post-ETF launch period where the global crisis would not cover more than half its duration. To that end, we opted for markets whose first ETF were launched not later than 2002.

Data were collected from Thomson-DataStream and Bloomberg on the daily observations of the following main spot market indices (country's name in brackets) for the 2/01/1990–12/12/2014 period: BEL20 (Belgium); OMXH25 (Finland); CAC40 (France); DAX30 (Germany); AEX (Netherlands); OMXS30 (Sweden); SMI (Switzerland); and FTSE100 (UK). The choice of 2/1/1990 as our start-date here was made to ensure consistency, since the BEL20 index was launched on that date with all other seven indices having been launched before 1990. The choice of the mentioned indices was based on the fact that each constituted the underlying index of each of our eight sample markets' first-ever launched ETFs. Our ETF-sample includes daily observations on the following (country's name in brackets) ETF-series[16]: LYXOR ETF BEL 20 (Belgium); SLG OMXH25 Index Shares ETF (Finland); Lyxor ETF CAC40 (France); DAX^{EX} (Germany); Street Tracks AEX Index ETF (Netherlands); XACT OMXS30 (Sweden); XMTCH ON SMI (Switzerland); and iSHARES FTSE100 (UK).

Table 19.1 includes descriptive statistics for the daily log-differenced returns of the sample market spot indices (Panel A) and their corresponding ETFs (Panel B). The statistics reported are the mean, the standard deviation, skewness, excess kurtosis, the normality (Jarque-Bera) test, and the Ljung–Box test statistic for ten lags. A first look at the statistics reported in Table 19.1 indicates that our sample's spot index series (Panel A) do not subscribe to normality. The spot indices of Finland, Germany, the Netherlands, Switzerland, and the United Kingdom are reflective of significant (1% level) negative skewness, the Swedish one is significantly (1% level) positively skewed, while all eight spot index series appear highly leptokurtic. These departures from normality are further evidenced by the uniformly significant (1% level) Jarque-Bera test-statistics for all eight spot indices. The above documented nonnormality is also apparent in the ETF-series' properties as outlined in Panel B.

This widespread rejection of normality can be partially attributed to temporal dependencies in the moments of the series. The Ljung-Box test-statistic is significant (5% level) for all spot and ETF series,[17] thus providing evidence of temporal dependencies in the first moment of the distribution of returns, possibly due to market frictions (e.g., thin trading). However, this statistic is incapable of detecting any sign reversals in the autocorrelations due to positive/negative feedback trading, as it can only confirm the presence of first-moment dependencies. Evidence on higher order temporal dependencies is provided by the Ljung-Box test-statistic when applied to squared spot and ETF returns. The latter is significant (1% level)[18] and higher

---

[16] Data on these series was again obtained from Thomson-DataStream and Bloomberg.
[17] With the exception of the Finnish ETF series.
[18] With the exception again of the Finnish ETF series where it appears insignificant.

Table 19.1: Descriptive statistics.

Panel A: Spot market returns

	BEL 20 (2/1/1990–12/12/2014)	OMXH25 (2/1/2990–12/12/2014)	CAC 40 (2/1/1990–12/12/2014)	DAX 30 (2/1/1990–12/12/2014)	AEX (2/1/1990–12/12/2014)	OMXS 30 (2/1/1990–12/12/2014)	SMI (2/1/1990–12/12/2014)	FTSE 100 (2/1/1990–12/12/2014)
μ	0.0069	0.0237	0.0080	0.0211	0.0140	0.0267	0.0206	0.0144
σ	1.17	1.54	1.41	1.46	1.37	1.51	1.19	1.14
S	0.0322	−0.1399[a]	−0.0209	−0.134777[a]	−0.149673[a]	0.157458[a]	−0.153008[a]	−0.1182[a]
$E(K)$	7.19452[a]	3,428.451[a]	4.81715[a]	5.017958[a]	6.660763[a]	3.954705[a]	6.2505[a]	6.3200[a]
Jarque-Bera	12,346.0123[a]	2,823.0669[a]	5,536.7283[a]	6,024.8404[a]	10,606.3108[a]	3,755.0301[a]	9,343.5617[a]	9,543.1603[a]
LB(10)	76.663[a]	29.46[b]	49.374[a]	21.752[b]	71.265[a]	25.856[b]	63.736[a]	87.3580[a]
LB^2(10)	3,620.314[a]	1,405.300[a]	2,600.058[a]	2,544.918[a]	4,615.734[a]	1,663.497[a]	3,419.23[a]	3,932.7120[a]

Panel B: ETF returns

	LYXOR ETF BEL 20 (2/10/2002–12/12/2014)	SLG OMXH25 (11/2/2002–12/12/2014)	LYXOR ETF CAC 40 (22/1/2001–12/12/2014)	DAX^{ex} (3/1/2001–12/12/2014)	AEXT STREETTRACKS (30/5/2001–12/12/2014)	XACT OMXS30 (30/10/2000–12/12/2014)	XMTCH ON SMI (15/3/2001–12/12/2014)	iSHARES FTSE 100 (28/4/2000–12/12/2014)
μ	0.0158	0.0073	−0.0218	−0.0053	−0.0252	−0.0075	−0.0079	−0.0032
σ	1.22	1.61	1.57	1.60	1.63	1.67	1.31	1.36
S	−0.0123	2.5761[a]	0.0663	0.0317	−0.2178[a]	0.0476	−0.1428[b]	−0.6752[a]
$E(K)$	7.1359[a]	50.3621[a]	4.7329[a]	4.9762[a]	6.6765[a]	3.1183[a]	5.5128[a]	14.0484[a]
Jarque-Bera	5,070.9611[a]	268,996.585[a]	2,652.8994[a]	2,944.1616[a]	5,023.1261[a]	1,176.1084[a]	3,557.7241[a]	25,030.7644[a]
LB(10)	22.033[b]	12.7170	52.835[a]	21.929[a]	53.57[a]	31.198[a]	44.224[a]	72.012[a]
LB^2(10)	734.959[a]	5.1060	1,388.581[a]	1,262.31[a]	1,990.169[a]	762.728[a]	2,090.305[a]	1,326.713[a]

$E(K)$, Excess kurtosis; LB(10), LB^2(10), the Ljung- Box test-statistics for returns and squared returns for 10 lags; μ, mean; S, skewness; σ, standard deviation. Dates in brackets refer to the sample window for each series. All spot indices bear 2/1/1990 as their start-date; ETF-series bear different start dates contingent upon the launch-date of each.

[a] Denotes significance at the 1% level.
[b] Denotes significance at the 5% level.

than the Ljung-Box test-statistic calculated for spot and ETF returns, suggesting that higher moment temporal dependencies are present.

19.3.2 Methodology

Our estimations are based on the empirical design proposed by Sentana and Wadhwani (1992) which assumes there exist two trader-types, "rational speculators" and "feedback traders." The demand function of the rational speculators is as follows:

$$Q_t = \frac{E_{t-1}(r_t) - \alpha}{\theta \sigma_t^2} \tag{19.1}$$

Where Q_t represents the fraction of the shares outstanding of the ETF (or, alternatively, the fraction of the market portfolio) held by those traders, $E_{t-1}(r_t)$ is the expected return of period t given the information of period $t-1$, α is the risk-free rate, θ is a coefficient measuring the degree of risk-aversion, and σ_t^2 is the conditional variance at time t.

The demand function of the feedback traders assumes they track returns one period back:

$$Y_t = \gamma r_{t-1} \tag{19.2}$$

Where γ is the feedback coefficient and rt_{-1} is the return of the previous period $(t-1)$ expressed as the difference of the natural logarithms of prices at periods $t-1$ and $t-2$, respectively. A positive value of γ implies the presence of positive feedback trading, while a negative value indicates the presence of negative feedback trading. In equilibrium, the aggregation of the above two demand functions yields:

$$Q_t + Y_t = 1 \tag{19.3}$$

$$E_{t-1}(r_t) = \alpha - \gamma r_{t-1} \theta \sigma_t^2 + \theta \sigma_t^2 \tag{19.4}$$

To estimate Eq. (19.4), we convert it into a regression equation, by setting $r_t = E_{t-1}(r_t) + \varepsilon_t$, where ε_t is a stochastic error term; substituting into Eq. (19.4) we obtain the following:

$$r_t = \alpha - \gamma r_{t-1} \theta \sigma_t^2 + \theta \sigma_t^2 + \varepsilon_t \tag{19.5}$$

Where r_t represents the actual return at period t and ε_t is the error term. To allow for autocorrelation due to market frictions (e.g., thin trading), Sentana and Wadhwani (1992) proposed the following specification of Eq. (19.5):

$$r_t = \alpha + \left(\phi_0 + \phi_1 \sigma_t^2 \right) r_{t-1} + \theta \sigma_t^2 + \varepsilon_t \tag{19.6}$$

Where ϕ_0 is designed to capture possible nonsynchronous trading effects and $\phi_1 = -\theta \gamma$. This suggests that a positive (negative) value of ϕ_1 would indicate the presence of negative (positive) feedback trading. As Eq. (19.5) shows, return autocorrelation is an increasing function of risk in the market (σ_t^2) as indicated by the term $\gamma r_{t-1}\theta\sigma_t^2$, whereas if positive (negative) feedback traders prevail, then the autocorrelation will be negative (positive). To test whether the estimated feedback trading bears asymmetries in its behavior contingent upon the market's direction, Sentana and Wadhwani (1992) modify Eq. (19.6) as follows:

$$r_t = \alpha + \left(\phi_0 + \phi_1\sigma_t^2\right)r_{t-1} + \theta\sigma_t^2 + \phi_2\left|r_{t-1}\right| + \varepsilon_t \tag{19.7}$$

According to Eq. (19.7), positive values of ϕ_2 indicate that positive feedback trading grows more significant following market declines as opposed to market upswings. Thus, the coefficient on r_{t-1} now becomes:

$$\phi_0 + \phi_1\sigma_t^2 + \phi_2 \quad \text{if} \quad r_{t-1} \geq 0$$
$$\phi_0 + \phi_1\sigma_t^2 - \phi_2 \quad \text{if} \quad r_{t-1} < 0$$

In order to evaluate whether there exists a significant difference in feedback trading between the period before and the period after the introduction of ETFs, we utilize the following specification proposed by Antoniou et al. (2005):

$$r_t = \alpha + \theta\sigma_t^2 + \left[\phi_{0,1}D_t + \phi_{0,2}(1-D_t)\right]r_{t-1} + \left[\phi_{1,1}D_t + \phi_{1,2}(1-D_t)\right]\sigma^2 r_{t-1} + \varepsilon_t \tag{19.8}$$

$$\sigma_t^2 = \beta_{0,1}D_t + \beta_{0,2}(1-D_t) + \beta\varepsilon_{t-1}^2 + \gamma\sigma_{t-1}^2 + \delta S_{t-1}\varepsilon_{t-1}^2 \tag{19.9}$$

Where $D_t = 1$ pre-ETF and $D_t = 0$ post-ETF.

Since the post-ETF period includes the ongoing global credit crisis in its duration, we rerun the set of Eqs. (19.8) and (19.9) for the post-ETF period alone, this time specifying $D_t = 1$ precrisis and $D_t = 0$ postcrisis. The purpose of this test is to examine the effect of the crisis over our post-ETF results; the pre-, postcrisis cut-off point here is defined as 1/9/2007, since it was around September 2007 that the subprime crisis started being reflected in most Western stock markets.

To control for the possibility that feedback traders bear a memory in their demand longer than the single-period one, we assume a second lag in Eq. (19.2) which now becomes:

$$Y_t = \gamma_1 r_{t-1} + \gamma_2 r_{t-2} \tag{19.10}$$

In this case, Eq. (19.6) will be extended as follows:

$$r_t = \alpha + \left(\phi_0 + \phi_1\sigma_t^2\right)r_{t-1} + \left(\phi_3 + \phi_4\sigma_t^2\right)r_{t-2} + \theta\sigma_t^2 + \varepsilon_t \tag{19.11}$$

Where $\phi_1 = -\theta\gamma_1$ and $\phi_4 = -\theta\gamma_2$. As with Eq. (19.6), negative (positive) values for ϕ_1 and ϕ_4 would indicate the presence of positive (negative) feedback trading based on the first and second lag of returns, respectively while a significant value of ϕ_0 and ϕ_3 would reflect the presence of inefficiencies through a significant first- and second-order autocorrelation, respectively.

We finally specify the conditional variance (σ_t^2) as an Asymmetric GARCH process (Glosten et al., 1993) to gauge whether there exists a link between the established (Bollerslev et al., 1994) volatility asymmetries and the feedback trading asymmetries tested through Eq. (19.7):

$$\sigma_t^2 = \omega + \beta\varepsilon_{t-1}^2 + \gamma\sigma_{t-1}^2 + \delta S_{t-1}\varepsilon_{t-1}^2 \tag{19.12}$$

Here δ captures the asymmetric responses of volatility in the aftermath of positive versus negative shocks. S_{t-1} is a binary variable equaling one if the shock at time $t-1$ is negative and zero otherwise. If δ is positive and statistically significant then negative shocks increase volatility more that positive shocks.

19.4 Results—Discussion

We begin the discussion of our results by first presenting the estimates from the original Sentana and Wadhwani (1992) model [Eqs. (19.6) and (19.12)] in Tables 19.2 (pre-ETF) and 19.3 (post-ETF). A first glimpse at these two tables reveals that ϕ_0 appears significantly (5% level) positive in six of the eight markets of our sample (with the exception of the Netherlands and the United Kingdom) pre-ETF, with this significance disappearing uniformly post-ETF. With ϕ_0 reflective of first-order return-autocorrelation, our results suggest that the evidence in favor of predictability in the return-structure of six out of our eight spot indices prior to the launch of ETFs dissipates afterward, thus implying that the introduction of ETFs has promoted efficiency in these markets. The ϕ_1 coefficient exhibits significance (5% level) pre-ETF only in Belgium and Finland, while its negative sign is indicative of significant positive feedback trading in both markets; feedback trading[19] appears insignificant in the rest of the markets pre-ETF. In the aftermath of the ETFs' introduction, ϕ_1 appears uniformly insignificant, thus suggesting that their introduction led to the depression of any pre-ETF significance of noise trading. As far as the conditional variance process [Eq. (19.12)] is concerned, volatility appears persistent, with the γ coefficient remaining highly significant (1% level) pre- as well as post-ETF. Calculating its half-life[20] confirms its persistence, since the impact of a shock over volatility is felt for a considerable number of trading days in all markets.[21] The half-life figures appear notably higher post-ETF (with the exception of the United Kingdom), indicating that the persistence of volatility grew post-ETF, something further confirmed through the higher values of the γ coefficient post-ETF (again with the

---

[19] With the exception of the UK where we observe the presence of insignificant *negative* feedback trading, France, Germany, the Netherlands, Sweden, and Switzerland maintain insignificant *positive* feedback trading pre-ETF.

[20] Volatility half-life is calculated as $HL=\ln(0.5)/\ln(\beta+\gamma+\delta/2)$; see Harris and Pisedtasalasai (2006).

[21] 7 (Switzerland) to 92 (UK) trading days pre-ETF; 40(Switzerland) to 75 (Netherlands) trading days post-ETF.

Table 19.2: Maximum likelihood estimates of the Sentana and Wadhwani (1992) model: pre-ETF spot market indices daily returns.

Conditional mean equation: $r_t = \alpha + (\phi_0 + \phi_1\sigma_t^2)r_{t-1} + \theta\sigma_t^2 + \varepsilon_t$

Conditional variance specification: $\sigma_t^2 = \omega + \beta\varepsilon_{t-1}^2 + \gamma\sigma_{t-1}^2 + \delta S_{t-1}\varepsilon_{t-1}^2$

Parameters	BEL 20 (2/1/1990–1/10/2002)	OMXH25 (2/1/1990–10/2/2002)	CAC 40 (2/1/1990–21/1/2001)	DAX 30 (2/1/1990–2/1/2001)	AEX (2/1/1990–29/5/2001)	OMXS30 (2/1/1990–29/10/2000)	SWISSMI (2/1/1990–14/3/2001)	FTSE 100 (2/1/1990–27/4/2000)
α	−0.0043	0.0498	−0.1085	−0.0038	0.0153	0.0625	0.0008	0.0035
	(0.0197)	(0.0427)	(0.0493)[b]	(0.0380)	(0.0262)	(0.0355)	(0.0328)	(0.0293)
θ	0.0171	−0.00750	0.0996	0.0356	0.0347	−0.0020	0.0462	0.0401
	(0.0245)	(0.0205)	(0.0361)	(0.0275)	(0.0277)	(0.0221)	(0.0341)	(0.0397)
ϕ_0	0.1812	0.2105	0.0782	0.0672	0.0331	0.1242	0.1040	0.0581
	(0.0239)[a]	(0.0314)[a]	(0.0384)[b]	(0.0339)[b]	(0.0288)	(0.0303)[a]	(0.0286)[a]	(0.0369)
ϕ_1	−0.0268	−0.0291	−0.0158	−0.0170	−0.0050	−0.0168	−0.0209	0.0016
	(0.0121)[b]	(0.0084)[a]	(0.0186)	(0.0132)	(0.0146)	(0.0096)	(0.0137)	(0.0324)
ω	0.0347	0.0877	0.0649	0.0458	0.0197	0.0473	0.0994	0.0062
	(0.0028)[a]	(0.0093)[a]	(0.0088)[a]	(0.0057)[a]	(0.0025)[a]	(0.0080)[a]	(0.0090)[a]	(0.0016)[a]
γ	0.8442	0.8658	0.9018	0.8951	0.9082	0.8732	0.7832	0.9559
	(0.0111)[a]	(0.0090)[a]	(0.0114)[a]	(0.0103)[a]	(0.0084)[a]	(0.0109)[a]	(0.0191)[a]	(0.0050)[a]
β	0.0573	0.0800	0.0145	0.0437	0.0474	0.0484	0.0322	0.0129
	(0.0099)[a]	(0.0074)[a]	(0.0086)[a]	(0.0093)[a]	(0.0078)[a]	(0.0071)[a]	(0.0115)[a]	(0.0057)[b]
δ	0.1209	0.0387	0.0737	0.0586	0.0493	0.1117	0.1729	0.0474
	(0.0141)[a]	(0.0118)[b]	(0.0119)[a]	(0.0112)[a]	(0.0085)[a]	(0.0139)[a]	(0.0157)[a]	(0.0082)[a]
$(\beta+\delta)/\beta$	3.1099	1.4838	6.0828	2.3410	2.0401	3.3079	6.3696	4.6744
Half life	17.9	19.5	14.4	21.4	34.7	30.4	6.7	92.1

Parentheses include the standard errors of the estimates.
[a]Denotes significance at the 1% level.
[b]Denotes significance at the 5% level.

Table 19.3: Maximum likelihood estimates of the Sentana and Wadhwani (1992) model: post-ETF spot market indices daily returns.

Conditional mean equation: $r_t = \alpha + (\phi_0 + \phi_1\sigma_t^2)r_{t-1} + \theta\sigma_t^2 + \varepsilon_t$

Conditional variance specification: $\sigma_t^2 = \omega + \beta\varepsilon_{t-1}^2 + \gamma\sigma_{t-1}^2 + \delta S_{t-1}\varepsilon_{t-1}^2$

Parameters	BEL 20 (2/10/2002– 12/12/2014)	OMXH25 (11/2/2002– 12/12/2014)	CAC 40 (22/1/2001– 12/12/2014)	DAX 30 (3/1/2001– 12/12/2014)	AEX (30/5/2001– 12/12/2014)	OMXS30 (30/10/2000– 12/12/2014)	SWISSMI (15/3/2001– 12/12/2014)	FTSE 100 (28/4/2000– 12/12/2014)
α	0.0496	0.0329	-0.0138	0.0091	0.0031	0.0043	0.0007	-0.0042
	(0.0224)[b]	(0.0286)	(0.0240)	(0.0249)	(0.0217)	(0.0288)	(0.0211)	(0.0198)
θ	(-0.0130)	-0.0023	0.0058	0.0039	-0.0054	0.0036	0.0017	0.0036
	(0.0175)	(0.0176)	(0.0135)	(0.0130)	(0.0126)	(0.0145)	(0.0176)	(0.0167)
ϕ_0	0.0079	0.0506	-0.0383	-0.0108	0.0183	0.0043	-0.0037	-0.0408
	(0.0262)	(0.0305)	(0.0261)	(0.0270)	(0.0259)	(0.0288)	(0.0231)	(0.0241)
ϕ_1	0.0004	-0.0057	0.0002	-0.0016	-0.0050	-0.0038	0.0027	-0.0022
	(0.0071)	(0.0088)	(0.0062)	(0.0059)	(0.0051)	(0.0070)	(0.0064)	(0.0074)
ω	0.0197	0.0190	0.0238	0.0265	0.0163	0.0224	0.0209	0.0161
	(0.0029)[a]	(0.0032)[a]	(0.0036)[a]	(0.0037)[a]	(0.0027)[a]	(0.0037)[a]	(0.0032)[a]	(0.0024)[a]
γ	0.8901	0.9239	0.9180	0.9180	0.9265	0.9325	0.9017	0.9156
	(0.0076)[a]	(0.0080)[a]	(0.0076)[a]	(0.0087)[a]	(0.0070)[a]	(0.0069)[a]	(0.0084)[a]	(0.0080)[a]
β	0.0092	0.0143	-0.0229	-0.0198	-0.0171	-0.0099	-0.0142	-0.0097
	(0.0083)	(0.0086)	(0.0067)[a]	(0.0085)[a]	(0.0078)[b]	(0.0066)	(0.0071)[b]	(0.0081)
δ	0.1740	0.1008	0.1850	0.1747	0.1628	0.1340	0.1905	0.1590
	(0.0158)[a]	(0.0125)[a]	(0.0140)[a]	(0.0135)[a]	(0.0123)[a]	(0.0118)[a]	(0.0143)[a]	(0.0120)[a]
$(\beta+\delta)/\beta$	19.9130	8.0490	-8.3434	-7.8232	-8.5205	-12.5354	-12.4155	-15.3918
Half life	50.2	60.5	55.6	47.6	75.0	66.3	39.8	47.1

Parentheses include the standard errors of the estimates.

[a]Denotes significance at the 1% level.

[b]Denotes significance at the 5% level.

exception of the United Kingdom). As regards the β coefficient, it appears significantly (5% level) positive in all markets pre-ETF indicating that volatility increased significantly as a result of the news-impact during that period. The impact of news over volatility seems to decline post-ETF, as the β coefficient is insignificant in half the markets post-ETF, while in the other half, it turns significantly (5% level) negative. δ is significantly (5% level) positive both before and after the launch of ETFs, thus denoting that volatility in our sample markets is strongly asymmetric; this asymmetry is also verified when calculating the asymmetric ratio $(\beta+\delta)/\beta$, which allows us to gauge intuitively the extent to which volatility is affected following positive versus negative shocks.[22] The above are confirmed when controlling for the directional asymmetry of feedback trading [Eqs. (19.7) and (19.12)], whose test-results are reported in Tables 19.4 and 19.5 for the periods before and after the introduction of ETFs, respectively. The ϕ_2 coefficient appears insignificant in all tests for both periods, suggesting the absence of feedback trading asymmetries. This is something perhaps to be expected given the scant evidence of feedback trading significance (significant positive feedback trading is again detected only in Belgium and Finland pre-ETF in Table 19.4).

We now turn to assess whether the differences in market dynamics are significant before as compared to after the launch of ETFs. Table 19.6 presents the estimates obtained from the set of Eqs. (19.8) and (19.9) which indicate a similar picture to that generated from the results in Tables 19.2–19.5. More specifically, the ϕ_0 coefficient appears significant (5% level) pre-ETF in Belgium, Finland, France, Germany, Sweden, and Switzerland with no sign of its significance detected anywhere post-ETF. The significance of the difference between the values of ϕ_0 before and after the ETF-introduction is evident at the 5% level in Belgium, Finland, France, Sweden, Switzerland, and the UK. Similarly, ϕ_1 is found to be significant (1% level) only in Belgium and Finland pre-ETF, indicative of significant positive feedback trading during that period there; conversely, feedback trading appears uniformly insignificant post-ETF, with no significant difference in feedback trading appearing pre- versus post-ETF. Another interesting finding here is that, with the exception of Belgium, the average level of volatility grows smaller post-ETF ($\beta_{0,1} > \beta_{0,2}$). As our Wald-tests indicate, the difference in that coefficient's values pre- versus post-ETF is significant (5% level) in most markets, with the exception of Belgium and the Netherlands.

To test for the robustness of the results presented in Table 19.6, we repeat the estimations using 2-, 3-, and 4-year windows around the ETF-introduction date; Table 19.7 presents the estimates for the ϕ_0 and ϕ_1 coefficients. The previously reported results on the significance of ϕ_0 pre-ETF are confirmed for Belgium (2-/3-/4-year windows) and France (2-/4-year windows), whereas the coefficient also appears now significant in the UK

---

[22] In the event of a positive shock, δ will equal zero and so the shock's effect will be reflected through β alone. If the shock is negative, its contribution will be reflected through the sum of β and δ. As Kallinterakis and Kaur (2010) noted, an absolute value of the asymmetric ratio in excess of unity implies that negative shocks contribute more to market volatility than positive ones.

Table 19.4: Maximum likelihood estimates of the Sentana and Wadhwani (1992) model: pre-ETF spot market indices daily returns.

Conditional mean equation: $r_t = \alpha + (\phi_0 + \phi_1\sigma_t^2)r_{t-1} + \theta\sigma_t^2 + \phi_2|r_{t-1}| + \varepsilon_t$

Conditional variance specification: $\sigma_t^2 = \omega + \beta\varepsilon_{t-1}^2 + \gamma\sigma_{t-1}^2 + \delta S_{t-1}\varepsilon_{t-1}^2$

Parameters	BEL 20 (2/1/1990–1/10/2002)	OMXH25 (2/1/1990–10/2/2002)	CAC 40 (2/1/1990–21/1/2001)	DAX 30 (2/1/1990–2/1/2001)	AEX (2/1/1990–29/5/2001)	OMXS30 (2/1/1990–29/10/2000)	SWISSMI (2/1/1990–14/3/2001)	FTSE 100 (2/1/1990–27/4/2000)
α	0.0024 (0.0205)	0.0486 (0.0431)	-0.1026 (0.0491)[b]	-0.0067 (0.0394)	0.0014 (0.0275)	0.0617 (0.0364)	0.0047 (0.0332)	0.0074 (0.0304)
θ	0.0322 (0.0284)	-0.0094 (0.0239)	0.1112 (0.0396)[b]	0.0306 (0.0303)	0.0091 (0.0313)	-0.0030 (0.0254)	0.0539 (0.0376)	0.0483 (0.0427)
ϕ_0	0.1870 (0.0242)[a]	0.2095 (0.0320)[a]	0.0837 (0.0392)[b]	0.0655 (0.0341)	0.0273 (0.0290)	0.1236 (0.0308)[a]	0.1079 (0.0293)[a]	0.0606 (0.0373)
ϕ_1	-0.0277 (0.0120)[b]	-0.0289 (0.0085)[a]	-0.0176 (0.0189)	-0.0165 (0.0133)	-0.0030 (0.0147)	-0.0167 (0.0096)	-0.0214 (0.0136)	0.0003 (0.0325)
ϕ_2	-0.0334 (0.0291)	0.0053 (0.0314)	-0.0259 (0.0328)	0.0124 (0.0358)	0.0583 (0.0323)	0.0028 (0.0327)	-0.0176 (0.0352)	-0.0159 (0.0332)
ω	0.0352 (0.0029)[a]	0.0877 (0.0095)[a]	0.0668 (0.0090)[a]	0.0453 (0.0056)[a]	0.0192 (0.0025)[a]	0.0472 (0.0081)[a]	0.1005 (0.0091)[a]	0.0063 (0.0016)[a]
γ	0.8422 (0.0112)[a]	0.8658 (0.0092)[a]	0.8994 (0.0116)[a]	0.8960 (0.0102)[a]	0.9096 (0.0084)[a]	0.8733 (0.0109)[a]	0.7810 (0.0193)[a]	0.9554 (0.0051)[a]
β	0.0572 (0.0099)[a]	0.0802 (0.0076)[a]	0.0152 (0.0088)	0.0434 (0.0093)[a]	0.0466 (0.0078)[a]	0.0484 (0.0072)[a]	0.0323 (0.0117)[a]	0.0132 (0.0058)[b]
δ	0.1243 (0.0143)[a]	0.0383 (0.0118)[b]	0.0745 (0.0121)[a]	0.0581 (0.0112)[a]	0.0487 (0.0083)[a]	0.1116 (0.0139)[a]	0.1749 (0.0162)[a]	0.0477 (0.0083)[a]
$(\beta+\delta)/\beta$	3.1731	1.4776	5.9013	2.3387	2.0451	3.3058	6.4149	4.6136
Half life	17.7	19.5	14.0	21.6	35.3	30.5	6.6	91.5

Parentheses include the standard errors of the estimates.
[a] Denotes significance at the 1% level.
[b] Denotes significance at the 5% level.

Table 19.5: Maximum likelihood estimates of the Sentana and Wadhwani (1992) model: post-ETF spot market indices daily returns.

Conditional mean equation: $r_t = \alpha + (\phi_0 + \phi_1\sigma_t^2)r_{t-1} + \theta\sigma_t^2 + \phi_2|r_{t-1}| + \varepsilon_t$

Conditional variance specification: $\sigma_t^2 = \omega + \beta\varepsilon_{t-1}^2 + \gamma\sigma_{t-1}^2 + \delta S_{t-1}\varepsilon_{t-1}^2$

Parameters	BEL 20 (2/10/2002– 12/12/2014)	OMXH25 (11/2/2002– 12/12/2014)	CAC 40 (22/1/2001– 12/12/2014)	DAX 30 (3/1/2001– 12/12/2014)	AEX (30/5/2001– 12/12/2014)	OMXS30 (30/10/2000– 12/12/2014)	SWISSMI (15/3/2001– 12/12/2014)	FTSE 100 (28/4/2000– 12/12/2014)
α	0.0482	0.0477	-0.0177	0.0164	0.0006	0.0119	-0.0015	-0.0062
	(0.0248)	(0.0318)	(0.0281)	(0.0289)	(0.0262)	(0.0320)	(0.0244)	(0.0233)
θ	-0.0142	0.0087	0.0043	0.0073	-0.0065	0.0079	0.0000	0.0022
	(0.0210)	(0.0191)	(0.0148)	(0.0143)	(0.0139)	(0.0159)	(0.0196)	(0.0182)
ϕ_0	0.0074	0.0537	-0.0391	-0.0089	0.0179	0.0064	-0.0044	-0.0411
	(0.0266)	(0.0304)	(0.0262)	(0.0270)	(0.0260)	(0.0287)	(0.0235)	(0.0241)
ϕ_1	0.0004	-0.0059	0.0002	-0.0017	-0.0050	-0.0040	0.0028	-0.0022
	(0.0071)	(0.0088)	(0.0062)	(0.0059)	(0.0052)	(0.0069)	(0.0064)	(0.0075)
ϕ_2	0.0041	-0.0385	0.0077	-0.0155	0.0055	-0.0171	0.0060	0.0050
	(0.0355)	(0.0353)	(0.0332)	(0.0334)	(0.0332)	(0.0317)	(0.0333)	(0.0321)
ω	0.0197	0.0194	0.0238	0.0264	0.0163	0.0225	0.0209	0.0161
	(0.0029)[a]	(0.0033)[a]	(0.0036)[a]	(0.0037)[a]	(0.0027)[a]	(0.0037)[a]	(0.0032)[a]	(0.0024)[a]
γ	0.8903	0.9225	0.9182	0.9177	0.9266	0.9320	0.9019	0.9158
	(0.0079)[a]	(0.0082)[a]	(0.0077)[a]	(0.0087)[a]	(0.0071)[a]	(0.0069)[a]	(0.0084)[a]	(0.0081)[a]
β	0.0091	0.0145	-0.0232	-0.0194	-0.0173	-0.0097	-0.0143	-0.0098
	(0.0084)	(0.0086)	(0.0067)[a]	(0.0085)[a]	(0.0079)[a]	(0.0066)	(0.0071)[b]	(0.0081)
δ	0.1739	0.1026	0.1849	0.1746	0.1627	0.1345	0.1903	0.1588
	(0.0160)	(0.0128)[a]	(0.0141)[a]	(0.0135)[a]	(0.0124)[a]	(0.0119)[a]	(0.0144)[a]	(0.0121)[a]
$(\beta+\delta)/\beta$	20.1099	8.0759	-6.9698	-8.0000	-8.4046	-12.8660	-12.3077	-15.2041
Half life	50.4	58.9	54.9	47.8	73.8	66.0	39.8	47.1

Parentheses include the standard errors of the estimates.
[a]Denotes significance at the 1% level.
[b]Denotes significance at the 5% level.

Table 19.6: Maximum likelihood estimates of the Sentana and Wadhwani (1992) model: test for parameter changes in the spot market indexes daily returns.

Conditional mean equation: $r_t = \alpha + \theta\sigma_t^2 + [\phi_{0,1}D_t + \phi_{0,2}(1-D_t)]r_{t-1} + [\phi_{1,1}D_t + \phi_{1,2}(1-D_t)]\sigma^2 r_{t-1} + \varepsilon_t$

Conditional variance specification: $\sigma_t^2 = \beta_{0,1}D_t + \beta_{0,2}(1-D_t) + \beta\varepsilon_{t-1}^2 + \gamma\sigma_{t-1}^2 + \delta S_{t-1}\varepsilon_{t-1}^2$

Parameters		BEL 20	OMXH25	CAC 40	DAX 30	AEX	OMXS30	SWISSMI	FTSE 100
α		0.0139	0.0531	-0.0246	0.0140	0.0199	0.0379	0.0048	0.0067
		(0.0140)	(0.0241)[b]	(0.0211)	(0.0207)	(0.0159)	(0.0223)	(0.0175)	(0.0152)
θ		0.0055	-0.0123	0.0224	0.0112	0.0031	-0.0004	0.0195	0.0107
		(0.0138)	(0.0132)	(0.0132)	(0.0124)	(0.0120)	(0.0124)	(0.0160)	(0.0158)
$\phi_{0,1}$		0.1750	0.2075	0.0837	0.0656	0.0486	0.1282	0.0968	0.0591
		(0.0229)[a]	(0.0294)[a]	(0.0350)[b]	(0.0324)[b]	(0.0280)	(0.0288)[a]	(0.0271)[a]	(0.0359)
$\phi_{0,2}$		0.0056	0.0537	-0.0397	-0.0147	0.0158	-0.0001	-0.0094	-0.0469
		(0.0266)	(0.0307)	(0.0263)	(0.0277)	(0.0263)	(0.0297)	(0.0236)	(0.0241)
$\phi_{1,1}$		-0.0234	-0.0275	-0.0146	-0.0135	-0.0083	0.0183	-0.0164	0.0080
		(0.0118)[a]	(0.0079)[a]	(0.0161)	(0.0122)	(0.0138)	(0.0100)	(0.0122)	(0.0306)
$\phi_{1,2}$		0.0006	-0.0090	-0.0012	-0.0032	-0.0060	-0.0051	0.0016	-0.0023
		(0.0068)	(0.0086)	(0.0064)	(0.0061)	(0.0052)	(0.0069)	(0.0065)	(0.0076)
$\beta_{0,1}$		0.0271	0.0500	0.0442	0.0400	0.0200	0.0347	0.0464	0.0151
		(0.0016)[a]	(0.0053)[a]	(0.0040)[a]	(0.0035)[a]	(0.0018)[a]	(0.0040)[a]	(0.0031)[a]	(0.0019)[a]
$\beta_{0,2}$		0.0278	0.0240	0.0267	0.0293	0.0172	0.0279	0.0305	0.0116
		(0.0027)[a]	(0.0031)[a]	(0.0032)[a]	(0.0034)[a]	(0.0024)[a]	(0.0037)[a]	(0.0032)[a]	(0.0017)[a]
γ		0.8690	0.9047	0.9174	0.9052	0.9103	0.9049	0.8776	0.9240
		(0.0066)[a]	(0.0053)[a]	(0.0054)[a]	(0.0057)[a]	(0.0052)[a]	(0.0059)[a]	(0.0072)[a]	(0.0053)[a]
β		0.0333	0.0492	-0.0013	0.0150	0.0246	0.0225	0.0059	0.0101
		(0.0060)[a]	(0.0047)[a]	(0.0046)	(0.0047)[a]	(0.0042)[a]	(0.0046)[a]	(0.0054)	(0.0055)
δ		0.1448	0.0593	0.1226	0.1164	0.1007	0.1169	0.1625	0.1044
		(0.0102)[a]	(0.0077)[a]	(0.0084)[a]	(0.0081)[a]	(0.0067)[a]	(0.0083)[a]	(0.0091)[a]	(0.0078)[a]
$(\beta+\delta)/\beta$		5.3483	2.2053	-93.3077	8.7600	5.0935	6.1956	28.5424	11.3366
Half life		27.0	41.8	30.3	31.7	46.6	48.6	19.3	50.2
Wald tests	$H_0: \phi_{0,1} = \phi_{0,2}$	23.3092[a]	13.2654[a]	7.9303[b]	3.5511	0.7217	9.6152[a]	8.8097[b]	6.0001[b]
statistics	$H_0: \phi_{1,1} = \phi_{1,2}$	3.2053	2.656312	0.6088	0.5725	0.0248	1.1810	1.8034	0.1089
	$H_0: \beta_{0,1} = \beta_{0,2}$	0.1214	46.2358[a]	44.5183[a]	17.873635[a]	2.2880	5.035845[b]	52.0386[a]	6.4387[b]

Parentheses include the standard errors of the estimates. Wald-test statistics are represented here through their chi-square values.
[a]Denotes significance at the 1% level.
[b]Denotes significance at the 5% level.

Table 19.7: Maximum likelihood estimates of the extended Sentana and Wadhwani (1992) model: tests for parameters changes using 2-/3-/4-year windows.

Conditional mean equation: $r_t = \alpha + \theta\sigma_t^2 + [\phi_{0,1}D_t + \phi_{0,2}(1-D_t)]r_{t-1} + [\phi_{1,1}D_t + \phi_{1,2}(1-D_t)]\sigma_t^2 r_{t-1} + \varepsilon_t$

Conditional variance specification: $\sigma_t^2 = \beta_{0,1}D_t + \beta_{0,2}(1-D_t) + \beta\varepsilon_{t-1}^2 + \gamma\sigma_{t-1}^2 + \delta S_{t-1}\varepsilon_{t-1}^2$

Parameters		BEL 20	OMXH25	CAC 40	DAX 30	AEX	OMXS30	SWISSMI	FTSE 100
2-year windows	$\phi_{0,1}$	0.1224	0.1326	0.1767	0.3320	0.1908	-0.0369	0.0841	-0.0434
		(0.0842)	(0.0592)[b]	(0.1319)	(0.1293)[b]	(0.1485)	(0.1183)	(0.1060)	(0.1218)
	$\phi_{0,2}$	-0.0288	-0.0739	0.0969	-0.0081	-0.0098	-0.0027	0.2543	-0.0201
		(0.0665)	(0.0639)	(0.1047)	(0.0759)	(0.0798)	(0.0760)	(0.1080)[b]	(0.0649)
	$\phi_{1,1}$	-0.0109	-0.0005	-0.0262	-0.1254	-0.0602	0.0210	-0.0363	0.0434
		(0.0460)	(0.0205)	(0.0267)	(0.0667)	(0.0618)	(0.0611)	(0.0328)	(0.1022)
	$\phi_{1,2}$	0.0154	0.0108	-0.0124	-0.0018	-0.0040	-0.0019	-0.0413	0.0142
		(0.0358)	(0.0150)	(0.0503)	(0.0165)	(0.0129)	(0.0102)	(0.0202)[b]	(0.0148)
Wald tests statistics	$H_0: \phi_{0,1} = \phi_{0,2}$	2.1432	5.6306[b]	0.2229	4.9150[b]	1.4142	0.0587	1.2687	0.0277
	$H_0: \phi_{1,1} = \phi_{1,2}$	0.2426	0.2064	0.0576	3.2370	0.7943	0.1378	0.0180	0.0792
3-year windows	$\phi_{0,1}$	0.1828	0.1591	-0.0110	0.1073	0.0419	-0.0053	0.0714	0.0170
		(0.0727)[b]	(0.0513)[b]	(0.0933)	(0.0707)	(0.0742)	(0.0596)	(0.0623)	(0.0518)
	$\phi_{0,2}$	-0.0541	-0.0181	0.0949	-0.0283	-0.0516	-0.0110	0.1793	-0.0645
		(0.0533)	(0.0490)	(0.0730)	(0.0652)	(0.0693)	(0.0604)	(0.0755)[b]	(0.0542)
	$\phi_{1,1}$	-0.0311	-0.0067	0.0076	-0.0091	0.0046	0.0193	-0.0158	0.0113
		(0.0408)	(0.0180)	(0.0188)	(0.0262)	(0.0231)	(0.0190)	(0.0164)	(0.0183)
	$\phi_{1,2}$	0.0028	0.0016	-0.0202	-0.0012	-0.0011	-0.0036	-0.0309	0.0167
		(0.0191)	(0.0130)	(0.0429)	(0.0147)	(0.0116)	(0.0091)	(0.0161)	(0.0142)
Wald tests statistics	$H_0: \phi_{0,1} = \phi_{0,2}$	6.9180[b]	6.1760[b]	0.808546	1.9647	0.8542	0.0044	1.1750	1.1769
	$H_0: \phi_{1,1} = \phi_{1,2}$	0.5883	0.1478	0.3589	0.0691	0.0507	1.2029	0.4110	0.0562
4-year windows	$\phi_{0,1}$	0.1508	0.1697	0.0122	0.1319	0.0806	0.0430	0.0540	0.0635
		(0.0590)[b]	(0.0461)[a]	(0.0687)	(0.0608)[b]	(0.0549)	(0.0539)	(0.0516)	(0.0480)
	$\phi_{0,2}$	-0.0924	-0.0019	0.0766	-0.0647	-0.0415	0.0208	0.0724	-0.0454
		(0.0493)	(0.0415)	(0.0601)	(0.0508)	(0.0540)	(0.0457)	(0.0567)	(0.0444)
	$\phi_{1,1}$	-0.0300	-0.0082	0.0020	-0.0211	-0.0093	0.0025	-0.0121	-0.0003
		(0.0386)	(0.0177)	(0.0137)	(0.0217)	(0.0150)	(0.0171)	(0.0145)	(0.0170)
	$\phi_{1,2}$	0.0056	0.0065	-0.0125	0.0034	-0.0029	-0.0078	-0.0163	0.0098
		(0.0183)	(0.0120)	(0.0398)	(0.0132)	(0.0103)	(0.0079)	(0.0137)	(0.0131)
Wald tests statistics	$H_0: \phi_{0,1} = \phi_{0,2}$	10.0273[a]	7.5660[a]	0.502729	6.1347[b]	2.5235	0.0981	0.0566	2.7858
	$H_0: \phi_{1,1} = \phi_{1,2}$	0.7069	0.0060	0.1220	0.9555	0.1245	0.3037	0.0439	0.2377

Parentheses include the standard errors of the estimates. Wald-test statistics are represented here through their chi-square values.

[a]Denotes significance at the 1% level.

[b]Denotes significance at the 5% level.

(3-/4-year windows); its values for these specific tests are insignificant post-ETF, while their difference pre- versus post-ETF is significant at the 5% level.[23] In terms of ϕ_1, it appears overwhelmingly insignificant in all tests, with the sole exception of Sweden in its 2-year window post-ETF test,[24] thus again confirming that feedback trading is not a significant element of our sample markets' dynamics.

As mentioned in the previous section, the post-ETF period accommodates the ongoing global crisis, whose reflection in Western markets began in September 2007, when they started to exhibit their first clear descending trends. Assuming 1/9/2007 as the cut-off point for the crisis, we repeat the set of Eqs. (19.8) and (19.9) for the post-ETF period only, in order to gauge whether the findings reported so far for that period persist when controlling for the crisis' impact. Table 19.8 presents the estimates from these tests and if there is one thing that appears obvious at first notice is the complete absence of significance of both ϕ_0 and ϕ_1, thus suggesting that the previously reported insignificance of first-order return-autocorrelation and feedback trading post-ETF remains robust when accounting for the impact of the ongoing crisis.[25] The outbreak of the crisis appears to have increased[26] the average level of volatility for all markets ($\beta_{0,2} > \beta_{0,1}$), with volatility itself maintaining its strong persistence and asymmetries.

To assess whether the changes in market dynamics following the ETFs' introduction are due primarily to an improvement in market efficiency or a reduction in the impact of noise traders, we run the set of Eqs. (19.11) and (19.12), where we account for a second lag in the feedback traders' demand function. Results are presented in Tables 19.9 (pre-ETF) and 19.10 (post-ETF) and show that both the first- (ϕ_0 and ϕ_1) and second-order coefficients (ϕ_3 and ϕ_4) exhibit much of their significance pre-ETF, with very little evidence of significance being documented post-ETF. To begin with, France, Germany, and the Netherlands are found to maintain insignificant values for these coefficients both before and after the launch of ETFs. Belgium and Switzerland bear significant ϕ_0 and ϕ_3 values pre-ETF which turn insignificant post-ETF, thus indicating that the change in market dynamics for both is the product of improvements in their efficiency. Finland is characterized by significant ϕ_0 and ϕ_1 values pre-ETF, while post-ETF it is the ϕ_0 only that appears significant; in this case, it is the reduction in noise trading that leads to changes in market dynamics following the introduction of ETFs, not changes in market efficiency. Sweden maintains significant inefficiencies pre-

---

[23] Exception here is Sweden, where ϕ_0 appears significant post-ETF using 2- and 3-year windows, with its difference from its respective pre-ETF values being however insignificant.

[24] Its difference from its respective pre-ETF value is insignificant.

[25] We repeated these tests using the 1/9/2008 as an alternative cut-off point (coinciding with the Lehman Brothers' filing for bankruptcy) with results confirming this insignificance in all markets before and after the crisis' outbreak, with the sole exception of ϕ_0 for Finland pre-crisis. Results are not presented here in the interest of brevity but are available from the authors upon request.

[26] The rise in average volatility levels is significant in Belgium, Finland, France, the Netherlands, and the UK at the 5% level and insignificant for the rest of the markets.

Table 19.8: Maximum likelihood estimates of the Sentana and Wadhwani (1992) model: test for parameter changes in the post-ETF spot market indexes daily returns pre versus postcrisis.

Conditional mean equation: $r_t = \alpha + \theta\sigma_t^2 + [\phi_{0,1}D_t + \phi_{0,2}(1-D_t)]r_{t-1} + [\phi_{1,1}D_t + \phi_{1,2}(1-D_t)]\sigma^2 r_{t-1} + \varepsilon_t$

Conditional variance specification: $\sigma_t^2 = \beta_{0,1}D_t + \beta_{0,2}(1-D_t) + \beta\varepsilon_{t-1}^2 + \gamma\sigma_{t-1}^2 + \delta S_{t-1}\varepsilon_{t-1}^2$

Parameters		BEL 20	OMXH25	CAC 40	DAX 30	AEX	OMXS30	SWISSMI	FTSE 100
α		0.0487	0.0267	-0.0177	0.0074	-0.0005	0.0015	0.0011	-0.0133
		(0.0225)[b]	(0.0289)	(0.0239)	(0.0250)	(0.0213)	(0.0289)	(0.0211)	(0.0192)
θ		0.0095	0.0009	0.0097	0.0054	-0.0004	0.0046	0.0030	0.0127
		(0.0178)	(0.0179)	(0.0135)	(0.0132)	(0.0126)	(0.0146)	(0.0177)	(0.0162)
$\phi_{0,1}$		0.0128	0.0931	-0.0465	-0.0055	0.0251	0.0353	-0.0181	-0.0428
		(0.0375)	(0.0486)	(0.0353)	(0.0350)	(0.0330)	(0.0375)	(0.0315)	(0.0307)
$\phi_{0,2}$		0.0238	-0.0019	-0.0144	-0.0071	0.0210	-0.0374	0.0230	-0.0234
		(0.0399)	(0.0526)	(0.0420)	(0.0439)	(0.0423)	(0.0493)	(0.0357)	(0.0425)
$\phi_{1,1}$		-0.0177	-0.0204	0.0002	-0.0057	-0.0089	-0.0111	0.0042	-0.0067
		(0.0124)	(0.0291)	(0.0109)	(0.0084)	(0.0071)	(0.0110)	(0.0116)	(0.0146)
$\phi_{1,2}$		0.0000	0.0012	-0.0016	0.0016	-0.0032	0.0023	0.0000	-0.0020
		(0.0085)	(0.0112)	(0.0073)	(0.0080)	(0.0069)	(0.0095)	(0.0074)	(0.0090)
$\beta_{0,1}$		0.0229	0.0204	0.0247	0.0257	0.0168	0.0213	0.0207	0.0177
		(0.0033)[a]	(0.0035)[a]	(0.0037)[a]	(0.0036)[a]	(0.0027)[a]	(0.0036)[a]	(0.0031)[a]	(0.0025)[a]
$\beta_{0,2}$		0.0513	0.0365	0.0415	0.0321	0.0290	0.0267	0.0253	0.0398
		(0.0099)[a]	(0.0096)[a]	(0.0082)[a]	(0.0060)[a]	(0.0050)[a]	(0.0056)[a]	(0.0052)[a]	(0.0058)[a]
γ		0.8769	0.9204	0.9145	0.9170	0.9233	0.9338	0.9012	0.9143
		(0.0104)[a]	(0.0089)[a]	(0.0080)[a]	(0.0089)[a]	(0.0074)[a]	(0.0069)[a]	(0.0088)[a]	(0.0084)[a]
β		0.0079	0.0130	-0.0259	-0.0202	-0.0202	-0.0110	-0.0149	-0.0242
		(0.0090)	(0.0086)	(0.0062)[b]	(0.0085)[b]	(0.0082)[b]	(0.0067)	(0.0072)[b]	(0.0086)[a]
δ		0.1764	0.1005	0.1884	0.1751	0.1671	0.1322	0.1895	0.1721
		(0.0169)[a]	(0.0127)[a]	(0.0146)[a]	(0.0138)[a]	(0.0129)[a]	(0.0116)[a]	(0.0148)[a]	(0.0131)[a]
$(\beta+\delta)/\beta$		23.3291	8.7308	-6.2741	-7.6683	-7.2723	-11.0182	-11.7181	-6.1116
Half life		25.3	42.0	40.0	43.9	51.6	62.1	36.2	28.7
Wald tests statistics	$H_0: \phi_{0,1}=\phi_{0,2}$	0.0400	1.764607	0.3448	0.0008	0.0056	1.3904	0.7515	0.1379
	$H_0: \phi_{1,1}=\phi_{1,2}$	1.4248	0.4885	0.0230	0.4382	0.3684	0.9152	0.1010	0.0775
	$H_0: \beta_{0,1}=\beta_{0,2}$	12.3482[a]	4.3937[b]	6.8175[b]	1.9546	9.9485[b]	1.7489	1.5009	23.9439[a]

Parentheses include the standard errors of the estimates. Wald-test statistics are represented here through their chi-square values.

[a]Denotes significance at the 1% level.

[b]Denotes significance at the 5% level.

Table 19.9: Maximum likelihood estimates of the Sentana and Wadhwani (1992) model: controlling for higher-order feedback traders' demand (pre-ETF).

Conditional mean equation: $r_t = \alpha + (\phi_0 + \phi_1\sigma_t^2)r_{t-1} + (\phi_3 + \phi_4\sigma_t^2)r_{t-2} + \theta\sigma_t^2 + \varepsilon_t$

Conditional variance specification: $\sigma_t^2 = \omega + \beta\varepsilon_{t-1}^2 + \gamma\sigma_{t-1}^2 + \delta S_{t-1}\varepsilon_{t-1}^2$

Parameters	BEL 20 (2/1/1990– 1/10/2002)	OMXH25 (2/1/1990– 10/2/2002)	CAC 40 (2/1/1990– 21/1/2001)	DAX 30 (2/1/1990– 2/1/2001)	AEX (2/1/1990– 29/5/2001)	OMXS30 (2/1/1990– 29/10/2000)	SWISSMI (2/1/1990– 14/3/2001)	FTSE 100 (2/1/1990– 27/4/2000)
α	-0.0053	0.0563	-0.1030	-0.0007	0.0182	0.0522	0.0042	0.0036
	(0.0200)	(0.0428)	(0.0516)[b]	(0.0394)	(0.0272)	(0.0363)	(0.0360)	(0.0299)
θ	0.01452	-0.0116	0.0936	0.0298	0.0297	-0.0003	0.0353	0.0358
	(0.0252)	(0.0207)	(0.0384)[b]	(0.0290)	(0.0297)	(0.0231)	(0.0388)	(0.0411)
ϕ_0	0.1671	0.2110	0.0708	0.0640	0.0290	0.1192	0.0975	0.0535
	(0.0247)[a]	(0.0316)[a]	(0.0383)	(0.0338)	(0.0295)	(0.0305)[a]	(0.0290)[a]	(0.0370)
ϕ_1	-0.0194	-0.0292	-0.0124	-0.0170	-0.0020	-0.0152	-0.0171	0.0079
	(0.0126)	(0.0083)[a]	(0.0188)	(0.0133)	(0.0148)	(0.0098)	(0.0137)	(0.0331)
ϕ_3	0.0581	0.0302	0.0583	0.0567	0.0261	0.0782	0.0586	0.0866
	(0.0265)[b]	(0.0341)	(0.0366)	(0.0334)	(0.0289)	(0.0292)[a]	(0.0279)[b]	(0.0359)[b]
ϕ_4	-0.0257	-0.0138	-0.0283	-0.0253	-0.0266	-0.0235	-0.0214	-0.0976
	(0.0136)	(0.0091)	(0.0179)	(0.0137)	(0.0156)	(0.0091)[a]	(0.0136)	(0.0337)[a]
ω	0.0345	0.0907	0.0630	0.0440	0.0195	0.0480	0.1019	0.0063
	(0.0028)[a]	(0.0096)[a]	(0.0087)[a]	(0.0056)[a]	(0.0025)[a]	(0.0084)[b]	(0.0092)[a]	(0.0016)[a]
γ	0.8450	0.8629	0.9040	0.8992	0.9084	0.8718	0.7761	0.9558
	(0.0111)[a]	(0.0093)[a]	(0.0113)[a]	(0.0101)[a]	(0.0085)[a]	(0.0115)	(0.0194)[a]	(0.0052)[a]
β	0.0558	0.0825	0.0140	0.0412	0.0481	0.0473	0.0343	0.0125
	(0.0099)[a]	(0.0077)[a]	(0.0087)	(0.0090)[a]	(0.0079)[a]	(0.0072)[a]	(0.0118)[b]	(0.0057)[b]
δ	0.1223	0.0370	0.0728	0.0576	0.0477	0.1158	0.1792	0.0484
	(0.0143)[a]	(0.0119)[a]	(0.0119)[a]	(0.0110)[a]	(0.0085)[a]	(0.0148)[a]	(0.0165)[a]	(0.0083)[a]
$(\beta+\delta)/\beta$	3.1918	1.4485	6.2000	2.3981	1.9917	3.4482	6.2245	4.8720
Half life	17.9	18.9	14.9	22.2	34.9	29.8	6.6	92.1

Parentheses include the standard errors of the estimates.

[a] Denotes significance at the 1% level.

[b] Denotes significance at the 5% level.

Table 19.10: Maximum likelihood estimates of the Sentana and Wadhwani (1992) model: controlling for higher-order feedback traders' demand (post-ETF).

Conditional mean equation: $r_t = \alpha + (\phi_0 + \phi_4\sigma_t^2)r_{t-1} + (\phi_3 + \phi_4\sigma_t^2)r_{t-2} + \theta\sigma_t^2 + \varepsilon_t$

Conditional variance specification: $\sigma_t^2 = \omega + \beta\varepsilon_{t-1}^2 + \gamma\sigma_{t-1}^2 + \delta S_{t-1}\varepsilon_{t-1}^2$

Parameters	BEL 20 (2/10/2002–12/12/2014)	OMXH25 (11/2/2002–12/12/2014)	CAC 40 (22/1/2001–12/12/2014)	DAX 30 (3/1/2001–12/12/2014)	AEX (30/5/2001–12/12/2014)	OMXS30 (30/10/2000–12/12/2014)	SWISSMI (15/3/2001–12/12/2014)	FTSE 100 (28/4/2000–12/12/2014)
α	0.0501	0.0814	-0.0103	0.0093	0.0011	0.0110	0.0055	-0.0013
	(0.0230)[b]	(0.0262)[b]	(0.0243)	(0.0251)	(0.0217)	(0.0292)	(0.0215)	(0.0202)
θ	-0.0165	-0.0181	0.0026	0.0022	-0.0062	-0.0004	-0.0027	0.0002
	(0.0187)	(0.0137)	(0.0139)	(0.0133)	(0.0128)	(0.0149)	(0.0182)	(0.0175)
ϕ_0	0.0068	0.0593	-0.0378	-0.0104	0.0173	0.0047	-0.0058	-0.0409
	(0.0262)	(0.0230)[b]	(0.0264)	(0.0271)	(0.0259)	(0.0288)	(0.0239)	(0.0246)
ϕ_1	0.0011	-0.0080	-0.0003	-0.0017	-0.0047	-0.0042	0.0037	-0.0027
	(0.0072)	(0.0060)	(0.0064)	(0.0061)	(0.0052)	(0.0070)	(0.0077)	(0.0081)
ϕ_3	0.0194	0.0217	-0.0016	0.0148	0.0288	-0.0135	-0.0104	-0.0059
	(0.0258)	(0.0243)	(0.0247)	(0.0249)	(0.0246)	(0.0260)[b]	(0.0249)	(0.0235)
ϕ_4	-0.0076	-0.0083	-0.0061	-0.0049	-0.0047	-0.0070	-0.0094	-0.0097
	(0.0074)	(0.0061)	(0.0057)	(0.0053)	(0.0046)	(0.0067)	(0.0080)	(0.0075)
ω	0.0194	0.0209	0.0232	0.0261	0.0161	0.0213	0.0205	0.0157
	(0.0029)[a]	(0.0031)[a]	(0.0036)[a]	(0.0037)[a]	(0.0027)[a]	(0.0037)[a]	(0.0032)[a]	(0.0024)[a]
γ	0.8913	0.9125	0.9191	0.9187	0.9279	0.9343	0.9025	0.9169
	(0.0076)[a]	(0.0051)[a]	(0.0076)[a]	(0.0087)[a]	(0.0070)[a]	(0.0068)[a]	(0.0083)[a]	(0.0079)[a]
β	0.0086	0.0526	-0.0221	-0.0195	-0.0189	-0.0093	-0.0128	-0.0091
	(0.0083)	(0.0060)[a]	(0.0068)[a]	(0.0085)[a]	(0.0078)[b]	(0.0066)	(0.0071)	(0.0081)
δ	0.1737	0.0561	0.1813	0.1734	0.1640	0.1297	0.1864	0.1556
	(0.0158)	(0.0086)[a]	(0.0137)[a]	(0.0134)[a]	(0.0125)[a]	(0.0115)[a]	(0.0141)[a]	(0.0117)[a]
$(\beta+\delta)/\beta$	21.1977	2.0665	-7.2036	-7.8923	-7.6772	-12.9462	-13.5625	-16.0989
Half life	52.0	100.8	55.8	48.8	76.7	67.9	40.2	47.8

Parentheses include the standard errors of the estimates.
[a] Denotes significance at the 1% level.
[b] Denotes significance at the 5% level.

ETF (both ϕ_0 and ϕ_3 are significant), with ϕ_4 being significant pre-ETF as well; post-ETF it is only ϕ_3 that remains significant, indicating that the change in market dynamics is due to the reduction of both noise trading and market inefficiencies (which do not disappear completely, as the second-order autocorrelation significance persists). Finally, the United Kingdom exhibits significance in the ϕ_3 and ϕ_4 coefficients pre-ETF, whose values turn insignificant post-ETF, thus implying that changes in its market dynamics following the introduction of ETFs was due to the reduction of both noise trading and market inefficiencies.

We now examine whether the overall documented depression of noise trading post-ETF can be ascribed to noise traders' migration toward the ETF-segment. Table 19.11 presents the results from the original Sentana and Wadhwani (1992) model run on our sample markets' ETF-series from where it becomes apparent that the migration hypothesis is overwhelmingly rejected, as the ϕ_1 values are insignificant for all markets. ETFs are characterized by efficiency (ϕ_0 values are insignificant) and by the volatility properties (persistence; asymmetries) reported for their underlying spot indices. Combined with the evidence presented in the previous tables, these results confirm that the introduction of ETFs has proved beneficial for capital markets, in line with the evidence presented by Kallinterakis and Kaur (2010). More specifically, our findings show that ETFs (1) are not dominated by noise investors, (2) enhance market efficiency, (3) dampen the significance of noise trading, and (4) produce no significant effect over market volatility.

19.5 Conclusions

The present study is motivated by concerns, both theoretical (related to the attractiveness of ETFs as products to retail investors from a behavioral perspective) and empirical (stemming from studies emphasizing the size of retail participation in ETF-volume), as to whether the introduction of ETFs promotes noise trading. Drawing upon a sample of eight European markets, we employ the established rational-feedback-trader framework proposed by Sentana and Wadhwani (1992) to assess the impact of ETF-introduction over market dynamics, in terms of noise trading, efficiency, and volatility. Our evidence lends little support to the above mentioned concerns, since it denotes that the launch of ETFs bears an overall beneficial effect over these markets as it leads to improvements in their efficiency and depresses any existing feedback trading. Its effect over market volatility appears rather limited, since volatility appears highly persistent and asymmetric both prior to and after the introduction of ETFs. These results are robust to the impact of the ongoing global crisis and are largely confirmed when accounting for longer memory in feedback traders' demand. Although feedback trading is eliminated in all markets post-ETF, there is no evidence to suggest that this is due to feedback traders migrating to the ETF-segment.

The above are obviously encouraging from a regulatory viewpoint, as they confirm earlier literature findings (Switzer et al., 2000; Kurov and Dennis Lasser, 2002) on ETFs' relation

Table 19.11: Maximum likelihood estimates of the Sentana and Wadhwani (1992) model: ETF daily returns

Conditional mean equation: $r_t = \alpha + \left(\phi_0 + \phi_1 \sigma_t^2\right) r_{t-1} + \theta \sigma_t^2 + \varepsilon_t$

Conditional variance specification: $\sigma_t^2 = \omega + \beta \varepsilon_{t-1}^2 + \gamma \sigma_{t-1}^2 + \delta S_{t-1} \varepsilon_{t-1}^2$

Parameters	LYXOR ETF BEL 20 (2/10/2002– 12/12/2014)	SLG OMXH25 (11/2/2002– 12/12/2014)	LYXOR ETF CAC 40 (22/1/2001– 12/12/2014)	DAX^{EX} (3/1/2001– 12/12/2014)	AEXT STREETTRACKS (30/5/2001– 12/12/2014)	XACT OMXS30 (30/10/2000– 12/12/2014)	XMTCH ON SMI (15/3/2001– 12/12/2014)	iSHARES FTSE 100 (28/4/2000– 12/12/2014)
α	0.0526 (0.0218)[b]	−0.1324 (0.0680)	−0.0041 (0.0252)	−0.0028 (0.0241)	0.0119 (0.0232)	0.0142 (0.0304)	0.0034 (0.0220)	−0.0022 (0.0204)
θ	−0.0133 (0.0205)	0.0593 (0.0288)[b]	0.0005 (0.0140)	0.0096 (0.0126)	−0.0140 (0.0131)	−0.0014 (0.0144)	0.0002 (0.0183)	0.0019 (0.0166)
ϕ_0	−0.0006 (0.0284)	0.0128 (0.0203)	−0.0413 (0.0263)	0.0062 (0.0271)	0.0064 (0.0253)	−0.0226 (0.0302)	−0.0139 (0.0240)	−0.0457 (0.0239)
ϕ_1	0.0082 (0.0098)	0.0000 (0.0156)	0.0008 (0.0064)	0.0008 (0.0060)	−0.0037 (0.0052)	−0.0017 (0.0077)	0.0028 (0.0072)	−0.0070 (0.0060)
ω	0.0176 (0.0027)[a]	0.1477 (0.1452)	0.0223 (0.0036)[a]	0.0267 (0.0030)[a]	0.0144 (0.0027)[a]	0.0170 (0.0031)[a]	0.0193 (0.0028)[a]	0.0162 (0.0024)[a]
γ	0.8972 (0.0083)[a]	0.8989 (0.0351)[a]	0.9189 (0.0077)[a]	0.9217 (0.0076)[a]	0.9300 (0.0073)[a]	0.9465 (0.0058)[a]	0.9118 (0.0079)[a]	0.9161 (0.0071)[a]
β	0.0062 (0.0080)	−0.0012 (0.0012)	−0.0184 (0.0071)[a]	−0.0280 (0.0078)[a]	0.0170 (0.0082)[b]	−0.0101 (0.0055)	−0.0157 (0.0071)[b]	−0.0028 (0.0076)
δ	0.1636 (0.0148)[a]	0.0886 (0.0276)[a]	0.1753 (0.0139)[a]	0.1820 (0.0130)[a]	0.1590 (0.0117)[a]	0.1104 (0.0100)[a]	0.1722 (0.0143)[a]	0.1442 (0.0110)[a]
$(\beta+\delta)/\beta$	27.3871	−72.8333	−8.5272	−5.5000	10.3529	−9.9307	−9.9682	−50.5000
Half life	46.5	11.6	58.1	45.0	−26.5	82.2	38.6	47.1

Parentheses include the standard errors of the estimates.

[a] Denotes significance at the 1% level.

[b] Denotes significance at the 5% level.

to price-efficiency and constitute evidence in favor of ETFs rendering capital markets more complete. What is more, these results also bear important implications for the investment community, since the insignificant noise traders' presence in ETF-trading enhances confidence in the role of ETFs as risk-management tools, thus helping them attract more investors and rendering their market more liquid. To that end, it would be useful to see this research extended in the future to emerging capital markets, where the ETF-industry is, in the vast majority of cases, either in its infancy or nonexistent. ETFs, for example, can prove useful when investing in emerging markets that are considered highly risky and ill-transparent, since a foreign investor with little faith in their information environment can opt for investing in these markets through an ETF instead of actively trying to collect information on individual stocks. Furthermore, an investor wishing to hedge his positions in an emerging market would find the presence of an ETF-industry in that market highly convenient in case overseas listed ETFs benchmarked against that market's stocks do not exist. In view of the increased integration of emerging markets in the global financial architecture and the concomitant rise in foreign investment, the above raise issues rendering the use of ETFs particularly relevant in these markets' context.

References

ASX investors' update newsletter, 2011. Where the ETF market is heading. Available from: http://www.asx.com.au/resources/investor-update-newsletter/201106-where-the-etf-market-is-heading.htm

Ackert, L.F., Tian, Y.S., 2000. Arbitrage and valuation in the market for Standard and Poor's depositary receipts. Financ. Manage. 29 (3), 71–88.

Anderson, T., 2008. US-listed ETF industry review and 2008 outlook. SPDRs State Street Global Advisors. Available from: http://www.ssgafunds.com/library/mkcm/Outlook_2008_01.15.2008REVCCRI1200502543.pdf

Antoniou, A., Koutmos, G., Pericli, A., 2005. Index futures and positive feedback trading: evidence from major stock exchanges. J. Empir. Finance 12 (2), 219–238.

Barber, B.M., Odean, T., 2000. Trading is hazardous to your wealth: the common stock investment performance of individual investors. J. Finance 55 (2), 773–806.

Barber, B.M., Odean, T., 2008. All that glitters: the effect of attention and news on the buying behavior of individual and institutional investors. Rev. Financ. Studies 21 (2), 785–818.

Barber, B.M., Odean, T., Zhu, N., 2009. Systematic noise. J. Financ. Markets 12 (4), 547–569.

Barberis, N., Huang, M., 2001. Mental accounting, loss aversion and individual stock returns. J. Finance 56 (4), 1247–1292.

Bollerslev, T., Engle, R.F., Nelson, D.B., 1994. ARCH models. Engle, R.F., McFadden, D.L. (Eds.), Handbook of Econometrics, Vol IV, Elsevier Science, Amsterdam.

Boyd, M., 2001. On ignorance, intuition, and investing: a bear market test of the recognition heuristic. J. Psychol. Financ. Markets 2 (3), 150–156.

Cherry, J., 2004. The limits of arbitrage: evidence from exchange traded funds. Working Paper. University of California-Berkeley.

Curcio, R.J., Lipka, J.M., Thornton, J.H., 2004. Cubes and the individual investor. Financ. Serv. Rev. 13 (2), 123–138.

Deloitte Research, 2009. Exchange traded funds: challenging the dominance of mutual funds? Available from: http://www.runtogold.com/images/Deloitte-ETF-report.pdf

Deville, L., 2008. Exchange traded funds: history, trading and research. Zopounidis, C., Doumpos, M., Pardalos, P.M. (Eds.), Handbook of Financial Engineering, Vol. 18, Springer, New York.

Ellis, R.J., 2009. Wealth management overview: top trends in client segmentation, products and delivery channels. Novarica Research Report.

Elton, E.J., Gruber, M.J., Comer, G., Li, K., 2002. Spiders: where are the bugs? J. Bus. 75 (3), 453–472.

Financial Times, 2011. ETF launches reveal investors want broader portfolios. Available from: http://www.ft.com/cms/s/0/3b1aeb5af40111e0b22100144feab49a.html#axzz1j46uPCi1

Glosten, L.R., Jagannathan, R., Runkle, D.E., 1993. On the relation between the expected value and the volatility of the nominal excess return on stocks. J. Finance 48 (5), 1779–1801.

Greenwich Associates, 2010. ETFs gain foothold in institutional market. Available from: http://www4.greenwich.com/WMA/greenwich_reports/report_abstract/1,1622,7300,00.html?rtOrigin=A&vgnvisitor=e6eYmaWLnJQ=

Harris, R.D.F., Pisedtasalasai, A., 2006. Return and volatility spillovers between large and small stocks in the UK. J. Bus. Finance Account. 33 (9–10), 1556–1571.

Hill, J., Teller, S., 2010. Hedging with inverse ETFs: a primer. J Indexes 13, 18–24.

Hirshleifer, D., Teoh, S.H., 2003. Limited attention, information disclosure, and financial reporting. J. Account. Econ. 36 (1–3), 337–386.

Hirshleifer, D., Lim, S.S., Teoh, S.H., 2011. Limited investor attention and stock market misreactions to accounting information. Rev. Asset Pricing Studies 1 (1), 35–73.

Ho, J., 2006. Myths and facts about exchange traded funds. Asian Investor. Available from: http://www.ishares.com.hk/pdf/Asian%20Investor_Myths%20Facts%20About%20ETF_JH_BGI%20version.pdf

Huberman, G., 2001. Familiarity breeds investment. Rev. Financ. Studies 14 (3), 659–680.

Kallinterakis, V., Kaur, S., 2010. On the impact of exchange traded funds over noise trading: evidence from European stock exchanges. In: Gregoriou, G.N. (Ed.), Handbook of Trading: Strategies for Navigating and Profiting From Currency, Bond, and Stock Markets. McGraw-Hill, New York, NY.

Kostovetsky, L., 2003. Index mutual funds and exchange-traded funds. J. Portfol. Manage. 29 (4), 80–92.

Kurov, A.A., Dennis Lasser, D.J., 2002. The effect of the introduction of cubes on the Nasdaq-100 index spot-futures pricing relationship. J. Futures Markets 22 (3), 197–218.

Luskin, D.L., 1988. Portfolio Insurance: A Guide to Dynamic Hedging. John Wiley and Sons, New York.

Osler, C.L., 2002. Stop-loss orders and price cascades in currency markets. Federal Reserve Bank of New York. Available from: https://www.newyorkfed.org/medialibrary/media/research/staff_reports/sr150.pdf

Park, T.H., Switzer, L.L., 1995. Index participation units and the performance of index futures markets: evidence from the Toronto 35 index participation units market. J. Futures Markets 15 (2), 187–200.

Sentana, E., Wadhwani, S., 1992. Feedback traders and stock return autocorrelations: evidence from a century of daily data. Econ. J. 102 (411), 415–425.

Skelly, A, 2011. Digging deeper: institutional ETF-investing in Australia—insights and implications. Russel Investment Management Ltd. Available from: http://www.asx.com.au/documents/products/Russell_Investments_ETF_Research_-_Australian_Securities_Exchange_-_ASX.pdf

Switzer, L.N., Varson, P.L., Zghidi, S., 2000. Standard and Poor's depository receipts and the performance of the S&P 500 index futures market. J. Futures Markets 20 (8), 705–716.

The Trade, 2011. TSE nears ETF target, but looks for institutional growth. Available from: http://www.thetradenews.com/newsarticle.aspx?id=5544

Ünal M (2009) The usage of ETFs by institutional investors. In: The Euromoney ETFs & Indices Handbook 2009. World Federation of Exchanges November 2011 Report (Chapter 1). Available from: http://www.funds-at-work.com/uploads/media/Funds_Work-Euromoney.pdf

The Behavior of Individual Online Investors Before and After the 2007 Financial Crisis: Lessons From the French Case

Daniel Haguet

EDHEC Business School, Nice, France; Institute of Business Administration, Nice Sophia Antipolis University, Nice, France

20.1 Introduction

If we look at the world stock capitalization between the end of 2007 and the end of 2008, we can observe a huge drop from 60,855 B\$ to 32,584 B\$, that is, −46% in just 1 year (Fig. 20.1). For investors in general, individual investors in particular, this change was extremely brutal.

The origins of the global financial crisis started in the United States when the real estate bubble started to burst. In July 2007, the Dow Jones index peaked at its maximum of 14,000 points but 418 securities issued by "big" names, such as Citigroup, Morgan Stanley, Merrill Lynch, and Bear Stearns were downgraded by the rating agency Standard & Poor's due to their exposure to the subprime loans. Ben Bernanke, Chairman of the Federal Reserve said in 2007,

> Some estimates are in the order of between \$50 billion and \$100 billion of losses associated with subprime credit problems.

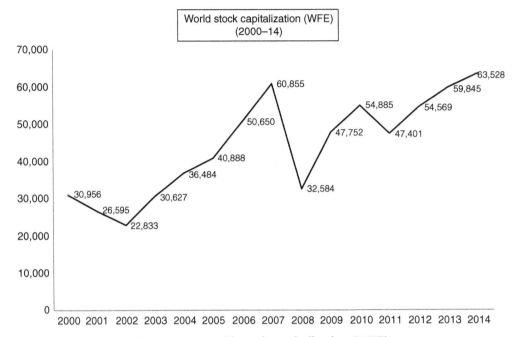

Figure 20.1: World Stock Capitalization (WFE).

European banks and some European funds were also struck by the shock through the securitization of the US subprime mortgage loans used as investment products. In France, a few money market funds from big asset management companies had to be reimbursed to clients because of the failure of securitization vehicles.

Since 1970, behavioral finance research has brought a new way to analyze the behavior of individual investors. The first fundamental papers (Tversky and Kahneman, 1974, 1981) based on cognitive psychology modified the basic hypothesis of traditional finance with a more accurate description of the decision process under risk. A few years later, empirical papers gave information on the main individual investors' biases on the financial markets (Odean 1998, 1999). This global framework gives concepts and tools to address the question of the individual investors trading behavior during financial crises, especially that of 2007.

The objective of this chapter is to look at the behavior of a sample of individual investors before and after the 2007 financial crisis. We use a sample of French individual online investors between the beginning of 2006 and mid-2008. We compare their trading behavior to the short-term performance and the long-term performance of the domestic market. We find an interesting discrepancy between their trading behavior before the financial crisis and their trading behavior after the financial crisis. Investors tend to be more sensitive to the return of the market after the financial crisis than before.

The structure of this chapter is as follows: we will begin by a literature review, then a sample description, and our main results. The last section will conclude.

20.2 Literature Review

To understand the behavior of individual online investors before and after the financial crisis, we need to look at the rationality of decisions, the specificities of online investors, and the research carried out on the financial crisis.

20.2.1 Rationality of Decisions

The fundamental article of Markowitz (1952) on Portfolio Theory assumed the individual to be fully rational. The same assumption is behind the CAPM model (Lintner, 1965; Mossin, 1966; Sharpe, 1964) and the Modigliani and Miller theorems (Modigliani and Miller, 1958, 1963). The agent of the traditional financial theory is considered to be entirely rational and follows a certain number of rules (Von Neumann and Morgenstern, 1953), such as maximization of his utility or certain axioms, such as transitivity, completeness, continuity, and independence. For this stream of academic literature in finance, individual rationality, capital markets efficiency, and the absence of arbitrage are the fundamental pillars.

The "homo econo micus" hypothesis was strongly questioned by the numerous papers published by Daniel Kahneman and Amos Tversky during the 1970s. In 1974, they present the main heuristics and biases (Tversky and Kahneman, 1974): representativeness, availability, adjustment, and anchoring. According to Kahenman and Tversky, these heuristics cloud the decision making process of individuals when they make an investment. For example, people believe that a baseball player is more likely to succeed his shot after one or two previous successes than after failing his previous shots (Gilovich et al., 1985). Then, Kahneman and Tversky developed the concept of framing (Tversky and Kahneman, 1981, 1986) which describes the fact that the positive or negative framing of the same question could lead to a different answer.

The next step was to present an alternative decision making theory: the Prospect theory (Kahneman and Tversky, 1979; Tversky and Kahneman, 1992). Prospect theory contributes a new analysis of the decision making process by taking into account

- a value function instead of a traditional utility function, the value function presents the pleasure and the pain following a positive or a negative change in the level of wealth,
- the asymmetry of risk aversion between gains and losses: the individuals are risk averse in a situation of gain and risk seekers in a situation of loss. In a casino, it means that they will stop gambling when they win and will go on gambling when they lose,
- the aversion to losses, individuals suffer twice as much for a loss than they feel pleasure when they win the same amount,
- and the transformation of objective probabilities into subjective probabilities.

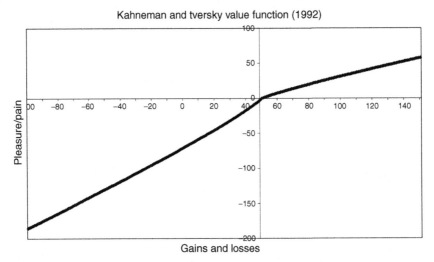

Figure 20.2: Example of a Kahneman and Tversky (Kahneman and Tversky, 1979; Tversky and Kahneman, 1992) Value Function.

Prospect theory is used in many cases to describe behaviors outside a finance framework. For example, the behavior of New York City cab drivers (Camerer et al., 1997) or that of golf players, such as Tiger Woods (Pope and Schweitzer, 2011) who exhibit an asymmetric reaction to a risky situation (risk aversion in a positive situation and risk seeking in a negative situation). We present an example of a Kahneman and Tversky value function in Fig. 20.2 and the differences between traditional finance and behavioral finance in Table 20.1. Behavioral finance is of interest because it leads to a valuable description of the behavior of individuals when they trade or manage their investments.

From the empirical point of view, based on a US broker database, Odean (1998, 1999) showed that most individual investors were prone to investment mistakes, such as disposition effect (Odean, 1998) and overconfidence (Shefrin and Statman, 1985; Odean, 1999). The disposition effect (Odean, 1998) is the tendency to keep losing stocks longer and to sell winning stocks faster. Individual investors' portfolios have fewer and fewer winning stocks and more and more losing stocks, which creates a growing underperformance compared to a benchmark. Overconfidence (Odean, 1999) drives individuals to a high turnover of their portfolios, more fees to pay on transactions and a decrease in the returns of their portfolios compared to that of the market.

Other authors have highlighted more investment mistakes. For example, we know that, according to Markowitz (1952), a diversified portfolio has a lower risk than a portfolio with a very low number of assets, but Goetzmann and Kumar (2008) showed that the average number of securities held in individual investor portfolios is around three or four. Beside underdiversification, French and Poterba (1991) also documented the existence of a "domestic

Table 20.1: Differences between traditional finance and behavioral finance.

	Traditional Finance	Behavioral Finance
Function	Traditional utility function	Value function
Risk	Risk aversion	• Risk aversion in situation of gain • Risk seeking in situation of loss
Rationality	The individual is fully rational	• Individual suffer from heuristics a biases
Derivative theories	• Markowitz (1952) efficient frontiers CAPM (Sharpe, 1964)	• Behavioral CAPM (Shefrin and Statman, 1994) • Behavioral portfolio theory (Shefrin and Statman, 2000)
Investment mistakes	None	• Disposition effect (Odean, 1998) • Overconfidence (Odean, 1999) • Domestic bias (French and Poterba, 1991) • Underdiversification (Goetzmann and Kumar, 2008)

bias" on aggregated data from different countries (United States, Japan, United Kingdom, France, Germany, and Canada) showing that individuals are reluctant to invest in foreign stocks and prefer domestic stocks.

Most of Odean's papers point out that individuals or retail investors should not trade directly on the market due to an extensive number of mistakes they make. Maybe they would be better off buying index funds or exchange trading funds (ETF's) and following a passive strategy.

20.2.2 Online Investors

Individual online investors are a subsample of individual investors. According to Barber and Odean (2002), they are younger, richer, and wealthier than traditional individual investors are.

Barber and Odean (2002) also show that individual online investors suffer more from overconfidence than other retail investors do. Comparing two matching samples of the US retail investors, one trading by phone and the other one switching from phone trading to online trading, Barber and Odean (2002) found out an excess of trading due to overconfidence, an excess of fees, and a dramatic decrease in the portfolios return compared to traditional individual investors on the US market.

In other countries, several papers presented the characteristics of online investors for Korea (Oh et al., 2008), Sweden (Anderson, 2007), USA (Choi et al., 2002), and Germany (Glaser, 2003). The main results are listed in Table 20.2.

Table 20.2: Main results on online individual investors by country.

Country	United States of America	Korea	Sweden	Germany
Author(s) (year)	Choi et al. (2002)	Oh et al. (2008)	Anderson (2007)	Glaser (2003)
Period	May 1997–March 2000	January 2001–December 2005	May 1999–March 2002	January 1997–April 2001
Type of data	Individual—Broker	Global—Market	Individuals—Broker	Individuals—Broker
Frequency of transactions	Twice more trades			Increase
Size of transactions	Lower		Low	
Percent portfolio turnover	No change		100% per year	30% per month
Number of securities in the portfolio	Nonapplicable (mutual funds)		2	Increase
Performance	No overperformance of online transactions compared to phone based transactions	Low performance of online individual investors compared to foreigners and institutions	Underperformance compared to the market due to the high turnover and the fees	

Results are quite heterogeneous due to the differences between databases but one of the most common results is the underperformance compared to the market of individual online investors compared to traditional individual investors.

20.2.3 Financial Crisis

A large stream of literature deals with the history, the characteristics, and the explanations of financial crises. The book *"Manias, Panics and Crashes"* by Kindleberger et al. (2005) is certainly one of the most famous. It describes the history and the anatomy of a financial crisis, focusing on the central role of credit. The 2008 financial crisis was extremely severe and Shefrin and Statman (2011) highlighted the need to incorporate behavioral finance (i.e., aspirations, cognition, emotions, and culture) into our economic and financial theories.

A few academic papers have been written on the behavior of individual investors during financial crises. Kim and Shang-Jin (1999) analyzed different categories of foreign portfolio investors in Korea. They found out that nonresident institutional investors are always positive feedback traders whereas resident investors were negative feedback traders before the crisis then turn into positive feedback traders during the crisis. Later, Hoffmann et al. (2013) showed that the investor perception changed the trading and risk-behavior during the 2008–09 financial crisis. Kallberg et al. (2014) used the trading records of a sample of Chinese individual investors between January 2005 and November 2008. They find that (1) individual investors did not withdraw their funds from the equity market during the crisis; (2) the net flow decisions were influenced by past positive returns; and (3) during the crisis, investors revised their portfolios to hold relatively safer, and more liquid stocks.

Kaniel and Sraer (2013) examined a French retail trader holdings and transactions database between January 1999 and December 2010 and documented the heterogeneity in the trading behavior. They found that sophisticated investors increased their demand for risky assets during the crisis and less sophisticated investors were prone to a flight to safety decreasing their investment in risky assets and experiencing the decline of their performance.

20.3 Sample Description

We use a sample of French individual online investors between January 2006 and June 2008. We have two files: one for the 1.3 M transactions and one for the 16,241 accounts. The first one contains the date, the amount, the name, and the ISIN code for each security traded, the fees, and a code for a purchase transaction or a sale transaction. We have 1.3 million of purchases and sales from January 1, 2006 to June 30, 2008 (Tables 20.3 and 20.4). Most of the transactions take place on the French stock market but we also have transactions on money market mutual funds. The average fee for buying and selling stocks is 0.18%.

Table 20.3: Description of the purchases and sales in volume.

Item	Total Database	French Stock Market	Percent French Stock Market (%)
Number of purchases	717,000	654,817	91.33
Volume of purchases	5,736,561,186 €	5,137,889,133 €	89.56
Average buy	8,000.78 €	7,846.30 €	98.07
Number of sales	610,960	565,703	92.59
Volume of sales	5,018,357,732 €	4 375,372,038 €	87.19
Average sell	8,213.89 €	7,734.40 €	94.16
Total number of trades	1,327,960	1,220,520	91.91
Total volume	10,754,918,918 €	9,513,261,171 €	88.45
Average volume	8,098.83 €	7,794.43 €	96.24
Number of accounts	16,241	12,594	77.54
Number of securities	17,236	14,112	81.88
Number of clients	13,516	10,407	77.00

Table 20.4: Characteristics of the trades.

Number of trades	1.327.960
Period	01/01/2006–30/06/2008
Percent purchases	54%
Percent sales	46%
Percent French stocks	92.13%
Percent internet transactions	91.63%

Our sample is quite homogeneous: French individual investors trading French stocks on the Internet.

The second file contains the description of the 16,241 accounts: gender, zip code, age, date of creation, fiscal profile (some French accounts called "PEA" have tax advantages). That gives a brief description of our sample based on demographic information. A major part of our sample is male (91.68%) and 97.91% is of French citizenship. The average age is 67 years old but the median is 53 years old (Table 20.5).

The main index on the French stock market is the CAC 40. It contains 40 stocks with the largest size of capitalization in France using a capi-weighted scheme. Fund managers and portfolio managers use this index as a benchmark for the performance of French stocks. The top 10 stocks in number and in volume traded by our sample are all part of the CAC 40 (Table 20.6).

20.4 An Empirical Analysis of the Trading Behavior of Our Sample

The objective of this section is to threefold. First, we will look at the general situation of the French market during this period. Second, we will give a general description of the trading behavior of our sample and we will verify if there has been a significant change in the selling behavior since June 2007 due to the financial crisis.

Table 20.5: Demographic characteristics of our sample.

Number of clients	13,517
Average age	67 years old
Median age	53 years old
Percent male	91.68%
Percent French citizenship	97.91%
Percent Paris and Paris region	36%

Table 20.6: Top 10 stocks traded by our sample.

	ISIN Code	Name
1	FR0000120354	VALLOUREC
2	FR0010220475	ALSTOM
3	FR0004025062	SOITEC
4	FR0000130007	ALCATEL-LUCENT
5	FR0000125486	VINCI
6	FR0000131104	BNP PARIBAS
7	FR0000120131	RHODIA
8	FR0000133308	ORANGE (France TELECOM)
9	FR0000120628	AXA
10	FR0000031122	AIR France KLM

It is worth noticing that the database used in the United States by some authors, such as Barber and Odean (2002) or Kumar (2007) is larger (77,000 clients) but older (1991-96) than ours.

20.4.1 The French Situation

The trend of the French stock index, the CAC 40, (Fig. 20.3) clearly shows a switch in June 2007 between a "bull" period (01/01/2006–01/06/2007) where returns were mostly positive and a "bear" period where returns were mostly negative. Table 20.7 indicates the differences in mean return and volatility between these two periods. Returns are positive during the first period and negative during the second one and volatility experiences a huge increase during the "crisis" period.

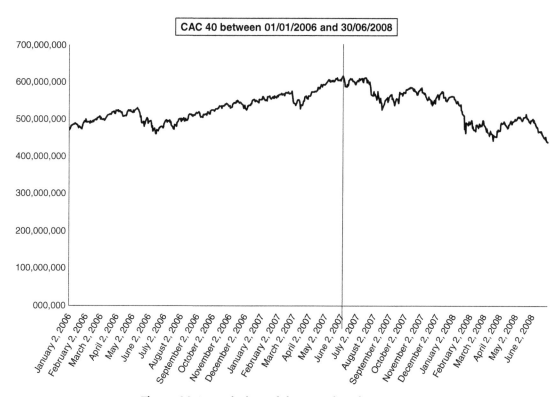

Figure 20.3: Evolution of the French Index CAC 40.

Table 20.7: Bull market and bear market on the CAC 40.

CAC 40	01/01/2006 01/06/2007 "Bull"	02/06/2007 30/06/2008 "Bear"
Annualized return	6.40%	−26.98%
Annualized volatility	11.50%	19.36%

20.4.2 General Behavior

Our file contains each individual trade per day. The total of the trades was summarized on a daily basis in order to have, for each day: the number of purchases, the number of sales, the volume of the purchases, and the volume of the sales. We have 766 daily observations from which we excluded Saturdays and Sundays and got 634 observations. We also have the breakdown between French stocks and money market mutual funds. Those could be of interest to look at the breakdown between the flows in risky assets and in nonrisky assets.

In the first part, we will look at the general behavior of our sample, then the breakdown between stocks and money market funds. The third part will present the buy and sell transactions by number.

1. General volume and number of transactions: Fig. 20.4 shows the volume of the purchases and sales on a monthly basis. The volume of purchases and the volume of sales are strongly correlated (correlation coefficient = 0.84) and the volume of buys is greater than the volume of sells each month.

2. Breakdown between risky assets and nonrisky assets: In this section, we also took the volume of purchases and sales in money market funds (as a proxy of nonrisky asset) to

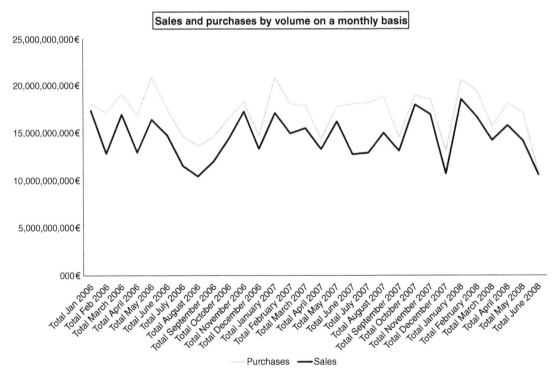

Figure 20.4: Evolution of the Purchases and Sales in French Stocks (Volume).

compare with the volume of purchases and sales in stocks (as a proxy of risky assets). We present in Figs. 20.4 and 20.5, the percentage of each asset class in the total flow of sales (Fig. 20.5) and purchases (Fig. 20.6).

On average, money market funds represent 10.18% of the purchase flows and 11.14% of the sale flows (the difference is nonsignificant) and a correlation coefficient equal to 0.39. We regressed the percentage of money market fund in purchase transactions and in sale transactions with two explaining variables. The first one is the daily change of the CAC 40 and the second one is a dummy variable equal to "one" after the financial crisis and "zero" before. Table 20.8 displays the coefficients.

The main result of Table 20.8 is that the flow of sales in money market funds is influenced by the binary variable "financial crisis" but we did not find a significant coefficient with the daily performance of the French market.

3. Number of sales and number of purchases: We use the number of purchases and the number of sales to measure the trading behavior of our sample (Fig. 20.7).

The two series are strongly correlated (correlation coefficient equal to 0.90) but we see that the number of purchases is always greater than the number of sales. We use the ratio between the number of purchases and the number of sales to measure the trading behavior compared to the market returns. Our two proxies for the French domestic stock market are the return of

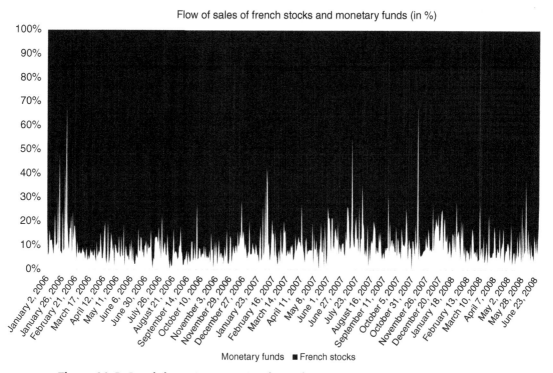

Figure 20.5: Breakdown Between Stocks and Monetary Funds (Flow of Sales).

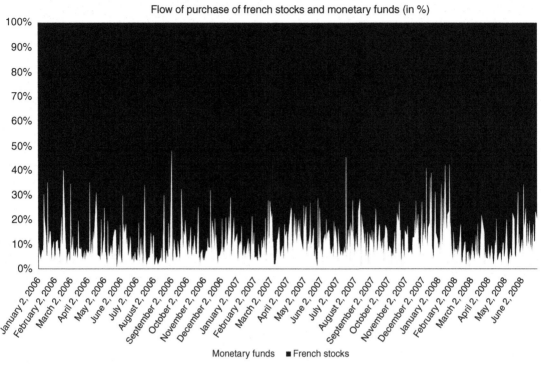

Figure 20.6: Breakdown Between Stocks and Monetary Funds (Flow of Purchases).

Table 20.8: Regression of flows of money market funds.

Explained Variable	Percent Money Market Fund in Purchase Transactions	Percent Money Market Fund in Sale Transactions
Explaining variables		
Constant (*t*-stat)	0.100 (24.331)	0.098 (24.938)
Daily changes of the CAC 40 (*t*-stat)	0.341 (1.253)	−0.709*** (−2.742)
Binary variable "crisis" (*t*-stat)	0.015 (2.394)	0.020*** (3.391)

** and *** denote significant at the 5% and 10% levels, respectively.

the CAC 40 on a daily basis and the same return of the CAC 40 on a continuous 12-months period (annual basis). The first one gives the influence of the short-term return of the market and the second one gives the influence of the long-term return of the market.

Our regression is as follows:

$$y_i = a_1 X_1 + a_2 X_2 + a_3 X_3 + \varepsilon_i$$

Where y_i is the ratio between the number of purchases and the number of sales, X_1 is the daily return of the CAC 40, X_2 the yearly return of the CAC 40, and X_3 is a binary variable equal to

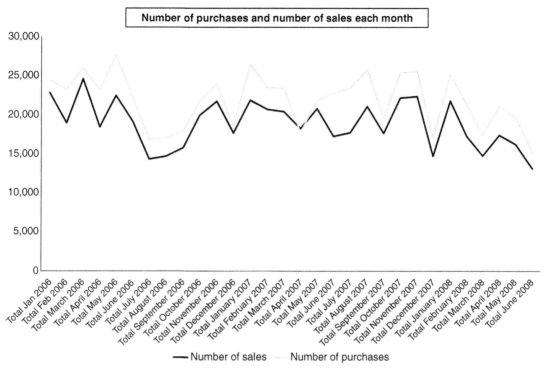

Figure 20.7: Evolution of the Number of Purchases and the Number of Sales.

Table 20.9: Regression on the sample as a whole.

Explained Variable	Number of Purchases/Number of Sales
Explaining variables	
Constant (*t*-stat)	1.116 (23.799)
CAC 40 daily (*t*-stat)	−14.258 (−9.097)***
CAC 40 12 months (*t*-stat)	49.598 (1.324)
Binary variable "crisis" (*t*-stat)	0.120 (2.209)**
Number of observations	634

** and *** denote significant at the 5% and 10% levels, respectively.

1 after June 2007 ("bear" period) and equal to 0 before June 2007 ("bull" period). Results are displayed in Table 20.9.

Only one coefficient of the regression is significant; it shows a negative correlation between the buying and selling behavior of the whole sample and the daily changes of the CAC 40 index. It means that when the return of the market increases, the number of sales increases compared to the number of purchases. When the market return decreases, we have more purchases than sales.

The long-term return of the CAC 40 is nonsignificant for the whole sample; the binary variable "crisis" is nonsignificant as well.

We will now look more closely at the selling behavior of our sample in the context of the financial crisis.

20.4.3 Impact of the Financial Crisis on the Selling Behavior

One of the main differences between behavioral finance and traditional finance is the selling behavior of individuals. Behavioral finance research and Prospect theory (Kahneman and Tversky, 1979; Tversky and Kahneman, 1992) show that, in situations of loss, people have a tendency to increase their risk (Fig. 20.2). Therefore, we decided to focus on the selling behavior of our sample compared to the return of the market.

We analyze the selling behavior based on the number of sales from which we take the logarithm. Therefore, our explained variable is log(number of sales). Our hypothesis is that there is a difference between the selling behavior of our sample before and after the beginning of the financial crisis.

Our objective will be to verify if the switch between positive and negative returns of the CAC 40 index has a significant impact on the selling behavior of our individual investor sample.

We wanted to analyze the impact of the switch between a "bull" period before June 2007 and a "bear" period after June 2007. The global sample was divided between two subsamples: the first one uses the daily trades from January 1, 2006 to the end of May 2007 ("bull" period). The second subsample uses the daily trades between June 2, 2007 and the end of June 2008 ("bear" period).

We use two measure of the CAC 40 index performance: the first one is simply the return of the index between the day of the trade and the day before; the second one is the return of the CAC 40 on a yearly basis showing a positive or a negative trend during the "bull" period and the "bear" period.

Our regression is as follows.

$$y_i = a_1 X_1 + a_2 X_2 + \varepsilon_i$$

Where y_i is the logarithm of the number of sales, X_1 is the daily return of the CAC 40, and X_2 the yearly return of the CAC 40. Results are displayed in Table 20.10.

Table 20.10 shows two regressions. The results are quite interesting. First, the two explaining factors (short-term return and long-term return of the CAC 40) are not significant before the financial crisis and become significant after the financial crisis. This information is of interest, showing that individuals are more sensitive to the return of the market when it falls.

Table 20.10: Regression on the two subsamples.

Explained Variable: Log (Number of Sales)	Before the Financial Crisis (01/02/2006–06/01/2007)	After the Financial Crisis (06/01/2007–06/30/2008)
Explaining variables		
Constant (*t*-stat)	6.882 (167.482)	6.702 (405.449)
CAC 40 daily (*t*-stat)	2.091 (1.329)	4.265 (3.617)***
CAC 40 12 months (*t*-stat)	−84.268 (−2.359)	95.985 (3.305)***
Number of observations	360	274

** and *** denote significant at the 5% and 10% levels, respectively.

Second, the coefficient for the daily return of the CAC 40 is positive and shows that our individual online investors increase their sales when the market is rising and decrease their sales when the market is falling. This behavior is in line with Prospect theory that states that individuals become risk seekers in loss situations.

The third and last comment is about the long-term return of the CAC 40. This factor becomes significant after the beginning of the financial crisis and has now a very high coefficient compared to that of the short-term return. Our interpretation is that individual investors become much more sensitive to the long-term tendency of the market after the financial crisis than before. In a "bear" market, they tend to decrease their sales.

20.5 Conclusions

The 2007 financial crisis was a difficult situation for all investors: the global wealth on the stock markets went down by more than 45%, causing massive distress for institutional investors, for example, defined-benefits pension funds. It was also very difficult for individual investors in every country.

Based on a sample of French individual online investors between the beginning of January 2006 and the end of June 2008, we show that the selling behavior of individual investors changes after the beginning of the financial crisis. The individuals exhibit a tendency to decrease the number of their sales when the market is going down. This result is supported by behavioral finance research that shows a high sensitivity to losses and previous losses (Thaler and Johnson, 1990). Our interpretation is that individual investors exhibit a higher sensitivity to the changes in the market returns during periods of financial distress.

In France, the statistics show that the number of individual investors went down from 7 million in 2002 to 3.7 million after the 2007–08 financial crisis. However, we do not have detailed statistics concerning individual online investors. Research shows that they are more sophisticated (Barber and Odean, 2002). We can assume that the remaining individual investors in France are online investors.

References

Anderson, A., 2007. All guts, no glory: trading and diversification among online investors. Eur. Financ. Manage. 13 (3), 448–471.

Barber, B.M., Odean, T., 2002. Online investors: do the slow die first? Rev. Financ. Studies 15 (2), 445–487.

Camerer, C.F., Babcock, L., Loewenstein, G., Thaler, R., 1997. Labor supply of New York City cabdrivers, one day at a time. Q. J. Econ. 112 (2), 407–441.

Choi, J.J., Laibson, D., Metrick, A., 2002. How does the internet affect trading? Evidence from investor behavior in 401(k) plans. J. Financ. Econ. 64 (3), 397–421.

French, K., Poterba, J., 1991. Investor diversification and international equity markets. Am. Econ. Rev. 81 (2), 222–226.

Gilovich, T., Vallone, R., Tversky, A., 1985. The hot hand in basketball: on the misperception of random sequences. Cogn. Psychol. 17 (3), 295–314.

Glaser, M., 2003. Online broker investors: demographic information, investment strategy, portfolio positions, and trading activity. Working Paper.

Goetzmann, W., Kumar, A., 2008. Equity portfolio diversification. Rev. Finance 12 (3), 433–463.

Hoffmann, A.O.I., Post, T., Penning, J.M.E., 2013. Individual investor perception and behavior during the financial crisis. J. Bank. Finance 37 (1), 60–74.

Kahneman, D., Tversky, A., 1979. Prospect theory: an analysis of decision under risk. Econometrica 47 (2), 263–292.

Kallberg, J., Liu, C.H., Wang, N., 2014. Individual investors and the financial crisis. Working Paper.

Kaniel, R., Sraer, D., 2013. Heterogeneity in retail investors behavior: evidence from the financial crisis. Working paper.

Kim, W., Shang-Jin, W., 1999. Foreign portfolio investors before and during a crisis. OECD Working Paper.

Kindleberger, C.P., Aliber, R., Solow, R., 2005. Manias, Panics and Crashes, fifth ed. Wiley Investment Classics, Hoboken, New Jersey.

Kumar, A., 2007. Do the diversification choices of individual investors influence stock returns? J. Finan. Markets 10 (4), 362–390.

Lintner, J., 1965. The valuation of risk assets and the selection of risky investments in stock portfolios and capital budgets. Rev. Econ. Stat. 47 (1), 13–37.

Markowitz, H., 1952. Portfolio selection. J. Finance 7 (1), 77–91.

Modigliani, F., Miller, M., 1963. Corporate income taxes and the cost of capital: a correction. Am. Econ. Rev. 53 (3), 433–443.

Modigliani, F., Miller, M., 1958. The cost of capital, corporation finance and the theory of investment. Am. Econ. Rev. 48 (3), 261–297.

Mossin, J., 1966. Equilibrium in a capital asset market. Econometrica 34 (4), 768–783.

Odean, T., 1998. Are investors reluctant to realize their losses? J. Finance 53 (5), 1775–1798.

Odean, T., 1999. Do investors trade too much? Am. Econ. Rev. 89 (5), 1279–1298.

Oh, N.Y., Parwada, J., Walter, T.S., 2008. Investors' trading behavior and performance: online versus non-online equity trading in Korea. Pacific-Bassin Finance J. 16 (1/2), 26–43.

Pope, D.G., Schweitzer, M.E., 2011. Is Tiger Woods loss averse? Persistent bias in the face of experience, competition and high stakes. Am. Econ. Rev. 101 (1), 129–157.

Sharpe, W.F., 1964. Capital asset prices: a theory of market equilibrium under conditions of risk. J. Finance 19 (3), 425–442.

Shefrin, H., Statman, M., 1994. Behavioral capital asset pricing theory. J. Financ. Quant. Anal. 39 (3), 323–349.

Shefrin, H., Statman, M., 2011. Behavioral Finance in the Financial Crisis: Market Efficiency, Minsky and Keynes. Santa Clara University, Mimeo.

Shefrin, H., Statman, M., 2000. Behavioral portfolio theory. J. Financ. Quant. Anal. 35 (2), 127–151.

Shefrin, H., Statman, M., 1985. The disposition to sell winners too early and ride losers too long. J. Finance 40 (3), 777–790.

Thaler, R.H., Johnson, E.J., 1990. Gambling with the house money and trying to break even: the effect of prior outcomes on risky choices. Manag. Sci. 36 (6), 643–660.

Tversky, A., Kahneman, D., 1974. Judgment under uncertainty: heuristics and biases. Science 185 (4157), 1124–1131.

Tversky, A., Kahneman, D., 1981. The framing of decisions and the psychology of choice. Science 211 (4481), 453–458.

Tversky, A., Kahneman, D., 1986. Rational choice and the framing of decisions. J. Bus. 59 (4), S251–S278.

Von Neumann, J., Morgenstern, O., 1953. Theory of Games and Economic Behavior. Princeton University Press, Princeton, NJ.

Further Reading

Tversky, A., Kahneman, D., 1992. Advances in prospect theory: a cumulative representation of uncertainty. J. Risk Uncertain. 5 (4), 297–323.

Behavioral Trading Strategies During Financial Crises

Simple Tactical Asset Allocation Strategies on the S&P 500 and the Impact of VIX Fluctuations

Constantinos E. Vorlow

IMAR, International Markets and Risk, Attika, Greece

Chapter Outline

21.1 Introduction

In his 1989 article Phillips (1989), addressing the findings of Brinson et al. (1986) highlights the importance of asset allocation, as this was demonstrated later, during the 1987 market crash (McKeon et al., 2009; Metz, 2003; Waldrop, 1987). "Black Monday," as it turned out to be known, wiped off the Dow 22.6% of its value, as the index dropped 508 points, eradicating $500 billion dollars of market capitalization (October 19, 1987). As expected, the crash urged investors to adopt a very short-term attitude toward the determination of asset combinations and fund allocations. Medium-to-long term "strategic" and "tactical asset allocation" views were blurred by significant noise and panic, leading to failures of informational efficiency (Brunnermeier, 2001; Grossman, 1995). Usually, after severe market crashes, such as the "Panic of 2008" (Soros, 2009), these investment attitudes are mistermed as "tactical asset reallocation," but are in fact, derivatives of "market timing" investment procedures, as identified by earlier work (Sharpe, 1975).

As Phillips (1989) suggested early on, in this article we investigate a market timing approach to determine the allocation mix between low and high risk assets. For the sake of clarity and simplicity, we allocate our portfolio's cash between the SPY[1] (Sharpe, 2010;) and TLT[2] exchange traded funds (ETF) (Ferri, 2011; Gastineau, 2008) to determine whether a simple signaling mechanism can lead fund managers to outperform the index or not. ETFs are especially suitable for passive investing, with low expense ratios and immediate mark-to-market pricing. These characteristics allow investors to mimic portfolios of certain assets, deploying a fraction of funds needed normally. They also allow low cost leverage and/or exposure to markets that cannot be traded easily by retail investors. Investing in ETFs also allows us to track certain total market or commodity indices and other nontradable indices (e.g., the VIX) and short these markets without the use of derivatives trading.

Our market-timing approach in this paper, suggests a more active investment style, where instead of using a traditional "passive" 60/40 allocation in US bonds and stocks (Gupta et al., 2016) to minimize portfolio risk, we use the CBOE VIX index (Brenner et al., 1984, 1989, 1993) to adjust our risk exposure, outperforming classic 60/40 and other passive investment styles via ETFs, while keeping risk and drawdowns to acceptable levels. In this earlier sense, we rather demonstrate an "Adaptive Asset Allocation" (AAA) policy's (Sharpe, 2010) superiority to buy and hold approaches. We also alter our target allocation weights to 70% S&P 500 versus 30% Bonds and vice-versa (instead of the traditional 60/40 allocation) to increase exposure to the risky asset during "calm periods" in order to achieve slightly higher returns.

21.2 Literature Review

While asset allocation plays a significant role toward portfolio performance, market timing is also of great importance as it lessens risk exposure and drawdowns. Academic literature suggests (Goldbaum, 1999; Bessembinder and Chan, 1995; Brock et al., 1992)[3] that market timing is a determinant of higher returns versus buy-and-hold investment strategies. The choice of the information to be used as a "leading indicator" or an "early warning system" for future market turbulence, is of crucial importance as is the choice of the tactical asset allocation style. The key elements in such an investment strategy is timing and correct application of the information via some kind of trading rule. The profitability of many technical trading rules is confirmed by research based on sign and volatility predictability

---

[1] The SPY or The SPDR® S&P 500® ETF Trust seeks to provide investment results that, before expenses, correspond generally to the price and yield performance of the S&P 500® Index. See also under https://www.spdrs.com/product/fund.seam?ticker=SPY

[2] The TLT or iShares 20+ Year Treasury Bond ETF seeks to track the investment results of an index composed of U.S. Treasury bonds with remaining maturities greater than twenty years. See also under https://www.ishares.com/us/products/239454/ishares-20-year-treasury-bond-etf

[3] Seminal work back in the 1980s and 1990s identified the importance of macroeconomic indicators for adjusting investment styles or strategies and timing the market (Breen et al., 1989; Fama and Schwert, 1977, 1979; Vandell and Stevens, 1989).

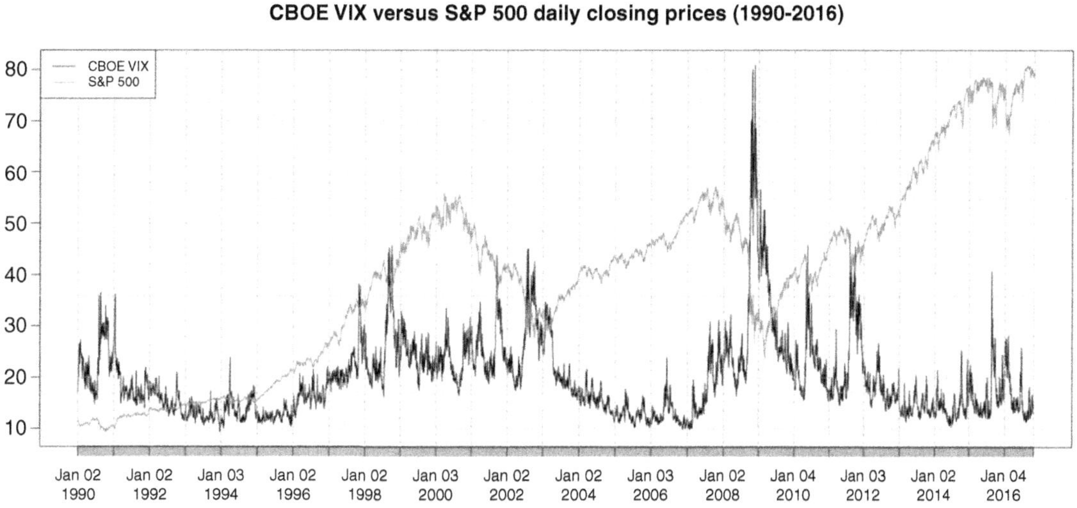

CBOE VIX versus S&P 500 daily closing prices (1990-2016)

Figure 21.1: CBOE VIX Versus S&P 500 Daily Closing Prices (1990–2016).

(Pesaran et al., 1994, 1995), as well as the ability of technical trading rules to beat efficient markets (Brock et al., 1992; Gençay, 1998; Neftci, 1991, among others).

Forecasting stock returns is a crucial exercise for all investors. It is directly linked to their risk tolerance as well as the search for arbitrage opportunities. Many factors are believed to affect future stock and stock index returns, contrary to the "market efficiency" concept (Fama, 1965a,b). Real economy factors and business cycles are directly linked to stock market performance and volatility (Hamilton and Gang, 1996; Moore and Visscher, 1993; Nyberg and Henri, 2011). However, since the stock market is accepted as a leading indicator of the overall performance of the economy, using macrofinancial variables to establish future paths for volatility and returns may be proven problematic if not a futile exercise. Investors are more well-informed and quick to react to any new information about the stage of the business cycle, reassessing their valuations, and rebalancing their portfolios or exiting entirely the markets. A more detailed inspection of Fig. 21.1 suggests that investors were already "bearish" well before the 2008 crash, despite the peak of commodity prices in the same summer. Since December 2007, the market (as reflected by the S&P 500) was already in a downward trending "bearish" state and macroeconomic variables (such as unemployment) were pointing toward a weaker real economy. Indeed, the NBER[4] (the National Bureau of Economic Research in the United States) later determined as the start of the "great recession" December 2007. Likewise, the bottoming of the market in early 2009, preluded the economic rebound, as the NBER identified June 2009 as the end of the recession (Rosenberg, 2012). Hence, it may be problematic to use lagging macroeconomic indicators, which are available

---

[4] See NBER website: http://www.nber.org/cycles.html

several weeks or months after their time stamp, to construct models based on real economy data that forecast stock price fluctuations. The answer most likely lies in more readily available and of higher frequency information sets than those of macroeconomic variables, which provide more timely trading information, such as the derivative or credit markets data.

Regarding credit market information, Thomakos et al. (2007) examine the predictability of stock index returns in the US market using a short-term interest rate. They conclude that the latter has market timing abilities over the relative performance of stock index returns, leading to profitable or benchmark outperforming investment strategies. Schizas and Thomakos (2013) using pairs of "passive" ETFs also show that rules based on relative pricing and volatility, lead to profitable rotation strategies against buy-and-hold positions, but at a higher risk. Research focusing on the yield spread (Resnick and Shoesmith 2002) has also shown that portfolios can be formed that beat the index while others focus in how style rebalancing outperforms passive investment strategies (Below et al. 2009).

Focusing away from the interest rates and credit-interest rates market based literature, the current paper investigates whether a market-timing procedure can be improved via the use of a volatility gauge based in forward looking derivatives markets, such as the VIX. This depends on the ability of the latter to identify bullish or bearish sentiment in the markets and translate it to a readable piece of information. As mentioned earlier, the notion of "efficient markets" contradicts the existence of a link between implied volatility and future stock returns. Contrary though to this theoretical framework, market participants view large spikes of implied volatility as signaling entry points for long positions, while panicking investors may overreact or calmer ones may as well close positions or rebalance their portfolios. This selling activity drives implied volatility upward and establishes an inverse relationship with the stock market trend. Academic research has already focused on how implied volatility can be used to explain realized historical volatility or future returns.

With respect to volatility forecasting, scientific research suggests that the VIX can improve predictions (Auinger, 2015; Fleming et al., 1995; Kambouroudis and McMillan, 2015; Liu et al., 2015). Existing work, though, has indicated (Canina and Figlewski, 1993; Figlewski, 1997; Fleming et al., 1995) that the VIX may not be as useful in forecasting future market volatility as opposed to historical volatility. Moreover, other papers suggest (Becker et al., 2006, 2007) that there are no efficiency gains in using the VIX to improve forecasting exercises. However, Becker et al. (2009) later discuss that the VIX encapsulates information of past historical (realized) volatility spikes, useful in explaining future positive jump activity of the S&P 500. The relationship between implied and realized volatility is also treated in a number of papers (Bandi and Perron, 2006; Christensen and Hansen, 2002; Christensen and Prabhala, 1998; Shu et al., 2003), which indicate that implied volatility is an efficient forecast of realized return volatility. Harvey and Whaley (1992) also find that market volatility is predictable via implied volatility in the S&P 100 index option market. For an extensive review of the volatility forecasting literature one can refer to Poon et al. (2003, 2005) and Poon (2005).

Using VIX to forecast realized volatility in an expost universe is the one side of the coin. The other side focuses on using the informational content of implied volatility, as this is reflected by the VIX, to forecast the S&P 500 price activity directly. Based on the observation that VIX spikes are corresponding to oversold conditions in markets that have bottomed, contrarian investors may be deploying assets in an attempt to establish long positions after a significant market drawdown. This activity may establish the VIX as a useful tool for market timing. The relationship between implied volatility and index or portfolio performance has been identified in many papers (Banerjee et al., 2007; Kambouroudis et al., 2016). These mainly focus on the relationship between increased levels of implied volatility and the contemporaneous drop of stock index levels or portfolio performance. Durand et al. (2011) using a Fama and French (1993) approach report that the market risk premium and the value premium are especially sensitive to changes in the VIX.

Existing studies (Banerjee et al., 2007; Doran and Kevin, 2010; Giot, 2002; Kambouroudis et al., 2016) conclude that implied volatility can be a predictor when it comes to market returns with varying degrees of success. Guo et al. (2006) find that implied volatilities and market returns are positively related. Research by Hsiao and Li (2010) also highlights that conditional volatility, as derived by options, predicts future returns and market timing can also be profitable if based on implied volatility information, hence, investors should increase exposure when volatility increases. Other research stresses the importance of volatility for market timing. Research by Christoffersen and Diebold (2006) and Christoffersen et al. (2007) suggests increased predictability of returns based on volatility. Johannes et al. (2002) show that a volatility timing strategy based on a simple stochastic volatility model "uniformly dominates market timing strategies." Similar volatility timing approaches are adopted in other research (Fleming et al., 2001, 2003), which concludes in the superiority of these over classic market timing practices. Style and size rotation literature (Copeland and Copeland, 1999; Dori, 2012; Efremidze et al., 2014; Lin et al., 2012) has also commented on the added value of volatility as a factor that improves the performance of rotation strategies, leading to positive returns or excess returns, even in higher frequencies. Copeland and Copeland (1999) show that through style rotation between value and growth portfolios, using the VIX for market timing, portfolio returns are improved with value stocks outperforming growth stocks, after a jump in the VIX index and vice versa. This indicates also how investors alter their mix of holdings during distressed markets. Other research in VIX based market timing (Boscaljon et al., 2011) also corroborates with the findings of Copeland and Copeland (1999) for longer holding periods, highlighting the benefits of switching to value stocks when volatility is heightened.

21.3 The VIX: History and Description

The VIX market volatility index[5] was introduced by the Chicago Board Options Exchange (CBOE) in 1993. It was initially conceived as a measure of the implied volatility of S&P 100 put and call options. In 2003, Goldman Sachs and the CBOE (Neftci, 2008) revised the index to use 30-day out-of-the money S&P 500 calls and puts, with inversely proportional weights to the squares of the strike price. By then, the S&P 100 options market was much more illiquid compared to the S&P 500 one and the latter was deemed a much more appropriate vehicle to estimate US stock market volatility, as this is reflected in the derivatives markets. The VIX today is calculated via a set of synthetic variance swaps using the prices of the S&P 500 index and tracks the Black-Scholes implied volatility of the SPX at-the-money options with expirations closest to 30 days.[6]

The VIX is quoted as a number (which refers to percentage change). For the market participants, a number of VIX of, say, 30% informs as a rule of thumb that the S&P 500 is expected to be 30% higher or lower 1 year from now, with a 68% probability (i.e., one standard deviation of the normal probability curve). This represents an expected annualized change within a year's time span. However, the VIX index does not indicate which direction that change could be. It could be either up or down, however, VIX spikes are always occurring during severe market drops and increased turbulence (see the historic market crashes of 2008 and late 1990s in Fig. 21.1). To calculate the expected volatility magnitude for a single month from this reading, we divide the VIX number of 30 by the square root of 12 and for a week by square root of 52. This implies that the S&P 500 may fluctuate within a range of ± 8.66% from its current price over the next 30-day period and ± 4.66% over the next week. This explains why VIX values close or below 20 are interpreted as more favorable by market participants as they are implying "acceptable" levels of risk and lower potential drawdowns.

Fig. 21.1 illustrates the daily closing prices of the VIX index against the S&P 500, since 1990 (the new index was backdated by the CBOE since its inception to provide a longer history of observations). The largest peak of the VIX index coincides historically with the "subprime" credit market crisis led crash of 2008 (November 20, 2008 closing price[7] VIX = 80.86). It was not though till the March 9, 2009 that the S&P 500 reached its lowest closing price of 676.53. The 2008 crash would not be though the largest value that the "new" VIX would have reached historically. The "Black Monday" crash of October 19, 1987, caused the "old" (original)

---

[5] For more on the CBOE VIX index one can refer to the CBOE's website: http://cfe.cboe.com/education/vixprimer/about.aspx

[6] The exact mathematical formulation of the VIX index is outside the scope of the current paper. However a good reference in how the index is calculated can be found online at the CBOE website under https://www.cboe.com/micro/vix/vixwhite.pdf. A good reference is also the book by Poon (Poon 2005).

[7] All-time highest VIX intraday value was 89.53 reached on 24 October 2008. The VIX closed at 79.13 on that day which was the third highest close in its history so far.

version of VIX (now called VXO) to reach a value of 150.19 and 1 day later, that of 172.79. The "new" VIX would have been over a 100 during the 1987 crash which is a gauge of the magnitude of "fear" and uncertainty dominating the markets at that time. Actually the VIX has been termed as "the Fear Index" by many investors (Auinger, 2015) as it tends to spike during volatile sessions where lack of investor visibility and risk aversion are heightened (Whaley, 2000).

Other VIX peaks were reached during 1997, 1998, 2001, and 2002 where market volatility due to increased uncertainty, had heightened. The periods 2002–07 and 2009–16 have been mostly characterized by a downward trend of the VIX from its peaks, due to the increased liquidity in the markets led by FED's quantitative easing policies, especially after the 2008 crash. However, the market frictions caused by the uncertainty of the debt crisis in Europe, led by the increased fears of Greece's prospective default in government debt and exit from the Eurozone, have also provided incidents where the VIX had locally peaked between 2010 and 2012. More recently in 2015 and the early 2016, the VIX has peaked again just above 40, due to investors being concerned about a referendum in Greece (Aug 24, 2015, VIX = 40.74) and a significant and abrupt slowdown of the Chinese economy that would hurl markets into a prolonged bear state and instigate a world-wide recession. Apparently, the lowest ever daily VIX closing value recorded was in 1993 (December 22, 1993 VIX = 9.31). In its more recent history, the VIX has "bottomed out" in July 3, 2014, reaching a low value of 10.32. Table 21.1 contains the basic (descriptive) statistics for the SPX (S&P 500) and the CBOE VIX indices. Fig. 21.2 also illustrates the distributions of the CBOE VIX daily closing prices and their first differences.

Table 21.1: Descriptive statistics of daily closing prices of the CBOE VIX Index (first column).

	VIX Levels	Difference(VIX)	S&P 500 Percentage Returns	TLT Percentage Returns
Minimum	9.31	−17.36	−0.0903	−0.0504
First quartile	14.04	0.64	−0.0046	−0.0046
Median	17.84	−0.06	0.0004	0.0005
Mean	19.71	0.00	0.0003	0.0001
Standard Deviation	7.85	1.53	0.0113	0.0087
Third quartile	23.09	0.57	0.0056	0.0053
Maximum	80.86	16.54	0.1158	0.0516
Annualized return	N/A	N/A	0.0754	0.0337
Annualized Standard Deviation	N/A	N/A	0.1536	0.1389
Standard error of mean	0.0956	0.02	0.0001	0.0001
Skewness	2.11	0.67	−0.0636	−0.0034
Kurtosis	7.72	17.97	8.7516	1.6924

The first differences of the VIX (second column), the SPX (S&P 500) index percentage daily returns (third column), and TLT ETF percentage daily returns (since 2002-07-30). The sample period is 1990-01-03 till 2016-10-27, a total of 6760 daily observations (3589 for TLT).

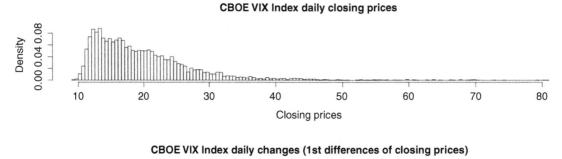

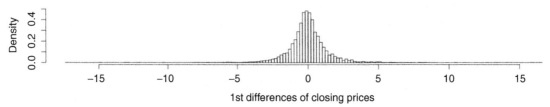

Figure 21.2: Histograms of CBOE VIX Daily Closing Prices and Day-to-Day Differences.

As it becomes evident from Fig. 21.1, the VIX tends to spike around strong, deep, or abrupt drawdowns of the S&P 500. Usually it exhibits a downward trend when the market has a steady bullish attitude but this is not always the case. For example, the VIX remained elevated throughout the 1998–2003 period with no downward momentum (although it was fluctuating between the 40 and 20 values, and 20 or below is not an indication of increased market turbulence, rather the opposite). As it stands in Fig. 21.1, it is not clear whether the VIX has a leading property over the SPX and whether it can be used, in a linear fashion, as an early warning indicator. However, diagrammatically, after strong spikes of the VIX index, when it drops below the 50% of its recent maximum, the market starts trending steadily upward.

As it can be seen in Table 21.1, the VIX closing prices, for its whole history so far, exhibit a mean of 19.71 and a median of 17.84, while only 25% of its values are above 23 (and below 80.86 which is its historical maximum). According to market participants, when the VIX drops below 20, as a rule of thumb, expectations are that the market has reached a medium-term top and a sell-off is imminent. When the VIX increases above 25, investors become increasingly nervous and adopt more risk averse attitudes. VIX can jump abruptly though, reaching higher prices within normal session hours due to events after the market close or during premarket, catching investors off guard. That usually happens when very negative news hit the market, outside the normal trading sessions. Also, it is not infrequent to see the VIX increasing while markets appear to be governed by "normal" levels of volatility, as investors seek insurance. Normally, the fluctuations of the VIX are negatively correlated to the S&P 500, but around 20% of the time it moves in the same direction as the market index.

Table 21.2: Cross-correlogram (XCF) between S&P 500 daily percentage returns and VIX daily differences.

Lag	XCF	Significance	Lag	XCF	Significance
−10	−0.0361	***	0	−0.792	***
−9	0.0105		1	0.0458	***
−8	−0.009		2	0.0545	***
−7	0.0549	***	3	−0.0094	
−6	0.0073		4	0.0231	*
−5	0.0274	**	5	0.0431	***
−4	0.0431	***	6	0.0042	
−3	0.0309	**	7	0.0124	
−2	0.0692	***	8	−0.0144	
−1	0.0751	***	9	−0.005	
0	−0.792	***	10	−0.0346	***

Note: Asterisks indicate statistical significance: ***, **, and * correspond to 0.01, 0.05, and 0.1 levels of statistical significance, respectively.

The linear correlation coefficient between VIX first differences and the percentage returns of the S&P 500 is −0.79 and statistically significant. Table 21.2 also shows that cross-correlations persist between VIX and S&P 500 daily fluctuations for at least 2 trading weeks (10 lags) and are statistically significant. Concluding, there is no mathematically established and straightforward inverse relationship between VIX and S&P 500 fluctuations but for strong changes, contemporaneously the VIX moves opposite the market (depending also on the time window through which we observe the market). According to Table 21.1, the daily mean changes of the VIX levels (close to close) are very small and close to 0, with a standard deviation of 1.53. The top 25% daily changes in magnitude (third quartile) range between 0.57 and 16.54. The maximum 1-day jump of the index occurred on 2008-10-22 while the maximum 1-day drop of −17.36 occurred on 2008-10-20, 2 days earlier, during the market turmoil of 2008.

21.4 Description of the Dataset and TAA Strategy

Our paper concentrates on whether there are outperforming strategies that reallocate funds in stocks and bonds during periods of market stress, as these are identified by the VIX index. Our portfolios consist of two ETFs, namely the SPY and the TLT which mimic the performance of the S&P 500 index and an index composed of US Treasury bonds with remaining maturities greater than 20 years. Figs. 21.3 and 21.4 illustrate the performance across time of the two ETFs, since their inception (daily closing prices and volumes). For our analysis, we use adjusted prices for dividends, stock splits etc. Fig. 21.5 contains the histograms of the daily percentage returns of each ETF while Fig. 21.6 compares the densities of these returns. Table 21.1 also includes the descriptive statistics for the TLT daily returns sequence.

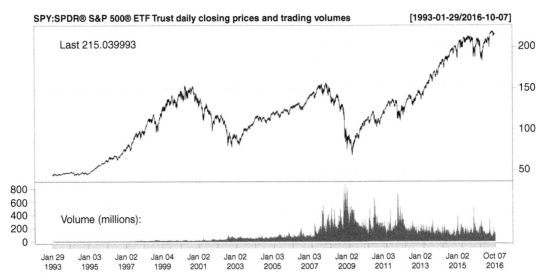

Figure 21.3: SPY (SPDR S&P 500 ETF Trust) Daily Closing Prices and Trading Volumes (1993–2016).

Figure 21.4: TLT (Ishares 20+ Year Treasury Bond ETF) Daily Closing Prices and Trading Volumes (2002–16).

In order to time the S&P 500 (SPX) market, we assume that we need a sensitive metric to stock price fluctuations and their volatility, as this is reflected in the VIX index. Ideally, we would use an indicator that combines information from both the S&P 500 and the VIX. By limiting ourselves to these two variables, we essentially mimic the attitude of a "conventional" investor who observes the level of the index and its volatility and decides to alter mix of his exposure to stocks and bonds accordingly.

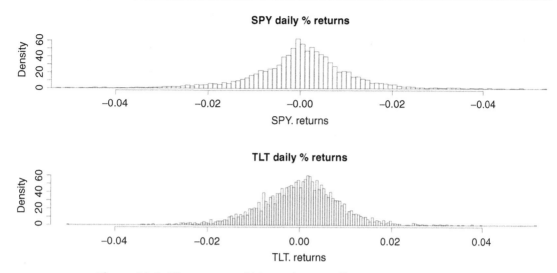

Figure 21.5: Histograms of SPY and TLT Daily Percentage Returns.

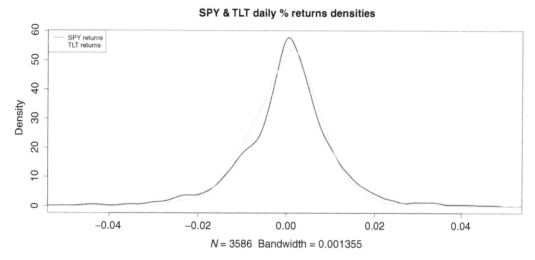

Figure 21.6: Densities of SPY and TLT Daily Percentage Returns. 🔳

Using a simple technical trading rule, we adopt an impulse "classification" approach to the design of our leading indicator sequence that depends on the S&P 500 and the VIX. We classify SPY returns and VIX spikes, according to their magnitude, in 10 incremental categories which coincide with their distribution deciles. Our logic is that investors will observe ranges of fluctuations for both SPY and VIX sequences and classify their values of both as "high" or "low" according to these ranges. If the SPY return is in a low range category, investors will react if VIX spikes and is classified in a top decile, rebalancing accordingly their portfolios, whereas if both VIX and SPY are classified in deciles that correspond to a calm and trending market, investors will adopt a more "steady as she goes" attitude, exposing themselves to higher risk. Essentially, we recode the whole range of SPY returns and VIX differences, creating a type of mapping and an "event profiler" which classifies events according to the magnitude of the sequences' fluctuations, on a daily basis. Our aim is to establish ranges within which, when SPY and VIX fluctuate, the allocation procedure yields superior returns at a lower risk.

We use specific time frames within which we classify VIX shocks and stock return fluctuations, according to their magnitude within the time frame's history, which spans between 2002 and 2016, since there are no pricing data for the TLT ETF before that time-frame (the TLT inception date is July 22, 2002). Using daily closing prices for the VIX and S&P 500, we compute the first differences (D(VIX)) of the daily VIX levels and daily percentage returns of the S&P 500 (via the SPY ETF). We then create deciles of the distributions of these two sequences and determine all the possible pairs of VIX and SPY decile limit combinations, 3025 of them. The idea is to create ranges within which SPY returns and VIX spikes are allowed to exist and create classifications according to these ranges. Hence, following the previous step, we run an iterative procedure that checks serially from the beginning of the sample, all these combinations of ranges against the SPY and VIX fluctuations. For days that SPY and VIX fluctuations fall into a category designated by the particular range, a signal is generated that contains 1, otherwise 0. Following the "contrarian" considerations of the existing academic literature and conclusions so far about VIX based market timing (Copeland and Copeland, 1999; Giot, 2002 and others), when the signal is 1, the asset allocation is arranged in 30% in the SPY and 70% in TLT. When the signal is 0, this allocation is swapped, that is, we hold only 30% of our funds in bonds. 3025 strategies are generated this way. The rebalancing signal is lagged 1 day to avoid the look ahead bias and we assume that all rebalances happen at the close (or close to). This could render our implementation impractical, however the procedure yields usually a couple of rebalances of the SPY/TLT portfolio a week during the sample history and investors remain fully invested and long only in both ETF assets. Such rebalances may not be costly for retail investors and algorithmic traders, however, for large funds this rebalance frequency may be unfavorable if we take into account commissions, slippages, and other trading costs.

For robustness and in order to test for how long after a particular VIX daily change, the shock resonates in the market psychology, we check the earlier procedure for lags of the VIX differences of up to 20 days. In other words, we observe the change of the VIX not in the current or previous day, but some days before (up to 20). In other words, we allow for a delay between the VIX impulse (positive or negative) and the reaction of the market. This allows for inertia in investment decisions, that is, investors observe information with some delay which allows for the delayed feedback loops documented in academic research (Kyrtsou and Terraza, 2008; Kyrtsou and Vorlow, 2009; Kyrtsou et al., 2004, 2009). At the end, we compute the profit and loss functions for every realization of the strategy, as well as annualized returns and standard deviations, maximum drawdowns, number of portfolio rebalances, and Sharpe ratios for the 20 lag structures, a total of 60,500 sets of statistics.

21.5 Results of the VIX/SPY Based TAA Strategies

Table 21.3 contains the best and worst results of all 60,500 TAA strategies realizations, one for every lag structure (our delayed VIX impulse consideration). The first 3 rows of each panel contain the performances of TLT and SPY ETFs as well as the "vanilla" 70% SPY and 30% TLT buy-and-hold strategies. The remaining rows contain the performance statistics of the "good" strategies in descending P&L order (Panel A) and the "poor" strategies in ascending P&L (Panel B). The best performance belongs to the strategy that observes the VIX daily jump 17 days ago, which furnishes 568% since 2002 against the 206% of buying and holding the S&P 500. This translates to an annualized return of 14.34% for the TAA dynamic strategy versus the 8.05% of the S&P 500, 7.09% of the TLT bonds ETF, and 8.65% of the 70%/30% static allocation between stocks and bonds. Clearly the dynamic strategy based on the VIX is outperforming the index. The strategy focuses on positive spikes of the VIX, that is, it checks whether the daily changes of the volatility index lay between -0.85 and 16.54 (in this case 17 days ago and the SPY or S&P 500 return of the previous trading day should be between -9.85% and -0.67%). Clearly, these are very large ranges corresponding to a very large chunk of the fluctuations' distributions as indicated in Table 21.1. For the top eight performing TAA strategies, only part of the VIX fluctuations distribution is being utilized by the strategy. For the rest though, the whole range between minimum and maximum values is being considered $[-17.36, 16.54]$. In other words, the TAA strategy is agnostic with respect to the VIX changes and decides solely on the magnitude of the S&P 500 (SPY) returns. However, on an average there are only 1.85% of strategies that are insensitive to VIX fluctuations and 20% of those, on an average, outperform the 70/30 passive strategy. In total and on an average, one out of three strategies outperforms the 70%/30% static allocation mix between SPY and TLT and all strategies, even the poor ones (as expected), have a positive P&L as shown in Table 21.3, Panel B. From Table 21.1, Panels A and B, it is obvious that the highest performing TAA strategies are the ones that consider, almost always, a negative previous day S&P 500 return, that is, a drop in the markets, while the poor performing ones are those that consider a positive (mostly) lagged return within the $[-0.67\%, 14.52\%]$ range. Maximum drawdowns for the best performing strategies range between 17% and 23%, compared to 55.19% of the SPY by-and-hold strategy and 36.81% of the 70%/30% static mix between stocks and bonds. The poor performing strategies exhibit similar maximum drawdowns to the 70%/30% benchmark. Moreover, the annualized standard deviation of the outperforming strategies is roughly half of that of the S&P 500 index.

Table 21.3: Results of highest (Panel A) and lowest (Panel B) performing TAA strategies according to P&L, for lags 0 through 20, period 2002-07 to 2016-10.

Panel A: Highest performing TAA strategies against buy and hold positions

LAG	Boundaries				TAA SPY/TLT Strategy Performance Statistics					Number of rebalances
	Lower SPY return	Higher SPY return	Lower D(VIX)	Higher D(VIX)	Total P&L	Annualized Return	Annualized Standard Deviation	Annualized Sharpe	Max Drawdown	
SPY Adj.	N/A	N/A	N/A	N/A	206.12%	8.05%	0.1917	0.4200	55.19%	1
TLT Adj.	N/A	N/A	N/A	N/A	162.41%	7.09%	0.1383	0.5125	26.59%	1
70%/30%	N/A	N/A	N/A	N/A	228.16%	8.65%	0.1229	0.7037	36.81%	1
17	−9.85%	−0.67%	−0.85	16.54	567.87%	14.34%	0.1037	1.3825	16.99%	939
15	−9.85%	1.20%	−0.85	0.77	555.96%	14.18%	0.0983	1.4422	17.33%	1365
0	−9.85%	−0.09%	0.39	16.54	547.61%	14.02%	0.108	1.2973	18.16%	1387
1	−9.85%	−0.68%	−1.51	16.54	543.83%	13.97%	0.1058	1.3209	21.89%	975
18	−9.85%	−0.67%	−17.36	1.54	533.41%	13.91%	0.1063	1.3088	19.17%	1028
10	−9.85%	−0.67%	−0.85	16.54	523.68%	13.76%	0.1031	1.3341	19.50%	924
9	−9.85%	0.45%	−1.51	1.54	519.88%	13.70%	0.1026	1.3359	17.31%	1588
16	−9.85%	1.20%	−17.36	0.39	519.16%	13.72%	0.1079	1.2721	20.12%	1646
20	−9.85%	−0.67%	−17.36	16.54	512.57%	13.65%	0.109	1.2528	22.97%	1105
4	−9.85%	−0.67%	−17.36	16.54	501.72%	13.45%	0.1096	1.2273	22.97%	1108
2	−9.85%	−0.67%	−17.36	16.54	497.46%	13.38%	0.1098	1.2186	22.97%	1107
11	−9.85%	−0.67%	−1.51	16.54	483.58%	13.23%	0.104	1.2726	20.93%	1036
12	−9.85%	−0.67%	−17.36	16.54	483.38%	13.23%	0.1091	1.2128	22.97%	1106
6	−9.85%	−0.67%	−17.36	16.54	483.19%	13.20%	0.1097	1.2035	22.97%	1108
19	−9.85%	−0.67%	−17.36	16.54	479.57%	13.21%	0.1094	1.2069	22.97%	1105
3	−9.85%	−0.67%	−17.36	16.54	477.38%	13.11%	0.1081	1.2129	22.97%	1109
8	−9.85%	−0.67%	−17.36	16.54	477.20%	13.13%	0.1097	1.1969	22.97%	1107
14	−9.85%	−0.67%	−17.36	16.54	475.81%	13.13%	0.1092	1.2023	22.97%	1107
7	−9.85%	−0.67%	−17.36	16.54	468.52%	13.00%	0.1095	1.1872	22.97%	1106
13	−9.85%	−0.67%	−17.36	16.54	465.63%	12.99%	0.1092	1.1891	22.97%	1106
5	−9.85%	−0.67%	−17.36	16.54	450.54%	12.74%	0.1079	1.1814	22.97%	1106

Panel B: Lowest performing TAA strategies against buy and hold positions

LAG	Boundaries				TAA SPY/TLT Strategy Performance Statistics					Number of rebalances
	Lower SPY return	Higher SPY return	Lower D(VIX)	Higher D(VIX)	Total P&L	Annualized Return	Annualized Standard Deviation	Annualized Sharpe	Max Drawdown	
SPY Adj.	N/A	N/A	N/A	N/A	206.12%	8.05%	0.1917	0.4200	55.19%	1
TLT Adj.	N/A	N/A	N/A	N/A	162.41%	7.09%	0.1383	0.5125	26.59%	1
70%/30%	N/A	N/A	N/A	N/A	228.16%	8.65%	0.1229	0.7037	36.81%	1
16	−0.67%	14.52%	−1.51	16.54	44.42%	2.63%	0.1024	0.2564	38.42%	1324
4	−0.67%	14.52%	−17.36	0.39	48.59%	2.82%	0.0981	0.2877	31.83%	1738
20	−0.67%	14.52%	−17.36	1.54	60.34%	3.39%	0.1018	0.3329	39.97%	1337
10	−0.67%	14.52%	−1.51	16.54	62.48%	3.48%	0.1013	0.3431	33.45%	1308
8	−0.67%	14.52%	−17.36	1.54	63.34%	3.51%	0.1007	0.3488	33.55%	1325
2	−0.67%	14.52%	−0.85	16.54	70.26%	3.81%	0.1004	0.3795	34.46%	1497
15	−0.67%	14.52%	−17.36	16.54	70.35%	3.83%	0.1056	0.3624	38.29%	1108
19	−0.67%	14.52%	−1.51	16.54	70.40%	3.83%	0.1014	0.3783	32.14%	1327
6	−0.67%	14.52%	−1.51	16.54	71.13%	3.85%	0.1009	0.3816	40.56%	1288
13	−0.67%	14.52%	−17.36	16.54	73.69%	3.97%	0.1055	0.376	38.29%	1106
14	−0.67%	14.52%	−17.36	0.77	74.58%	4.01%	0.0991	0.4042	29.38%	1545
11	−0.67%	14.52%	−17.36	16.54	75.55%	4.04%	0.1055	0.3834	36.92%	1110
17	−0.67%	14.52%	−17.36	16.54	75.70%	4.06%	0.1055	0.3844	38.29%	1103
18	−0.67%	14.52%	−17.36	16.54	76.17%	4.08%	0.1053	0.3871	36.51%	1104
7	−0.67%	14.52%	−17.36	1.54	76.25%	4.07%	0.099	0.4109	34.12%	1306
1	−0.68%	14.52%	−1.51	16.54	77.30%	4.10%	0.1002	0.4094	28.40%	1401
12	−0.67%	14.52%	−17.36	16.54	77.97%	4.14%	0.1056	0.3925	37.84%	1104
9	−0.67%	14.52%	−17.36	16.54	83.35%	4.36%	0.1054	0.4135	36.93%	1109
5	−0.67%	14.52%	−17.36	16.54	84.68%	4.41%	0.1058	0.4167	38.29%	1108
0	−0.67%	14.52%	−17.36	16.54	86.62%	4.48%	0.1058	0.4233	37.40%	1108
3	−0.67%	14.52%	−17.36	16.54	90.45%	4.63%	0.1055	0.439	37.26%	1107

21.6 Conclusions

In this paper, we consider whether a dynamic Tactical Asset Allocation long-only investment procedure based exclusively on VIX and S&P 500 historical fluctuations, can be designed to outperform passive investment strategies, which buy and hold the Index or allocate a fixed 70% and 30% of the portfolio funds in the Index and bonds, respectively. Testing our approach with portfolios that hold only the SPY and TLT ETFs post 2002, with daily data, we conclude that taking into consideration information from the implied volatility of the S&P 500 via the VIX index, results in more superior portfolio performances than simply holding the Index or some static mix between stocks and bonds. Positive VIX spikes and drops in the S&P 500 provide signals for shifting the allocation weights between stocks and bonds. Outperforming strategies are also characterized by much smaller or manageable drawdowns and almost half of the annualized standard deviation of the market. However, a small set of high performance strategies disregards the contribution of the VIX information and produces profits only from technical trading decisions based on the market index returns. This warrants further research and may indicate that a "linear" decision rule, such as the one we adopt in this paper, about which VIX fluctuations should be influencing effective TAA decisions, may not be appropriate.

References

Auinger, F., 2015. The Causal Relationship Between the S&P 500 and the VIX Index: Critical Analysis of Financial Market Volatility and Its Predictability. Springer, Gabler Verlag.

Bandi, F.M., Perron, B., 2006. Long memory and the relation between implied and realized volatility. J. Financ. Econom. 4 (4), 636–670.

Banerjee, P.S., Doran, J.S., Peterson, D.R., 2007. Implied volatility and future portfolio returns. J. Bank. Finance 31 (10), 3183–3199.

Becker, R., et al., 2007. Does implied volatility provide any information beyond that captured in model-based volatility forecasts? J. Bank. Finance 31 (8), 2535–2549.

Becker, R., et al., 2006. On the informational efficiency of S&P500 implied volatility. North Am. J. Econ. Finance 17 (2), 139–153.

Becker, R., et al., 2009. The jump component of S&P 500 volatility and the VIX index. J. Bank. Finance 33 (6), 1033–1038.

Below, S., Kiely, J., Prati, R., 2009. Style index rebalancing for better diversification: lessons from broad market and equity style indexes. Financ. Serv. Rev. 18, 231–248.

Bessembinder, H., Chan, K., 1995. The profitability of technical trading rules in the Asian stock market. Pacific-Basin Finance J. 3, 257–284.

Boscaljon, B., Filbeck, G., Zhao, X., 2011. Market timing using the VIX for style rotation. Financ. Serv. Rev. 20, 35–44.

Breen, W., et al., 1989. Economic significance of predictable variations in stock index returns. J. Finance 44 (5), 1177–1189.

Brenner, M., Menachem, B., Dan, G., 1993. Hedging volatility in foreign currencies. J. Deriv. 1 (1), 53–59.

Brenner, M., Menachem, B., Dan, G., 1989. New financial instruments for hedge changes in volatility. Financ. Anal. J. 45 (4), 61–65.

Brenner, M., Menachem, B., Dan, G., 1984. On measuring the risk of common stocks implied by options prices: a note. J. Financ. Quant. Anal. 19 (4), 403.

Brinson, G.P., Randolph Hood, L., Beebower, G.L., 1986. Determinants of portfolio performance. Financ. Anal. J. 42 (4), 39–44.

Brock, W., et al., 1992. Simple technical trading rules and the stochastic properties of stock returns. J. Finance 47 (5), 1731–1764.

Brunnermeier, M.K., 2001. Asset Pricing Under Asymmetric Information: Bubbles, Crashes, Technical Analysis, and Herding. Oxford University Press, New York.

Canina, L., Figlewski, S., 1993. The informational content of implied volatility. Rev. Financ. Studies 6 (3), 659–681.

Christensen, B.J., Hansen, C.S., 2002. New evidence on the implied-realized volatility relation. Eur. J. Finance 8 (2), 187–205.

Christensen, B.J., Prabhala, N.R., 1998. The relation between implied and realized volatility. J. Financ. Econ. 50 (2), 125–150.

Christoffersen, P., et al., 2007. Direction-of-change forecasts based on conditional variance, skewness and Kurtosis dynamics: international evidence. J. Financ. Forecasting 1 (2), 3–24.

Christoffersen, P.F., Diebold, F.X., 2006. Financial asset returns, direction-of-change forecasting, and volatility dynamics. Manag. Sci. 52 (8), 1273–1287.

Copeland, M.M., Copeland, T.E., 1999. Market timing: style and size rotation using the VIX. Financ. Anal. J. 55 (2), 73–81.

Doran, J.S., Kevin, K., 2010. Implications for asset returns in the implied volatility skew. Financ. Anal. J. 66 (1), 65–76.

Dori, F., 2012. Does volatility allow for style rotation? Evidence from international stock market returns. SSRN Elect. J. Available from: http://dx.doi.org/10.2139/ssrn.2190586

Durand, R.B., Dominic, L., Kenton Zumwalt, J., 2011. Fear and the Fama-French factors. Financ. Manag. 40 (2), 409–426.

Efremidze, L., et al., 2014. Using VIX entropy indicators for style rotation timing. J. Invest. 23 (3), 130–143.

Fama, E.F., 1965a. Random walks in stock market prices. Financ. Anal. J. 21 (5), 55–59.

Fama, E.F., 1965b. The behavior of stock-market prices. J. Bus. 38 (1), 34.

Fama, E.F., French, K.R., 1993. Common risk factors in the returns on stocks and bonds. J. Financ. Econ. 33 (1), 3–56.

Fama, E.F., Schwert, G.W., 1977. Asset returns and inflation. J. Financ. Econ. 5 (2), 115–146.

Fama, E.F., Schwert, G.W., 1979. Inflation, interest, and relative prices. J. Bus. 52 (2), 183.

Ferri, R.A., 2011. The ETF Book: All You Need to Know About Exchange-Traded Funds. John Wiley & Sons, Hoboken, New Jersey.

Figlewski, S., 1997. New York University & Salomon Brothers Center for the Study of Financial Institutions. Forecasting volatility.

Fleming, J., et al., 1995. Predicting stock market volatility: a new measure. J. Futures Markets 15 (3), 265–302.

Fleming, J., et al., 2001. The economic value of volatility timing. J. Finance 56 (1), 329–352.

Fleming, J., et al., 2003. The economic value of volatility timing using "realized" volatility. J. Financ. Econ. 67 (3), 473–509.

Gastineau, G.L., 2008. Exchange-Traded Funds. In: Handbook of Finance, 6, 61.

Gençay, R., 1998. The predictability of security returns with simple technical trading rules. J. Empir. Finance 5 (4), 347–359.

Giot, P., 2002. Implied Volatility Indices as Leading Indicators of Stock Index Returns? CORE Discussion Paper, Facultés Universitaires Notre-Dame de la Paix, (2002/50). Available from: http://dx.doi.org/10.2139/ssrn.371461

Goldbaum, D., 1999. A nonparametric examination of market information: application to technical trading rules. J. Empirical Finan. 6, 59–85.

Grossman, S.J., 1995. Dynamic asset allocation and the informational efficiency of markets. J. Finance 50 (3), 773.

Guo, H., Hui, G., Whitelaw, R.F., 2006. Uncovering the risk-return relation in the stock market. J. Finance 61 (3), 1433–1463.

Gupta, P., Skallsjo, S.R., Li, B., 2016. Multi-Asset Investing: A Practitioner's Framework. John Wiley & Sons, New York.

Hamilton, J.D., Gang, L., 1996. Stock market volatility and the business cycle. J. Appl. Econom, 11 (5), 573–593.

Harvey, C.R., Whaley, R.E., 1992. Market volatility prediction and the efficiency of the S & 100 index option market. J. Financ. Econ. 31 (1), 43–73.

Hsiao, P., Li, M., 2010. Implied volatility and future market return. Insurance Markets Companies Anal. Actuarial Comput. 1 (2), 52–60.

Johannes, M.S., Polson, N. and Stroud, J.R., 2002. Sequential Optimal Portfolio Performance: Market and Volatility Timing. Available from: SSRN: https://ssrn.com/abstract=304976 or http://dx.doi.org/10.2139/ssrn.304976

Kambouroudis, D.S., McMillan, D.G., 2015. Does VIX or volume improve GARCH volatility forecasts? Appl. Econ. 48 (13), 1210–1228.

Kambouroudis, D.S., McMillan, D.G., Tsakou, K., 2016. Forecasting stock return volatility: a comparison of GARCH, implied volatility, and realized volatility models. J. Futures Markets 36 (12), 1127–1163.

Kyrtsou, C., Labys, W.C., Terraza, M., 2004. Noisy chaotic dynamics in commodity markets. Empir. Econ. 29 (3), 489–502.

Kyrtsou, C., Terraza, M., 2008. Seasonal Mackey-Glass-GARCH process and short-term dynamics. SSRN Elect. J.

Kyrtsou, C., Catherine, K., Michel, T., 2009. Seasonal Mackey–glass–GARCH process and short-term dynamics. Empir. Econ. 38 (2), 325–345.

Kyrtsou, C., Vorlow, C., 2009. Modelling non-linear comovements between time series. J. Macroecon. 31 (1), 200–211.

Lin, Y.-N., Yueh-Neng, L., Jeremy, G., 2012. Nature of VIX jumps on market timing of hedge funds. SSRN Electron. J.

Liu, Q., et al., 2015. VIX forecasting and variance risk premium: a new GARCH approach. North Am. J. Econ. Finance 34, 314–322.

McKeon, R., Ryan, M., Netter, J.M., 2009. What caused the 1987 stock market crash and lessons for the 2008 crash. SSRN Electron. J.

Metz, T., 2003. Black Monday: The Stock Market Catastrophe of October 19, 1987. Beard Books, Washington, DC.

Moore, G.S., Visscher, S.L., 1993. Stock returns, inflation, and the business cycle. J. Bus. Econ. Stat. 8 (1), 45–50.

Neftci, S.N., 1991. Naive trading rules in financial markets and Wiener-Kolmogorov prediction theory: a study of "technical analysis". J. Bus. 64 (4), 549.

Neftci, S.N., 2008. Tools for Volatility Engineering, Volatility Swaps, and Volatility Trading. In: Principles of Financial Engineering. Academic Press, US. pp. 415–437.

Nyberg, H., Henri, N., 2011. Risk-return tradeoff in U.S. stock returns over the business cycle. J. Financ. Quant. Anal. 47 (01), 137–158.

Pesaran, M.H., Hashem Pesaran, M., Allan, T., 1994. Forecasting stock returns an examination of stock market trading in the presence of transaction costs. J. Forecasting 13 (4), 335–367.

Pesaran, M.H., Hashem Pesaran, M., Allan, T., 1995. Predictability of stock returns: robustness and economic significance. J. Finance 50 (4), 1201.

Phillips, D., 1989. Differentiating tactical asset allocation from market timing. Financ. Anal. J. 45, 14–16.

Poon, S.-H., 2005. A Practical Guide to Forecasting Financial Market Volatility. John Wiley & Sons, England.

Poon, S.-H., Ser-Huang, P., Clive, G., 2005. Practical issues in forecasting volatility. Financ. Anal. J. 61 (1), 45–56.

Poon, S.-H., Ser-Huang, P., Granger, C.W.J., 2003. Forecasting volatility in financial markets: a review. J. Econ. Lit. 41 (2), 478–539.

Resnick, B.G., Shoesmith, G.L., 2002. Using the yield curve to time the stock market. Financ. Anal. J. 58 (3), 82–90.

Rosenberg, J.M., 2012. The Concise Encyclopedia of The Great Recession 2007-2012. Scarecrow Press.

Schizas, P., Thomakos, D.D., 2013. Market timing using asset rotation on exchange traded funds: a meta-analysis on trading performance. 10(2), 166–173.

Sharpe, W.F., 2010. Adaptive asset allocation policies. Financ. Anal. J. 66 (3), 45–59.

Sharpe, W.F., 1975. Likely gains from market timing. Financ. Anal. J. 31 (2), 60–69.

Shu, J., Jinghong, S., Zhang, J.E., 2003. The relationship between implied and realized volatility of S&P 500 index. Wilmott 2003 (1), 83–91.

Soros, G., 2009. The Crash of 2008 and What It Means: The New Paradigm for Financial Markets. Scribe Publications, New York.

Thomakos, D.D., Tao, W., Jingtao, W., 2007. Market timing and cap rotation. Math. Comput. Model. 46 (1–2), 278–291.

Vandell, R.F., Stevens, J.L., 1989. Evidence of superior performance from timing. J. Portf. Manag. 15 (3), 38–42.

Waldrop, M.M., 1987. Computers Amplify Black Monday: the sudden stock market decline raised questions about the role of computers; they may not have actually caused the crash, but may well have amplified it. Science 238 (4827), 602–604.

Whaley, R.E., 2000. The investor fear gauge. J. Portf. Manag. 26 (3), 12–17.

CHAPTER 22

Investors' Behavior on S&P 500 Index During Periods of Market Crashes: A Visibility Graph Approach

Michail D. Vamvakaris*, Athanasios A. Pantelous*, Konstantin Zuev**

*Institute for Risk and Uncertainty, University of Liverpool, Liverpool, United Kingdom;
**California Institute of Technology, Pasadena, CA, United States

22.1 Introduction

The *efficient market hypothesis* (EMH) is one of the milestones in the modern financial theory. It was developed independently by Samuelson (1965) and Fama (1963, 1965), and in a short time, it became a guiding light not only to practitioners, but also to academics. In brief, EMH states that in an efficient market, stocks incorporate instantly all publicly available information useful in evaluating their prices and, thus no one can consistently outperform the overall market without accepting higher risk. Since information arrives randomly, the stocks' future price trajectories are as predictable as a sequence of cumulated random numbers. In other words, price increments (decrements) are *independent*, which implies that no one can predict stocks' price future paths based on their history. Although, EMH has been developed and discussed extensively since then, the concept that price increments are independent, uncorrelated, and unpredictable was initially introduced by Louis Bachieler. Bachelier (1900) claimed that a security price sequence can be modeled by a *stationary* Gaussian random walk and, consequently, price increments do not contain autocorrelation. This idea was further developed by Osborne (1959), who proposed that the logarithm of price changes behave similarly to particles in Brownian motion.

On the other hand, by studying cotton price series, Mandelbrot (1967, 1997) observed that the distribution of price increments was *not* Gaussian, but rather stable Paretian, which implies that the distribution is more peaked around the mean and has fatter tails, which actually means that outliers are more frequent compared to those supported by the normal distribution frame. Furthermore, his research concluded that cotton price series are not stationary and that there is dependence among the price increments. This latter finding led him to conclude that stock price series should be best modeled by a *fractional Brownian motion* (fBm) (Mandelbrot and Van Ness, 1968), which is a long-memory version of the standard Brownian motion (sBm) process characterized by the Hurst exponent, *H*. Even though, Fama (1963, 1965) studied stock price series and he also exhibited the distinguishing leptokurtosis that characterizes the distribution of stock price increments, and he was adamant that price changes are independent and uncorrelated.

Since then, bulk of literature focuses mainly on studying whether the EMH is valid, that is, whether there is a random walk in the markets, then based on the analysis of different empirical data, contradictory evidences have been demonstrated. Obviously, since EMH should not be approached as an *all-or-nothing* question (Lim, 2007), several studies have demonstrated the dynamic character of markets' efficiency (Alvarez-Ramirez et al., 2008; Barunik and Kristoufek, 2010; Cajueiro and Tabak, 2004a; Grech and Mazur, 2004; Grech and Pamuła, 2008; Lim, 2007; Lim et al., 2008; Wang et al., 2010). What is more, Campbell et al. (1997) claimed that it is better to study the relative efficiency of a market, since the hypothesis of existence of an efficient market seems to be a utopia in practice, thus it is better to distinguish between more and less efficient periods or markets.

In this chapter, we have been motivated by Grech and Mazur (2004) and Lim et al. (2008) who showed that DJIA index became more *"nervous"* before some major market crash events and that stock market crashes deteriorate temporarily the market efficiency in Asian countries, respectively. Under this frame, since the stock markets' time series are the mirror of the investors' behavior, we study how particular financial crashes, such as the Dot.com crisis in 2000 and the Subprime Mortgage crisis in 2007 affected the behavior of S&P 500 price-index using high frequency data by quantifying the degree of index series persistency, as well as quantifying the memory in the index series. It is the first time that instead of just using tests to reject or confirm the random walk hypothesis, we take advantage of the recently introduced Visibility Graph method to identify changes of investors' behavior throughout periods of financial crashes by studying, how the local properties of the index series evolve over the course of time.

By using high frequency data, our results provide stronger evidence that stock markets have a dynamic character and thus, properties of financial time series might vary over time. In particular, we find that the impact of two specific financial crashes in the S&P 500 index series, and actually on its investors' behavior, is only temporal while we also provide evidences that the index time series exhibit "nervousness" before those events occurred. To the best of our knowledge, this is the first attempt to study the Hurst exponent of stock indexes using high frequency data. Finally, we report that there is a link between the Hurst exponent and the degree of irreversibility of a series.

The paper is structured as follows. In Section 22.2, we analyze the properties of the Hurst exponent and what the irreversibility in financial time series suggests. In Section 22.3, the proposed method is explained in order to calculate the Hurst exponent and to quantify index series irreversibility. Section 22.4 describes the data we use and Section 22.5 provides the methodology followed. Finally, in Section 22.6, the empirical results are presented and Section 22.7 concludes the whole discussion.

22.2 Literature Review

22.2.1 Hurst Exponent

In 1956, the hydrologist Harold Edwin Hurst (Hurst, 1956) investigated a novel method for calculating the long-range dependences within observations of a time series. In fact, Hurst exponent, H, estimates the autocorrelations of a series as well as the rate at which autocorrelations diminish as the time delay between pairs of values increases.

The values of the index, H, range within [0,1]. Values in the interval $H \in (0.5, 1]$ indicate *a positive auto-covariance coefficient at all lags* which points out a persistent behavior (Mandelbrot and Van Ness, 1968). Interpreting persistency in terms of financial time series, it implies that an increment (decrement) is, statistically speaking, more probable to be followed by another increment (decrement). According to Greene and Fielitz (1977), persistency is not the result of an ordinary serial dependence, but rather its' root can be traced on a special kind of dependence with an infinite memory which is called "*noncyclic, long-run statistical dependence.*" Time series that are characterized as persistent contain long-memory and thus, they exhibit "*trends*" and "*cycles*" of varying length.

On the other hand, $H \in [0, 0.5)$ characterizes time series, which have *negative* autocovariance at all lags and series exhibit an antipersistent behavior (Barkoulas et al., 2000). This means that a decrement (increment) is more probable to be followed by an increment (decrement). In other words, an antipersistent series reverts more frequently than a random one

(Kristoufek, 2010). Finally, when $H = 0.5$, we deal with a process which does not contain dependences, such as a sBm process.

The EMH states that technical analysis cannot help the markets' investors to gain additional information that facilitates them to predict future movements of prices, since prices' future paths are not dependent on their history. Consequently, if a market was efficient, then its behavior could be modeled by a random walk, that is, $H = 0.5$, which indicates that the series do not contain autocorrelation. Consequently, any deviation from $H = 0.5$ is an indication of presence of autocorrelation in the series which in turn indicate a violation of the EMH. According to Morales et al. (2012), due to the finite size of financial time series, it is also possible to obtain a Hurst exponent different than $H = 0.5$, even for random series. So, in most cases there is a small interval near the value $H = 0.5$, where we can assume that the series increments are independent and uncorrelated. Fractal Brownian series with higher values of Hurst exponent are found to be smoother in comparison with lower values of the exponent. In Fig. 22.1, we plot fBm for different values of the Hurst exponent in order to present clearly the additional information gained.

Along these lines, rich literature in finance has been developed to study the Hurst exponent and connect it with the existence of EMH (Alvarez-Ramirez et al., 2008; Barunik and Kristoufek, 2010; Cajueiro and Tabak, 2004a,b; Di Matteo, 2007; Grech and Mazur, 2004; Grech and Pamuła, 2008; Lim et al., 2008; Wang et al., 2010). In more details, Cajueiro and Tabak (2004a,b) calculated the time-varying local Hurst exponent using daily data of 11 emerging and 2 developed stock indexes from January 1992 till December 2002. Even though, the Hurst exponent for the emerging markets was found to be considerably higher than 0.5, the long-term trajectory of H was decreasing eventually toward 0.5, which indicates

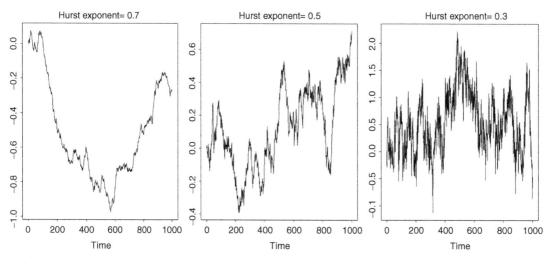

Figure 22.1: Fractional Brownian Motion with (Right to Left) $H = 0.7$, $H = 0.5$, and $H = 0.3$, Respectively.

that the efficiency of these markets was increasing over the course of time. On the other hand, the efficiency of developed markets appeared not to have serious changes over time, and to fluctuate around $H = 0.5$. The same conclusion was also confirmed by Wang et al. (2010) who studied the efficiency of Shanghai stock market. On the other hand, Di Matteo (2007) examined 32 stocks' market indexes for 1 time-period in order to study the multiscaling properties of financial time series and her results illustrate that developed stock markets were characterized by H close to 0.5, while in the emerging markets, the estimated Hurst exponent was much higher. Grech and Mazur (2004) used the concept of local Hurst exponent as a tool for forecasting a market crash. Using daily data, they analyzed three major market crashes, such as the market crashes of 1929 and 1987 in the United States and of 1998 in Hong Kong. They reported that the local Hurst exponent dropped sharply before the crashes, which is an indication that the market becomes more *"nervous"* and *"volatile"* before some major events. On contrary, throughout the crashes, the values of H increased significantly indicating a ramped-up inefficiency. The same conclusion was also reported by Grech and Pamuła (2008) for the Polish stocks' market. Using again daily data, Alvarez-Ramirez et al. (2008) studied the evolution of S&P 500 price-index and DJIA index as well. Their results also exhibited a time-varying evolution of market efficiency. Furthermore, Lim et al. (2008) studied the impact of financial crises on markets' efficiency. Particularly, they found that Asian crisis of 1997 adversely affected the efficiency of most stocks' markets, though markets' efficiency recovered to precrisis level. Ranking the markets' inefficiency, they found that markets were most efficient during the postcrisis period, followed by precrisis period while during the crisis, markets showed high inefficiency.

Commenting the work conducted by previous researchers and by recruiting a *new* methodology for estimating the Hurst exponent, in this chapter we report how the Hurst exponent evolves over time and, particularly, we are interested in how financial crashes affect the behavior of S&P 500 index using *high frequency* data during 1996–2010 as it will be discussed in Section 22.4.

22.2.2 Irreversibility

Reversibility is a property of time series which, informally, states that if we reverse the time evolution of a time series its statistical properties do not change which means that the series do not contain asymmetries.

According to Zumbach (2009), a rigorous formulation of time reversal invariance is that the transformation $t \rightarrow -t$ is an exact symmetry of the system under consideration. A formal definition of time invariance is that a dynamic process $\{X_t\}$ is time reversible if for every positive integer n, the process $X = \{x_{t_1}, x_{t_2}, \ldots, x_{t_n}\}$, and its time reverse process $X^- = \{x_{-t_1+m}, x_{-t_2+m}, \ldots, x_{-t_n+m}\}$ have *asymptotically* the same joint distribution (Ramsey and Rothman, 1996). Based on this definition, reversibility requires stationarity, and since

X and X^- are equally probable then, any random process is reversible. For instant, a linear Gaussian random process or even a monotonic transformation of a linear Gaussian random process are reversible while nonlinear processes, non-Gaussian linear processes as well as linear ARMA models are time irreversible processes (Lacasa and Flanagan, 2015; Lacasa et al., 2012).

Generally speaking, financial markets are characterized by different types of asymmetry, that is, *information asymmetry* between buyers and sellers, *perception asymmetry* which implies that not all investors react to news in the same manner, *behavioral asymmetry* meaning that price upswings are longer and slower than downswings, etc., and thus the financial time series are irreversible. Indeed, as stated in Ramsey and Rothman (1996), Zumbach (2009), and Xia et al. (2014), financial time series are inherently irreversible. Although, irreversibility is basically an all-or-nothing property, which means that a series is either reversible or not, we can also discriminate different degrees of time reversibility via the methodology described in Section 22.3.3. The closer the properties of an irreversible process are with a reversible process, the lower the degree of irreversibility is. Jiang et al. (2016) found that emerging markets are more time irreversible in comparison with developed markets and they have related predictability with irreversibility to some extent.

Studying the properties of the S&P 500 price-index from 1871 to 1988, Ramsey and Rothman (1996) found that the index series was irreversible and, in addition, the source of the irreversibility could be attributed to the underlying nonlinear dependences. Further, Cox et al. (2005) claimed that *"irreversibility is the symptom of nonlinearity."* Although financial time series are inherently irreversible, studying the local irreversibility, Flanagan and Lacasa (2016) identified subperiods where the properties of stock series could be characterized as reversible. This phenomenon led them to conclude that *"general stock price series are irreversible but periods of quasireversibility are not uncommon."* Moreover, they asserted that there was a strong link between irreversibility and predictability where higher degree of irreversibility indicated more predictable series. Studying 35 companies listed in the NYSE for the time interval from 1998 to 2012, they showed that the financial crisis of 2008 coincided with increasing values of irreversibility for all stocks.

Puglisi and Villamaina (2009) showed that memory acts as a hidden dissipative external force in a process and thus, its presence implies irreversibility. This assertion did not contrast with the findings of previously cited works which claimed that nonlinear dependences were the source of irreversibility in the financial time series. As a final remark, we would like to point that Xia et al. (2014) showed that the presence of noise resulted a loss of irreversibility.

Therefore, quantifying the degree of irreversibility of a time series is actually an implicit way for quantifying the degree of nonlinear dependences (memory) underlying in a time series, and consequently, the degree of predictability of a series.

In this chapter, we study irreversibility as an alternative measure which can help us identify nonlinear dependences among time series observations. This can be used as a complimentary method for quantifying index memory which will either validate the results obtained by calculating the Hurst exponent or give different results indicating the existence of a more complicated structure.

22.3 Visibility Graph Method for Hurst Exponent and Time Irreversibility

This section describes the method employed to calculate the Hurst exponent and quantify the time irreversibility of a series. Although statistics and econometric modeling are the most broadly used tools in economics and finance for analyzing data sets, there are cases that they do not perform well or the assumptions made do not correspond to reality. For these reasons, in this Section, we exploit the ability of methods proposed in the field of statistical mechanics to facilitate the analysis of the S&P 500 price-index.

22.3.1 Visibility Graph Approach

Visibility graph (VG) is a novel method that maps a time series into a network according to a simple geometric criterion (Lacasa et al., 2008). It is shown that the associated graph inherits several properties of the initial time series and consequently, we can extract useful information regarding the properties of the initial time series by means of analysis conducted on the associated graph.

The geometric criterion that maps a time series into a network is mathematically rather simple. Let $\{X_t\}_{,t=1,2,...n}$ be a series with n observations. Each observation of the original time series is transformed into a vertex in the associated network, and two random vertices i and j are "*visible*" to each other, if we can draw a straight line that connects the series data, and thus they are adjacent in the associated graph given the fact this line does not intersect any intermediate data height.

In Lacasa et al. (2008), there is a mathematically strict definition of VG method: Let $X = \{x_{t_1}, x_{t_2}, \ldots, x_{t_n}\}$ be a time series with n observations. Any two arbitrary observations (t_a, x_a) and (t_b, x_b) will be adjacent in the associated graph if for any other observation (t_c, x_c) such that $t_a < t_c < t_b$ the following criterion is fulfilled:

$$x_c < x_b + (x_a - x_b) * \frac{t_b - t_c}{t_b - t_a}.$$

In Fig. 22.2, there is a graphical illustration of the VG method. A periodic time series with period four is depicted in the upper part of the figure while in the bottom we plot

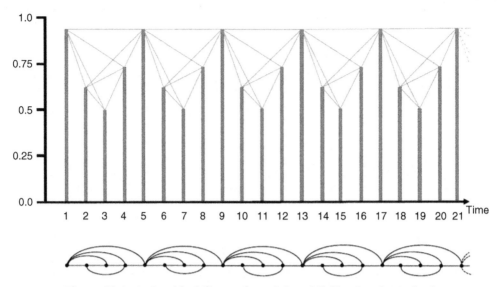

Figure 22.2: A Graphical Illustration of the Visibility Graph Method.
In the upper part, there is a plot of a period time series while on the bottom it is plotted the corresponding visibility graph.

the associated graph extracted following the aforementioned procedure. Some remarks regarding the properties of the associated graph should be made before proceeding with explaining how we calculate the Hurst exponent through this method. Any visibility graph is always:

1. A connected graph since any arbitrary data series observation (t_a, x_a) is connected at least the previous one (t_{a-1}, x_{a-1}) and the following one (t_{a+1}, x_{a+1}).
2. Invariant under affine transformation of series data.

In the next subsection, the estimation of the Hurst exponent is illustrated by mapping a time series into a network.

22.3.2 Estimating Hurst Exponent

In the corresponding literature, there is a variety of methods for estimating the Hurst exponent, each of them with its own advantages and drawbacks. The most broadly used methods are the *detrending moving average*, the *detrended fluctuation analysis*, the *generalized Hurst exponent approach*, the *classical rescaled range analysis*, and the *modified rescaled range analysis*. In our methodology, an approach recently introduced by Lacasa et al. (2009) is implemented, which overcomes many of the drawbacks that other methods have. Based on the discussion in the previous sections, our only assumption made is that the time series under study follow fBm.

Most of the properties of a network can be revealed by calculating its degree distribution. It is shown in Lacasa et al. (2009) and Ni et al. (2009) that fBm series map into scale-free networks with a power law degree distribution in form of:

$$P(k) = k^{-a},$$

where k is the degree of a node. It is also shown that there is a linear relation between the Hurst exponent (H) of an fBm and the exponent a of the degree distribution of the associated graph. The relation that binds H with a is:

$$H = \frac{3.1 - a}{2}.$$

Thus, the Hurst exponent of fBm can be estimated by mapping the series of the process into a network via the VG method and by calculating the exponent a of the degree distribution of the associated graph.

22.3.3 Quantifying Time Irreversibility

As it was described in Section 22.2, a time reversible process is the one whose properties remain invariant under time reversal. As shown in Lacasa et al. (2012), Donges et al. (2013), Lacasa and Flanagan (2015), and Flanagan and Lacasa (2016), the VG method is capable of separating reversible and irreversible series as well as quantifying the degree of irreversibility for time variant series. This can be done by introducing the notion of VG irreversibility which implies that the properties of the associated graph remain invariant when we change the arrow of time.

In order to examine if a process is invariant under time reversal, first we have to introduce the notion of time in the associated graph. Thus, we divide the degree of a node k into in-degree k_{in} and out-degree k_{out} such that $k = k_{in} + k_{out}$. In-degree is the number of series data from the past that has visibility on a node i while out-degree is the number of future series data that a particular node i has visibility on.

According to Lacasa and Flanagan (2015), if a series is reversible then, the in-degree and the out-degree distributions should coincide asymptotically. If the process is irreversible then, the two distributions diverge and the higher the divergence, the more irreversible the series is. So, under these circumstances, a mathematic tool is implemented that can assist to examine whether the two distributions coincide and if not, then, to give a quantification of the divergence. In the context of this work, the Hellinger distance is used as a measure of distance between the two distributions.

Mathematically speaking, Hellinger (1909) distance between two discrete distributions $P(p_1, p_2, ..., p_n)$ and $Q(q_1, q_2, ..., q_n)$ can be calculated by the following formula:

$$H(P,Q) = \frac{1}{\sqrt{2}} \sqrt{\sum_{i=1}^{n} \left(\sqrt{p_i} - \sqrt{q_i}\right)^2}.$$

For reversible series of infinite length, the two distributions coincide asymptotically. In fact, none of real life series is of infinite length and thus we expect that the distance between the two distributions has a nonzero value even for reversible series, and as the length of the series increases, the two distributions converge asymptotically.

22.4 The Data

The dataset we use for the purpose of this research consists of tick data from Thompson Reuters Tick History (TRTH) for the S&P500 price-index starting on the January 2, 1996 until June 10, 2010. Although, higher frequency leads inevitably to a larger microstructure noise, as it has been suggested by Hansen and Lunde (2006), we aggregate the data constructing a dataset that contains 5-min data points which has more than 320,000 observations. In Fig. 22.3, we plot the daily closing prices of the index for the corresponding time interval. The red shadowed areas denote the two major financial crashes that happened between 1996 and 2010, while some other minor stock market crash incidents are also being marked.

Figure 22.3: Plot of the Daily Closure Points of the S&P 500 Price-Index for the Period January 1996–June 2010.

22.5 Methodology

As it has already been described in Section 22.1, the microbehavior of the S&P 500 price-index is investigated during the financial crises occurred. In order to accomplish this, we have to study the properties of the index series locally, that is, to split the initial series into shorter overlapping periods of interest and study the properties of each subperiod (window). Conclusions can be drawn by comparing how properties of the index series vary over the course of time.

An important issue we have to address is to specify the length of windows. A long window will inevitably incorporate the impact of past events into the results which is not desirable, while a short window is probable to provide misleading results due to the small number of observations. Thus, in our case 10,400 observations are elaborated which correspond to 130 trading days or 6-month period. The number of increments between successive rolling windows is 240 observations or 3 trading days. Then, we apply the rolling window method into the index series to achieve continuity and for each window we estimate the values of Hurst exponent and calculate the degree of irreversibility via the VG method. In total, there are 1,290 subperiods of interest covering the period of January 1996 till June 2010.

At this point we specify the major crises that took place in the United States during the time interval 1996–2009. In Table 22.1, the two major financial crises are reported.

Both financial crashes elaborated in this chapter are related to an index crash following a prolonged period of index rally. The beginning of the crisis is the day where the index reaches its maximum value before starting a downward sloping trajectory. On the other hand, the end of the crisis is considered as the day where the index reaches its lowest value before rebounding again.

In the next section, we present the empirical results obtained after processing with the data and the methodology described earlier.

22.6 Empirical Results

Hurst exponent is an index for quantifying the degree of persistency (or antipersistency) of a time series and is broadly used for measuring the degree of efficiency in a market. The results of the analysis conducted on the original index series are presented in Figs. 22.4 and 22.5. In

Table 22.1: Sample period.

Sample Period	
Subperiod 1 (Dot.com bubble collapse):	March 15, 2000–October 1, 2002
Subperiod 2 (USA subprime crisis):	October 1, 2007–March 10, 2009

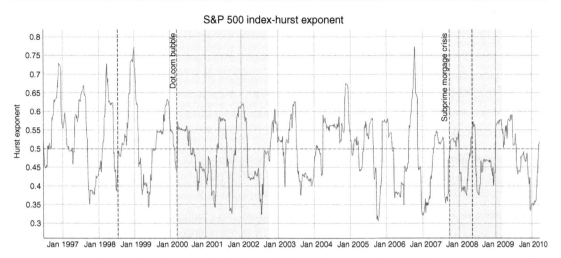

Figure 22.4: Plot of the Estimated Hurst Exponent for all Windows.
Dark shadowed regions denote periods of financial crisis. The *red line* corresponds to the values
$H = 0.5$ which characterizes the Brownian motion.

Fig. 22.4, we plot the values of the Hurst exponent for all subperiods, while in Fig. 22.5, the values of the Hellinger distance are plotted. The red shadowed regions in both plots denote periods of major financial crashes.

Compared with several other references (see Section 22.2 for more details), since our study contains high frequency data, the Hurst exponent inevitably varies significantly indicating that the properties of the index series are not constant but rather evolutionary over the course of time. We also report that only 4.4% of all windows calculated have an estimated

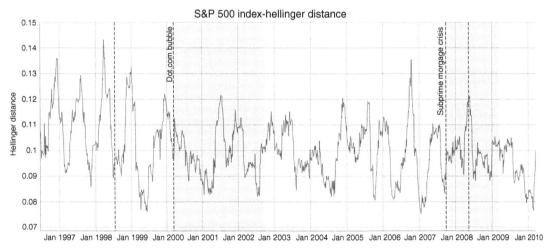

Figure 22.5: Plot of the Hellinger Distance for all Windows.
Dark shadowed regions denote periods of financial crisis.

Hurst exponent which lies within the interval $0.495 < H < 0.505$, that is, it is very close to $H = 0.5$, and thus, we can assume that these subseries have the same properties with a random walk. In total 49.16% of all subseries exhibit persistency, while 46.44% can be characterized as antipersistent. Actually, these results indicate that an fBm process is valid, since a high portion of subseries studied appears to have an estimated Hurst exponent far different from $H = 0.5$. In particular, the maximum value of Hurst exponent is 0.773 and the minimum is 0.306, fact that exhibits that the Hurst exponent varies from extreme high to extreme low values. Furthermore, in Fig. 22.4, we observe that the Hurst exponent "*jumps*" from high to low values and opposite, which indicates that the behavior of the S&P 500 Index fluctuates between a high degree of persistency and antipersistency. This also becomes visible if the summary statistics of the Hurst exponent are calculated. In this direction, in Fig. 22.6 we plot the distribution of the Hurst exponent for all subperiods. We report that the distribution is slightly right skewed and its tails are fatter than those of normal distribution. The mean value of the Hurst exponent is 0.501 and the standard deviation is 0.0873, which indicate the existence of large movements in the values of the exponent. This becomes obvious also in Fig. 22.4, where the Hurst exponent does not appear to follow any long-term trend but it fluctuates rather constantly around $H = 0.5$. This observation exhibits the abrupt movements of investors' behaviors and these changes are mirrored in the index time series.

In Gençay et al. (2001), it was mentioned that stock market is a place where heterogeneous agents interact with each other while agents are distinguished mainly by the frequency they operate in the market. This result implies that by the use of high frequency data, we allow to integrate the behavior of all types of investors varying from fundamental to high frequency speculative investors. For instance, events, such as the flash crashes that happened in May

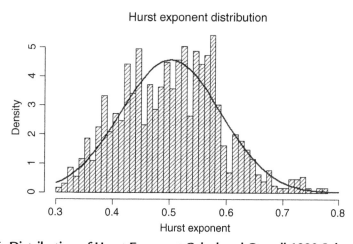

Figure 22.6: Distribution of Hurst Exponent Calculated Overall 1290 Subperiods.

6, 2010 which was caused by crashes of high frequency trading algorithms and lasted for 30 min can also be captured in our analysis. Interactions among heterogeneous investors are the main reason why our results differ from those already presented in the corresponding literature. Although the results presented in Fig. 22.4 are in line with Cajueiro and Tabak (2004a), who showed that the Hurst exponent was fluctuating around the value $H = 0.5$ for S&P 500 price-index series throughout January 1992 and December 2002, the Hurst exponent appears to be much more volatile in contrast with results presented in other papers using daily data (Cajueiro and Tabak, 2004a,b, 2005; Grech and Mazur, 2004; Grech and Pamuła, 2008; Lim, 2007; Lim et al., 2008). Moreover, we do not observe prolonged trends on the plot of the Hurst exponent, but rather the value of the exponent fluctuates intensely.

These fluctuations become particularly obvious throughout the period 1996–2000, when the Hurst exponent reaches its' maximum values, $H > 0.65$, and then it drops abruptly losing more than 0.3 points in all cases. The same phenomenon took place at the end of 2006. It appears that high degree of persistency destabilizes the index series such that *highly persistent* periods are followed by *highly antipersistent* periods.

Nevertheless, some more concrete patterns are observed in the local Hurst exponent series before the major index crashes. We observe that before both financial crises, that is, Dot. com bubble crisis in 2000 and the Subprime mortgage crisis in 2007, the Hurst exponent peaks at its highest level, $H > 0.75$. This peak corresponds to the index boom that happened between the second half of 1998 and the first half of 1999 as well as between the second half of 2006 and first quarter of 2007 as shown in Fig. 22.3. The period of extreme increase in the index value is followed by a period where the index value is decreasing below 0.5 (high antipersistency) before starting booming again. Generally speaking, antipersistency indicates "*nervousness*" and we usually observe antipersistency before shift points in the index series. Grech and Pamuła (2008) confirmed that Hurst exponent can be used as predictive tool of market crashes. In particular, they demonstrated that markets exhibit an antipersistent behavior before the crash, while afterward its' behavior becomes persistent.

About a year before each of those two crashes considered earlier, as it is observed from Fig. 22.4, the Hurst value fell temporarily below $H < 0.35$. However, after these two short periods, index series exhibit again an increasing persistency which was not as strong as it was before and it had a lower volatility. The onset of both financial crises is associated with quite prolonged periods of small fluctuations of the Hurst exponent at a level between $0.505 < H < 0.57$ indicating weak persistency. However, the index crash does not seem to alter investors' behavior in a long-term. What we observe is a short-living effect of the onset of the index crash and there is no sign of any repeated pattern throughout the crash.

In order to illustrate further that the Hurst exponent can be linked with index crashes, we have additionally marked with dash lines on Figs. 22.1, 22.2, and 22.3, some minor index crashes and we study the Hurst exponent throughout these crashes. The first crash happened on July 1998 and the second on May 2008. Even though the onset of both crashes finds the Hurst exponent lying in the antipersistency band, it is followed in both cases by an increase in the Hurst exponent value which reaches the persistency band. Once again, an index crash is preceded by antipersistency in the index series indicating "nervousness" in its investors' interactions.

Summarizing what we have discussed so far, except for the temporal effect that the onset of financial crisis has on the index behavior, the existence of financial crisis does not appear to affect considerably the properties of the index series. Stock market is an open dynamic system, which is adaptable on different disturbances happening in its environment and thus, the effect of most events has only short term duration.

In Fig. 22.5, we plot values for the Hellinger distance which gives a quantification of the degree of irreversibility of a series. As stated in Section 22.2, irreversibility is strongly related with the presence of nonlinear dependences and memory, and consequently, by quantifying the degree of irreversibility, we can implicitly measure the degree of memory underlying in the series. Interestingly, the shape of the plot in Fig. 22.5 is close to Fig. 22.4. This is not just a coincidence, but it means that the correlation between the Hurst exponent and the presence of memory in the series is high. In fact, except for the value $H = 0.5$, where increments of series are independent and uncorrelated, when $H \in [0, 0.5) \cup (0.5, 1]$, there is a form of dependence among increments and thus, a form of memory is also present. In particular, as we have already mentioned, when $H \in [0, 0.5)$, the time series under study can be characterized by long-term switching between high and low values in adjacent pairs while a value of Hurst exponent within the interval $H \in (0.5, 1]$ is an indication of a series which contain long-term positive autocorrelation.

The link between the Hurst exponent and the memory is also depicted in Fig. 22.5, where the irreversibility of the S&P 500 price-index series is studied. The correlation between Hurst exponent and Hellinger distance is 0.83, which means that higher (lower) values of Hurst exponent are associated with higher (lower) values of Hellinger distance. In particular, these results reveal that a persistent behavior of the index series is associated with a higher degree of irreversibility while antipersistency is associated with lower levels of irreversibility. Based on what other researchers have stated on this topic (see Section 22.2.1 for more details), relating the level of irreversibility of a series with its predictability, higher levels of irreversibility exhibit higher degree of predictability and so, we have some evidences that subseries whose Hurst exponent is $H > 0.5$ are more predictable than subseries where $H < 0.5$.

22.7 Conclusions

In this contribution, the local properties of the S&P 500 price-index series are calculated as a way to investigate how the financial crashes that took place throughout the time interval from January 1996 to June 2010 have affected the behavior of the index series. By using high frequency data and the VG methodology, the local Hurst exponent is estimated as a way to measure the persistency as well as to quantify the local degree of irreversibility of the S&P 500 price-index. We find that the properties of the index series vary over the course time and that both the Dot. com crisis in 2000 and the Subprime mortgage crisis of 2007 affected those properties only temporarily. Moreover, we provide evidence that the index series are linked with antipersistent behavior before the crashes incident while after the onset of the crash, the index series exhibit persistency. Irreversibility is in close relation with Hurst exponent which makes it a valuable tool that gives us an insight about the memory dynamics (linear and nonlinear) underlying in a series and periods characterized as antipersistent are found to contain less asymmetries.

Acknowledgments

The authors would like to acknowledge the gracious support of this work by the EPSRC and ESRC Centre for Doctoral Training on Quantification and Management of Risk & Uncertainty in Complex Systems & Environments (EP/L015927/1). This paper benefited from the comments of participants at the 2nd Quantitative Finance and Risk Analysis (QFRA) Symposium, Rhodes, Greece. Warm thanks are due to Prokopios Karadimos who read very carefully a preliminary version of our paper and who has afforded us considerable assistance in enhancing both the quality of the findings and the clarity of their presentation.

References

Alvarez-Ramirez, J., Alvarez, J., Rodriguez, E., Fernandez-Anaya, G., 2008. Time-varying Hurst exponent for US stock markets. Physica A 387 (24), 6159–6169.

Bachelier, L., 1900. Théorie de la spéculation. Gauthier-Villars, France.

Barkoulas, J.T., Baum, C.F., Travlos, N., 2000. Long memory in the Greek stock market. Appl. Financ. Econ. 10 (2), 177–184.

Barunik, J., Kristoufek, L., 2010. On Hurst exponent estimation under heavy-tailed distributions. Physica A 389 (18), 3844–3855.

Cajueiro, D.O., Tabak, B.M., 2004a. The Hurst exponent over time: testing the assertion that emerging markets are becoming more efficient. Physica A 336 (3), 521–537.

Cajueiro, D.O., Tabak, B.M., 2004b. Ranking efficiency for emerging markets. Chaos Solitons Fractals 22 (2), 349–352.

Cajueiro, D.O., Tabak, B.M., 2005. Testing for time-varying long-range dependence in volatility for emerging markets. Physica A 346 (3), 577–588.

Campbell, J.Y., Lo, A.W.C., MacKinlay, A.C., 1997. The Econometrics of Financial Markets, Princeton University Press, Princeton, NJ, pp. 149–180.

Cox, D.R., Hand, D.J., Herzberg, A.M., 2005. Foundations of Statistical Inference, Theoretical Statistics, Time Series and Stochastic Processes. Cambridge University Press, first ed., UK.

Di Matteo, T., 2007. Multi-scaling in finance. Quant. Finance 7 (1), 21–36.

Donges, J.F., Donner, R.V., Kurths, J., 2013. Testing time series irreversibility using complex network methods. Europhys. Lett. 102 (1), 10004.

Fama, E.F., 1963. Mandelbrot and the stable Paretian hypothesis. J. Bus. 36 (4), 420–429.

Fama, E.F., 1965. The behavior of stock-market prices. J. Bus. 38 (1), 34–105.

Flanagan, R., Lacasa, L., 2016. Irreversibility of financial time series: a graph-theoretical approach. Phys. Lett. A 380 (20), 1689–1697.

Gençay, R., Dacorogna, M., Muller, U.A., Pictet, O., Olsen, R., 2001. An Introduction to High-Frequency Finance. Academic Press, first ed., California, USA.

Grech, D., Mazur, Z., 2004. Can one make any crash prediction in finance using the local Hurst exponent idea? Physica A 336 (1), 133–145.

Grech, D., Pamuła, G., 2008. The local Hurst exponent of the financial time series in the vicinity of crashes on the Polish stock exchange market. Physica A 387 (16), 4299–4308.

Greene, M.T., Fielitz, B.D., 1977. Long-term dependence in common stock returns. J. Financ. Econ. 4 (3), 339–349.

Hansen, P.R., Lunde, A., 2006. Realized variance and market microstructure noise. J. Bus. Econ. Stat. 24 (2), 127–161.

Hellinger, E., 1909. Neue Begründung der Theorie quadratischer Formen von unendlichvielen Veränderlichen. J. Reine Angew. Math. 136, 210–271.

Hurst, H.E., 1956. The problem of long-term storage in reservoirs. Hydrol. Sci. J. 1 (3), 13–27.

Jiang, C., Shang, P., Shi, W., 2016. Multiscale multifractal time irreversibility analysis of stock markets. Physica A 462, 492–507.

Kristoufek, L., 2010. On spurious anti-persistence in the US stock indices. Chaos Solitons Fractals 43 (1), 68–78.

Lacasa, L., Flanagan, R., 2015. Time reversibility from visibility graphs of nonstationary processes. Phys. Rev. E 92 (2), 022817.

Lacasa, L., Luque, B., Ballesteros, F., Luque, J., Nuno, J.C., 2008. From time series to complex networks: the visibility graph. Proc. Natl. Acad. Sci. 105 (13), 4972–4975.

Lacasa, L., Luque, B., Luque, J., Nuno, J.C., 2009. The visibility graph: a new method for estimating the Hurst exponent of fractional Brownian motion. Europhys. Lett. 86 (3), 30001.

Lacasa, L., Nunez, A., Roldán, É., Parrondo, J.M., Luque, B., 2012. Time series irreversibility: a visibility graph approach. Eur. Phys. J. B 85 (6), 1–11.

Lim, K.P., 2007. Ranking market efficiency for stock markets: a nonlinear perspective. Physica A 376, 445–454.

Lim, K.P., Brooks, R.D., Kim, J.H., 2008. Financial crisis and stock market efficiency: empirical evidence from Asian countries. Int. Rev. Financ. Anal. 17 (3), 571–591.

Mandelbrot, B., 1967. The variation of some other speculative prices. J. Bus. 40 (4), 393–413.

Mandelbrot, B., 1997. The variation of certain speculative prices. Springer New York, USA.

Mandelbrot, B.B., Van Ness, J.W., 1968. Fractional Brownian motions, fractional noises and applications. SIAM Rev. 10 (4), 422–437.

Morales, R., Di Matteo, T., Gramatica, R., Aste, T., 2012. Dynamical generalized Hurst exponent as a tool to monitor unstable periods in financial time series. Physica A 391 (11), 3180–3189.

Ni, X.H., Jiang, Z.Q., Zhou, W.X., 2009. Degree distributions of the visibility graphs mapped from fractional Brownian motions and multifractal random walks. Phys. Lett. A 373 (42), 3822–3826.

Osborne, M.F., 1959. Brownian motion in the stock market. Operat. Res. 7 (2), 145–173.

Puglisi, A., Villamaina, D., 2009. Irreversible effects of memory. Europhys. Lett. 88 (3), 30004.

Ramsey, J.B., Rothman, P., 1996. Time irreversibility and business cycle asymmetry. J. Money Credit Bank. 28 (1), 1–21.

Samuelson, P.A., 1965. Proof that properly anticipated prices fluctuate randomly. Ind. Manag. Rev. 6 (2), 41–49.

Wang, Y., Liu, L., Gu, R., Cao, J., Wang, H., 2010. Analysis of market efficiency for the Shanghai stock market over time. Physica A 389 (8), 1635–1642.

Xia, J., Shang, P., Wang, J., Shi, W., 2014. Classifying of financial time series based on multiscale entropy and multiscale time irreversibility. Physica A 400, 151–158.

Zumbach, G., 2009. Time reversal invariance in finance. Quant. Finance 9 (5), 505–515.

Further Reading

Clark, P.K., 1973. A subordinated stochastic process model with finite variance for speculative prices. Econometrica 41 (1), 135–155.

Fama, E.F., 1995. Random walks in stock market prices. Financ. Anal. J. 51 (1), 75–80.

Malkiel, B.G., Fama, E.F., 1970. Efficient capital markets: a review of theory and empirical work. J. Finance 25 (2), 383–417.

CHAPTER 23

Illiquidity as an Investment Style During the Financial Crisis in the United Kingdom

Husaini Said, Evangelos Giouvris

Royal Holloway, University of London, Egham, United Kingdom

Chapter Outline

23.1 Introduction

Market efficiency signifies that obtaining abnormal returns is not possible but over the years, researchers found evidence to contradict the *efficient market hypothesis (EMH)* and various investment styles (or strategies) have been developed in order to beat the market. Style investments were recommended by Sharpe (1978) who looked at general styles, such as passive and active management. This was further extended to include more specific and generally accepted investment styles of size, value/growth, and momentum/contrarian. For instance, Banz (1981) mentioned that average returns are found to be inversely related to size while Fama and French (1992) highlighted that value was considered superior than growth investing. However, there are contradictory findings as well, which will be discussed in the literature review.

The financial crisis of 2007 has resulted in the emergence of studies of its impact on financial markets and instruments. Ivashina and Scharfstein (2010) studied bank lending[1] while Ben-David et al. (2012) studied hedge fund stock trading.[2] Moreover, the study of illiquidity has gained importance, probably due to the financial crisis[3] (Brunnermeier, 2009) and financial sector development (Rajan, 2006). General evidence seems to indicate that asset returns will increase with illiquidity, such as bid-ask spread (Amihud and Mendelson, 1986). The relationship between returns and illiquidity is quite obvious as Ibbotson et al. (2013) mentioned that investors clearly want more liquidity. Hence, illiquidity should be compensated with additional returns. Surprisingly, even though it is so apparent, for some reason illiquidity is rarely used as a control variable and is not a common investment style, as most studies, generally use the other three styles (Subrahmanyam, 2010). Only lately, research on illiquidity as an investment style has been undertaken [Chang et al. (2013) on the *Taiwanese stock market (TSM)* and Ibbotson et al. (2013) on the *United States (US)* market, who both found evidence to support illiquidity as an investment style].

Given the lack of more recent evidence for other well-known markets, we decided to investigate the potential of illiquidity as a reliable and consistent investment style during the financial crisis. We believe that the *United Kingdom (UK)* market provides a good opportunity because the *London Stock Exchange (LSE)* is considered as one of the largest stock markets by capitalization, signifying that the market is quite liquid and hence the results will be as immune as possible from biases, such as infrequent trading (Galariotis and Giouvris, 2007). We also agree with Galariotis and Giouvris (2007) that the results on the UK market will be of great interest to the international scientific, corporate, and investment community. This is further strengthened by our usage of precrisis and postcrisis data that will allow us to assess the extent to which illiquidity is a good trading strategy pre and postcrisis.

Using Ibbotson et al. (2013) framework and Sharpe (1992) four benchmark portfolio criteria,[4] our research starts by investigating whether the respective investment styles' premium[5] including illiquidity premium exist within the UK market. This will be followed by investigations on double sorted quartile portfolios, which are the intersection between illiquidity and the other investment styles. Lastly, stock migration analysis is conducted to investigate the stability of the portfolios.

---

[1] Ivashina and Scharfstein (2010) shows that during the peak period of the financial crisis, new loans to large borrowers fell.

[2] Ben-David et al. (2012) highlighted that hedge fund investors are more sensitive to losses compared to mutual fund investors during the financial crisis.

[3] Brunnermeier (2009) mentioned that the financial market turmoil in 2007 and 2008, due to liquidity and the credit crunch, has led to the most severe financial crisis since the Great Depression.

[4] Sharpe (1992) established that a benchmark portfolio should be (1) identifiable before the fact, (2) not easily beaten, (3) a viable alternative, and (4) low in cost.

[5] An investment style premium happens when one specific style performs better than its relevant antagonist style. For example, value premium (value portfolio returns > growth portfolio returns) and growth premium (value portfolio returns < growth portfolio returns).

Overall, our research for the UK market shows that with the exception of momentum premiums, the other investment styles do generate positive and significant premiums. The illiquid portfolios also consistently outperform the benchmarks and are quite stable during both periods. Nonetheless, illiquidity appears to meet Sharpe (1992) four benchmark criteria precrisis only and not postcrisis. This signifies that illiquidity can be classified as a reliable investment style precrisis but it is highly correlated to size.

The remainder of this paper is organized as follows. Section 23.2 presents the literature review while Section 23.3 describes the data and variables. In Section 23.4, the methodology, empirical results, and analysis of the research are discussed followed by our conclusion in Section 23.5.

23.2 Literature Review

23.2.1 Investment Styles

Chang et al. (2013) define investment style as the combining of stocks with the same characteristics to construct style portfolios and make investments in the stock markets. They also highlighted that the most common type of investment styles are *"value versus growth"* stocks, *"small versus big"* stocks, and *"momentum versus contrarian"* stocks. Therefore, we will first discuss the most common type of investment styles.

23.2.1.1 Value versus growth

Value and growth are two popular fundamental investment styles whereby value style looks for stocks that are undervalued according to companies' financial statements while growth style involves identifying long-term potential and performance. Past literature seems to indicate that value style is an antagonist to growth style, as researchers tend to compare the two styles with each other, by using suitable variables, such as *book to market ratio (B/M ratio)* and *price earnings ratio (P/E ratio)*.

Most research appears to conclude that value style is considered superior to growth style in the US market resulting in value premium (Basu, 1983; Fama and French, 1992). Daniel et al. (2001) also found value premium within the Japanese market, while Capaul et al. (1993) who studied six international markets including UK obtained consistent results to US market studies.

In contrast, a mixed outcome was obtained by Ding et al. (2005) who looked into East Asia markets. Value premium appears to be significantly negative in Thailand and in Indonesia it is insignificant. Gonenc and Karan (2003) discovered that there is no value premium within the *Istanbul Stock Exchange (ISE)*, signifying growth superiority. However, Beneda (2002) highlighted that the research period is important, as it is shown that over a short period of 5 years, value style is found to be more profitable but for a longer period (at least 14 years), average returns for growth stocks are superior.

23.2.2.2 Size effect

Banz (1981) highlighted that average returns are negatively related with size. This widely recognized anomaly is known as either small-firm or size effect and is also supported by researchers, such as Keim (1983). Such a relationship is expected as small firms are usually considered riskier than large firms and their returns are expected to be higher. Chan et al. (1985) confirmed this as they stated that within an efficient market, the higher average returns of smaller firms are justified by the additional risks borne by such firms.

Nevertheless, studies on size effect are less optimistic after the early 1980s as Van Dijk (2011) highlighted that past empirical studies declared the size effect to be dead since then. Gonenc and Karan (2003) actually obtained opposite findings whereby firms with larger capitalization were considered superior while Horowitz et al. (2000) reported no consistent relationship between size and realized returns, and their results show that the widespread use of size in asset pricing is unwarranted. Amihud (2002) highlighted that the size effect was partially due to market illiquidity, as times of dire illiquidity will cause flight-to-liquidity, resulting in preference for larger stocks and hence small stocks are actually subjected to higher illiquidity risk premium. Nonetheless, there is still recent evidence of a size effect within the UK (Dissanaike, 2002) and the US (Van Dijk, 2011) but Van Dijk (2011) also mentioned that more empirical research needs to be conducted to examine the robustness of size effect on the US and international stock markets.

23.2.2.3 Momentum versus contrarian

De Bondt and Thaler (1985) in their behavioral finance research on stock market overreaction discovered that loser stocks (or contrarian style) perform exceptionally well in comparison to winner stocks (or momentum style) over extended time periods of 3–5 years horizons. Nonetheless, in contrast, Jegadeesh and Titman (1993) document that investment styles that combined buying winner stocks and selling loser stocks generate significant positive returns of about 1% per month over 3–12 months holding periods. Jegadeesh and Titman (2001) revisit the subject and their evidence indicates that momentum profits have continued in the 1990s, suggesting that the original results were not a product of data snooping bias.

However, Conrad and Kaul (1998) emphasized that contrarian style is profitable for long-term horizons, while the momentum style is usually profitable for medium-term holding periods of between 3 and 12 months. Shen et al. (2005) findings agree with Conrad and Kaul (1998), who show that contrarian profits in the US market are very dependent on the period examined. In the UK, Dissanaike (2002) showed results that contrarian style outperformed momentum style and their *loser-winner effect (or contrarian premium)* results are significant. Nonetheless, Galariotis et al. (2007) demonstrated that both momentum and contrarian profits are available for the LSE.

23.2.2.4 Illiquid versus liquid

General evidence seems to indicate that returns will increase with illiquidity (Amihud and Mendelson, 1986; Brennan and Subrahmanyam, 1996) and Acharya and Pedersen (2005), also highlighted the importance of liquidity on asset prices. Nevertheless, there are some contradictory results, which showed that illiquid stocks do not necessarily provide consistently higher returns. Eleswarapu and Reinganum (1993) found evidence to suggest that "the January effect" and "size effect" are significant, indicating that the return for illiquidity may be a result of seasonal and size effect. Brennan et al. (2013) who analyzed the Amihud (2002) measure of illiquidity and its role in asset pricing, state that in general, only the down-days element commands a return premium. Furthermore, Ben-Rephael et al. (2008) who studied the *New York Stock Exchange (NYSE)* found evidence that the profitability of trading strategies based on illiquidity premium has declined over the past 4 decades, rendering such strategies virtually unprofitable.

However, unlike Eleswarapu and Reinganum (1993), Datar et al. (1998) finds a strong positive relationship between stock returns and illiquidity. The illiquidity premium is not restricted to the month of January alone and is prevalent throughout the year. Additionally, using three liquidity measures in the UK, Said and Giouvris (2015) reveal that illiquid portfolios consistently earn higher returns compared to liquid portfolios and the zero-cost portfolio returns[6] are statistically significant for at least two of the illiquidity measures used.

23.2.2.5 Returns between different investment styles

Past literature shows that there are links between different investment styles. Asness et al. (2013) highlighted that value and momentum are inversely correlated to each other, within and across asset classes. However, Bauman et al. (1998) who initially believed that the value premium was attributed to small-firm effects, discovered that the superiority of value style was actually genuine.

There are also studies that connect illiquidity with other styles, such as Asness et al. (2013) who found significant evidence that funding liquidity risk is inversely related to value but positively related to momentum globally across asset classes. Similarly, Pastor and Stambaugh (2003) measures of liquidity risk are positively related to momentum in the US stocks. One of the most common style connections is between illiquidity and size, as Eleswarapu and Reinganum (1993) highlighted that the illiquidity premium was a result of size effect. In contrast, Elfakhani (2000) mentioned that the returns of small-firms were larger due to the liquidity hypothesis, as small-firms were considered to be less liquid and thus should obtain higher return premiums. This is contradictory to Ibbotson et al. (2013) study on the US market, who highlighted that the returns obtained of illiquidity based portfolios are sufficiently different from those of the other styles. Considering the research earlier, one can see that the relationship between illiquidity and size is not clearly defined.

---

[6] Zero-cost portfolio = long the Illiquid portfolio and short the Liquid portfolio.

23.2.2 Potential of Illiquidity

Due to the recent crisis,[7] the study of liquidity has become more prominent and researchers have noticed the potential and importance of illiquidity as an investment tool. Yan (2008) in their research of US mutual funds found evidence to suggest that liquidity is an important reason why size erodes fund performance indicating the importance of liquidity in investment management. Moreover, Idzorek et al. (2012) mentioned that on average, mutual funds that held illiquid stocks performed significantly better than funds that held more liquid stocks. Thus, signifying the potential of liquidity as investment strategy or style particularly during the financial crisis. Even Ibbotson et al. (2013) suggested that liquidity should be given equal standing to the other investment styles.

23.2.2.1 Illiquidity as an investment style

Nowadays, it is normal for different investment styles to be made a *benchmark portfolio*,[8] *such as S&P/BARRA Growth stock index* and *S&P/BARRA Value Stock index* (Capaul et al., 1993). Therefore, similar to Ibbotson et al. (2013), we felt that the best way to explore whether illiquidity can be chosen as a reliable investment style during the crisis, is to investigate if a dependable *benchmark portfolio* can be created based on illiquidity. According to Sharpe (1992), a *benchmark portfolio* should meet four criteria namely (1) *"identifiable before the fact"*, (2) *"not easily beaten"*, (3) *"a viable alternative"*, and (4) *"low in cost"*.

23.3 Data and Variables

23.3.1 Data

In order to capture the UK stock market, the sample that we use consists of stocks listed under the *FTSE All-Share index* for the 14years period from January 2001 to December 2014. Although the financial crisis happened around August 2007, we decided to divide the 14 years sample period equally into half, namely precrisis (January 2001 to December 2007) and postcrisis period (January 2008 to December 2014). All data used in this paper are obtained from Datastream.

23.3.2 Investment Styles' Measures

To determine *"value versus growth"* investment style, Gonenc and Karan (2003) use B/M ratio while Beneda (2002) suggests using P/E ratio and Bauman et al. (1998) use dividend

---

[7] Crotty (2009) highlighted that the financial crisis happened when investors ran for liquidity and safety.

[8] A benchmark portfolio is a portfolio consisting of a list of securities that has been constructed based on specific criteria, which can be compared to an actual portfolio's performance. So if the investment style of "illiquidity" appears to be attractive in the UK then we will be seeing benchmark portfolios, such as "S&P illiquidity index" in the future.

yield. We use *price to book ratio (P/B ratio),* which is just the inverse of B/M ratio, because it is one of the most widely recognizable variables and allowed us to obtain data for more companies compared to P/E ratio. Determining the *"small versus big"* investment style is simpler, as we felt that using the *market value (MV)* of each firm is the most appropriate measure as in Dissanaike (2002). Similarly, choosing the most appropriate variable for *"momentum versus contrarian"* investment style is also straightforward as we will be using *monthly returns* as in De Bondt and Thaler (1985).

For illiquidity, we have decided to choose the *Amihud illiquidity measure*[9] (Amihud, 2002) as it is a well-known measure and has been extensively used in past literature. Moreover, we also thoroughly considered two other liquidity measures namely the Roll estimator (Roll, 1984) and High Low spread by Corwin and Schultz (2012) and we find that *Amihud* provided results that are more consistent to past studies. We have chosen *FTSE All-Share index* and *UK 3 months London Interbank Offered Rate (LIBOR)* as benchmarks for market returns and risk-free rate, respectively.

23.4 Methodology, Empirical Results, and Analysis

23.4.1 Illiquidity as an Investment Style Based on its Ability as a Benchmark

As highlighted earlier, exploring whether illiquidity can be made into a dependable portfolio benchmark seems to be the best way to investigate illiquidity's potential as a reliable investment style and how the financial crisis affects it. Thus, we feel that we should follow Ibbotson et al. (2013) framework, whereby they based it on Sharpe's (Sharpe, 1992) specification of a *portfolio benchmark*, which should be (1) *"identifiable before the fact,"* (2) *"not easily beaten,"* (3) *"a viable alternative,"* and (4) *"low in cost."*

To meet the *"identifiable before the fact"* criterion, we will be constructing quartiles (or portfolios) based on the prior year $(t-1)$ measure of the relevant investment style, which is then used to calculate the results of the portfolios for a given year (t). Therefore, the portfolios are *"identifiable before the fact."* The next criterion for us to fulfil is the *"not easily beaten."* This will be achieved by investigating if the returns of the illiquidity portfolios can provide positive returns (if any) and then compare it with the chosen benchmarks and other investment styles. This will be followed by *"a viable alternative"* criterion, which will be achieved by applying the method used by Ibbotson et al. (2013), who distinguished illiquidity from the other styles by constructing double-sorted portfolios. The double-sorted portfolios will allow us to study whether illiquidity is able to enhance the performance of the more

---

[9] It is calculated for each stock, s, every month as follows:

$$Amihud_{sm} = \frac{1}{t}\sum_{t}\frac{1,000,000 \times |return_t|}{price_t \times volume_t}$$

where t is each trading day.

recognized styles. Lastly, similar to Ibbotson et al. (2013), we investigated the *"low in cost"* criterion by exploring stock migration, which will allow us to consider whether illiquidity can be managed passively and at low cost.

23.4.2 Comparison of Investment Styles' and Risks

Our research starts with the investigation of portfolio performance across different investment style quartiles. This section will also allow us to determine whether illiquidity will be able to meet the first two benchmark criteria of *"identifiable before the fact"* and *"not easily beaten."* More importantly, this section will also confirm whether an illiquidity premium[10] exists in the first place.

Table 23.1 shows the equally weighted average annualized monthly returns and risks of the investment styles based on quartiles. Over the 14years period, the selection period is between 2000 and 2013 (inclusive), while the performance period is between 2001 and 2014 (inclusive). The two portfolios that are ranked top 25% and bottom 25% are classified as either Q1 or Q4 quartiles and the stocks are rebalanced annually.

The final column in Table 23.1 shows the zero-cost portfolio returns (or applicable investment style premium), which takes a long position on Q1 portfolio and short position on Q4 portfolio. Thus, for *"value versus growth"* investment style, it would be the *value premium* if *"high value portfolio (Q1)"* outperforms *"high growth portfolio (Q4)"* and *growth premium* if *"high growth portfolio (Q4)"* is found to perform better than *"high value portfolio (Q1)."*

The zero-cost portfolio[11] in Table 23.1 shows the existence of *value premium, small-firm premium*, and *illiquidity premium*,[12] consistent with Capaul et al. (1993), Dissanaike (2002), and Amihud and Mendelson (1986), respectively for both periods. As expected, all three premiums dropped in value postcrisis. The best result is achieved by value premium and small-firm premium precrisis and postcrisis, respectively. *Momentum premium* is not statistically significant for both periods, which is not akin to past research, such as Jegadeesh and Titman (1993). Dissanaike (2002) who studied the UK market discovered that contrarian performed better while Galariotis et al. (2007) mentioned that both momentum and contrarian profits are available within UK, which may explain the insignificant results for both periods. In fact, Fig. 23.1, shows the growth of *value premium, small-firm premium, and illiquidity premium* consistently over the 14years period while *momentum premium* noticeably dropped in value after the financial crisis of 2007, performing worse in comparison to the other premiums and even the two benchmarks (FTSE All Share Index and 3 months LIBOR).

---

[10] Illiquid quintile provides higher returns compared to liquid quintile.

[11] *Q1–Q4* (e.g., *value–growth quartile*).

[12] Q1 is greater than Q4.

Table 23.1: Cross-sectional annualized returns and risks of the investment styles pre and postcrisis.

Cross-Section	Result	Precrisis Period (2001–07)					Postcrisis Period (2008–14)				
		Q1	Q2	Q3	Q4	Q1 – Q4	Q1	Q2	Q3	Q4	Q1 – Q4
Value effect Value versus growth (Q1 = Value, Q4 = Growth)	Arithmetic mean	19.66%	7.22%	13.34%	6.05%	**13.61%** **(0.0352)**	16.80%	4.07%	10.46%	9.58%	**7.22%** **(0.0119)**
	Standard deviation	17.13%	22.21%	21.15%	22.83%	11.16%	40.77%	28.81%	29.28%	27.56%	15.67%
	Beta (FTSE All-Share)	0.86	1.16	1.12	1.33	−0.47	2.07	1.51	1.53	1.44	0.63
	Average number of stocks	113	113	113	112		140	140	140	139	
Size effect Micro versus big (Q1 = Micro, Q4 = Big)	Arithmetic mean	18.34%	11.78%	9.21%	6.32%	**12.02%** **(0.0280)**	16.20%	10.31%	8.36%	5.30%	**10.91%** **(0.0005)**
	Standard deviation	21.53%	21.62%	21.81%	17.41%	9.77%	35.07%	35.40%	29.80%	26.34%	10.58%
	Beta (FTSE All-Share)	1.04	1.17	1.21	1.01	0.03	1.81	1.85	1.56	1.37	0.44
	Average number of stocks	115	115	115	115		142	142	142	141	
Momentum effect Momentum versus contrarian (Q1 = Momentum, Q4 = Contrarian)	Arithmetic mean	12.42%	12.75%	10.35%	10.07%	2.35% 0.3412	10.75%	10.98%	8.36%	10.36%	0.39% (0.9463)
	Standard deviation	19.36%	16.07%	19.15%	29.80%	17.60%	28.45%	28.01%	28.38%	46.31%	29.57%
	Beta (FTSE All-Share)	0.97	0.92	1.08	1.48	−0.51	1.44	1.45	1.47	2.25	−0.81
	Average number of stocks	115	115	114	114		142	141	141	141	
Illiquidity effect Illiquid versus liquid (Q1 = Illiquid, Q4 = Liquid)	Arithmetic mean	17.12%	11.32%	9.52%	6.56%	**10.55%** **(0.0135)**	14.13%	10.97%	9.91%	5.17%	**8.96%** **(0.0002)**
	Standard deviation	21.36%	21.21%	22.53%	17.43%	7.56%	33.30%	33.07%	32.94%	27.37%	7.68%
	Beta (FTSE All-Share)	1.11	1.16	1.23	1.01	0.10	1.75	1.71	1.71	1.42	0.33
	Average number of stocks	113	113	114	112		142	142	142	141	

(Continued)

Table 23.1: Cross-sectional annualized returns and risks of the investment styles pre- and postcrisis. (cont.)

Cross-Section	Result	Precrisis Period (2001–07)					Postcrisis Period (2008–14)				
		Q1	Q2	Q3	Q4	Q1–Q4	Q1	Q2	Q3	Q4	Q1 – Q4
FTSE All-Share index	Arithmetic mean	2.67%					2.75%				
	Standard deviation	16.71%					18.97%				
3 months LIBOR	Arithmetic mean	4.66%					0.98%				
	Standard deviation	0.76%					0.84%				

This table shows equally-weighted, annualized returns (in percentage format) for quartile portfolios formed based on the investment styles briefly described. Although the financial crisis happened around August 2007, we decided to equally divide the 14 years return sample periods into half, namely, Precrisis (January 2001 to December 2007) and Postcrisis period (January 2008 to December 2014). Quartile portfolio ranks are determined by the value of the investment style measure in the year ($t-1$) prior to the year (t) in which returns are calculated and are rebalanced annually. Therefore, the style measure for the year 2000 is used to construct the quartiles and then calculate the returns for the year 2001, where the stocks will be held for at least 1 year. The "Q1–Q4" portfolio is a portfolio that takes a long position in the quartile of stocks (Q1) and a short position in the quartile of stocks (Q4). For example, in relation to *illiquid versus liquid investment style*, "Q1–Q4" takes a long position in the quartile of *illiquid stocks (Q1)* and a short position in the quartile of *liquid stocks (Q4)*. The table also shows two benchmarks namely *3 months LIBOR* and *FTSE All-Share index*. It also shows the total and systematic risks of the portfolios measured based on standard deviation and beta, respectively. Beta is calculated based on *FTSE All-Share index*. Newey-West *p*-values are reported in brackets for the arithmetic mean of the "Q1–Q4" portfolio, whereby bold figures denote a statistically significant coefficient at least at 10% level. The bandwidth parameter for the Newey-West *p*-value was calculated using the Newey-West automatic lag selection.

1. *Value effect (value versus growth investment style)* uses the end of year *price-to-book value (P/B) ratio*.
2. *Size effect (micro versus big investment style)* uses the *end of year market value (MV)*.
3. *Momentum effect (momentum versus contrarian investment style)* used the *annualized monthly returns*. It is also commonly known as *winners versus losers' investment style*.
4. *Illiquidity effect (illiquid versus liquid investment style)* uses the *Amihud illiquidity measure (Amihud)*.

Source: All data were obtained from Datastream.

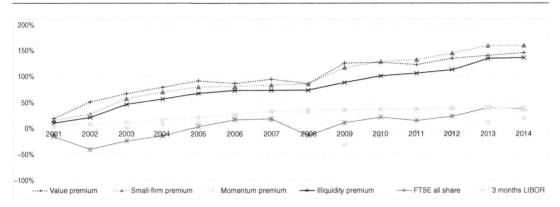

**Figure 23.1: Comparison of the Growth
of the Respective Investment Style Premiums Pre and Postcrisis.**
This figure shows the growth of the respective investment style premiums over the 14years study period (7 years pre and 7 years postcrisis). The investment premiums included are *value premium, small-firm premium, momentum premium,* and *illiquidity* premium. The percentage growth for investing in the benchmark of *FTSE All-Share index* and *3 months LIBOR* are also included in the figure. *All data are obtained from Datastream.*

Similar to Ibbotson et al. (2013) study on the US, Table 23.1 shows that the best performing top[13] investment style is achieved by *"high value portfolio (Q1)"* for both periods. The worst performing portfolio is the bottom investment style of *"high growth portfolio (Q4)"* for the precrisis period but postcrisis, it is the *"mid value portfolio (Q2)"*. One interesting finding is that regardless of periods, all the top and bottom investment styles show higher returns relative to the benchmarks of *FTSE All-Share index* and *3 months LIBOR,* indicating that any of the simple investment styles, allow investors to outperform the market.

In terms of risk, the highest standard deviation and beta is reported by the *"high contrarian portfolio,"* which is not consistent with the traditional theory of *"higher returns comes with higher risk,"* as it did not produce the highest returns. Nevertheless, the crisis obviously resulted in higher risks, as observed in the postcrisis results.

Overall, portfolios constructed based on illiquidity can generate positive returns. Moreover, with the exception of *"high value portfolio"* and *"micro portfolio,"* the *"high illiquid portfolio"* performed better in comparison to the other styles and the two benchmarks for both periods. Hence, it can safely be concluded that illiquidity had met the second benchmark criterion of *"not easily beaten."* Since the portfolios are constructed based on the prior year (*t*−1) measure, this automatically also satisfies the first criterion of *"identifiable before the fact."* Also as expected, investment styles seem to be superior precrisis.

---

[13] Top investment style means the top 25% ranked based on the relevant investment style or Q1 and it is expected to be Value, Micro, Momentum, and Illiquid portfolios. Bottom investment style means the bottom 25% ranked based on the relevant investment style or Q4. It is expected to be Growth, Big, Contrarian, and Liquid portfolios.

23.4.3 Intersection of Illiquidity Portfolios with Other Investment Styles

Although our results in the last section appear to indicate that illiquidity is *"not easily beaten"* for both periods, some researchers highlighted that the positive performance of illiquidity is actually due to other styles. Asness et al. (2013) found significant evidence that funding liquidity risk is inversely related to value but positively related to momentum globally, whereas Eleswarapu and Reinganum (1993) highlighted that the illiquidity premium is a result of size effect. Therefore, we will implement the *double sorting technique* used by Ibbotson et al. (2013), as this technique will allow us to test whether illiquidity is able to enhance the other styles and hence meeting the third benchmark criterion of *"a viable alternative."*

23.4.3.1 Intersection of illiquidity and value/growth investment styles (portfolios)

The first double sorted portfolios are constructed by independent sorting, based on Amihud and P/B ratio, to produce 16 intersection portfolios as can be seen in Table 23.2. As before, the prior year $(t-1)$ intersection measure is used to construct and calculate the portfolio performance for a given year (t). The stocks are also rebalanced annually.

Unfortunately, due to the limited number of stocks available for the UK market, the number of stocks significantly reduce after segregation into 16 intersection portfolios. Therefore, we have to ensure that each portfolio is diversified. Past studies have different opinions on the number of stocks required to properly diversify a portfolio, such as Evans and Archer (1968) who highlighted that 10–15 stocks are required. Nevertheless, Reilly and Brown (2012, p. 201) highlighted that based on past studies, such as Evans and Archer (1968) and Tole (1982) *"…major benefits of diversification were achieved rather quickly, with about 90 percent of the maximum benefit of diversification derived from portfolios of 12 to 18 stocks."* Thus, we consider portfolios that have at least 12 stocks as *"acceptable portfolios"* because achieving 90% of the maximum benefit of diversification is more than satisfactory for us.

Panel A of Table 23.2 shows only one portfolio has less than 12 stocks precrisis while for postcrisis, all portfolios are considered acceptable. Both precrisis and postcrisis periods show results that are less consistent, as across value portfolios (rows), illiquid stocks do not consistently generate higher returns relative to more liquid stocks. Similarly, across illiquidity (columns), value portfolios also do not perform consistently better compared to growth portfolios.

However, although the highest return is not generated by the intersection of *"high value & high illiquid portfolio,"* its return of 20.93% is higher than the return of 19.66% of the *"high value portfolio (Q1)"* in Table 23.1 for precrisis period. This can also be seen postcrisis, signifying that illiquidity did enhance the value investment style.

Table 23.2: Annualized returns and risks of value/growth and illiquidity intersection portfolios pre and postcrisis.

Cross-Section	Precrisis Periods (2001–07)				Postcrisis periods (2008–14)			
	High Illiquid	Mid Illiquid	Mid Liquid	High Liquid	High Illiquid	Mid Illiquid	Mid Liquid	High Liquid
High value								
Arithmetic mean	20.93%	21.66%	15.51%	11.81%	17.60%	18.90%	13.84%	10.51%
Standard deviation	19.00%	16.72%	18.59%	12.78%	34.21%	43.58%	46.79%	41.11%
Beta (FTSE All Share)	1.01	0.72	0.97	0.58	1.78	2.11	2.33	2.06
Average number of stocks	43	32	25	10	56	44	28	15
Mid value								
Arithmetic mean	8.78%	7.81%	3.47%	7.03%	4.65%	5.25%	3.47%	0.47%
Standard deviation	22.72%	21.32%	22.88%	25.02%	28.40%	24.08%	34.06%	36.09%
Beta (FTSE All Share)	1.18	1.14	1.08	1.21	1.48	1.25	1.77	1.86
Average number of stocks	29	30	31	18	33	49	31	22
Mid growth								
Arithmetic mean	20.38%	12.63%	15.40%	7.29%	18.35%	12.42%	8.74%	5.27%
Standard deviation	26.27%	21.17%	27.17%	16.63%	33.26%	32.47%	28.54%	25.15%
Beta (FTSE All Share)	1.21	1.09	1.34	0.98	1.73	1.66	1.48	1.31
Average number of stocks	22	26	25	37	32	27	37	43
High growth								
Arithmetic mean	17.28%	3.86%	4.05%	5.21%	18.45%	8.77%	12.86%	5.09%
Standard deviation	25.99%	31.21%	28.12%	16.74%	38.21%	35.78%	28.40%	22.48%
Beta (FTSE All Share)	1.18	1.73	1.53	0.98	1.98	1.84	1.46	1.16
Average number of stocks	17	21	29	45	18	19	42	59

The table shows the results of intersection quartiles between value/growth and illiquidity investment styles. The portfolios are constructed by independently sorting the portfolios into quartiles based on the two investment styles and then by taking the intersection sets of portfolios to produce 16 intersection groups. As before, the prior year (t−1) intersection measure is used to construct the portfolios, which are then used to calculate the portfolio returns and risk for a given year (t). The portfolios are rebalanced annually. Thus, the *sorting* period is from January 2000 to December 2013 while *performance* period is from January 2001 to December 2014 and the stocks are held for at least 1 year. The 14 years performance sample periods are divided into half, namely, Precrisis (2001–07) and Postcrisis period (2008–14). Due to the limited number of stocks and to ensure that the results are significant, we only considered portfolios that meet our diversification requirements of at least 12 stocks on average. Thus, acceptable portfolios with 12 or more stocks on average are in bold.
Source: All data were obtained from Datastream.

23.4.3.2 Intersection of illiquidity and size investment styles (portfolios)

Unlike Ibbotson et al. (2013), Table 23.3 seems to show that within the UK, investing in illiquid stocks is almost similar to investing into small firms because the intersection of the portfolios resulted in a limited number of stocks for some portfolios. This is particularly noticeable for the *"Micro & High Liquid portfolio,"* where the average number of stocks is only 1 for both periods. This is not surprising since it is expected that micro stocks are less liquid compared to other size related portfolios.

Among the "acceptable portfolios," Table 23.3 shows conflicting results as both illiquidity and size do not show clear enhancing ability, indicating that illiquidity does not provide additional benefits when combined with portfolios based on size for both periods. Therefore, signifying that size does appear to capture illiquidity, as suggested by Eleswarapu and Reinganum (1993).

23.4.3.3 Intersection of illiquidity and momentum/contrarian investment styles (portfolios)

Table 23.4 which combines illiquidity and momentum/contrarian style is more evenly segregated for both periods, suggesting that the two styles are quite independent of each other. Across momentum portfolios (rows), illiquid portfolios generally produce higher returns compared to more liquid portfolios and the highest return is generated by the enhanced portfolio of *"high contrarian & high illiquid portfolio"* and *"high momentum & high illiquid portfolio"* precrisis and postcrisis, respectively.

Nonetheless, across illiquidity portfolios (columns), highly momentum portfolios sometime generated better returns compared to contrarian styles but it is less consistent for both periods. In fact *"high contrarian & high illiquid portfolio"* produces higher returns than the *"high momentum & high illiquid portfolio"* precrisis. Furthermore, compare to the *"high momentum portfolio (Q1)"* and *"high contrarian portfolio (Q4)"* in Table 23.1, Table 23.4 also shows that illiquidity does manage to enhance the returns of the two portfolios for both crisis periods.

Overall, Tables 23.2, 23.3, and 23.4 show that risks have consistently increased after the crisis but returns can be higher, probably as a compensation for the higher risks. Nevertheless, the essential finding is that with the exception of size, so far our results appear to meet the third benchmark criterion of *"a viable alternative"* as illiquidity managed to enhance both value and momentum investment styles for both periods.

23.4.4 Illiquidity as a Factor in Comparison to Other Investment Factors

Since illiquidity seems to be able to enhance value and momentum styles, similar to Ibbotson et al. (2013), we conducted further investigation on the ability of illiquidity as an investment style by looking at the risk factors (zero cost or dollar neutral) of the styles. Nevertheless, instead of using annual data, we will be using monthly data for the correlation and regression analysis to ensure more meaningful results.

Table 23.3: Annualized returns and risks of size and illiquidity intersection quartiles pre and postcrisis.

Cross-Section	Precrisis Periods (2001–07)				Postcrisis Periods (2008–14)			
	High Illiquid	Mid Illiquid	Mid Liquid	High Liquid	High Illiquid	Mid Illiquid	Mid Liquid	High Liquid
Micro								
Arithmetic mean	**18.26%**	17.40%	19.63%	11.66%	**16.02%**	**14.75%**	**37.26%**	−46.99%
Standard deviation	**20.60%**	28.06%	23.42%	N/A	**33.76%**	**38.31%**	**80.87%**	N/A
Beta (FTSE All Share)	**1.04**	1.29	2.69	N/A	**1.77**	**1.84**	**2.92**	N/A
Average number of stocks	**80**	29	2	1	**103**	**38**	**2**	1
Small								
Arithmetic mean	15.69%	9.53%	12.89%	19.31%	**9.82%**	**9.59%**	**10.95%**	−25.94%
Standard deviation	23.68%	20.73%	25.92%	15.04%	**33.33%**	**32.23%**	**54.09%**	N/A
Beta (FTSE All Share)	1.26	1.17	1.15	1.22	**1.73**	**1.69**	**2.66**	N/A
Average number of stocks	27	66	19	1	**36**	**82**	**24**	1
Medium								
Arithmetic mean	13.77%	8.21%	8.79%	9.87%	8.19%	8.95%	**8.36%**	**6.62%**
Standard deviation	19.09%	22.15%	22.20%	23.83%	28.56%	28.86%	**28.86%**	**39.75%**
Beta (FTSE All Share)	1.02	1.09	1.23	1.36	1.35	1.51	**1.51**	**1.94**
Average number of stocks	6	17	82	9	4	22	**100**	**16**
Big								
Arithmetic mean	−3.17%	**16.44%**	7.30%	**6.26%**	64.09%	16.66%	**10.53%**	**4.74%**
Standard deviation	25.79%	**42.05%**	24.48%	**16.73%**	N/A	68.39%	**27.55%**	**26.26%**
Beta (FTSE All Share)	1.21	**2.70**	1.37	**0.97**	N/A	6.90	**1.41**	**1.37**
Average number of stocks	1	**1**	11	**103**	1	1	**16**	**126**

This table shows the results of intersection quartiles between size and illiquidity investment styles. The portfolios are constructed by independently sorting the portfolios into quartiles based on the two investment styles and then by taking the intersection sets of portfolios to produce 16 intersection groups. As before, the prior year ($t-1$) intersection measure is used to construct the portfolios, which are then used to calculate the portfolio returns and risk for a given year (t). The portfolios were rebalanced annually. Thus, the sorting sample period is from January 2000 to December 2013 while *performance* sample period is from January 2001 to December 2014 and the stocks are held for at least 1 year. The 14 years performance sample periods are divided into half, namely, Precrisis (2001–07) and Postcrisis period (2008–14). Due to the limited number of stocks and to ensure that the results are significant, we only considered portfolios that meet our diversification requirements of at least 12 stocks on average. Thus, portfolios with 12 or more stocks on average are in bold.
Source: All data were obtained from Datastream.

Table 23.4: Annualized returns and risks of momentum/contrarian and illiquidity intersection portfolios pre and postcrisis.

Cross-Section	Precrisis Periods (2001–07)				Postcrisis Periods (2008–14)			
	High Illiquid	Mid Illiquid	Mid Liquid	High Liquid	High Illiquid	Mid Illiquid	Mid Liquid	High Liquid
High momentum								
Arithmetic mean	16.37%	11.19%	8.34%	12.44%	17.64%	7.17%	11.29%	9.05%
Standard deviation	23.25%	22.19%	19.78%	16.54%	29.91%	32.11%	27.68%	25.00%
Beta (FTSE All Share)	0.91	1.11	1.00	0.92	1.47	1.62	1.43	1.24
Average number of stocks	28	31	31	22	35	32	39	37
Mid momentum								
Arithmetic mean	17.63%	17.08%	12.57%	5.36%	13.69%	11.34%	10.07%	8.69%
Standard deviation	17.07%	11.84%	21.23%	15.65%	32.34%	28.91%	26.51%	23.36%
Beta (FTSE All Share)	0.91	0.65	1.21	0.88	1.69	1.51	1.36	1.15
Average number of stocks	28	27	28	30	36	41	32	32
Mid contrarian								
Arithmetic mean	15.17%	7.44%	9.51%	6.77%	10.50%	9.85%	9.41%	2.53%
Standard deviation	19.14%	24.07%	21.70%	16.58%	30.44%	27.65%	27.78%	29.40%
Beta (FTSE All Share)	1.03	1.37	1.20	0.97	1.60	1.42	1.42	1.46
Average number of stocks	27	25	29	30	38	38	33	32
High Contrarian								
Arithmetic mean	17.77%	8.77%	7.06%	4.10%	15.04%	13.07%	8.78%	5.29%
Standard deviation	29.49%	29.55%	34.53%	27.15%	42.12%	48.75%	50.06%	43.34%
Beta (FTSE All Share)	1.44	1.51	1.71	1.43	2.15	2.24	2.44	2.08
Average no. of stocks	30	28	23	31	33	31	37	41

This table shows the results of intersection quartiles between momentum/contrarian and illiquidity investment styles. The portfolios are constructed by independently sorting the portfolios into quartiles based on the two investment styles and then by taking the intersection sets of portfolios to produce 16 intersection groups. As before, the prior year ($t-1$) intersection measure is used to construct the portfolios, which are then used to calculate the portfolio returns and risk for a given year (t). The portfolios were rebalanced annually. Thus, the sorting period is from January 2000 to December 2013 while *performance* period is from January 2001 to December 2014 and the stocks are held for at least 1 year. The 14 years performance sample periods are divided into half, namely, Precrisis (2001–07) and Postcrisis period (2008–14). Due to the limited number of stocks and to ensure that the results are significant, we only considered portfolios that meet our diversification requirements of at least 12 stocks on average. Thus, portfolios with 12 or more stocks on average are in bold.
Source: All data were obtained from Datastream.

23.4.4.1 Correlation of the investment styles (factors) with each other and the market

The correlation analysis is conducted to see the relationship of the respective factors with each other and the market. Results in Table 23.5 are almost similar for the two periods. The illiquidity factor is positively related with size and value factor. It is worth noticing that the illiquidity factor is not significantly correlated with the market precrisis but it is negatively correlated postcrisis. We also obtain contradictory results for value, size and momentum factors in relation to the market for the two periods.

The strongest positive correlation was observed between the illiquidity factor and size factor, which comes into contrast with Ibbotson et al. (2013) who found a negative correlation between the two factors. The positive correlation obtained here between the two factors is not surprising as our earlier results in Table 23.3, show that there is a close relationship between illiquidity and size. This provides further evidence to indicate that size captures illiquidity in the UK. However, postcrisis, the illiquidity factor is slightly less correlated to size.

23.4.4.2 Regression analyses of various illiquidity portfolios

Similar to Ibbotson et al. (2013), we will use three asset pricing models (univariate CAPM, Fama-French 3 Factor model, and Carhart 4 Factor model) to further explain the average returns of various relevant illiquidity portfolios that were discussed earlier.

Table 23.6 shows the regression results for two portfolios namely the zero-dollar *"illiquidity factor portfolio"* (Panel A) and long only *"high illiquid portfolio"* (Panel B). The table shows that based on CAPM, both portfolios (Panel A and Panel B) report positive and statistically significant monthly alpha for both periods. The Fama-French 3 factor model shows that after including the value factor and size factor, the monthly alpha disappears for the *"illiquidity factor portfolio."* However, the long only *"high illiquid portfolio"* monthly alpha remains precrisis but it disappears postcrisis. Surprisingly, although slightly reduced, the monthly alpha of the long only *"high illiquid portfolio"* remains even after the introduction of the momentum factor signifying that investing into illiquid portfolios can generate positive returns and thus poses a challenge to the EMH, as it should have resulted in no significant monthly alpha. Nevertheless, this can only be observed for the precrisis period, as the financial crisis seems to have cause the monthly alpha to disappear postcrisis.

23.4.4.3 Regression analyses of various enhanced illiquidity portfolios

Using the three asset pricing models, Table 23.7 shows the regression results of three enhanced intersected illiquidity portfolios (net of risk free rate). The three enhanced portfolios are (1) *"High Value & High Illiquid portfolio,"* (2) *"Micro & High Illiquid portfolio,"* and (3) *"High Momentum & High Illiquid portfolio."* Although the three portfolios did not produce

Table 23.5: Correlation and descriptive statistics of the monthly returns of the respective factors with each other and the market pre and postcrisis.

Precrisis Periods (2001–07)

Correlation	Illiquidity Factor	Market	Value Factor	Size Factor	Momentum Factor
Illiquidity factor	1.0000	−0.1346	0.3763	0.9418	0.0461
	—	(0.2221)	(0.0004)	(0.0000)	(0.6771)
Market	−0.1346	1.0000	−0.2259	−0.1885	−0.2528
	(0.2221)	—	(0.0388)	(0.0860)	(0.0203)
Value factor	0.3763	−0.2259	1.0000	0.4911	−0.0516
	(0.0004)	(0.0388)	—	(0.0000)	(0.6408)
Size factor	0.9418	−0.1885	0.4911	1.0000	−0.0217
	(0.0000)	(0.0860)	(0.0000)	—	(0.8445)
Momentum factor	0.0461	−0.2528	−0.0516	−0.0217	1.0000
	(0.6771)	(0.0203)	(0.6408)	(0.8445)	—

Postcrisis Periods (2008–14)

Correlation	Illiquidity Factor	Market	Value Factor	Size Factor	Momentum Factor
Illiquidity factor	1.0000	−0.2381	0.1995	0.8416	−0.0939
	—	(0.0195)	(0.0514)	(0.0000)	(0.3628)
Market	−0.2381	1.0000	0.3074	−0.0837	−0.1619
	(0.0195)	—	(0.0023)	(0.4177)	(0.1151)
Value factor	0.1995	0.3074	1.0000	0.6004	−0.8653
	(0.0514)	(0.0023)	—	(0.0000)	(0.0000)
Size factor	0.8416	−0.0837	0.6004	1.0000	−0.5366
	(0.0000)	(0.4177)	(0.0000)	—	(0.0000)
Momentum factor	−0.0939	−0.1619	−0.8653	−0.5366	1.0000
	(0.3628)	(0.1151)	(0.0000)	(0.0000)	—

This table shows the correlation of the monthly returns of the respective factors with each other as well as the market. The *p*-values of the correlations are reported in brackets under each respective correlation coefficient, whereby bold figures denote a statistically significant coefficient at least at 10%. The sample uses stocks that are listed on *FTSE All-Share index* between January 2001 and December 2014 (168 months) divided further into pre (84 months) and postcrisis periods (84 months).

Source: All data were obtained from Datastream.

Table 23.6: Regression analyses of monthly returns of the zero-cost illiquidity factor and high illiquid portfolio pre and postcrisis.

	Precrisis Periods (2001–07)							Postcrisis periods (2008–14)						
	Monthly α (%)	Market Beta	Value	Size	Momentum	Adjusted R² (%)	N	Monthly α (%)	Market Beta	Value	Size	Momentum	Adjusted R² (%)	N
Panel A *Illiquidity factor portfolio (illiquidity effect)*														
CAPM	**0.86%** (0.0020)	−0.0863 (0.2340)				0.52%	84	**0.76%** (0.0048)	−0.1373 (0.0188)				5.41%	84
Fama-French 3 factor	0.01% (0.9125)	0.0195 (0.4233)	**−0.1251** (0.0110)	**1.0123** (0.0000)		89.38%	84	0.06% (0.6027)	−0.0032 (0.9048)	**−0.3252** (0.0000)	**0.9726** (0.0000)		84.17%	84
Carhart 4 factor	−0.01% (0.9144)	0.0333 (0.1810)	**−0.1161** (0.0162)	**1.0140** (0.0000)	**0.0656** (0.0420)	89.80%	84	−0.10% (0.3146)	−0.0357 (0.1286)	−0.0490 (0.4129)	**0.9599** (0.0000)	**0.1935** (0.0000)	88.68%	84
Panel B *Long only high illiquid portfolio*														
CAPM	**1.25%** (0.0003)	**1.0378** (0.0000)				61.99%	84	**0.99%** (0.0025)	**0.9502** (0.0000)				68.90%	84
Fama-French 3 factor	**0.46%** (0.0307)	**1.1376** (0.0000)	**−0.3147** (0.0020)	**1.1643** (0.0000)		88.80%	84	0.19% (0.2821)	**1.0122** (0.0000)	−0.0625 (0.3484)	**0.9140** (0.0000)		91.04%	84
Carhart 4 factor	**0.41%** (0.0487)	**1.1685** (0.0000)	**−0.2945** (0.0031)	**1.1682** (0.0000)	**0.1467** (0.0261)	89.35%	84	0.15% (0.4285)	**1.0029** (0.0000)	0.0164 (0.8847)	**0.9103** (0.0000)	0.0553 (0.3899)	91.01%	84

This table shows results from the following three regression models on zero-cost (or dollar neutral) *Illiquidity factor portfolio* (Panel A) and *long only High Illiquid* portfolio (Panel B). *Illiquidity factor portfolio* (or *illiquidity effect*) takes a long position in the portfolio of *high Illiquid* stocks and a short position in the portfolio of *high liquid* stocks. The p-values are reported in brackets under each respective coefficient, whereby bold figures denote a statistically significant coefficient at least at 10%. The sample uses stocks that are listed on *FTSE All-Share index* between January 2001 and December 2014 (168 months) divided further into pre (84 months) and postcrisis (84 months).

1. *Capital asset pricing model (CAPM)*

$$R_p = \alpha_p + \beta_p\left(R_m - R_f\right) + \varepsilon_p \qquad (23.1)$$

2. *Fama-French three factor model*

$$R_p = \alpha + \beta_p\left(R_m - R_f\right) + V_p\left(R_v - R_g\right) + S_p\left(R_s - R_b\right) + \varepsilon_p \qquad (23.2)$$

3. *Carhart four factor model*

$$R_p = \alpha + \beta_p\left(R_m - R_f\right) + V_p\left(R_v - R_g\right) + S_p\left(R_s - R_b\right) + M_p\left(R_{mom} - R_z\right) + \varepsilon_p \qquad (23.3)$$

Source: All data were obtained from Datastream.

Table 23.7: Regression analyses of monthly returns of the enhanced illiquidity portfolio pre and postcrisis.

Precrisis Periods (2001–07)

	Monthly α (%)	Market Beta	Value	Size	Moment-um	Adjusted R² (%)	N
Panel A High value & High illiquid							
CAPM	1.57% (0.0000)	1.0422 (0.0000)				61.49%	84
Fama-French 3 factor	0.43% (0.0544)	1.1810 (0.0000)	0.1489 (0.1560)	0.9946 (0.0000)		87.72%	84
Carhart 4 factor	0.35% (0.0938)	1.2316 (0.0000)	0.1819 (0.0647)	1.0009 (0.0000)	0.2403 (0.0004)	89.40%	84
Panel B Micro, & High illiquidi							
CAPM	1.34% (0.0003)	1.0512 (0.0000)				59.53%	84
Fama-French 3 factor	0.38% (0.0696)	1.1721 (0.0000)	−0.2255 (0.0231)	1.2447 (0.0000)		89.75%	84
Carhart 4 factor	0.33% (0.1081)	1.2048 (0.0000)	−0.2042 (0.0345)	1.2488 (0.0000)	0.1555 (0.0168)	90.35%	84
Panel C High momentum & High illiquidi							
CAPM	1.18% (0.0121)	1.0005 (0.0000)				44.42%	84
Fama-French 3 factor	0.57% (0.1401)	1.0809 (0.0000)	−0.6528 (0.0005)	1.3624 (0.0000)		70.72%	84
Carhart 4 factor	0.38% (0.2533)	1.1985 (0.0000)	−0.5762 (0.0004)	1.3771 (0.0000)	0.5591 (0.0000)	78.17%	84

Postcrisis Periods (2008–14)

	Monthly α (%)	Market Beta	Value	Size	Moment-um	Adjusted R² (%)	N
Panel A High value & High illiquid							
CAPM	1.28% (0.0020)	1.0108 (0.0000)				61.21%	84
Fama-French 3 factor	0.32% (0.1540)	1.0100 (0.0000)	0.1801 (0.0311)	0.9343 (0.0000)		89.21%	84
Carhart 4 factor	0.21% (0.3537)	0.9882 (0.0000)	0.3649 (0.0099)	0.9258 (0.0000)	0.1295 (0.1016)	89.44%	84
Panel B Micro, & High illiquidi							
CAPM	1.15% (0.0010)	0.9428 (0.0000)				65.88%	84
Fama-French 3 factor	0.27% (0.1107)	1.0011 (0.0000)	−0.0351 (0.5757)	0.9841 (0.0000)		92.28%	84
Carhart 4 factor	0.23% (0.1964)	0.9923 (0.0000)	0.0396 (0.7104)	0.9806 (0.0000)	0.0523 (0.3876)	92.26%	84
Panel C High momentum & High illiquidi							
CAPM	1.29% (0.0006)	0.9278 (0.0000)				62.04%	84
Fama-French 3 factor	0.65% (0.0337)	1.0783 (0.0000)	−0.3927 (0.0007)	0.9460 (0.0000)		76.05%	84
Carhart 4 factor	0.34% (0.2419)	1.0150 (0.0000)	0.1454 (0.4096)	0.9213 (0.0000)	0.3770 (0.0003)	79.48%	84

This table reports results from the three regression models of enhanced illiquidity portfolios. There are three enhanced illiquidity portfolios based on its intersection with other investment styles namely Micro & High illiquidity, High value & High Illiquid and High momentum & High illiquid portfolios. The p-values are reported in brackets under each respective coefficient, whereby bold figures denote a statistically significant coefficient at least at 10%. The sample uses stocks that are listed on FTSE All-Share index between January 2001 and December 2014 (168 months) divided further into pre (84 months) and post crisis periods (84 months).

Source: All data were obtained from Datastream.

the highest returns, we decided to use those to provide consistent comparison between precrisis and postcrisis periods. Besides, with the exception of size, illiquidity did manage to enhance the other two investment style returns. Furthermore, Ibbotson et al. (2013) used similar portfolios.

Based on CAPM, all three portfolios generated significant positive monthly alpha whereby the *"High Value & High Illiquid portfolio"* produced the highest alpha for both periods. All portfolios are found to be positively related to the market but interestingly, the relationship seems weaker postcrisis signifying that the respective portfolios have lower systematic risk. Using the Fama-French 3 factor model, the monthly alpha remains for *"High Value & High Illiquid portfolio"* and *"Micro & High Illiquid portfolio"* for precrisis periods but it disappears for postcrisis periods. The alpha of the *"High Momentum & High Illiquid portfolio"* remains only postcrisis.

Fascinatingly, Panel A of Table 23.7 shows that the monthly alpha of the *"High Value & High Illiquid portfolio"* remains positive and significant precrisis, even after the inclusion of all three factors confirming that illiquidity has improved the value portfolio as reported earlier. The table also shows that the portfolio is positively related to value, size, and momentum factor precrisis. The monthly alpha of the *"Micro & High Illiquid portfolio"* and *"High Momentum & High Illiquid portfolio"* disappears precrisis and postcrisis, respectively.

Overall, although our results are not similar to Ibbotson et al. (2013) in relation to the illiquidity factor, the significant positive results for the long only *"high illiquid portfolio"* in Panel B of Table 23.6 for the precrisis period does confirm that illiquidity is *"not easily beaten"* and can even be considered as *"a viable alternative."* Furthermore, the ability of illiquidity to enhance the value portfolio in Panel A of Table 23.7 with a positive and significant monthly alpha does confirm illiquidity as meeting the third portfolio benchmark criterion of *"a viable alternative."* Our results also show the substantial effect of the crisis on the portfolios as the monthly alpha disappears postcrisis after the inclusion of all three factors.

23.4.5 Illiquidity Stability and Migration

The fourth and last benchmark criterion of Sharpe (1992) is whether the illiquidity investment style can be managed at *"a low cost,"* which will be assessed by using the technique developed by Ibbotson et al. (2013). It is important to consider costs as Carhart (1997) highlighted that investment costs of expense ratios, transaction costs, and load fees, all have a direct, negative impact on funds' performance. Furthermore, Kaplan and Schoar (2005) highlighted that although private equity partnerships earn returns (gross of fees) exceeding the S&P 500 over the entire sample period (1980–97), average fund returns net of fees are roughly equal to those of the S&P 500, signifying the negative impact of fees.

Ibbotson et al. (2013) highlighted that illiquidity has a cost as the stocks may take longer to trade and even have higher transaction costs but trading costs can be mitigated through longer horizons and less trading, which translates into higher returns for the less liquid stocks. Nevertheless, less liquid portfolios are more risky to liquidate in a crisis compared to more passively held portfolios which can largely mitigate this risk. Therefore, studying migration of the stocks in a portfolio would allow us to understand if any of the portfolios can be managed at a low cost or passively.

23.4.5.1 Migration of stocks of various investment styles

Table 23.8 shows the migration of stocks from each quartile in *year* (*t*) (sorting year) to other quartiles in *year* (*t* + 1) (performance year) for all investment styles. As before, the quartiles are only rebalanced annually meaning that the stocks are held for at least 1 year while diagonal results (underlined and *italics)* represent stocks that remain in their respective quartiles after 1 year.

Panel A of Table 23.8 shows that overall 77.66% of the illiquid stocks remain in the same quartile, precrisis. For the *"high illiquid portfolio"* (Quartile 1), 75.54% remain in their quartile while the rest migrated to other quartiles, with the next quartile (Q2) receiving the most stocks (22.21%). However, the most stable quartile is the *"high liquid portfolio"* (Quartile 4) as 93.83% of stocks remain within their quartile.

Precrisis, size is considered the most stable as overall 84.20% of stocks remain within their quartile while momentum resulted in the lowest stability of only 30.87%. Value portfolios are also relatively stable, whereby overall 67.29% remained in the same quartile. Similar results are obtained postcrisis. Table 23.8 signifies that generally the transaction costs in maintaining illiquidity based portfolios are relatively low. Therefore, along with the stable returns and risks reported earlier, illiquidity styles can be regarded as a stable strategy. Moreover, Table 23.8 shows that the *"high liquid portfolio"* (Quartile 4) is the most stable (low transaction costs), although the portfolio still generates positive returns with lower risks (Table 23.1). However, a fascinating finding is that postcrisis, overall illiquidity portfolios increased in stability while other investment styles decreased in stability, suggesting the preference of illiquidity based portfolios postcrisis.

To summarize, the results in Table 23.8 indicate that portfolios based on illiquidity can be managed at *"a low cost,"* meeting the fourth and final benchmark criterion. The improved stability of illiquid portfolios postcrisis, signifies that investors can even reduce transactions costs by using illiquid portfolios. This means that at least precrisis, illiquidity has met all four of Sharpe (1992) benchmark criteria signifying that it can be made into a benchmark portfolio and can be categorized as a viable investment style in line with the other more traditional styles, such as value style.

Table 23.8: Migration of stocks 1 year after portfolio construction for all investment styles pre and postcrisis.

	Precrisis Periods (2001–07)				Postcrisis Periods (2008–14)			
	Panel A-Illiquidity Migration (Overall 77.66% Remains in the Same Quartile)				*Illiquidity Migration (Overall 82.16% Remains in the Same Quartile)*			
Year t (Illiquidity)	*Year t + 1 (Illiquidity)*				**Year t + 1 (Illiquidity)**			
	Q1	*Q2*	*Q3*	*Q4*	*Q1*	*Q2*	*Q3*	*Q4*
Quartile 1	**75.54%**	22.21%	2.13%	0.13%	**83.56%**	15.93%	0.50%	0.00%
Quartile 2	19.71%	**64.08%**	16.21%	0.00%	16.49%	**71.28%**	12.03%	0.20%
Quartile 3	0.85%	12.32%	**77.17%**	9.67%	0.50%	11.00%	**80.52%**	7.98%
Quartile 4	0.11%	0.00%	6.06%	**93.83%**	0.11%	0.00%	6.62%	**93.27%**
	Panel B-Value Migration (Overall 67.29% Remains in the Same Quartile)				*Value Migration (Overall 66.14% Remains in the Same Quartile)*			
Year t (Value)	*Year t + 1 (Value)*				*Year t + 1 (Value)*			
	Q1	*Q2*	*Q3*	*Q4*	*Q1*	*Q2*	*Q3*	*Q4*
Quartile 1	**67.07%**	27.10%	2.70%	3.12%	**64.49%**	27.35%	5.55%	2.61%
Quartile 2	29.36%	**56.88%**	13.11%	0.65%	28.85%	**56.72%**	13.90%	0.53%
Quartile 3	2.53%	13.67%	**67.42%**	16.38%	5.29%	13.71%	**63.68%**	17.32%
Quartile 4	2.26%	1.94%	18.03%	**77.78%**	2.53%	0.64%	17.15%	**79.68%**
	Panel C-Size Migration (Overall 84.20% Remains in the Same Quartile)				*Size Migration (Overall 82.95% Remains in the Same Quartile)*			
Year t (Size)	*Year t + 1 (Size)*				*Year t + 1 (Size)*			
	Q1	*Q2*	*Q3*	*Q4*	*Q1*	*Q2*	*Q3*	*Q4*
Quartile 1	**86.31%**	13.45%	0.24%	0.00%	**86.83%**	12.86%	0.21%	0.10%
Quartile 2	12.34%	**76.20%**	11.46%	0.00%	12.17%	**74.60%**	12.83%	0.40%
Quartile 3	0.51%	9.95%	**81.27%**	8.27%	0.62%	11.74%	**78.54%**	9.09%
Quartile 4	0.00%	0.13%	6.84%	**93.03%**	0.20%	0.32%	7.66%	**91.82%**
	Panel D-Momentum Migration (Overall 30.87% Remains in the Same Quartile)				*Momentum Migration (Overall 29.39% Remains in the Same Quartile)*			
Year t (Momentum)	*Year t + 1 (Momentum)*				*Year t + 1 (Momentum)*			
	Q1	*Q2*	*Q3*	*Q4*	*Q1*	*Q2*	*Q3*	*Q4*
Quartile 1	**31.21%**	25.33%	19.93%	23.53%	**29.89%**	22.44%	21.03%	26.64%
Quartile 2	25.32%	**29.34%**	26.34%	19.00%	25.08%	**28.87%**	26.25%	19.81%
Quartile 3	21.34%	25.60%	**31.22%**	21.85%	19.96%	27.99%	**29.79%**	22.26%
Quartile 4	24.74%	21.19%	22.36%	**31.71%**	26.14%	21.33%	23.53%	**29.00%**

The table shows the migration of stocks from each quartile in *year (t)* (sorting year) to other quartiles in *year (t + 1)* (performance year) for all investment styles. The sample uses companies that are listed on *FTSE All-Share index* between January 2000 and December 2014. As before, the quartiles are only rebalanced annually meaning that the stocks are held for at least 1 year. Diagonal results (underlined and *italics*) represent stocks that remain in their respective quartiles after 1 year. *Source: All data were obtained from Datastream.*

23.5 Conclusions

Investors have always wanted to find ways to beat the market and thus various investment styles have been established, such as value (Fama and French, 1992) and momentum styles (Jegadeesh and Titman, 1993). Recently, illiquidity has gained importance due to the financial crisis. Although researchers, such as Amihud and Mendelson (1986) found evidence to suggest that returns are an increasing function of illiquidity, it was never classified as a separate investment style. Ibbotson et al. (2013) even stated that illiquidity has the most obvious connection to valuation, as investors will pay more for liquid and less for illiquid stocks. Thus, we felt that it is time to conduct such a study on the UK market as well as on the style's response toward the crisis, using Ibbotson et al. (2013) framework, which is based on Sharpe (1992) benchmark criteria of (1) *"identifiable before the fact"*, (2) *"not easily beaten"*, (3) *"a viable alternative"*, and (4) *"low in cost"*.

The first criterion of *"identifiable before the fact"* is met by using the prior year ($t-1$) related style measure to obtain the results of the quartiles (or portfolio) for a given year (t). For the traditional style measures, we have decided to use P/B ratio (value), MV (size), and annualized returns (momentum). For measuring illiquidity, we use the *Amihud illiquidity measure* (Amihud, 2002). '

The second criterion is *"not easily beaten"* and our results showed that value premium, size premium, and even illiquidity premium exists but momentum premiums are insignificant for both periods. The *"high illiquid portfolio"* also performed better than the two benchmarks and other styles, with the exception of *"high value portfolio"* and *"micro portfolio."* Similar to Ibbotson et al. (2013), we use CAPM, Fama-French 3 factor model, and Carhart 4 factor model for estimating alpha. The results showed that the long only *"high illiquid portfolio"* is able to generate significantly positive monthly alpha on all three models precrisis only. Thus, we consider the *"high illiquidity portfolio"* as *"not easily beaten"* but not for postcrisis.

Since illiquidity is able to outperform the benchmarks, it can be considered as satisfying the third criterion of *"a viable alternative"* but the illiquidity premium might also be due to the other styles. To shed light on this, we constructed double sorted illiquidity portfolios with the other styles. Illiquidity is able to enhance the returns of both value and momentum styles. Moreover, using CAPM, all enhanced portfolios are able to generate positive and significant alpha for both periods. The *"high value & high illiquid portfolio"* is even able to generate positive and significant alpha for all three models precrisis only. Thus, meeting the third benchmark criterion of *"a viable alternative"* but again not for the postcrisis period.

Illiquid stocks were also found to be overall more stable than value and momentum portfolios for both periods, signifying that illiquid portfolios can be managed at low cost, meeting the fourth criterion of *"low in cost."* Furthermore, illiquid stocks stability actually improved postcrisis, indicating the preference for illiquid stocks after the financial crisis.

To summarize, our results show that precrisis, illiquidity as captured by *Amihud illiquidity measure*, was able to meet the four criteria of Sharpe (1992) benchmark requirements or at least show its profitability as an investment style. Thus, we agree with Ibbotson et al. (2013) that illiquidity can be considered as an alternative investment style in equal standing with the other styles and our *"high value & high illiquid portfolio"* is the best strategy for fund managers to utilize in UK, precrisis.

As expected, there was a detrimental effect on the illiquidity portfolios due to the crisis; the portfolios performance postcrisis was almost consistently worse relative to precrisis. Interestingly, although illiquidity is not as successful after the crisis, it did provide steady profits as it was able to perform better than the benchmarks. Furthermore, it is more stable, signifying potential of profit opportunity.

Nevertheless, even though our results appear to confirm illiquidity as a profitable style, one must keep in mind that there is a strong relationship between size and illiquidity. This comes into contrast with Ibbotson et al. (2013), signifying that the favorable performance of illiquidity may actually be due to size. Eleswarapu and Reinganum (1993) also highlighted similar results but Elfakhani (2000) believed that the size premium may actually be due to illiquidity. Moreover, our results are weaker in comparison to Ibbotson et al. (2013), probably due to the shorter periods and different liquidity measure used. Another reason might be the different characteristics of the UK and US markets, such as the lower volatility in the UK market relative to the US market (Bartram et al., 2012), since the lower level of volatility will definitely affect asset prices and liquidity. Stoll (1978), showed that liquidity is positively affected by return volatility while Vayanos (2004) mentioned that investors reduce their willingness to hold illiquid assets during volatile times.

Further studies need to be conducted in different geographical areas and over longer periods. However, we feel that illiquidity still has its merits as an investment management tool and choosing an investment style actually depends on investors' preference. In fact, it was shown that the migration stability of illiquid stocks has improved after the crisis, signifying lower transaction costs. Besides since the crisis was partly attributed on the illiquidity of financial markets, it is expected that investors would expect more compensation for the illiquidity risk of holding stocks longer, indicating profit opportunities with lower transaction costs.

References

Acharya, V.V., Pedersen, L.H., 2005. Asset pricing with liquidity risk. J. Financ. Econ. 77 (2), 375–410.
Amihud, Y., 2002. Illiquidity and stock returns: cross-section and time-series effects. J. Financ. Markets 5 (1), 31–56.
Amihud, Y., Mendelson, H., 1986. Asset pricing and the bid-ask spread. J. Financ. Econ. 17 (2), 223–249.
Asness, C.S., Moskowitz, T.J., Pedersen, L.H., 2013. Value and momentum everywhere. J. Finance 68 (3), 929–985.
Banz, R.W., 1981. The relationship between return and market value of common stocks. J. Financ. Econ. 9 (1), 3–18.

Bartram, S.M., Brown, G., Stulz, R.M., 2012. Why are US stocks more volatile? J. Finance 67 (4), 1329–1370.

Basu, S., 1983. The relationship between earnings' yield, market value and return for NYSE common stocks: Further evidence. J. Financ. Econ. 12 (1), 129–156.

Bauman, W.S., Conover, C.M., Miller, R.E., 1998. Growth versus value and large-cap versus small-cap stocks in international markets. Financ. Anal. J. 54 (2), 75–89.

Ben-David, I., Franzoni, F., Moussawi, R., 2012. Hedge fund stock trading in the financial crisis of 2007-2009. Rev. Financ. Studies 25 (1), 1–54.

Ben-Rephael, A., Kadan, O., Wohl, A., 2008. The diminishing liquidity premium. CFS Working Paper.

Beneda, N., 2002. Growth stocks outperform value stocks over the long term. J. Asset Manage. 3 (2), 112–123.

Brennan, M., Huh, S.W., Subrahmanyam, A., 2013. An analysis of the Amihud illiquidity premium. Rev. Asset Pricing Studies 3 (1), 133–176.

Brennan, M.J., Subrahmanyam, A., 1996. Market microstructure and asset pricing: on the compensation for illiquidity in stock returns. J. Financ. Econ. 41 (3), 441–464.

Brunnermeier, M.K., 2009. Deciphering the liquidity and credit crunch 2007-2008. J. Econ. Perspect. 23 (1), 77–100.

Capaul, C., Rowley, I., Sharpe, W.F., 1993. International value and growth stock returns. Financ. Anal. J. 49 (1), 27–36.

Carhart, M.M., 1997. On persistence in mutual fund performance. J. Finance 52 (1), 57–82.

Chan, K.C., Chen, N.F., Hsieh, D.A., 1985. An exploratory investigation of the firm size effect. J. Financ. Econ. 14 (3), 451–471.

Chang, K., Wang, G.Y., Lu, C., 2013. The effect of liquidity on stock returns: a style portfolio approach. WSEAS Trans. Math. 12 (2), 170–179.

Conrad, J., Kaul, G., 1998. An anatomy of trading strategies. Rev. Financ. Studies 11 (3), 489–519.

Corwin, S.A., Schultz, P., 2012. A simple way to estimate bid-ask spreads from daily high and low prices. J. Finance 67 (2), 719–760.

Crotty, J., 2009. Structural causes of the global financial crisis: a critical assessment of the 'new financial architecture'. Camb. J. Econ. 33 (4), 563–580.

Daniel, K., Titman, S., Wei, K., 2001. Explaining the cross-section of stock returns in Japan: factors or characteristics? J. Finance 56 (2), 743–766.

Datar, V.T., Naik, N.Y., Radcliffe, R., 1998. Liquidity and stock returns: an alternative test. J. Financ. Markets 1 (2), 203–219.

De Bondt, W.F., Thaler, R., 1985. Does the stock market overreact? J. Finance 40 (3), 793–805.

Ding, D.K., Chua, J.L., Fetherston, T.A., 2005. The performance of value and growth portfolios in East Asia before the Asian financial crisis. Pacific-Basin Finance J. 13 (2), 185–199.

Dissanaike, G., 2002. Does the size effect explain the UK winner-loser effect? J. Bus. Finance Account. 29 (1–2), 139–154.

Eleswarapu, V.R., Reinganum, M.R., 1993. The seasonal behavior of the liquidity premium in asset pricing. J. Financ. Econ. 34 (3), 373–386.

Elfakhani, S., 2000. Short positions, size effect, and the liquidity hypothesis: implications for stock performance. Appl. Financ. Econ. 10 (1), 105–116.

Evans, J.L., Archer, S.H., 1968. Diversification and the reduction of dispersion: an empirical analysis. J. Finance 23 (5), 761–767.

Fama, E.F., French, K.R., 1992. The cross-section of expected stock returns. J. Finance 47 (2), 427–465.

Galariotis, E.C., Giouvris, E., 2007. Liquidity commonality in the London stock exchange. J. Bus. Finance Account. 34 (1–2), 374–388.

Galariotis, E.C., Holmes, P., Ma, X.S., 2007. Contrarian and momentum profitability revisited: evidence from the London Stock Exchange 1964-2005. J. Multinat. Financ. Manage. 17 (5), 432–447.

Gonenc, H., Karan, M.B., 2003. Do value stocks earn higher returns than growth stocks in an emerging market? Evidence from the .Istanbul Stock Exchange. J. Int. Financ. Manage. Account. 14 (1), 1–25.

Horowitz, J.L., Loughran, T., Savin, N.E., 2000. Three analyses of the firm size premium. J. Empir. Finance 7 (2), 143–153.

Ibbotson, R.G., Chen, Z., Kim, D.Y.J., Hu, W.Y., 2013. Liquidity as an investment style. Financ. Anal. J. 69 (3), 30–44.

Idzorek, T.M., Xiong, J.X., Ibbotson, R.G., 2012. The liquidity style of mutual funds. Financ. Anal. J. 68 (6), 38–53.

Ivashina, V., Scharfstein, D., 2010. Bank lending during the financial crisis of 2008. J. Financ. Econ. 97 (3), 319–338.

Jegadeesh, N., Titman, S., 1993. Returns to buying winners and selling losers: implications for stock market efficiency. J. Finance 48 (1), 65–91.

Jegadeesh, N., Titman, S., 2001. Profitability of momentum strategies: an evaluation of alternative explanations. J. Finance 56 (2), 699–720.

Kaplan, S.N., Schoar, A., 2005. Private equity performance: returns, persistence, and capital flows. J. Finance 60 (4), 1791–1823.

Keim, D.B., 1983. Size-related anomalies and stock return seasonality: further empirical evidence. J. Financ. Econ. 12 (1), 13–32.

Pastor, L., Stambaugh, R.F., 2003. Liquidity risk and expected stock returns. J. Polit. Econ. 111 (3), 642–685.

Rajan, R.G., 2006. Has finance made the world riskier? Eur. Financ. Manage. 12 (4), 499–533.

Reilly, F., Brown, K., 2012. Analysis of Investments and Management of Portfolios, tenth ed., International ed. South-Western, Cengage Learning.

Roll, R., 1984. A simple implicit measure of the effective bid-ask spread in an efficient market. J. Finance 39 (4), 1127–1139.

Said, H., Giouvris, E., 2015. Inter-temporal variation in the illiquidity premium and its relationship with monetary conditions within the United Kingdom market. Paper presented at the Fifth International Conference of the Financial Engineering and Banking Society, Audencia Nantes School of Management, Nantes, France.

Sharpe, W.F., 1978. Major investment styles. J. Portf. Manage. 4 (2), 68–74.

Sharpe, W.F., 1992. Asset allocation: management style and performance measurement. J. Portf. Manage. 18 (2), 7–19.

Shen, Q., Szakmary, A.C., Sharma, S.C., 2005. Momentum and contrarian strategies in international stock markets: further evidence. J. Multinat. Financ. Manag. 15 (3), 235–255.

Stoll, H.R., 1978. The supply of dealer services in securities markets. J. Finance 33 (4), 1133–1151.

Subrahmanyam, A., 2010. The cross-section of expected stock returns: what have we learnt from the past twenty-five years of research? Eur. Financ. Manag. 16 (1), 27–42.

Tole, T.M., 1982. You can't diversify without diversifying. J. Portf. Manag. 8 (2), 5–11.

Van Dijk, M.A., 2011. Is size dead? A review of the size effect in equity returns. J. Bank. Finance 35 (12), 3263–3274.

Vayanos, D, 2004. Flight to Quality, Flight to Liquidity, and the Pricing of Risk. National Bureau of Economic Research, London, Available from: http://eprints.lse.ac.uk/archive/00000456/

Yan, X., 2008. Liquidity, investment style, and the relation between fund size and fund performance. J. Financ. Quant. Anal. 43 (3), 741–768.

CHAPTER 24

On the Pricing of Commonality Across Various Liquidity Proxies in the London Stock Exchange and the Crisis

SungKyu Lim, Evangelos Giouvris

Royal Holloway, University of London, Egham, United Kingdom

Chapter Outline

24.1 Introduction

Empirical evidence is mixed regarding the relationship between liquidity and stock returns. Amihud and Mendelson (1986) investigate the influence of liquidity on stock returns on New York Stock Exchange (NYSE) stocks over the period 1961–80. They use bid-ask spread as a liquidity measure, which shows a strong positive relationship with stock returns. Eleswarapu and Reinganum (1993), however, argue that a positive relationship between liquidity and returns exists in January only. Moreover, different conclusions are drawn when different

447

liquidity measures are used, such as turnover and volume. Brennan et al. (1998) find a negative relation between returns and trading volume for both NYSE and NASDAQ stocks while Jun et al. (2003) find a positive correlation between stock returns and market liquidity. Datar et al. (1998) use turnover ratio as a liquidity measure and find a negative correlation between liquidity and returns for NYSE stocks. Similarly, Dey (2005) support a negative relation between returns and turnover but this relationship is valid for developed markets only as the emerging markets show a positive relationship.

Since liquidity is not a simple concept to explore and not directly observable, a number of liquidity measures have been proposed; bid-ask spread (Amihud and Mendelson, 1986), turnover and volume (Brennan et al., 1998), price impact (Amihud, 2002; Korajczyk and Sadka, 2008), and zero return (Bekaert et al., 2007; Lesmond, 2005). Even though, these liquidity proxies are widely used in asset pricing research, there is no such thing as a superior proxy that is able to capture all facets of liquidity. Chai et al. (2010) emphasizes the multidimensional characteristics of liquidity by looking at relations between six liquidity proxies and stock characteristics in the Australian stock market. The six liquidity proxies employed are proportional spread, turnover, the Amihud measure, returns reversal measure, zero returns, and turnover adjusted number of zero daily volume[1] and stock characteristics are stock prices, trading volume, and volatility. They report low correlations between adopted liquidity proxies which imply that the proxies used represent different dimensions of liquidity. Also, they point out that the turnover measure shows a rather different pattern compared to all other liquidity proxies and there is no evidence that the return reversal measure depends on stock characteristics. Brown et al. (2008) show that the main determinants of commonality in liquidity are different for each market because each of the markets they look into has different trading mechanisms and the traders' behavior is different. These two fundamental differences (dimensions of proxy and market structure) could lead to different conclusions. Therefore, it is crucial to analyze markets using a type of liquidity measure, which captures as many facets of liquidity as possible in order to reconcile the different relations observed.

In order to capture the different facets of liquidity proxies, Korajczyk and Sadka (2008), (hereafter K&S), investigate commonality in liquidity using a latent factor model. K&S

---

[1] Return reversal measure is obtained by running the following OLS regression:
$r_{i,t+1}^{e} = \gamma_0 + \gamma_1 r_{i,t} + \gamma \left[\text{sign}\left(r_{i,t}^{e}\right) \times vol_{i,t} \right] + \varepsilon_{i,t}$ where $r_{i,t+1}^{e}$ is the excess return with respect to the value-weighted market index return, $r_{i,t}$ is the return for firm I on day t, $\text{sign}\left(r_{i,t}^{e}\right)$ is the sign of the excess return with respect to the market index return for firm I on day t, and $vol_{i,t}$ is the trading volume. They estimate Zero return following Lesmond et al. (1999). Finally, turnover-adjusted number of zero daily volume is defined as:

$$LM_{i,t} = \left[NoZV_{i,t} + \frac{\dfrac{1}{\overline{turnover_{i,t}}}}{Deflator} \right] \times \frac{21}{NoTD_t}$$ where $NoZV_{i,t}$ is the number of zero daily trading volume, $turnover_{i,t}$ is

stock turnover, and $NoTD_t$ is the total number of trading days in the market in month t, and the *deflator* is set to 480,000.

obtain common factors from different liquidity proxies. They apply an asymptotic principal components method to estimate a measure of systematic liquidity risk across a set of eight measures for NYSE-listed stocks. They obtain within-measure and across-measure common factors. They investigate relations between market-wide within-measure factors and across-measure using canonical correlation. They show that there is commonality across assets for each measure of liquidity. They also find common factors across all eight liquidity measures and that liquidity shocks are contemporaneously correlated with return shocks for the United States. Since the across-measure is correlated with various liquidity proxies and it is confirmed as a priced factor in the US stock market, we assume that the across-measure may be a better measurement of liquidity in terms of its accuracy because it contains multidimensional characteristics of liquidity. We apply K&S's framework to investigate if their findings apply to other markets as well, such as the United Kingdom which is the third most important market in the world following the United States and Japanese markets with market capitalization equal to USD 3266 billion.[2] To the best of our knowledge the extent to which liquidity risk is priced in the UK market is still unexplored. In particular, we investigate: (1) the degree of commonality in liquidity for the UK stock market for each measure of liquidity (within-measure) and systematic common liquidity factor (across-measure), (2) persistence of liquidity shocks for within-measures and the across-measure, (3) the lead-lag relation among all liquidity measures and predictability between liquidity shocks and stock returns, and (4) if systematic liquidity risk is a priced factor in the United Kingdom.

We find strong liquidity commonality for the United Kingdom, which is consistent with the result of Galariotis and Giouvris (2007, 2009) and Gregoriou et al. (2011). Also, our study shows that changes in liquidity measures are correlated. They are also contemporaneously correlated with returns in the UK stock market. Even though persistence of liquidity shocks in the UK stock market is weaker, we find a strong two-way relationship between liquidity and returns. For instance, shocks to returns can predict future liquidity levels and returns can be predicted by past liquidity shocks in our empirical study. K&S, however, find a one-way relationship. Shocks to returns can predict future liquidity but the opposite does not hold. We obtain strong evidence regarding the pricing of the across-measure liquidity in the United Kingdom. The remainder of this paper is organized as follows. Section 24.2 present the literature review and Section 24.3 describes the data and the measures of liquidity proxies and methodology. In Section 24.4, we present our findings and we conclude in Section 24.5.

24.2 Literature Review

24.2.1 Commonality in Liquidity

Several studies identify systematic components in measures of liquidity which has evolved over time as an important concern to many investors and markets. Chordia et al. (2000) find

---

[2] www.world-stock-excahnges.net

evidence of systematic components in the market and in the industry in daily bid-ask spreads and quoted depth. Pastor and Stambaugh (2003) use AMEX and NASDAQ stocks to look into commonality. The liquidity measure used in this study is order flow which shows significant commonality across stocks. Also, smaller stocks are less liquid and are more sensitive to market liquidity and stocks sensitive to market liquidity tend to have higher expected returns. Further investigation by Kamara et al. (2008) shows that commonality in liquidity has increased over time for large firms and declined for small firms. They point out institutional investing and index trading as the main source of commonality in liquidity and it is more prevalent in large stocks than in small stocks. All the earlier studies concentrated on the US market.

There are some papers focusing on the United Kingdom and other markets. Galariotis and Giouvris (2007) look into commonality in the UK market across different trading regimes using FTSE100 and FTSE250 stocks. They find that commonality is quite strong for FTSE100 stocks at individual and portfolio level, while for the FTSE250, it is strong only at portfolio level. Overall commonality is on average similar across trading regimes, irrespective of the nature of the provision of liquidity. Gregoriou et al. (2011) apply the methodology adopted by Chordia et al. (2000) in the UK market and confirm the existence of commonality in liquidity in the UK market before and after the financial crisis. They use relative and effective bid-ask spreads as proxies for liquidity. Moreover, a few other studies have attempted to explore systematic liquidity risk and its relation to expected returns for other countries. Commonality is also present in smaller markets. In particular, Galariotis and Giouvris (2008) show that commonality is also present in smaller markets, such as the Athens Stock Exchange which has more than 50% of its stocks owned by international investors, 77% of which is institutional ones, but it is not priced and not as strong as in the United Kingdom and United States, while it comes in waves and appears more pertinent in high capitalization companies. Additionally, Kuntar and Visaltanachoti (2008) examine commonality in liquidity in the Thai stock market. The study confirms strong market-wide commonality in liquidity across all size-based portfolios. However, the effect of commonality in liquidity for Thailand is generally less than the evidence of the US market.

These empirical studies provide strong evidence of commonality in liquidity. Also, the level of commonality in liquidity is varying over time based on market conditions.

24.2.2 Inconclusive Empirical Findings Regarding the Relation Between Liquidity and Returns

Empirical findings of the impact of liquidity on stock returns are not always consistent. According to Amihud and Mendelson (1986), there is a positive relationship between bid-ask spread and returns. Eleswarapu and Reinganum (1993) find that a positive relationship between liquidity (bid-ask spread) and returns exists only in January. Different conclusions are drawn when different liquidity measures are used, such as turnover and volume. Brennan et al. (1998)

find a negative relation between returns and trading volume. Datar et al. (1998) examine the liquidity (turnover)-return relationship. They find a strong negative relation between stock returns and liquidity. Dey (2005) supports a negative relation between turnover and returns using 48 stock exchanges. They find that turnover is significant for emerging market portfolios only while it is insignificant for developed market portfolios but volatility is significant for developed market portfolios only. Thus they conclude that "The intuition behind these results is that in developed markets, which are already liquid markets, liquidity is not a concern for investors, price volatility is; but in emerging markets many of which are thin and lack liquidity, liquidity risk is the principal source of risk" (p. 63). Similarly, Jun et al. (2003) investigate the relationship between stock returns and liquidity measures, such as turnover ratio, trading volume, and turnover-volatility ratio. They show that stock returns in emerging countries are positively correlated with liquidity measures. This positive correlation holds in both cross-sectional and time-series analysis. They argue that "if emerging markets are not fully integrated with the global economy, then lack of liquidity will not function as a risk factor, and thus cross-sectional returns will not necessarily be lower for liquid markets" (p. 3). Hence, a potential explanation of this positive relation in emerging markets could be the low degree of global integration.

24.2.3 Multidimensional Characteristics of Liquidity and Determinants

As we mentioned previously, there are many liquidity proxies widely used in the literature. However, there is no such thing as a superior proxy. In the study of Chai et al. (2010), six liquidity proxies are used to investigate how they relate to each other and to stock price, volatility, and trading volume. They report low correlations between the adopted liquidity proxies which imply that each of the proxies represents different dimensions of liquidity. They also find that stock price, volatility, and trading volume are important determinants of liquidity, the only exception being the return reversal measure which does not depend on any of the stock characteristics discussed. Moreover, Brown et al. (2008) argue that the pattern or behavior of liquidity risk is different between markets and the main determinants of value premium are different for each market. More recently, Karolyi et al. (2012) investigate the effect of demand side factors (trading behavior of investors, investor sentiment, and incentives to trade individual securities) and supply side (funding liquidity) factors on commonality in liquidity (captured by the Amihud-measure). They show that the degree of commonality in liquidity varies across the 40 countries and over time. They also find that demand side factors are the main determinants of commonality in liquidity in many of the countries under examination while funding liquidity (supply-side factor) is the main driver of commonality in liquidity in the United States during the recent crisis.

24.2.4 Systematic Liquidity Risk and Pricing

Systematic liquidity risk and pricing is another strand of literature which has received a lot of attention. Martinez et al. (2005) analyze the Spanish stock market following

Pastor and Stambaugh (2003). Their findings show that systematic liquidity risk is priced in the Spanish stock market. Lam and Tam (2011) look into the Hong Kong stock market and confirm that liquidity is a priced factor in the Hong Kong market however momentum is not priced. More importantly, the level of commonality in liquidity tends to vary significantly over time in emerging markets, such as China, India, and Malaysia depending on market conditions.[3]

Considering the well established presence of commonality in liquidity (see Section 24.2.1), the inconclusive evidence regarding the relation between liquidity and returns (see Section 24.2.2), the different facets of liquidity (see Section 24.2.3), and the more recent trend in testing whether liquidity risk is priced (see Section 24.2.4), we decided to examine all those issues concentrating on the London stock exchange using the K&S methodology.[4]

24.3 Data and Methodology

24.3.1 Data Sources and Liquidity Proxies

We focus on the UK stock market using FTSE100 and FTSE250 from March 1999 until December 2011. We use daily data to construct monthly time series liquidity variables. All data are obtained from Datastream. After filtering the data set and synchronizing individual firms' trading days, we construct a monthly time series of six different measures of liquidity which are used widely in the literature.

1. Amihud measure: The daily average of absolute value of return divided by Pound (£) volume for asset i in month t.

$$A_{i,j} = \sum_{i=1}^{d_t} \frac{|r_{i,j}|}{£vol_{i,j}} \tag{24.1}$$

Where $r_{i,j}$ is the absolute return on asset i on day j of month t, £ $vol_{i,j}$ is the £ volume traded in asset i on day j of month t, and d_t is the number of trading days in month t. We require asset i to have at least 15 days observation in month t to include in the sample. In order to remove the downward trend in the series, we rescale $A_{i,j}$ by the ratio of market capitalization of FTSE100 market index at $t-1$ and at a reference date (31/3/1999).

---

[3] Karolyi et al. (2012).

[4] In an earlier study, Hasbrouck and Seppi (2001) examine Dow Jones 30 stocks using Principal Component Analysis and extract common factors across returns, order flows, and liquidity, such as bid-ask spreads, depths, and quote-slope measures. They provide evidence for the existence of market-wide common factors in order flows and stock returns but liquidity measures, such as spread, log size, and quoted depth show weak or little evidence of commonality.

2. Proportional spread: The quoted percentage spread, measured for each trade as the ratio of the quoted bid-ask spread and the midpoint of bid-ask spread.

$$Proportional_{i,t} = \frac{1}{n_{i,t}} \sum_{j=1}^{n_{i,t}} \frac{Ask_{i,j} - Bid_{i,j}}{m_{i,j}} \tag{24.2}$$

Where the midpoint is estimated as follows: $m_{i,j} = \left(Ask_{i,j} + Bid_{i,j} \right) / 2$. $Ask_{i,j}$ and $Bid_{i,j}$ are the closing ask and bid quotes prevailing at the time of the jth trade of asset i in month t, and $n_{i,t}$ is the number of eligible trade of asset i in month t.

3. Turnover: The ratio of monthly volume divided by shares outstanding.

$$TO_{i,t} = \frac{\sum_{j=1}^{d_t} Vol_{i,j}}{SO_{i,t}} \tag{24.3}$$

Where SO_t is share outstanding at the end of month t and $Vol_{i,j}$ is the volume of asset i.

4. Pastor and Stambaugh spread (hereafter PS): We use the reversal-measure of illiquidity based on Pastor and Stambaugh (2003). It is estimated in the following way.

$$r_{i,d+1,t} - r_{M,d+1,t} = \alpha_{i,t} + \beta_{i,t} + \gamma_{i,t} sign\left(r_{i,d,t} - r_{M,d,t} \right) \times vol_{i,d,t} + \varepsilon_{i,d,t} \tag{24.4}$$

Where $r_{i,d,t}$ is a return of stock i on day d in month t, $r_{M,d,t}$ is a market return on a day d in a month t, and $vol_{i,d,t}$ is a pound trading volume. The coefficient of signed trading volume ($\gamma_{i,t}$), the liquidity measure, is expected to be negative reflecting price reversals due to large trading volume.

5. Roll measure (Roll): Roll (1984) propose a parsimonious model for estimating spread, using the time series of bid-ask bounce. This model is also called the effective bid-ask spread and is measured by calculating the first-order autocovariance of the returns for each stock.

6. Corwin and Schultz (2012)'s spread (hereafter CS): They use the daily high-low prices to estimate the spread. It assumes that: the mid-price follows a random walk; the spread is fixed; and the highest (lowest) midprice corresponds with the highest (lowest) transaction price and the buy (sell) order.

24.3.2 Methodology

Following Korajczyk and Sadka (2008), we use principal components analysis (PCA) to extract and analyze common factors in returns and various liquidity proxies. PCA explains the variance-covariance structure of the underlying data using linear combinations of the original variables. In PCA one must look for a maximum, because the first component has to extract maximum variance from the set of variables and each next component is also at maximum from the remaining variance.

We extract the first three principal components for each liquidity measure. In order to explore the strength of commonality across assets for each liquidity measure, we run a time-series regression for each individual stock's liquidity on the extracted factors. We report the R^2 of regression and p-value of the factor loadings. The regression estimated is

$$L^i_{j,t} = B^i_j \hat{F}^i_t + \hat{\varepsilon}^i_{j,t} \tag{24.5}$$

Where $L^i_{j,t}$ is a standardized liquidity variable for security i at time t. For example, in our case, $L^i_{j,t}$ represents standardized Amihud, proportional spread, PS, CS, Roll, and turnover. $\hat{F}^i_t$ is the $K \times 1$ vector of factor estimates for month t. The cross-sectional average of R^2 and adjusted R^2 values for $K = 1,2,3$ are reported in Table 24.1.

Additionally, we estimate systematic factors across all six liquidity measures defined as the across-measure factor. We also change signs of these extracted factors as Korajczyk and Sadka (2008) refer to liquidity rather than illiquidity. For within-measures and across-measure, we set it as negatively correlated with the time series of the cross-sectional mean

Table 24.1: Diagnostics of within-measure common factors.

		Degree of Commonality			Eigenvalues and Explained Variance (%)		
Variable	Statistic	Factor 1	Factor 2	Factor 3	1st	2nd	3rd
Return	R^2	0.302	0.338	0.363	57.82	9.91	6.20
	Adjusted R^2	0.298	0.330	0.350	(31.088%)	(36.418%)	(39.753%)
Amihud	R^2	0.168	0.295	0.322	50.05	22.36	10.82
	Adjusted R^2	0.163	0.285	0.308	(21.563%)	(38.935%)	(44.756%)
Proportional	R^2	0.177	0.258	0.305	78.752	21.52	14.37
Spread	Adjusted R^2	0.172	0.248	0.291	(42.340%)	(53.913%)	(61.643%)
Turnover	R^2	0.239	0.303	0.326	59.14	9.35	5.97
	Adjusted R^2	0.289	0.294	0.313	(31.798%)	(36.828%)	(40.041%)
CS spread	R^2	0.206	0.277	0.427	92.59	24.67	9.07
	Adjusted R^2	0.201	0.268	0.416	(51.16%)	(64.76%)	(69.81%)
PS	R^2	0.012	0.030	0.031	178.1	0.96	0.15
	Adjusted R^2	0.006	0.018	0.012	(98.94%)	(99.48%)	(99.58%)
Roll	R^2	0.121	0.222	0.318	10.12	2.50	1.49
	Adjusted R^2	0.116	0.211	0.305	(36.17%)	(45.09%)	(50.44%)

This table reports the degree of commonality across assets for each liquidity measure. Common factors are extracted separately for returns and different measures of liquidity using principal component analysis. The liquidity proxies used are Amihud, proportional bid-ask spread, turnover, PS measure, CS measure, and Roll measure. We regress each stock's liquidity on the three extracted factors ($L^i_{j,t} = B^i_j \hat{F}^i_t + \hat{\varepsilon}^i_{j,t}$). Then we save the R^2 and the adjusted R^2. The table presents the average R^2 and the average adjusted-R^2 from the regression associated with one, two, and three factors. The sample includes FTSE100 and FTSE250 firms between March 1999 and December 2011 (154 months).
Source: All data are obtained from Datastream.

of that measure except turnovers (positively correlated). Thus changes in sings imply a positive relationship between each liquidity factor and liquidity.

24.4 Empirical Results and Analysis
24.4.1 Degree of Commonality

In order to illustrate the degree of commonality, we extract the first three principal components for each liquidity measure (within measure) and then we run the following regression.

$$L^i_{j,t} = B^i_j \hat{F}^i_t + \hat{\varepsilon}^i_{j,t} \tag{24.6}$$

Where $L^i_{j,t}$ is the individual firm's liquidity and $\hat{F}^i_t$ represent the first three extracted factors of each liquidity proxy. We report the R^2 value and the adjusted R^2 value in Table 24.1.

According to Corwin and Lipson (2011), if there were no common components in the original variables, each eigenvalue would equal 1 and the first three principal components would explain $3/N$ of the total variation. We report eigenvalues of the first three components and the percentage of variance explained by the first three eigenvalues. While Corwin and Lipson (2011) examine the US market and report an eigenvalue of 8.43 for returns and the first three components explain approximately 11.7%, we obtain an eigenvalue of 57.82 for returns and the first three components explain 39% of variance. For liquidity, the percentage of explained variance ranges from 21% to 99%.

Table 24.1 also shows the average R^2 and adjusted-R^2 values for 1, 2, and 3 factors. For all liquidity variables, R^2 values increase as we increase the number of factors and the value of adjusted R^2 is slightly smaller than the R^2. For a 1-factor model, the R^2 ranges approximately from 1% to 30% and returns have the highest R^2 value (30%) and PS shows the smallest R^2 values (1%). For a three-factor model, CS spread shows the highest R^2 values (42%) while the PS has the lowest level of commonality (3%). These results are consistent with the results of Chordia et al. (2000), who find commonality among quoted and effective spreads. Also, the degree of commonality (R^2 value) for some variables is very similar and some of them are even greater than those reported for the US market by Korajczyk and Sadka (2008). Based on a 3-factor model, for instance, we obtain commonality of 35% for returns while K&S report 23% for returns. The level of commonality in turnover in our study is much greater than K&S's finding (33% and 23%, respectively). However, proportional spread in our study shows a commonality of 17% while it is 25% in the K&S study. The Amihud measure in the K&S study shows greater commonality (44%) than the Amihud measure in our study (32%). The weakest commonality is associated with the PS measure in this study.

24.4.2 The Time Series Properties of Systematic Liquidity Factors

We examine the persistence of liquidity factors in this section. Following K&S, we fit AR(2) models to the liquidity factors and apply impulse response function to estimate the persistence of liquidity shocks 6 and 12 months afterward. Table 24.2 shows the result of impulse response estimation for within-measures as well as across-measure. The coefficient of AR(1) is statistically significant for all measures while the coefficient of AR(2) obtained for proportional spread, and across-measure is statistically insignificant. All of the liquidity variables show stronger persistence of shocks at 6 months compared to shocks at 12 months. The strongest persistence occurs for turnover followed by the Amihud measure. The Roll measure presents the weakest persistence at 6 and 12 months. These results show that UK stock market presents milder persistence of liquidity shocks compare to the findings of K&S for the United States. This could be because of the smaller sample.

Fig. 24.1 shows residuals from an AR(2) specification for each of the individual liquidity measures and the systematic factor (the across-measure). The factors are signed so that positive changes are associated with increasing liquidity. In Fig. 24.1, we can observe the behavior of our liquidity proxies over time. First, proportional spread shows relatively milder volatility overall and the most volatile period of time is in 2000 (dot com bubble) while the Amihud measure, Roll, and CS are clearly capturing both the dot com bubble crisis (in 2000) and recent financial crisis (in late 2007). Turnover shows the most consistent level of volatility over the whole sample period. The across-measure which has been extracted from these six liquidity proxies shows consistent fluctuation over the sample period and it is very similar to the behavior of turnover.

Table 24.2: Persistence of aggregate liquidity.

Persistence of Liquidity Variables				
Variable	AR(1)	AR(2)	Shock After 6 Months	Shock After 12 Months
Amihud	0.5282(0.0000)	0.2312(0.0057)	0.1576	0.0453
Proportional	0.8345(0.0000)	−0.0370(0.6028)	0.0759	0.0181
Turnover	0.6158(0.0000)	0.3354(0.0000)	0.2434	0.1950
PS	0.2083(0.0098)	0.2474(0.0022)	0.0317	0.0015
CS Spread	0.3542(0.0000)	0.2511(0.0016)	0.0718	0.0090
Roll	0.1474(0.0555)	0.2834(0.0003)	0.0314	0.0014
Across	0.4821(0.0000)	0.0789(0.3413)	0.0383	0.0019

We extracted within-measure factors separately for different measures of liquidity using the PCA method and across-measure common factors are extracted for all the liquidity measures jointly. Then we fit an AR(2) model for each first principal component in order to demonstrate the persistence of liquidity shocks. The 6-month and 12-month values of the impulse response function applied to each time series are reported. AR(1) and AR(2) in the table represents the coefficient of first-order and second-order autocorrelation, respectively. We report p-value in brackets.
Source: All data are obtained from Datastream.

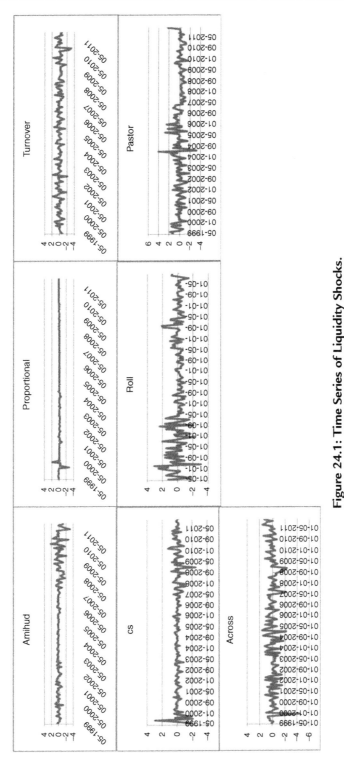

Figure 24.1: Time Series of Liquidity Shocks.

The first common factor is extracted separately for different measures of liquidity using the PCA method. Additionally, we extract across-measure common factors for all liquidity measures jointly. We fit an AR(2) model for each first principal component and then plot the residuals as factor shocks. All data are obtained from Datastream.

24.4.3 Contemporaneous Canonical Correlations of Liquidity Factors

The most advantageous point of this methodology is extracting common factors from each liquidity variable and all liquidity measures together and testing correlations. None of the previous studies extracts common factors from all measures together.

We analyze several different measures of liquidity and the extent to which liquidity shocks are systematic across all measures. In this section, we start with estimating three canonical correlations between individual liquidity measures (within-measure), and across-measure using the first three extracted factors across each pair of variables. We also look into canonical correlation between returns, within measure, and across-measure. Panel A of Table 24.3 presents results of pair-wise canonical correlation with unadjusted factors (raw data set) and Panel B presents results of pair-wise canonical correlation from prewhitened [using an AR(2) model] factors.

Canonical correlations between each within-measure and across-measure are all statistically significant at 5% in Panel A of Table 24.3. The correlation between the CS spread and across-measure is about 67% and is the strongest one while the across-measure shows a weaker correlation associated with Roll measure and Turnover (38.18% and 38.38%, respectively). The correlation between liquidity and stock returns is consistent with US findings. The first column in panel A shows the contemporaneous correlation between liquidity and stock returns. The Amihud, proportional spread, and PS are statistically significant at 1% and turnover, CS, Roll, and across-measure are statistically significant at 5%. Evidence from Panel A shows that within-measures are contemporaneously correlated with across-measure and all liquidity measures including across-measure are contemporaneously correlated with returns.

Panel B in Table 24.3 presents results of canonical correlations. These correlations are obtained after prewhitening with an AR(2) process. Comparing Panel A (raw data) and Panel B [fitting AR(2)], the level of correlations between returns and liquidity measures do not change a lot but proportional spread and CS spread becomes statistically insignificant after fitting AR(2). The canonical correlations between the within-measure factors and the across-measure factors tend to be lower. Also proportional spread, turnover, and the Roll measure become statistically insignificant after the AR(2) process. The within-measures are strongly correlated with the across-measure. The canonical correlations between the within-measure factors and the across-measure factors tend to be lower after the AR(2) process. Our findings for the United Kingdom are consistent with K&S's findings for the United States. The evidence suggests that since the across-measure based on various measures of liquidity is consistently correlated with stock returns, it may improve the accuracy of estimating systematic liquidity shocks to returns than estimating systematic liquidity shocks based on a single liquidity measure.

Table 24.3: Canonical contemporaneous correlations.

Panel A	Return	Amihud	Proportional	Turnover	CS	PS	Roll
Amihud	0.3363 0.8372 (0.0020)						
Proportional	0.3448 0.8505 (0.0040)	0.6712 0.5312 (0.0000)					
Turnover	0.2483 0.8909 (0.0460)	0.3118 0.8828 (0.0300)	0.2082 0.9478 (0.5380)				
CS	0.3031 0.8842 (0.0320)	0.4319 0.7932 (0.0000)	0.7344 0.4581 (0.0000)	0.1653 0.9624 (0.7700)			
PS	0.3448 0.8505 (0.0040)	0.3874 0.7823 (0.0000)	0.2263 0.9369 (0.3770)	0.4939 0.7395 (0.0000)	0.2646 0.9046 (0.0940)		
Roll	0.3253 0.8784 (0.0230)	0.5896 0.6075 (0.0000)	0.5016 0.7211 (0.0000)	0.4372 0.7851 (0.0000)	0.5657 0.6569 (0.0000)	0.3448 0.8356 (0.0020)	
Across	0.3251 0.8671 (0.0120)	0.6697 0.4555 (0.0000)	0.6010 0.5998 (0.0000)	0.3838 0.8084 (0.0000)	0.6733 0.5162 (0.0000)	0.4532 0.7871 (0.0000)	0.3818 0.7602 (0.0000)
Panel B	Return	Amihud	Proportional	Turnover	CS	PS	Roll
Amihud	**0.2927** **0.8472** **(0.0040)**						
Proportional	0.2505 0.9344 (0.3610)	0.1779 0.9406 (0.4460)					
Turnover	**0.4564** **0.7576** **(0.0000)**	0.2220 0.9124 (0.1480)	0.1341 0.9783 (0.9560)				
CS	0.2533 0.9164 (0.1760)	**0.5016** **0.7346** **(0.0000)**	0.2065 0.9536 (0.6460)	0.1514 0.9581 (0.7180)			
PS	**0.2652** **0.8985** **(0.0760)**	0.2154 0.9221 (0.2240)	0.1890 0.9448 (0.5090)	**0.2907** **0.8604** **(0.0090)**	0.1924 0.9501 (0.5910)		
Roll	0.3513 0.8648 (0.0120)	0.3497 0.8624 (0.0100)	0.4414 0.7962 (0.0000)	0.3335 0.8354 (0.0020)	0.3689 0.8353 (0.0020)	0.3558 0.8712 (0.0170)	
Across	0.36507 0.8674 (0.0140)	0.5760 0.6456 (0.0000)	0.2463 0.9051 (0.1050)	0.2597 0.9226 (0.2290)	0.5943 0.6436 (0.0000)	0.2901 0.9031 (0.0960)	0.1928 0.9522 (0.6250)

Three common factors are extracted separately for returns and different measures of liquidity using PCA method. This table reports the first canonical correlation (contemporaneous) between each two groups of common factors. We report canonical correlations (first row), the Wilks' lambda (second row), and p-value in parentheses. Panel A uses raw time series while Panel B uses the residuals of a AR(2) model for each factor.

24.4.4 The Temporal Relation Between Liquidity and Asset Returns

As we have seen in the previous section, several within-measures and the across-measure are contemporaneously correlated with each other and stock returns, thus we could expect that there is a relation between liquidity risk and returns. If this is so, then liquidity shocks may be able to predict future returns or vice-versa. So in this section, we look into this by performing a pair-wise canonical correlation analysis where one of the variables lags one period. The results are reported in Table 24.4, Panel A (raw common factors) and Panel B (prewhitened factors).

The first column in Panel A of Table 24.4 shows that 1 month lagged within-measures (the Amihud and proportional spread) and the across-measure can predict future returns while turnover, CS, PS, and Roll measure do not predict future returns. Also, the first row shows that the returns seem to predict most of the liquidity measures, the exceptions are CS and PS. Interestingly, the one period lagged across-measure can predict returns and all within-measures at time t (bottom row in Panel A).

In Panel B, the lead-lag correlations between returns and liquidity measures have changed compared to the findings in Panel A. Shocks to liquidity (absolute and proportional spread) can predict future stock returns and returns can predict liquidity measures.

Noticeably, lagged returns can predict across-measure. Generally speaking, we obtain strong evidence of lagged liquidity shocks being able to predict returns and of lagged returns being able to predict liquidity shocks. K&S find that shocks to returns can predict most of the liquidity measures but shocks to liquidity do not predict future returns.

24.4.5 The Pricing of Liquidity Risk and Liquidity Characteristics in the Cross-Section

In this section, we investigate whether liquidity risk is priced in the cross-section. In particular, we are asking if the different liquidity measures are priced and if this is the case whether the six measures we use capture a different aspect of liquidity or the same. Even though running a multiple regression with all the liquidity variables is quite appealing, there is a very high possibility that we will be unable to draw any inferences because of lack of power in the tests. Therefore, we decompose liquidity shocks into those driven by across-measure liquidity shocks and within-measure liquidity shocks.

24.4.5.1 Constructing across-measure and measure-specific liquidity factors

In order to investigate the relative importance of the across-measure liquidity factor against the measure-specific liquidity factor in explaining the time variation of firm level liquidity, we need to run a number of regressions at two different stages. First, we want to assess whether there is additional information in the individual liquidity factors. For this reason, we

Table 24.4: Canonical lead-lag correlations.

Panel A t−1/t	Return	Amihud	Proportional	Turnover	CS	PS	Roll	Across
Return	**0.4156**	**0.3540**	**0.3526**	**0.3108**	0.2284	0.1986	**0.4155**	**0.3317**
	0.7818	**0.8184**	**0.8329**	**0.8927**	0.9238	0.9485	**0.7853**	**0.8526**
	(0.000)	**(0.000)**	**(0.001)**	**(0.051)**	(0.227)	(0.549)	**(0.000)**	**(0.005)**
Amihud	**0.3184**	0.6539	0.6582	0.9059	0.6841	0.3956	0.5429	0.4602
	0.8742	0.4113	0.5509	0.1651	0.5144	0.8305	0.6175	0.7508
	(0.018)	(0.000)	(0.000)	(0.000)	(0.000)	(0.001)	(0.000)	(0.000)
Proportional	**0.3007**	0.5264	0.9182	0.2425	0.7815	0.2462	0.4954	0.5272
	0.9018	0.7054	0.0485	0.9311	0.3852	0.9355	0.7395	0.6937
	(0.082)	(0.000)	(0.000)	(0.305)	(0.000)	(0.359)	(0.000)	(0.000)
Turnover	0.2727	0.2958	0.3271	0.9155	0.1962	0.4778	0.5226	0.3901
	0.9074	0.8967	0.8893	0.1582	0.9509	0.7607	0.6854	0.8142
	(0.108)	(0.063)	(0.043)	(0.000)	(0.588)	(0.000)	(0.000)	(0.000)
CS	0.2574	0.9368	0.7144	0.1998	0.8060	0.3374	0.5068	0.6807
	0.9263	0.1036	0.4849	0.9508	0.3383	0.8708	0.7049	0.3646
	(0.251)	(0.000)	(0.000)	(0.586)	(0.000)	(0.015)	(0.000)	(0.000)
PS	0.1759	0.3723	0.2778	0.5011	0.2303	0.3039	0.4678	0.4408
	0.9595	0.8332	0.9059	0.7155	0.9167	0.9008	0.7637	0.7855
	(0.726)	(0.001)	(0.100)	(0.000)	(0.167)	(0.078)	(0.000)	(0.000)
Roll	0.2882	0.5190	0.4023	0.3237	0.4807	0.3574	0.6809	0.3844
	0.9091	0.6854	0.7928	0.8848	0.7532	0.8632	0.4546	0.7212
	(0.117)	(0.000)	(0.000)	(0.033)	(0.000)	(0.009)	(0.000)	(0.000)
Across	**0.2427**	0.4212	0.5998	0.7013	0.6906	0.4191	0.3855	0.7230
	0.8904	0.7785	0.6057	0.4643	0.4594	0.8193	0.7664	0.3995
	(0.045)	(0.000)	(0.000)	(0.000)	(0.000)	(0.001)	(0.000)	(0.000)

Panel B t−1/t	Return	Amihud	Proportional	Turnover	CS	PS	Roll	Across
Return	**0.3391**	**0.3168**	**0.3106**	0.2895	0.2318	0.1766	**0.4093**	**0.2985**
	0.8572	**0.8384**	**0.8954**	0.9046	0.9262	0.9523	**0.8223**	**0.8699**
	(0.0080)	**(0.0020)**	**(0.0650)**	(0.1030)	(0.2660)	(0.6260)	**(0.0010)**	**(0.0160)**
Amihud	**0.2953**	0.1755	0.0854	0.9226	0.3445	0.2339	0.3405	0.3009
	0.8967	0.9514	0.9884	0.1421	0.8669	0.9079	0.8530	0.8932
	(0.0700)	(0.6120)	(0.9950)	(0.0000)	(0.0140)	(0.1210)	(0.0060)	(0.0580)
Proportional	**0.3469**	0.3021	0.0904	0.1778	0.1902	0.1898	0.3479	0.1385
	0.8738	0.9039	0.9879	0.9678	0.9625	0.9555	0.8398	0.9777
	(0.0200)	(0.1000)	(0.9950)	(0.8550)	(0.7830)	(0.6760)	(0.0030)	(0.9520)
Turnover	**0.3075**	0.1678	0.8125	0.1937	0.2453	0.2676	0.4869	0.0707
	0.8855	0.9588	0.3276	0.9615	0.9361	0.9176	0.7041	0.9923
	(0.0390)	(0.7290)	(0.0000)	(0.7690)	(0.3840)	(0.1860)	(0.0000)	(0.9990)
CS	0.2181	0.8936	0.0959	0.1929	0.5162	0.2771	0.2449	0.5959
	0.9724	0.2002	0.9901	0.9495	0.6343	0.9102	0.9036	0.6201
	(0.4720)	(0.0000)	(0.9980)	(0.5810)	(0.0000)	(0.1340)	(0.0980)	(0.0000)
PS	0.1525	0.2768	0.3083	0.3030	0.1975	0.1550	0.4035	0.3227
	0.9668	0.8834	0.8778	0.9026	0.9558	0.9703	0.8024	0.8834
	(0.8430)	(0.0350)	(0.0250)	(0.0945)	(0.6820)	(0.8840)	(0.0000)	(0.0350)
Roll	**0.3052**	0.2872	0.2587	0.1571	0.1881	0.1976	0.4148	0.2857
	0.8825	0.8781	0.9088	0.9588	0.9329	0.9479	0.8039	0.8922
	(0.0330)	(0.0260)	(0.1260)	(0.7270)	(0.3420)	(0.5560)	(0.0000)	(0.0550)
Across	0.2659	0.5119	0.2313	0.6034	0.3107	0.2170	0.2292	0.3928
	0.8811	0.7194	0.9357	0.6235	0.8962	0.9326	0.9325	0.8263
	(0.0310)	(0.0000)	(0.3780)	(0.0000)	(0.0680)	(0.3380)	(0.3370)	(0.0010)

Three common factors are extracted separately for returns and different measures of liquidity using PCA method. This table reports the first canonical autocorrelation and cross-correlations (one lag) between each two groups of common factors. We present canonical correlations (first row), the Wilks' lambda (second row), and p-value in parentheses. Panel A uses raw time series while Panel B the residuals of an AR(2) model for each factor.

orthogonalize each of the individual liquidity factors (the first component). We do this by running the following regression (first stage):

$$\hat{F}_{1,t}^i = \mathbf{b}_0^i + \mathbf{b}_1^i \hat{F}_{1,t} + \hat{u}_{1,t}^i \tag{24.7}$$

Where $\hat{F}_{1,t}^i$ is the within-measure nonorthogonalized systematic factor (the Amihud measure, proportional spread, PS, CS, Roll, and turnover) and it is prewhitened using AR(2). $\hat{F}_{1,t}$ presents the first common factor of the across-measure systematic factor [also prewhitened using AR(2)] and $\breve{u}_{1,t}^i$ is the within-measure orthogonalized systematic factor. At a second stage, we regress each firm's liquidity on the across-measure and projected within-measure. The regression is as follows (second stage):

$$\hat{F}_{1,t}^i = b_0^i + b_1^i \hat{A}_{1,t} + b_2^i W_{1,t}^i + \hat{u}_{1,t}^i \tag{24.8}$$

Where $\hat{F}_{1,t}^i$ is each firm's liquidity for liquidity proxy i, $\hat{A}_{1,t}$ is the across-measure, and $W_{1,t}^i$ is the orthogonalized within measure from the previous regression. Superscript i represents our six liquidity proxies, such as the Amihud measure, proportional spread, PS, CS, Roll, and turnover.

The importance of across-measure and within-measures in cross-sectional analysis is shown in Table 24.5. We report the percentage of firms in the sample that exhibit significant coefficients at the 1% and 5% levels. Also Table 24.5 shows joint significance (*F*-statistic), average R^2, and adjusted R^2. At 1% and 5% significant level, the percentage of significant coefficient for across-measure is lower than within-measure for the Amihud, proportional spread, CS, and turnover. Associated with Roll measure, 50% (60.7%) of coefficients for across-measure are significant at 1% (5%) level which is higher than within-measure. Individually the across-measure and within-measure factors are statistically significant at frequencies much greater than the test size. Also, rejection rates of the joint null at frequencies are much greater than the test size.

Overall, it shows that both across-measure and within-measure are important factors but within-measure is relatively more important than across-measure in our study. This could be drawn by errors associated with individual assets, as K&S emphasize that "the factor loadings are likely to be estimated with much error for individual assets" Korajczyk and Sadka (2008, p. 66).

24.4.6 Liquidity Risk, Liquidity Characteristics, and Average Returns

We estimate systematic liquidity risk of assets in a five-factor model that includes the across-measure liquidity factor in addition to the Fama-French three factor model and momentum. First of all, to estimate factor betas, we regress returns for each stock on the across-measure

Table 24.5: Percent of firms with significant exposure to across measure and within measure factors.

Variable	Statistical sig level (%)	Intercept	Across Measure	Within Measure	Joint Sig.	Average R^2	Average Adjusted. R^2
Amihud	1	69.7	28.1	50.2	59.4	0.1011	0.0891
	5	72.9	38.4	62.1	68.1		
Proportional	1	83.9	86.7	89.4	91.7	0.6145	0.6094
	5	92.8	88.3	90.0	91.7		
PS	1	100	0.55	0.55	0.55	0.0178	0.0046
	5	100	0.55	1.11	0.55		
CS	1	84.4	13.9	55.6	57.8	0.0844	0.0721
	5	87.8	31.1	66.7	77.2		
Roll	1	42.8	50.0	42.8	60.7	0.1238	0.1120
	5	53.6	60.7	42.8	71.4		
Turnover	1	47.3	3.76	47.3	42.5	0.0601	0.0475
	5	56.4	10.7	66.7	60.7		

This table presents distribution statistics of time-series regressions. Within-measure common factors are extracted separately for different measures of liquidity using the PCA method. In addition, across-measure factors are extracted for all liquidity measures jointly. Then, for each liquidity measure of each stock, a time-series regression for the variable on the across-measure common factor (the first principal component) and the within-measure common factor (the first principal component) of the particular liquidity measure is executed (the within-measure common factor is first projected on the across-measure common factor to orthogonalize). The table reports the percentage of firms in the sample that exhibit significant coefficients at the 1% and 5% significance levels, as well as the joint significance (F-statistics). The average R^2 and the average adjusted R^2 of these regressions are also reported.

liquidity factor, market portfolio, high minus low (HML), small minus big (SMB), and momentum.[5] The first stage multiple time series regression is given as follows:

$$R_{i,t} = \beta_{0,i} + \beta_i' f_t + \varepsilon_{i,t} \tag{24.9}$$

Where f_t is a vector of factors. From this regression, we obtain a coefficient of the across-measure which we use to assign stock to portfolios. Namely, every month we rank stocks based on their beta relative to the across-measure using the past 36 months of data.[6] We create 12 portfolios and 15 assets are allocated to each portfolio. Then, returns for each portfolio are calculated. We calculate excess returns by deducting risk free rate for each portfolio and run a second stage regression. The purpose of this second stage regression is to estimate the beta of the liquidity risk portfolio (*i*).

Table 24.6 shows the average portfolio return in excess of the 1-month risk-free return, Jensen alpha relative to a four-factor model where the factors are MKT, HML, SMB, and UMD and the post ranking liquidity betas excess returns. Coefficients of excess returns are

---

[5] The momentum factor represents the difference in returns between the top and bottom third of all ordinary stocks. We obtain the four factors from the University of Exeter's website: http://xfi.exeter.ac.uk/researchandpublications/portfoliosandfactors/disclaimer.php

[6] It requires 24 months of data out of the past 36 months in order to include an asset.

Table 24.6: Performance of across-measure liquidity loading sorted portfolios.

FTSE100 and FTSE250 (01.2002 ~ 12.2010)			
Portfolio Ranking	**Excess Return**	**FF4 Alpha**	**FF4 + All Loadings**
P1 (low)	−0.0651 (0.0750)	−0.00005 (0.6849)	−0.00006 (0.5675)
P2	0.3273 (0.0000)	−0.00107 (0.0002)	0.00007 (0.3637)
P3	0.2818 (0.0001)	0.00097 (0.0005)	0.00008 (0.2272)
P4	0.0175 (0.8199)	0.00025 (0.3819)	−0.000005 (0.9503)
P5	−0.0212 (0.6643)	−0.00029 (0.1410)	−0.00011 (0.2188)
P6	0.0749 (0.1672)	0.00047 (0.0320)	−0.00017 (0.0756)
P7	0.0851 (0.1166)	0.00059 (0.0004)	0.00006 (0.4920)
P8	0.4202 (0.0000)	0.00138 (0.0000)	0.00010 (0.2730)
P9	0.0559 (0.4681)	0.00065 (0.0229)	−0.00007 (0.5466)
P10	−0.1082 (0.0405)	0.00011 (0.5102)	−0.00005 (0.6572)
P11	0.5362 (0.0000)	0.00175 (0.0000)	0.00016 (0.1305)
P12 (high)	0.7282 (0.0000)	0.00233 (0.0000)	0.00016 (0.1317)
12-1 (high-low)	0.9631 (0.0000)	−0.00021 (0.3672)	−0.00007 (0.7590)
12-2 (high-low)	−0.5609 (0.0000)	−0.00037 (0.0617)	−0.00005 (0.7927)

Across-measure common factors are extracted jointly for different measure of liquidity measures using PCA method. Twelve portfolios are sorted each month by the across-measure liquidity loading estimated using the past 36 months (the loading is computed while controlling for Fama-French four factors). The time-series mean return (excess of risk-free rate) and risk-adjusted returns (using Fama-French four factors) of each portfolio are presented. The number in brackets is the *p*-value.

positive except P1, P5, and P10. We obtain negative coefficients of FF4 alpha for P1, P2, and P5, while others are positive. Alpha is mostly statistically significant except P1, P4, P5, and P10. Across-measure betas are mostly statistically insignificant except P6.

Fig. 24.2 shows a plot of the four-factor alpha against the portfolio systematic liquidity beta of the 12 portfolios. If liquidity risk is priced independently of the four factors in the asset pricing model (MKT, HML, SMB, and UMD) then we can expect a statistically significant positive relationship between the alpha and the liquidity beta. Our result shows in Fig. 24.2 that there is a significant relation between the alpha and the liquidity beta in the UK stock market which is consistent with findings in the US market.

24.4.7 Cross-Sectional Regressions

Since a significant relation exists between FF4 alpha and across-measure liquidity as shown in the previous section, we test explicitly for the pricing of liquidity in the cross-section. The asset pricing models used are the following:

$$R_{i,t} = \gamma_{0,t} + \gamma_t' \beta_{i,t} + \delta_t' Z_{i,t-1} + \varepsilon_{i,t} \tag{24.10}$$

Where $R_{i,t}$ denotes the return of portfolio i (excess of risk-free rate), β_i is the vector of factor loadings of asset i relative to several different risk factors, such as SMB, HML, MKT, UMD, the across-measure, and within-measure liquidity factors. γ is a vector of factor premia, Z_i

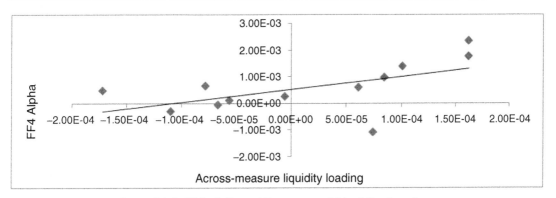

Figure 24.2: Risk-Adjusted Returns and Liquidity Loadings.
Across-measure common factors are extracted jointly for different measure of liquidity measures
using the PCA model. The risk-adjusted returns of each portfolio p, alpha, are calculated using
Fama-French four factors. In addition, the loading of each portfolio on the across-measure liquidity
factor is calculated using a time series regression on returns including the Fama-French four factors.
The line plots the fitted regression model. The number in bracket is the p-value.

$$\alpha_p = 0.0005 + 4.8492\ \beta_{LIQ,p} + \varepsilon_p$$

[0.0453] [0.0450]

are characteristics (in month $t-1$), such as the raw liquidity measures, size, and the book-to-market equity ratio, and δ is a vector of characteristic premia. We use the beta relative to the across-measure liquidity which is estimated in the previous section. Also, we use Newey-west t-statistics for hypothesis testing. First, the CAPM is examined using MKT including unstandardized level of the liquidity measure as a characteristic premium. Second, we run the model with three factor premiums, such as MKT, across-measure, and within-measure (orthogonalized factor to across-measure) but exclude the illiquidity characteristic. The third model specification includes MKT, the liquidity factors, and the illiquidity characteristic. Then, we repeat with addition of the SMB, HML, and UMD factors in the model. Finally, we add two additional characteristics, the logarithm of the stocks' market capitalization (size) and the book-to-market equity ratio.

The results of the cross-sectional regressions are presented in Table 24.7. Model 1 (M1) shows that the coefficient for MKT is positive and significant for all measures. The premium for illiquidity measures as characteristic is also significant. Model 2 (M2) shows that the coefficients for MKT remain significant even after including across-measure and within-measure. The coefficients for across-measure are statistically significant for proportional spread and CS. The coefficient of projected within-measures associated with proportional spread is statistically significant. As illiquidity is included in the model (see Model 3), the result of regression is slightly altered. MKT remains significant for all measures, the across-measure is significant for the Amihud, proportional spread, and CS. The coefficients of

Table 24.7: Pricing liquidity in the cross-section.

Measure		Factor Premium						Characteristic Premium		
		MKT	SMB	HML	UMD	Across-Measure	Within-Measure	Illiquidity	Size	B/M
M1	Amihud	0.0564 (0.0000)						0.0014 (0.0000)		
	Proportional	0.0572 (0.0000)						−0.0048 (0.0238)		
	Turnover	0.0571 (0.0000)						−0.6601 (0.0000)		
	PS	0.0775 (0.0000)						0.0018 (0.0115)		
	CS	0.0576 (0.0000)						0.3018 (0.0006)		
	Roll	0.0575 (0.0000)						0.0003 (0.0433)		
M2	Amihud	0.0559 (0.0000)				0.0003 (0.1042)	0.000099 (0.5891)			
	Proportional	0.0544 (0.0000)				0.0003 (0.0725)	0.0044 (0.0352)			
	Turnover	0.0551 (0.0000)				0.0002 (0.1659)	−0.0002 (0.5482)			
	PS	0.0561 (0.0000)				0.0003 (0.1081)	−0.0002 (0.1836)			
	CS	0.0575 (0.0000)				0.0003 (0.0701)	−0.0005 (0.3187)			
	Roll	0.0549 (0.0000)				0.0002 (0.1882)	−0.0003 (0.2320)			
M3	Amihud	0.0553 (0.0000)				0.0003 (0.0388)	0.0002 (0.3081)	0.0015 (0.0035)		
	Proportional	0.0548 (0.0000)				0.0003 (0.0700)	0.0039 (0.0551)	−0.0036 (0.1850)		
	Turnover	0.0559 (0.0000)				0.000059 (0.5454)	−0.0003 (0.4061)	−0.6539 (0.0000)		
	PS	0.0571 (0.0000)				0.0002 (0.2203)	−0.0002 (0.2427)	0.0014 (0.0914)		
	CS	0.0577 (0.0000)				0.0003 (0.0961)	−0.0003 (0.3457)	0.2741 (0.0140)		
	Roll	0.0553 (0.0000)				0.0002 (0.2392)	−0.0004 (0.0955)	0.0004 (0.1301)		

Model	Measure									
M4	Amihud	0.0538 (0.0000)	0.0236 (0.0012)	-0.0099 (0.0391)	-0.0004 (0.6034)			0.0014 (0.0007)		
	Proportional	0.0534 (0.0000)	0.0235 (0.0007)	-0.0091 (0.0798)	-0.0028 (0.5485)			-0.0049 (0.0329)		
	Turnover	0.0532 (0.0000)	0.0182 (0.0111)	-0.0109 (0.0381)	-0.0061 (0.1758)			-0.6241 (0.0001)		
	PS	0.0546 (0.0000)	0.0247 (0.0004)	-0.0110 (0.0199)	-0.0023 (0.5473)			0.0021 (0.0106)		
	CS	0.0553 (0.0000)	0.0239 (0.0002)	-0.0089 (0.0637)	0.0007 (0.6078)			0.2851 (0.0039)		
	Roll	0.0546 (0.0000)	0.0245 (0.0002)	-0.0091 (0.0837)	-0.0004 (0.6514)			0.0004 (0.1021)		
M5	Amihud	0.0525 (0.0000)	0.0253 (0.0000)	-0.0107 (0.0354)	-0.0019 (0.6098)	0.0003 (0.0629)	-0.0002 (0.2983)			
	Proportional	0.0506 (0.0000)	0.0215 (0.0010)	-0.0082 (0.0858)	-0.0034 (0.4786)	0.0004 (0.0279)	0.0037 (0.0912)			
	Turnover	0.0498 (0.0000)	0.0239 (0.0007)	-0.0096 (0.0471)	-0.0034 (0.4732)	0.0002 (0.1346)	-0.0006 (0.1517)			
	PS	0.0525 (0.0000)	0.0229 (0.0013)	-0.0105 (0.0358)	-0.0028 (0.5343)	0.0003 (0.0557)	-0.0002 (0.2992)			
	CS	0.0528 (0.0000)	0.0231 (0.0007)	-0.0097 (0.0527)	-0.0024 (0.5279)	0.0003 (0.0524)	-0.0002 (0.3721)			
	Roll	0.0526 (0.0000)	0.0247 (0.0012)	-0.0103 (0.0347)	-0.0023 (0.6416)	0.0003 (0.0417)	0.0001 (0.4286)			
M6	Amihud	0.0519 (0.0000)	0.0213 (0.0001)	-0.0070 (0.1054)	0.0039 (0.3074)	0.0002 (0.0687)	0.00004 (0.3219)	-0.0003 (0.3427)	0.0032 (0.1378)	0.00001 (0.0118)
	Proportional	0.0512 (0.0000)	0.0212 (0.0003)	-0.0068 (0.1467)	0.0030 (0.4372)	0.0003 (0.0579)	0.0019 (0.2306)	-0.0019 (0.2248)	0.0014 (0.4491)	0.000008 (0.0649)
	Turnover	0.0517 (0.0000)	0.0198 (0.0023)	-0.0084 (0.0836)	0.0003 (0.6467)	0.0001 (0.3182)	-0.0002 (0.5310)	-0.3116 (0.1174)	0.0020 (0.1982)	0.000006 (0.0423)
	PS	0.0520 (0.0000)	0.0217 (0.0009)	-0.0072 (0.1295)	0.0038 (0.3118)	0.0003 (0.0535)	0.00001 (0.5018)	-0.0001 (0.5622)	0.0030 (0.1674)	0.000009 (0.0546)
	CS	0.0510 (0.0000)	0.0215 (0.0000)	-0.0076 (0.0700)	0.0037 (0.3074)	0.0002 (0.0421)	0.00009 (0.4352)	-0.1021 (0.2701)	0.0033 (0.1292)	0.00001 (0.0027)
	Roll	0.0514 (0.0000)	0.0207 (0.0011)	-0.0074 (0.1080)	0.0035 (0.3546)	0.0002 (0.0502)	-0.00005 (0.4681)	-0.0001 (0.1696)	0.0033 (0.1832)	0.00001 (0.0739)

We extracted within-measure factors separately for different measures of liquidity using the PCA method and across-measure common factors are extracted for all liquidity measures jointly. Factor loadings are calculated using time-series regressions of returns of 12 portfolios on the Fama-French four factors. The results of Fama-Macbeth regressions of stock returns on the factor loadings are reported. (p-values associated with Newey-West adjusted t-statistics are in parentheses).

within-measure for proportional and Roll are significant. The Amihud, turnover, PS, and CS as illiquidity characteristics become significant. Overall, the CAPM beta is positive and statistically significant and remains unchanged when we include additional variables, such as across-measure, within-measure, and illiquidity characteristics. Illiquidity becomes significant as across and within-measure is included in the model. Across-measure is consistently significant for proportional spread and CS over Models 2 and 3.

Now, we run the Fama-French four factor model with characteristic variables. The factors are MKT, SMB, HML, UMD, and the characteristic variables are illiquidity measure, size, and book-to-market ratio. Model 4 shows that MKT, SMB, and HML factor premium are statistically significant for all measures except UMD factor premium. Also, illiquidity as characteristic is significant for all measures except Roll. Model 5 (M5) contains FF4 factors and across-measure and within-measure. Results of FF4 factor premiums remain unchanged. The coefficients of across-measure are statistically significant for all measures except turnover.

Only proportional within-measure is significant while other within-measures are statistically insignificant. Finally, Model 6 (M6) shows the results associated with all variables in the model. As we include all variables in the model, the across-measure is statistically significant for all cases except turnover. The coefficients of within-measure are all insignificant. MKT and SMB are all significant. HML is also insignificant except in the cases of turnover and CS. Also, illiquidity and size characteristics become insignificant for all measures while B/M characteristic premium is significant for all measures.

To compare with Korajczyk and Sadka (2008), our results show that the premia relative to MKT, SMB, and HML are significant while the Fama-French four factors are insignificant in their study.

The across-measure liquidity factor behaves similarly to the US market (Korajczyk and Sadka, 2008) and earns consistently a statistically significant premium regardless of the specification. Results obtained for illiquidity premia as characteristic is consistent with K&S who report statistically significant premia, however, this pattern breaks when we include all variables, such as FF4 factors, across and within measure, and characteristics (Model 6). The premium for size characteristic is insignificant while book-to-market equity characteristic is significant for all measures. Thus, book-to-market equity characteristic is priced, but size and illiquidity as characteristics are not priced in the cross-section.

Liquidity risk for the UK market is priced. More specifically, coefficients of non-risk illiquidity characteristics and within-measures are becoming insignificant while systematic liquidity risk (across-measure) is persistently and strongly priced as we include more variables in the model.

24.5 Conclusions

Since liquidity is not a simple concept to explore and not directly observable, a number of liquidity measures have been proposed. Even though, various liquidity proxies are widely used in asset pricing studies, there is no such thing as a superior proxy that is able to capture all facets of liquidity. Following Korajczyk and Sadka (2008), we estimate an across-measure which is obtained by extracting common factors across a number of different measures of liquidity in order to combine as many different dimensions of liquidity as possible for the UK market.

Our results are consistent with evidence from the US market (Korajczyk and Sadka, 2008). We find that there is strong commonality across assets for each individual measure of liquidity (consistent with Galariotis and Giouvris, 2007, 2009 and Gregoriou et al., 2011) and that these common factors (within measure) are correlated across different liquidity measures. The relation between within measure and across-measure is statistically significant and these measures are contemporaneously correlated with returns. Also our study shows that changes in liquidity measures are correlated with each other and with the across-measure. Shocks to returns can predict future liquidity levels and lagged liquidity shocks can predict future returns.

Finally, we examine if liquidity is priced using different specifications (CAPM benchmark and Fama-French four factor benchmark) with across-measure liquidity factor as well as within-measures which are orthogonalized to the across-measure. The study shows that liquidity risk for the UK market is priced. More specifically, coefficients of nonrisk illiquidity characteristics and within-measures are becoming insignificant while systematic liquidity risk (across-measure) is persistently and strongly priced as we include more variables in the model.

References

Amihud, Y, 2002. Illiquidity and stock returns: cross-section and time-series effect. J. Financ. Markets 5 (1), 31–56.

Amihud, Y., Mendelson, H, 1986. Asset pricing and the bid-ask spread. J. Financ. Econ. 17 (2), 223–249.

Bekaert, G., Harvey, C.R., Lundblad, C, 2007. Liquidity and expected returns: lessons from emerging markets. Rev. Financ. Studies 20 (6), 1783–1832.

Brennan, M.J., Chordia, T., Subrahmanyam, A, 1998. Alternative factor specifications, security characteristics, and the cross-section of expected stock returns. J. Financ. Econ. 49 (3), 345–373.

Brown, S., Du, D.Y., Rhee, S.G., Zhang, L, 2008. The returns to value and momentum in Asian markets. Emerging Markets Rev. 9 (2), 79–88.

Chai, D., Faff, R., Gharghori, P, 2010. New evidence on the relation between stock liquidity and measures of trading activity. Int. Rev. Financ. Anal. 19 (3), 181–192.

Chordia, T., Roll, R., Subrahmanyam, A, 2000. Commonality in liquidity. J. Financ. Econ. 56 (1), 3–28.

Corwin, S.A., Lipson, ML, 2011. Order characteristics and the sources of commonality in prices and liquidity. J. Financ. Markets 14 (1), 47–81.

Corwin, S.A., Schultz, P, 2012. A simple way to estimate bid-ask spreads: theory and evidence. J. Financ. Quant. Anal. 23 (2), 219–230.

Datar, V.T., Narayan, Y.N., Radcliffe, R, 1998. Liquidity and stock returns: an alternative test. J. Financ. Markets 1 (1), 203–219.

Dey, MK, 2005. Turnover and return in global stock markets. Emerging Markets Rev. 6 (1), 45–67.

Eleswarapu, V.R., Reinganum, MR, 1993. The seasonal behaviour of the liquidity premium in asset pricing. J. Financ. Econ. 34 (3), 373–386.

Galariotis, E., Giouvris, E., 2007. Liquidity commonality in the London stock exchange. J. Bus. Finance Account. 34 (1), 374–388.

Galariotis, E., Giouvris, E., 2008. Systematic liquidity and excess return: evidence from the Athens Stock Exchange. J. Money Invest. Bank. 1 (2), 81–97.

Galariotis, E., Giouvris, E., 2009. Systematic liquidity and excess returns: evidence from the London Stock Exchange. Rev. Account. Finance 8 (3), 279–307.

Gregoriou, A., Ioannidis, C., Zhu, K., 2011. Commonality in Liquidity of UK Markets: Evidence From Recent Financial Crisis. University of Bath. Working Paper. Available from: http://people.bath.ac.uk/ci200/Commonality%20in%20Liquidity_v1.pdf

Hasbrouck, J., Seppi, D.J., 2001. Common factors in prices, order flows, and liquidity. J. Financ. Econ. 59 (3), 383–411.

Jun, S.G., Marathe, A., Shawky, H.A., 2003. Liquidity and stock returns in emerging equity markets. Emerging Market Rev. 4 (1), 1–24.

Kamara, A., Low, X., Sadka, R., 2008. The divergence of liquidity commonality in the cross-section of stocks. J. Financ. Econ. 89 (3), 444–466.

Karolyi, G.A., Lee, K.H., Van Dijk, M.A., 2012. Understanding commonality in liquidity around the world. J. Financ. Econ. 105 (1), 82–112.

Korajczyk, R.A., Sadka, R., 2008. Pricing the commonality across alternative measures of liquidity. J. Financ. Econ. 87 (1), 45–72.

Kuntar, P.Le., Visaltanachoti, N., 2008. Commonality in liquidity: evidence from the Stock Exchange of Thailand. Pacific-Basin Finance J. 17 (1), 80–99.

Lam, L.S.K., Tam, L.H.K., 2011. Liquidity and asset pricing: evidence from the Hong Kong stock market. J. Bank. Finance 35 (9), 2217–2230.

Lesmond, D.A., 2005. Liquidity of emerging markets. J. Financ. Econ. 77 (2), 411–452.

Lesmond, D., Ogden, J., Trzcinka, C., 1999. A new estimate of transaction costs. Rev. Financ. Studies 12 (5), 1113–1141.

Martinez, M.A., Nieto, B., Rubio, G., Tapia, M., 2005. Asset pricing and systematic liquidity risk: an empirical investigation of the Spanish stock market. Int. Rev. Econ. Finance 14 (1), 81–103.

Pastor, L., Stambaugh, R.F., 2003. Liquidity risk and expected stock returns. J. Political Econ. 111 (3), 642–685.

Roll, R., 1984. A simple implicit measure of the effective bid-ask spread in an efficient market. J. Finance 39 (4), 1127–1139.

Index

Printed in the United States
By Bookmasters